Tactics and Techniques of Community Practice

Fred M. Cox
Michigan State University

John L. Erlich
California State University, Sacramento

Jack Rothman
John E. Tropman
University of Michigan

F. E. PEACOCK PUBLISHERS, INC.
ITASCA, ILLINOIS 60143

Preface

It was not easy to select the articles for this book. We tried hard to choose practical, concrete, and down-to-earth materials; a number of the pieces were recommended by our students and practitioner friends. With the help of work drawn from little known and fugitive sources, we believe that a strong and pervasive emphasis on "how-to-do-it" has been achieved. However, this is neither a "cookbook" nor a "road map." The characteristics of the particular user, his or her agency, the community in which the action is taking place, and the client population involved must all be taken into account if tactics and techniques are to be successfully initiated. The increasingly interorganizational context of human service work at the community level also needs to be considered.

With any practice-oriented book of this kind, there is always a question about what is *really* meant by evocative words like "tactics" and "techniques." What is the intended difference (if any) between tactics and techniques and strategy? We view strategy as "an orchestrated attempt to influence a person or system in relation to some goal which an actor desires."[1] Tactics and techniques may be regarded as specific interventive devices or means that contribute to the operationalization of a strategy. Thus the key differences between strategy and tactics and techniques involve scope and duration. Tactics are generally more modest in these respects. For example, a strategy to achieve an affirmative action plan in a community mental health agency may involve coordinated approaches to the community, a board of directors, the staff, and the clientele. Once designed, tactics and techniques contributing to realization of the affirmative action plan strategy might include organizing Third World and women's caucuses among staff, preparing a position paper for the board, or conducting an open forum in the community.

Because of the clear and important relationship between strategy and tactics,

---

[1] Fred M. Cox, John L. Erlich, Jack Rothman, and John E. Tropman, eds., *Strategies of Community Organization*, 2d ed. (Itasca, Ill.: F. E. Peacock Publishers, 1974), p. 162. An elaboration of this definition follows in that source.

we believe that students and practitioners will need to give attention to the nature and dimensions of strategies which the material in this book might augment and support. Our experience suggests that *Strategies of Community Organization,* another book prepared by the authors, may assist in this process.[2] The notion of three practice models—social action, social planning, and locality development—has been a fruitful conceptual design for many practitioners.[3] Also, a detailed step-by-step problem-solving schema may prove useful.[4] However, the important point is not which text might be used, but rather the need to explore potentially useful treatments of strategy in community practice.

Finally, the editors would like to add a personal note. As practitioners and teachers we have struggled with the need for more disciplined, planful, and responsible approaches to practice, whether it be organizing, planning, policy-making, or administration. Our students and practitioner-colleagues have struggled with us. Each of us knows the degree to which we have "flown by the seat of our pants." It is our feeling that the material in this book can help to reduce that flying time.

**Fred M. Cox, John L. Erlich,
Jack Rothman, and John E. Tropman**

---

[2] Op. cit.
[3] Op. cit., pp. 22–39.
[4] Op. cit., pp. 425–454.

Contents

Introduction

Most people have a great deal of difficulty thinking in ways that are different from the ways they were taught or learned from personal experience. Practitioners of community organization—organizers, planners, administrators—are no exception. In fact, when viewed from some distance, the general impression is that the majority of practitioners use a rather narrow range of tactics and techniques to achieve their chosen objectives. However, this is scarcely surprising in a field whose major successes are frequently short-lived and whose fundamental value as an approach to social intervention is still a subject of controversy. "Go with that you know" is how street wisdom would have it. These limitations, often self-imposed, may include the following factors: personal ideology; the time, place, or modalities in which the practitioner was trained; fragile funding; client suspicion of the practitioner; organizational constraints; the local "political" climate; or the practitioner's degree of "battle fatigue."

But recent experience and the continuing expansion of the knowledge on which community practice can be based tells a different story. Never have the range and variety of available techniques been so broad and rich. And in an era of disillusionment and pessimism, perhaps the need to use them effectively in the cause of positive social change has never been greater. This book is an attempt to bring together some of what we believe to be the most useful tactics and techniques currently available to human service practitioners working in the community arena. This potential is not easily realized. Perhaps more than anything else, it needs to be considered in the context of a conception of community.

Within recent decades, community organization has been a powerful concept, used both as a term describing what is lacking in contemporary American communities and as an approach to training people in strategies, tactics, and techniques of organizing, planning, policy-making, and administration. Yet even today, after more than 50 years of work in the field of community organization, many theorists and practitioners are not sure what a "community" is (or ought to be) and what the focal point of their work should be. Some argue for functional communities, such as the "aging community" which does not have all of its members living in one geographic space. Other practitioners especially consider the geographic community, neighborhood, and—by extension—the city or rural area as a whole. And, though workplace organizing has been the focus of a great deal of attention in union activities and professional associations (though with little reference to the word "community"), this perspective is often overlooked.

Yet there is the widespread feeling that "community"—however defined—is being weakened and is without direction. People point to the decline of the city, and predict (as they have since the emergence of cities) its ultimate collapse. Books like *Eclipse of Community* (Stein, 1960) or *Quest for Identity* (Wheelis, 1958) give the impression that the more intimate, closer, and informal relationships which seemed to characterize earlier communities have given way to a more formalized, more calculating, more distant set of relationships. Tonnies' (1957) classic dichotomy between community and society has grown in the eyes of many, to the point where we are seen as having no communal relations—only societal ones. The shift has left the family and other small groups prey to media manipulation and exploitation. The "decline" of the family has been, in part, attributed to this development.

We think the situation is less grim, although there are a host of problems to be addressed. First among these problems, however, is how to develop an adequate theoretical picture of the arenas within which change and development have taken place in our society, how these shifts have led to some new sets of dilemmas, and how these developments in turn lead to change in the potential roles for the community worker. Without this consideration, tactics and techniques are grabbags of tricks whose use will be guided largely by chance or whim.

Metropolitan Society

Contemporary society may be characterized as metropolitan society. Much of the population lives in large metropolitan areas. While there are boundaries of sorts between black and white, rich and poor, upper middle and working class, suburb and inner city, these groups are all tied together in a large geographic space and are dependent upon one another. For the decade of the seventies, metropolitan problems—and metropolitan organization—have become the relevant systems in which reform goes on and which influence much of our life choices and chances.

Metropolitan society is one in which a variety of forms of social differentiation have evolved, and this development poses a fresh and challenging set of problems for those in community organization. Basically, these changes are (1) the development of greater vertical differentiation within the society, (2) the development of greater horizontal differentiation within the middle layer or segment of the vertical axis (i.e., family, workplace, and culture), and (3) the emergence of the family as a more distinctive and more important unit of orientation.

Vertical Differentiation: The Emergence of Community

What historically has been referred to as a once narrow continuum between community and society is now expanded among family, various geographic, functional, and organizational communities, and society or, as Kornhauser has suggested, among primary, secondary, and tertiary relationships (1959). Most important is the family, whether nuclear—husband, wife, children—or "modified extended"—including an additional generation or other close relatives (Litwak, 1961). The pattern of differentiation has made families increasingly nuclear and thus smaller. One of the reasons why some of the income support programs, for example, did not do more to relieve poverty is that the additional income given to extended family units was apparently used to create more families (Lipset, 1975). For example, when additional monies came to an older person, that person would be able to move out, creating a new "family" (and often one living in poverty). Younger people, too, have established their own "families" at increasing rates. The difficulties, stresses, and isolation of many of these new families have been well documented. Responsive community practitioners must take such consequences of differentiation into account as they work.

Secondary relationships are those intermediate interactions—not as intimate as the family or as impersonal as with the society—between the individual and his or her church, work group, service club, civic association, recreation center, political organization, and so on. The pattern of differentiation has resulted in a proliferation of these associations. Political groups, for example, are often subdivided along conservative, moderate, and liberal orientations, and more recently also distinguished by caucuses made up of people of the same race, ethnicity, sex, age, or sexual preference. The range of secondary relationship options is both a problem (e.g., how does the individual locate the most beneficial one) and an opportunity (e.g., because of the variety of potentially rewarding involvements). Clearly, the area of secondary relationships has been a major focus of community practice effort and will continue to be.

Tertiary, or societal, relationships are the most formal and impersonal of interactions and entitlements. These relations stem from basic rights of citizenship which have nothing to do with evaluations, judgments, or qualities of the persons involved. Everyone reaching a certain age can vote; whether they are kind or cruel, wealthy or impoverished is irrelevant. In the sixties, there was a substantial increase in the access to public entitlements enjoyed by citizens. The whole arena of equality-advancing activity illustrates this trend (Tropman, 1975).

In past analyses, family and community were seen as part of a common relationship. The social differentiation in metropolitan society has, we believe, separated these two into primary and secondary relationships. The greater the amount of differentiation, the greater the need for professional intervention, both within levels and between them. We judge that reintegration is probably one of the central issues today, and certainly one of the key problems at the community level. For example, coordination of services has become a catchword at the metropolitan level.

Horizontal Differentiation: The Triple Community

In years gone by, family and community were often similar—one an extension or version of the other, and located in close proximity. Similarly, one's cultural compeers were geographically nearby, and the workplace was either immediate (as on a farm) or near at hand (as in the neighborhood factories). Advances in technology separated home and work, and it was this separation which was especially bothersome to Marx. If anything could be said to be the hallmark of an industrial society, it is the separation of the homeplace from the workplace. The urbanization of industrial society forces additional separations. It not only requires more extensive separation of the homeplace from the workplace; it removes the workplace from the locus of common culture and the locus of common culture from the homeplace. Perhaps the most striking example of the separation of these three parts of the modern "community" occurs when a family of ethnic identification moves into the suburbs. As a territory the suburb is important. It supplies schooling, neighbors, and prestige. But, it may contain no people who share a common culture. Cultural compeers may have remained in the central city but may also be widely scattered in various suburban rings or rural areas. The workplace may be located in still a third spot with some people from the geographic area, some people from the culture, and many strangers. Thus the family in question has three elements of the "community" system to which it must relate located in geographically separate areas.

The vitality of these differentiating community systems has not, however, developed at the same rate. The organizational (or work) community is one which has grown vigorously, in fact almost overwhelming the other aspects of community. The ethnic community—the cultural community—has been in a somewhat defensive position but is now flourishing with the advent of racial and ethnic pride and a variety of rights-oriented groups such as those composed of women, homosexuals, ex-prisoners, and the like. Perhaps the weakest entity is the geographical community—the neighborhood or district—which cannot seem to garner enough resources to become an effective systemic unit.

Therefore, it is especially ironic to think of community-based treatment services and community mental health programs as relying so heavily upon the geographical community. Nonetheless, these recent emphases, plus the development in psychology of a "community" focus, point to the need for expanded attention to the whole area of community, with attention to its cultural and geographic elements. From a somewhat different perspective, perhaps more scrutiny should be given to ways of reducing (or holding in check) the influence of their jobs on people's lives.

Relationship to Traditional Definition. Defining three communities rather than one may raise some questions about the more "traditional" approaches to defining community. An example of the traditional definition is the one adapted by Gideon Sjoberg from that proposed by Talcott Parsons in *The Social System* (1951), p. 91: "A community is a collectivity of actors sharing a limited territorial area as the base for carrying out the greatest share of their daily activities" (Sjoberg, 1964, p. 114).

Some would argue that Parsons's definition stands for some specific entity.

Perhaps, in the historical past, it did indeed represent some single locus in the social system. We are suggesting that today "community" must be understood as embracing three contexts, similar to the three elements contained within the Parsonian definition—collectivity, territoriality, and "the greatest share of daily activities." Specifically, we can consider community as formal organization, community as territory, or community as subculture. Each of these social subsystems has only some of the qualities of the more traditional notion of community. One central element is solidarity. Parsons notes that a collectivity involves solidarity.

It is only when an action system involves solidarity that its members define certain actions as required in the interest of the system itself, and others as incompatible with that integrity—with the result that sanctions are organized about this definition. Such a social system will be called a "collectivity" (Parsons, 1951, p. 97).

He adds that "A collectivity is a system of concretely specific interactive roles" (Parsons, 1951, p. 39). From Parsons's viewpoint, then, a collectivity is definitely not an "aggregate" of unrelated parts but combines specific roles with solidarity. In this sense, a collectivity could be regarded as either a subculture or an organization, depending upon whether the solidarity derives from shared values arising naturally through close interaction or from planned and goal-directed interdependencies (Parsons, 1951, p. 15).

Among other things collectivities share is the occupation of a territorial (or domainlike) area. Naturally, both subcultures and organizations have territories. For these two communities, there is a center, often subcenters, and usually peripheral elements—all of which contribute to their vitality. The typical application of the term "community" limits its use and tends to make a specific geographical area the sole criterion.

Advantages of the Triple Community Concept.   There are several advantages of the triple community perspective. First, it specifies a level of interaction between the primary group (or family) and the formal, societal relationship. Second, it begins to sketch out what some of the key structures are in that secondary system. From a practitioner's perspective, it specifies in a coordinated scheme the major units with which he or she will be working. Each type of community may lack some of the elements of the other types, and these other elements may well serve as a focus of professional community organization work.[1] So, for example, since the neighborhood has a common geography but its members may have little in the way of common values or purpose, the development of some semblance of shared interests and joint projects might well be the focal point of work. Territorial communities often organize around school and housing problems (organization-related) because those are key elements of a commonly shared fate with respect to geographic areas.

Similarly, the organization, seen as a community, had the advantages of its members spending considerable time together and carrying out an important

---

[1] It is well to emphasize again here that in the contemporary "triple community" system no one of the communities is complete. This approach is in contrast to a more typical formulation which suggests communities as "whole" relationship centers as opposed to "partial" ones.

segment of their daily activities there. On the other hand, members may become too dependent upon the organization. A prime example is suggested by the concept of an "organization man," whose life is dominated by the organizational community.

Yet, as human service union organizers know, there is much to be done in humanizing the workplace, even though the organizational community is the most "organized," and has perhaps the greatest clarity of membership (rights, responsibilities, etc.) of the three types. Some of the most salient questions arise from the control the organization has over the worker's life. It is perhaps because of the strength and pervasiveness found in the workplace that fresh organizational efforts there are so laden with conflict. Measures of power, money, or prestige are often at stake.

Finally, the culture—or common experience and belief system—represents a third area of "community." People may have a common territory or may make their living in similar ways and in common locales. But culture needs to be focused and fused into sets of common goals and purposes, and a sense of peoplehood and common fate may need to be enhanced. Perhaps the most basic form of community organizing effort in this respect is "radicalizing" or "consciousness raising," in which people's perspectives are changed and their perception of their common fate is developed and strengthened. This approach has been used in arenas ranging from welfare rights to Grey Panthers.

In sum, the metropolitan region has undergone increased differentiation—a fractionalization which has divided the functions performed by the "community" in days gone by into three sectors which overlap but which usually have different focuses and geographical boundaries. The tasks the worker performs in each of these communities, or among them—those, for example, that link the organizational system with the societal system or the family system—may be of great importance in our complex, distrustful society.

The Reemergence of the Family

Today it may seem incongruous to speak about the reestablishment of the family, but we feel this point deserves strong emphasis. The differentiation which has occurred—the three communities to which the family must relate—means that the family may occupy a strategically more significant position than was true in the past. While the family may no longer be the major dispenser of important life chances, it is crucial in its consolidating, coordinating, and integrating aspects (i.e., as among competing values, personal role options, and so on). In this context, for example, the high rate of divorce may represent not so much the dissolution of the family as a reaffirmation of the family structure— but a structure which must perform new and more sophisticated integrative functions. Certainly the family can be viewed as having lost some of its traditional ability to link work, home, and subculture. But if our analysis is even partially correct, the family is in the process of establishing innovative roles and functions as a linking agent, such as family participation in politics, the family unit serving as the organizational base for ethnic celebrations, or family member involvement in work as it relates family needs to demands and opportunities of the "triple community." The rising rate of remarriage (Epstein, 1974) may represent additional evidence of the validity of this line of reasoning. Perhaps the most notorious application of the "family disorganization" theory was contained in Moynihan's analysis of the black family and the celebrated controversy it precipitated (Rainwater and Yancy, 1967). A major portion of the disagreement centered around differing definitions of family and the functions it does (or should) perform. For our purposes, it is important to recognize that Moynihan failed to adequately address the strengths of the black family, strengths that enabled its members to survive in a largely hostile, externally dominated environment. Tactics and techniques which can aid a practitioner in supporting the efforts of minority (or poor) communities to sustain their family structures are clearly of interest.

One additonal piece of evidence supporting our perspective rests directly on a study of families in their neighborhoods. Donald Warren (1976) has been engaged in a series of researches which indicate that a "Middle American (white) Radical" group is politically important—strong enough to have launched George Wallace and prompted Jimmy Carter in their campaigns for presidential nomination. The families in this group, according to Warren, value the country as a whole as well as the sanctity of their neighborhoods, yet they feel victimized by a "coalition" of the poor and the rich. In our terms, they have been unable to cope with the increasing differentiation and have not formed effective links with a newly emerging set of organizational, geographical, and subcultural communities. Indeed, these are the people, according to Warren, who are most likely to take to the streets in a busing crisis. The busing issue, especially given the interlinked problems of residence, zoning, and urban-suburban shifts, illustrates the significance of the metropolitan "community" (Tropman & Lind, 1972). Thus these families are in some ways active and potent, yet need assistance in forging a set of links to metropolitan society and the communities which make it up.

Eclipse of City and Nation

The sixties was a period in which great hope was held out for the role that the national government could play in resolving some of our key social problems. Yet now the federal government has largely divested itself of its substantive leadership role in most social programs. The federal role tends more to be one of raising money which is returned to the states in various forms of revenue sharing. These funds are allocated in ways determined largely at the local level.[2]

---

[2]Beer (1976) characterizes this situation as a shift from private-sector politics to public-sector politics, in which a host of demands rise from the subnational governments. Government itself becomes a source of "demands." He notes that this obtains because the subnational governments have become the center for "the delivery of a multitude of services originating with professional elements and mandated by the central government as a condition of its financial aid" (Beer, 1976, p. 131). He notes also that in the United States, as in other countries, there is a tendency to "spread money around without much regard for merit or need . . . " (Beer, 1971, p. 132), and he calls this tendency "distributive localism."

Perhaps the notion of "eclipse" is too strong in view of the current rise in economic and political control exercised by localities. This tendency suggests that localities—metropolitan areas—should be getting stronger.

However, while policy control by subnational governments has been increasing, the cities, which (along with the states) might be thought of as the main beneficiaries, are not faring well either. There are several reasons for this development; they were demonstrated perhaps most keenly by the troubles New York City went through in its recent (and continuing) financial crisis. The cities have always been somewhat disliked and mistrusted. Ancient poems by the Roman satirist Juvenal entitled "Against the City of Rome" document this assertion. In the medieval period, cities were a refuge for those who fled the existing social order, a role which won them more enemies than friends (Pirenne, no date). For some the excitement and opportunities of the urban area are still an almost irresistible magnet (Howe, 1973).

The current dislike of cities has not simply emerged from these historical trends. There are certain recent manifestations of the disfavor in which cities are held. One, of course, is the response to the civil disturbances of the sixties, an enflaming of the general suspicion of cities as a source of disorder. A second is the trend toward suburbanization, which has created a situation in which the relatively disadvantaged poor and minority oppressed—never the politically strongest groups—have become either the majority or a larger proportion of the central cities' population. Thus the political and economic clout of cities has diminished as new suburban areas have grown and taken much of the economic base with them. It is becoming increasingly clear that cities, in and of themselves, cannot sustain the diversity of population necessary to maintain the political base of support which will, in its own turn, command adequate resources. It is paradoxical but clearly accurate that as needs are increasing, as they have been in the cities, the means by which those needs can be met are decreasing.

The fact that most cities are impoverished and getting poorer creates—at least in this country—a further problem. Because of our ethics of individualism and "self-reliance," we seem to feel that the cities should somehow support themselves. Indeed, the paucity of urban policy at the time of the fiscal crisis in New York was indicated by the fact that the old "Vietnam vocabulary" was dusted off and applied as the phrase mongers went to work on the problem. The "domino theory" indicated that if New York fell, so would other cities. "No," it was argued, "we can contain the crisis." If the "infrastructure" of the New York municipal system really wanted to succeed—had the "will to win" (including cutting unnecessary services and staff)—then there would be no crisis ... and so on. The point is that the American society—out of guilt, fear, confusion, and the like—becomes discomfited in the face of need. We tend, in Ryan's (1971) classic phrase, to "blame the victim." The fact that cities were broke did not call forth sympathy; it called forth rebuke.

Roles for Community Practice

Never before in our history has the need for community practice been so great. Communities lie at the strategic crossroads between society and the family. The metropolitan structure of contemporary society points to the ecological interdependence of city and suburb. Yet we have not fully taken account of the crucial role the metropolitan region has come to play. Intervention strategies for practitioners operating at various levels—city planners; grass-roots organizers; interagency policy-makers, administrators, and program directors; unit supervisors, and so on—have become more elaborate and refined (Brager & Specht, 1976). More often than in the past, we have available basic approaches to metropolitan problems (be they transportation, health care, or discrimination) which may be effective. We can sketch out what such techniques as organizing service consumers, planning with professionals around improved delivery systems, or developing new policy perspectives may entail in relation to a single issue or question. The problem, however, is often how to move from one step to another in the general strategy.

Thus for practitioners, tactics which can tie the elements of strategy and goals together may be of foremost importance. At the same time, different settings and arenas (from the city block to public hearings at the state level) suggest the use of certain techniques. Documented experience and research now warrant collection and collation of materials on tactics and techniques of community practice. And surely the need for these tactics and techniques to be applied effectively is clear. What can the conceptual framework we have developed tell us about where, when, and how they might be used?

The Geographic Community

The territory provides a place or space around which community organization occurs. The special focus is organizing within locations and forging links across territorial boundaries. For example, in metropolitan society, community practitioners should keep in mind possible links between city and suburb. Notice that we did not use "merge" or "unite" or any other verb which suggests any specific form of relationship. The organizational and cultural communities in specific territories may have concerns (like racism) and hesitations (like economic exploitation) which must be taken into account. Nonetheless, neither the city nor the suburb can survive alone; greater integrity and strength must be developed within each, and this integrity and strength may be used as a new basis for forming cooperative relationships.

There are a host of specific problems—such as schooling, recreation, sewage, transportation, employment, crime, pollution—which do not respect political boundaries. These problems can be the focus of cooperation and interlinking. Community organizers, armed with a knowledge of the interdependence of the two systems, can establish the tactical means to provide the links.

The Subcultural Community

Subcultural communities, in which the unity that the members share results from a set of common beliefs and identifications, is a second focus of work. Common beliefs may arise from joining an association. More likely, though, they arise from membership in a group which shares a common experience. The cultural communities which are most familiar are religious, racial, ethnic, and those based upon sexual preference. The sense of commonality often comes from sharing an oppressed or ignored status. Often, an initial task in working with subcultural organizations is to expose and examine the link between social structure and the subcultural constellation of beliefs and values. Enhancing recognition of the similarity of positions in a subculture (i.e., women as housewives, sex objects, etc.) is another task of the community organizer within the cultural context. The achievement of this goal often comes through collective social action which serves to increase the resources of the group (i.e., marching for gay liberation). Joint action also encourages a sense of oneness and enhances competence in the ability of the group to influence events and decisions that affect them. Cultures and subcultures, of course, are not uniquely located in single territories, although they may be centered there. Thus, working with a subcultural group provides opportunities for territorial contacts (i.e., ethnic groups with major constituencies in both central cities and suburbs).

One reason the strengthening of local as contrasted with national subcultural groups is so important is that increased resources have become available to local groups as a result of recent national policy shifts. In spite of federal requirements demanding local participation in planning, little has been forthcoming. The generation of some new resources would provide the stimulus to further subcultural organization. As yet, a net increase in resources through federal revenue sharing and block grant programs, in the context of double digit inflation, has been minimal to nonexistent.

The Organizational Community

It might seem strange to consider that disorganization—or reorganization—is a role for community practitioners, but that is one of the roles the worker in a formal organization must consider. The benefits and resources available to (and through) formal organizations have led some to speculate that they would be the next major form of fundamental social structure, replacing the nation-state as a basis for loyalty and commitment, much as the nation-state replaced the feudal lord and his manor during the Middle Ages. While that seems to be a remote possibility, there is little question that the formal organization regularly exercises the most power among the three communities. Indeed, it is often so tightly organized that it has almost swamped the other structures with which it coexists and those that exist below and above it—the family and the society.

Thus, reorganization and creating countervailing organizations (e.g., in the form of unions or professional associations) become the key elements which may characterize community work in connection with formal organizations. The worker in the formal organization, rather than developing a sense of common linkage or raising consciousness and an emerging sense of potency, needs to emphasize the redistribution of benefits and powers in decision making, plus the development of a sense of community itself. Organizations do not think of themselves as communities; indeed, the word tends to convey to many organizational participants something which is antithetical to the crucial organizational values of profit making or competitive position. Yet the organization, as we have indicated, may be viewed as a powerful community which has an important effect on the lives of the members and others who are associated with it. It is perhaps not so clear that the organization affects those around it in the same sense that the territorial community does. As organizational analysts point out, the boundary of the organization is not limited to those who are employed by it or consume its services or products, but rather may include politicians, organizations providing similar goods or services, organizations providing the goods or services which the initial organization uses, the fiscal bodies which benefit (or do not benefit) from the taxes which it pays (or does not pay), and so on. While the limits of these territorial effects are not fully specified or clear, there can be little question that their impact may be quite serious and must be considered by the practitioner operating at the organizational or interorganizational level.

Linkages

We have referred to three communities and to a set of important areas in which community organizers should gain access. It now becomes clear that there is another important arena—providing linkages between territories, subcultures, and organizations, or the enhancement of the community system itself. It is here that a practitioner might well perform his or her most valuable function. As we have indicated, the three have crucial and important connections. Yet organizations tend to be unconcerned about territories or cultures, except to the extent that they have some rather short-range dollar or status implications. Many cultures are only beginning to realize their structural position within the organizational and territorial system (i.e., in relation to labor markets for Third World people and women). Finally, territories, which have been sensitive to the importance of other communities, are only now beginning to exploit this situation. With federal resources available on a geographic basis, metropolitan organizations, such as councils of governments, have more of a bargaining position than they had in the past.

Intercommunity links are only one of three sets of links which are necessary, however. These horizontal relationships must be matched by links between the community system and the family and societal systems. Litwak and Meyer (1974), for example, explored a portion of these linkages in their work on formal organizations and primary groups. This pioneering effort suggested that the importance of these relationships (in this particular case, between schools and families) had been overlooked. Yet we have only begun to develop the same perspective with respect to subcultural membership and families and territories and families. Interestingly, there is now a project, centered in George Washington University, which will attempt to see whether a link between the federal system and the family system can be developed through the mechanism of a "family impact statement." Such a statement, analogous to an environmental impact statement, would be developed as federal policy is proposed. While this idea may be long in coming to reality, it seems fundamentally sound and one which is firmly based on the need to consider potential relationships between communities and families.

Conclusion

In this introduction, we have suggested some of the processes of specialization and differentiation which are occurring in the American social system, and argued that the community is a structurally crucial part of it. The need for community integration, development, and change has never been greater. As keynoter Barbara Jordan put it at the Democratic National Convention in 1976, our belief in ourselves can be restored "if we restore the belief that we share a common national endeavor, if we restore our sense of national community. We are a people in search of a national community to fulfill our national purpose, to create and sustain a society in which all of us are equal." For practitioners—as planners, organizers, administrators, and policy-makers—who want to work in this direction, we offer this book as an aid to small steps along the road.

References

Beer, Samuel. "The Adoption of General Revenue Sharing." *Public Policy,* 24:2 (Spring 1976).

Brager, George, & Harry Specht. *Community Organizing.* New York: Columbia University Press, 1973.

Epstein, Joseph. *Divorced in America.* New York: E. P. Dutton, 1974.

Howe, Irving. "The City in Literature," in I. Howe, ed., *The Critical Point.* New York: Delta, 1973.

Humphries, R., Jr. *The Satires of Juvenal.* Bloomington: Indiana University Press, 1959.

Kornhauser, William. *The Politics of Mass Society.* Glencoe, Ill.: Free Press, 1959.

Lind, Roger, & John E. Tropman. "Delinquency Planning and Community Competence." Report to the Office of Juvenile Delinquency and Youth Development, Department of Health, Education and Welfare, No. 68–15. 1968.

Lipset, S. M. Talk Given at Greenfield Village, Dearborn, Michigan, Spring 1975.

Litwak, Eugene. "Geographic Mobility and Extended Family Cohesion," *Human Sociology Review,* 25 (June 1960). (a) "Occupational Mobility and Extended Family Cohesion." *Human Sociology Review,* 25 (February 1960). (b)

Litwak, Eugene, & Henry J. Meyer. *School, Family and Neighborhood.* New York: Columbia University Press, 1974.

Parsons, Talcott. *The Social System.* Glencoe, Ill.: Free Press, 1951.

Pirenne, Henri. *Medieval Cities.* New York: Anchor Books, n.d.

Rainwater, Lee, & William Yancy. *The Moynihan Report and the Politics of Controversy.* Cambridge, Mass.: M.I.T. Press, 1967.

Ryan, William. *Blaming the Victim.* New York: Pantheon, 1971.

Sjoberg, Gideon. "Community," in J. Gould and W. L. Kolb, eds., *Dictionary of the Social Sciences*. Glencoe, Ill.: Free Press, 1964.

Stein, Maurice. *Eclipse of Community*. Princeton: Princeton University Press, 1960.

Tonnies, Ferdinand. *Community and Society*. (trans. C. P. Loomis). East Lansing: Michigan State University Press, 1957.

Tropman, John E. "The Welfare Calculus." *Journal of Sociology and Social Welfare* II: 4 (Summer 1975).

Warren, Don. "The Middle American Radical." *Detroit Free Press,* May 9, 1976.

Wheelis, Alan. *The Quest for Identity*. New York: Norton, 1958.

**John E. Tropman, John L. Erlich,
and Fred M. Cox**

CHAPTER I

What's Going On: Assessing the Situation

Introduction

Getting started on a new job, perhaps in an unfamiliar community, is one of the most difficult—and most exciting—parts of community organizing and social planning. Getting one's bearings before being thrown into the full responsibilities of a job should be a top priority for the organizer or planner beginning work in a new neighborhood or community. There must be a period for orientation, relatively free from programmatic demands, with time to inquire in some depth about the kind of community one is confronted with, the problems it faces, the resources available to it, and the organizations serving its citizens. Without such time for reflection, practice is apt to be governed entirely by preconceived ideas, expedience, past habits of work, stereotyped attitudes, the insistent demands of a vocal minority, and accidental encounters with atypical situations.

It is our hope that the articles in this first chapter will help the practitioner make good use of that period when he or she is getting started in a new job or a new program. The late Robert K. Lamb, a member of the Department of History and English at the Massachusetts Institute of Technology, prepared a memorandum for his students entitled "Suggestions for a Study of Your Hometown" which was originally published about 25 years ago. His advice is as fresh and timely as the day it was written. His suggestions were used by such diverse groups as sales engineers in the fifties and Students for a Democratic Society in the sixties as a way of gaining an understanding of the social and, especially, the economic forces in a community. Though they are most readily applied in smaller communities, Lamb's suggestions have general application in communities of all sizes.

All practitioners, both organizers and planners, must get a grip on the needs of the communities they will serve. One way is simply to talk to people where they shop and work, go to school and play, and where they relax of an evening.

There is no real substitute for firsthand knowledge of people and their problems, their needs and hopes. But sometimes community workers, especially when planning a new program, applying for a grant, or convincing a sponsor to continue financial support, must go beyond the impressions and informal talk to demonstrate in a systematic way the existence of a problem, the prevalence of negative attitudes, or the effectiveness of a program. Under these conditions, a survey may be in order. Although he does not get into the technical aspects, Roland Warren describes the different ways in which surveys may be used and suggests a step-by-step guide for conducting a survey which uses ordinary citizens to do the work, with special emphasis on the human relations aspects of carrying out this complex task. It should be clear to every community organizer that conducting a survey may be one method of involving people with local problems and heightening and spreading a sense of concern and a desire to take corrective action.

A typical response of a community organizer to the question, "Where can we get the resources to carry out our program?" is "Apply for a grant." In these days of shrinking public resources for community work and most social programs, that answer may no longer be feasible. However, it may be possible to examine existing resources and develop plans for their redeployment. We are not suggesting that public or private social agencies and other organizations lightly drop programs and take on new ones, or divert resources from one program area to another casually. But there may be possibilities in the existing pattern of organizations and services that are untapped, and Michael Murphy provides a useful guide in exploring them.

As the practitioner gets closer to the organizations providing services, Yeheskel Hasenfeld's guide to exploring their potentialities and limits will have obvious utility. His detailed guide to the external relationships and internal features of human service organizations is an invaluable tool in assessing an agency's capabilities. With some experience the skillful practitioner will be able to adapt Hasenfeld's guide to other types of organizations in which there may be some interest—e.g., funding agencies and neighborhood associations.

A major library is a bewildering place for most organizers and planners. Most of us have little special training in using the library to obtain descriptions of communities or neighborhoods, to locate funding sources, or for any of the countless other purposes to which a well-equipped library may be put by a resourceful practitioner. Anne Beaubien, in a piece specially commissioned for this volume, has done a masterful job in pulling together the major library resources of interest to the community practitioner and detailing what the practitioner can expect to find in each resource. Organizers as well as planners should find this a very practical tool.

Assessment turns full circle when programs are put into operation and monitored. Questions of impact, cost, efficiency, and the like arise in every community effort. These matters are of such importance that a separate chapter of this book is devoted entirely to evaluating programs.

Fred M. Cox

1. Community Life: How to Get Its Pulse

Robert K. Lamb

SUGGESTIONS FOR A STUDY OF YOUR HOMETOWN

This memorandum is written as if you were visiting Hometown for the first time and as if your company or organization had instructed you to arrive as quickly as possible at a comprehensive knowledge of Hometown so that you might effectively represent it there. Towards the end of the memorandum I shall have something to say about the advantages you, with your long experience in the community, would have over a newcomer in your *own* Hometown.

To do this job of community-analysis there are certain tools you will obviously need. A map of Hometown is your first tool, for a brief glance at it will provide the trained eye with more facts than could be secured from any other source. (This of course depends upon the map; most street maps are featureless without an accompanying street directory).

Once upon a time, about 1890 or before, American street directories were even more useful than they are today, but they are still an indispensable part of any such investigation as this. There are three principal divisions of the average directory: (1) the alphabetical name section for individuals and business firms, organizations, etc.; (2) the street directory listing each house or building, and usually each separate family or business occupant of such buildings; (3) the classified advertising section. Most, if not all such directories also contain an introductory section in narrative style, containing facts about the town sta-

tistically arranged from the census and other sources; there is usually also a section devoted to the city government, giving the principal office holders, and often a great deal of detail about the personnel of the various city services.

For the fastest orientation it is ideal if you can find a series of older maps of the city (usually accessible at the public library) so that you can trace the characteristics of the city's growth.

Before you have gone much further with your investigation it will be advisable to learn more about the earlier inhabitants. For this purpose you will need another tool: one or more volumes of local history, usually to be found in the form of county-wide accounts of the history and biographies of the area, with sections devoted to the towns and cities in each county.

Other tools will be suggested later, but we shall start with those mentioned and see whether after a week in town we could arrive at any understanding of its social structure.

Let us start first with the county history. Here we shall assign fictitious names to typical characters. Sooner or later in the county history we will come across the name of Jedediah Early who was connected with the Early Trust Company; perhaps we shall also be able to establish that William A. Newcomer married one of the Early girls. If we can also connect the Early and Newcomer families with the foundation of the Hometown Manufacturing Company we have a good running start on a reconstruction of the way people have earned their living in Hometown for

Reproduced by permission of the Society for Applied Anthropology from *Human Organization* 11(2), 1952.

many years. This is, of course, a round-about way of approaching the matter. There are probably in the county history many names of families who have moved away, and others whose names have died out, at least in the direct line, although middle and even first names may survive.

The quickest way to find out where the major economic decisions are made in Hometown is to go to the public library and ask to see a copy of Rand-McNally's *Banker's Register* (if the library does not have it, go to one of the local banks). There you will find the names of all the Hometown banks as of the year of publication; however, because of the mortality of banks after 1929 there are great advantages in looking up two volumes: the current one and one prior to 1929. Take this list of banks and look up another publication, Moody's *Banks.* Here you will find the names of the directors of your Hometown banks, together with the history of the mergers which have taken place and which have contributed to the present condition of these banks. In this book there will also be found a current bank statement of assets and liabilities, and probably the dividend record.

Another set of tools becomes necessary: a card file. Some people prefer 3" x 5" cards because they are handy to carry; others use 5" x 8" because they provide more space for notations. Use one card for each bank and record the names of the directors on the ruled side and the history of the bank on the reverse, unruled side. Then make a separate card for each bank director, with his name (last name first) in the upper left-hand corner. Put his address if it is available on the top right, and his directorships (with his principal connection on top) in the middle. On the reverse side of the card record his personal history, date of birth and parentage at the top, marriage, children, education, etc.

These cards should be alphabetically filed in the boxes in which the cards were bought, thus dispensing with the added expense of buying special files.

Card files become your most important source of information, and you will find that it is necessary to cross-reference them constantly. They constitute the basic difference between our approach and that of the census-taker: we are primarily interested in individuals and their patterns of relationship, while he is interested in the overall statistical aggregates.

With the list of bank directors in hand, turn now to another tool volume: Poor's *Register of Directors.* Here are listed all the most important corporate directors in the United States. These men do not always record their directorships, but the listing is as complete as the editors are able to make it on the basis of their investigations. From Poor's *Register* you can find the *other* corporate directorates held by Hometown bank directors. This will lead you at once to the names of all important Hometown businesses, for banks tend to accumulate to themselves the leading financial and business talent in town. This method of analysis will be successful provided Hometown's bank is not part of a chain of banks which merely maintains a manager in your town. But unless your town is very small it did once have a bank, and not so very long ago, so that a study of earlier editions of the volumes cited above will reveal the names of Hometown's bank directors.

Such volumes as these may not be available in many cities and towns but if there is a university in the neighborhood its library may carry them; they should also be found in large city public libraries. In many cities there are often business libraries attached to the Chamber of Commerce, or elsewhere, and usually your Hometown banks subscribe to some or all of these publications. If, among its successful sons who have moved away, your town numbers a broker in some big city or a metropolitan banker, a letter to him may bring your library a copy of one or more of these volumes which although perhaps a few years out of date will still be useful for your general purposes. The names of the directors of your banks for the current year can be ascertained by asking the local bank for a copy of its annual statement, which is usually published in a small folder on the back cover of which is a list of the directors. Business connections which are not corporate, such as partnerships or firms, will usually be found in your street directory.

Turn now to the Hometown Manufacturing Company in your directory where the names of its officers and chief supervisory employees will probably appear. This will enable you to plot on the map the residences of superintendents or foremen, and operating management. You will find that while only the top men live on High Street or in "Hills and Dales," the others often tend to live as close to these neighborhoods as they can afford, the older men nearer High Street, the younger nearer "Hills and Dales."

A number of directories also designate the place of employment of those who work in the Hometown Manufacturing Company by some such mark as "Hometown Mfg.," for example. This will enable you to plot on the map the residences of those employed at the factory. When the craft or special skill of the worker is also indicated, as it is in most directories, you can find out where the several grades of workers live. (It should be understood that the word "grades," as used here, has a purely technical usage, such as "machinist" or "foremen," and is a means of distinguishing the probable wage received, since this tends to determine what rent workers can pay, and other economic facts we are trying to establish.)

Once you have begun to accumulate cards for individual residents in different parts of the city, and have marked their cards according to their occupations, you are on the way to the preparation of a residential map of the city. It will be advisable to devise a system of symbols to designate the different income grades and occupational groups, and attach them to individual residents on the map in order to show the approximate location of their homes on the streets of the city.

Incidentally, if you are enterprising, one map bought from the local bookseller who handles the Hometown street directories will enable you to trace any number of copies on transparent paper. Once you have plotted on your maps the location of your bank directors, corporation directors, superintendents, foremen, and workers in the factory, you are ready to branch out into a neighborhood-by-neighborhood investigation of Hometown; this will include its churches, neighborhood and nationality clubs, formal and informal social groups, political and business groups, etc.

Such an investigation will lead you back in the direction of your census materials, which are also to be found in the public library. But the model for the investigation is not to be found in the census, but in the publications of social workers. For information about census tracts it will be necessary to approach someone connected with a public or private charity, or a governmental office dealing with welfare or relief. In many cities (and their number is increasing), students have made area studies of the different neighborhoods, showing the number of cases of one sort or another falling in a given area; types of sickness, law violations, social maladjustments such as juvenile delinquency, have been indicated area by area on city-wide maps. This is one of the most fruitful parts of any study you may make of Hometown. However, these findings must be considered very carefully and you should avoid arriving at a hasty conclusion on the basis of any one type of case as it appears on the map.

From this wealth of material, a comprehensive pattern of neighborhood distribution of these various groups will emerge. By turning to the street section of your Hometown directory you may be able to discover whether or not the resident is a home-owner and sometimes whether he has a telephone. This information will help to confirm your guesses about income status. By working back and forth between the street section and the alphabetical section of your volume, you will be able to verify your sampling on a street by street basis. In this way you will soon know a great deal about the distribution of Hometown population—group by group—and income—class by class. If your company were interested, for example, in a door-to-door selling campaign, this information would be of considerable help.

For some purposes it may be necessary for your company to know the national origins of different groups in the community. In past times many of these groups tended to live in their own separate neighborhoods and to develop separate national institutions, such as churches, parochial schools, clubs and organizations of one kind and another. Increasingly these distinctions arising from national origin are breaking down in this country. The younger generation is tending to move out to newer suburban developments where they mingle with people of other national origins. This is part of the "melting pot" of which the Americans are so properly proud. A study of your Hometown map as prepared by the method described above will reveal, however, that the "melting"

process is far from complete in many communities.

Any study of local politics will reveal that politicians are highly aware of group differences of all kinds, including those just described, and that they are a factor in the political, social and economic life of the community. By turning to the first section of your Hometown directory where information about City Hall and other city services is listed, a card file can be made on the political structure of Hometown. A study of this file will show that it reflects some of the divisions within the community, as already indicated in the foregoing.

The life of most communities is still dominated to a large extent by the oldest inhabitants and their descendants. Usually they exercise the chief influence on the boards of local banks, and insofar as businesses are locally owned they tend to retain a controlling interest. But today this is by no means a universal pattern since the influence of out-of-town corporations has become more and more important in all but the leading cities of the country. As a first approximation we can say that the social system of a community (with its various organizations, such as the Community Chest, Red Cross, etc.) leans heavily upon the families of those long established in the community; the economic leadership is drawn from the ranks of newer individuals and groups; and the political leadership is even more frequently in the hands of the representatives of newer groups.

To understand the social system of the community insofar as it can be distinguished from the political and economic systems, it is usually necessary to begin with the churches as the oldest, local, social institutions. These are in turn distributed throughout the community, and a map showing their location will be very instructive and assist in pointing up some of your other findings. Since most churches are not only religious but neighborhood social organizations, incorporating many non-religious activities, a study of the leadership of these sub-groups within the church will also contribute to your understanding of the community.

Any young businessman coming to the city for the first time and expecting to establish residence there will want to know about the other social and charitable organizations, their functions and their representation of various groups. Some of these can be called "total community" organizations, for instance the Community Chest, or, within the business community, the Chamber of Commerce. Others are representative of special groups in the community. One of the most significant keys to the social grading system is to be found in the structure of the more exclusive clubs. There is usually a club to which only the older inhabitants are admitted, and their method of choosing even among this older group displays their attitude as to the necessary qualifications for membership in the inner circle of their group. If you can secure a list of their membership and compare it with other parts of the social structure, such as leadership in total community organizations, churches, charities, and clubs, you will have a useful key to the relationship between the older and newer groups in town.

In this type of study it is easy to lose sight of the fact that getting a living is the backbone of community life and that the jobs held by men and women are bound to be the ruling factors in their lives. The increase of absentee ownership of factories and stores, and even of newspapers and banks in towns and cities of the United State, makes it more and more difficult to understand the patterns of organization of individual communities. To find out what is happening to these plants and businesses

you need new tool volumes. For industries, consult Moody's (or Poor's) *Industrials*. One or the other of these will give you a picture of the extent to which your local factory is still locally controlled, or to what extent control has passed to out-of-town groups. While these sources are adequate for our present purposes, if a really extensive study of these matters were being made, it would be necessary to consult the records of the Securities and Exchange Commission in Washington. If the language used is unfamiliar, some acquaintance who has experience with reading such source material should be called upon for help. Here you may find that the local company (though still locally owned) has perhaps undergone a series of mergers prior to arriving at its present size; if you are interested in the historical aspects of the community it will be worthwhile studying the companies that merged to form the existing one. The story of your local industries is paralleled by what has happened to your local, privately-owned electric light, gas, water, and street transportation system or systems. A similar tool volume is available for investigation of these companies in Moody's (or Poor's) *Public Utilities*. All of these facts should be recorded on file cards and properly catalogued.

In a short space of time you will now have gathered a very comprehensive picture of the life of Hometown. (The size of the community will of course determine the length of time this job will take, although much will depend upon your previous experience in making such studies.) I venture to say that you will know many things about the community which might have escaped your notice even if you had lived there all your life. Nevertheless there are many things you cannot find out by these mechanical methods. The most important facts which tend to elude this approach are of a personal order. It is essential to live long years in a community in order to be aware of some of the most important of these facts. As an outside observer, or even one who has had a short residence in the community, you cannot hope to find a completely adequate substitute for this experience. However, as the representative of your company, you are expected to find a short-cut which will be the best possible substitute for such long residence.

The best substitute for your own long residence is to gain access to certain of the oldest inhabitants. Experience will show that there are certain people in the community, not always members of the socially elect group but frequently drawn from among them, whose type of mind reproduces the patterns we have just described, without resort to our complicated methods. Frequently these individuals have recently retired from the most influential positions in the community and are still active in the local historical society. If you are properly introduced and they respect you as a scientific investigator and believe you have the best interests of the community at heart, they will often be of invaluable assistance to you in providing that type of information which can generally come only from a lifetime knowledge of their town or city. You will do well to try to find at least one such person (and if possible several) who is willing to assist you and who will talk to you freely. By working with more than one of these individuals you will be able to triangulate your results and so avoid some of the inevitable effects of bias. Even the most objective of these persons is bound to see the life of his community from a slightly different vantage point than would any other such observer. You must learn to make allowances for these differences of point of view.

If you, the reader, are yourself a lifelong resident of Hometown, you will be able to supply the same sort of information as this oldest inhabitant, and will want to correct your bias by the methods I have described. Nevertheless a lifelong resident will have a great advantage over our supposed representative of an out-of-town company. You will know, for example, who married whom, and what the grandparents and even the great-grandparents of many of your fellow residents contributed to the life of the community. Without having to make maps of the historical growth of the community, you will know at what point in time which suburbs developed, and just when different local businesses came under out-of-town control.

Without referring to the files of the local newspapers (which by the way are indispensable to our visitor-observer) or having to talk to the local newspaper editors, you will know just which events in the life of Hometown are of the greatest importance in the estimation of its citizens. You will know when crises arose in the life of the community and how they were solved. You will know what effect the depression and mass unemployment had on the town or city and what happened when labor tried to organize the local plants and businesses. Above all, you will know the personalities and dispositions of the human beings who make up Hometown, and you will realize what an important part such personal traits can play in the average community. In short, these mechanical methods I have recommended are bound to produce a de-humanized picture. It is essential for the observer to try to restore the characteristics of a living community, with its hopes and fears, its shared pleasures and its sorrows.

One of the most elusive things you must try to understand is "community spirit," and in this connection you must attempt to discover what individuals or groups in the community hold the symbols of community leadership at any given time.

Outside of the churches there are two places to look for the symbols of community integration. One of these focal points is the cemetery and the other is the patriotic organization. No community, modern or ancient, can be understood without reference to these two sets of facts. It has been said that "the most important people in Hometown are dead." Even to American society, with its gaze fixed upon expansionism and the future, ancestors are of great symbolic importance. If ancestors in general are important, those who participated in our military history are of great significance. Certain patriotic organizations in each community tend to be regarded by the rest of the community as safeguarding the symbols of patriotism. It is necessary to study the structure of these patriotic organizations as an important

factor in the advancement of Hometown life, to be present on the day of their most symbolic activity, Memorial Day, and watch the course taken by the parade— from High Street down through the business section of the town and out to the oldest cemetery. This will usually contribute many useful facts about the nature of community spirit.

All this is bound to sound like an overwhelming job; for the largest cities, of course, it is much too great an undertaking for any single individual to carry out in a reasonable period of time, even as a first approximation. Nevertheless, if you will re-read these proposals with care you will find ways and means for short-cutting and sampling, depending upon the size of your community; after operating with this outline for only a few weeks, the characteristics of your community will take on new significance even if you have lived there all your life.

2. Community Needs: How to Identify And Understand Them

Roland L. Warren

ORGANIZING A COMMUNITY SURVEY

Often during the discussion of a community problem, someone suggests, "Let's have a survey," and the other members of the group, perhaps knowing no other positive course of action, give their assent. A survey may or may not be indicated for the type of program you have in mind. We present below some considerations which

Reproduced by permission of the publisher, Russell Sage Foundation, New York, New York. From Roland L. Warren, *Studying Your Community,* © 1965, pp. 306–322.

might be weighed before reaching a decision.

1. Are the facts you need already available in usable form? If so, the time and money and energy spent in making a survey might possibly be put to better use in an action program, that is, in doing something to improve the existing conditions.

2. Is the survey likely to be a substitute for action? Often a survey is merely a

mode of temporizing about a problem which everyone knows exists and about which there is adequate factual information to form a basis for an action program. People sometimes choose a survey so as to postpone or avoid action. Occasionally the survey is undertaken with a view toward action, but so much time and effort are spent in making an exhaustive survey that there is little energy remaining to do anything about the results.

3. Is your group an "action group"? If it wants to see definite results and to work hard in a constructive program of community action, then perhaps it should confine itself to a brief survey. In one type the procedure is simply to ask the people of a community to fill out slips stating what they think are the worst things about the community, and what they think might be done to improve it. This simple procedure often yields interesting suggestions and indicates how widely held are some of the viewpoints expressed. The suggestions received are often sufficient to keep an active group occupied for years in community improvement projects, although there may be a need for modifying the program to meet changing situations.

If your group is eager to go into action, it is important that the action be carefully thought out. Often more extensive study of the situation is required than is at first apparent. For example, some people may suggest the need for a local mental health clinic. It may be unwise to embark immediately upon a campaign to raise the necessary funds, for a survey may show that there is not a large enough population to support such a clinic, or that the clinic would actually cost many times more than was originally supposed. It may be possible to join forces with some other community and share a clinic, or there may be other ways of securing the needed services.

The point here is that premature action in carrying out suggestions may be highly wasteful and inopportune.

The survey is not, and should not be, an end in itself. If the purpose is merely to assemble useful information for referral by anyone who cares to consult it, then the survey should be so planned and conducted. If it is to be part of an action program, then it should be so oriented, and only the material necessary should be solicited. Knowledge about the community has value if it is used only as an aid in the normal discharge of the duties of citizenship; or it may lead to more definite, enterprising action toward community betterment. In any case, the survey is not the end product; it is a tool to work with. The end product is a healthy, vital, growing community whose citizens are alert to its needs and possibilities and active in building the type of community they want.

DIFFERENT KINDS AND USES OF SURVEYS

The term "survey" is used with a variety of meanings. It can denote an extensive study of the needs and resources of a large community involving a large staff and extending over many months' duration, or it can denote a brief and superficial study of the "situation" of a particular organization or agency. Between these extremes lie a multitude of possibilities, and the person who is interested in making a survey will want to have a clear idea of just what he hopes to accomplish.

Experience has shown that surveys usually involve much more work and time than is anticipated. Even surveys of relatively small communities often occasion surprise on the part of laymen when they learn that their community is so complicated, or that it supports so many organizations, business establishments, and so on. And a survey of a metropolitan community may involve scores of volunteer workers headed by a professional staff of survey consultants over a period of months and even years.

The reader may want to consider some of the possibilities in survey work. He can thus measure his own or his group's resources against the size of the community and breadth of the proposed survey, and make a reasonable disposition of effort.

Surveys Can Be Primarily For Information or For Action

Surveys are often conducted with no particular end in view. Groups of high-school or college students in social studies classes occasionally study their local community as a sort of social laboratory. Or members of a women's club may set out to study the local community to inform themselves on its government or some other aspect.

Such surveys have definite value. They provide learning experience for the participants, stimulate awareness of community conditions and problems, and afford a useful body of factual knowledge for those interested in learning more about their community. It is not at all unusual for such studies to lead to action as needs are uncovered and possibilities for remedial measures present themselves. Indeed, some survey chairmen find that their survey committees have become so absorbed in a particular problem which they have uncovered that they prefer to remedy this problem than to complete the survey. There is no reason why a survey group must refrain from action completely, but, of course, care should be taken that the energies of the participants do not become diffused with every new problem which presents itself.

Usually the purpose of surveys of any

size is to stimulate remedial programs to correct such serious deficiencies in the community structure as are found to exist. A long history of social surveys indicates that if action is considered a primary objective of the survey, early planning is necessary. It is not essential to foresee the survey results, but it *is* important to develop citizen interest that will bring about action. Many excellent factual surveys gather dust because the broad base of citizen support, or the organizational and agency base for action programs, was not developed. One of the best ways to avoid this is to involve in the survey process the people and agencies that will be called upon later to support and implement the survey findings.

Sometimes a community survey is one of the first activities of a new community betterment organization. Although the survey has no specific end in view, the thought is that from it will come definite programs of action which the new organization can stimulate. Community councils have a long record of such stimulation. One such organization in Kentucky reported a list of 115 different activities, large and small, which were initiated as citizens organized, surveyed their needs, and took action.[1]

A term which is often applied to a somewhat different type of survey-action program is the "community self-survey." Used in this narrower sense, the term denotes a study of discriminatory practices in the community with remedial action as an integral part of the program. Of course, the term is also used in its broader meaning to denote any community self-study activity.

There is a continuous line of possibilities

---

[1] The London-Laurel County Development Association. See *Start Now . . . A Community Development Program,* 2d ed. (Louisville: Kentucky Chamber of Commerce, 1951).

between two extreme types of survey activity. At the one extremity is a survey conducted by outside experts, which is scientifically accurate and reliable, but is destined only for the library shelves. At the other, is an unscientific, hastily put-together survey of community needs; a survey short on facts and long on generalizations but enthusiastically carried into action by a well-organized, high-spirited citizens' group. But there is no reason why widespread, interested participation and support should be separated from scientific accuracy, and no reason why an enthusiastic desire for action should militate against the validity of the study.

Surveys Can Cover the Whole Community or Merely One Aspect of It

A decision will have to be made as to whether the community is to be studied in its manifold aspects or whether the survey is to be confined to only one area of community activity, such as economic conditions, welfare, or education.

It is well to keep in mind that the more extensive the survey is, the more people or time will be needed. Also, generally speaking, the larger the community, the more time-consuming is the survey task. If the purpose is simply to help the surveyors learn more about their community, they may choose between an extensive but somewhat superficial survey and a more intensive survey limited to one particular field. However, if the material gathered is to be used as a valuable source of facts about the community, if important decisions are to be made on the basis of the survey findings, or if the desire is to become thoroughly familiar with some aspect of the community, a limited but intensive survey may be indicated. In any case, a certain amount of general data

about the community will have to be gathered.

Many surveys which are thought to be comprehensive are actually somewhat limited in scope. They may comprise data which are chiefly of an economic nature, or they may be limited to needs and resources in the health, welfare, recreation, and education fields, omitting important economic or physical aspects of the community.

Even a single aspect of the community, such as health, may be too broad as a survey topic. If so, the effort may be confined to a study of public health facilities, or hospitals, or medical care, or facilities for and care of the chronically ill, or children. Obviously such limited topics can be studied adequately only by considering their setting in the whole health picture, and indeed in the whole community picture. It is simply a question of emphasis and the degree of intensiveness desired.

Surveys Can Be Designed to Canvass a Particular Need

Some surveys arise as part of the program of an interested group to improve the community's facilities in one or another of its aspects. A women's group may be interested in determining whether it should go ahead in promoting a child day care center, or a citizens' organization may be studying the desirability of a new school building program, or another group may be studying the problem of juvenile delinquency with a view toward improving the probation system. Early determination of the specific purpose of the survey can be of great help in formulating the survey plan so that it will yield the type of information desired without needless excursions into by-roads which are not relevant to the problem. However, in perhaps no other type of survey is there greater possibility of inaccurate information or biased conclusions. The temptation is to be like the club president who said, "We want to make an objective study and prove why we need a new clinic!" Such studies should always be undertaken tentatively, with the strong possibility that as the study progresses those interested may find that their earlier conception of what the community needed is not warranted by the facts.

One of the chief advantages of such a study, over and above the information gathered, is that the study itself often becomes part of an action program. That is to say, the interested participation of many citizens in ferreting out the facts, their experience in "seeing the conditions with their own eyes," and the publicity given to the problem by the study procedure itself, may all contribute to stimulating public interest in the needs and assuring that action will result from the study.

Surveys Can Be Made by Volunteers or Professionals

The advantages of volunteer surveys are that they are generally less expensive; many citizens have an opportunity to learn more about their community; the results may be more readily accepted because they are not the work of "outsiders who don't understand that this community is different"; and enthusiasm and interest may be generated during the course of the survey which will help carry over into action.

The advantages of the professional survey are that there is less waste of time, much more likelihood of getting the type of information which is available and needed without overlooking important sources of relevant data, and above all, scientific validity. Professional survey personnel are usually well equipped for fact-gathering and making analyses. This fact of itself does not assure their competence in *evaluation* of services in any particular field such as child welfare or education. Some professional survey specialists are, of course, well qualified for evaluation in specific fields of community services.

Where a survey is to be made in a community of any considerable size, a large number of workers will be needed unless the work is to be extremely superficial. A growing practice is to have the survey conducted by local people, with an outside survey specialist giving expert advice. Such a professional consultant can help the survey group formulate its plans and organize for the undertaking, assure that the data gathered will be objective and in usable form, and also help in evaluating the findings. In addition to the help given by the consultant the fact that he is an "outsider" fosters confidence generally in the impartiality of the survey and reassures the survey group itself. Nevertheless, there are limitations to what the consultant can accomplish. The bulk of the work must still be done by local people. Caution should be exercised in regard to accepting "package plans" for surveys, plans made up in advance and utilized elsewhere, which may or may not be feasible for the local community.

Since nationally affiliated organizations often conduct larger surveys, they may be able to obtain professional consulting service from their national headquarters. Examples would be a local welfare council, which could get help through any number of national organizations, or a local League of Women Voters or chamber of commerce. If there is no such national affiliation involved, it is possible, depending on the type of survey, to get help from the appropriate department or agency of the state government. This is particularly true of the state or agricultural college, or the state department of commerce. Various state or national private organizations may be willing to lend a hand. The survey conducted by volunteer citizens with professional leadership often combines the advantages of the volunteer survey with those afforded by the professional research team.

There are three aspects of the community in which the gathering of facts for planning is widespread. They are: (a) industrial development, (b) planning the physical aspects of the community, and (c) health and welfare planning.... In all such activity, community survey work is called for.

The existence of the three types of planning described above is important for several reasons. First, much information about one of these aspects of the community may be available through the local industrial development commission, city planning commission, or health and welfare council. Second, an organization in one or all of these three fields may, itself, be the appropriate body to carry out the particular survey in which the reader is interested. At least, the organization exists, and presumably it is equipped for factgathering in its field. It should not be ignored. Third, the reader should keep in mind that each of these organizations is typically concerned with only a limited aspect of the community, so that in a sense there is no assurance that any of them represents a communitywide point of view. With this in mind, the reader is less likely to be deflected into following the conventional pattern of community study carried on under any of these auspices unless it suits his purpose.

STEPS IN A CITIZENS' SURVEY

This section is designed for readers in small or medium-sized communities or in neighborhoods or districts of large communities who want to survey the whole community in comprehensive fashion with a view toward making recommendations and encouraging community action on such recommendations. The plan given here should be considered merely as a series of suggestions based on experience. Considerable modification may be advisable in adapting it to any particular community.

Determining the Scope and Size

Here are some of the questions you will want to consider:

What is the size of the "community" you want to study?

How many people can you count on to help with the work of the survey?

How much time do you want to devote to the survey?

How thorough do you want it to be?

An intensive survey of even a small community, say, a village of 1,500 people and its surrounding area, should keep many people occupied over a period of several months. If your survey seems too extensive a task for your group, you can expand the group, get additional help, study a smaller geographic area, or narrow the topic of your survey.

The Sponsorship of the Survey

It is important that some organization sponsor the survey, for the following reasons:

1. To lend the survey prestige and give it some standing in the community;
2. To organize and launch the survey committee;
3. As a source of volunteer workers;

4. To provide funds for survey expenses and to provide for possible publication and distribution of the survey report.

The sponsoring organization can be a local service club, the local chamber of commerce, or a church, women's club, farm bureau, or like organization. Frequently the question of who will sponsor the survey answers itself because the idea develops within a particular organization which more or less automatically comes to be the sponsor. Sometimes the organization which develops the idea may not be the proper one to sponsor the survey, for it may be too small or insufficiently representative of the community, or it may not have sufficient prestige, or it may be without adequate funds to undertake the responsibility, and so on. Careful thought should be given to the sponsoring organization, for community attitudes toward the organization may be transferred to the survey. Is the organization considered to represent only one particular economic group? Is it considered to prefer its own selfish interests to those of the larger community? If this organization is sponsor, will large segments of the community feel alienated? Can this organization act as sponsor without "taking over" the survey and using it merely for its own aggrandizement or to promote the special economic interests of its members?

Sometimes no organization exists which adequately reflects the various interests and groups in the community and which can act for the community because it is broadly representative of it. As a result, it may seem wise to form an organization along the lines of a "community council." Such an organization, whatever it is called in the local community, is a logical sponsor for a community survey, and indeed the survey committee may be a committee of this community council. If such an organization does not exist, it is often formed as part of the process of organizing a survey.

The Cost of the Survey

Surveys of small communities conducted by groups of local volunteers need not be costly. Two major items should be kept in mind. Even though the services of a survey consultant may be given free by a national agency or the extension service of the state university or a department of the state government, it may be necessary to pay the consultant's expenses, which may be considerable over a period of time. This matter should be ascertained, and plans should be made accordingly. Another sizable item may be the publication of the survey report. If the survey findings are to be given wide attention, it is definitely advisable to plan for a mimeographed or printed report.

Below is an outline suggested for use in estimating the expenses of the small survey:

Postage, paper, and other supplies
Secretarial work, such as typing, mimeographing, filing, mailing, unless such service is to be donated
Travel, perhaps to gather data at the county seat, or to canvass farmers within the trade area, or for other reasons
Expenses or fees for a survey consultant
Expenses, if any, of renting meeting halls for such communitywide meetings as may be held
Expenses of publishing and mailing the survey report
Other expenses

Organizing the Survey Committee

Certain principles should be kept in mind in organizing the survey committee itself.

First, it should be comprised of persons

who represent different groups in the community, and who, if possible, are familiar with the general aspect of the community under study.

Second, the survey committee should be divided into subcommittees according to the major outlines of the study. Thus, there may be one subcommittee for the economic aspects of the community, another for government, another for health, another for welfare, another for education, and so on. Perhaps six or seven such topical categories would be a good number. The chapter topics of the present book can be combined into the number desired. If the study is limited to one of these topics, the subcommittees can each be responsible for one aspect of the topic.

Each subcommittee may consist of several persons, with one acting as chairman. In larger communities, it may be judicious to turn over each separate topic to an appropriate organization within the community, and let it take responsibility for gathering the information. Thus, the topic of health may be assigned to a health organization; the topic of economic activities, to the chamber of commerce or a service club; the topic of education, to a parent-teacher association; and so on. In this process, care must be taken to safeguard the accuracy and objectivity of the survey, and to avoid any distortion of it by groups who want to promote their own objectives. In smaller communities an individual, rather than a subcommittee, may be charged with gathering the facts in each branch of the survey.

The Survey Chairman

The chairman of the survey should see that each committee has clearly in mind the purpose and procedure of the whole study and its own part in it, ascertain that the various subcommittees are assembling their information according to schedule, help to iron out any personality clashes, bolster up any branch of the survey that bogs down, and, finally, assemble the results and perhaps draft the final report, subject to the approval of the whole committee. Needless to say, it is advisable that the chairman of the survey committee should be someone experienced in survey work or at least in some field of endeavor where objectivity and accuracy are called for, someone whose point of view is broad rather than that of some special group, and one who commands wide respect and is skillful in human relations.

A professional survey expert may be called in to direct the survey, or such a person may be engaged as a consultant. Where a special expert is asked to direct the entire study, he will take over the direction of the actual mechanics of the survey, while the local chairman of the survey committee will function administratively as committee chairman.

Preparing the Survey Forms

The survey forms list the questions which are to be answered and the information which is to be filled in. These forms should be prepared in advance of the actual field work. Each subcommittee chairman should have a complete set of forms to be filled out by his subcommittee, in such quantities as are needed. For example, the subcommittee on churches will solicit certain information from each church. All the kinds of information to be solicited from each church should be assembled in question form and then sufficient copies made so that a worker can fill one out for each church. The effort spent in planning these forms to facilitate tabulation will be well rewarded. Care should be taken that a suitable amount of space is provided for the answers.

It is probably needless for any community to start completely from scratch in making up its forms. There are many different survey outlines available for certain aspects of the community, such as health, recreation, delinquency, and so on. . . .

Unevenness of intensity in the survey should be avoided, unless there is special reason for studying one aspect of the community more thoroughly than others. Since all of the data will be gathered according to the forms which are prepared, the survey committee can assure itself even before the field work commences that it is covering each aspect of the community with the appropriate degree of intensity.

Conducting the Field Work

If adequate time and care have been devoted to preparation and to getting the various parts of the community behind the survey effort, the field work will be facilitated. Organization of the survey around the principle of joint participation by various organizations in the community should assure the cordial reception of the field workers as they go from one center of information to another. Nevertheless, it is important that the field workers be given careful instructions as to how to conduct their work. Sources of information already compiled should first be combed and the available material recorded insofar as possible before the field interviews commence. This will enable the interviewers to be reasonably well informed and will avoid bothering busy people unnecessarily. Material gathered in interviews should be recorded as precisely as possible. This will be easier if most of the survey forms are of such a nature as to request definite answers to specific questions, rather than requiring extensive comment and interpreta-

tion. However, care should be taken not to record purely categorical answers, such as "yes" or "no," when they are misleading unless qualified.

It should be impressed upon the field workers that accuracy is not only desirable but necessary if the survey results are to be worthwhile.

The matter of neatness in the recording of data is much more important than it may seem. Frequently the temptation is to scribble so as not to prolong the interview, or to copy figures too rapidly so as to speed up the tedious job of extracting material from official records. Illegibility makes for wasted time in retraced steps, and militates against accuracy. All material should be labeled sufficiently so that any member of the survey group can identify and use it. Unidentified data are a menace to the accuracy of the survey and a constant source of frustration to all concerned. All figures and facts should be checked against the original source after they have been recorded.

When all the forms which will require tabulation are completed, the work of tabulation can begin. Tables should be clearly labeled. They should be checked when completed, and any individual item on which there was a question concerning the way it should be classified should be marked and indication given as to how it actually was tabulated. When the statistical work has been completed, the total amounts, averages, and other statistical measures can be incorporated into the report, along with such tables as are thought desirable to reproduce.

Writing the Survey Report

In the case of a small survey, the survey director or someone who has been directly connected with the entire survey process should write the report. In larger surveys, each subcommittee chairman may draft the report of the work of his subcommittee. The report should be written in a simple, direct style without the use of technical jargon but also without "talking down" to the reader. Charts and other illustrations often help to clarify important points.[2] Documentary photographs are particularly effective in presenting to the reader some of the conditions which the report seeks to emphasize. The various charts in this book are designed to furnish the reader with suggestions for graphic illustration of the survey report. The numerous plot maps which have been suggested in connection with various chapters may in some cases become a valuable graphic supplement to the verbal report.

Presumably, the facts gathered will be much more voluminous than can be handled in a summary report; therefore careful selection of data should be made so as not to obscure any of the important findings.

Depending on the purposes and nature of the survey, there may be a section on "chief findings" or "recommendations," or both. One possibility would be to put a brief section on "chief findings" at the beginning, right after the acknowledgments, and a section on "recommendations" at the end. Some prefer to start out with the recommendations, then give the supporting data as the body of the report. Another possibility is to have a section on appropriate recommendations at the end of each topic covered in the report. Sometimes both "findings" and "recommendations" are briefly summarized at the beginning of the report.

Whatever acknowledgments of help and cooperation are appropriate should be

[2] See Modley, Rudolf, and Dyno Lowenstein, *Pictographs and Graphs: How to Make and Use Them,* (New York: Harper and Bros., 1952).

made at the beginning of the report. Mention may be made of the participating organizations, the survey committee, the field workers and other helpers, the government officials and agency heads on whom great demands for help were made, any outside agency which lent aid, and so on.

It is highly desirable that all major findings and recommendations be reviewed by the officials and organization or agency heads to whose work they pertain, and that they approve of the manner in which these findings and recommendations are presented. Sometimes this desirable result cannot be brought about, but it should be sought earnestly.

Publicity and Follow-Up

Publicity is important particularly at the beginning of the survey process and at the end. At the beginning, publicity will aid in achieving communitywide support or participation. It will prepare the way for the field workers, in that their informants will already know about the survey and will receive them graciously.

During the survey, publicity can serve to sustain interest, to give credit to individuals and organizations that are actively helping in one phase or another, and to prepare the community for the report. Publicity should not be thought of only in terms of newspapers, but also radio, TV, letters and speeches to organizations, and so on.

As the survey is brought to a conclusion, sometimes a meeting or a series of meetings is held to acquaint the interested individuals and organizations in the community with the findings and recommendations.

A plan to be recommended is the holding of a communitywide meeting to coincide with the distribution of copies of the survey report. This makes an occasion of the distribution of the reports, and brings together the people and organizations that are most interested, for it is upon them that follow-through depends. Such a meeting may be a dinner meeting. In any case, the chairman of the survey committee or some other appropriate person can give a speech reviewing briefly the history of the survey and then the major findings and recommendations can be presented. Copies of the report itself can be distributed. The press should be invited to this meeting.

If the sponsoring agency or the survey committee intends to follow through and try to stimulate action on the recommendations, this meeting can be part of the initial stages of the follow-up. Whatever organizational steps are indicated may be taken. The survey committee may be terminated at this point, and a follow-up organization activated. The survey committee and the sponsoring organization may see their job only as one of fact-finding. In this case the carrying out of the recommendations will be left to the appropriate community agencies and organizations.

Plans should be made to mail the report to certain persons who did not attend the meeting but should be apprised of the survey findings, and to publicize the fact that copies of the report are available on request.

If it is possible to interest the newspapers or radio or TV stations in publicizing different aspects of the findings and recommendations over a period of time, this will do much to get the findings before the people who might not otherwise be informed. Copies of the report should be displayed, if possible, in schools, libraries, and other places where they may be consulted.

HUMAN RELATIONS IN SURVEY WORK

Whether intentionally or not, community surveys are all ventures in human relations, an aspect of survey work which can be ignored only at the surveyor's peril. This section will give some suggestions on human relations specifically related to the survey task. They are derived from generally accepted principles of human relations which have arisen out of the experience of countless community workers. They are merely applications of certain basic truths about human beings, in our culture at least. We all like a little praise; we all want to keep and enhance our self-respect; we have our own group loyalties and cultural values; we like to have the situation fully explained to us; and we usually respond when we feel our contribution is really wanted.

Obtain Broad Representation on the Survey Committee. Most communities show broad groupings of interest and association. They should not be ignored. For example, in a rural community it is easy to forget the farmers. Be sure the Grange, Farm Bureau, Home Bureau, and such organizations are represented. Similarly, do not let your committee be composed exclusively of any particular income or education group.

Use the Principle of Participation. People usually throw themselves into a project when they have made a contribution to it that is considered important. Let it be their survey, let them help plan it, determine its goals, carry out the procedures, review the findings, consider the recommendations, and they will be more likely to support it actively.

Understand the Role of Leaders. Try to put the "natural" leaders in positions of actual leadership. Avoid "cliquishness" if possible. Don't assign someone to leadership who is not capable of fulfilling the task. Not all people take leadership naturally. Avoid people who antagonize their associates by being domineering. Democratic leadership does not involve doing things for people who are able to do these things for themselves. On the other hand, democratic leadership does not demand chaos. There is often a tendency to equate ineffectiveness with democracy. People in a group need clarity of purpose, a common "definition of the situation." In this, the leader must take responsibility.

Be Patient in Encountering Resistance. You may find people who do not want to cooperate, who want to withhold the required information, who deprecate the study, or who in other ways show resistance. Patience and forbearance in doing what is called for will often win their support. They may need reassurance that no one is out to "get" them or their department. They may simply be taking their own way of showing their resentment at having been ignored in the planning stages, or at this intrusion on their time. Straightforward and patient interpretation of what is being done, acknowledgment of any affronts, and willingness to see the other fellow's point of view will usually be rewarded.

Observe the Informal Groupings in Your Own Committee and in the Community. On your own committee, see that people who are congenial to each other are assigned as members. In the community, work through the natural "networks" of informal groupings. Very likely many of the official leaders will be on your committee. Also, win the support of people of prestige. These may or may not be the same persons as the official leaders. See that you get the backing of some of the unofficial leaders as well. The local groceryman may wield more influence than the president of the women's club. Natural leaders are found in every neighborhood, and their influence is often wider than that of the official leaders.

Use People Where They Can Help the Most. Some people are especially clever at drawing. They can make maps, posters, or charts. Some people have a tremendous enthusiasm for one little segment of the community's activities. They will ring doorbells for cancer but not for juvenile delinquency. Some people will make excellent interviewers, others will not. Often, the latter can perform valuable service in noninterview activities.

Be Sure Everybody Knows Where His Task Fits in With That of Other Workers. The subcommittee chairman should have a clear picture of what his group is responsible for accomplishing. Individual field workers are entitled to definite and clear assignments. Leaders should have a clear idea of the problems that can be settled on the level of their own group and of which ones should be referred back to the larger group for a decision. Instruction sheets can be drawn up, particularly for the field workers, who will want to know where they stand and what is expected of them.

Keep Open the Channels of Communication. People like to know what is happening. Field workers should report significant events to subcommittee chairmen, and so on. Developments may call for modifications which should be known by other people taking part in the survey. New decisions reached in the course of administering the survey should be relayed to those who should know of them. People are rightfully resentful when they discover, sometimes under embarrassing circumstances, that they have been acting according to a procedure which was changed two weeks ago without their being informed. Similarly, the community should be informed of the progress of the survey. People who will be interviewed should have some idea when to expect a call. Suggestions made for improving methods should be communicated to those who are charged with that part of the survey.

Conduct Meetings Effectively. Among other things, this means preparing carefully the agenda for the meeting and holding the meeting in as informal a manner as is consistent with the accomplishment of the business at hand. Generally speaking, the larger the group, the more formally must the meeting be conducted. Parliamentary procedure can be used as an aid; it should not become a straitjacket.

Adapt To Your Own Community. In one sense, every community *is* different. Each community has its own "flavor". It differs slightly in what is accepted as "the thing to do" and who are "the people to know" if you want to get things done, and whose approval has to be given to a project if it is to receive wide acceptance in certain groups. Some communities are not used to working together; others have a long history of intergroup cooperation. Some are conservative; others are ready for anything that sounds reasonable. Some will "go for" a clam bake; others will have nothing to do with it. In some, the political party officials are more important than governmental officials; in others, it is the other way around. In one community, it is a particular church which "runs" things; in another it is the "Garden Club"; and in still another it is the Volunteer Fire Department. Flexibility of approach is important. No hard and fast "system" can be applied to every community with equal success. Adapt your program to the organization and tone and general climate of your community.[3]

3. Community Resources: How To Find And Use Them

Michael J. Murphy

UTILIZING EXISTING COMMUNITY RESOURCES

INTRODUCTION

We are all aware that the field of the aging, like that of mental retardation, has only recently come to the front of our national conscience. The 1960 Census records almost 20 million people over 65 years of age—better than 10 percent of our national population. This enormous population calls for a retooling and a reassessment of our community priorities to assure that their "twilight years" are, indeed, their "golden years."

The basic concepts discussed in this paper apply to all communities, whether they are a San Francisco, a Madison, Wisconsin, a Bangor, Maine, or a Struthers, Ohio. They are general concepts

---

Excerpted from "Community Organization, Planning and Resources for the Older Poor," a monograph published in March 1970 by The National Council on the Aging, Inc.

[3] An excellent guide to this and other aspects of community betterment work is Irwin T. Sanders, *Making Good Communities Better*, 2d ed. (Lexington: University of Kentucky Press, 1953).

geared toward opening our minds to our communities, toward giving us a different perspective of these communities, toward exploring resources existing in our community in a new way, and, finally, toward the effective use of community resources in relation to our aged population.

While the concepts are applicable to all communities, the techniques suggested will vary with the size of the community. We urge you not to accept these ideas as infallible solutions but rather as suggestions with the emphasis on:

1. Thinking before doing.
2. Analyzing your objectives.
3. Taking logical, sound, and proven steps to secure your objectives.

ANALYZING OUR COMMUNITY

It has been simply stated that a community involves an aggregation of people in a geographic area. Such a simple definition does not connote the most salient feature of a community—its multidimensionality. There have been studies that have more than taken this feature into account. One study identified 323 "major" characteristics in any community. There seems to be an "overkill" of characteristics in such a study. For our use, we will explore a community from a series of standpoints. The outline below should bring some closure on our ideas when we adapt it to our own communities. We must view the community as a dynamic organism embracing individuals, groups, and many institutions in ever-changing patterns of relationships. When attempting to utilize community resources for a particular program, we should be aware of this view and the facts found in the following outline. This information is useful for a quick identification of the major characteristics of a community and is not intended for detailed, elaborate research.

I. IDENTIFICATION
1. Name of community.
2. State in which community is located.
3. What is the population?
4. Does the community correspond approximately with a governmental unit: city, county, village, etc.?
5. If so, give name and type of unit.
6. Classification: type of community (metropolitan center, industrial, etc.).
7. What are the major geographical characteristics of the community?
8. Note any major foreign-born or racial groups in the community.
9. What are the main economic bases in the community?
10. What is the form of local government?
11. What is the political party setup in this community?

II. RESOURCES IN THE COMMUNITY
12. Note any special items of interest in regard to the following types of community resources:
  a. Educational
  b. Health and medical
  c. Recreational and leisure time
  d. Welfare and civic
  e. Religious
  f. Housing and community facilities (transportation, utilities, etc.)

III. PROBLEMS IN THE COMMUNITY
13. Are there problem areas within the community (e.g., slums, etc.)? Describe.
14. Are there special problems connected with any minority groups? Describe.
15. Are there significant conflicts or tension situations in the community? Describe.
16. Are there any economic problems within the community? Describe.

IV. COMMUNITY APPRAISAL
17. What would you say are the dominant social value characteristics of the community (interests, traditions, attitudes, etc.)?
18. Does the community have a positive sense of identity, loyalty? Describe.

19. Is the community characterized by having a great deal, a fair amount, or hardly any autonomy in control over its specific organizations? (Include whether the community's "horizontal pattern" is strong or weak.) Describe.
20. In respect to health and social welfare, what are the major strengths and weaknesses of this community?

ANALYZING COMMUNITY RESOURCES

A resource, Webster tells us, is "a new or a reserve source of supply or support; the available means; computable wealth in money, products, property, etc.; immediate and possible sources of revenue." Three words stand out: support, immediate, and possible. All too often, when we are considering the resources available for a particular project, we understand what we mean by "support" and we understand what we mean by "immediate" but we limit ourselves to what we mean by "possible." Seldom or hardly ever do we consider all the possible resources we have at hand or within our grasp. For example, in working with community programs for the aged, we spend a great deal of time exploring possible sources of support from health and welfare agencies and public departments, and neglect such areas as good government leagues, union counseling groups, religious groups, service clubs like the Rotary, Kiwanis, Lions, etc. This is a real tragedy because each of these associations is a marked feature of life in American communities. As such, they should be considered as local community resources.

Another point to remember is we cannot consider "resource" in a vacuum. The use or potential use of the resource depends upon the use to which it will be put. A Rotary Club may be a valuable resource if one wishes to spread information about

the needs of the aged. However, the Rotary Club would not be useful as a "drop-in center" for the aged, primarily because Rotary Clubs do not own buildings. A better resource in this case might be a social agency, church or synagogue, a United Fund, a Community Action Agency, or a host of other resources.

The resource, then, is defined as a valid means to an end. Community resources can always be better utilized and can sometimes be better mobilized and enlarged. We should not limit our conception of resources to social, health, and welfare agencies, but should include a myriad of other entities: such as lay leadership volunteer participation, staff facilities (i.e., buildings, land, etc.), physical equipment, funds, statutes and laws, newspapers, radio-TV, and so on. A resource, or the utilization of resources, is limited only by imagination.

Let us consider the following resources for meeting the needs of the aging: a senior citizens center is organized in a community where one has not existed before; a family service agency earmarks a caseworker for giving specific services to the aged in a small suburb; a Lions Club promotes better services for the aged by forwarding contributions from their "Light Campaign" to a rehabilitation agency serving aged people having problems with their eyesight; a public assistance worker enlists the interest of a dynamic transportation company executive to promote low-cost transportation for the elderly to service centers; a combination recreation and reading room is added to a community center building, greatly increasing the program possibilities for the aged; an area druggist association is persuaded to give discount prices on drugs to people 55 and over; a still dynamic 70-year-old man is elected to the board of directors of a poverty program agency, thus ensuring a voice and active representation of the aged on program deliberations; the annual amount raised by the local United Fund increases and additional funds are allocated to programs for the aged.

The list could go on and on, limited, we repeat, by our imagination. Let us now consider the organizational resources within our communities. Any community, whether a small coastal village, a suburb, or a huge metropolitan center, has within it a number of organizations. These organizations can range from a small Grange or recreation association in the small coastal village to the more than 900 clubs and organizations found in Cleveland.

Social work has a fine initial premise: in order to help, the worker must start WHERE the individual, or the group, or the community, IS. This complements our earlier comments on having knowledge before we act.

We will discuss two general thoughts that should prove helpful in relation to groups or organizations:

1. Each community, regardless of size, is the locale for an "ecology" of civic and economic activities. By this we mean that there are mutual relationships between individuals, organizations, and their environment within every community. These activities take place at various levels of status, and community projects offer individuals a means to strive upward. Without a detailed description of stratification, with all its sociological implications, we can say that Americans are the most organized people in the world and that their organizations often serve as vehicles for upward mobility.

2. A brief discussion of the differences between "primary" and "secondary" groups will be helpful. In studying organizations, groups, and associations, sociologists use the term "formal groups" and/or "secondary groups" as opposed to the term "primary groups." Primary groups, according to Charles H. Cooley, are small, close, face-to-face groups like the family or the neighborhood, and are called "primary" because of their "primary" influence on the individual's personality. A "secondary group" is more formal in structure and less intimate than the primary group; for example, a civic improvement organization. As used in this paper, a formal group means a secondary group, with a name, officers, general purpose, a fairly regular time and place to meet. In this country, we have seen a tremendous increase in social participation in secondary groups (with all their formal rules, regulations, delineation of responsibilities, etc.) at the expense of primary groups. We must recognize, however, the informal network of associations based on family, friendship, and neighborhood patterns; these primary relationships often encourage mutual association between those on the same social level and discourage it between those on different levels.

Bearing the aforementioned two points in mind, we can begin to determine what organizational resources are available within a given community. This listing will give a general picture of group or organizational life within a community. It is not all-inclusive but should indicate the types of organizational resources present in American communities. It is not concerned with "primary groups," as such. Some of these organizations will be present in most communities; others only in particular communities, dependent upon size, location, degree of urbanization, industrialization, etc. It should not be too difficult to classify the organizational resources within our community because Americans tend to compartmentalize various aspects of their lives and to affiliate themselves with a variety of groupings. Each of these groupings can exist on several participation levels (i.e., local, communitywide, district, county, state, or national). Each of these groupings is further interconnected by a complex net of interrelationships. Functionally, it does not seem difficult to categorize these groupings. Consensus on these categories is fairly general among social scientists and community researchers.

Omitting the primary group, we can delineate eight types of organizations in American communities. We will describe the types and then list various organizations that fit the pattern.

1. *Economic Organizations.* Those organizations with the most direct and considerable economic stake in the community; e.g., profits, jobs, wages, attracting new industry.

2. *Government Organizations.* Those governmental units, departments, field offices, etc., that are public agencies, supported by tax funds and represent city, county, state, or Federal activities within the community; e.g., F.H.A., City Planning Department, State Division of Family Services, Social Security, the County Welfare Department, the School Department, etc.

3. *Education Organizations.* Those organizations concerned with better education in the community; e.g., PTA's.

4. *Religious Organizations.* Those organizations primarily related to spiritual, religious, or ethical needs; e.g., churches, synagogues, Ecumenical Commissions.

5. *Cultural, Fraternal, and Recreational Organizations.* Those organizations meeting the cultural, nationality, fraternal, and recreational needs of the community; this ranges from lodges to athletic clubs to art societies, to organizations meeting the needs of specific groups (e.g., Italian-American Clubs).

6. *Civic Organizations.* That whole range of organizations devoted primarily to civic, neighborhood, and community improvement; e.g., Neighborhood Improvement Associations, League of Women Voters, Kiwanis, veterans associations.

7. *Health and Welfare Organizations.* Those volunteer organizations designed to meet the health and welfare needs in the community; e.g., social agencies, cancer society, welfare associations.

8. *Community Organization and Planning Organizations.* Those organizations devoted to coordinating and planning, assisting agencies, providing central services, research, and fund-raising; e.g., United Appeals, Community Action Agencies, Community Councils.

With the concept of these eight general types of organizations fresh in our minds, let us now refer to a general listing of the organizational resources within our communities.

UTILIZATION OF THE COMMUNITY'S RESOURCES

We may now wish to consider the organizations themselves. It is not enough to know what organizations exist in a particular community; we need to know more specific facts about them. These organizations should not be considered in a vacuum; we should examine them in relation to their particular use or potential use. Before analyzing specific organizations, we need to know our goal. Our particular objective dictates whether a resource is of potential value in helping us secure that goal. Once clear on what we wish to do, we can study what resource offers the best potential. This involves planning; specifically, evaluating all the alternatives for action. It means formulating our need into a systematic, logically coherent plan.

We offer a general worksheet that may be helpful (Figure 3.1). It suggests a compact plan for assessing where we are going. It is similar to the reporter's key questions: "Why? What? Who? Where? and How?"

FIGURE 3.1
Worksheet for Analyzing Our Needs

1. *Why* is the endeavor to be undertaken?
2. *What* is to be done?
3. *Who* is/are to perform the activities?
   a. Any interrelationships to each other?
4. *Where* is the endeavor to be carried out?
5. *When* is the endeavor to be initiated and effected?
6. *How* is the endeavor to be effected?
   a. What methods?
   b. What standards
   c. What financing?

Necessary Components

1. Objectives of the Endeavor
2. Program (activities, services, etc.)
3. Structure and Personnel of the Organization
4. Territory covered
5. Time schedule
6. Methods, Standards, and Budget

Analyzing our needs, complemented by a general plan, is really "problem-solving." The analysis is the breaking up of the problems; the plan is the synthesizing of proposals for future action. Once we have made an analysis of our needs (problem), logically we should be led to adopt a plan that would contain six components: (1) objectives; (2) program; (3) structure and personnel of the organization; (4) territory to be covered; (5) time schedule; (6) methods, standards, and budget (see Figure 3.1).

It may help clarify this complementary relationship if we briefly look at a hypothetical objective: We are members of a CAP agency in a community of approximately 40,000 people. After a joint study by our agency, the Community Council, the Family Services Agency, and the City Recreation Department, the results are known; to wit: there is a large gap in services to the aged in our community and there is a definite need for a Senior Citizens Center. Consulting our worksheet, we might fill it out accordingly:

1. *Why?* The Joint Study reflected that 19 percent of our population is over 65 years of age and there is a substantial lack of services, meeting places, etc.
2. *What* is to be done? Lease, rent, or preferably be given a facility for a Senior Citizens Center, with appropriate cultural, social, and recreational services provided by volunteer and paid staff for a majority of our aged population.
3. *Who?* The CAP agency will provide a coordinator for the program; Family Services will provide casework staff; City Recreation Department will provide a staff member; the Council will provide outreach workers. The staff members of the agencies will be responsible to the Coordinator during the activity time of the center, approximately 11:00 A.M. to 3:00 P.M., four days a week.
4. *Where?* Southern "downtown" area, preferably in the Harlow Street School Area, where the major percentage of the community's elderly population lives.
5. *When?* Program to begin in August with the full program to be effected in the late Fall.
6. *How?*
   a. Methods—joint staff conferences, a publicity buildup to attract members, etc.
   b. Standards—free services, periodic evaluation procedures, etc.
   c. Financing—through possible funding from a combination of sources: United Fund, City Recreation Department, State Department of Health and Welfare.

Continuing our hypothetical case, we now refer to the planning worksheet. This example refers to a rather extensive project; therefore, it might be necessary for our plan to embrace all six components corresponding to our six questions in our "Need Analysis." We will leave the plan up to your imagination. We reiterate that this worksheet is one example of many possible working tools that may be used as

FIGURE 3.2
Worksheet for Analyzing Pertinent Community Organizations

Item	Organization 1	Organization 2
1. Name	United Community Services of Penobscot Valley, Bangor, Maine	
2. Purposes	*a.* To serve as the coordinating, planning, and fund-raising social welfare organization in Eastern Maine *b.* To assure public and private co-operation in serving area citizens *c.* Etc.	
3. Major Activities	*a.* Comprehensive health planning; social planning in four-County area *b.* Fall United Fund Campaign to deficit support 31 agencies *c.* Functional budgeting system for 31 agencies	
4. Number of Active Members	33 board members; 450 other members of Committees, etc.	
5. Type of Member (Restrictions?)	No restrictions	
6. Meeting Time	Board on 3rd Thursday of month	
7. Key Leaders	*a.* John Smith, President *b.* William Prince, Chairman, Social Planning Division *c.* E. Savings, Chairman United Fund Division *d.* R. Jones, board member	
8. Organizations with Which It Cooperates	*a.* CAP *b.* State Department of H.E.W. *c.* Area Community Council *d.* Etc.	
9. Type of Auspices	Voluntary association	
10. Funding Source (if applicable)	Gifts, fees, etc.	
11. Formal Locus of Its Decisions	Board of Directors	
12. Ultimate Authority	Board of Directors, members	
13. Major Community Controls	Patterns of gifts	
14. Other Interesting Data	*a.* Currently expanding area served *b.* Recently signed contract with state Division of Aging *c.* Etc.	

a direction-finder. Remember that analysis and planning go hand in hand, each a complement to the other.

Let us now return to our earlier considerations of the organizations present in our communities. If we know our goals, (and the foregoing worksheets were designed to uncover those goals), we now ask ourselves, "What organizations are relevant to our needs?" We cannot answer this question without obtaining additional data about our local organizations, more than the fact that this or that particular organization exists in our community. We have prepared another sample worksheet (See Figure 3.2 on p. 41) which can be used to analyze some of the organizations that will be pertinent to our use. An organizational card file, with this type of data, is indispensable in analyzing local organizations for their potential as resources.

Given this information, we should be able to tell whether a particular program can best be promoted by working through an existing organization or organizations. By answering questions such as: what is the purpose, who are the key leaders, what are the cooperative relationships, what are the funding sources, who makes the decisions, and where are the major community controls—we are able to determine whether the organization is a possible resource. In this manner, we can be quite selective in our utilization. We do not have to make a series of false starts. We do not have to waste our time working on organizations that have little or no value to our endeavor. Once again, we emphasize strongly that our need or objective is to determine whether a resource has potential utilization. An organization may not be a potential resource for one objective but may have potential for another, different objective.

4. Organizations: How to Analyze and Understand Them

Yeheskel Hasenfeld

ANALYZING THE HUMAN SERVICE AGENCY'S INTERORGANIZATIONAL RELATIONS AND INTERNAL CHARACTERISTICS

INTRODUCTION

The outline and questions that follow are designed to guide the practitioner in understanding organizations engaged in providing human services. A careful attempt to answer the questions posed will provide the basis for a relatively complete

Source: Unpublished, Yeheskel Hasenfeld, "Analyzing the Human Service Agency's Interorganizational Relations and Internal Characteristics," March 1976.

understanding of the agency and the context in which it operates.

The first part focuses on the agency's interorganizational relations and includes sections on the agency environment, market relations, and regulatory groups. The second part directs attention to the internal features of human service organizations: their structure, technologies, and processes; their domain and goals; clients;

and resources. Technical terms are defined at the point in the text where they are introduced.

THE AGENCY AND INTERORGANIZATIONAL RELATIONSHIPS

I. AGENCY ENVIRONMENT

To understand the behavior of any agency, it is necessary to be knowledgeable about the community in which it functions. A wide array of factors may influence agency behavior, but it is expected that these will vary among agencies and communities.

A. Locate, study, and summarize demographic data relevant to understanding the environment in which this agency exists. Included would be data about population composition and mobility, economic base, tax policy and situation, governmental, welfare, business and industrial structures, housing, medical facilities, and so forth. (Sources for the above data include: U.S. Census and Department of Labor reports, courts, city planning commissions, school census and planning reports, Chamber of Commerce, university library, etc.)

B. As far as possible, map the "organization set" for the agency being studied. Indicate differential types of relationships such as

formal authority, regulatory, complementary, informal, etc.

1. Of these relationships, which ones are perceived by the agency as most important in the transactions? Why? Which ones the least? Why?

2. With which additional groups, organizations, institutions, etc., would the agency like to develop relationships? Why?

3. Identify any major problems the agency has encountered in developing linkages with other groups.

C. What is the nature of the communication system between the agency and its "organizational set"?

1. What mechanisms has the agency used or developed to secure and process information from its organizational set and the general environment?

2. Identify formal and informal channels of communication.

3. What is the quality of the information exchanged?

4. What barriers and gaps to communication can be identified?

D. What planning, coordinating, or governing bodies exist between the agency and its organizational set?

1. Does the agency have delegated representatives to such bodies? If so, to which groups? How are representatives selected?

2. Is content from these activities considered in agency meetings or is the representation only of a pro forma type?

E. Identify the principal sources of material resources for the agency (e.g., taxes, fees, contributions, endowments).

1. What strategies has the agency developed to secure and maintain resources?

2. What problems has the agency encountered in this area?

F. Identify any major areas of conflict between the agency and members of the "organizational set." How has the agency handled such conflict?

G. As far as possible assess the relative power position of the agency to other groups in the organizational set.

1. How much influence does the agency seem to have?

2. What coalitions, if any, has the agency joined? Why?

H. Identify the principal sources of legitimation for the agency (e.g., political

groups, governmental units, public at large, professional organizations, special interest groups).

In all of the above, indicate the impact of the various environmental characteristics upon the activities of the agency. For example, do certain characteristics of the "organization set" facilitate or constrain agency decision-making?

From the perspective of the organization, what type of external pressures and forces have interfered most in the organization accomplishing its goals? What modes of influence and adaptation has the organization used to minimize such pressures?

II. MARKET RELATIONS

Market relations are: (1) the complex of arrangements, exchanges, and contingencies the target agency (i.e., the agency under study) encounters in disposing of its output. The units which receive the agency's outputs are "receiving units" (questions A–J). (2) Its relations with other agencies offering complementary and similar (competing) services (questions K–T). Complementary services are those services provided by external units which assist the target agency in achieving its tasks with the clients, services given to clients concomitantly with those of the target agency, and services given to clients upon referral by the target agency.

A. Identify the major external units (families, communities, agencies, etc.) which import, purchase, or use the agency's outputs; in so doing, indicate the nature and proportion of the agency's output marketed to each of these units.

B. How does the target agency identify external units as actual or potential "receiving units"?

1. Is information about the receiving units (e.g., their address, contact personnel, input criteria) readily available in codified form for appropriate staff in the target agency?

   a. If "no," how do staff know about potential receiving units?

   b. If "yes," provide illustrative examples and indicate how such information is maintained "current."

C. Where possible, for each of the units receiving the outputs of the agency, identify:

1. The amount of freedom they have in accepting or rejecting the output.

2. The nature of the preconditions, if any, they set up for accepting certain outputs.

D. Can you discern how these preconditions were set up and by whom?

E. What type of information, if any, is requested by each of these units about the output and in what form is it furnished

to them? (For example, what information is given to a halfway house that accepts a client from a state hospital?)

F. Who in the agency is in charge of marketing the agency's outputs to these units? What is their training and status in the agency?

G. From interviews with these staff and analyzing clients' characteristics upon exit from the agency, estimate the extent to which the agency takes into account the preconditions and specifications made by the units receiving the outputs.

H. Are there any indications of difficulties, strains, and problems on the part of the agency in meeting these preconditions? Describe them.

I. What are the possible and actual reactions of the receiving units if some preconditions are not met?

J. Summarize the patterns of the relations between the target agency and each of its receiving units.

K. Identify the units which provide *complementary* services to the target agency. In so doing, describe:

1. The nature of the service given.

2. The kinds of clients (or staff) receiving it.

3. The frequency by which these services are provided.

L. Identify the preconditions, if any, that the target agency must meet to secure these services.

M. How do staff evaluate the importance of securing each of these services in terms of accomplishing their tasks?

N. What services, payments, or other resources does the target agency provide, if any, to each of these units?

O. Identify those agencies in the community which provide services *similar* to the target agency. Indicate the extent of the similarity in terms of services given and clients served.

P. How does the executive core of the target agency compare the agency vis-a-vis these agencies in terms of:

1. Tasks performed by staff?
2. Desired goals to be achieved?
3. Characteristics of clients?
4. Staff-client relations? Indicate in the comparison what is perceived to be unique to the target agency by the executive core.

Q. Rank these agencies and the target agency in terms of budget size, number of clients served per year,

and number of line personnel. (In the case of multifunction agencies, compare the subunits engaged in the same kinds of services.)

R. Does the target agency have any form of contact, arrangement, etc., with these agencies? If so, describe their content.

S. Is there competition for clients among these agencies? If so, how is it manifested?

T. Are there efforts underway to move toward complimentarity, combines, or other forms of organization where the target agency and one or more other agencies provide similar services for clients?

III. REGULATORY GROUPS

Regulatory groups are all the major organizations, legislative or legal bodies, associations, boards, etc., toward which the target agency must be *accountable* and from which it must receive approval, formal and informal, for its domain and the legitimacy of its activities. Such units may certify the agency, review operations of the agency as a whole or subunits of it, enact rules the agency must adopt, etc.

A. Identify the major units and organizations that periodically inspect, review, and evaluate various aspects of the agency's activities. In so doing classify the various units according to:

1. The regulatory func-

tion that each unit performs (e.g., certifies, accredits, makes recommendations, legislative review, etc.)

2. The aspect of the agency's activities of concern to each of these units.

3. The kinds of mechanisms each unit uses to maintain relations with the agency and vice versa (e.g., representative from an agency's board, periodic meetings, etc.).

B. What criteria, if any, are being used by each unit to evaluate the agency's activities?

C. Were these criteria agreed upon mutually by the agency and the unit, imposed on the agency, suggested by the agency, or established in other ways? What is the agency's view of the legitimacy and utility of the regulatory unit's regulatory efforts?

D. What specific kinds of information are requested by these units and in what form is information furnished to them? Analyze the nature of the information given in terms of:

1. Is it intrinsic to the nature of the activities reviewed; that is, does the information directly describe the nature of the activi-

ties reviewed, or provide some indirect assessment of them?

2. Does each unit requesting the information specify the kind of questions, data, and analysis it wants, or are these left to agency personnel to decide?

3. Is the information provided on a continuous or discontinuous basis?

4. Does the information provided lend itself to further analysis beyond that done by the agency? If so, does the agency receive any feedback from the regulatory units about comparative performance, etc., vis-a-vis other similar agencies?

E. Who in the agency is in charge of maintaining relations and working with these units? In each of the regulatory units who is in charge of maintaining contact with the target agency, and how is it done?

F. What are the possible sanctions that each of these units can impose on the agency? Rank the units in terms of severity of sanctions each can potentially impose. Can the unit freely impose the sanctions?

G. By interviewing the

agency's executive core, find out which of these units they consider the agency is most dependent upon in terms of continuation of services and what reasons they give for their assertions.

H. Based on your observations, review of reports, etc., estimate the amount of effort, resources, and personnel time spent by the agency to meet the requirements of each unit.

I. For each of these units, what do the agency's staff conceive to be the regulatory group's expectations re:
1. The characteristics of the clients?
2. The desired changes to be achieved?
3. The appropriate intervention techniques that need to be utilized?

J. What is the nature of any discrepancies between each unit's expectations and those of other units or the staff's expectations?

K. Assess the impact of the regulatory functions of each of these units upon the effectiveness and efficiency of the provision of services to clients by the agency.

L. Identify any civic groups which, though they do not carry regulatory functions, have been involved in supporting, challeng-ing, or expressing concern about the mandate of the agency.
1. Estimate the resources (financial, personnel, prestige, connections with other organizations, etc.) that each of these groups has or can mobilize.
2. What types of pressures or support have they brought on the agency?
3. Identify any conflicting expectations these groups may have in relation to the agency's operations.
4. How does the agency handle its relations with each of these groups?

ORGANIZATIONAL ANALYSIS

I. ORGANIZATIONAL STRUCTURES, TECHNOLOGIES, AND PROCESSES

A. Structure
1. Outline the organizational chart of the agency, identifying the major formal structural components which can be used to characterize the organization.
2. What various informal structures can be identified in the organization, and what effects, if any, have these structures had on organizational technologies and processes?

B. Technology
1. Describe the various types of

technologies in the organization.

  a. The organization's standards governing the performance, control, and specification of that technology.

  b. The kind of feedback mechanisms that exist or have been established to assess the technology.

  c. The manner in which that technology is linked with other components of the organization.

  d. The method of evaluating the output.

C. Decision-Making. Identify issues that have significant consequences for the service delivery of the agency.

  1. Describe the factors that have led to the emergence of each issue.

  2. Identify the roles and positions of the key participants in the decision-making process.

  3. Evaluate the relative influences or power of each participant.

  4. What position toward the issue did each participant take? What assumptions and ideologies underlay them?

  5. Identify the processes and procedures through which decisions were reached or attempted.

  6. What relations (i.e., locations, bargaining, competition) were formed among the participants in arriving at each decision?

  7. Assess the degree of partici-

pation in the decision process of various staff groups and clients.

  8. What organizational constraints played a role in affecting the nature of the issue and the resulting decision?

  9. What mechanisms were developed to implement the decisions?

  10. How will the decisions affect services?

D. Control-Coordinating. Describe the formal and informal process of socialization and control of individual staff members, divisions or departments, and clients in the organization.

E. Conflict-Communication

  1. Identify and describe major areas of internal and external conflict.

  2. What strategies and tactics have been used by the organization to resolve these conflicts?

  3. What type of conflict has been viewed by the organization as functional, why? What type as dysfunctional, why?

  4. What systems have been developed for transmitting information within and outside of the organization?

  5. How does the agency evaluate the effectiveness of the received and transmitted information, both within and outside of the organization?

II. ORGANIZATIONAL DOMAIN AND GOALS

A. Organizational domain means the claims which the organization stakes out for itself in terms of: (1) the range of human problems, issues, and concerns it purports to handle. (These may include concerns about problems of malfunctioning as well as concerns about enhancement and improvement of individual and social functioning); (2) the services offered; and (3) the population entitled to use the service.

1. Identify and list the specific human problems and concerns that this agency is set up to handle. In so doing, classify these by (a) the unit to which the problem or concern is related (e.g., individual, family, community, etc.) and (b) what in the unit is the target of concern (e.g., occupational role of the individual, parent-child relations, organization of community health services, etc).

2. Identify and list the services that the agency offers vis-à-vis the problems and issues it attempts to handle.

3. Identify those units which are eligible for the services offered by the agency. In so doing enumerate the conditions and qualifications they have to meet in order to be officially eligible for services.

B. Organizational Goals. The concept of organizational goals generates different meanings and different guides for action in various parts of the organization, varying with the frames of reference and objectives of those who define or interpret organizational goals. Yet, they should be distinguished from organizational domain. The domain defines the areas in which the organization will function, but not the desired ends and outcomes its members aim at achieving in these areas and the corresponding services. Such definitions are the function of goals.

1. Cite the official statements, if any, which describe the mission and goals of the agency. Have there been major changes in the content of such statements in the agency's recent past?

2. As a result of interviewing the executive core of the agency, how would you describe their perspectives on the organization's goals?

   a. What do they see as the agency's objectives in relation to the clients? What priorities do they establish among the several goals?

   b. What perceptions do they have about the relevant characteristics of their clients as they define them?

   c. What roles do they see the agency playing in the larger community?

   d. What aspects of the agency's programs do they see as best reflecting their objectives?

   e. What do they identify as the major problems or tasks that require prompt solutions?

3. Summarize the ideological commitments of the executive core, that is, their belief systems about the characteristics of the clients; the na-

ture and purpose of the intervention technologies; the desired changes to be achieved in the clients and the role of line personnel vis-à-vis clients.

4. From interviews with line personnel answer the following:

   a. What do they perceive as their major objectives in relation to clients?

   b. Can you discern a priority ranking among the various objectives mentioned?

   c. What perceptions do they hold about the relevant characteristics of their clients?

   d. What perceptions do they hold about the proper staff-client relations?

   e. What role do they see the agency playing in the larger community?

5. From interviews with clients, answer the following:

   a. What do they see as the major objectives of the agency?

   b. What expectations do they have of staff?

   c. What would they like the agency to do which it does not do currently?

6. Summarize the similarities and discrepancies among the perspectives of the executive core, line staff, and clients about agency's goals.

7. From observations of staff-clients relations, what are your conclusions as to actual tasks that staff perform?

8. From reviewing the agency's allocation of personnel, budget, and other resources to various work units, which tasks and objectives receive more priority?

9. Compare the existing priority given to various tasks based on allocation of resources to that purported by the executive core and other staff.

III. CLIENT INPUTS

A. Present a profile of the clients served by this agency.

   1. If the clients are individuals or families describe:

      a. Age, sex, and race

      b. Socioeconomic status

      c. Place of residence

      d. Most frequent presenting problems or concern

   2. If the clients are other organizations or associations, describe:

      a. The stated goals and functions of these organizations

      b. The major services they provide to achieve their goals

      c. The characteristics of their constituent population (see 1)

      d. The amount of resources (financial, personnel) these organizations have

B. What is the rate or extent of the problem in the community which the agency is designed to serve? What proportion of this possible case load is served by the agency?

C. What admission criteria do clients have to meet in order to benefit from the services of the agency?

D. How were these criteria established (e.g., were they externally imposed, based on individual staff decision, etc.); and how much control did the agency's staff have in setting them?

E. Observing staff, analyzing data on the clients characteristics, and comparing those accepted for services vs. those rejected, identify the *actual* mechanisms staff use to select and screen clients.

F. How do these compare to the formally stated admission criteria?

G. Identify and chart the different routes that clients can take in the agency, and indicate some of the major criteria used to route clients at each juncture (e.g., initial routing to major divisions in the agency, further routing to specific services, movement from one work unit to another, etc.). Develop a flow chart of initial client case processing.

H. In assigning clients to services, can you differentiate subcohorts of clients, each of which is characterized by a common client profile and a common service (e.g., all clients of a certain age, race, income, and problem receive a certain kind of service)?

I. By interviewing and observing staff and clients, analyze the extent to which clients can actively negotiate their admission for services and be actively involved in decisions about the kinds of services that will be provided for them.

J. Can you identify what types of clients have better chances of negotiating successfully with staff as compared to those who have little

chances of doing so?

K. What other alternatives do clients have in seeking the needed services?

L. To what extent is the agency dependent on clients for financial support?

M. To what extent is cooperation on the part of the client essential for staff to perform their tasks?

N. Are clients referred to the agency by other organizations (or individual professionals)? If so,
   1. Describe the organizations engaged in referral and the extent of their referral.
   2. Analyze the extent to which the target agency is dependent upon each of these organizations for receiving clients, financial support, professional services (e.g., testing, diagnosis, supporting services, etc.) and personnel.
   3. To what extent is the target agency free to accept or reject referrals?
   4. What kinds of services, if any, does the target agency reciprocate for referrals?

O. Identify any pressures exerted on the agency to accept and reject certain client cohorts:
   1. What are the agency's responses to these demands?
   2. What do you consider to be the organizational reasons for such responses?

P. Identify the people in the agency in charge of client intake, their professional status and their position in the agency.

Q. What is the ratio of clients per line staff (e.g., average case load)?

R. Can you infer from observations

and other information what types of clients the agency seems to prefer?

S. In some agencies clients are given some form of representation (e.g., P.T.A. membership, advisory board, etc.). Do clients in the target agency have any form of representation? If so, describe:
1. The criteria used and the ways clients are recruited to such roles
2. The formal tasks assigned to such a body
3. The nature of the decisions made by this body
4. The role of staff vis-à-vis this representation
5. The amount of influence such a body has on the agency's policies and the amount of control staff have on the decisional processes of this group

T. Are there any segments of the agency's clients who are organized in some formal pattern, yet not represented in the agency governance structure (e.g., welfare recipients associations)? If so,
1. Describe the characteristics of the clients belonging to that association
2. How did it come into being?
3. What are its major objectives?
4. What strategies are being utilized to achieve these objectives?
5. How does the executive core react and respond to this association?
6. Can you discern any influence such association has over the agency's policies?

U. What are the various methods used by the agency to assess clients' needs?

V. From the perspectives of the executive, various other staff, client community residents, or others outside the organization, what are the areas of conflicts and gaps in client services and types of service delivery patterns in the organization? What steps have been taken to resolve conflicts and close such gaps?

IV. RESOURCES INPUTS

By resources inputs we refer mainly to those external units which provide the target agency with its financial basis and those units which provide its personnel. You should note that many units will assume a number of functions in relation to the target agency, such as combining regulatory and funding functions. Hence there may be considerable overlap in your analysis of these units.

A. Financial
1. Identify the major units which provide the agency with its financial resources.
   a. What proportion of the total agency's budget is contributed by each of these units?
   b. To what extent does each supporting unit specify the activities for which the funds are to be allocated?
2. What criteria are being used by each of these units in determining their allocation of resources to the agency?
3. Can you discern whether these criteria have been de-

termined by the unit exclusively, by negotiation with the target agency, or what?

4. What types of information are requested by these units, and in what forms are they furnished to them? Provide examples.

5. Who in the agency is in charge of maintaining relations and working with the target agency?

6. In each of the funding units, who is in charge of maintaining contact with the target agency?
   a. What forms do such contacts take?
   b. Does such a person participate in the policy decision-making processes in the agency?

7. Through interviewing agency's staff in charge of contact with each unit, what do they perceive to be the specific preconditions and requirements that the agency has to meet in order to secure funds from each unit?

8. Based on your observations, review of reports, etc., estimate the amount of efforts, resources, and personnel time spent by the agency to meet the requirements of each unit.

9. Are there any indications of difficulties or strains on the part of the agency to meet the preconditions set by the funding units?

10. How do these external units check whether their requirements have been met

by the agency?

11. Can agency's staff identify any expectations or beliefs on the part of each funding unit regarding:
    a. The characteristics of the clients?
    b. The desired changes to be achieved?
    c. The appropriate intervention techniques?
    d. The role of staff vis-à-vis clients?

12. How do these beliefs compare with those of the agency's staff?

13. Assess the impact that each funding unit has on the ways in which the agency renders its services (e.g., type of service given, nature of personnel agency can afford to hire, number of clients served, etc.), through the requirements each makes, the amount of resources given, restrictions on their use, and the like.

14. What external units are considered to be the agency's immediate competitors for resources vis-à-vis each of the fund providing units?

15. Does the target agency provide any services to each of the funding units? Are there other agencies which provide similar services to these units?

16. Describe the budgetary process in the agency in relation to such factors as planning programs, determining cost, securing funds, allocating funds, etc.

17. Describe the method(s) the agency has used in an attempt to measure benefits (outcome). To what extent is the planned program congruent with the organization's outputs? What problems have been encountered internally and externally in justifying its program and budget?

B. Personnel

1. Identify the units from which the agency's personnel are recruited.

2. What criteria are used by the agency for hiring personnel for each major work unit (excluding building maintenance staff)?

3. Analyze staff characteristics in terms of their formal education, training for current task, and prior experience.

4. What methods are used by the agency to recruit its staff? What problems does the executive core encounter in recruitment efforts?

5. In the eyes of the executive core what kinds of demands, questions, and contingencies are expressed by potential staff as conditions for employment?

6. How are these met and handled by the agency?

7. Are there any direct relations between the agency and the units which provide staff?

a. Describe the nature of these relations.

b. Does the agency provide any services (e.g., training, research, etc.) to these units?

8. Identify the major professional and occupational associations with which staff affiliate. Does their affiliation serve a regulatory function? If so, how?

9. Are there conflicts among staff groups with different professional and organizational affiliations in relation to their beliefs? How are these expressed in the agency?

10. From the perspectives of the executive core, which of these associations has had the greatest influence on the agency's ideologies in working with clients?

11. What formal and informal criteria are used for evaluating the performance of staff?

12. What is the agency's orientation to the use of paraprofessionals?

13. If there are paraprofessionals in the agency, what mechanisms, if any, are or have been used to integrate professional and paraprofessional staff?

14. Has the agency experienced any particular positive and negative consequences as a result of employing paraprofessionals?

5. Library Sources: How to Locate and Use Them

Anne K. Beaubien

LIBRARY RESOURCES FOR THE COMMUNITY ORGANIZER: SURVEY AND BIBLIOGRAPHY

This article is designed to alert professional community organizers to some of the most common and useful library resources for their field. Specifically, it will focus on the types of materials and services one can expect to find in the reference department of all but the smallest libraries, works to help identify socioeconomic characteristics of a community, and sources of grant funds. This discussion is designed for people unfamiliar with basic reference and government publications and does not attempt a full or complete coverage. Those interested in a more thorough survey of general reference materials should see Carl White's *Sources of Information in the Social Sciences* (1) and Eugene Sheehy's *Guide to Reference Books* (2). Numbers following the titles refer to the bibliography at the end of the article, which provides complete citations for the items discussed.

STANDARD SOURCES IN THE REFERENCE DEPARTMENT

Libraries, like social service agencies, are oriented primarily toward public service of an immediate kind. Not only college and university libraries but also most public libraries contain a wealth of current information of vital interest to the community organizer. Reference librarians, themselves specially trained professionals, are willing and eager to help others find the

exact information they need. One has only to ask in order to receive expert assistance in identifying potential sources of information, in understanding the utility and format of a particular work, or in exploring alternative approaches to specific data. For example, sometimes interlibrary loan may be necessary to obtain materials which are unavailable in the local library. The following are some of the most important types of reference works for background research in social service with specific titles to illustrate each type.

Essential for background research on virtually any topic are the numerous general and specialized encyclopedias ranging from the familiar, all-purpose *Encyclopedia Britannica* (3) to the scholarly and comprehensive *International Encyclopedia of the Social Sciences* (4) to the very specific *Encyclopedia of Social Work* (5). Just as an encyclopedia provides survey articles on topics, concepts, or theories, a dictionary gives a brief identification of terms and ideas. In addition to English and foreign language dictionaries there are numerous specialized subject dictionaries such as the *Dictionary of the Social Sciences* (6) and *Black's Law Dictionary* (7). Dictionaries can be used profitably together with the encyclopedias for a quick overview of a field or movement. The *Acronyms and Initialisms Dictionary* (8) is helpful for decoding organizations' abbreviations.

Bibliographies on specific topics are readily available and list sources for indepth reading. *Bibliographic Index* (9) is

Source: Unpublished, Anne K. Beaubien, "Library Resources for the Community Organizer: Survey and Bibliography."

a good place to start to identify bibliographies which have appeared in books or journal articles or which have been separately published. The *Council of Planning Librarians Exchange Bibliography* (10) series offers timely and current bibliographies on all aspects of urban planning including environment, community organization, and the black community. Other bibliographies may be located by looking in the card catalog under the subject in which one is interested subdivided by "bibliography," e.g., Abortion—Bibliography.

Journal indexes are a type of bibliography which lead you by subject and usually by author to articles which have appeared in major journals. Like the card catalog, journal indexes will sometimes use the subdivision "bibliography" after subject headings, thus leading one to other relevant material. The *Reader's Guide to Periodical Literature* (11) indexes general, popular magazines like *Time* and *Psychology Today*. *Social Sciences Index* (12) is similar to *Reader's Guide* but covers scholarly social science journals. *Public Affairs Information Service Bulletin* (P.A.I.S.) (13) indexes journals, government documents, pamphlets, and books on all social science topics including administration, social welfare, statistics, economics, and political science. In a large public or college library one can also expect to find *Psychological Abstracts* (14), which focuses on psychological journals, conference proceedings, books, and technical reports and includes a short description of each item. *Sociological Abstracts* (15) provides similar coverage for the field of sociology but with less complete indexing than *Psychological Abstracts*. Other specialized indexes include *Human Resources Abstracts* (16), *Public Administration Abstracts* (17), and *Abstracts for Social Workers* (18).

The reference department will probably have a complete set of state laws and, in a large library, a set of the *U.S. Statutes at Large* (19) and the *U.S. Code* (20), a rearrangement of federal laws under fifty subject headings called titles.

Directories provide identification and addresses for people and organizations, and a variety of them are useful in social work. A most important reference work, the *Public Welfare Directory,* (21), is a guide to federal and state agencies in the United States and Canada concerned with public welfare. A section on federal agencies describes their organization, administration, and programs. For each state there is indicated which agencies take administrative responsibility for public welfare, services and assistance, and where to address correspondence regarding such matters as institution cases, records of births and deaths, and private nursing home licensing. Various bureaus, divisions, and sections of state agencies are listed giving directors and phone numbers. Also included are the addresses of related state agencies and the directors and addresses for all county departments of social services. Symbols are used to indicate the type of programs offered by each agency.

Another key directory, the *National Directory of State Agencies* (22), covers 66 functional agency categories (such as Aging, Human Rights, Juvenile Delinquency, and Social Services) for all 50 states and the District of Columbia, and is arranged by state and by function. The information given for each agency includes the name of the bureau or division and overall agency, name of administrator, exact address including room number, and telephone number. The *Public Welfare Directory* is more detailed for public welfare than the *National Directory of State Agencies*. For example, the latter lists only each state's department of social services while the *Public Welfare Directory* indicates the various offices and bureaus within that department.

The *United Way Directory* (23) gives statistics on the fund raising campaigns of the United Way and Community Health and Welfare Councils by state and by city. Information listed includes the goal and the amount raised together with the telephone number, address, and name of the executive. More specialized reference collections will also have the *NASW Directory of Professional Social Workers* (24) and the *Directory of Member Agencies and Associates of the Child Welfare League of America.* (25)

Biographical information is provided by regional directories such as *Who's Who in the Midwest* (26) or by profession-oriented directories such as the *Official Congressional Directory* (27) and the *Directory of Rehabilitation Consultants* (28). Although limited to giving an individual's place of employment and address, the *NASW Directory of Professional Social Workers,* mentioned above, may be helpful.

Occasionally one may need more general directories. The annual *U.S. Government Manual* (29) describes the agencies of the legislative, executive, and judicial branches of the federal government as well as many commissions, boards, and committees. In addition to the agency address, it gives information on the current officials, organizations, and activities. Most states also have a similar manual for the state government. A list of state publications was compiled by Charles Press and Oliver Williams (30) and updated by Peter Hernon (31 and 32).

The *Zip Code Directory* (33), as well as telephone directories (both white and yellow pages) from around the state and country, are staple items in all reference

departments. There are also directories describing universities and colleges, including their address and enrollment, such as *American Universities and Colleges* (34), and periodical directories like *Ulrich's* (35) and newspaper directories like *Ayer's* (36), which provide addresses, editors, and subscription prices of magazines and newspapers, respectively. The *Encyclopedia of Associations* (37) lists United States and some Canadian associations including address, telephone, purpose, and publications.

The *Statistical Abstract of the United States* (38) is the basic place to start to find statistics on most topics. Over 1,400 tables summarize social, political, and economic statistics for the United States. The emphasis is on national data but some state and regional statistics are included, some of them unpublished. There is a detailed subject index to the statistical data, some of which are derived from governmental and nongovernmental sources. At the bottom of each table the source of the statistics is cited, but there is no way of knowing what the exact breakdown of the expanded statistics will be. In addition, many states publish their own statistical abstracts. To determine if there is one for your state check Press and Williams (30) and Hernon (31 and 32). Some libraries will also have the *American Statistics Index* (39), which leads you to federal statistics appearing in journals, series, annuals, and the like. The index is detailed and indicates the exact form of the statistics. *American Statistics Index* is limited to published sources, however, and has only been published since 1973 so its value will increase as time progresses.

THE COMMUNITY

Socioeconomic characteristics of a community can be invaluable in the initial decision of whether to move to a community, in helping plan and design social service programs that will meet the needs of the community, and, in general, in helping acquaint the community organizer with the environment and potential problems. The *Editor and Publisher Market Guide* (40) provides information on cities in which at least one daily newspaper is published. It gives location of the city; number of households; income per household; estimate of the population for the current year; principal industries of the area (with number of employees and average weekly wages); climate; names of shopping centers with number of stores in each; and names of department, discount, and chain food stores. The *Rand McNally Commercial Atlas* (41) has detailed information on each state as well as special subject maps on the entire United States' for example, telephone area code map and railroad distance table between United States' cities. Each state has a map showing counties, rivers, and cities and an index of physical features such as mountains, creeks, and lakes. A separate city index provides additional information about the community. Symbols indicate if there is a post office, the zip code, coordinates on the map, whether there are railroads and airlines servicing the town, and an indication of whether the community is incorporated. This is followed by the 1970 census population figure and population estimate as of January 1 of the current year. Of the two sources, the *Commercial Atlas* gives more complete population estimates since *Market Guide* is limited to cities large enough to support a daily newspaper.

The most detailed and comprehensive socioeconomic statistics are available from the U.S. Census Bureau. When people refer to "the census" they usually mean the *Census of Population* (42), taken decennially since 1790. The Census Bureau

also publishes a census of governments and economic censuses such as agriculture, manufacturers, and retail trade. Most of these began as part of the decennial Census of Population and Housing and later developed into separate publications taken during intercensal years. This discussion of the census will center on the major parts of the Census of Population and Housing. As one would expect, the most detailed statistics are available for the most densely populated areas. The smaller the place, the less detailed the information. Those interested in a more complete treatment of the topic should consult the *Bureau of the Census Guide to Programs and Publications* (43).

The most reliable approach to census publications is through the *U.S. Census Bureau Catalog* (44), which is issued monthly with quarterly and annual cumulations. It is a complete record of the published census reports. Each series has a note indicating the scope of coverage. There are separate indexes by subject and geographic areas. Thus one can determine which reports give information by state, city, and/or county although one cannot look up the name of a specific city. A cumulation of the catalog has been published for the period 1790–1972 (45).

Characteristics of the Population (46) comprises the first part of the 1970 Census of Population. There is one volume for each state and a summary volume for the entire United States. The exact definition of terms used is given in the front of each volume. A list of tables appears at the front of each section. The inside cover of bound volumes indexes the tables by subject and size of place. Each volume is divided into four chapters:

Part A: Number of Inhabitants
    Population by size of place
Part B: General Population Characteristics
    Demographic characteristics such as sex,

age, race, marital status and household relationship

Part C: General Social and Economic Characteristics

Educational attainment, ethnic characteristics, occupations, employment status, income

Part D: Detailed Characteristics

Family composition, years of school completed, more detailed data on occupations, income, poverty

The *Subject Reports* (47) series compiles data on many topics of interest to community organizers, data which are not readily available from other sections of the 1970 census. These statistics are more detailed but generally they give only national figures and do not cover individual localities. Over 35 *Subject Reports* have been issued from the 1970 census, for example, "Puerto Ricans in the United States," PC (2)-1E; "Mobility for Metropolitan Areas," PC (2)-2C; and "Family Composition," PC (2)-4A.

The *Census of Housing* (48) is part of the decennial census. There is a United States summary volume and one volume for each state. Statistics include median value of dwelling and rent, size of household, and duration of vacancy. Separately published reports provide similar housing data for individual city blocks within urbanized areas (49). Statistics correspond to city block numbers provided on the accompanying maps.

Data found in both parts of the decennial census are combined in the *Census of Population and Housing* (50). Statistics are for Standard Metropolitan Statistical Areas. An SMSA is a core city of over 50,000 and the closely surrounding area. To date, the Census Bureau has defined 268 such SMSA's. SMSA's are subdivided into census tracts, geographic areas of approximately 4,000 people created for comparative statistical purposes. It is necessary to consult an accompanying map to determine the number of tract or tracts in which one is interested. Statistics on both housing and socioeconomic characteristics are given for each tract as well as for the entire SMSA.

The *1970 Census User's Guide* (51) defines terms and lists all the questions used but it does *not* give complete listings of all subject reports and parts of the census. The *Census Catalog* cited above, will be far more useful in identifying the parts of the census available.

There is nothing that approaches a complete update of the census between decades. However, the *Current Population Reports* (52) series serves as a valuable supplement to the census. These reports are issued frequently and offer continuing up-to-date statistics on population counts, characteristics of the population, and other special studies on the American people, for example, income, educational attainment, and birthrates. Each subject subseries has its own separate number:

P–20 Population characteristics (national figures)

P–23 Special studies

P–25 Population estimates and projects

P–26 Federal-State cooperative program for population estimates

P–28 Special censuses

P–60 Consumer income

P–65 Consumer buying indicators

Sample titles from the P–20 series include "Characteristics of the Population by Ethnic Origin" and "Birth Expectations of American Wives," and from the P–23 series, "Some Demographic Aspects of Aging in the United States" and "Social and Economic Status of the Black Population in the United States."

The *County and City Data Book* (53) is a handy compendium of statistics on United States counties, cities, and SMSA's based on the censuses of agriculture, business, governments, housing, manufacturers, mineral industries, and population, as well as data from governmental and private agencies. It is published every five years.

Congress has appointed several libraries in each state to serve as depository libraries. These libraries automatically receive publications of the U.S. Government Printing Office provided they make the documents readily available to the people in that state. Academic and major public libraries are usually depositories and census publications should be available in them. A smaller library may have the parts of the census relevant to that geographic region. Selection policies will vary on this, so it is wise to check with the reference department about the extent of documents holdings.

The *Monthly Catalog of United States Government Publications* (54) is a listing of U.S. government publications (both depository and nondepository) arranged by issuing agency. There is an index by title of documents and by subject which is cumulated annually. Although the *Monthly Catalog* is not a complete list of all government publications, it is the best place to start to identify them.

Government bookstores located in several cities stock the most frequently used documents in their respective areas. A list of bookstores appears on the cover of the *Monthly Catalog.*

To supplement statistical data one should file collection. Such files can provide information on community resources, services, and institutions. They can help provide both background and very recent information on issues or programs in the community.

There may also be information on local grants, on parks and recreation, or biographical background on prominent individuals.

GRANTS

Since money for project development; in-service training; attendance at seminars, courses, and conferences; equipment and/or construction; and publication is not always available in the regular budget, it is sometimes necessary to seek additional funds through grants to support these types of activities. Most of the funding for grants comes from governmental agencies and from international, national, or private organizations including foundations, business, and professional associations.

The *Annual Register of Grant Support* (55) is an up-to-date guide to a wide variety of financial aid for applicants from the United States and Canada. Each program description contains the organization's name, address, and telephone number; the purpose, type, and duration of the grant; financial data; instructions for applicants, including eligibility requirements and deadline; and any special stipulations. The *Register* is divided into ten broad subject fields, for example, social sciences and race minorities, and has four separate indexes: subject, organization and program, geographic, and personnel. The *Grants Register* (56) is a biennial publication designed for citizens of the English-speaking countries of the world. Approximately one third of the grants are international in scope. Using the separate subject index under nationality one should check the general listings and subject headings such as social development and welfare, professions and occupations. The entry for each program gives the address of the organization, purpose of the grant, value, eligibility, closing date, and address for applications. Symbols indicate awards limited to women, men, or persons with a doctoral degree.

The *Foundation Directory* (57) and its quarterly supplements (58) describe grants available from foundations, corporations, and charitable trusts in the United States. Major national, state, and regional foundations are included. Foundations are listed alphabetically by state with separate indexes to the foundations by field of interest; state and city; donors, trustees, and administrators; and names of foundations. Information in each entry lists the name and address of the foundation, its purpose and activities, financial data on number of grants and their total value (when known), officers and trustees, and the name of person to whom correspondence should be addressed. The fifth edition (1975) has two essays of interest: "What Makes a Good Proposal?" by F. Lee Jacquette and Barbara L. Jacquette (pp. 424–426) and "What Will a Foundation Look for When You Submit a Grant Proposal?" by Robert A. Mayer (pp. 427–429). Judith B. Margolin has written a pamphlet entitled "About Foundations: How to Find the Facts You Need to Get a Grant" (59) in which she discusses the best sources for obtaining information about foundations.

Additional information on foundations can be obtained from *Foundation News* (60). This bimonthly publication contains articles on foundations such as "What Foundations Should be Saying to Congress" and "Do's and Don'ts for Development Officers" (volume 16). There is also a regular section "Foundation Grants Index" in which foundation grants of $5,000 or more are listed geographically by state. Each entry includes the granting foundation's name and state, amount donated, name of recipient, and in most cases a sentence describing the purpose of the grant. There are separate indexes by recipients and by key words and phrases, for example abortion services, study, race relations, or mental health. The indexes are not, however, cumulated for the year. It could be very helpful to discover which foundations have awarded grants on a topic similar to the project you are considering. The *Foundation Grants Index* (61) is a cumulation of the section appearing in *Foundation News* and lists " . . . grants of $10,000 or more made by foundations, charitable trusts or corporations" (Introduction). The grants are arranged under broad subjects such as welfare, with subcategories such as community development or social sciences. An article by Karin Abarbanel entitled "Using the Grants Index to Plan a Funding Search" (62) discusses the best use of this tool. The *Foundation Center Source Book* (63) provides detailed information on national and regional foundations including statements of policies, programs, and fiscal data. One can write the Foundation Center (64) for information about microform publications and computerized data bank.

Some states have a directory of their own foundations. To discover if there is a directory for a specific state, check with the library's reference department.

CONCLUSION

Libraries are much more than a repository for books and journals. Every library has its own unique public service program which one will want to investigate. Perhaps the most significant resource of all is the professional librarian; the larger the library the more likely it is there will be a librarian specially trained in the social sciences and a separate social sciences department. Other typical library services including meeting rooms, photocopy equipment, sound recordings, movies, interlibrary loan, and subscriptions to current magazines and newspapers. Large libraries may also have computer data bases which permit the user to search an index like *Psychological Abstracts* by author or subject. There is usually a charge for the computer time.

This article has attempted to point out the major types of tools and services available in most libraries. It should be remembered that there are many more reference sources than can be covered in an overview article such as this. Most topics, particularly in the social sciences, are interdisciplinary. It is important to consider what other fields may be concerned with the same or similar phenomena and to investigate the literature of those fields for additional data and new perspectives.

The author hopes this survey of library resources will motivate readers to become familiar with these basic concepts and tools and will inspire them to discover the countless other information sources at their command.

BIBLIOGRAPHY

1. White, Carl. *Sources of Information in the Social Sciences; a Guide to the Literature.* Chicago: American Library Association, 1973.
2. Sheehy, Eugene P. *Guide to Reference Books.* 9th ed. Chicago: American Library Association, 1976.
3. *New Encyclopedia Britannica.* 15th ed. Chicago: Encyclopaedia Britannica, 1974.
4. *International Encyclopedia of the Social Sciences.* New York: Macmillan, 1968.
5. *Encyclopedia of Social Work.* New York: National Association of Social Workers, 1929– .
6. Gould, Julius, and Kolb, William L. *A Dictionary of the Social Sciences.* New York: Free Press, 1964.
7. Black, Henry Campbell. *Black's Law Dictionary.* 4th ed. rev. St. Paul: West Publishing Co., 1968.
8. *Acronyms and Initialisms Dictionary.* 5th ed. Detroit: Gale Research, 1976.
9. *Bibliographic Index.* New York: H. W. Wilson Co., 1938– .
10. *Council of Planning Librarians. Exchange Bibliography.* Urbana, Ill., 1956– .
11. *Reader's Guide to Periodical Literature.* New York: H. W. Wilson Co., 1901– .
12. *Social Sciences Index.* New York: H. W. Wilson Co., June 1974– . (Supersedes in part the *Social Sciences and Humanities Index* 1965–1974 which was entitled *International Index* from 1907–1965.)
13. *Public Affairs Information Service Bulletin* (PAIS). New York: Public Affairs Information Service, 1915– .
14. *Psychological Abstracts.* Washington, D.C.: American Psychological Association, 1927– .
15. *Sociological Abstracts.* New York: Sociological Abstracts, Inc., 1953– .
16. *Human Resources Abstracts.* Beverly Hills: Sage Publications, 1966– . (Entitled *PHRA: Poverty and Human Resources Abstracts* from 1966–1974.)
17. *Sage Public Administration Abstracts.* Beverly Hills: Sage Publications, 1974– .
18. *Abstracts for Social Workers.* Albany, N.Y.: National Association of Social Workers, 1965– .
19. *United States Statutes at Large.* Washington, D.C.: U.S. Government Printing Office, 1789– .
20. *United States Code.* 1970 ed. Washington, D.C.: U.S. Government Printing Office, 1971. Supplement. 1972– .
21. American Public Welfare Association. *The Public Welfare Directory.* Chicago: American Public Welfare Association, 1940– .
22. *The National Directory of State Agencies.* Washington, D.C.: Information Resources Press, 1974/75– .
23. *United Way Directory.* New York: United Way of America, 1932– .
24. National Association of Social Workers. *NASW Directory of Professional Social Workers.* New York: National Association of Social Workers, 1960– .
25. Child Welfare League of America. *The Directory of Member Agencies.* New York: Child Welfare League, 1948– .
26. *Who's Who in the Midwest.* Chicago: Marquis Co., 1949– . (Other regional directories are *Who's Who in the East, Who's Who in the South and Southwest,* and *Who's Who in the West.*)
27. U.S. Congress. *Official Congressional*

Directory. Washington, D.C.: U.S. Government Printing Office, 1809–   .

28. *Directory of Rehabilitation Consultants.* Gainesville, Fla.: Regional Rehabilitation Research Institute of University of Florida, Gainesville for the U.S. Social and Rehabilitation Service, 1971.

29. *United States Government Manual.* Washington, D.C.: U.S. Government Printing Office, 1935–   .

30. Press, Charles, and Williams, Oliver. *State Manuals, Blue Books, and Election Results.* Berkeley: Institute of Governmental Studies, University of California, 1962.

31. Hernon, Peter. "State Publications: A Bibliographic Guide for Academic (and other) Reference Collections," *Library Journal, 97* (April 15, 1972), 1393–98.

32. Hernon, Peter. "State Publications: A Bibliographic Guide for Reference Collections," *Library Journal, 99* (November 1, 1974), 2810–19.

33. United States Postal Service. *National ZIP Code Directory.* Washington, D.C.: U.S. Government Printing Office, 1965–

34. *American Universities and Colleges.* 11th ed. Washington, D.C.: American Council on Education, 1973.

35. *Ulrich's International Periodicals Directory.* New York: Bowker, 1932–

36. *Ayer's Directory of Newspapers and Periodicals.* Philadelphia: Ayer Press, 1880–   .

37. *Encyclopedia of Associations.* 10th ed. Detroit: Gale Research, 1976.

38. U.S. Bureau of the Census. *Statistical Abstract of the United States.* Washington, D.C.: U.S. Government Printing Office, 1878–   .

39. *American Statistics Index.* Washington, D.C.: Congressional Information Service, 1973–   .

40. *Editor and Publisher Market Guide.* New York: Editor and Publisher Co. Inc., 1943–   .

41. *Rand McNally Commercial Atlas and Marketing Guide.* New York: Rand McNally and Co., 1911–   .

42. U.S. Bureau of the Census. *Census of Population: 1970.* Washington, D.C.: U.S. Government Printing Office, 1973.

43. _____. *Bureau of the Census Guide to Programs and Publications: Subjects and Areas, 1973.* Washington, D.C.: U.S. Government Printing Office, 1974.

44. _____. *Bureau of the Census Catalog.* Washington, D.C.: U.S. Government Printing Office, 1946–   .

45. _____. *Bureau of the Census Catalog of Publications, 1790–1972.* Washington, D.C.: U.S. Government Printing Office, 1974.

46. _____. *Census of Population: 1970. Characteristics of the Population.* Washington, D.C.: U.S. Government Printing Office, 1973.

47. _____. *Census of Population: 1970. Subject Reports.* Washington, D.C.: U.S. Government Printing Office, 1973–   .

48. _____. *Census of Housing: 1970. Housing Characteristics for States, Cities, and Counties.* Washington, D.C.: U.S. Government Printing Office, 1972.

49. _____. *Census of Housing: 1970. Block Statistics.* Washington, D.C.: U.S. Government Printing Office, 1971.

50. _____. *Census of Population and Housing: 1970. Census Tracts.* Washington, D.C.: U.S. Government Printing Office, 1972.

51. _____. *1970 Census Users' Guide.* Washington, D.C.: U.S. Government Printing Office, 1970.

52. _____. *Current Population Reports.* Washington, D.C.: U.S. Government Printing Office, 1947–   .

53. _____. *County and City Data Book.* Washington, D.C.: U.S. Government Printing Office, 1949–   .

54. U.S. Superintendent of Documents. *Monthly Catalog of United States Government Publications.* Washington, D.C.: U.S. Government Printing Office, 1895–   .

55. *Annual Register of Grant Support.* Orange, N.J.: Academic Media, 1969–   .

56. *The Grants Register 1975–1977.* New York: St. Martin's Press, 1975.

57. *The Foundation Directory.* New York: Russell Sage Foundation, 1960–   .

58. *Foundation Center Supplement.* New York: Russell Sage Foundation, 1975–   . (Entitled *Foundation Center Information Quarterly* 1972–1974).

59. Margolin, Judith B. *About Foundations: How to Find the Facts You Need to Get a*

Grant. New York: Foundation Center, 1976.

60. *Foundation News.* Baltimore: Foundation Library Center, 1960–   .

61. *Foundation Grants Index 1974.* New York: Foundation Center, 1975.

62. Abarbanel, Karin. "Using the Grants Index to Plan a Funding Search,"
Foundation News, 17 (Jan/Feb 1976), 44–53.

63. *Foundation Center Source Book.* Rev. ed. New York: Foundation Center, 1975.

64. Foundation Center Associate Program, 888 Seventh Avenue, New York, New York, 10019.

CHAPTER II

Planning with the Community

Introduction

The community organization practitioner often uses planning skills, but too frequently these skills are seen as being narrow and technical, and in the province of a trained few. Often, too, they are seen as being heavily quantitative in orientation, so that scientific and engineering principles become the basis for planning tasks. Part of this tradition stems from the heavy involvement of the physical planners in urban work; with physical planning comes a heavy technical component of skill. Further, the mathematical models of the policy planners of places like the Rand–New York City Corporation give the patina of "operations research" to human services planning.

We would not deny, and have indeed been supporters of, this technical component of the planning process. Yet if that component is seen as the whole process, two drawbacks are created. The first is that more common skills, which are nonetheless critical, tend to be left by the wayside; the second is that the technical skills (perhaps "formal," or "quantitative," would be a better word) create a chasm between the planner and the people. Since many in any community cannot relate to or comprehend the complex quantitative-formal approach, community members often feel left out and excluded. Some of these elements were covered in the previous chapter. This chapter develops a range of techniques of planning which are in some sense common in everyday life and which we all use on one occasion or another. They are techniques which build links between the professional and the people, between the community organizer and the community.

Many of these techniques, however, are not performed very well. Take, for example, planning a conference. How many times have we all been at conferences which were shabbily organized and indifferently run? And yet many important community issues are addressed at such conferences. For this reason we present a piece on conference planning (Reading 10), which covers this important tactic from A to Z. While solid planning and meticulous attention to detail will not assure positive interaction of the conference with the community, it is a certainty that a poorly designed conference will not be an effective device for dealing with community issues.

Another common area of professional practice is committee staffing and the making of studies. Despite many courses in community organization in schools of social work, there is little material on how to be a "staff" person. Here we are using "staff" in its transitive sense, not as a member of an organization but as someone hired to assist in the functioning of a committee. The staff person is often instrumental in conducting studies of one kind or another on behalf of community interests. The articles by Elmer Tropman on planning tools and by Yeheskel Hasenfeld on policy analysis point to the importance of good analysis and suggest ways in which it might be undertaken.

Time after time a community organizer will be called upon to pull together a "representative group" which can comment on some matter or effect some change. Yet there is little available material on how this task might be accomplished or what some of the requisites might be. Jack Rothman's article on using representative committees hits directly at this point. Suggestions are made as to what to do and how to do it.

The need for a conceptual overview is always present for the planner. Such an overview can assist the planner to integrate technical-quantitative aspects with community-based "people" aspects, and both of these with professional aspects and substantive knowledge in a particular area. The social system model is a handy tool for this purpose; we are fortunate to have an especially good sample in the work of Jack Bloedorn, Elizabeth Mac Latchie, William Friedlander, and J. M. Wedemeyer.

In sum, the tactics and techniques presented in this chapter are ones which all community organizers and social work practitioners will use at one or another time. They are planning techniques because they are ways in which the professional can involve the community in anticipating the future; they are perhaps even more needful of systematic treatment because of their nature.

John E. Tropman

6. Understanding the Issues: Policy Analysis

Yeheskel Hasenfeld

POLICY ISSUES AND INTERORGANIZATIONAL RELATIONS

GENERAL

1. Which are the major groups, organizations, institutions, etc., concerned and involved with the problem or issue (political, public, private, community, etc.)?
   a. Map the structural arrangements between these groups.
   b. How have these arrangements been negotiated? Identify special obligations or allegiances that have been formed.
   c. What is the nature of the interaction between these groups (exchanges, communications, etc.)?
   d. What are the forces, if any, impelling these groups toward or preventing them from working together?
2. How do the various groups define the problem or policy issue?
   a. Identify historical, ideological, and value orientation of these groups.
   b. What role do these orientations play in the groups' perception, reaction, and response to the problem or issue?
3. What parties have been identified as the major actors involved in the problem or issue?
   a. Which persons or groups have been identified as:

1. being most affected by the problem or issue?
2. providing support?
3. causing opposition?
   b. What effect have such groups had on the problem?
4. What general approaches have been used toward resolving the problem or issue?
   a. What seem to be the varying priorities established by different groups?
   b. What program strategies have been developed around the problem or issue?

POWER DISTRIBUTION

Identify major power groups, both formal and informal, that are involved with the problem or issue.
1. Which groups seem to have more influence?
2. How is the influence of these groups exercised?
3. How accessible are those in power to other persons or groups working with the problem or issue?
4. What effect do these groups have on the direction and action taken regarding the problem or issue?
5. What groups seem to have the least amount of influence?
   What major role do these groups play?

Source: Unpublished, Yeheskel Hasenfeld, "A Problem or Policy Issue and Interorganizational Relationships," March 1976.

6. How have the various groups approached building constituencies to support their position?
7. What evidence, if any, is there of attempts to redistribute the power base?

RESOURCES

1. When are the major sources of material and nonmaterial resources directly related to the problem or issue?
   a. What special pre-conditions and criteria, if any, exist regarding the use of these resources?
   b. How, if at all, are resources monitored?
2. What resources are currently being utilized for the problem or issue?
   a. How effectively are the resources being utilized?
   b. What are the gaps in resources? What additional resources are needed?
   c. What potential resources can be mobilized?

d. What plans and strategies have been or are being developed to secure and maintain resources?

IMPLEMENTATION OF POLICY OR PROGRAM

1. Which groups working with the problem or issue have developed specific policies and programs toward resolution of the problem?
   a. How have these groups tried to operationalize their goals?
   b. What major problems have they encountered?
   c. Identify evidence of conflict and competition between groups working on the problem or issue.
   d. What environmental demands have been made on these groups regarding their policies or programs?
2. What alternative solutions have been developed or could be developed? Which alternatives appear to be more acceptable? Why?

7. Interorganizational Cooperation: Using Representative Committees

Jack Rothman

HOW TO ORGANIZE A COMMUNITY ACTION PLAN

In presenting guidelines to community action it should be clear that this is not a master plan to be adopted routinely by all communities.

Every community is different and its peculiarities have to be weighed in designing an appropriate action program. The way the problem of drug abuse presents itself will vary in different locales. In some communities marijuana may be used freely while heroin is absent. In other communi-

Source: Unpublished, Jack Rothman, "How You Can Help Fight Drug Abuse: The Next Step: What to Do To Serve Your Community."

This report was prepared for the Governor's Office of Drug Abuse by Dr. Jack Rothman, Professor of Community Organization, School of Social Work, University of Michigan.

ties the reverse may be true. Still other communities may have frequent usage of both.

Use of drugs by middle class teenagers in the suburbs for kicks presents a different problem than usage by adults in the inner city to escape the harshness of life.

There may be different degrees of involvement of organized crime in the drug picture from area to area. And the existence of an institutionalized drug culture differs from neighborhood to neighborhood based on the length of time drug abuse has persisted, the numbers of individuals involved, and the function served by drug abuse for the takers.

In addition, different communities may to varying degrees have already existing treatment-rehabilitation services or enforcement procedures. Resources available to apply to the problem by way of funds and professional expertise are uneven among communities. And citizens will desire to give their own emphasis to ameliorative programs, reflecting the particular value position of their community.

AN OPEN MIND

In embarking on a drug abuse program it would be well for a community to recognize that it is entering a highly complex and uncertain area of endeavor. It should be prepared to study the problem objectively and respond with frankness to facts about drug abuse as they become available locally and nationally.

The importance of truth and honesty in confronting drug abuse cannot be stressed enough.

Here is how the Kiwanis' "Operation Drug Abuse" plan explains it:

The whole field of drug abuse education is fraught with misinformation, superficial conclusions, emotionalism, and conjecture. A program cannot rest its case on obviously specious reasoning—for example, that marijuana must have chemical properties or produce pharmacological effects comparable to those of heroin, morphine, and opium because its use is regulated under the same state or federal statutes ... or that if most heroin addicts admit to having used marijuana before they used heroin, it must follow from this reason alone that marijuana use leads to the use of heroin ... or that if the percentage of drug addicts who have criminal records is higher than the percentage of non-addicts with criminal records, this must be proof of a drug-crime relationship.

Any respected authority who has reached any of these conclusions has not done so for these reasons alone, yet these are common place observations we hear in lay conversations. If a program is based on this level of reasoning, it will most certainly be exposed as a superficial one by even a young audience. The valid and factual information against drug abuse is so abundant that the well-informed participant will have no need to resort to the crutch of unsubstantiated dogmatism and authoritarianism. This is the reason for self-education. ...

Also if from the information available, we select only the horrifying, the tragic, the bizarre examples of drug abuse and present these as the total and true picture of contact with the drugs with which we are primarily concerned, we will lose the respect of those who know or will later find out that we have deliberately avoided the whole truth.

We will be dishonest with youth, furthermore, if we give the impression that today's drug abuse problem is just another youth problem, symptomatic of a generation gap or youth rebellion. It is our adult generation which has produced an estimated six and a half million alcoholics.

Our generation created a pill-oriented society in which United States physicians issued in 1968 alone 167 million prescriptions for amphetamines and barbiturates. Identifying youth as our primary audience in a drug education program must not confuse the fact that drug abuse cuts across all age groups in our society.

VARYING PROGRAM DIRECTIONS

In light of community variability and scientific uncertainty concerning the drug problem it would be presumptuous to prescribe a uniform community solution.

Instead it is recommended that the problem be placed on the community agenda as a number one priority concern and various mechanisms should be considered by which citizens and relevant agencies and professionals can talk and work together in coming to grips with local drug abuse problems.

Steps to be taken include at least:

1. Research and fact finding concerning social and medical dimensions of the problem locally and in the nation.
2. Development of specific program of prevention and rehabilitation based on local community needs and resources.

These programs may vary a great deal in emphasis and objectives.

Some typical programmatic approaches include the following:

a. A public discussion program to "loosen people up" to examine the drug abuse problem in an objective way, in a calm atmosphere. Here the intention in part might be to foster cross-generational dialogue.
b. Alternatively, a public education campaign geared to arousing the populace to the extent of drug abuse and to a program of curtailing all usage.
c. Work with young people to warn them of the dangers of drugs and change their attitudes about experimenting with them (educational, guidance and counselling programs).
d. Promote a crackdown on distributors and users of drugs. Encourage programs to support and aid the police in surveillance and enforcement. Encourage stiffer penalties for distributors and users. Root out organized crime.
e. Alternatively, change legal statutes to lessen penalties, particularly in connection with less dangerous drugs. Move drug abuse programs from the legal to the medical and social arena.
f. Develop new treatment-rehabilitation services.
g. In services that already exist, help improve them through expansion, bringing in newer techniques, or improving communication and cooperation among the agencies and professionals involved in the work.
h. Create or strengthen local research programs on medical and/or social aspects of drug abuse.

As the reader can see, program alternatives are diverse and are not always compatible with one another. A rational approach would require an open mind, a desire to study new scientific evidence as it becomes available, and a balance and experimental posture in program directions in light of the inconclusive state of scientific evidence.

Balance implies some equilibrium between preventive and rehabilitative approaches, between legalistic and educational ones, between short range and long range strategies. It is obvious that a purely punitive, legalistic approach which denies rehabilitation for those who are already addicted and in need of help, and which does nothing about attacking the underlying *causes* of the massive outbreak of drug abuse in America is doomed to failure.

STAGES IN ORGANIZING FOR COMMUNITY ACTION

Just as there are many approaches to the drug problem, there are various ways for communities to organize to do something about it. Following is an outline of an organizing format which has been successful in some communities and which presents a logical sequence of steps. It suggests establishment of a community-wide, broadly representative Drug Abuse Council. It is not offered as a blueprint, however; communities should be encouraged to adopt variations that seem better to suit local situations.

1. A Small Information Initiation Group

Most community action programs start small and snowball, including more and more people and organizations as they develop. A useful first step is for a group of interested people (citizens and/or professionals) to come together to test the extent of their own commitment and to ascertain generally whether a community program is needed. If there truly is a group that is willing to "start the ball rolling" and to provide manpower and encouragement through the early organizing stages, then additional organizational effort is in order.

2. Larger Representative Sponsoring Group

A larger planning group is necessary to survey the local scene and initiate the program formally. This group should represent wide community interests, including citizens, youth, interested parties (such as addicts and/or their families) and professionals engaged in drug abuse programs.

Such a group can test the feasibility of a unified community approach, share perspectives on the extent and nature of the problem in the community and legitimate the whole venture. In the earliest stage this group may want to engage in a period of self-education in order to be able to provide knowledgeable leadership (see Committee on Research and Evaluation under No. 4 for suggested activities).

Representatives from among the following kinds of groups might be invited to participate in this sponsoring group:

Parents
School representatives (High & Jr. High), administrators, faculty, students
Courts (juvenile, family, felony—judges, probation officers, service personnel)
Professionals in rehabilitation agencies (social workers, psychologists, psychiatrists)
Law enforcement agencies
Local drug or narcotics control commission
Clergymen (ministerial association) and church organizations
Kiwanis and other service clubs (Kiwanis has a Drug Abuse program)
Youth organizations
Medical Association chapter
National Association of Social Workers chapter
Pharmacists and pharmacologists
Mayor's office and city council members
Health Department
Civic groups such as League of Women Voters
Chamber of Commerce
United Community Services
Present and former drug users
College students and college professors

If a Drug Education Council or similar group already exists in the community (this should be checked), contacts should be made in order to discuss mutual interests. Possibilities include a cooperative venture, working through the structure of the existing organization to strengthen it, dividing tasks among two groups, or replacing the existing organization.

As a result of its deliberations this initial sponsoring group should arrive at some *tentative* understanding as to the nature of the problem locally, and the kind of programmatic measures necessary to deal with it. It should also be prepared to recommend a tentative organizational structure for proceeding with the work—that is an executive structure, necessary committees, means of funding the operation, etc.

It should plan the presentation of these preliminary recommendations to an open community meeting at which time the Drug Abuse Council would be officially established. Interim officers to preside at this meeting should be selected. A listing of possible committees that might be included in these initial recommendations is listed later in this report.

While preparing for the large public meeting, the sponsoring committee should work with news media in order to alert people to the problem locally and build up interest for the open public meeting.

3. Official Launching at an Open Public Meeting

The opening public meeting or "community mobilization" signals the official launching of the local Drug Abuse Council.[1] It is important to invite members of the community at large in addition to the general membership of organizations listed in No. 2.

Tentative recommendations concerning program and organizational arrangements should be presented for discussion and

[1] In some communities it may be desirable to establish the Council on the basis of Sponsoring Group Action alone suggested in No. 2 and forego the large public meeting.

either approval or modification. Some open-ended time should be allowed for people to "sound off" about the drug issue. A speaker or event of some educational, inspirational or entertainment character might be included to enliven the program (a panel of users, police and social workers in a "confrontation", a display of narcotic devices, etc.) Tentative officers could be elected. Individuals should be asked to sign up for specific committees on which they would like to work. Dues or financial contributions could be solicited. Sign-up sheets could be passed around in order to obtain names of potential members and participants, and to take an inventory of interest. Literature tables might be set up for purposes of community education.

4. Program Committee Structure

Form follows function, and committee structure should follow the specific goals and philosophy of a given organization. That is to say, there is no established committee organizational chart to suit all organizations. Committees can only be viewed in terms of the purposes of an organization and the programs which are desired to meet those goals.

A listing of possible committees follows. These are presented suggestively, to be selected among by the Local Drug Abuse Council, according to the requisites of the local situation and the Council's own priorities. *Few communities will have the manpower and resources to undertake all these committee activities at once, especially in the early stages.* It would probably not be desirable to undertake all of them in any instance because the efforts of the Council would become too diffuse. Most organizations tend to overstructure, that is, to establish too elaborate and ambitious an organizational framework.

Modesty and simplicity would be the desirable direction to lean at the beginning. Also, it is well for an organization to be somewhat fluid in its structure in the beginning so that a natural pattern may emerge from the interests and personalities of the membership. Committees to consider include:

COMMITTEE ON COMMUNITY INFORMATION

Establish close working relationships with newspapers, radio stations, and TV stations

Establish an Adult Speakers' Bureau

Write and promote "spot announcements" for local radio stations to use under the public service requirement of the FCC

Prepare news releases for the total program

Prepare a newspaper series on drug abuse for the local newspapers

Sponsor study sessions, seminars, and informational meetings for adults in the community

Prepare and disseminate "fact sheets" periodically on drug abuse

Establish a telephone "dial access" system on drug abuse for adults in the community

Serve in the role of disseminator for other committees

Form liaison with churches and synagogues

Form liaison with adult community organizations encouraging these organizations to: (*a*) conduct their own drug abuse programs, (*b*) contribute manpower, funds and other resources to the community program.

Literature distribution possibilities for this committee include:

1. Door to door to residences
2. To heavily visited offices and public places —doctors' and dentists' offices, public libraries, employment offices, welfare offices, etc.
3. Business locations—drug stores, bank lobbies, barber shops; places frequented by young people should be emphasized— sandwich shops, snack bars, "Y" 's, dance halls, etc.
4. Public reading racks in train stations, bus depots, churches, etc.
5. At public functions such as forums, conferences, school assemblies, etc.
6. To welfare and youth service agencies such as recreation programs, child guidance agencies, vocational guidance services, etc.
7. To police departments, juvenile court judges, sheriffs' offices, etc.
8. Through Civic Groups such as PTA's, Kiwanis, Chamber of Commerce, women's clubs, civic improvement associations, etc.

COMMITTEE ON PARENT RELATIONSHIPS

Conduct parent education programs—incidence of drug abuse, how to recognize it, what to do about it in the family.

Use a variety of means of presentation—
1. Authoritative presentation by a speaker
2. Panel discussion (physician, psychologist, student, police official, etc.)
3. A film and then discussion
4. Combined meeting of parents and youth
5. Conduct a series of such meetings

Develop literature programs aimed at parents

Establish family counselling service on drug abuse (by phone or personal conference)

COMMITTEE ON CURRICULUM DEVELOPMENT

Prepare a comprehensive status report on current instructional efforts

Determine whether or not current programs are appropriate and effective

Consider the desirability and feasibility of a formal, sequential instructional program— kindergarten through twelfth grade

Prepare additional instructional units for new grade levels as deemed appropriate

Determine the proper placement of instructional units in junior and senior high schools in terms of subject matter area

Determine the teacher qualifications necessary for instruction on the subject

Encourage extensive use of material and human resources in the program

Plan for and implement summer workshop programs as a prerequisite to instituting new units of study

Consider augmenting classroom programs with assemblies, student seminars, field trips, and guest speakers

It is important that all phases of this program should be conducted with the cooperation of local school boards and principals. The Michigan Department of Education is implementing its own drug abuse programs, and care should be exercised to avoid duplicating efforts.

COMMITTEE ON MULTIMEDIA MATERIALS

Preview and evaluate multimedia materials on drug use and abuse including films, film strips, film loops, booklets, pamphlets, books, periodicals, audio tapes, video tapes, recordings, slides, pictures, exhibits, etc.

Prepare annotated bibliographies on materials and recommend grade level use or adult use

Consider feasibility of establishing a mobile and/or stationary Drug Library

Set up and circulate drug displays in cooperation with other committees

Provide assistance in the development of multimedia materials for use in the schools

COMMITTEE ON SCHOOL PROFESSIONAL STAFF DEVELOPMENT

Work with local school districts and help provide inservice training programs for the general teaching staff of all schools

Help provide specialized training programs for counselors, nurses, social workers, assistant principals, and principals of all schools (public and nonpublic)

Secure and/or prepare materials for professional staff members on symptoms of drug usage, and effects of drug usage

Develop a statement on practices and procedures for teachers to follow when a drug user is detected or suspected

Plan and implement summer workshops to prepare staff members as trainers to serve in leadership roles for inservice activities of other staff members during the school year

Identify and/or prepare training films, audio tapes, and video tapes for use with staff members

Again, to avoid duplication, close cooperation with local school boards and principals is necessary to carry out these objectives

COMMITTEE ON RESEARCH AND EVALUATION[2]

Attempt to determine the extent of drug usage and abuse among all people in the community

Attempt to determine the nature of drug abuse

Attempt to determine the sources of drugs and how they are made available

Review, digest, and disseminate research findings in the area of drug abuse

Design evaluation instruments to be used to determine impact of program activities for total program

Work on the problem of contributing factors and/or "personality types" that relate to susceptibility to drug usage

COMMITTEE ON CLINICAL SERVICES

Determine the desirability of establishing a drug clinic in the community

Determine the feasibility of establishing a drug clinic

Study the appropriate functions a drug clinic should serve relative to prevention and/or rehabilitation services (and types of needed personnel)

Prepare a cost analysis of a clinic in terms of location, space requirements, staffing, equipment, furniture, materials, and supplies

Study the funding problem in terms of community support of such a facility

Study the existing and projected facilities for this area and the State of Michigan in light of need

Study and evaluate existing clinic facilities in this area in terms of services offered and impact of their efforts

COMMITTEE ON POLICE AND COURT RELATIONSHIPS

Form liaison with agencies of law enforcement and administration of justice

Compile up to date information on incidence of investigations, arrests and convictions in the drug abuse area

Recruit police and court officials who can participate in community programs

Become and remain informed about drug statutes—be prepared to inform the organization and the community

Evaluate current legal and enforcement situation in terms of—
1. Are the laws adequate or inadequate?
2. If adequate, are they adequately and appropriately enforced?
3. Are laws so severe that juries and courts are reluctant to convict violator?
4. Does enforcement harass the small violator and ignore the bigger organized crime elements?

---

[2]In the earliest stage the Council as a whole may wish to attend primarily to these tasks in order to provide a basis for all further activities. The committee would then supplement and continue these early research efforts.

The work of this committee overlaps to some degree the Committee on Legislation. The two could be combined.

COMMITTEE ON LEGISLATION

Review, study, and evaluate current legislation, in the area of drug abuse

Attempt to influence legislators to revise or change current legislation that is inappropriate

Identify limitations in current laws and attempt to initiate new legislation

Support legislation designed to provide institutional rehabilitation facilities for drug addicts

Support and/or initiate legislation designed to adequately fund programs and facilities to combat the problem of drug abuse

Organize a political action campaign to support and influence improved drug legislation

Work with other task force committees to gather supportive data and reactions to legislative proposals

COMMITTEE ON PROGRAMS AND RESOURCES IN OTHER COMMUNITIES

Establish liaison relationships with agencies, institutions, and programs in Michigan and the nation

Visit other programs for the purpose of gathering ideas and data to strengthen the local program

Share ideas, programs, and materials from the local program with others

Identify human resources in the State and nation that might be used on a consultant basis to strengthen the local program

Share promising materials and practices with the other appropriate committees

Prepare a compendium of promising programs based upon data gathered

A SEPARATE YOUTH-TO-YOUTH PROGRAM OR COMMITTEE

Many activists in the drug abuse field have concluded that the most effective way to make an impact on young people is through other young people. One means of attempting this is through the establishment of a Mayor's Youth Committee on Narcotics (MYCON).

Dearborn Heights [Michigan] has conducted such a program over the recent past. The experience of that community might be a useful guide to others. A MYCON type of program could be conducted through the auspices of a Drug Abuse Council. Here is a resume of the program in Dearborn Heights:

The Dearborn Heights Experience

Purpose: The main purpose is to establish a group of dedicated young people (primarily high school, junior high school, and college students) who, through a program of education, will first learn about the dangers of drugs, and then in turn create a forum of communication with their peers.

"The first thing we have to set straight," explains the MYCON chairman, "is that we're not informants. If we ever squealed on users, we might as well forget about any of these kids trusting us.

"But if we can convince those who are tempted to try drugs how dangerous it is . . . if we can persuade at least one of our friends to stop using them before it is too late, or to seek help from those who want to help . . . then we are really accomplishing our goal."

The first step the Mayor of Dearborn Heights took was to appoint an adult advisory commission (voluntary) to serve as a foundation for MYCON.

The Advisory Commission immediately began (1) an evaluation of the problem in Dearborn Heights, and (2) self-education program on drugs.

The next step was to contact all the school districts in the city and advise them of the problems facing the community. A meeting was scheduled and each district was invited to send a representative (senior student) from their schools. The concept of MYCON was presented at this first meeting.

The following meeting included school officials and eight students from each school, and a discussion of ideas which could be applicable to the situations in each of the areas (school districts) represented. Those who expressed a genuine interest in MYCON "signed up" as members of the committee.

Education of this original MYCON group included:

1. Study of local needs.
2. Review of available films on drugs.
3. Study of drug display kit (visual aid) created and maintained by the police department.
4. Study of reference sheets with description and classifications of drugs, explanation of effects and use and relative danger.
5. Field trips to Synanon.
6. Discussing clinical information from Lafayette Clinic.
7. Review first-hand another city's MYCON program to determine how it could be adapted locally.
8. Devising a plan (contacts, meetings, workshops) for educating the community (youth and adults) on the dangers of drug abuse.
9. Establishing a speaker's bureau of informed students who can accept invitations to speak about MYCON at school assemblies and to concerned adult organizations.

The response of this core group (about 20 teens) was one of enthusiasm, dedication and commitment. After the above steps in their education were completed and the students were ready "to go out on their own", the adult advisors stepped back to allow the students to take over the program. The adults do attend MYCON meetings and programs as consultants and advisors. But it is the young people themselves who are maintaining the program. THIS IS THE MOST IMPORTANT ASPECT OF THE MYCON PROGRAM and should be emphasized right at the start. It is a youth to youth program, or student to student program if one chooses to use these terms.

MYCON representatives have spoken to high school and junior high school assemblies, PTA's, Boys Club, service organizations, home and civic improvement associations, and other interested groups.

While the presentations vary according to the audiences, they generally consist of:

1. *Student speaker* first showing need for education and action by citing examples (local and neighboring communities) of bad trips, deaths, suicides and other physical and mental damage resulting from the abuse of drugs.
2. *Guest speaker or film* (Guest speaker at a number of assemblies was former high school football star, decorated serviceman *and* former "user" and ex-convict, Mr. George B., who "tells it like it is").
3. *Display* (accompanying MYCON is a police officer who has a display of drugs and photographs and answers questions).
4. *Explanation of MYCON* and its aims and *invitation* to students to join MYCON. (A table is placed somewhere in the rear of the room with membership applications and a drop box.)

Another important phase of the program are the seminars for students who are interested in becoming members of MYCON. This involves a more thorough study of drug abuse and the MYCON program.

The evidence of the success of the above format for a MYCON program is in the response of the students attending the programs. This dialogue of student to student, of friend to friend is the key to success.

Students know what the problems are. Students know what drugs their friends are experimenting with. They are in a position to convey to other students the message of the dangers of drug abuse.

Adult guidance, technical knowledge, and legal counsel are necessary . . . but only as foundation, moral guidance and background leadership. Nothing will turn a youngster "off" as quickly as an adult lecture on a youth-oriented problem.

But on the other hand, students will listen and believe one of their own when they "tell it like it is". The student who has seen with his own eyes a human destroyed by drugs . . . one who has technical and legal knowledge about drug abuse . . . is the most convincing speaker one can get for a MYCON program.

Pitfalls to be avoided include the use of outdated films and technical data that become boring.

Long-winded speeches, however good, tend to distract rather than educate. Over-anxious adults who interject themselves into MYCON also can hurt the program. *MYCON must be student operated.* Adults should exercise background leadership and guidance only.

Special requirements and areas of cooperation include:

1. Working with school officials and availability of school facilities for assembly programs and presentations to PTA's.
2. Permission to be excused from classes is necessary when a student member of MYCON is scheduled to speak at another school assembly or to other interested groups during school hours.
3. Cooperation of Police Department is vital.
4. Dedication of adult advisors is essential.

They must not only be available for MYCON meetings and seminars, but also for presentations to student assemblies and other interested groups.
5. Cooperation of city officials and service clubs. Funds are necessary to maintain such a program.

ADMINISTRATIVE AND FINANCIAL COMMITTEE STRUCTURE

Program is the heart of any organization, but the organization must also set up an appropriate administrative structure to perform ongoing maintenance functions. A set of officers is ordinarily required, including the usual chairman or co-chairman, one or more vice-chairmen, secretary and treasurer. This group, together with all committee chairmen, should sit as a steering committee to direct the overall policies and programs of the organization.

To the program committees already listed it might be useful to also add a membership committee and a finance committee.

If the general program becomes moderately large it would be useful or even necessary to add a paid clerical worker or to acquire professional staff assistance.

A professional staff administrator may be hired directly by the organization (full or part-time), or perhaps might be obtained on loan from a community agency with an ongoing strong interest in drug abuse.

There are a number of organizations and agencies in the community with regular programs, personnel and budgets whose functions include concern about drug abuse problems. Such organizations may include the mayor's office, the board of education, the police, a local drug clinic service, United Community Services, the courts, the Chamber of Commerce, etc.

If the aid of one or more of such groups can be enlisted, they may offer funding as well as staff service to the Drug Abuse Council. Such agencies might view such a community approach as a beneficial extension of enrichment of their own program—in a sense, a way of fostering a broader implementation of their mandate.

One precaution is in order here. An agency providing such assistance might want to put its own personal stamp on the community program, and thus make it parochial or one-sided. Thus, board of education sponsorship might entail pressure to concentrate only on youth, police sponsorship to focus exclusively on stricter enforcement, etc. If it's possible to obtain sponsorship from one of these agencies, the officers of the community Drug Abuse Council should explore thoroughly with the director of the agency whether he is willing to commit its resources to a broad-based community structure and a multi-faceted community approach.

If he is, the resources of the agency (money and/or staff assistance) can be powerful in getting the organization started and sustaining it. If there is no such commitment it would probably be better to seek other sources of funding. (Some agencies such as United Community Services and the Chamber of Commerce generally approach problems in broad community terms rather than from the standpoint of narrower program interests).

Other funding possibilities include:

Membership fees for participating in the organization (individual or organizational)

Voluntary contributions from individuals and organizations

Fees obtained from distribution of literature, films, speakers, etc.

United Fund

Foundations

Grants from federal sources

CONCLUSION

We have attempted to lay out some guidelines for community action approaches to the drug problem. Again, we would like to underline that communities should view this text as a series of suggestions rather than a formula to be copied.

In developing these activities it should be recognized that an outbreak of widespread taking of drugs must be viewed as a symptom of broader problems in our society.

Drug abuse in the inner city may be seen as a reaction to the poverty and discrimination to which our racial minorities are subjected.

Drug abuse by teenagers may well represent a reaction to the materialism and value normalness that they find around them.

As communities attack the manifestations of drug abuse through programs such as those which have been suggested, they should recognize that eventual elimination of the affliction will depend on solutions to broader problems such as these. It may be necessary to direct energies in both directions if real progress is to be made.

8. Planning Tools: A Social Systems Model

Jack C. Bloedorn, Elizabeth B. MacLatchie,
William Friedlander, and J. M. Wedemeyer

DESIGNING SOCIAL SERVICE SYSTEMS

THE APPROACH

In very few fields is it more apparent that the sum of the parts doesn't add up to the whole, yet traditionally social planners —Federal, state, and local—have poured enormous amounts of time and money into piecemeal efforts to improve the social service structure. What is now being suggested, and we believe receiving some cognizance by social planners at long last, is the systemic character of the social service structure and the resulting necessity to consider systemic diagnosis and treatment of administrative and structural problems.[1] Some describe this approach as the systems analysis or operation research approach to problem solving. Whatever it is called, action in terms of the whole system rather than piecemeal on its parts is an important, perhaps fundamental, underpinning not only to our approach in proposing a new social service system, but to continued responsive operation of such a system over time, in the face of environmental and/or legislative changes. Thus our proposal includes not only reconceptualization of key areas around approaches to social services, but also ac-

counts for the fact that a systemic structure must also be provided by which these concepts can be made viable (put into practical, effective operation) and kept viable, responsive, and effective over time.[2]

Because it is precisely the systematic manner or approach to social problems which we wish to recommend to planners as part of this treatise—in addition to the reconceptualization results we present for public social services—it may be interesting and useful to outline briefly here the fundamental process we put ourselves through which resulted in the material contained herein.

We first identified the problem area with which we would concern ourselves— public social service systems, and how to improve them. Our knowledge of the elements and dimensions of the problem and the performance of the present public social service system led us to ask ourselves which of two general lines of approach we should follow:

1. Carefully analyze each identified problem in the present structure and then develop proposed solutions for each of them, or

2. Redefine the fundamental objectives of public social service and work from

Reproduced by permission of the publisher, American Public Welfare Association, Washington, D.C. From Jack C. Bloedorn, Elizabeth B. MacLatchie, Wm. Friedlander and J.M. Wedemeyer, *Designing Social Service Systems,* © 1970, pp. 2–4, 66–90.

[1] Helen O. Nicol comes relatively close to taking a total systemic view, albeit at a level which would require much clarification before being operationally useful. See "Guaranteed Income Maintenance: A Public Welfare Systems Model," *Welfare In Review,* Vol. 4, No. 9 (November, 1966).

[2] For examples of recognition of this need, and appeals to the systemic view of social problems. see N. E. Golovin. "Social Change and the Evaluation Function In Government," *Management Science.* Vol. 15. No. 10 (June, 1969), and also Walter Burkley, *Sociology and Modern Systems Theory* (Englewood Cliffs, N.J.: Prentice-Hall, 1967).

there to develop a conceptual system design independent of the present structure.

Essentially we chose to proceed with the second approach line, principally because of our strong convictions about the need for systemic treatment of the whole social situation, and our strong convictions about the fruitlessness of trying to patch up in piecemeal fashion the existing structure. In reality, of course, one never makes a clean break from approach one to approach two—in our case precisely because the present structure in fact exists and it is this present structure which is the principal source of facts, experience, problems, needs, etc., which underpin developments in the second approach. The important point is, however, that we early-on dedicated ourselves to reconceptualization rather than simple "patching," and this brought us a long way toward realization of the systemic approach.

Having decided to take this approach, we next asked ourselves, "How shall we achieve a redesigned public social service system?" Considerable experience fortified by a modicum of literature research convinced us that the answer lay in formulation of a new set of concepts, ideas and methods together with a new operational, functional framework. This conclusion, of course, triggered the next question, namely, "How do we arrive at such a new formulation?" Our conclusion was that to do so required prior development of a thorough set of criteria by which we felt the successful development of a new public social service system should be measured —in other words, development of a fundamental set of principles, attributes, and desirable characteristics against which to test the applicability of various alternative concepts, ideas, methods, and structures toward redesign.

This led quite naturally, and rightly, to the final question, "On what shall we base such a criteria-set?" Our conclusion was that development of a criteria-set must depend upon a prior assignment of overall objectives for a public social service system.

Having gone through this question-and-answer exercise, our steps for development became quite clear, namely:

1. Formulate overall objectives for a public social service system.
2. Develop desirable criteria and characteristics of a public social service system by repeating the overall objectives down through layers of subobjectives to criteria using an objective-means iterative approach.[3]
3. Using the criteria then developed, select the subset of alternative concepts and ideas pertinent to social services which best meet the criteria.
4. Using the criteria, select the functional, organizational structure which best translates the select concepts and ideas into practical, implementable form.[4]

---

[3] The "objective-means" approach is an iterative procedure to develop alternatives for meeting given objectives. Starting with the overall objective, gross means of meeting that objective are created. Each such "means" is then itself treated as an objective, and a sublayer of more detailed means created to meet it. Each "means" in the sublayer is similarly treated as an objective and another layer of means created, and so forth, to any desired level of detail.

[4] We should emphasize that the overall objective, criteria, concepts and ideas, and functional structures developed represent our view of what these should be. Although we have strong convictions about them, we recognize that the reader may wish to assign a different overall objective and thus develop a different set of criteria, concepts, ideas, and functional structures. Thus, while we feel our overall objective is valid and our subsequent reconceptualization is highly relevant and useful, we wish to underline that perhaps the most important issue is *not* whether our redesign is better than another, but *is* whether a consistent, logical, systemic approach has been employed to arrive at redesign conclusions.

PUBLIC SOCIAL SERVICES AS A SYSTEM

Building upon the basic concepts and ideas described earlier, we have now constructed the general, functional framework of an operating model of the public social service system. But the technically oriented reader—especially if he is a specialist in management science, operations research, public administration or whatever—will probably have sensed a gap or jump between our two discussions. There is indeed, as we implied in our introductory remarks about the use of the systems approach to redesign, an intermediate step. It consists of the analysis of the requirements of the system in gross terms and the construction of a series of models at a high level of generality which will fulfill them. We took that step and will describe it here, rather than in its actual sequence in time, because we recognize that it is of interest primarily to the kinds of specialists we have identified above.

The reader will note that the organizational functions described earlier are not direct translation of generic systemic functions we will be discussing below. This "discrepancy" is not surprising since the two sets were developed for different purposes—one to establish fundamental criteria, the other to make the criteria operational. Thus some function criteria translate directly, one-for-one, while for others there is no translation at all. For example, while "basic community research" is a direct, one-for-one translation between the criteria set and the organizational set, "advocacy" does not translate at all since it is a "posture" of the system rather than an organizational unit. For other criteria, translation will be across many organizational functions as, for example, the mapping of "community relations" into parts of "mobilization," "liaison and coordination," and "outreach." Still others will be divided with respect to applicability at state or local level. For example, "distribution" at state level is articulated in "technical assistance," while at local level it deals with "client processing" and "service delivery."

An Input-Output Social Service System Model

In order to lay the proper foundation for development of specific planning criteria, we begin by outlining a very generalized input-output model of a public social service system. Diagrammatically, the model is displayed in Figure 8.1. Such a model accomplishes several things in terms of arriving at a set of desirable social service system attributes and functions [5] which in turn lay the foundation for reconceptualization and organizational planning. First, it emphasizes our basic contention that a public social service system behaves in a manner not dissimilar to most service or even product delivery systems. That is, it can be seen as a cyclical phenomenon whose operations consist of a circular chain of events which are continuously dependent upon preceding events around the chain. This is a fundamental principle in terms of the organization and management posture required to successfully operate a public social service system over time.

Second, the model demonstrates graphically the importance of "feedback" in terms of systemic operations. Most social planners already know or suspect that "feedback" is basic reaction to systemic operations and that no matter how a pub-

---

[5] Throughout the discussion which follows, we will use the terms "criteria," "authorities" and "principles," and to some extent "functions" as generally descriptive of the same thing, namely, the characteristics we feel are the important measuring-stick in the meaningful redesign of a public social service system.

FIGURE 8.1

Human Services Administrative System Cycle

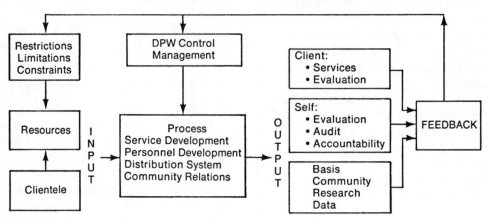

lic social service system is designed, there will always be such a reaction. The principal challenge posed by such a truism, of course, is how to take advantage of the feedback phenomenon so that consumer reaction is actively sought and constructively and continuously employed to plan and replan operations over time. Such controlled feedback might well be exemplified by the encouraged, managed feedback system used in the state of Pennsylvania's Governor's Branch Office operations (essentially field representatives of the Governor stationed in the center of social problem areas and available for immediate reaction to problems, needs, desires, and frustrations of the social welfare constituency), and the more common use of citizens' advisory boards, counsel with leaders of the need community, and even simple suggestion systems. The objective, of course, is to provide and encourage use of a vehicle for usefully and constructively reacting to social welfare operation. On the other hand, most of us are familiar with the negative side of such controlled feedback. First, if it is "too" controlled (if its sources are completely a part of the

system or under its effective influence) it becomes dysfunctional by feeding back only what the administrators want to hear. And, second, this control raises the issue of cooptation,[6] as it is now called, which in turn often results in feedback of a most uncontrolled variety. The problem is how to maintain control of the feedback *system* while not allowing the system to control the content of the feedback itself. Our approach to that problem has already been described.

Finally, this overall input-output model provides a useful vehicle for a starting point since it begins to provide insights into the elements which will need to be addressed in ascribing attributes, criteria, and functions to a public social service delivery system. This should be evident in the following discussion of the model.

The input-output model shown in Fig-

---

[6] T! 's phenomenon of "institutionalizing conflict" or "buying off militant leadership" (depending on your viewpoint) has now been widely discussed, but the reader who is unfamiliar with it is referred, among many other sources, to Alan Haber, "The American Underclass," *Poverty and Human Resource Abstracts,* Vol. II, No. 3 (May–June, 1967), pp. 5–20.

ure 8.1 demonstrates the overall flow of activity, both explicit and implicit, in a public social service system. Input to the system is composed of three elements:

1. *Resources* provided by the community either directly or through formalized tax and revenue allocation methodology, together with human resources in terms of the labor market.
2. *Restrictions,* limitations, and constraints imposed by Federal, state and local governments, as well as less direct limitations implied by public opinion, morals, attitudes, etc.
3. The *clientele* or ultimate recipients of the social service benefits. (Note the link established between clientele and resources.) To the extent that people of the need or target community are themselves used or employed in the system (in addition to being beneficiaries of it), they become resources input in terms of manpower.

Given inputs of *restrictions, resources,* and *clientele,* a public social services system may be viewed as a process which transforms these elements into (hopefully) desirable products. Such a process is composed of many component processes, five of the most important of which are:

1. The process of community research by which information is gathered in order to meaningfully develop resources into trained personnel and useful services. (The process includes and accounts for the "feedback" reaction phenomenon previously highlighted.)
2. The process by which resources are developed into the service produced for the consumer.
3. The process by which personnel resources are developed into a service delivery capability.

4. The process by which personnel and physical resources (plant and equipment) are deployed (distributed) to render the developed services.
5. The process by which the needy community is made aware of the existence and availability of the service product.

Controlling the process is the overall management element, in this case operative at Federal, state and local levels, and therefore subject to the restrictions and limitations imposed by legislation and general public opinion, as well as related to the direct feedback resulting from distribution of the outputed services.

Outputs of the model shown on Figure 8.1 are of three major types:

1. *Client output*—the services physically consumed by clients, the evaluation by the client of the quality of services together with system performance in delivering them, and the dissemination of information to clientele about what is available to them.
2. *Self-output*—meaning the social service establishment's self-evaluation of its own performance in quality of services, delivery performance and statutory compliance. Such compliance also implies accountability for funds as well as classification of what was done, to whom, when, how, and why (i.e., statistical accountability).
3. *Basic community research*—the output of information about the size, location, needs, changes and other characteristics of the risk population and related economic and social data.

Each of these outputs, in part or in whole, feeds back to the beginning of the cycle, namely to management control, to restrictions, and to resources. This is to say, the resulting output of the system is ultimately evaluated by several entities involved and made known (in one way or another) to the resource base, to the legislative base, and to the management-control base.

Starting with this broad and general view of a public social service system, the next step will be to focus on the major areas of concern in the development of a functional cycle model for a public social service system.

A Functional Cycle Model for a Public Social Service System

Maintaining the cyclical characteristics of the Figure 8.1 Input-Output model, Figure 8.2 transforms the generic input-output cycle into functional activity form, with major functional areas replacing the input, output and process elements. The model again alludes to resources, and restrictions flowing as input to the process which is broken down into the five major functional areas shown: personnel development, service product development, community relations, distribution and evaluation. The inputs flow into two main developmental functions, *personnel development* and *service-products planning and development*. Out of personnel and service development, service products, and trained people flow to a distribution function which services the clientele (also who are an input to the distribution function). Resulting from distribution, the evaluation function occurs and as a result feeds back performance information to the initial input of restrictions and resources as well as to the overall management-control function. The management-control function is shown quite properly as controller of each of the process elements—personnel development, service-products planning and development, community relations, distribution and evaluation. Finally, separate and apart, there exists the community research function which is shown to be basically clientele input and feedback to management-control, restrictions, and resources.

Figure 8.2 therefore serves to isolate for further consideration the eight major functional areas we consider to be essential for the operation of the service system on the state and local level. They are: (1) community research; (2) service-product planning and development; (3) distribution; (4) evaluation; (5) community relations; (6) personnel training and development; (7) accountability and fiscal coordination; (8) general management and control.

As a further step in the development of a service system that can ultimately be operated, we will treat the eight major functions (or means) as objectives themselves and for each develop alternative "submeans." Submeans will then be treated as objectives, through several iterations until a fairly specific set of detailed principles, attributes, activities, and criteria are evident.

The Community Research Function

The main objective of this function is effective and continuing investigation into the service needs and resources available to the clientele for which the system is responsible. Three major activities are necessary to achieve this objective:

1. Identification of the composition of the community of need.
2. Identification of what services are most wanted and needed by the need community.
3. Identification of services which are available, and the conditions of their availability, to the need community.

Identification of the Composition of the Need Community. Identifying the com-

FIGURE 8.2
Functional Cycle Scheme for Human Services Administrative System

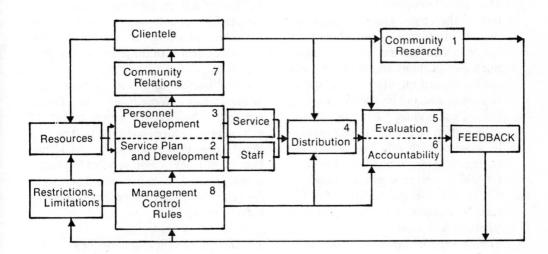

Functions (Means) under our Control:
1. Community Research
2. Service Planning and Development
3. Personnel Training and Development
4. Distribution
5. Evaluation
6. Accountability and Fiscal Coordination
7. Community Relations
8. Overall General Management and Control

position of the need community is a means of achieving the stated goals of effective and continuing community research. It is itself an objective which must be accomplished by a set of submeans, namely, obtaining specifications about composition such as:

1. *Type*—specification of the composition of the target community in terms of principal classification of eligibility.
   a. The risk population—the gross current and potential group needing

service because of their economic or situational status.
   b. The several target populations—subsets of the risk population who can be identified in terms of the relationship between their specific needs, personal objectives, and concrete services.

2. *Size and Location*—specification of the size and location of the need community. Rural-urban variations are substantial in all the states we have examined, and information on this

topic is essential for making planning decisions with respect to service delivery methods, locations, and required capacity.

3. *Mobility Transportation*—specification of the target group in terms of their ability to move from where they are to where services are available. Such specifications are an obvious extension of, and qualifier to, the specification of size and location of need.

4. *Other Demographic Characteristics*—specification of the target community in terms of such other categories as: *(a)* age and sex; *(b)* problem type (i.e., for which service might be helpful); *(c)* families versus individuals; *(d)* race; *(e)* number of children involved; *(f)* others, as appropriate.

5. *Timing*—specification of the need community in terms of when over time, problems may be anticipated, or when by virtue of chronological aging the public assistance group may expand dramatically, etc. It is not sufficient to take one "cut" at classification of the need community as of today: proper planning must account for future possibilities.

Having specified the composition of the need community, we may move to the next level and ask, by what means should the objective of composition specifications be met? We suggest several as follows:

1. Use of advice and counsel from the need community itself including advisory groups, individual leaders from within the group, and other interested members of the need group, such as the welfare rights leaders.

2. Use of professionally contracted, or employed, demographers and researchers on a regular, continuing basis.

3. Use of other staff members who are not necessarily trained in research but who have ready access to sources of field data.

4. Use of advice, information and counsel from counterpart research staff in other planning or service systems which deal with the need community.

Identification of What Services Are Wanted and Needed by the Target Groups. The second major means of achieving effective community research may be described as comprehensive identification of what human services the target community wants and needs. The means for achieving such comprehensive identification are two-fold:

1. *Obtain specifications on new service activities wanted and needed, including clear understanding of such items as:*

   a. Kind of service (probably in descriptive terms).

   b. From among several new services wanted, the priority the need community assigns to each—which should precede the other in the view of the need community.

   c. How should new services be delivered; that is, what sort of physical arrangements should be made to place the benefits of the service into the hands of the needy?

   d. The timing of the new service; that is, trade-offs between emergency requirements of here-and-now versus phased-in activity or even long range new services to be installed when demography, age, or other factors come into a particular juxtaposition.

2. *Obtain critiques of current services* including an understanding of how these services relate to current needs,

the desirability of currently employed delivery techniques, and the relative priority of current services taken in the context of all service needs.

To obtain specification on new service wants and needs and on critiques of current services, these five principal means are suggested:

1. *Use of advice and counsel from formally established community advisory groups.* The principle of formal establishment here is considered to be equally as important as the use of the counsel obtained.
2. *Seek advice and counsel from public welfare employees themselves.* Frequently, the "man on the firing line" can reveal much about what new services are needed as well as what's wrong (or right) with current services.
3. *Counsel with other groups operating in the target community* such as OEO offices, local church leaders, local offices of state employment services, welfare rights movement leaders, and the like.
4. *Provide for and encourage ad hoc suggestions and criticisms* about welfare social services and delivery patterns from employees, from recipients, or from anyone interested. The principle is to make private, anonymous communication available, desirable, and effective for anyone who has an interest in expressing his view.
5. *Finally, increase the use of "need community" personnel in the administration of the community research effort itself.* More and more we are learning that acquisition of reliable information is a function of whom the inquirer is or represents. This principle of maximizing use of needy people themselves in the research ef-

fort recognizes the fact that, at least as conditions exist today, perhaps only they can truly get at identification of services and service delivery systems which will satisfy root problems.

Identification of Services Available in the Community. The third means of achieving the community research objective is by identifying the services in the community which are already available to the system's current or potential clientele. To do this fully, involves several activities or subobjectives:

1. Identification of the nature of the services.
2. Determination of the actual capacity (in terms of numbers of clients) of each service which has been identified.
3. Determination of the actual availability and accessibility of each service for the system's clientele. (This involves information regarding topics such as costs, fees, hours, locations, personal eligibility restrictions, etc.).
4. Estimation of the possibility of changes in the nature, capacity or availability of these services.

In order to carry out these activities several submeans will have to be employed:

1. In the instance of services which are already operated by the welfare system, appropriate administrators will have to be interviewed or otherwise involved in data collection.
2. Similar officials in other agencies will have to be contacted to secure information about their services.
3. Officials of planning, coordinating and funding bodies who do not operate the services but are familiar with

them will need to be solicited for additional information and expert opinion.

4. Welfare clients or other service consumers also will be very useful informants, especially regarding the actual nature and availability of service.

Service Planning and Development Function

The second of eight major functional areas deals with the planning and development of services. We first identify two major activities in the achievement of comprehensive product planning and development:

1. Identification of legislative and other regulations and restrictions which inhibit, control, or otherwise regulate the nature of services or their delivery. This will include formal legislative statements as well as pertinent information in explanation and clarification of legislative intent.

2. Determination of services and service methodology: which services should be delivered, in what quantity and according to which delivery method—direct operation, compact, or contract with another agency?

Identification of Legislative and Other Regulations. In order to plan and develop services for public social service system delivery, considerable effort will be required in the clarification of Federal and state statutes, memoranda, regulations, and restrictions as they apply to services. This must include sifting through voluminous memoranda in order to clarify the intent of what are often obtusely written policies. In order to perform adequately in planning services, this effort must, of course, address itself to staying with regulations but more importantly, a concerted effort is necessary to clarify what can be

done as opposed to what cannot—what the real enabling intent of statutes or regulations are, rather than the simple execution of rules and procedures. A considerable amount of innovation and imagination together with checking, verifying, and keeping up-to-date are all clearly involved.

Determination of Service and Service Methodology. In the identification of services that will be made available to the need community, comprehensive product planning and development will be involved in three subactivities:

1. *Budgeting*—deciding what each service proposed will cost, what each will yield in social objectives, what priorities should be established, and how available resources should therefore be allocated to a particular service.

2. *The Creative Process*—invention of the structure of services in response to needs including evaluation and re-evaluation of existing services continuously against expressions of need and against desirable attributes of services. Other creative functions include physical modification of existing services based on analysis of adequacy, justification for deletion of services, and detailed specifications drawing for additions, modifications or deletions.

3. *Implementation Planning*—the setting of time phasing for installation of new services or modifications or deletions of services. In connection with time phasing, this includes the complete specification of the implementation plan including who is responsible for what, when and where.

Budgeting, the creative process, and implementation planning are means for achieving the determination of service objectives. The desirable attributes of a public social service system which enables the budgeting, creative, and implementation-planning processes are suggested to be the following:

1. *Analysis of Community Research.* Given a sound, thorough community research program, vital data should be forthcoming which together with evaluation data set the patterns of activity in service planning and development. Statistical analysis and probability theory appear to be necessary requisites for quality analysis in this area.
2. *Utilization of All Funding Possibilities.* By combining all community research data regarding who needs services, who receives service, and who is eligible to receive service, with what Federal/state matching provisions apply in each instance, it should be possible to rechannel existing client and funding streams in order to increase the financial support level of the service system.
3. *Counsel With Other Service Systems.* In even the most rural, impoverished regions, the public social service system does not exist in a vacuum. Services-planning must therefore be undertaken with the knowledge and advice, if not always the consent, of other service systems.
4. *Involvement of Members of the Need Community.* Both the proper interpretation of community research as well as the cogent planning of resulting services suggest that members of the need community may be able to make a significant contribution. It would appear desirable to use personnel from the need community in several roles in this connection:
   a. in training and development of public social service employees who will ultimately be responsible for delivering the newly created or modified services;
   b. in interpreting the meaning of community research and assisting to articulate such research into meaningful programs;
   c. in the general planning and administration and carrying-out of the service planning and development function.

The Distribution Function

The third major function relating to the effective public administration of social services concerns distribution of the services planned and developed for consumption. By distribution is meant the massive, high-impact dissemination of services available to the target community. Two major means are suggested toward achieving this objective: (1) an inventory of services demanded; (2) a high-volume oriented supplier.

Inventory of Services Demanded. In order to supply services to consumers, a public social service system must obviously have available a stock of services. Further, the stock must be of services which the needy community feels it needs and wants —that is, those services which are in demand. To try to satisfy consumers with products in which they are not interested is a traditional welfare folly which inevitably drives consumers to alternative means of satisfaction of their wants or to disenchantment, frustration, and sometimes disorder. In public welfare, consumers do not really have alternative means of satisfying their wants, so that traditional offers of service products unrelated to their needs and wants may begin to explain consumer disenchantment with the relevance of public welfare service programs. Therefore, a second level objective of high impact, massive distribution of services necessarily is the availability of an inventory of services which are in consumer demand.

In order to achieve this objective, sufficiency of inventory and easy acquirability are the primary means.

1. *Easy acquirability.* Services offered in a high impact, massive turnover kind of distribution situation must be easily and quickly attainable by the consuming community. The scale of the distribution operation alone dictates that quick, efficient disposition be made of individual requests. To achieve such an objective, we suggest three desirable attributes of the social services system:

   a. *Simple, easy access.* Statement of problem (or request for service) and establishment of entitlement (eligibility) are, of course, prerequisites to giving service to consumers. What is important is that such a process be as straightforward, simple, quick, and easy as possible. In public welfare terms it should be the antithesis of the traditional access (intake) process for public assistance.

   b. *Acquisition should be dignified.* The distribution of public social services should be no different for the consumer than buying a quart of milk at the corner grocery. The general public has made the decision to care for its dependent people, and therefore acquisition of services is a right of such people, not subject to undue scrutiny or degradation by another person. The consumer is the central figure in public social service programs and should be treated with a dignity consistent with that role.

   c. *No post-facto strings attached.*

Contributing to the objective of easy acquirability is the "after the fact" treatment of the consumer. With but a few special case exceptions (for example, consumer evaluation surveys), the guiding principle we suggest is to leave the consumer alone after he has acquired the service desired except to determine periodically with him whether the service is helping him meet his own objectives.

2. *Sufficiency of inventory.* The second major objective in achieving inventory availability is concerned with the sufficiency or quantity and type of inventory of service available to the consumer. This may be thought of in two categories: those services which are high-volume-demand services, and those which are of a special-demand nature.

   a. *High-volume-demand services.* A desirable attribute of a social service distribution system will be the availability of those services in high demand by the consumer. In response to such demand, we suggest that the distribution system have two principal attributes:

      (1) The ability immediately to supply the service in demand from immediate inventory—that is, satisfy the demand by immediately and physically performing the service in question using public service agency staff, funds or other service products;

      (2) The ability to refer high demand service requests to agencies, public and private, for satisfaction, i.e., where public service agency per-

sonnel either cannot or will not perform a high-demand, high-volume service using their own immediate capability, the ability should at least exist to refer the consumer to someone who can satisfy the demand.

b. *Special demand type service.* The second desirable attribute under sufficiency of inventory is the ability of public social service agencies to handle special situations, special demands. Two principal attributes of a public social service system capable of handling such demands are:

(1) The ability to respond to emergency or crisis situations. This should include community assistance in the wake of general disaster as well as special and unusual response to individual disaster problems, unrelated to the community as a whole. Rules and procedures will only state the principle of such response, since it is impossible to stipulate all the possible situations to which it might be applied. In no case should simple-minded rule-following preclude response to emergency situations, either community or individual.

(2) The ability to provide services of a long-term nature or highly specialized, low-volume nature. Whereas the public social service system we envision will be most desirably geared to massive, high-impact, high-volume service dissemination, an important attribute of such a system is its ability, nevertheless, to develop and deliver services in response to the relatively few consumers having relatively long-term problems. An example of such a capability might be specialized long-term psychiatric care.

High-Volume-Oriented Supplier. The second major means by which it is proposed to achieve massive, high-volume service distribution is concerned not so much with the availability of services for dissemination as with the nature of the agency actually doing the supplying. Given the sufficiency of services, as described in previous paragraphs, it is proposed that the necessary corollary is a volume-oriented supplier organization. These two elements together constitute the means for massive, high-volume distribution of services in a public social service framework. Such an organization must have three characteristics:

1. *The supplier must be highly accessible and immediately available to his clients.* Regardless of the quantity of service available and its quality in terms of the wants and needs of the clients; and in spite of the suppliers' desire to distribute widely, it is obvious that the volume of distribution will be a function of the accessibility and availability of the supplier to the clients. We therefore conclude that high accessibility and availability are desirable objectives of public social service delivery systems. In achieving these subobjectives, there are three principal attributes which are considered extremely desirable to such a system. They are:

a. *Long hours.* A high impact distribution system is in many ways geared to the accessibility, in time, of the supplier. Appropriate studies will reveal the optimum office hours of operation for social service agencies in particular locales. It will not be surprising if these optimal hours fail to coincide with usual government employees' working hours. In any event, at the point of distribution of social services, an important attribute of a successful operation will be hours of operation which correspond to the needs of the target community, including evening hours, weekend hours, and total weekly hours potentially in excess of the usual 40-hour standard.

b. *Convenient location.* Community research programs will tell the social service system much about the mobility of the target community and something of how much the community is willing to pay for transportation to obtain wanted services. With due consideration of this research, a desirable attribute of a successful distribution system will be the location of the supplier as close to the target community as possible for at least the most wanted and needed (highest volume) services.

c. *Attractiveness.* The office surroundings of the public social service supplier should be attractive and comfortable in atmosphere for the consumer. It should not reek of either government or poverty as so many public welfare offices do, but should be as attractive a representation of the community in which it resides as possible.

2. *The supplier should be organization-ally mass-distribution oriented.* The second attribute of a high volume supplier of social services is that the supplier be organizationally geared for mass distribution. To achieve such an objective involves three principal attributes:

a. *The supplier should be highly responsive.* Being highly responsive is a function composed of three elements: (1) *contact with the consumer on a direct one-to-one basis;* i.e., meeting and dealing with applicants personally and directly when they come to the sources of service; (2) *provision of immediate service;* i.e., giving immediate attention to the consumer and taking on-the-spot action against his stated problem; (3) *acceptance of the potential client's expression of his problem as the "real problem."* The principle here is that the client is, in the vast majority of cases, smart enough to pinpoint his own problem and that, for mass distribution in high volume, the public social service supplier must take a sort of calculated risk in accepting the client's analysis of his own situation and needs. Unless the vast majority of cases are handled in this manner, it will be difficult to achieve the volume, mass distribution objective deemed desirable.

b. *The supplier must be flexible to the specifics of consumer demands.* The principle of flexibility is an important attribute of a high-volume, high-impact service distribution system. It is not enough that there are quantities of services available and that the public service agency is highly responsive to customers. The traditional infraction which creeps into such an arrangement in governmental-operated bureaucracies is "pettiness" in rule following. Of course, there must be rules for entitlement and eligibility, and rules for filling out forms, and rules for service application, etc., but a respectable high-impact distribution system will never permit the existence of such rules to overshadow the fact that people are not as standardized as are forms and procedures. There can never be a set of rules so comprehensive as to cover every human situation —and yet—an effective service distribution system must be able to do just that; cope with every type and kind of special human consideration without being encumbered by an inflexible set of rules and regulations.

c. *The supplier must have the capacity for volume.* The capacity for handling volume, both in terms of services, and in terms of service consumers, is a function of the physical facilities in which staff must operate. Suffice to say in current context, that the physical facility must be engineered carefully in order to assure adequate space and appropriate layout to handle a large volume of people yet provide a degree of privacy for discussions of problems and assignments of services. Suffice also to say with respect to staff in this context, that adequate numbers of skilled personnel must be available to deal with the consumer such that there is a minimum of delay in getting attention to his problem.

3. *The supplier must be of reliable repute.* The reputation for reliability is the essence of trust and confidence, and the baseline for high-volume, high-impact distribution of social services. It represents a key objective of any public social service system to be designed. Rightly or wrongly, there appears to be a universal distrust, a universal lack of confidence—in short, a universal challenge to the validity of governmental operating agencies—a feeling that in some way the agency exists for the sake of itself rather than for the sake of the people to which it is supposed to be of service. It is no surprise that this appears to be particularly true with respect to the public welfare social service establishment.

Desirable attributes of a service delivery system which can earn a reasonably good reputation among the consumer public will include such items as:

a. *Demonstration of knowledge and interest in the service consumer.* Very simply stated, public social service agency personnel delivering services must be encouraged to take an interest in the need community in which they serve. They must have depth knowledge of the community and be able to empathize with its problems and vacillations. To the service consumer, the public servant representing the agency must be considered "one of us," at least in the sense of understanding and feeling the conditions of life in the area involved, if not physically from the area.

b. *Client follow-up.* A desirable attribute of a service system is its ability to keep in touch with those it has served. The purpose of such follow-up is the seeking of additional opportunities to serve as well as evaluation of services rendered. By no means is the purpose to be confused with the continuous reinvestigations for eligibility which are normally and obnoxiously associated with public assistance.

c. *Practice of the philosophy that the "customer is always right."* A simple but important principle which contributes to good reputation is practice of the philosophy that the service recipient is both right in what he says and has the right to say it. It is the client's prerogative to reject, to change his mind, to complain, and to demand. It is the responsibility of the public social service system to ensure that he is encouraged to exercise these rights, and to render direct response to consumer specification of problems and needs, and in a manner consistent with his desires.

The Evaluation Function

The fourth major function contributing to an effective public social service system is that of evaluation. We view evaluation in the public social service setting as a multidimensional activity involving several different kinds of action by several different bodies. We thus define an evaluation function objectively as "thorough, multi-aspect quality control and feedback." The context, as shown previously in Figure 8.1 and Figure 8.2, is that of the flow of reaction to services and service delivery modes back to the original points of resource input and back to the overall management control of the system. In this context, we view evaluation as a set of three basic principles: (1) self-evaluation; (2) consumer evaluation; (3) other evaluation (from outside the agency or need community).

Self-evaluation. By self-evaluation we mean the process by which the public social service system attempts to regulate itself in terms of evaluating its own activities against its own standards and evaluating its results against its own objectives. Given a reasonable set of standards and a reasonably objective quality control mechanism, this form of evaluation can be the most effective self-improvement and self-correctional tool possible. No one really knows nor can evaluate the system operators themselves, we believe. Therefore, given reasonable levels of integrity among the personnel of a public social service agency, self-regulation can effect the most powerful and the most meaningful modifications, corrections, and improvements possible to the structure and delivery of social services, both new and ongoing.

In the context of a public social service entity, at least three major activities are involved in self-evaluation.

1. *Evaluation of the quality and uniformity of services rendered.* In this context, desirable evaluation attributes will include:

    a. The testing of services rendered against the criteria of establishing needs, the objectives being to assure that the expressed needs and wants of the clientele are being met in terms of quantity, quality, and timeliness.

    b. Examining both the service development and the service delivery functions against the criteria of need and the criteria of desirable attributes of service-planning and service-distribution. Services developed and delivered by either the public social service agency, or by contractual agencies should all be subject to such examination.

2. *Compliance or rule-following audits.* An onerous, but necessary attribute of effective self control is the audit of detailed procedural compliance. We have mentioned several times that there will always exist formal sets of rules and regulations governing the administration of a public agency. It is the audit of compliance to these rules that is involved here.

3. *Impact evaluation.* An integral part of performance evaluation is evaluation of the impact of the public social service system on the target community; i.e., regardless of what was delivered or how it was delivered, what was the impact on the recipient population? Two principal attributes of a system of self-impact evaluation in this context are:

   a. The existence of mechanisms to measure macrocommunity impact. By this is meant measures such as the total employability of the community after installation of a program of services to train large segments of the target group for employment; or total school dropout rates for the community in question; or average income level for the target group; and the like. There are obviously problems with such types of measures, including the difficulty of getting statistics, and most importantly, the difficulty of finding out how much of a contribution to an overall measure can be assigned to public social service systems in light of a proliferation of causes and effects operating simultaneously in the target community.

   b. The existence of mechanisms to collect and evaluate point-of-service data. By this is meant mechanisms to collect data about present problems, about classifications made, about service actions taken, and about the results of individual service actions.

Consumer Evaluation. Thorough quality control and feedback will necessarily include evaluation by the clients of the public system. In the context of a public social service system, we define two levels of consumer evaluation activity:

1. *Formal consumer evaluation.* A desirable attribute of an effective quality control system will involve formal consumer evaluation initiated jointly by the consumer populace and by the public service agency itself. Formal evaluation should probably include, but not necessarily be limited to:

   a. Formal surveys conducted jointly by the public service agency and established community groups. The purpose of the survey is to solicit commentary from the recipient community in terms of reaction to the services program and delivery mechanisms of the agency. This activity should not be confused with or substituted for that of community research even though there are some similarities. The fundamental difference is in who conducts the survey.

   b. Obtaining formal counsel and advice from community-based advisory boards.

2. *Informal consumer evaluation.* As pointed out earlier in this section, the public social service agency is going to hear about the need community's

reaction to social services of the agency one way or another, whether the agency likes it or not. Earlier we advocated a system which provided for an orderly means of securing information without attempting to control its content. In the context of consumer evaluation, therefore, several desirable attributes of such an informal reaction-information system will include:

a. A capability to "tune in" to local "word-of-mouth" in the target community. This may be a source of evaluative information unavailable by any other means.

b. The practice of encouraging and attending ad hoc community group sessions specifically intended for evaluation and discourse on the effectiveness of the local public service system.

c. The provision of a client suggestion system which permits him to communicate his feelings about public social service systems both in private and in writing, to a responsible level of state or local government which he knows will take action.

Other Forms of Evaluation. Outside of self-evaluation and consumer evaluation there must inevitably be some independent evaluation of the social service system from sources not directly involved with its activities. In this context we define two forms of outside evaluation.

1. *The Federal or State Auditor General.* For purposes of fiscal responsibility and legislative control, a desirable attribute of the social service system will include Federal and/or State Auditor General evaluations of the public social service system.

2. *General public reaction.* The reaction of the general public will inevitably be felt with respect to public social service agencies. A desirable attribute of a well-controlled feedback system in public social services will be the capability of the system to elicit public reactions by both formal (such as surveys) and informal means (such as "town meetings"). Since the ultimate source of resources for support of a public social service system is the general public, it will be of some importance to keep abreast of public attitudes and to conduct a modicum of public relations, image-improvement activity.

The Community Relations Function

The fifth major function contributing to an effective public social service system is a comprehensive and effective community relations program. By community relations is meant the dissemination of information among the risk populations and others concerned with what public social service programs are, and how to obtain them.[7] Two major means for accomplishing community relations are defined: (1) comprehensive information dissemination; (2) "moving with" the community.

Comprehensive Information Dissemination. Since public social service systems involve more than just the caseworker and consumer, comprehensive-information dissemination will need to take

---

[7]It is pertinent to. note that we believe that the most effective community relations program is really the implementation of a massive distribution system. That is, the best community relations program comes from meeting the consumer's needs as he expresses them with an effective and timely delivery of service. Word of mouth about the impact of good distribution is an invaluable means of communicating information about the system which no special community relations program can achieve by itself.

into account a whole gamut of direct and indirect participants. In this context, we group the major participants into four categories: per se public social service personnel, consumer personnel, non-consumers, and other public and private agencies.

1. *Information dissemination within the social service agency.* A desirable attribute of a comprehensive, information dissemination program will include thorough briefings of public social service personnel about what service and what delivery vehicles are available or are in stages of planning. It is nearly axiomatic that public social service employees be more knowledgeable about service availabilities than any other single group, not only to better provide them to the target groups, but to be able to make reference to them in contacts with the general public and the target community in a consistent, whole-picture framework.[8]

2. *Information dissemination to the risk population.* Desirable attributes of an information-dissemination program to the risk population will include at least the following elements:
   a. *What.* Descriptions of what services are available from the public social service agency as well as specifications of entitlement or eligibility requirements and how the services may be obtained (or at least how information about access may be obtained). Such descriptions most desirably will present public social services programs in a coordinated, consistent package rather than a proliferation of pamphlets or by any other fragmented manner of presentation.
   b. *How.* The package of coordinated information about public social services can be disseminated in many different ways. (Elsewhere in this paper and in one of the Supplements to the *Challenge to Validity* we have dealt with this subject in great detail which need not be repeated.)

3. *Information dissemination to nonconsumers.* An important attribute of a successful public social service agency will be its ability to marshal the general public behind its efforts by demonstrating that it is doing a worthwhile job in an effective, efficient manner. This is basically a problem of image which can be built by carefully cultivating understanding and support on the part of the general public.
   a. *What.* Basically, the public social services system should inform the general public about what public social service is as a whole—i.e., description of the integrated package of services, something about how the resources allocated by the general public are being efficiently employed in the effort, and to whom benefits accrue.
   b. *How.* Information dissemination should probably be the traditional methods of distribution of written materials, together with speeches, and hopefully, good press and general media. An important attribute of materials distributed will be the consistency and coordination of the materials—i.e., the whole story carefully folded together rather than presentation of only fragmented pieces.

---

[8] Field experience has pointed up an appalling lack of knowledge among welfare agency personnel with respect to the range of service possibilities available or planned, both within the agency and within the community as a whole.

4. *Information dissemination to other public and private agencies.* An important attribute of the dissemination program will be its ability to reach other participants in the social welfare framework. This will include churches, voluntary agencies, other government agencies and the like. Information dissemination among these groups will have two basic attributes:

  a. It will tell in integrated, consistent terms what it is that the public social service system offers and what it is in fact, doing in the community.

  b. It will elicit reaction in terms of ways and means for the public social service agency and other agencies to work together toward solving the problems of the target community—either in complementary manner, by joint participation, or both.

"Moving With" the Community. By "moving with" the community we mean those community relations and participation activities of the system which support the basic purpose of providing a set of social services but which also tend to transcend it. "Moving with" has two principal attributes:

1. *Advocacy.* An important attribute will be the public social service system's ability to act for the need community, as in a partnership, to assist the community to obtain the services and delivery modes to which it is entitled.

2. *Community Planning and Participation.* Another demonstration of the public social service agency's readiness to move with the community is provided by its willingness to take part with other service agencies and systems in wider community planning ac-

tivities, demonstration programs, special projects, and the like. "Moving with" the community in these ways has value in and of itself, but it also constitutes an excellent form of community relations (a type of "institutional advertising") for the agency.

The Personnel Training and Development Function

The sixth major function of an effective social services system is the training and development of services personnel. The overall objective of such a function is the provision of well-trained staff in adequate numbers to effectively operate a public social services system. For such a system, personnel programs and personnel objectives are not viewed as much different than for any organization. Only the subject matter and the general environmental context are different. For purposes of this exposition, therefore, we shall simply describe the principal attributes of a generalized personnel model with the assumption that it will apply quite well to a public social service system.

There are four principal means of achieving the objectives of a well-trained staff of adequate size: *training programs, employment programs, development programs,* and *deployment programs.*

Training Programs. Desirable attributes of a personnel training program in a public social services context will include:

1. *The existence of standards.* By standards is meant both standard-training materials and standards of proficiency of training which must be met by those being trained.

2. *Existence of various types of training.* Training must obviously address itself to various categories of personnel for the purpose of specialized training to

meet specialized objectives. A redesigned service system will require training for three categories of personnel:

a. *Influx training.* The training of newly hired employees for various beginning roles in the public social service framework.

b. *Retraining.* The retraining of current employees in the new philosophy and procedures of the service system; in new job requirements and skills; and, in some cases, in new administrative requirements and techniques.

c. *Preparation programs.* In a public social services context, a specialized kind of training may well be the preparation of personnel from the target community to take a role in the system. In such cases, it is conceivable that specialized elementary preparation programs may be necessary before such people are ready for ordinary influx training, or even retraining.

Employment Programs. The provision of adequate numbers of trained personnel will obviously be influenced largely by the nature of service system recruitment programs. Acquisition of personnel to operate a newly conceived public social service system will clearly require mounting of both professional and clerical recruiting programs. In a typical setting such programs should be able to draw on a labor pool that is enlarged in two dimensions beyond the traditional boundaries:

1. It will be able to recruit personnel for a variety of service jobs from the need community itself—a largely untapped source and one that is desirable in several ways.

2. It will need and therefore be able to recruit from several professions other than social work, as well as commercial sources.

Development Programs. The continuing development of personnel in any organization is a vital mechanism for keeping the organization up-to-date and viable. A public social service system no less than any other organization requires careful development of its personnel on a continuing basis.

There are innumerable forms of personnel development programs and voluminous literature in the personnel field about the alternative ways and means available. Suffice to say, in the current context, that the principal attributes of a sound personnel development program for a social service system will include:

1. *Incentives (physical or psychological) for experimentation, inventiveness,* and *innovation* in serving the target community both in terms of type of service and in terms of delivery methodology.

2. *Incentives for personnel growth.* There must be recognition of the desire and potential for employees to expand their realm of responsibility and the understanding that this is a most desirable phenomenon in any organization. The public social service system must therefore assure that incentives exist which encourage such development.

3. *Availability of specialized developmental training programs,* particularly supervisory training, and general administrative training. Many years of industrial experience have told us that simple tenure (years of service), is no criterion for selecting effective

supervisors, administrators, or agency managers.

4. *Existence of promotion standards, personnel evaluation and guidance.* In terms of standards for promotion, the road to advancement must be defined and made clear to employees. An inevitable corollary is the existence of competent personnel counseling and evaluation capability. The two go hand-in-hand since standards are applicable to the groups of employees as a whole while application of standards is inevitably an interpersonal, individualistic proposition requiring skillful counsel and evaluation by professional personnel officers.

Deployment Programs. The final major aspect of a comprehensive personnel program deals with deployment planning. Public social service systems, like most organizations, are cursed with problems of limited resources, especially manpower resources. It is therefore an important attribute of an effective system that it carefully consider manpower deployment in terms of allocation of a scarce and valuable resource. In the context of a social services system, there are three desirable attributes of effective deployment planning:

1. *An effective manpower deployment plan* that will carefully spell out the plan for deployment of current staff on current service programs. It will also take into account the work of planning and development groups and community research groups in plotting the course of manpower deployment over the next several years. As services shift and change over time, the manpower deployment plan will have anticipated such shifts with alternative deployment plans to account

for new personnel needs. Present and alternative manpower deployment plans will also be useful to developers of new service packages in terms of what it takes to implement service proposals from a manpower or staffing point of view.

2. *Maximum usage of all available manpower resources,* expecially the largely untapped manpower reserves available in the target community.

3. *Stationing of the right person at the right level.* Effective personnel deployment will carefully identify and write specifications for each kind of role to be played in the social service organization and will, to the extent possible, place personnel with the proper qualifications in these roles. In a public social service agency context, particular attention may well be paid to careful specifications of the kind of manpower most suitable for client contact. Special mention is made of this issue because of the potential usage of need-community personnel in such roles.

The Accountability and Fiscal Coordination Function

The seventh major function in a public social service system involves fiscal and accounting operations. We may distinguish between the two operations by defining *fiscal* as dealing with the acquisition and allocation of dollar resources, and *accounting* as classifying and reporting the results of operations both in terms of dollars, manpower, services delivered, and clients served.

Fiscal Coordination. There are four principal criteria for the realization of the objective of achieving adequate fiscal coordination:

1. *Maximization of Federal matching provisions.* This activity has already been discussed in some detail. Here we simply warn against the familiar temptation to permit the criterion of fiscal adequacy to determine *a priori* the content of the service inventory. Although it will always be one factor in service planning, the danger is that much-needed services may be omitted simply because they cannot capture as great a proportion of Federal funds as some other service which is less important to the clientele.

2. *Fiscal coordination with other agencies.* A major problem in any human service system is the overlapping responsibilities of agencies, both public and private, and the ramifications of competition for Federal and state-support dollars. The solution or amelioration of this problem requires not only careful service planning within the social service agency but also planning and coordination with others with respect to who shall be responsible for what and, therefore, who shall be responsible for obtaining financial resources. We suspect, incidentally, that much greater use of interagency contracts which we discussed earlier, might provide a practical means of achieving the always-elusive goal of coordinated services.

3. *Creative funding.* In harmony with the two previous points, it is suggested that adequate fiscal coordination will also include some degree of creativity or ingenuity in finding dollars to pay for public social services. For example, a form of creative funding might be convincing a local industry to take on the responsibility for certain kinds of employment training programs—paid for and administered by the local industry under the aegis

of the public social services framework. The desirable attribute here is the capability and willingness of the public social service organization to seek out innovative ways and means of achieving the services which community research indicates are important —ways and means outside the traditional allocation of Federal and state funds.

4. *Budgeting and fiscal allocation.* A principal activity of fiscal coordinators will be the allocation of available resources to programs of service and modes of service delivery. The principal desirable attribute to be observed here is application of scarce resources to the service indicated by the need community as most necessary and wanted, with due consideration of maximization of cost-effectiveness.

Contract Standards and Arrangements. To the extent that the public social service system responds to expressed needs by contracting for service from outside organizations, careful attention will need to be paid to the formulation of contractual arrangements with such organizations. Of note in this context is the desirable contractual attribute that follow-up communication be an important element of the contract. By referring clients to a contracted service, the public social service agency cannot abdicate its responsibility for the welfare of the client. In order to assure that the service agency remains attuned to the progress of the client, a desirable attribute of any contractual arrangement will be that regular reports to the service agency be required.

Accounting. Effective accounting of the results of public social service operations is a necessary means for controlling the entire framework. The desirable attributes of an effective accounting program in a public social service context include: (1) *financial accounting*—provision of the traditional accountability for resources and expenditures; (2) *administrative accounting*—formal mechanisms to account for manpower in terms of numbers, levels, time percentages, and other standard formulations; (3) *client-service accounting*—accounting for the service operation itself in terms of numbers of cases handled, kinds of problems expressed, type of service rendered, follow-up results reported, and similar items which demonstrate the physical activity of the public social service program, and lay the groundwork for evaluative systems.

General Management and Control Function

The eighth major function of an effective public social service system—general management and control—has as its main objectives the provision of overall management coordination and control, long range planning, and administrative services to the system itself. Inasmuch as they are largely the same as those for any organization, with the possible exception of the role of long range planning, we will discuss each of them very briefly.

Control. By control is meant the internal, interventional reaction of general management to solve problems or correct situations based on regularly received and analyzed control reports.

Organization Planning. By organization planning is meant the responsibility of the general management structure to for-mulate organization charts, to draw up and publish operating unit charters of responsibility, and attendant definitional duties in regard to new offices, new services, new units, new policies and procedures, etc.

Systems and Procedures. By systems and procedures is meant the responsibility of general management to specify in writing, the procedures, rules, regulations, policies, forms, etc., by which the public social service system shall operate. It is an attendant responsibility to continuously update such specifications, and prepare detailed clarifications and interpretations as required for smooth operation of subordinate units.

Long Range Planning. By long range planning is meant responsibility of general management to both formulate the strategies by which ultimate policy will be achieved, and to coordinate on the highest level the interplay of outside major participants in the system. In our context this will include contact, coordination, and liaison at the highest level with the general public, state legislatures, the Federal government, county administrations, other arms of state and local government, and other organizations participating in or even interested in social welfare.

Decision Making. It is the obvious responsibility of general management to promptly make the decisions requested of it by subordinate units. In addition, general management decision-making extends to formulation of overall policy for the service system as well as final decision of the allocation of resources.

9. Planning Tools: Committees and Data Collection

Elmer J. Tropman

STAFFING COMMITTEES AND STUDIES

ELEMENTS, TASKS, AND TOOLS OF PLANNING

Perhaps a better insight into planning—what it is, what is involved, what is required—can be obtained through exploration of its elements and the relationship to these elements of typical tasks that planning is called upon to perform and some of the tools available and required by the planner in the performance of those tasks. The latter, of course, involves knowledge of the tools and the technical skill in their use. The four elements identified in the working definition of planning include:

- Goal determination
- Program development
- Program implementation
- Program evaluation

Some of the typical tasks and tools identified with each of these elements are outlined below.

Goal Determination

Typical tasks:
  Assessment of needs and resources
  Analysis of problems and programs
  Social forecasting
  Priority determination
  Ideological assessments of:
    Individuals
    Organizations
    Communities
Tools related to data collection and management:
  Research methods and techniques

Collection, analysis, synthesis, and presentation of data
Methods for assessing needs and problems
Information systems
Data banks
Computer techniques
Methods for studies of:
  Agencies
  Geographical areas
  Fields of service
  Total community
Social indicators
Methods of social forecasting (such as Delphi method)
UWASIS
Tools related to the process for citizen involvement, education, and communication:
  Committee management
  Citizen participation
  Community organization
  Public information hearings
  Forums
  Conferences
  Negotiation
  Conflict resolution
  Methods and techniques for memo and report writing and presentation

Program Development

Typical tasks:
  Development of alternative approaches for achievement of goals—covering such items as auspices, administrative arrangement, program elements, staffing patterns, cost estimates, and methods of financing
  Strengthening, changing, rearranging service patterns and auspices
Tools related to data collection and management:
  Budget and cost analysis
  PERT

Source: Unpublished, Elmer J. Tropman, "Introduction to Planning," 1975.

Program standards
Knowledge of community resources
Tools related to the process of getting understanding, agreement, and acceptance of the program:
  Committee management
  Citizen participation
  Negotiation
  Conflict resolution
  Community organization
  Coalitions
  Self-help groups
  Methods and techniques of memo and report preparation and presentation

Program Implementation

Typical tasks:
  Developing or changing public policy
  Securing the understanding and support of plans and programs by public officials and other community leaders, administrators, and institutions
  Developing understanding and support of plans and programs by groups and individual citizens
  Facilitating priority development and reserved allocation
  Furthering interorganizational coordination and communication
  Developing and promoting the funding of projects
  Delineating public and voluntary funding responsibility
  Proposal writing
  Strategy development
Tools related to data management:
  PPBS
  MBO
  Interpretation and promotion
  Accounting and financial reporting
Tools related to the process of cooperation, coordination and support:
  Public hearings
  Forums
  Conferences
  Coalitions
  Committee management
  Community organization
  Mediation
  Advocacy
  Methods and techniques of memo and report preparation and presentation

Program Evaluation

Typical tasks:
  Development of methods and systems for public accountability
  Monitoring program operations
  Assessment of the efficiency and effectiveness of programs
  Preparation and distribution of information
  Communication with financial and other supporters
Tools (evaluation tools are still rather limited and lack the scientific base that this complicated process requires):
  Accounting and financial reporting
  Service statistics reporting
  Studies of agency programs (either by self-study or outside organizations) focusing on:
    Level of effort
    Level of performance
    Efficiency review
    Process review
  Reaction to program by:
    Users
    Constituency
  Measurement of impact in terms of stated objectives
  Management study of the agency
  Methods and techniques of memo and report preparation and presentation

The Total Effort

Although planning involves the four elements just described, it should not be inferred that every project of a voluntary community planning organization necessarily encompasses all of them. A given project might be primarily concerned with establishing a goal through a needs and resources assessment, or developing a program for an already established need, or providing the know-how and influence to implement a plan, or evaluating a program that has already been in operation. Some planning organizations have given more emphasis or developed greater skills in one or more of these areas than others. Consequently, a given organization's community image may be of a technical consulting agency or a community organization social action agency. But even though the voluntary community planning agency is involved in only one of the elements in the planning process, all four should be covered in some way by some organization if the planning process is to be a complete one. Further, the total process involves both technical analytical tasks and process relationship or interactional tasks.

TWO BASIC TOOLS

Perhaps two of the tools most frequently used by the planner are (a) committee management and (b) collection, analysis, synthesis, and presentation of data. Frequently, the initial suggestions of individuals or a group interested in a problem are:

- Let's appoint a committee.
- Let's make a study.

In view of the popularity and prevalence of these tools of planning, special attention is given to them here.

Committee Management

We are living in an age of committees. Committees are almost a way of life in our society. The human services field has a long history of working through boards and committees, but even industry, which for many years was operated in a more direct "line of authority," is now increasingly using committees. In view of their extensive use and popularity, one would expect our knowledge and handling of committee activity would be rather sophisticated and that, generally, committee activity would be satisfying and productive. But, all too frequently, the exact opposite seems nearer the truth. The critics of the committee process have described a committee as:

A group of the unfit appointed by the unwilling to do the unnecessary.

[A] process that takes "minutes" to waste "hours."

A group of individuals who alone can do nothing and then get together to decide that nothing can be done.

Why the dissatisfaction, the disillusionment, the dissipation of all these efforts that go into committee activity? The reasons are many. Perhaps most fundamental is the failure to appreciate that committee operation is not a simple process. It is not just a matter of getting a group of people together (there is no magic in numbers); it is not just a forum; it is not just conversation. Alfred Sheffield, in his book *Creative Discussion,* says a committee is "[A] test tube in social dynamics. Its success all centers on making differences mutually enhancing instead of mutually thwarting."

A committee is a complex operation involving the orchestration of three key elements (the chairman, the members, the staff) and the adequate handling of committee dynamics and committee mechanics. Committee mechanics and dynamics are not just things that occur when people are assembled for a meeting but include such things as:

1. The decision that the job to be done can be better done through a committee process than any other approach or process.
2. A clear statement of the committee's charge.
3. Careful selection of an appropriate chairman.
4. Careful selection and recruitment of members.
5. Adequate attention to premeeting activities.
6. Adequate handling of the committee meeting process.

7. Adequate postcommittee activities.
8. Especially important is the role of the staff person in the entire process.

The committee process should be used when we need people's judgment, when we want to create new ideas or common ideas out of the interplay of people, when we want to translate "like interests" into "common interests," when we want to bring about understanding, agreement, and clarification.

The committee process is often thought of as an isolated event or a series of events, namely, the committee meeting or meetings. But, actually, much of the activity involved in the committee process takes place before and after the committee meeting itself. Perhaps as much as four to five times as much effort goes into this "behind-the-scenes" process. Also, because of this emphasis or attention to the committee meeting itself, there is a tendency to be more concerned with the dynamics of the meeting and especially with the personalities involved than with concern for preparation and procedures for the total dynamics of the committee process, including what happens before and after the committee meeting, as well as what takes place during the meeting.

Following are some principles or guidelines for the handling of the committee activity:

- Be focused:
  The clarification and understanding of the committee's purpose is basic and essential to the performance of its task.
- Be selective:
  The leadership of the chairman is the single most important ingredient in successful committee activity.
  The selection of the committee members must be thoughtfully and carefully done, using as a guideline the purpose to be achieved by the committee activity.
- Be prepared:
  The quality of the committee operation is related to the adequacy of planning and preparation for all aspects and phases of the committee process.
  The progress and movement of the committee meeting itself is directly related to the adequacy of the preparation that preceded the meeting and the follow-through after it.
- Be involved:
  Participation is the keystone for a productive and effective committee operation.
  There must be balance between thorough preparation for and control of the committee meeting in the interest of covering a maximum amount of work in a minimum amount of time, and provision for adequate discussion and the creation of the feeling by committee members that they are helpful participants, not just window dressing or rubber stamps.
- Be a leader:
  Leadership and not manipulation should be the approach of all who participate in the committee process.
  The staff person should support and not supplant the leadership work of the chairperson or individual committee members.
- Be communicative:
  Keep committee members and other individuals or organizations with a legitimate interest informed of the committee activity, clearing with them plans and proposals or positions before final action is taken.
- Be dynamic:
  A sense of progress, movement, and accomplishment is essential for committee members' morale and satisfaction.

Data Management

The principle that things should be undergirded with sound, factual information is well accepted. It reflects an understanding that planning is a complex decision-making process in which the values of the participants exercise considerable influence. Factual information tends to increase the "rationality" of the entire process. The importance of data in the planning process and guidance to its collection and use are reflected in a two-volume booklet, published by the Community Chests and Councils of America in 1942, entitled "Let's Make a Study."

Range of Data Collection and Research Activities. Data collection ranges from simple inventories of services or operation information to more complex studies of needs and resources in a functional field, community surveys or efforts to measure the claims of agencies or the impact of effectiveness of agencies' services. Some of the more typical data collection efforts of the planning agency include:

1. Establishment, identification, or measurement of need for services.
2. Measurement of services offered.
3. Evaluation of the results or outcome of services.
4. Administrative studies of individual agencies or comparative studies of agencies relative to some specific factor, such as costs, personnel practices, and so forth.
5. Priorities studies.
6. Characteristics of clientele.
7. Volume and cost of services and source of income.

With the increased demand for accountability and the increased complexity of the human services field and the related difficult policy decisions related to fund allocations, the need for sound and adequate information has become more apparent. Likewise, the need for greater knowledge, skill, and sophistication in research on the part of planners has become essential.

Regular vs. Specific Collection of Data. A troublesome question is how much data should be regularly and continuously collected by the voluntary community planning agency. As pioneers in the human services planning field, many voluntary planning agencies stimulated the regular collection and centralization of social data. They launched the first effort to report service and cost data and several made extensive analyses of census data and other related social information on a census track basis. However, the complexity, cost, and even the wisdom of a voluntary agency attempting to collect basic social information regularly has resulted in the elimination or modification of such factual collection programs. In recent years there also has been the trend for some social information to be regularly collected by regional planning agencies, city and county planning departments, and agencies with interests in specialized fields such as comprehensive health planning, criminal justice, and so forth. In addition, state departments of social welfare and health, federal departments like H.E.W., H.U.D., Labor, and so forth, and national voluntary agencies all collect data on a regular and continuing basis. Unfortunately, there is no one place where all these human service data are centralized and analyzed. There are some efforts to develop significant and sensitive indices in the human services field similar to indices in the economic field but these efforts are still in the exploratory and developmental stage.

Experience also indicated that the routine collection of social data can be costly and wasteful. Frequently, despite the volumes of data collected, it fell short of providing the information needed in connection with a given problem. The result was a shift in data collection from the general to the more specific. Data are now more frequently collected routinely if they are needed for a specific purpose, such as agency cost and service statistics. Other data collecting is related to the specific question under consideration in a specific study. This had led to an increased effort to clarify at the beginning of a study the questions it is trying to answer. Data collection is then specifically related to these questions. This shift in approach to data collection means that planners must be (1) knowledgeable about sources of information that are collected through other organizations and (2) knowledgeable and skillful in the application of research techniques essential to the collection of pertinent data.

Pressures to Make Studies. A review of the programs of voluntary planning councils indicate a considerable emphasis on "studies." The pressure to undertake studies sometimes evolves from our naiveté that studies will lead us to our desired goal, but sometimes it relates to a Machiavellian device to keep us busy or to slow us down and, therefore, prevent us from moving toward a desired goal. Studies usually are undertaken to help solve problems and problems related to matters of policy and fund allocation. These are basically political issues which, in the last analysis, will depend on the judgments of the people involved. This should not detract from the importance of studies, but make us appreciative of the fact that studies are only one of the inputs in this decision-making process.

Studies are appropriate input into the decision-making process:

1. If the regular channels for decision-making (e.g., United Way Allocating Committee) seem unable, or need help, to cope with change.
2. If there is need to reflect broader and different perspectives or to facilitate modification of established programs for service delivery systems.

But studies should not be undertaken:

1. If the timing seems unsuitable for implementation of study findings.
2. If the funding sources (e.g., the board, allocating committee, legislating body, government administrators, and so forth) have no or limited interest or commitment to the study.
3. If there is no power base for follow-through on the study.
4. If the study contains no plan or potential for implementation.
5. If the study process is being used as a diversionary device to delay action.

In brief, studies should not be separated from implementation or should not be undertaken if implementation is left entirely to chance. For this reason, some planning agencies use as a guiding principle that they will not undertake a study unless it is requested, preferably by people with authority or who are in a position to do something with the study findings. This is a sound approach, with the exception that sometimes a planning agency observes a problem that needs community thought and attention, but no one has requested that it be made. In such instances, the planning agency might want to give community leadership in its exploration. However, it might be wisest to generate and cultivate interest in the problem through community organization efforts before undertaking any formal study.

Closely related to the above is the matter of studies of a community's total human services system. This is an extensive and an expensive undertaking. It usually generates a long list of recommendations, varying from specific ones to the very general. Implementation becomes a major problem. Perhaps such studies must be viewed somewhat differently from the more limited studies focused on a given agency, field of service, age group, or problem. Such broad community studies do help us reassess our goals and directions, provide for input from a broader cross section of the community than is possible through our established processes of decision-making, generate an interest and enthusiasm in the human services field and its problems that is not always possible through the more limited approaches. Therefore, a community should understand the values and limitations of such studies and be realistic in its expectations of what they can accomplish.

Synthesis and Presentation. Perhaps the most difficult and challenging aspect of data collection is its analysis, synthesis, and presentation. Too much data can be as useless as too little data if they are not ordered, classified, and integrated in a way that provides insight into the questions being explored. Data are *not* useful themselves. They must be so arranged and analyzed as to clarify and not complicate their use. It is easy to be overwhelmed with the volume of data relative to a given problem. It is difficult to select the wheat from the chaff, the pertinent from the nonessential. It is difficult to maintain an objective position in the selection and interpretation of information. It is difficult to be brief and succinct in presenting a mass of complex material for consideration by a study committee. This is the responsibility of the planner. This is the skill and discipline that must be brought to the task. The goal must always be to maximize the effective use of the factual data.

10. Conference Planning

League of Women Voters Education Fund

HOW TO PLAN AN ENVIRONMENTAL CONFERENCE

This manual on planning land and water use seminars for citizen leaders draws on the League of Women Voters Education Fund experience gained through seventeen such seminars. It updates information on governmental and in-

Reproduced by permission of the publisher, League of Women Voters of the United States, Washington, D.C. From League of Women Voters Education Fund, *How to Plan an Environmental Conference—A Technique for Developing Citizen Leadership*, pp. 3–48.

This handbook for planning environmental conferences was published under Training Grant #1TT1-

stitutional tools useful to citizens seeking solutions to their water resource problems. Organizational techniques outlined in it are adaptable to small local conferences, multicounty or statewide projects, or conferences of national scope. They are also useful in arranging meetings for leadership training on any environmental problem.

WP-46-01 from the Office of Water Programs, Environmental Protection Agency. The League of Women Voters Education Fund gratefully acknowledges the continuing financial assistance which has made the series of land and water seminars possible.

INITIATING THE PROJECT

Goals and Scope

In undertaking a project on environmental quality or any other subject, a group must first decide on its objectives in relation to an identified need, determine what kind of project would best fulfill those objectives, and then draw up a plan of operation, including a budget.

The basic format the Education Fund has used to these ends is a series of three-day seminars for participants drawn from diverse groups throughout the geographic area of concern. Fifty participants has proved to be a good number—large enough to be stimulating and representative and to establish a nucleus of informed leadership for future educational activities throughout an area, yet small and flexible enough for group discussion and easy social mixing. Participants are not asked to pay their expenses, for two reasons: planners are free to choose participants for potential leadership rather than ability to pay, and participants feel responsible for follow-up activity.

Each seminar to date surveys water resource problems specific to a basin or region, outlines governmental functions and legal framework relating to water management in the area, and presents examples and techniques of citizen action. To encourage a spirit of genuine inquiry and uninhibited exchange of views, no votes are taken, no resolutions passed.

To stimulate interest in follow-up and spark ideas between regions, LAND AND WATER ROUNDUP, an informal newsletter, is sent to seminar attendees for two years.

Funding a Seminar

If a proposed project requires funding

from outside sources, the organizing group should inquire of prospective donors whether they will entertain a request for a grant. The organizing group will then prepare its proposal in the format preferred by the interested foundation, government agency, corporation, or individual, following any guidelines the prospective donor suggests.

A proposal describes the nature and source of the problem to be addressed, points out the need for the project, states the objectives, lists the anticipated accomplishments, and presents a budget. The plan of operation should be outlined in some detail.

The contributions which the applicant is prepared to make in money and volunteer time and skills should be stated and financial needs explained.

Drawing Up a Budget Proposal

The estimated budget accompanying applications for funds for three-day seminars should include travel, meals, and lodging for seminar participants, committee, and speakers; printing and mimeographing, long-distance telephone, clerical work, postage, other local expenses for planning the seminar and for encouraging follow-up activities; and cost of guidance and help needed from the sponsoring group, including travel, staff salary and office expenses, long-distance telephone calls, mailings, etc.

All local committee members for land and water seminars have been volunteers, but postage, printing, travel, and other expenses they incurred for the seminars and follow-up activity were part of the project budget.

Selecting an Appropriate Area

In selecting areas for specific projects,

consider questions like these: Is there one outstanding common problem which recurs over a wide area? Is there public concern about a regional environmental problem? Is there an issue that provides a focus for citizen concern? Can a region be defined large enough to encourage a regional approach yet compact enough so that seminar participants can keep in touch without prohibitive travel expenses? Is there need to bring together widely dispersed residents or opposing interests for discussion of watershed on which they all depend and which they all affect?

The intensified effort possible in a small area is tempting, but this advantage should be weighed against the need to find basin-wide or regional solutions to environmental problems or against the wisdom of serving a larger area within which problems are similar. Travel facilities and costs must also be considered. Are travel connections within the area reasonably good?

For most local organizations, the geographic area of concern is already established. A national organization wishing to initiate a project in a particular region must make sure that local leadership is available. A competent general chairman able to devote substantial time to the project is essential.

THE PLANNING COMMITTEE

Setting Up the Planning Committee

Let us assume that you—the sponsoring group or organization—have decided to hold a seminar, have roughly defined the geographic area and the theme, and have found a general chairman. Careful selection of the planning committee is the most important of the general chairman's first tasks.

The key ingredient of League of Women Voters Education Fund seminars, the bringing together of diverse and sometimes conflicting interests in a working situation, is applied first in formation of the planning committee.

A planning committee for a seminar should include both sponsor and nonsponsor members—men and women—with a range of occupational and avocational interests, all drawn from the geographic area covered by a seminar.

A total of 15 to 20 members has proved to be effective. Too large a group becomes unwieldy; too small a group lacks the variety of viewpoints and the manpower needed to do the planning job. A few well-known persons lend prestige, but the committee is essentially a working group, with each member expected to do his share.

For an interstate seminar, each state involved should be represented on the planning committee, preferably by both a member and a nonmember of the sponsoring organization. The major areas within a region, too, should be represented if possible. This representation helps in recruiting participants from each location, in gathering background data, in obtaining speakers, and especially in planning program content and in follow-up.

Committee members should know who are the local civic leaders, who helps to form opinion, and how key elements of their governments work. Each member should be sensitive to the needs, interests, and prejudices of the area he represents but be willing to cooperate with other groups.

In the search for nonsponsor members of the planning committee, the chairman will have the advice and help of the sponsoring organization and should seek suggestions from university, civic, conservation, and official contacts. From these recommendations, several experts from the region to be covered by the seminar, representing various interests concerned with water quality and water resources (or whatever the subject may be), are then asked to serve on the planning committee. Later they attend the seminar as members of the committee. They bring different points of view, and their participation assures broad support.

Members of a university faculty, conservationists, and representatives of state or regional agencies can be helpful in developing the program. So can representatives of important businesses or industries in the area, whose help in recruiting participants from the business community will be indispensable. A newspaper editor has useful sources of information and publicity outlets. If there is a present or potential human health problem, include a medical doctor. Several skills, much knowledge, and considerable effort go into a successful conference, and planning committee members need to understand that in accepting the invitation to serve on the committee, each is agreeing to accept and discharge particular responsibilities.

Meeting of the Planning Committee

Two meetings of the full planning committee are necessary, with a third if it will be productive and the budget permits. A full day should be allotted to each. The first meeting should take place about six months before the probable date for the seminar.

To settle many details and save planning committee time, the committee members belonging to the sponsoring organization should meet the day before for preliminary planning, tentative assignments, discussion of the budget, and briefing on guidelines and administrative network.

The first full planning committee meeting is the time to discuss project goals, firmly establish the geographic boundaries, and elicit both expert and lay views

on the nature and dimensions of the problem(s) the seminar is to deal with. Topics to be covered and names of good speakers should be proposed. Recruitment should be discussed thoroughly and apportionment of places among the geographic areas decided by the committee. Members should be asked to suggest organizations and individuals to be considered in recruitment and kit material to be solicited. Initial recommendations for publicity, public relations, and recording the seminar should be sought, and there must be some discussion of follow-up aims.

In this first meeting the location and firm dates of the seminar should be settled if possible, subcommittee assignments made, the budget outlined, and committee work schedule set up. At its conclusion, everyone should know who is going to do what.

FIGURE 10.1

A Checklist for the General Chairman

Help select a balanced, representative planning committee

Make all subcommittee assignments

Establish workable lines of communication with all committee members

Set up a time schedule and see that it is followed

Make final decisions on motel, letterhead, printing and mimeographing, date, location and agenda of all planning meetings, etc.

Supervise and coordinate all mailings

Attend all program committee meetings

Sign recruitment letter

Conduct meeting of planning committee on night before seminar opens to review all program and arrangement details

Establish adequate method to handle seminar's finances and keep accurate records

At seminar, be available to greet participants, open and close the program, introduce a speaker, or whatever is required

See that thank-you notes are written.

At the second full meeting three or four months later, but no later than two months before the seminar, the committee will select participants from the list of nominees, review the program, and plan for publicity and kits. Decisions on whether to tape the conference and about whether to publish a summary or report are made final at this time. Here is a good opportunity to discuss follow-up opportunities, plans, and arrangements, and perhaps to set a date for a post-seminar evaluation session. With all members up to date on seminar prospects, any required policy decisions may be made by the committee at this time.

General Chairman's Duties

The *general chairman* will want to have probable committee assignments and a tentative work plan in mind before the first planning meeting. Indeed, he should, in consultation with his organization, insure that needed talent or experience from the sponsoring organization will be available on the committee and that certain key members are willing to assume specific responsibilities, particularly for program, recruitment, follow-up, and publicity.

The general chairman should send out an advance agenda, well before the first planning committee meeting, and ask committee members to come prepared with certain information.

The general chairman will maintain close supervision over all activities of the planning committee, chiefly by mail or telephone. In consultation with the sponsoring organization, the chairman makes final decisions on all matters of policy and on important details. As an ex-officio member of each subcommittee, he should receive copies of all correspondence. As project coordinator, he will keep members up to date on what each subcommittee is doing. This intercommunication is imperative where committee members live in different states.

The chairman should have administrative ability but need not be a specialist in water resources. (Such specialists are essential, of course, on the program subcommittee.) He will probably need some paid secretarial help to handle the correspondence and should have access to mimeographing, addressing, and mailing services.

The chairman approves all local expenditures and keeps an accurate record of the running budget balance.

SUBCOMMITTEES AND THEIR DUTIES

These subcommittees are recommended:

Recruitment Committee
Program Content Committee
Follow-up Committee
Arrangements Committee
Kits Committee
Publicity Committee
Printing and Mimeographing Committee

There will also be secretarial and financial duties to assign.

Work on subcommittee assignments must begin promptly after the first planning committee meeting and continue throughout the planning period, during which time the program, recruitment, and follow-up subcommittees will need to meet separately.

Committee chairmen are normally selected from members of the sponsoring organization who are on the planning committee. Other planning committee members serve primarily on the program and recruitment subcommittees, although sometimes one of these members will volunteer to check motels in his vicinity or help get wider press coverage, etc. Non-sponsor members help in other ways, too —for instance, by recommending material for kits, obtaining materials in quantity, and providing audiovisual equipment and operators.

Committee assignments may have to be adjusted after the planning committee has decided on the location for the seminar. The arrangements chairman, for example, should live near the selected site. If the site is in or near a large city, usually the public relations chairman should be from that area.

There will be paper work for all, much correspondence, many telephone calls. At least one crisis is inevitable for every big project. But past committee members have found the returns well worth the work. Newly aroused leadership inspires new thinking and activity in the area. The local sponsoring organization receives new recognition and finds its contacts greatly broadened. Individual committee members widen and deepen their own knowledge and background while developing new skills. Most important, new alliances are forged.

RECRUITMENT: WHO AND WHY

On his committee, the *recruitment chairman* needs at least one person from each state or locale. The chairman also needs access to a mimeographing or photocopying machine, stationery, and lots of stamps.

Who Should Be Invited

Solutions to resource problems often entail social and political decisions with wide implications that need to be understood in the community. Seminar recruitment systems are designed to locate and attract citizen leaders from diverse segments of the community, leaders who can benefit from an opportunity to learn more about land and water, governmental structure, or citizen effectiveness; who will also benefit from an increased understanding of the conflicts among each other's interests; and who will in turn stimulate their own colleagues and constituents to take an active and concerned role.

Getting the right participants is vital to the success of this type of project. They should be present or potential community leaders representing varied economic, occupational, geographic, and avocational interests, with varied approaches to land and water resource use. They should have follow-up activity outlets that will enable them to reach business, labor, civic, professional, industrial, or agricultural groups, the news media, and educational services.

Examples of lay participants whose organizations have an interest in related matters might include a manufacturer whose industry requires water; a developer whose business involves land use, requires water supply and sewers, and affects land and water resources; a labor leader; a professional whose affiliations are with planning, design, or engineering of land or water projects; an editor whose newspaper neglects such issues; an officer of a preservation or garden society that has not become involved or effective in broader environmental affairs; a mayor; a teacher; an inner-city resident; a law student; a rancher; a retailer; a banker.

An expert, too, may benefit from insight into the social and economic aspects of competing demands on available land and water or into the workings of government or the dynamics of citizen action. A state legislator who serves on a committee deciding on any aspect of land- and/or water-use policies usually appreciates the opportunity to view the whole scope of

FIGURE 10.2

Countdown for Major Planning Steps

SUBCOMMITTEES

Arrangements	First meeting full Planning Committee Decision on location, definition of scope, organization of subcommittees	6 MONTHS
Program Content	Preparation of recruitment brochure, nomination form Reservation of meeting space Assembling of recruitment list Decision on program framework, follow-up Budget	5 MONTHS
Recruitment	Send out recruitment brochure w/ nominating form, tentative program outline Collect possible kit materials	4 MONTHS
Finance	Deadline for nominations Secure all speakers, order visual aids	3 MONTHS
Secretary	Choose participants--send them acceptance form, room reservation slip, list of participants Notify individuals not selected and all organizations Select and order kit materials, advance study materials	2 MONTHS
Kits	Draft problems for discussion sessions Mail to participants: publicity request, financial instructions Final arrangements, menus, etc. Print program	1 MONTH
Printing & Mimeographing	Send out advance study materials	2 WEEKS
Publicity	Prepare final kits News announcements to media	1 WEEK
Follow-up	Planning Committee arrives	1 DAY
		SEMINAR

problems presented. He can put the information to good use as well as leaven the discussions. Young people and representatives of minority groups may add important points of view. In short, the committee should try to reach beyond the water and conservation "establishments."

Good questions to ask about each suggested participant are: "What can he bring to the seminar? What can he take away?"

Choice of participants must be related to goals of a particular seminar. Each planning committee should adapt and expand these guidelines to fit its own situation, trying to avoid having too many experts, officials, industrialists, or conservationists. The committee should bear in mind that these categories will assuredly be represented on the faculty, too.

Selecting the Participants

Developing a List of Organizations within the Seminar Area. The first step in recruitment is to collect names of organizations active in the seminar area and interested in land and water issues. In this, the recruitment chairman needs everyone's help. Before the first planning committee meeting, someone from each state should be asked to assemble a current, comprehensive list of organizations in his state. If organizations are to be asked to send names of nominees, the current president's name and address will also be needed.

Among the obvious organizations are chambers of commerce, garden clubs, industrial groups, sportsmen's clubs, farm groups, labor unions, conservation organizations, student and other youth groups, teachers, and service clubs.

The Conservation Directory, issued annually by the National Wildlife Federation, the three-volume *Encyclopedia of*

Associations—available at university and large city libraries—state yearbooks or public affairs directories put out by the General Federation of Women's Clubs and chambers of commerce, local library listings, and the women's, state, business, and farm pages of local newspapers are all sources of this kind of information.

The list of organizations interested in land and water use in a river basin may number 250 or more, from which fifty seminar participants will be chosen. The selection can be made in a number of ways.

Obtaining Nominations

Nominations from the Recruitment and the Planning Committees. The planning committee can assume responsibility for nominating the participants. Each committee member suggests names of organizations and individuals to be considered, accompanying his suggestion with the fullest possible information on each, plus his reasons for the nomination. The recruitment committee seeks out supplementary information and then meets to select participants and alternates to recommend for the full committee's consideration. At its second meeting, the planning committee makes the final decisions. Invitations are then sent promptly to the individuals chosen.

Nominations from Selected Organizations. In a variation of the first method, the planning committee—individually and collectively—investigates each organization on the list to learn whether it has leaders who would be promising participants. The planning committee then selects fifty organizations and asks each to nominate someone to attend the seminar. These nominees are then invited.

Nominations from Many Organizations. Where the planning committee does not know the area's organizations or individual leaders well enough to make direct selections, many organizations can be asked to nominate participants from whom the planning committee can choose.

A letter, signed by the general chairman, asks each organization to nominate one of its leaders on an enclosed form. An attractive recruitment brochure and a tentative outline of the program explain the project, stimulate the organization's interest, and guide its selection of a nominee. Include a list of planning committee members with their affiliations. Remember the name and address of the recruitment chairman for returns.

Each of these pieces should have the approval of the general chairman. Mail them *at least four-and-a-half months* before the seminar. State the deadline for return on the form and in the letter or brochure and set it *at least two-and-a-half months* before the seminar date and two weeks before the second planning committee meeting.

If, as nominations come in, some categories are underrepresented, the recruitment committee suggests nominees. The recruitment chairman compiles information received about those nominated and presents it to the planning committee, which selects the fifty names to whom invitations are sent.

The advantage to this procedure is that it alerts whole groups to the project and confers organizational backing on the persons selected. The disadvantage is that many nominees must be rejected simply because the number of participants is strictly limited and geographic and occupational variety is sought. As these reasons have little to do with a nominee's qualifications, misunderstanding and resentment may result.

Preparing the Lists. Whatever the source of nominations, the recruitment chairman prepares a list of nominees for recruitment committee and full planning committee consideration. Nominees are grouped by states or localities, with a thumbnail sketch of each—occupation, background, interests, and organization or person nominating him. Thorough background information about nominees who are members of state, local, and regional boards and commissions is especially needed, so that the planning committee can decide whether an official's thinking will be so strongly determined by his private interests that he will not benefit from or add to the balance of the seminar. If possible, send the list to committee members before the second planning meeting.

Recruitment chairmen find it helpful to assemble information about each nominee on a separate card with space for home town, occupation, professional training, official and volunteer posts held, avocation, and affiliations. By sorting the cards as nominees are considered, a recruitment chairman can quickly check on geographic, occupational, or organizational balance of the group.

Choosing Those to Invite. In selecting the participants, the planning committee will take into account these factors:

Is the nominee a leader of the organization?

Does he have good organizational connections or potential for effective follow-up?
Does he already have some interest?
Does his organization agree to cooperate?
If he is already an expert, should he be considered as a speaker or panel member instead?
Is he receptive to new information and different points of view?

About some nominees, there will be immediate agreement. When the list approaches 30 or so, pause to look at the overall picture. Is the list geographically balanced? Is it balanced for occupations and interests? Special attention may be re-

FIGURE 10.3

LEAGUE OF WOMEN VOTERS EDUCATION FUND

COMMUNITY LEADERS' CONFERENCE

CITIZENS' SEMINAR

Coastal Lands and Waters of New England

APRIL 7, 8, 9, 1970

Sheraton-Hyannis Inn, Hyannis, Massachusetts

Dear Community Leader:

We are seeking your help in recruiting responsible men and women to participate in a conference for community leaders, CITIZENS SEMINAR: COASTAL LANDS AND WATERS OF NEW ENGLAND, to be held on April 7, 8 and 9, 1970 at the Sheraton Motor Inn in Hyannis, Mass. All expenses of the selected participants for travel, food and lodging will be assumed by the League of Women Voters Education Fund under a training grant from the Federal Water Pollution Control Administration, Department of the Interior.

Will you submit the names of one or more persons from your organization or community who are interested in exploring and understanding the many interrelated problems of land and water development in the coastal areas of Maine, New Hampshire, Massachusetts and Rhode Island? They must be willing and able to share this information widely in their own communities following the seminar. We ask that you recommend persons who have an interest in land and water use problems; they need not be experts in the field.

From the total list of nominees suggested by organizations such as yours, forty participants will be selected. Although the size of the group must be limited, the nominees who are not chosen will be asked to participate in follow-up activities. A report of the conference will be sent to all nominees.

At the seminar, a faculty of experts will deal with the problems and the potential of the coastal area, as noted in the tentative program outline. To achieve the purpose of the seminar for wide citizen understanding of and participation in decisions affecting the multiple uses of the area, each participant will be expected to carry on follow-up activities in his community.

A nominating form is enclosed which will give you an idea of the qualifications we seek in candidates for the seminar. Nominations must be received by January 10, 1970. We look forward to hearing from you soon.

Sincerely yours,

Barbara Fegan

Mrs. James Fegan, Chairman

FIGURE 10.4

League of Women Voters Education Fund

NOMINATING FORM

For Participation In

The Seminar on Land and Water Use

ARKANSAS-WHITE-RED RIVER BASINS - Middle and Lower Sections
March 17, 18, 19, 1970
Fort Smith, Arkansas

The _____
        (Name of Organization)

_____
(Address of Organization)

proposes as a Participant -

Name _____ Phone _____

Address _____

Nominee's Background:

A. Present Occupation _____

B. Experience in community projects, government, other organizations (professional or voluntary) _____

Will your nominee agree to -

1. Do preliminary reading for the seminar? Materials will be furnished in advance _____

2. Attend all sessions of the seminar? _____

Participants will be expected to carry the information gained at the Seminar back to their communities and to report on local activity to the planning committee from time to time for inclusion in a newsletter to be sent to all participants.

Is your nominee able and willing to carry out this plan? _____

Is your organization able to offer him assistance? _____

(Please continue on the other side.)

IN YOUR OPINION, WHAT ARE THE NOMINEE'S SPECIAL QUALIFICATIONS?
(Please answer fully.)

Is your nominee concerned with a particular land or water problem in your area? If so, what is it?

Please return not later than January 15, 1970
To: Mrs. Paul W. Andreas
    3549 West 11th Street,
    Wichita, Kansas 67203

After the planning committee has selected about 35 participants, considering answers to questions like those on the above nomination forms, it pauses to check whether the desired balance of interests is being achieved (see page 122).

FIGURE 10.4 Continued

PTA- Youth- Fish- 4H-Petroleum
Recreation- Education- Lawyer- Real Estate

AAUW II
Citizen River Group II
University Extension I
Chamber of Commerce I (Vol.) 2 or 3 Prof.
Bank I   Economic Dev I
LWV II   " Commission II
Farm Bureau I   Churchwomen I
Architect + Landscape Planner I
Politician III
Industry IIII
Attorney I
Conservationist (amateur) II
Farmer-, Rancher II
Journalist III
Federation of Women's Clubs I
Water Prof. (Govt.) IIII
Education - Adult (Sec) II
Petroleum Engineer (Polit) I
Timber I   Poultry I
Red River I   Broadcaster I
Youth II   Hydrologist I

quired to obtain representation from certain areas or interests. Changes may be necessary to round out the coverage.

Don't expect 100 percent acceptance and do anticipate a few inevitable last-minute cancellations. Therefore, to have 50 participants, send invitations to 60 persons and authorize the recruitment chairman to select last-minute additions from a reserve list.

Inviting the Participants

When the invitation list is firm, the recruitment chairman notifies those selected. Letters to them include:

1. Acceptance form, to be sure they un-

derstand their commitment to attendance for the full three days and to follow-up activity. Participants sign this form and return it to the recruitment chairman.

2. Room reservation slip. Participants fill out this form and return it to the recruitment chairman, who turns it over to the arrangements chairman.

3. Mimeographed list of all selected participants, with their addresses and the names of organizations they represent. (This list facilitates car-pooling. It can be sent with a later preseminar mailing.)

4. A more detailed list of speakers or program, if ready and funds permit.

If nominations were requested from organizations, the recruitment chairman also notifies:

Individuals not selected, by a personal letter

Each organization whose nominees were not selected, with a courteous explanation of the reasons

Organizations whose nominee was selected

FIGURE 10.5

Check List for the Recruitment Chairman

Coordinate with general chairman of planning committee on all mailings

Collect names and addresses of interested organizations, with name of current president or executive officer of organizations to be asked to nominate

Send recruitment letter or brochure, with nominating form (if this method selected), or

Collect names and addresses of individual nominees and coordinate research of recruitment committee (if this method selected)

Make list of nominees, with thumbnail sketch of background and affiliation

Help planning committee choose 50 participants

Invite those selected (and notify those not selected if third method used, as well as the organizations which nominated)

Enclose brochure, reservation and acceptance forms

Compile lists of participants with addresses and organizational affiliation, to mimeograph for kits

List for follow-up chairman those not selected

Work with general, publicity, arrangements chairmen, give lists to kits and follow-up chairmen

Help with registration at seminar

Adapting Recruitment Procedures to Needs

All recruitment procedures can be altered in several ways. For example, to reach more widely into the community, nominations of members of the sponsoring organization are strictly limited, though its local chapters should be asked to nominate people from their towns. However, particularly well qualified members from the sponsoring organization may be accepted as nominees.

Geographic balance is desirable, but for some seminars it may be appropriate to weight representation toward a particular locale.

Each planning committee should adopt the recruitment method suitable for its members and its area, bearing in mind that the goal is to achieve leadership representation from diverse and conflicting interests.

PROGRAM: WHAT, HOW, AND WHO

The Program Committee plans the seminar program and invites the speakers. Project goals and program topics discussed at the first meeting of the planning committee guide the program committee, which presents its plan for discussion and suggestions at the second planning committee meeting. Frequent revisions of the proposed program, formal letters to speakers, and communication with planning committee members responsible for printing, public relations, and arrangements are part of the program subcommittee's challenging work.

The committee has an immediate assignment: to draw up a general outline of program topics to be incorporated into the recruitment brochure or enclosed with the recruitment letter. An interesting outline which captures the essence of the seminar and suggests its content will enhance the appeal of the invitation. Obviously, at this stage it will be impossible to list speakers' names.

The *program chairman* should be a member of the sponsoring organization and must be knowledgeable about the sub-

FIGURE 10.6
Sample Recruitment Letters

LAND AND WATER SEMINAR

ACCELERATED GROWTH—ACCELERATED EROSION

Sediment, Our Wasted Wealth

April 13, 1971

Dear xxxxxxxx:

We are pleased to invite you to a Land and Water Seminar at the Baltimore West Holiday Inn, starting at 9:00 A.M. Tuesday, May 25, and ending at 3:00 P.M. Thursday, May 27. The Seminar is financed under a grant from the Water Quality Office of the Environmental Protection Agency.

Enclosed is a general outline of the proposed program which will concern urban-suburban erosion and sedimentation problems and solutions.

A distinguished faculty has agreed to serve as stimulators of discussion, and you are one of fifty community leaders from Maryland, Virginia and the District of Columbia who have been selected to participate. The invitation list is deliberately small and carefully chosen to allow a free flow of ideas from individuals with a wide variety of interests.

We are happy to add that our budget permits us to provide transportation and accommodation expenses. To facilitate the making of final arrangements, we ask that you reply to our invitation on the enclosed card by Tuesday, April 20.

We look forward to your attendance at this Seminar on May 25. Your presence will help assure its success.

Sample Letters

The wording of invitations sent to participants will vary with the selection process and with each seminar's purpose (See above). Letters sent to organizations that have made nominations will also need to be tailored to each group (see below).

GULF OF MEXICO COASTAL WATERS SEMINAR

January 20, 1970

Dear Community Leader:

Thank you for your expression of interest in the Gulf of Mexico Coastal Waters Seminar to be held in Pensacola in March.

As we anticipated in our brochure, we have had many more nominees than we can accept. We are giving priority to several categories: those who represent organizations or interests not already represented in the Seminar and those who may not already have a background of experience in the problems of coastal water development and management. I am sure you understand that we are trying primarily to expand citizen comprehension of the problems, rather than gather together a group of experts to talk to each other, in the hope that real grass roots action will result.

Regretfully, we have to turn down your nomination. However, we hope we shall have your continuing interest. Following the Seminar, each participant will be planning a program or programs in his own community. We hope you will help in planning and carrying out these programs.

Sincerely yours,

FIGURE 10.7

REGISTRATION INFORMATION

I plan to attend the Snake River Basin Seminar in
_____ Boise, June 3, 4, 5

_____ I will be able to pay my own travel costs.

_____ I will be able to pay my own lodging costs.

I am unable to attend the Snake River Basin Seminar
_____ in Boise, June 3, 4, 5

Please make reservations for me at the Rodeway Inn

    _____ to be assigned by the Seminar (two participants
    to a room)

    Roommate preference, if any _____

    _____ single room for which I agree to pay $3.00 extra
    each day

I will arrive _____ at _____
        (Day)   (Time of day)

Registration is Thursday morning, June 3, from 10:00 a.m.
to 11:30 a.m.

The first full meeting of the seminar will be at the Thursday
Luncheon.

Participants will be expected to stay for the full length
of the seminar.

        _____
          Signed
        _____
          Address

RETURN TO: Mrs. Samuel H. Day, Jr., Recruitment Chairman
            2001 North 19th
            Boise, Idaho 83702

          Phone: 344-3954

BIOGRAPHICAL INFORMATION TO BE USED FOR SEMINAR ROSTER AND
FOR NEWSPAPER RELEASES

Name: _____

Address: _____

Occupation: _____

Community Activities: _____

_____

_____

Special interests - achievements - affiliations:

_____

_____

_____

    _____ I enclose a photo that could be used in the
    local paper.

    _____ I do not have a photo available to the press
    at this time.

    The following newspaper and/or newspapers, radio or tele-
vision serve this area and might carry stories on the Snake
River Basin Seminar: _____

RETURN TO: Mrs. Samuel H. Day, Jr., Recruitment Chairman
            2001 North 19th
            Boise, Idaho 83702

          Phone: 344-3954

Forms to be completed and returned, enclosed with the invitations to participants, are informal
in tone yet convey firmly that those who attend accept the serious purpose of the seminar.

ject of the seminar. For the LWVEF land and water seminars, for example, a present or past League of Women Voters state water resources chairman usually handles this assignment. The general chairman, the follow-up chairman, and several experts from the planning committee serve on the program committee, as do the public relations and kit chairmen, if geography and funds allow.

Program Content

To make experts of the participants is not the goal of the seminar program. Rather, the seminar should be designed to leave the participants with a sense of the breadth of the problem; the complex interrelationships of its environmental, social, and economic factors; and the importance of public participation in decisions.

The challenge is to cover the highlights in three days in ways that awaken or enlarge a participant's interest, impel him to make effective use of the information provided by the program and the kits, put him in touch with other people of like interests, and show him how and where to find further information and help.

Program Format

Although no format will guarantee a successful program, certain conditions are necessary: able speakers, a clear structural relationship between the parts, variety and change of pace, ample audience participation.

A successful plan can be built around two major speakers, one philosophical and one informational. The first—the keynoter —will set the local or regional situation or the problem (if the seminar focuses on one problem) in broad perspective; the second will deal, from his expert knowledge, with one major facet of the seminar theme. For the rest of the program, vary the format. Use shorter talks, panels, films and slides, and small-group sessions.

After-dinner sessions are an accepted part of a seminar, but they should not be too heavy or run too late. Everyone is grateful to have his time used to full advantage, but enough is enough. A major talk by a noted speaker will be well received on the first evening. A short, lively talk, small group discussions, a film, or a series of inspiring and informative case histories might be a happy choice for the second evening. Or that evening could be used to bring together small groups of participants from the same locality to discuss its needs and how they can work together at home.

Because *participants should have a chance to participate,* provide plenty of time throughout the program for questions and discussion from the floor. List these periods on the printed program. Exchanges between panelists liven up a program. Encourage them!

In planning the program format, ample time must be allowed for coffee/coke breaks in both morning and afternoon sessions.

The program committee considers seating arrangements for meals. Plans could be made to seat participants according to area at one meal and to mix them at another. Packets of table assignments could be given out at registration time. Or the committee may prefer not to make any assignments except to see that speakers and committee distribute themselves widely. Topics for discussion can be placed at each table if you wish to emphasize the problem-solving orientation of the seminar, or one meal could be reserved for discussion of their problems by area groups. However, mealtimes are really not satisfactory for sessions at which decisions are to be taken about goals or follow-up.

Elements of a Good Program

In the Education Fund land and water seminars dealing with a basin or region, program content falls into three categories: information about water and the area, about governmental and legal institutional arrangements for water quality management, about techniques of effective citizen action.

Selecting Speakers

To make the complexities and conflicts of a land and water situation clear to your audience, use seminar speakers of many viewpoints. Avoid filling the program with conservationists or overweighting it with industrialists and officials. Do use speakers from different sections of your area.

Try to choose speakers who are expert in their fields. Try, too, to choose speakers who value citizen effort and welcome new techniques and subjects for community and regional action. If you approach a federal agency or a corporation or business organization for a speaker, make clear your preference for a person who actually deals with the problems on which you want him to speak yet is knowledgeable in the whole field. A big name is not important; the man with the title may or may not have the information you are seeking. Nor is the public relations officer usually the kind of speaker you want.

Consider the budget before inviting speakers. Will bringing someone from a great distance use up too much of the money budgeted for speakers? Will the government agency pay the travel costs of its speakers? Federal departments, and some states and cities, can pay travel expenses when their people speak, but requests often exceed agency funds. Will the senator expect a large honorarium? A member of the U.S. Congress may be willing to speak without payment in his own area. A congressman from elsewhere will expect a fee, the size increasing with his prominence.

Planning committee members will be able to suggest professors, businessmen, association people, etc., who will talk over seminar plans with the program chairman and recommend possible speakers. Some subjects can be covered by faculty members from area universities or officials of local, state, or regional agencies. Some parts of the program can be handled by planning committee members. Speakers can help with more than one topic; for example, in addition to giving his talk a speaker can serve on a panel, act as moderator, or be a resource person during the problem-solving sessions. Don't overlook good speakers from the sponsoring organization or other civic groups.

Try to check with someone who has heard the proposed speaker. Do his manner and his presentation hold the interest of his audience? Does he speak to his topic and make his ideas clear? Will he bring fresh ideas for the seminar or give an old speech? Don't depend on the fact that he wrote a good book on the subject.

When inviting a speaker, explain the purpose of the project, outline the program, and describe the size and make-up of the audience. Enclose a copy of the recruitment brochure. In the first letter tell what you wish the speaker to discuss or what point of view you wish him to represent and approximately how much time he will have on the program. State unambiguously whether or not your organization will pay his travel and seminar expenses. If prepared to offer an honorarium, state the amount you are prepared to pay or inquire what he will expect to receive. The LWVEF practice is to pay travel and living expenses for speakers whose agencies, companies, or organizations do not absorb the cost, but not to pay honoraria.

Urge each speaker to come for the entire three days, or, if he cannot do this, to stay as long as possible. Whether or not he fills more than one spot on the program, his continued presence will be valuable in informal discussions and in answering participants' questions. He may become keenly interested, decide to stay longer than he planned, and take part in subsequent activities!

In your correspondence after a speaker accepts, outline as specifically as possible what you wish him to deal with in his presentation and the exact time allotted for it. Send him a tentative program outline showing what others will cover before and after his talk. If he is to be on a panel, let him know who else is on it and, in some detail, what you have asked each to cover. Tell panelists the name of the panel moderator. Ask each speaker whether he will need any special equipment such as a projector, and if so what kind (and tell the arrangements chairman). Ask him to send or bring 85 copies of his speech (this need not apply to the "citizen action" and follow-up speakers) plus any reference material he wishes to distribute.

Request his biography immediately and *keep after him or his secretary* until you get it. Request a photograph of the keynoter for newspaper use just before the seminar. Then send these to the public relations chairman and the person in charge of the printed program and supply a copy for the person who will be introducing him.

Before the seminar, speakers will need a hotel reservation slip, instructions for reaching the hotel, and any other advance information which is going to the participants. Take care that the arrangements chairman and program chairman do not each think the other is sending this material to the speakers. Both chairmen need to know how long each speaker expects to stay.

After the seminar, the program chairman or the general chairman writes a thank-you letter to each speaker.

Planning Problem-Solving Sessions

If—as training for effective citizen action—the program is to include problem-solving group sessions, the program committee should draft the problems well in advance of the seminar. Problems should not be too fanciful or too complex but should resemble real situations that participants might face in their own communities. However, problems should not be identical with any well-known, controversial issue. Frame questions accompanying the problem to stimulate discussion about what facts people need to have, where and how to get the information, which government agencies and private interests are involved, and how to initiate a course of action.

Arrange for an experienced discussion leader and a resource person for each group of ten. Brief the discussion leaders in advance; ask each to be ready with an approach to guide participants. At the Education Fund seminars, League members from the planning committee or present in other capacities serve as discussion leaders; speakers and expert committee members serve as resource people. Because group participants always ask for more information about the fictitious communities described in the problems, a speaker or committee member might be assigned to each group to make up hypothetical answers to such questions. The three leaders in each group, but no one else, need copies of the problems in advance.

Setting up the Problems. Problem-solving sessions are an opportunity to be creative—in planning the sessions and in working on the problems. As a rule, each group is assigned a different problem, for which it tries to work out a suitable and effective citizen response.

One variation is to assign the same problem, with several alternative solutions briefly outlined, to all groups. Each group discusses the implications of the alternatives, fleshes out what citizens will need to do to implement each, and chooses one.

Another effective approach to problem-solving sessions is to assign participants to small groups according to place of residence. To make this structure work, have each group, early in the seminar select, through discussion, and list the major environmental problems in its area. Later on, nearer the end of the substantive part of the program, each group meets again to revise its list and to focus on issues most needing citizen attention. These preliminary sessions lead easily into discussion of "What to do when we get back home."

In a seminar concentrating on a single subject, each problem-solving group might work on a plan for problem analysis and a step-by-step strategy for problem solving, keeping in mind the goals of citizen organizations and the technological, financial, legal, administrative, and other constraints on them.

Reports from the Groups. After problem-solving discussion is well under way, each group appoints one of the participants (not a speaker or committee member) to report orally to the entire seminar. Reporting, usually presented with humor and imagination, stimulates groups to earnest application and changes the pace.

Four minutes per group is ample time for each report, perhaps with a short period for comment by the whole seminar and the moderator on the groups' decisions.

Remember These Details. Where groups work on different problems, each group receives copies of only the one prob-

FIGURE 10.8

Two Problem-Solving Samples

At the New England Coastal Waters Seminar, each small group examined a *different* problem. This was one group's problem:

"To handle projected demands for inexpensive electricity in your area, your regional electric company plans to build a nuclear power plant. The proposed site is on your town's tidal marshland, and considerable acreage will be dredged, filled, or otherwise altered from its natural condition. Various groups disagree as to how much, if any, change and/or damage to the environment will result from the rise in water temperature of the estuary as a result of the power plant's use of salt water for cooling. A number of schemes have been advanced for turning the heat to constructive use. Fishing interests, conservationists, ecologists, power people all cite different sets of facts in support of their views."

These were the accompanying questions: How could citizens get and evaluate facts, including information on possible accidents, disposal of nuclear wastes, etc.? What are the alternatives for more and cheaper power? Are economic or biologic results of existing plants known? What local benefits or drawbacks might the nuclear plant bring? Who will make the final decisions? How could citizens influence decisions?

At the seminar on urban sediment and erosion, all the small groups examined the *same* problem, on the basis of these alternatives:

1. Do nothing
2. Local erosion control ordinances
3. State law with local implementation
4. Strong state law affecting all jurisdictions equally
5. National law requiring states to set federally approved standards.

Each alternative was on a separate page. Advantages and disadvantages for each were listed, with generous space for notes and comments.

lem it is to analyze. Number and mimeograph each problem separately. Leave about fifteen copies of each problem unassembled for distribution to the group assigned to it. Just before the reporting session distribute assembled sets to everyone so reporters need not waste time reading each problem aloud.

Each participant's group assignment should be included in his kit or marked on his name tag. Unless group discussions are intended to bring people from the same area together, the program and the recruitment chairman try to put stimulating combinations of unlike interests in each group.

Holding small-group sessions early in the program helps participants get acquainted and start thinking about solutions to their environmental problems. On the other hand, problem-solving sessions scheduled on the second afternoon or evening make a welcome change from concentrated listening.

Planning the Citizen Action Session

As citizen action is so closely related to follow-up, the program chairman may wish to ask the follow-up chairman to help plan this portion of the program. This last session is extremely important because it offers guidance on what each participant is expected to do on returning home. However, it competes with fatigue and with the rush of departure. Plan it, therefore, to be dynamic, and let it be known throughout the three days that this final session is *all*-important. An enthusiastic moderator who can send participants home full of ideas and determination is, of course, one key to success.

Consider the Participants' Experience. If the participants' experience in citizen action is modest, include talks and the opportunity for questions on basic to-

pics such as how to get the facts, reach the public, build a committee, work with public officials, use media, develop effective spokesmen.

If most participants are experienced in citizen action, gear this part of the program to their more advanced needs. How to create and work with a coalition of organizations or how to get official recognition or quasi-official status for a state or local citizen environmental advisory board will interest some groups. How to lobby effectively will be useful to many. Tips on how to prepare persuasive testimony and arrange for appearances at hearings could be helpful. Ways and types of situations in which citizens may use the courts, as individuals or in class action suits, might be offered. Discuss how civic groups can communicate and coordinate simply, without violating each group's independence and mode of operation.

"How-to" sessions can be presented to an entire seminar or can run concurrently, each participant electing to attend the one most useful to him. Or a brief outline of all "how-tos" can be presented, followed by work sessions.

Some Suggestions from Past Seminars. Land and water seminars have used these devices, among others, in the citizen action session and found they worked well:

A lawyer knowledgeable in environmental matters, spotlighting those provisions in applicable laws that citizens can use to accomplish their ends.

What other states or other groups of citizens in the general region are doing, or what other seminar groups have done, followed by discussion of how to arouse and focus the public's concern.

Discussion sessions with the group divided by areas or jurisdictions, with each section reviewing where its area stands now, the gaps or weaknesses, what needs to be done, and where the pressure points are. One way to structure this kind of area session is to ask a panel made up of a legislator, an official, a specialist, and an experienced citizen leader, with a moderator, to lead discussions for each jurisdiction.

Analyzing weaknesses and examining strengths in past programs of groups represented at the seminar so that future effectiveness could be increased.

The stage is then set for reporting the immediate follow-up plans of each area group.

FIGURE 10.9

Checklist for the Program Chairman

Coordinate with general chairman of planning committee

Call first program committee meeting early

Draft outline of topics to be discussed at seminar, to be part of recruitment mailing

Develop a balanced program in detail

Present outline, and, later, proposed program in detail, to planning committee for comments and suggestions

Send invitations to speakers as early as possible, obtaining biographies and information on equipment required by each

Plan small group sessions and draft "problems"

Give special attention to sessions on citizen action and follow-up activity

Detail for each speaker his allotted subject, time, and place in program framework

Supply on time all details for printed program

Be sure publicity chairman is fully informed on all details regarding program and speakers

At seminar, keep close contact with speakers, help moderators arrange briefings for their panels, and handle any program adjustments

FOLLOW-UP: THE MULTIPLIER

If the momentum of the seminar is to carry forward, follow-up must be emphasized from the beginning—in the planning committee, the subcommittees, and the seminar sessions. Throughout the seminar program follow-up activity should be suggested wherever need for citizen activity is mentioned. Information on upcoming hearings, on reports and surveys soon to be released or currently under official consideration should include how citizens can use them. Reference to what other states and other citizens are doing should carry the connotation of follow-up possibilities. Planning committee members must be especially attuned to making this connection during discussion periods and informal conversations. The general chairman, the program chairman, and the follow-up chairman work together to keep follow-up constantly before the planning committee.

The seminar budget should contain a definite sum for follow-up activities. An absolute minimum is money enough for preparation, reproduction, and postage for two mailings. If a substantial amount of follow-up money is available, the planning committee should make provision for deciding how it is to be spent.

The *follow-up chairman* should be—or become—well informed on the seminar's subject and on pending issues, be well acquainted with governmental processes, and understand effective action techniques.

As a member of the program committee, the follow-up chairman will become familiar with issues suggested for seminar examination and will help plan the seminar sessions on citizen action and follow-up.

The follow-up chairman's work begins early—at the first meeting of the full committee. As the program shapes up and opportunities for productive citizen action are seen, the follow-up committee considers ways to stimulate and help all participants to work effectively after the seminar.

The follow-up chairman has numerous avenues for working with community leaders. Generally, the impetus for their activities comes from the participants themselves, in the fields where they themselves see a need. The follow-up chairman keeps in touch with participants and encourages — and occasionally prods—them to carry out their pledge on follow-up.

The chairman cannot, of course, be drawn into every undertaking of the participants but is primarily a coordinator and source of information. However, a creative and imaginative chairman and committee see many potentialities for effective action and through timely suggestions and encouragement help new projects off to a good start. Follow-up chairmen, for example, have been catalysts in formation of environmental coordinating committees and action councils or coalitions.

Preparations for Follow-Up

For effective follow-up, the chairman works with a committee of two or three others at least. If a seminar includes several states, a follow-up chairman and committee for each is essential. The follow-up chairman can enlarge the committee after the seminar by adding interested seminar faculty, participants, or members of the sponsoring organization.

Before arriving at the seminar, the follow-up chairman tries to become acquainted with the name, city, and background of each participant, having obtained a complete list from the recruitment chairman as early as possible. Participants meet the follow-up chairman when, near the start of the seminar, the general chairman introduces the subject of follow-up and its chairman from the platform.

During the seminar the follow-up chairman will want to talk with everyone present, making friends and building lines of communication, learning as much as possible about participants' interests, capabilities, and community needs. During these three days the state or city follow-up chairman and other members of the follow-up committee meet to flesh out follow-up plans. They set an early date for a post-seminar evaluation session, to be attended by all with responsibilities for follow-up. At this session, while impressions are fresh, the follow-up committee can consider the aims and interests expressed by seminar participants, decide what is to be done, and who is to do it.

Where follow-up funds are available, the follow-up committee evaluates proposals for use of such funds. Usually participants and their organizations willingly support incidental expenses of follow-up work, and seminars that open significant new vistas often generate financial support for more substantial follow-up activities. At first, though, the chairman plans to operate within the sum originally reserved for follow-up in the overall seminar budget.

Recording the Seminar

The follow-up chairman and her committee will find a record of the talks *and* of discussion periods valuable. In deciding whether to *publish* a summary or report on the seminar, the planning committee considers:

Its cost compared to the benefits derived from publication
Who will use it
Who will prepare it.

If a summary is to be published, who is to be in charge and who will take the notes should be decided early.

The most satisfactory system is to utilize both notes and tape recordings. Notes supplement available copies of speeches, are easier to work with (a tape has to be listened to and transcribed) and will be reliable if taken by two persons for each session.

Tapes, *well-indexed* as they are being made so that the desired part can be located easily, are a precaution for review of the discussion periods and are useful to fill in gaps in the notes.

FIGURE 10.10

Checklist for the Follow-Up Chairman

Attend planning and program committee meetings
Help plan program session on follow-up
Become familiar with participants' backgrounds
Consider desirability of and best format for a summary of the seminar
At seminar, get to know participants
Meet with follow-up committee during seminar to assess potentials, make any adjustments in schedule for follow-up session
Hold post-seminar evaluation session at earliest possible time to firm up initial plans
After seminar, prepare and send follow-up questionnaires, mailings; help with newsletter
After seminar, be available for suggestions
If funds available, evaluate with follow-up committee proposals for their use

ARRANGEMENTS: WHERE AND WHAT?

Choosing the City

In choosing the city for the meeting, the planning committee should give high priority to accessibility for both speakers and participants. This is very important, for it will affect the budget. Will most attendees be driving? Will the majority fly?

Come by train or bus? If distances are long, avoid a locale served only by infrequent connections.

Choosing the Meeting Place

The *arrangements chairman* should contact several motels to compare rates and facilities, keeping the convenience of travelers in mind. If most will be flying, an airport motel which is also easily accessible to participants who are driving may be the most convenient. Local participants should be discouraged from going home overnight, for this breaks the feeling of group solidarity and causes them to miss the benefits of continuous discussion and the opportunity to establish new connections. If most attendees will be driving, an inn well away from city distractions may best serve the group's needs. Recommendations should be sought from the committee for motels and inns whose price will lie within the project budget.

If a local university has formal conference facilities, investigate them. They are usually reasonable in cost. However, a dormitory offered during a school holiday may not provide the comfort or proper atmosphere for a good conference. Poor hotel facilities may save money but they will dampen the whole project. About 85 people (participants, speakers, and planning committee) will be giving their time for two nights and three days. They should be comfortable.

Before You Select a Motel

1. Check the meeting room being offered. Is it big enough for about 90 people (there will be speakers, press, and a few visitors to provide for), with at least 50 participants sitting at tables, facing the speakers' platform? Participants, of course, have priority in all arrangements, and chairs for speakers, committee mem-

FIGURE 10.11

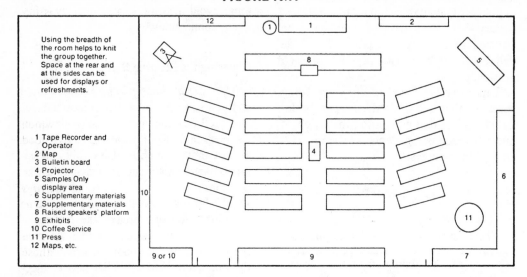

Using the breadth of the room helps to knit the group together. Space at the rear and at the sides can be used for displays or refreshments.

1 Tape Recorder and
  Operator
2 Map
3 Bulletin board
4 Projector
5 Samples Only
  display area
6 Supplementary materials
7 Supplementary materials
8 Raised speakers' platform
9 Exhibits
10 Coffee Service
11 Press
12 Maps, etc.

bers, and any visitors can be furnished at the rear or sides of the room.

Is the meeting room pleasantly designed and decorated? Do pillars block the view? Are acoustics good?

A slightly raised platform along one wall large enough to hold a panel of speakers is a *must*. Is there room for it? Can the motel supply one? Is there room near the door for a press table? Is there room for tables where pamphlets and copies of speeches may be put out? Will the displays be secure overnight?

Check the ventilation or the air conditioning. An interior room dependent on air conditioning can be very stuffy between seasons; a room without a thermostat, regulated only by an on-off switch, is very likely to alternate between being very cold and very hot. Two or three days before the conference, the arrangements chairman should personally make sure the ventilation system is in good, and quiet, working order. On the day of the meeting it will be too late.

2. Check the dining arrangements. A separate dining room, away from other motel guests, is needed, preferably not too far from the meeting room and equipped with round tables for no more than six or eight if possible. Long banquet tables stifle good conversation. If the dining room is adjacent to the meeting room, is the partition between the two thick enough so that the noise of clearing and setting up tables will not interfere with the meeting? Can this dining room be available for small problem-solving groups in the afternoon or evening?

3. Check the menu possibilities and prices. With the exception of breakfast, all menus should be selected by the arrangements chairman ahead of time. Within the project budget, what does the motel suggest for lunch and dinner?

4. Check facilities for no-host social hours, away from other motel guests. Social hours, reserved for the group, are an essential part of the seminar. They foster group feeling and draw the more retiring participants into discussions. Are there problems connected with serving or charging for liquor at the meeting site? Can special arrangements be made?

5. Check sleeping accommodations. Are bedrooms clean and adequate? Will heat-

ing and cooling arrangements be satisfactory? You will need twin-bed double rooms, which are less expensive per person, and a block of singles for participants who wish to pay extra for privacy, as well as for faculty and special guests.

Final choice of motel is left to the arrangements chairman in consultation with the general chairman of the planning committee. This decision should be made as soon as possible. *Specific details should be confirmed by the management in writing.* Then the arrangements chairman should obtain all the facts necessary to prepare mimeographed room reservation forms and travel directions to the motel.

The arrangements chairman, with the finance officer, works out the procedure for handling the hotel bills for the seminar (see section on "Money Matters"). The kit given to each seminar attendee contains a sheet explaining the procedure clearly.

Other Arrangements Responsibilities

Arrangements also include registration table, name tags, coffee, tea and coke breaks, microphones, speakers' table, lectern, bulletin board, projectors, screen, ash trays, drinking water, display tables, blackboard if desired, and a typewriter for the press plus one for the committee. Panel mikes are desirable for panel discussions. Do various speakers want different kinds of projection equipment? Are they providing their own projectors and operators? If the meetings are to be taped, provide a tape recorder, tapes, and a competent operator. Some hotels offer mimeograph services, handy for last minute lists, for room numbers of committee members, or for program amendments, for example. If not in the hotel, is reproduction service available nearby?

Insist on verification from the hotel, two

or three days before the meeting, that *all equipment* to be supplied by them is actually in working order.

Name tags can be prepared as soon as registration forms are returned. Tags can be keyed by color or ribbon for faculty, committee, or participants. States also may be differentiated if the area covered is large. A "convention typewriter," which has extra-large letters is particularly good for name tags. If not available ask someone with large, clear printing to make them by hand with a felt pen. *Name tags are useless unless easy to read.*

Name tags should give the home town and state as well as the name, as area notation helps a participant locate those with whom he will want to work on local follow-up. But it is usually a good idea *not* to include on the tags the name of the organization represented. Informal exchange is easier and freer when unaffected by preconceived ideas.

A chart showing who will be present for each meal and for each night, costs included, will be invaluable to the arrangements chairman. Participants will, with almost no exceptions, be present the full time, but speakers come and go and so do a few local committee members.

Other useful worksheets can be drawn up and posted for easy reference to show who will be at the door, who is to be on the platform when, who will introduce each speaker, who will lead and who will be resource person for each discussion group. Such work sheets will help all committee members know exactly where they are to be during the seminar.

At the seminar itself, the arrangements chairman keeps the restaurant management advised of last-minute changes in numbers to be served at each meal and checks bills for group meals and coffee breaks. The chairman is available for questions about expenses or room assignments and checks all room bills before forwarding them for payment.

The main function of the arrangements chairman, though, is to see that everything runs smoothly and to settle any difficulties unobtrusively.

FIGURE 10.12

Checklist for the Arrangements Chairman

Work closely with general planning chairman
Select motel or hotel early. Get firm commitment in writing regarding prices, accommodations, facilities, and services
Draft room reservation form, and travel directions if desirable, to be mailed to participants
Work with program chairman on special equipment for speakers
Arrange for microphones, raised platform, tables, and so forth
Choose menus
Arrange for name tags
With general chairman prepare clear written instructions regarding payment of hotel bills for management, cashier, committee and participants (see "Money Matters")
Check working order of equipment before seminar
Handle all details at seminar (see "At the Seminar")

KITS AND OTHER MATERIALS

Having enough publications at the seminar need cause no worry. Rather, the problem is to select the few best and most useful items from the wealth of pamphlets and flyers available, avoiding the temptation to put into the seminar kit an item on each subject of interest to the seminar group.

The astute *kits chairman* will hold down the size of the kits by persuading the planning committee to include only the choicest materials that relate directly to the theme of the conference and supplement information given in the seminar sessions. Participants have little time for reading during the seminar. Therefore, kit materials should be chosen mainly with an eye to follow-up activity after participants return home.

Kits also contain seminar information:

The program
Biographies of speakers—unless in program
Lists—name, address, telephone number— of participants and planning committee, and sometimes of nominees who could not be invited but may be drawn into follow-up
Financial instructions
Travel reimbursement forms
Check-out information
Information about the hotel
Evaluation questionnaire

It is the kits chairman's job to write for samples and for price and quantity information and to place the orders. Planning committee members help by lending sample copies of items they suggest for kit materials and arranging for quantity copies of items at no cost or at a discount. Many organizations are willing to give sufficient copies of their publications for seminar use.

The kits chairman writes national organizations, such as the League of Women Voters, key industries, and conservation organizations, explaining the nature of the project and requesting samples of publications suitable for kits. Professors, local industrialists, and associations are asked for suggestions. State and federal agencies can furnish publications. Regional offices of the Environmental Protection Agency, the Departments of Agriculture, Interior, Housing and Urban Development, and the Corps of Engineers have materials relating to land and water use.

Participants are no more likely than other people to read long and entirely technical pamphlets, but they will be eager for factual, accurate material, well presented by reliable sources. Include at least one light piece.

As soon as the planning committee approves the selection, the kits chairman starts to collect needed quantities of the items, for it is almost inevitable that one will be out of print, another won't be free after all, and that some misadventure will befall a third. A large volume of material must be stored, so decide early on the address for delivery.

Assemble kits at least the day before the seminar, one for every person present, including faculty, committee, special guests, and press. If kits are not identical—if, for example, people are to receive only their own state's water quality standards and regulations—label each kit with the individual's name and present it to him when he registers.

Supplementary Materials

Some attendees will bring publications for distribution at the seminar. Place these along with supplementary materials obtained by the kits chairman on display tables where those who wish may take them. They will! A separate table can be reserved for copies of speeches if there is not room at the press table. If some items are being lent and are for examination only, put them in a special area, conspicuously marked.

Displays

Displays are also the responsibility of the kits chairman. Some are solicited, and others are offered. Displays add to the attractiveness of the setting, but because of space limitations, the chairman needs to place some restriction on the size or number that can be accepted.

Do put a large, clearly marked map at the front of the principal meeting room. If one can't be borrowed, make a huge rough outline map on newsprint, with lettering that can be read from the back of the room.

FIGURE 10.13

Advance Homework

A mild assignment of advance homework stimulates participants to think about the coming seminar. It also provides background and vocabulary which they would otherwise not share.

Therefore, the kits chairman mails one or two, but no more than three, fairly simple items to arrive about a week before the seminar.

Among the publications suitable for this purpose are the following titles published by the League of Women Voters of the United States:

Population + Production = Pollution
Who Pays for a Clean Stream?
Where Rivers Meet the Sea
So You'd Like to Do Something about Water Pollution.

FIGURE 10.14

Checklist for the Kits Chairman

Select pamphlets and reports for inclusion in kits
Order 85-100 copies of each
Send advance homework if desired
Compile bibliography or list of films, if desired
Purchase kit covers. If desirable, label individually for every participant, faculty member and planning committee member
Obtain seminar materials (e.g., biographies, instructions) for inclusion in kits from subcommittee chairmen
Have kits stuffed and ready day before the seminar
See that kits are delivered to hotel
Arrange display tables, exhibits, and map
Arrange tables with other literature for examination or taking by participants
At seminar, handle distribution of speeches and any supplementary material

PUBLICITY

News about the seminar can stimulate public interest in land and water decisions, emphasize the citizen's role, and identify the problems of a region. The seminar gives representatives of the press an opportunity to get acquainted with community, industrial, and professional leaders active in environmental affairs and to discover new information, outlooks, or leads for future articles on water quality and land use.

At the first meeting of the whole planning committee, the *publicity chairman* starts to compile a list of newspapers and radio and TV stations to receive news releases before and during the seminar. Ask planning committee members for names and addresses of media in their areas and names of the best person to reach—editor, news editor, environmental reporter. Don't overlook area magazines and weekly newspapers, college papers and stations, public broadcasting stations, talk programs, and—if the region is large—media from urban centers not represented on the planning committee.

The publicity chairman works with the general chairman and the recruitment and program chairmen. As the seminars are not open to the general public, advance publicity that makes people want to attend is undesirable. Concentrate on news releases about participants and on media coverage of the seminar sessions.

During the Planning Period

After the first planning committee meeting, the publicity chairman sends a release to the home newspapers of each planning committee member, announcing that he or she is serving, explaining the purpose, scope, and sponsorship of the seminar, and giving the title, approximate dates, and place of the meeting.

When participants have accepted, prepare a similar release on each participant and send it to his local papers. To help the publicity chairman, ask participants to list on their acceptance forms the names, addresses, and environmental reporter or editor of the newspapers (including weeklies) in their areas.

Later, when the program is virtually complete, the publicity chairman goes in person to newspapers and to television and radio stations, talks with the environmental reporter or news editor (or the editor on smaller papers), asks to have reporters assigned to cover the entire seminar, or—if that is impossible—specifically recommends two or three particularly newsworthy highlights.

Possibilities for interesting the radio or television stations in some facet of the seminar program are numerous. Educational broadcasting stations may be interested in taping the program. Both they and the commercial stations can record interviews or provocative discussions set up between two or more of those attending.

A brief news story, which can be dated for release, naming two or three of the principal speakers, their topics, and something of interest about the participants is left with the paper or broadcasting station and sent to those that cannot be visited personally.

In urban centers these contacts should be made a week to ten days before the seminar. A much earlier approach is better for dailies and weeklies in smaller towns. For a regularly scheduled television show (not news) that might be interested in covering the seminar or interviewing one of the participants, start advance work almost six weeks before the seminar.

Make a reminder telephone call to all media a day or two before the seminar.

It's worth the effort to ask major speakers for advance texts and to prepare releases on the most newsworthy for distribution during the seminar. For an advance story on the day the seminar opens, furnish papers in the seminar city with a release focusing on a major speaker, probably the keynoter, with biographical data and a photograph.

Dealing with the Press

Broadcasting and press people work on deadlines. They appreciate being notified in advance of a function, but find out the person's schedule and never interrupt him when his deadline is nearing. Organize your information and present it concisely; highlight interesting features and names.

Since it is expensive to assign a reporter to one meeting for three days, a news editor will need some persuasion to give maximum coverage to the seminar. If a new study is to be unveiled, fresh facts presented, or new proposals for regional cooperation made, point these out.

Bear in mind that 10:00 a.m. to 3:00 p.m. are the best working hours for reporters. Find out the deadlines for morning and evening papers and TV programs. Remember that unless something is extremely interesting, the time it takes place will strongly affect whether it is covered and the story published.

If a paper sends a reporter to cover the full seminar, it will expect to pay his expenses, but it is customary to invite reporters who do not stay overnight to be seminar guests at group meals, and the publicity chairman extends this invitation.

At the Seminar

The publicity chairman greets reporters, sees that each has a kit, helps them meet people and get their material.

Reserve a suitable table for the press in the seminar meeting room. The publicity chairman or one of his committee should be at the press table at all times, ready and able to answer reporters' questions.

Although these seminars are not large enough to require a regular press room, provide a typewriter and have in mind some place for the reporters to use a phone. Provide copies of a general release or a fact sheet about the seminar for reporters to take. Give them copies of a speech as the speaker begins.

If a speaker is a national figure, the local press, radio, or television will probably wish to interview him. Throughout the seminar the publicity chairman and her committee members watch for leads for local-interest stories arising from presentations and discussions and alert the media to interesting local personalities. The publicity chairman encourages and arranges interviews and provides a suitable place for them.

If possible, prepare a final conference wrap-up on the spot, for immediate distribution to media unable to attend. Give copies of this overall wrap-up to participants and committee members to use with their local media as the first step in follow-up when they return home.

PRINTING AND MIMEOGRAPHING

The general chairman of the planning committee needs to be in close touch with printing and mimeographing, so arrangements should suit her convenience. These services should be budgeted for, though nonprofit organizations are sometimes fortunate recipients of contributed art services or of discount or at-cost work from commercial printers.

For reproducing materials to be sent to the committee, photocopying may be easiest. Most cities, and many public libraries, have centers or businesses where copies may be made at 5 cents per page. When

FIGURE 10.15

Two Samples for Newspapers

To Announce Planning Committee

(Name), of *(residence),* has been appointed to the planning Committee for "Sediment, Our Wasted Wealth," a seminar on land and water use problems to be held May 25–27. *(Name), (organization, title),* joins other professional and lay experts and leaders of the League of Women Voters in the region in the organization of the three-day seminar.

The meeting will focus on soil erosion and silting caused by urbanization. Building construction and roadbuilding are major problems in all rapidly developing areas and are especially severe in Maryland, Virginia and the District of Columbia.

Noting that sediment is by volume the principal water pollutant, Mrs. *(general chairman)* said, "Uncontrolled development and urbanization is pouring over a million tons of sediment into the Potomac River per year. Sediment has destroyed half the oyster grounds in the Upper Chesapeake Bay."

The seminar will be the 16th in a series which began six years ago under a grant to the League of Women Voters Education Fund from the Office of Water Programs in the Environmental Protection Agency. The others have dealt with major river, lake or coastal basins of the country. Their purpose is to stimulate citizens to take an effective part in land and water resource decisions.

To Stimulate Coverage of the Seminar

(Name, title, and residence) will keynote the Snake River Basin Seminar to be held June 3–5 in Boise, *(name of chairman)* announced.

During the three-day event some 90 community leaders, speakers, and planning committee members will interact in an effort to bridge the gap of understanding between citizens and the land and water use experts.

(Program chairman) called faculty outstanding and explained that views presented in panels and discussions will conflict . . .

"Meeting in small groups, participants will define basin-wide land and water use problems, then set priorities for action in their own areas."

A Tuesday panel on *(subject)* will feature . . .

Thursday participants will question how the Snake can be kept a healthy river through citizen action and use of the 1969 National Environmental Protection Act. Topics include legislation, testifying, enforcement, and citizen input.

Faculty members from the Boise area are *(names).* Out-of-Idaho faculty includes *(names).*

FIGURE 10.16

Checklist for the Publicity Chairman

Send press releases:
    to their local papers announcing appointment of committee members
    to participants' local newspapers
Arrange any preseminar publicity advisable
Help program chairman compile biographical briefs on speakers for printed program
Notify area media of dates, speakers, program content, purpose of project; urge coverage
Prepare fact sheet for reporters covering conference
Prepare release(s) based on advance text(s) of major speaker(s), if desirable
At seminar:
Greet reporters; see that they have kits, texts of speeches before delivery
Help them get facts and interviews; provide typewriter and space
Advise arrangements chairman about reporters' meals
If newsworthy developments occur, write and dispatch release
Prepare wrap-up release on entire seminar, if feasible

only a few copies are needed the cost will usually be less than the cost of cutting and running a mimeograph stencil.

For mimeographing or multilithing, line up someone on whom you can depend and give him advance notice of quantities and deadline for each work order.

It is recommended that at least 100 extra copies of the recruitment brochure and the final program be printed. Both are useful in follow-up activity and in answering queries about the project or about the work of the sponsoring organization. The Education Fund, for example, asks for 100 copies of brochure and program from each of the land and water seminars it sponsors —and never seems to have enough.

List of Items to be Reproduced

Special stationery, if desired
Agenda for each meeting
Minutes, including list of committee, with addresses
Notices of each planning committee meeting and final instructions, if any, to committee before seminar
Recruitment brochure, usually printed (otherwise multilithed or offset program outline and names of planning committee members to accompany letters of invitation to participants)
Nominating form, if used
Letter to organizations requesting nominations (if one of these methods is used)
Lists giving thumbnail sketch of each nominee
Letters to nominees selected as participants
Individualized letters to nominees not selected as participants
Individualized letters to all organizations that nominated participants, whether or not nominees were selected (if this method was used)
Acceptance form
Room reservation form
Draft program (two or three will usually be drawn up)
Press releases
Problems for small group discussion (100 copies of each)
Final program
List of selected participants who accept, with home address, affiliation, and name of nominator
List of those nominated but not selected, with address and nominating organization (for use in follow-up)
Financial and check-out instructions

SECRETARIAL DUTIES

Some sponsoring organizations will be able to detail a paid secretary to handle work for the seminar and to allow use of office facilities. Others will be less fortunate. In these, a planning committee member conveniently near the general chairman is needed to assume duties of the secretary, such as arranging for mimeographing and sending notices of meetings, preparing other mailings (agendas, draft programs, instructions, etc.) as proposed by the committee, preparing minutes of some committee meetings, and helping write thank-you notes to all faculty and planning committee members at the close of the seminar. At the seminar itself, she may act as recorder, with help from other planning committee members.

Since it is difficult, time-consuming, and risky to mail materials back and forth between a chairman and a secretary, if no nearby secretary can be recruited from the planning committee the chairman should make other convenient arrangements. Typing help for the general chairman and the recruitment, program, and perhaps the publicity chairmen should be in the budget.

MONEY MATTERS

In money matters the pattern is cut according to the cloth. Whether you can offer all, or only part, of all attendees' expenses will depend on the funds available for your seminar. Decisions between mimeographing, printing, ditto, and photo-offset, on the quality of stationery, and on reimbursement to committee members for such expenses as long-distance telephone calls, postage and local travel (taxis, parking, mileage) depend on your budget.

Preparing the Budget

Consider the following expenses in preparing a seminar budget. Will seminar funding cover them? Must they be omitted? Can they be met in some other way?

Travel

Planning committee meetings: transportation; food and lodging

Subcommittee meetings: transportation; meal

Seminar: transportation for participants, committee, and speakers; meals and lodging for participants, speakers, and committee

Miscellaneous local travel

Other

Consumable supplies, including printed stationery, if desired

Printing

Reproduction

Clerical help

Postage

Long-distance telephone

Rental of projectors, etc.

Kit covers

Publications for kits and for the committee's research

Follow-up

Report or summary of proceedings, if desired

Newsletter? Other mailings? Postage

Evaluation-cum-follow-up session for committee

Other meetings? Hall rental?

Overhead. If the project is conducted under the auspices of a central organization which has received and is administering a grant, the sponsor will require a percentage for its indirect costs (overhead) and for expenses incurred in connection with the project.

Costs of meals and lodging are relatively easy to calculate after the location and approximate number of persons is known. Include gratuities and taxes in your multiplication.

To estimate travel costs, get round-trip fares from air, rail, or bus lines, and automobile mileage from a representative selection of cities to your site. Terms of most grants require that less-than-first-class travel must be used when available. Follow your central organization's guidelines when setting a per-mile figure for automobile travel reimbursement. Then figure the cost of the likely mode of transportation from each place, not forgetting tips and taxis and connecting travel, and multiplying by the number you think may come from that general area. This will give you a working budget which may be refined later when more specifics are known.

Be sure to make these initial calculations *before* you promise an all-expenses-paid seminar.

Handling the Money

For a one-time project of a local organization, it is advisable to establish a project bank account and appoint one person to act as budget officer and treasurer. This person pays the bills, staying within the budget, and makes a full financial report when the project is completed.

The central organization will probably allocate a set figure for the total expenses of the project and will assign the local portion to the planning committee to budget. The Education Fund provides budget guidelines, indicating kinds and extent of allowable expenses, and instructions for record-keeping and for accounting; designates the procedure for requesting reimbursement; and pays the major bills for the seminars it sponsors.

Such an arrangement, like the first, requires assignment of financial responsibility to a member of the local planning committee. In Education Fund seminars, the chairman usually assumes this responsibility. All bills, requests for reimbursement and any requests for advances must be sent to the chairman or his designee for approval and forwarding to the central office for payment. A running account of ex-

FIGURE 10.17

Financial Instructions

Community Leaders Conference
Coastal Lands and Waters of New England

The League of Women Voters Education Fund will pay expenses as follows for participants and committee members at the seminar.

HOTEL ACCOMMODATIONS

A shared double room is allowed for each person for Tuesday and Wednesday nights, April 7 and 8.

MEALS

Meals provided by the Education Fund include luncheon and dinner Tuesday, April 7; three meals Wednesday, April 8; and breakfast and luncheon Thursday, April 9. All luncheons and dinners will be group meals. A $1.50 breakfast is allowed; pay any amount over $1.50, sign the breakfast check, and have $1.50 placed on your hotel bill.

WHEN YOU CHECK OUT OF THE HOTEL

Check out time is 12 noon. Ask for your bill at the desk and pay any charges over those allowed by the Education Fund. For example, the difference between a single and double room if you asked for and received a single room ($3.18 per night), telephone calls, room service, and extra nights, etc. Sign the bill and leave it with the hotel.

IF YOUR AGENCY OR ORGANIZATION WISHES TO PAY YOUR EXPENSES

Some organizations and participants have asked if they may cover a participant's expenses. All unexpended funds in the conference budget will be used later on for follow-up projects in local communities. Special arrangements may be made if you wish contribution of your expenses to be deductible for income tax purposes.

If you or your organization pays conference expenses, please handle your hotel bill in your usual manner. If you wish to arrange for tax deductibility, see Mrs. Richard Roberts, who will advise you of the proper procedure.

TRAVEL EXPENSE

Round trip–actual plane or bus fare; 9 cents per mile for the driver of a car.

Should you require reimbursement for travel expenses, pick up a travel voucher at the seminar registration desk. Fill out and return to Mrs. Richard Roberts before the end of the conference. Please note any participants who drove with you if you came by car. A check will be sent to you.

Planning Committee Members will handle their expenses as they have in the past. Speakers who need expense vouchers may pick them up at the conference registration desk. Please note this one exception to the above arrangements: the Education Fund provides single rooms for faculty members.

---

penditures must be kept, as it will be referred to frequently.

For Education Fund environmental projects the national office supplies vouchers to be used in requesting payment. Other organizations should prepare forms, in duplicate at least, on which to request reimbursement or account for advances, if they are not furnished by the sponsor. One copy is for the member of the local committee with financial responsibility (referred to as "finance officer" in the following paragraphs).

The form should carry instructions for itemization and receipts, bills, or memoranda required.

Include two copies of the form in each seminar kit. Persons to be reimbursed fill out and return both copies to the finance officer, who verifies and pays or keeps one copy and forwards the other to the sponsoring organization, if it is handling payment. The finance officer should be at the seminar to answer questions and to collect the vouchers.

Procedures for Paying the Hotel Bills

Arrangements can usually be made with the hotel management for each seminar guest to sign his hotel bill, which may then be charged to a master account for the seminar. In this way only travel expenses, breakfasts, and meals en route need be reimbursed to the individual. A similar arrangement, with a master account, should be made for meetings of the full planning committee. The arrangements chairman and the finance officer should have a clear understanding with the management, confirmed in writing, on items (telephone calls, room service, extra meals) to be paid by individuals and those to be charged to the master account.

If it is the planning committee's policy to allow only the cost of a shared double room, then arrangements for payment for the difference between single and double rates, by individuals desiring single rooms, must also be clear and firm.

It should also be settled in advance that the arrangements chairman and the finance officer will receive from the hotel the total bill for all meals and lodging, with individual room bills and restaurant checks for each group meal attached. After the bill has been checked and approved, it is paid by the finance officer or forwarded for payment by the sponsoring organization, whichever plan the latter has approved.

Clear instructions for handling the above matters should be prepared for the cashier and desk personnel. Clear instructions should be included in each kit on how to sign the hotel bill and how to request reimbursement for other expenses.

Keeping Records and Accounting.

All committee members should be instructed at the beginning of the planning period to keep all bills, vouchers, stubs, receipts, telephone bills, mileage records, etc., for which they will ask reimbursement.

Accounting for monies received under a grant must be made in the format required by the donor. For its environmental projects, for example, the Education Fund maintains the official books and prepares formal accountings for submission to the granting agency.

The chairman needs to know what has been spent and how much remains in the various categories in the budget and therefore also keeps accurate records.

The task will be eased for both the project chairman and the central office if local recordkeeping is set up so that individual items may be recorded under category headings corresponding to those in the budget. The finance officer will want to differentiate between bills forwarded for payment, itemization of expenditures for which reimbursement will be requested, and requests for advances.

To sum up, bookkeeping procedures should be as simple as possible, but detailed enough to:

1. Record which payments have been requested or made.

2. Give current balance in each budget category.

3. Provide records needed for the formal financial report to sponsor or donor, convenient to the format required for the submission.

AT THE SEMINAR

The Afternoon and Evening Before

An air of excitement prevails as the climax of months of preparation nears. This is the time to check all arrangements and set all signals at "go." Each committee chairman is busy with final preparations. The arrangements chairman goes over all details with the hotel management and makes sure that procedures for billing are set up as planned. The kits and display

FIGURE 10.18

Checklist for the Finance Officer

Draw up budget

Set up procedures for approval of expenditures, financial record-keeping, and paying bills

Check and submit bills to central organization

With arrangements chairman, have clear written understanding with hotel management on arrangements for payment

With arrangements chairman, draw up financial instructions to go in each kit, with copies for hotel manager and cashier

Be sure reimbursement request forms are in kits, if those attending are to be reimbursed

At seminar, be available for questions, check hotel and meal bills

Make detailed financial accounting

---

committee arrange supplementary and sample publications tables and displays. The program and recruitment chairman check periodically with the hotel management to learn if any speakers or participants have arrived and can be welcomed.

The general chairman and the full planning committee meet to run through the whole plan, making sure all details are arranged and each member's seminar duties understood.

Physical Arrangements to Double-Check

1. Are tables in meeting room arranged in rows, with chairs at each place?

2. Is the raised platform for speakers in place? Is it long enough for a panel group? Wide enough for a curved or "v" arrangement of the panel?

3. Do the microphones and projectors work? Is the screen placed where all can see it easily?

4. Is air conditioning working properly? Are there curtains to shield the group from the sun?

5. Is the registration table set up? Are name tags arranged alphabetically? Are the mechanics set to run smoothly?

6. Are kits stuffed and in alphabetical order?

7. Are display tables arranged? Is extra space available and an area with sample items for display or examination only conspicuously marked? Is each such item marked?

8. Will coffee service and setting up and clearing for meals be handled quietly without disturbing seminar sessions?

9. Are PRESS and DISPLAY tables marked?

10. Are mimeographed problems ready for the problem-solving session? Are complete sets ready for distribution at the reporting session?

11. Will arrangements for the no-host social area afford all attendees a pleasant place to mix freely and talk informally? How will drinks be paid for?

12. Where will the small groups meet?

Details for Final Review at a Preseminar Committee Meeting

1. Is a committee member assigned to be major-domo, keeping everything on time (starting sessions, getting people back from coffee breaks, meals)?

2. Who is to man the registration table? (Two the first day and one through the second day.)

3. Who is greeting each arrival?

4. Who is extending greetings to open the program? Who is introducing the first speaker? Subsequent speakers? Who chairs each session?

5. How are you letting speakers know their time is running out?

6. Will the general chairman or the program chairman explain to moderators the points they need to know about conducting their panels?

7. Who is to lead the discussion at each

small group session? Who will be serving as resource persons? How are discussion leaders being briefed?

8. How are participants to be assigned to small groups?

9. How and when are state groups being brought together?

10. Are there some important questions that should be asked of the speakers by the committee members if an issue has not otherwise been aired? Who will ask the questions?

11. Who are assigned as note-takers for each session?

12. Who is going to operate tape recorders, projectors, and lights?

13. Can the kits chairman or someone on his committee remain near the display section?

14. What is the plan for seating at meals?

15. Who is to be at the dining room door to suggest seating and see that speakers and experts do not cluster?

Curtain Up!

Expect a few crises; it is a rare function that comes off without at least one. But all details have been taken care of before opening day and everyone's duties have been reviewed at the planning committee meeting directly prior to the seminar, so the chairman is free to cope.

Greeting Participants, Speakers, and Guests. An informal and friendly tone can be set by greeters at each door; if several, so much the better! Post one welcomer near the hotel registration desk. Coffee and rolls available during registration help people meet one another. Recruitment committee members should be near the registration and coffee tables. They know names and organizations of participants and can do much to make them feel welcome. Program chairman

and committee members should be watching out for speakers.

Instructing the Moderators. Unless all moderators can meet together, the general chairman or the program chairman (as decided earlier) explains to each moderator, soon after he arrives, how the committee expects his session to operate. Ask each moderator to get his speakers or panel members together briefly before their segment so all hear the ground rules and duplications can be eliminated. But such a meeting must not become a dress rehearsal, for this detracts from the liveliness of the panel presentation.

Sessions are exciting when speakers and panelists engage with one another and when spirited interchanges develop from the audience. Ask moderators to encourage interchange, especially of unlike views, but to move the discussion along before it becomes acrimonious. Ordinarily, moderators should not allow the same participants or faculty to speak repeatedly or at great length from the floor.

Remind moderators not to forget the coffee breaks. Sometimes a short stand-up break during each morning, but especially in the afternoons, is useful. Remember what Confucius say: "The mind can absorb only what the backside can endure."

Keeping on Schedule. The general chairman, the program chairman, and the arrangements chairman will be watching the time closely, but it is best to avoid much mention of keeping on schedule. Participants should not feel pressed, though they must be reminded of when to be where and that sessions will start on time.

Keeping on schedule will call for a firm hand on the speakers, but there is perhaps no single other duty so important to the success of the conference. Speakers will not resent having to relinquish the floor at the expiration of their allotted time *if time limits are enforced for everyone and with good humor.* Using a timekeeper preserves program balance, is a courtesy to speakers scheduled late in the session, and preserves time for discussion sessions.

Encourage speakers to make comments from the podium and from the floor during audience participation periods, for these experts are often aware of relationships not apparent to laymen. However, the moderator will need to avoid letting the experts monopolize the discussion. One of the main purposes of the seminar is to bring the participants together for exchange of views, and they will be scattering once the seminar is over. Try to preserve the full time you planned for the discussion sessions.

Be flexible. Not only may last-minute adjustments in the program be necessary, but they may be desirable. If, for example, a participant shows some special insight pertinent to the discussion, let him have a minute or two on the platform. This kind of informal use of participants strengthens the cohesiveness of the group, though flexibility should not be allowed to totally disrupt the schedule.

And, finally, the chairman needs to allow about five minutes during each day for announcements. These will include financial instructions, location and hours of meals, check-out instructions, where to get copies of speeches. Most of this information will be in the kits, but some people will neglect to read it. Copies of speeches should not be distributed before the talks are given, except to members of the press, as noted in the preceding chapter, and to the seminar's note-takers.

FOLLOWING UP

Informed and effective follow-up by participants in their own communities is really the whole goal of the seminar.

Follow-up is emphasized from the beginning—in planning committee, subcommittees, and seminar sessions. Suggestions on how to carry on citizen action are built into the program. At the seminar, state and area groups make plans for keeping in contact, for getting and sharing information. Before departing from the meeting, each state and local group considers what is to be done next and who is to do it. Participants leave the seminar ready to impart their concern to others.

Helping participants see and recognize immediate and potential needs and opportunities for follow-up is an important responsibility of all members of the planning committee. It will occupy many informal conversations as well as those formal sessions devoted to citizen action and follow-up.

What Is Follow-Up?

The range of possible and feasible types of citizen activities is rapidly growing, and many opportunities to act on levels not previously accessible to citizens are emerging. Simultaneously, the interrelationship between water quality, air pollution, land use, energy production, agriculture, industry, and transportation has become evident. Major resource and pollution problems have a large social and political content, and consequently, in our democracy, the natural environment is everybody's business.

Opportunities for acting to protect or improve the quality of our water resources and our environment extend well beyond the immediate role of the voting citizen and member of civic or conservation groups. Businesses, industry councils, banks, religious denominations, labor unions are other organizations that can influence government decisions affecting the environment. Company executives, engineers, or employees can act more directly by persuading their corporations to manage their own waste water more effectively and to safeguard environmental values in their operations. Some participants will be drawn from these fields; all have such organizations in their communities.

The paragraphs which follow may be useful not only to the follow-up committee but to other committee members in their guidance to participants.

Keeping in Touch

A newsletter is one of the best tools for passing along new information and ideas as well as for keeping everyone informed of participants' activities. The Education Fund, for example, prepares and mails *Land and Water Roundup* twice a year to attendees of the latest series of seminars. Through brief notes on what various participants are doing, it reports a variety of activities which in turn give ideas to other groups. As space permits, *Roundup* includes short reports of new legislation on water subjects, major governmental appointments, studies or reports, notices of meetings or hearings, and reviews of books and films.

A newsletter used for follow-up for a more local audience could include much the same sort of information but cover local matters, hearing schedules, and so forth, in more detail.

If funds for postage, publications, or reproduction are available, the chairman can mail reprints of important new articles, pamphlets, citizen guides, data on regional plans and projects or bond issues, summaries of issues slated for public hearings, or notices of important meetings to participants.

If a follow-up conference is being organized, even very preliminary plans make exciting news for the seminar group.

A questionnaire, sent to each attendee a couple of months following the seminar and every few months thereafter, makes it easy for participants to report to the follow-up chairman and also reminds them that others are interested in their progress.

Choosing a Course of Action

In the course of the seminar, participants will discuss specific water quality and land resource problems in their area and the region's immediate needs. These may be sewers, a new treatment plant, enforcement of zoning ordinances, financing enforcement of an adequate plan, more funds for enforcement staff, pollution from an important factory, excessive runoff or pollution from roads, sedimentation from road-building, from housing development, from bad agricultural practices, logging or overgrazing, runoff from feedlots.

Next, groups should ask themselves what they see as long-term goals for their region. A land use plan? Regional planning? Flood plain zoning? Urban renewal? River basin planning? An improved water supply? Protection of ground water? Adjustment of principles governing water management?

Should civic groups focus on one specific goal or work across the board? Some groups face clear-cut local problems, easy to define. Other groups face broader problems requiring a state-wide or regional solution.

In either case, having selected their problem, those who have attended the seminar will inevitably need to gather more facts—an excellent assignment for a committee. In addition to the technical, scientific, social, economic, and political factors of any issue, they should know the applicable laws, regulations, and procedures and should get acquainted with the administrators. It will help them if the problem can be examined first-hand with people of differing viewpoints. Community leaders will want to find out what studies and planning projects are underway and get the reports. They must investigate where the power to remedy or improve lies, learn about the people who have decision-making power. They can get help, reports, and information about programs from state personnel. They could make a survey of open space, sources of pollution, conservation or aesthetic values, etc. They should understand the opposition and its sources.

Weighing these various considerations lights the way to the most productive courses of action; whether to

Build public awareness
Encourage discussion and try to resolve conflicts
Support (or oppose) a specific proposal
Continue to back an existing program, appropriation, enforcement, etc.
Prod officials to attack a problem
Encourage an official study or planning project
Support steps in implementing such a study or plan.

Building Public Concern

If the initial course of action chosen by a participant or his group is to build public concern about a problem, they must next choose their audience and their means.

Meetings can be planned: for leaders whose support they hope to win; for the public, with elected officials present to observe support for the issue; an organizing meeting, with reporters present. One-, two- or three-day conferences for a selected group, perhaps state legislators and officials; workshops; briefings; go-see tours; a series of programs or extension courses in conjunction with university, museum, library, water resources institute,

or state or local agencies—all are follow-up possibilities.

No list of ways to communicate can pretend to be complete, but any group planning a program of action will consider speakers for meetings, slide presentations, radio or television programs, interviews and spots, documentary films, literature stalls, portable displays, mailings of pamphlets and flyers, answers to common objections, legislative information, newspaper and newsletter stories, and background information for press use.

Help participants appreciate that through these activities they are helping to inform the public by offering scientific and technical information in terms people can understand, and that—through the seminar—they are acquainted with many articulate persons who bring a wide variety of points of view to the issue.

Opportunities are everywhere!

Taking Part in the Processes of Government

Committee members can encourage participants, and they in turn other citizens, to demonstrate the public interest in an issue through attendance at hearings and meetings of boards, legislative committees, city councils, or other responsible bodies when environmental matters are to be discussed. Citizen leaders should ask to be put on lists to be notified of hearings—both local and regional—and should urge local media to publicize and cover them.

Maintaining contact with officials at all levels enables civic leaders to feed them ideas, information and citizen views. If the citizen group establishes itself as reliable and responsible, officials may well come to seek its views on matters before them. Questionnaires to candidates for office are useful in getting information to the voter and as a basis for going back to the person elected.

Encourage citizen groups to make the governor or mayor aware of their concern when he is appointing members to an environmental council, water board, or zoning commission; they may suggest nominees for these positions. Help them see why citizen groups that have a plan for solving a particular problem should go first to their mayor or council, to consult them and ask for their support. They will have a better chance of success if the officials can make the plan their own!

The Coalition or Coordinating Council

The follow-up committee can help participants see the value of the interorganization coalition, whether it be a continuing organization or an ad hoc arrangement, whether it be geared for action or serves primarily to collect and disseminate information.

The coalition or coordinating council can be a powerful instrument, multiplying the effect and dividing the work. An effective coalition includes not only a nucleus of the principal conservation organizations in the region but a variety of organizations whose differing interests give it broader appeal. Such a coalition could in time receive quasi-official status as advisor to the executive of the area.

A coalition makes it possible to enlist more helpers, make more news, reach more people, use officials' time more efficiently. Its larger resources may make it possible to keep up with the meeting schedule of all agencies dealing with stream or air control, to publish a fact sheet about state agencies and laws, to prepare a digest of bills, to retain counsel, to commission an independent engineering report, to finance an ecological inventory or a scientific study of the region.

An adjunct of the coalition is the technical advisory committee comprising experts of several disciplines. Such a committee can evaluate the scientific and technical aspects of major water resource proposals for the coalition, for example, and the results of its studies can be presented to the appropriate government body and the press.

A major advantage of the coalition is that it facilitates citizen representation at hearings, which are becoming more numerous and more technical. The coalition can draw on its pool of resources in translating scientific, technical, and legal information into a lay explanation of how the citizens' interests will be affected by a given proposal. The coalition can provide to members who wish to testify information on procedures to be followed and, if the subject is a technical one, can conduct workshops on the subject matter or on preparing appropriate testimony. The coalition is in a position to bore in on the topic from many sides. It can line up panels to testify on different aspects, recruiting specialists on each, and at the same time earn the gratitude of legislators and other officials for reducing repetition.

Still another advantage of a coalition arises from the scale and complexity of environmental problems. Even for local problems, solutions must often be regional and interdisciplinary. The larger, more heterogeneous group can cultivate the wider support required for the larger scale solution.

To encourage formation of interorganization groups a follow-up chairman can tap her own sources (not forgetting seminar committee and speakers) for information to pass along on organizing and on what other citizen coalitions or coordinating councils are doing.

Through the Courts

New concepts also are evolving in the law and in the use of the courts, and more environmental issues are being referred to the courts.

The developing principle that the public is an interested party in legal actions involving such matters as pollution from an industrial plant or structural alterations of bodies of water has opened a new channel for expression of citizen opinion and influence. As environmental law evolves, citizen organizations may increasingly decide to join together for purposes of litigation.

There is a further trend in legislation and in court decisions to establish the principle that an individual citizen may file as a party likely to suffer environmental injury. Individuals in some instances may file class action suits on behalf of a large class of similarly affected citizens.

Another technique, which does not involve the substantial costs that must be borne by the party to any suit and which is often appropriate, is to file a brief as *amicus curiae,* that is, "friend of the court," presenting the citizen group's point of view on an environmental charge or complaint, usually in agreement with and with the consent of the plaintiff. A brief filed in this way may raise questions not posed in the plaintiff's brief, which reflect the particular concern of the group and to which answers are needed. A group must seek permission of the court to file as *amicus curiae.*

A lawsuit has many audiences: the court, regulatory agencies, the press, the public, other environmental organizations, the scientific, business, and industrial communities, elected officials and legislative bodies. In its larger context it can be viewed as part of the political process.

Litigation may often not be appropriate, but if no other alternatives seem to be effective, citizens should consult lawyers in their own state for guidance. If a group receives apparently contradictory advice from different sources, it should consider its goal carefully and let that guide the decision, keeping in mind that a lawsuit is a long process, requiring not only funds but scientific evidence, witnesses, and much volunteer time to assist the lawyer in preparation of the case.

The Importance of Financing Environmental Protection

Financing water pollution abatement and water quality protection is a subject on which citizen wishes should be expressed more vigorously. The citizen role in passage of bond issues for sewer lines and sewage treatment plants is well known. It has undoubtedly been due to the public's voice that bankers in one state adopted a pollution code; that in another they now offer antipollution bonds; and that in a third they established a public interest fund from which to make low-interest loans for public interest purposes including pollution control installations by industries. Seminar participants should be encouraged to examine tax policies which encourage land and water development rather than watershed protection and to support appropriations for water pollution abatement programs.

State and Local Action Is the Key

It has become increasingly clear that despite the many important federal programs designed to achieve environmental quality much of the job must fall on state governments. In nearly all federal environmental programs, the task of implementing and enforcing pollution control plans is a state or local function. Federal water and air pollution laws require public hearings where citizens may voice their wishes regarding the quality of air and water they desire and ways to achieve that level. How his state organizes itself for water quality protection, whether the power to regulate an activity is to be separated from the power to promote it, how legislative, police, and enforcement authorities are to be divided—all these are very much the citizen's concern. Yet passage of a law is only the first step. Implementing the law, monitoring its application and enforcing its provisions—and financing each of these processes—are the long, hard chores.

Citizen action in water quality matters ranges from stuffing envelopes with notices of a meeting, or carrying placards at that meeting, to developing and supporting a complex regional plan based on scientific and legal studies, to promoting needed alterations in basic national policies. As seminar participants think about

what they should do, they may be tempted to feel that some kinds of problems and some kinds of effort are small and insignificant, that others are beyond their strength and competence. It is true that opportunities and talents vary widely. However, citizens should remember that just as they often need professional help in developing solutions to their communities' environmental problems, expert solutions require popular support to be put into effect. To control pollution effectively, officials need the backing of the citizenry as much as they need an efficient plan to execute.

The effectiveness of the national efforts to safeguard and improve the quality of the environment rests on shared responsibility among government and business as well as among the various levels of government. It rests equally firmly on citizen support and action.

CHAPTER III

Organizing for Change

Tactics means doing what you can with what you have.

—Saul Alinsky

Introduction

The search for a set of organizing tactics that will regularly contribute to successful strategies of social change has accelerated since the early sixties. Riddled with the constraints of rival ideologies, competing theoretical "schools," and change programs fighting for survival, the search has been anything but placid. Unrealistic expectations about the rapidity of change and the significance of its impact on people's lives have often placed an almost impossible burden on those suggesting tactics that must be implemented over many months or years and offer very modest potential improvements.

At the same time, there can be little question that the entrenched resistance to change—particularly change that involves a shift in power arrangements—has stiffened and become more sophisticated in mobilizing counterforces. Middle- and lower-middle-class groups have been stimulated to oppose demands of the poor on the grounds that they will be the ones to pay for changes. Black, Latino, Asian, and native American organizations are increasingly placed in the position of having to battle each other over the reduced resources being made available to them. Traditional and newer, more innovative social welfare programs have also been put in situations where they must compete against each other for limited human service dollars.

In this context, it is hardly surprising that authors and demonstrators of tactical innovations are regarded with more than a little suspicion. However, there is a growing recognition of the fundamental value of organizing as a social change approach.[1] Despite the limitations noted above and the very modest record of successes, new and existing organizing efforts not only survive but

---

[1] For example, see George Brager and Harry Specht, *Community Organizing* (New York: Columbia University Press, 1973).

continue to grow as well.[2] Chapter III attempts to briefly explore, review, and summarize some of the tactics (and the broader strategies in which they have played a part) that have made this possible. There are a number of factors which have contributed to the relative strength of many recent change efforts based largely on organizing tactics.

1. THINKING SMALL

Among successful organizing efforts—whether in health, housing, delinquency, labor, or welfare—the pattern has been to set modest goals and propose to achieve them in reasonable time limits. Larger objectives are usually broken down into much smaller components that can be realized in a period of months. Often the "retreat" from radical rhetoric represents not so much a general withdrawal from major fields of battle (like a guaranteed annual income), but rather a tactical shift that recognizes the importance of not holding out promises of change that far exceed the possibilities for delivery in the immediate future. Small gains are now more likely to be given the acknowledgment they deserve. Some "big" solutions, it is now clearly understood, may contribute to a worsening of the problems they set out to attack (like Head Start, which promised so much more than it could possibly deliver).

2. RECRUITING HARD WORKERS RATHER THAN IDEOLOGUES

In order to support and sustain their organizing efforts, many organizers have come increasingly to the conclusion that a person's willingness to put in long, hard hours is more important than the purity or consistency of his or her ideological rhetoric. Cool commitment is valued above impatient militance. The "alternative institutions" that emerged out of the sixties and early seventies— like halfway houses, community-based medical clinics and diversion programs, and neighborhood co-ops—require approval and sustenance from a wide variety of community groups and organizations. Posturing about "decentralization" and "consumer participation" is not enough. Another aspect of the swing toward less ideologically outspoken workers is a reduction in the amount of (often unavoidable) resistance generated by the slashing combative style of previous organizers.

3. BECOMING MORE INTERDISCIPLINARY

Along with a general emphasis on pragmatic tactics has come a recognition that many organizing efforts can best be accomplished through interdisciplinary efforts—with doctors, lawyers, psychologists, school counselors, probation officers, business people, and the like. For example, organizing work with Grey Panthers, community mental health programs, and consumer advocacy groups is often most successful as a joint enterprise with non–social workers.

---

[2]For example, see *Just Economics* (monthly magazine of the Movement for Economic Justice), Vol. 4, No. 4 (May, 1976).

Also, programs aimed at protecting or extending the rights of ethnic and racial minorities, women, children, gays, and the physically handicapped have increasingly depended upon cooperating legal advisors.

4. BUILDING ALLIANCES

The need to build new structures of support for organizing efforts has become obvious (often painfully) to most organizers. Various political, economic, and religious leaders must be wooed, involved, or coopted. The "We'll go it alone" approach of the recent past seems foolhardy rather than heroic. With moral imperatives of social justice and equality on the decline as a force for change, the old (and newer) power politics is often the only game in town. In much the way that a political campaign is put together, organizers are mapping out whose support, and how much of it, will be needed to put a program across. Affirmative action initiatives to achieve opportunities for women are a particularly good illustration in that political support (with a small or large P) is almost always required to get them accepted. As Piven points out: "The sense of powerlessness, of fatefulness, has its sources in an American political system that bars the poor from effective influence."[3]

It is not only the poor that suffer this sense of inability to influence the forces by which they feel themselves controlled. Indeed, in the post-Watergate era this lack of efficacy runs throughout the middle classes. But the organizing goes on. It remains one of the few ways that people can participate in changing the things they want to see changed. In this sense, the tactics that can contribute to these changes are extremely important. The readings which follow explore and elaborate some of these tactics.

The article by Jack Rothman, John Erlich, and Joseph Teresa focuses on the step-by-step implementation of innovation as an essential (and perhaps the most basic) organizing tactic. However big or small the change being attempted, however radical or conservative the goal, a carefully planned out innovation is one of the ways to get there. Joyce Welsh's article, "Operation Independence," provides both an illustration of innovation and an approach to organizing around the needs of older people for services so they can remain in their own homes. This article also exemplifies many of the recent shifts in tactical orientation described above.

The California Homemakers Association is the subject for John Erlich's description of the making of a grass-roots organization. The association has taken as its major mission the securing of rights for those workers who provide attendant care and chore services for elderly, blind, and disabled welfare recipients. An epilogue details the tactical components which he feels have contributed most heavily to its success. In "Organizing the Consumer Cooperative" Merlin Miller explores tactics from a very different perspective. The context is how the cooperative organizer can bring lawyers into the effort. Some basic interdisciplinary issues are touched on as Miller lays out what basic facts must be ex-

---

[3]Frances F. Piven in Lawrence Bailis, *Bread or Justice* (Lexington, Mass.: D. C. Heath, 1974), p. xiii.

plained to the lawyer who knows little or nothing about poor people's co-ops. Finally, Gene Sharp explores and illustrates from the American past seven basic tactics of nonviolent intervention. These vary from establishing new social patterns to the utilization of guerrilla theater. As Walton notes: "When they are used, tactics of nonviolence are effective at least in part because the other group perceives this method as an alternative to violence. The option of violence is indirectly suggested *by advocating nonviolence.*"[4]

Taken together, these articles suggest a broad range of contexts in which organizing tactics may be effectively used. At the same time, they offer a number of different potential roles for those who might attempt to use them—from directing antiestablishment confrontations to coordinating social agencies serving the aging.

John L. Erlich

---

[4]Richard Walton, "Two Strategies of Social Change and Their Dilemmas," *The Journal of Applied Behavioral Science,* Vol. 1, No. 2 (April–May–June, 1965), p. 179.

11. Innovation: How to Bring It About

Jack Rothman, John L. Erlich, and Joseph Teresa

ADDING SOMETHING NEW: INNOVATION

Organizing demands innovation. The practitioner who cannot utilize tactics of innovation is not likely to be very successful. New programs, new delivery systems, and new groups almost always require the development, adoption, and diffusion of innovations. In this sense, the innovation may be something entirely new or, more often, new to the particular situation in which it is to be tried. However, whether the new introduction is a course in kung fu at a senior center, "meals on wheels" delivered by individual volunteers, or an effort to set up a grievance committee to provide advocacy support to welfare recipients, the basic elements are similar.

The material which follows was drawn from the "field test" experiences of a wide range of practitioners who participated in a research project undertaken by the authors.[1] The innovations were carried out in the context of their regular job responsibilities by practitioners in settings ranging from Catholic Social Services to an area health planning council, from a school district human relations office to a social welfare workers union. All were based in the State of Michigan.

Generally speaking, an innovation may be viewed as any program, technique, or activity perceived as new by a population group, institution, or organization. An innovation, as the term is most often used in research studies, refers to new technical, professional, and commercial ideas and practices, such as contraceptive devices, new medical equipment, and farming techniques. From a number of different disciplines and professions in these studies, the following generalization was drawn:

Innovations which are amenable to trial on a partial basis will have a higher adoption rate than innovations which necessitate total adoption without an anticipatory trial.[2]

This concept of partialization can be applied in what Everett Rogers characterizes as "observability." That is, an innovation is more likely to be adopted by an individual or group if there is an opportunity to first see the innovation in action and witness its results. In utilizing this approach one typically subdivides the target population. Research has shown that the likelihood of an innovation's being adopted by a larger population is increased if it is first utilized by a smaller group of opinion leaders. This smaller initiating group may be characterized by such terms as style setters, information disseminators, key communicators, etc. Thus innovations are frequently spread in a two-step sequence, from a small subsystem of early adopters and opinion leaders to a larger population or system.

Reproduced by permission of the publisher, John Wiley & Sons, Inc., New York, New York. From Jack Rothman, John Erlich, and Joseph Teresa, *Promoting Innovation and Change in Organizations and Communities,* © 1976, pp. 22-57.

[1]For a full description of this project, see Jack Rothman, John Erlich, and Joseph Teresa, *Promoting Innovation and Change in Organizations and Communities* (New York: John Wiley & Sons, 1976).

[2]Everett Rogers of Michigan State University has codified much of the research on innovation in his two books, *The Diffusion of Innovations* (New York: The Free Press, 1962): rev. ed., with F. Floyd Shoemaker, *The Communication of Innovations* (New York: The Free Press, 1971).

The following action guideline is derived from the principle of partialization:

Practitioners wishing to promote an innovation in a general target system should attempt to have it experienced initially by a partial segment of that target system.

A target system is defined as a particular group, organization, community, or society toward which an innovation is directed. In the context of our guideline we are dealing largely with the organizational and subcommunity level. The guideline conveys an incremental, stepping-stone process; success on a small scale with a limited group is used as the basis for promoting a new idea, or having it spread spontaneously, across a wider population grouping. There are a large number of familiar analogs—the demonstration project, the pilot program, the modeling of new roles or behavior, the free sample.

OPERATIONALIZING THE GUIDELINE

The selection of an appropriate, facilitative partial segment of the target system is crucial in carrying out the guideline. That is, the partial system chosen should enhance the probability of the innovation's success on a limited scale. An organizer in a welfare workers union, for example, wanted to introduce a system of implementing the union's programs at the individual welfare office level. He took into account many factors in selecting an initial target building:

The basic consideration for the successful application of this guideline, at least in my case, was the selection of the target subpopulation. I was able to employ the following factors: Geographic location, history of organizational activity leading to cohesiveness (how long had the folks been relating to each other organizationally), leadership (both actual and potential) within the partial target population; level of skill and experience within the target population.

It may be useful to illustrate in chart form (Figure 11.1) some other instances of innovation promotion, in order to show a range of types of innovations to which this guideline has been applied, as well as to demonstrate how other practitioners have applied the concepts of a general target system and partial target system. The chart also indicates the mechanisms by which the transfer was made from the smaller to the larger target system.

IMPLEMENTATION PATTERNS

There were two important variations in the patterns of implementation of the guideline in the field test. In the first pattern, which we call a "spontaneous" contagion model, the action proceeds from the practitioner (P) to the partial target system to the general target system. This pattern is typical of the agricultural extension approach in which one farmer uses a new seed and is successful, and his neighbors see the results and then plant the same seed. It can be depicted as: [see *First Pattern* below].

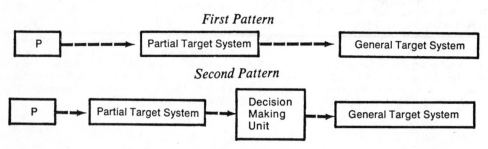

First Pattern

| P | ----→ | Partial Target System | ----→ | General Target System |

Second Pattern

| P | —→ | Partial Target System | —→ | Decision Making Unit | —→ | General Target System |

FIGURE 11.1

Setting	Innovation	General Target System	Partial Target System	Transfer Mechanism
Traditional settlement house serving a largely black population	Introducing an intensive educational focus into a program that had been largely recreational	Entire school age membership of the settlement house	A group of teen members were involved in two educational counseling sessions	Board of directors voted an allocation for hiring an educational director to serve the membership
A regional planning council serving several counties	Have the planning council gain responsibility for advising HUD on housing applications from all regional municipalities	All municipalities in the region	With HUD approval, reviewed and assessed trial applications from four municipalities	HUD approved review procedure for all municipality applications
A community mental health center in a semi-rural county	Stimulate local unions to accept the function of community care-givers for their members	All local unions in the county	A limited number of union members and leaders participated in a workshop on community care giving	The countywide (all inclusive) AFL-CIO Labor Education Committee voted sponsorship of a follow-up workshop to be offered to all county locals
A social welfare employees union in a metropolitan community	Decentralize program implementation through building level unit committees	All building level units in the union (thus, the total membership)	Shop stewards at a single building location were involved successfully in union program implementation functions	The union executive board instituted a policy of building level program implementation

In the second pattern, the action moves from the practitioner to the partial target system, and then to a relevant decisionmaking unit and finally to the general target system. In other words, a decision-making unit is involved between the partial and general target systems. This process typically is used in a *decision-making unit model* requiring organizational approval. See *Second Pattern,* bottom of page 158.

In the spontaneous contagion process the general target system accepts the innovation directly. In the decision-making unit arrangement a transfer mechanism or agent authorizes the carry-over from the smaller to the larger group. The authorization may involve carrying out the program either with or without the prior acceptance of the general target system.

Variations on the pattern of Practitioner → Partial Target → Decision-making Unit → General Target

are many. Sometimes the practitioner needs initial approval from a supervisor or the agency director. Occasionally he or she first receives approval from the Decision-making Unit to carry out the demonstration, completes it, and returns to the Decision-making Unit for authorization to spread to the general target. In some instances there are two Decision-making Units involved. Some practitioners arrange to have the Decision-making Unit experience the demonstration directly, as for example attending a conference at which a new technique or medium is employed.

Practitioners in the field study followed both of the basic patterns. An illustration of the spontaneous contagion model is contained in the experience of a president of a social workers union who wished to institute a training program for his executive board, using a method whereby case examples and sharing personal experiences are used to enhance effectiveness in dealing with grievance problems. He obtained approval from the board before he began the process.

I then contacted a select group of four board members, requesting them to participate on the committee. I asked them to present a case example for the meeting and scheduled a committee time with them.

I chaired the committee meeting, suggested the rationale for the model to be used, and assumed responsibility for following up on specific tasks. The committee decided to conduct the training session in front of the board following the format of the committee meeting. Individual contacts were made to publicize the training session. The model was used at the training session, and the response was most favorable as the board had directly seen and experienced what I was trying to get across.

The general target system, the executive board, participated with interest in the training session with positive evaluative comments ("we were really able to share problems in a new way"; "it was really helpful to know that other people had some of the same problems"; etc.).

The key suggestion—at the training session —was that a next target system, for the future, could be the general membership with the same model being applied.

The decision-making unit pattern was followed by a community worker in a traditional family service agency who was attempting to develop the concept of outreach services. She believed the agency should work directly with clients in a low-income housing project, rather than requiring them to come to the agency offices. The problem was to convince the agency board to provide this type of service and the housing manager to clear the way for it to operate within the project.

My use of the guideline involved a small group of residents living on a court in a low-cost housing project. We were able to convince the Housing Authority that social work intervention could make a difference in the social problems in the housing project; reduce the social causes for eviction. A subgoal was the introduction and sustaining of an outreach program by our agency to housing project residents. We selected one court (5 families) out of the entire project as a demonstration; set up a time limit for evaluative purposes; promised progress reports at specific intervals; and met with the residents regularly as well as just "dropping in." This plan was submitted in writing to the board along with my periodic progress reports.

The plan worked almost too well in that it was constantly referred to in agency Board meetings; the outreach idea was new here but it really impressed the Board and the Housing Director, and was accepted as a legitimate and appropriate agency program. The results with the residents were not as spectacular, but represented at least a beginning, and we gradually expanded to other courts.

In the great majority of cases in our study a formal decision-making unit was necessary in order to foster or legitimate the transfer and broadening of the innovation. This is of particular note because in much of the diffusion literature such mechanisms are not acknowledged. Clearly, most human services practitioners are organizationally based, and this generally requires rather formal and structured procedures in order to execute processes similar to those carried out by agricultural extension agents.

Another difference in implementation concerned the amount of effort expended by the practitioner in diffusing the innovation from the partial to the general targets. In some instances the practitioner was highly active in promoting the spread. For example, a community center worker demonstrated an intensive guidance program for unwed mothers within one high school. She then set out to have the same format introduced throughout the school system:

I now had to involve additional individuals and groups. I proceeded to develop a proposal and arrange for meetings with the following:

my Center's Board of Directors, School Age Parents Advisory Board, Episcopal officials (for funds), school administrators, teachers, and students. After a number of meetings and a month and a half we were able to gain administrative approval and a verbal commitment for funding of the program so all relevant students might benefit.

These patterns might be distinguished as a spontaneous process, on the one hand, and a directed process, on the other. In the spontaneous process, the practitioner is active in securing the adoption of the innovation by the partial target, but leaves the diffusion of the innovation to the general target in the hands of the partial target. The diffusion is thus carried out by the partial target, either by active promotion or by "inactive" modeling or example.

By contrast, the directed process involves the practitioner both in the adoption phase of the partial target and the diffusion phase to the general target system. It may involve the practitioner's "supervision" or encouragement of the partial target system in the diffusion to the general target system, or it may involve the practitioner as the sole "line of communication" between the partial and general target system.

The innovations being promoted by the practitioners fell into two categories. On the one hand, some of the practitioners had a fairly concrete detailed "product" to promote—a policy or program for adoption:

The development of a policy statement calling for an increase in the number of psychiatric beds for children in the metropolitan area.

To establish the Curriculum Poverty and Social Problems in six high schools in the tri-county area.

A rotating toy library for the use of six child care facilities.

On the other hand, some practitioners had a more fluid "process" of participation or involvement as an innovation to be promoted:

A subcommittee or task force of the eight private agencies in Wayne and Oakland Counties involved in institutional work with children to work cooperatively with three representatives of the public sector.

Small groups of black and white students who will meet together in one junior high school.

There were also differences in the practitioner's attitudes toward the innovation. Some practitioners were convinced of the validity of the new program. Others, however, were less certain and saw the guideline as a basis for "testing" rather than "selling." In this illustration a mental health worker describes what can be characterized as a feasibility study:

My first experience involved a program designed for mentally retarded adults to prove that such services could be delivered with volunteer help, and that response from volunteers would be forthcoming. Up until that time the agency had resisted using volunteers to any extent. Two small groups of adults were selected initially by using some Department of Social Services community care homes and their residents. Eventually we had other home operators asking that their residents be allowed to participate, and ultimately we used our experiences in this program to write a proposal to the public school's Adult Education Department for a weekly socialization program for 200 mentally retarded adults. All of this took planning in great detail initially because we could not afford for those first few programs to fail.

We recruited and trained volunteers; we selected the initial group with some care; and tried to monitor everything constantly.

Through demonstrating with a small portion of the target population, we could then open up the program to the larger target population—which we did. If we had not limited the group initially we would have had disaster, because we did not have the volunteers, the space, the equipment, nor the "know how" to handle a large group. In addition, we did not have the acceptance of the agency that this was a viable way to proceed in this program.

In the discussion thus far we have spoken of dichotomous categories—with or without a decision-making unit, spontaneous or directed diffusion, etc.—but the processes of social change are more complex than that. If we trace the steps of a practitioner in action, perhaps we can correct any tendency to oversimplification. The director of a mental health association for example, lists the steps he followed in getting the county mental health board (the general target) to endorse a policy statement calling for the provision of more psychiatric beds for emotionally disturbed children (the partial target was the Children and Youth Committee of the Board):

1. Collect basic data identifying the scope of the problem.
2. Renew active support of my own organization by presenting the problem to the Board of Directors at its December 2nd meeting.
3. Discuss the problem informally with Mental Health Act staff.
4. Discuss the problem informally with selected members of the Children and Youth Committee.
5. Present the issue formally to the Children and Youth Committee.
6. Discuss the problem informally with representatives of the State Department of Mental Health.
7. Encourage suggestions to meet the problem from members of the Children and Youth Committee, and from Mental Health Act and State Department staff.
8. Encourage site visits to prospective facilities.
9. Elicit a formal recommendation from the Children and Youth Committee to the full Mental Health Act Board.
10. Move to secure support of the full Mental Health Act Board.

Excerpts from his final report convey some of the flavor of this activity:

I first discussed the need for additional beds informally with several Committee members and with the Committee staff person. These contacts were with people whom I did not feel were resistive on doctrinaire grounds. These people encouraged me to bring the issue to the Committee for general discussion.

During the following two weeks, I again talked informally with several Committee members, and also spent some time meeting personally with mental health board staff in an effort to help them understand the nature of the need and the more desirable options available. The key staff person agreed that it would be helpful for me to present basic information to the Committee at its next meeting, and informed the Committee Chairman that I was going to prepare some helpful information.

With staff assistance from my own agency, I researched some of the issues related to inpatient care . . . . It was possible to prepare materials that provided valid answers . . . .

Prior to the actual Committee meeting, I again discussed the matter informally with several Committee members. I discussed the data I was collecting and asked them for their thoughts and suggestions.

At the December 15 meeting I presented the information that had been collected. Surprisingly (to me) there was general agreement about the validity of the data, and little support for the notion that there were alternatives to hospital care for the children in question. Inasmuch as the time seemed right to suggest a formal policy statement, I did so. After some discussion, the policy statement was adopted.

The Committee, through its chairman (a member of the full Board), made its recommendation to the Mental Health Board at its late December meeting. The Board adopted the policy statement and directed the Committee to work for its implementation.

USING THE GUIDELINE:
PROSPECTS AND LIMITATIONS

Several practitioners commented that the guideline helped them to be more systematic in their work, and some found the guideline easy to understand and apply. For example:

The guideline serves the purpose of breaking down in concrete terms a specific method for initiating and implementing change. I think it is useful to be specific, purposeful, and sequential in pursuing a goal. This guideline suggests such an orientation.

Given some clarity as to support for its use, the guideline is sensible, practical, do-able, and realistic.

It is one that I can put into use in a number of situations with little or no difficulty on my part.

Other practitioners noted that it is useful in terms of long-range (and medium-range) planning because operational problems can be seen on a small scale before the innovation is attempted on a large scale. They also felt that the initial experience by a limited portion of the target system was helpful in determining the potential success or failure of the innovation itself.

You do have an opportunity to work out problems of the innovation and to test its value before trying it on the total target system.

It allows for a test of the idea or change for the practitioner as well as a strategy for gaining acceptance.

While the practitioners expressed enthusiasm for the idea behind this mode of action, however, they pointed out a wide range of problems related to its execution. The perennial problem of time was noted, as was the related factor of the need to select a feasible, moderate-sized proximate goal:

I had little time to do the implementation of the guideline.

I guess it was having to be patient before things started happening. Assessment had to constantly take place along with the incredible amount of public relations. At first the pay off is small but it makes the professional more credible.

The guideline is still valid but there has to be a caution of thinking small and clearly—and limiting the goal sufficiently.

The selection of the partial target system was described as both a very important and a difficult task.

The most difficult thing is defining the appropriate "limited portion" of the target population.

It is important to choose a partial target system that will carry out with the total target.

Two general recommendations regarding the selection of a partial target group can be drawn from the experience of the field test. First, the group should be so constituted as to ensure the success of the limited demonstration. That is, it should have some of the following characteristics: receptive to the innovation, generally accepting of change, good relationship with or willingness to work with the practitioner, good motivation, special qualification such as education, skills, or experiences which would facilitate a successful demonstration, etc.

Second, the partial group should be respected by the general target population (or at least not be a deviant, disapproved segment). There should be strong linkages and good means of communication between the partial and general targets.

Action implications are suggested from other practitioner comments, such as "Give attention to interpersonal factors."

Practitioners stressed the degree to which this guideline called for the exercise of interpersonal skills: with board members, clients, the agency executive, etc.

One needs to be clear about the nature and quality of interpersonal relationships involved in the process of trying to reach the goal.

This suggests that the guideline entails modes of influence such as persuasion, example, and communication.

GETTING STARTED

In attempting to use this guideline for the first time you might follow a thought-action process roughly as follows:

1. Think of some new program, project, or other activity that you have been planning to carry out, or that ties in with general tasks and objectives of your current position or assignment.

2. Attempt to set this down as a goal, but of moderate scope and of short-range time dimension, something that could be completed in a minimum of about four and a maximum of twelve weeks.

3. Conceptualize the general or "total" target system at which this innovation is directed, who are the people collectively who would be benefiting from, utilizing, or participating in this innovation.

4. Think through a smaller segment of that target system, a more delimited subgroup:

   a. Who might relatively easily be drawn into a trial or demonstration of the innovation.

   b. With whom there is high likelihood of success in an initial trial.

   c. Whose success would likely have an impact on the larger target system or on a relevant Decision-Making Unit that could legitimate or authorize transfer of the innovation to the larger target system.

5. Our review of patterns of implementation suggests that early in the game, authorization or legitimation is often needed in order to proceed. This may be obtained from a superior (supervisor, agency director, etc.) or from the agency board. Also quite early, persons or organizations may need to be approached who can provide resources to carry through the small-scale demonstration, or can offer access to the smaller target system. Think

through those individuals, groups, or organizations whose acceptance needs to be gained.

6. When you have worked the issue through in your mind to this point, begin to fill out the Initial Log Form (below). This is meant to assist you in laying out on paper some prospective steps that you might take in starting to carry out this guideline.

INITIAL LOG FORM

Now as a further step toward getting started we suggest that you put down your tentative thoughts regarding implementation of the guideline. The Initial Log Form (Figure 11.2) we developed for the field test was helpful to practitioners in that connection. The Initial Log is a tool for ordering your thinking in a systematic way. It is geared especially to helping you think through your goal, ways of operationalizing the guideline, key individual and community groups to involve, and facilitating and limiting factors in the situation (personal, agency, client, community).

FIGURE 11.2

Initial Log: A Preliminary Guide For Action

1. Describe the circumstances (conditions, events, assignments, requests, etc.) which led you to use this guideline.

2. Look back at the intervention guideline. How would you begin to define or concretize *each* element of the guideline in your immediate practice situation (that is to say, how might you operationalize these components)?

   a. What is your *innovation?*

   b. What is the *General Target System?*

   c. What is the *Partial Target System* (specifically)?

   d. How will you *promote acceptance*—forms of linkage, communication, promotion, etc., you will use *to diffuse from the Partial to the General System?*

3. List the *major* steps you anticipate going through in order to utilize this guideline. Describe specific behaviors in the order in which you expect they will occur.

☐

☐

☐

☐

☐

☐

4. What *key* community groups will you probably involve (if any)?

Group   Reason for Contact

_____   _____
_____   _____
_____   _____
_____   _____

5. What *key* individuals will you probably involve (if any)?

Individual(s)   Title and/or Affiliation   Reason for Contact
(initials)

_____   _____   _____
_____   _____   _____
_____   _____   _____
_____   _____   _____

6. In general, to what degree do you feel community, client, agency or personal (related to yourself) factors may be *facilitating* as you attempt to implement this guideline?

7. In general, to what degree do you feel community, client, agency or personal (related to yourself) factors may be *limiting* as you attempt to implement this guideline?

12. Coalition Formation and Development

Joyce C. Welsh

OPERATION INDEPENDENCE

ORGANIZATION OF A COMMUNITY COALITION

Operation Independence is a major effort within the voluntary sector to stimulate the development of services within the community for the most vulnerable older persons who need supportive services to live alone or to return to their homes after hospital or institutional care. Operation Independence places emphasis on a collaborative planning process and partnership between service providers from the public and voluntary sectors to meet this need in a community.

So that older persons may have the option of continuing to live in their own homes or other places of residence for as long as they wish, a variety of community-wide services are necessary to maintain social well-being, to enhance mental and physical health and to supplement self-care whenever necessary. Operation Independence is designed to encourage local communities and groups to develop and strengthen such services where needed.

Many older adults who are vulnerable due to factors of health, isolation, or frailties which sometimes accompany old age may be able to function adequately with the help of a single supportive service available to them either in their own homes or readily accessible in the community. However, for some older adults living alone or as couples, the chances are that

Reproduced by permission of the publisher, The National Council on the Aging, Inc., Washington, D.C. From Joyce C. Welsh, *A Guidebook for Local Communities Participating in Operation Independence,* 1975, pp. 1-2, 4-6, 14-17, 19-20, 22-24.

one or more additional services are required to keep open their option of continued independent living at home. Thus, it is essential that public and voluntary agencies committed to the goal of assisting older adults to remain in or return to their own homes work together so that the services of each, as well as those which can be provided through voluntary organizations, are appropriately related to one another. Many different clusters of services are possible, whether established under public, private nonprofit, or commercial auspices. The clusters will involve different combinations of professional, nonprofessional, and volunteer personnel in accordance with the types of services offered.

For example, a homemaker-home health aide program involves basically a combination of paraprofessional homemakers and professional supervisors. The team for a given case may include a homemaker, a social worker or a nurse, perhaps a physician, a nutritionist, a physical therapist, or others; or it may consist only of the homemaker and her supervisor. Usually the homemaker is on a part-time basis. Consequently, it is necessary in many situations for contacts on days when the homemaker does not visit; a need that can be met by an organized telephone program, staffed by volunteers. Often there is need for chore service, including minor household repairs, which can be supplied by either an employee of an agency providing chore service (frequently the local homemaker-home health aide agency) or by a volunteer from such an agency. Other supportive services may be added or substituted, which give the plus to the basic health and welfare service designated nationally as homemaker-home health aide services.

Another example of a widely needed service is a *friendly visitors program,* staffed by volunteers under professional supervision. The friendly visitors help to reduce isolation and stimulate continued social relations. Such visitors may observe the need for a variety of other services in the homes they serve. This may call for close ties with an information and referral service regarding public services or for development of a transportation service to take the older adults to health services, to the grocery store, etc.

The national nutrition program sponsored by the Administration on Aging under Title VII of the Older Americans Act uses the provision of meals as the core service. The congressional intent of Title VII envisions a wide-ranging cluster of related services to promote the health and welfare of individuals receiving the meals service.

Any group offering or planning to offer services to older adults in their own homes should evaluate the multiplied effect of a cluster of services on the well-being of those served and concomitantly the economies—in time, money, effort, staff—of multiservice programs as contrasted with single service operations. Inevitably one program will lead to others, so that the agency concerned with an initial service can hopefully provide a variety of protective and preventive services when and as needed in individual situations.

Services cannot "just grow" for persons in their seventies and eighties. They *must be carefully planned,* community by community, so they are readily available and accessible throughout a given geographic area—and, hopefully, throughout a state. They will not meet full need unless they serve all economic and social groups, whether on a free basis, a sliding scale of fees, or purchase at full cost. They must be adequate not only in quantity but also in quality.

It is important to note the complementary relationship between Operation Independence and national programs of the Administration on Aging of the U.S. Department of Health, Education and Welfare plus the regionalized planning and coordination efforts of state units on aging and area agencies on aging. The program objective of Title III of the 1973 Older Americans Act Comprehensive Service Amendments is to strengthen or develop at the state and area levels a system of coordinated and comprehensive services for older persons—services to enable older persons to live in their own homes or other places of residence as long as possible. Area agencies on aging are charged with:

1. Becoming focal points for aging.
2. Serving as advocates for older persons in connection with all issues confronting their lives.
3. Developing a cooperative network to serve older persons by providing comprehensive coordinated services to meet their needs.

Also, Title XX of the Social Security Act, effective October 1, 1975, and administered by state social services agencies, mandates three specific services for the aged. Operation Independence, with its mobilization of voluntary resources focused on the most vulnerable older people and the in-home, supportive services they need to maintain their independence, complements and cooperates with the broader focus of the area agencies on aging and of state agencies administering Title XX.

A local cooperative effort can result in the development of a service delivery system enabling older persons to live independently in their own homes by

1. Focusing or concentrating attention on that objective.
2. Planning more fully.
3. Eliminating unnecessary duplication of effort.
4. Filling unmet service needs.
5. Sharing responsibilities and resources.

There must be a specific focus on the vulnerable and handicapped older adults; those most in danger of unnecessary institutionalization. Priority in service delivery must be given to older persons with physical, mental or emotional conditions that may handicap their functioning capability or their ability to fully care for themselves. In addition to community services, these people also frequently need in-home services to maintain maximum functioning ability and to prevent further deterioration and loss of independence. They are:

• Homebound and isolated
• Neighborhood bound and lonely
• Visually handicapped or blind
• Physically, mentally or emotionally handicapped
• Deinstitutionalized and convalescing
• Subject to frailties

A community coalition promotes independent living for older adults through services that make it possible for the more vulnerable to continue to live in their own homes or other places of residence in the community as long as possible. The coalition is an advocacy group. While growing in its own awareness of the needs of this specific segment of the aging, the coalition in turn informs and educates the community at large.

COALITION DEVELOPMENT

Community coalitions that form around the objectives of Operation Independence will follow two patterns:

1. In communities where there is an organization(s) with well-developed planning responsibility and capability, this organization and/or its advisory council, board, or committee will logically assume the Operation Independence coalition role. Operation Independence does not aim to set up competing planning and service mechanisms in any community.

2. The establishment of a new Operation Independence coalition will occur in communities where there are high proportions of older persons and no well-developed planning instrumentalities. New coalitions will be formed more frequently in small towns and rural areas; here there tend to be few, if any, formal planning structures, and large percentages of older persons are struggling to remain in their own homes with few public or voluntary agency services readily available to help them.

Step I

It is important, then, to determine first who, if anyone, in the community is engaged in planning services for older persons. Typically, this function is carried out by specific types of organizations. The following observations should be made before attempting to form a new coalition:

1. Is there an area agency on aging serving the locality? (If you are uncertain,

your county governmental structure or state commission on aging can provide this information.)

2. Is there a council on aging serving your community?

3. Does your Community Health and Welfare Council or local United Way (United Fund or Community Chest) have a committee with focus on aging?

4. Is your council of governments or local planning district involved in planning for the aging?

5. Are there any other organizations with planning capability now delivering services to older persons (county social services department, community action agencies, parks and recreation departments, voluntary action centers, private agencies such as senior centers, Senior Citizens' Services, Inc., etc.)?

Step II

If a planning mechanism for older persons does exist in your community, that organization and/or its advisory council, board, or committee may well assume the role of an Operation Independence coalition. If it is part of a planning and service area with a designated area agency on aging, the latter may wish to encourage formation of a local coalition in a rural county with many older persons but few services. Operation Independence encourages such organizations to undertake this role, requiring that two criteria be met:

1. Adoption of specific focus on the more vulnerable older person and the in-home and supportive services they need to maintain their independence. This could be accomplished by expanding an existing community service to include a priority

with respect to the more vulnerable older person or by initiating a new program either within one or more of the participating agencies or directly under auspices of the coalition.

2. Representation of public and voluntary groups. This could be accomplished by appointing a subcommittee or task force.

You or your organization can act as a catalyst and encourage organizations with existing planning structures to undertake leadership in the two action steps outlined above.

Step III

If there is no area agency on aging in your planning and service area—and no other planning structure exists in your community—the next step is to convene an initial meeting of representatives of public and voluntary agencies/organizations to accept a commitment to the goal of Operation Independence and to agree on a plan for action. To develop an effective membership, care should be taken to invite all public and voluntary agencies with a service which is, or might be, provided to older persons plus representatives of churches, service clubs, and fraternal organizations, etc., who have the authority to make group decisions.

Examples of agencies and organizations to be invited to the initial meeting are:

Community Health and Welfare Council
County/City Council on Aging
Area Agency on Aging
Council of Governments
County/City Health Department
County/City Department of Social Services
Social Security
Housing Authority
Parks and Recreation Department
Local affiliates of national voluntary organizations which are members of National Volun-

tary Organizations for Independent Living for the Aged (NVOILA), such as professional associations of doctors, home economists, librarians, etc.

Voluntary health and social welfare agencies, such as the American Red Cross, Visiting Nurses Association, Family Service Agency, Homemaker Service, etc.

Civic and fraternal organizations, such as Rotary, Lions, Kiwanis, Pilot, Altrusa, women's clubs

Religious organizations, such as ministerial alliances, churches, synagogues

Union organizations

Local institutions of higher education, community colleges

Senior citizen organizations and centers, including programs sponsored by civil rights and ethnic groups

Make certain that organizations serving the rural areas of your county or community have been approached:

Farm Bureau
County agents
Grange
Home demonstration agents
State Extension Service
Future Farmers of America
Future Homemakers of America
National Farmers Union
Green Thumb

EXAMPLE OF A COMMUNITY COALITION

BOULDER (COLORADO) COUNTY STEERING COMMITTEE ON AGING

Purpose:
1. To provide a representative group in Boulder County for research and development of the needs of the aging.
2. To act as an advocacy group which makes an effort to assure equitable distribution of Federal and state funds for aging.
3. To act as a coordinator of grant application for services for the aging.

Structure:
1. The membership is limited to a maximum of 25 persons.
2. The set meeting date is the second

Wednesday of each month at 1:30 P.M. Special meetings may be held as needed.
3. Council membership is composed of department or agency heads or persons designated by such organizations to insure authority to make group decisions. An alternate is appointed by each member organization to insure continuity of action.
4. The chairperson is expected to request consumer representation when appropriate.
5. The chairperson and vice-chairperson are elected each January 1 on a rotating basis.
6. A secretary, recruited from outside the group, prepares a record of discussions and decisions (summary of actions taken).
7. Summaries of discussions and decisions made are communicated to three county commissioners, county representatives, state legislators and congressmen, as well as to mayors and/or city managers in Boulder County.

Composition (current membership):
Boulder Senior Citizen Center
Volunteer and Information Center—Information and Referral
Boulder County Health Department
Boulder County Department of Social Services
Nutrition programs
R.S.V.P.
City housing
County Commissioners
Church liaison representative
Senior Citizens Coordinating Committee
Nursing homes
Retirement housing
Senior Opportunities and Services section of Boulder
Economic Opportunity Council, Inc.
Mental health
Community Nurse Coordinator
Lafayette Parks and Recreation
American Red Cross
Broomfield Parks and Recreation
St. Vrain Council of Agencies, Senior Task Force
Residential Care Facility.

Program accomplishments:
1. Development of the group from a steering committee to the Boulder County Council on Aging. Once it became clear that the area agency on aging expected to organize county councils in each county, the Boulder Steering Committee went to the county commissioners and

asked that it be recognized officially as the County Council on Aging. This clear linkage with the area agency on aging has added a significant dimension to the council's effectiveness.

2. Development of a countywide coordinating and planning instrumentality that includes representatives of existing service providers. This group works cooperatively and jointly plans for future services.
3. Establishment of a directory of senior services for Boulder County.
4. Telephone reassurance program.
5. Adult health care conference (screening).
6. Development of the steering committee into a grant review committee for all funding proposals for senior programs in the county submitted by agencies within the coalition. The committee established and coordinated a comprehensive package of five service proposals for submission to the area agency on aging.

Formation process (1971):

1. The coordinator of the Volunteer and Information Center and the director of the Boulder Senior Citizen Center were invited to be co-convenors of an initial meeting by the National Steering Committee. They sent out invitations to all agency people in the community that dealt with older persons. One hundred and thirty-eight national voluntary organizations elected to become part of an action program growing out of the 1971 White House Conference on Aging called the Steering Committee of National Voluntary Organizations for Services to Older Persons in Their Own Homes or Other Places of Residence. The Plan for Action of the Steering Committee called for designated individuals/organizations in over 400 communities to convene a meeting of representatives of private and public service deliverers and voluntary organizations. The meeting's purpose was to consider the possibility of working together for the planning, coordination, and provision of services to enable older persons to live independently in their own homes or other places of residence. Positive results were effected in more than half of the 400 communities, either in the encouragement of further efforts towards activities already under way or in the initiation of new coalitions for action.
2. Sixty persons responded and attended the first meeting, where the following actions took place:

a. Identification of the needs of older persons at the local level.
b. Identification of existing community services.
c. Identification of gaps in services and unmet needs.
d. Selection of an executive committee as a policy committee (directors of major agencies).

3. The Executive Committee met and determined 11 priority areas of need from the list identified at the initial general meeting (transportation, homemaker and home health care, adult health care, residential care, communication coordination and education regarding senior services, spiritual well-being, home renovation and repair, adult day care, housing, telephone reassurance, and nutrition).
4. A second general meeting was called, where the following actions took place:
a. Division of the general group into subcommittees.
b. Assignment of separate priorities to subcommittees
c. Initial work begun on coordinating existing programs and services/and developing new services to fill unmet needs.

Note: For the first two years there was no attempt to formally structure the group, which made the coalition less threatening, enabling it to remain operational through three stages: A city coalition to a countywide coalition to the County Council on Aging.

SELECTED PROGRAMS AND SERVICES HELP OLDER ADULTS REMAIN IN OR RETURN TO THEIR OWN HOMES

The goals of national, state, and local organizations, however varied, can include specific services to older Americans and, of course, they frequently do. Most organizations can provide a specific service directed toward helping older persons to remain in their own homes or other places of residence. In Operation Independence, public and private agencies serving the elderly join with affiliates of national organizations to promote and develop programs which enable older persons to live independently in their own homes.

The following is an attempt to list a number of action programs in which organizations can participate in some way. The participation may take place variously. The organizations may use their facilities for program headquarters, their publications to communicate program ideas; they may urge their membership to become involved on a paid or voluntary basis, use their funds to support such programs, or they may take the leadership role in organizing community action. Many of these programs offer an opportunity to enlist the skills and energies of older persons themselves, in itself a contribution to their continued health and well-being. Also, many programs can provide opportunities for older and younger persons to work together, bridging the generations.

A. Programs of Information and Referral

Through public media, newsletters, information centers, volunteer programs and other means, organizations can provide older persons with information to help them remain in their own homes, including:

1. Social Security
2. SSI (Supplemental Security Income)
3. Social service program
4. Protective services
5. Consumer services
6. Counseling services
7. Health programs
8. Food stamp eligibility
9. Housing relocation
10. Employment assistance
11. Volunteer programs

B. Programs of Direct Service

These programs can include service to older persons in their own homes or in group settings, as in a senior center. Bear in mind the multiplier effect of a cluster of services on the well-being of those served. [See below.]

I. Consumer Issues
  Consumer education
  Cooperative buying

II. Creative/Leisure Activities
  Adult education
  Arts and crafts
  In-home library services
  Recreation activities
  Talking books, reading
    services for the blind

III. Health
  Health education/counseling
  Home health services
  In-home physical therapy
  Mail order drug services
  Multiphasic health screening

IV. Housing
  Home repair services
  Housing counseling

V. Legal Services
  Conservatorship/guardianship programs
  Financial counseling

  Legal aid
  Tax counseling

VI. Nutrition
  Congregate meals
  Food stamps
  Home-delivered meals
  Nutrition education

VII. Social Support Services
  Adult day-care centers
  Chore services
  Counseling services
  Equipment loan
  Escort services
  Foster home care
  Friendly visitors
  Homemaker–home health
    aide services
  Personal grooming
  Shopping services
  Telephone reassurance
  Transportation services—
    reduced bus fares
  Driver refresher courses

C. Programs of Advocacy

National organizations and their local affiliates, in conjunction with local public agencies, can help older persons remain in their homes by serving as their advocates. For instance, their members can work for the development of housing authorities. They can influence local school boards to provide facilities and vehicles for nutrition and transportation programs.

In many cases, this advocacy role can mesh with other special concerns of an organization. An organization concerned with the physically handicapped could work to influence rehabilitation agencies to focus on the elderly's rehabilitation needs. All organizations can underline and obtain support for the selection of the special issues that confront the elderly who are members of minority groups or who have special handicapping conditions.

13.   Organizing the Poor: Cooperatives

Merlin Miller

ORGANIZING THE CONSUMER COOPERATIVE

If in every community where cooperatives are organized among the poor there could be efficient legal services for the poor consumer, the problems of these cooperatives would be very much less. Unfortunately, most lawyers are as unfamiliar with the problems of cooperatives as most cooperative organizers and educators are with the problems of the poor. What the cooperative organizer can suggest to the lawyer can be condensed into four topics: First, what is a cooperative? second, the problems of the poor in organizing cooperatives; third, the legal problems; and fourth, steps in organizing a cooperative.

Reproduced by permission of the publisher, Ohio State Legal Services Association, Columbus, Ohio. From Merlin Miller, "Organizing The Consumer Cooperative," from *Course on Law and Poverty: The Consumer* 8.01 (1968), © 1968, pp. 392–399.

WHAT IS A COOPERATIVE?

First, what is a cooperative? To a New Yorker a cooperative is a high-rise apartment building owned by the tenants. To a grain farmer from Kansas a cooperative is a tall grain elevator with the word CO-OP in bold letters across the top. They're both right and they're both wrong. "Cooperative" is used commonly—and loosely—to describe a business enterprise operated on a cooperative basis. Still more loosely it is used to describe the business buildings and facilities of such an enterprise. But, in its essence, a cooperative is the group of people who have banded together to carry on a business enterprise for the benefit of all of them, which acting as individuals they could not do, or could not do as well. The cooperative, then, is the organized group of people who have provided their own self-help, user-owned, group business enterprise. Every word of this functional definition is important; *self-help, user-owned, group business enterprise.*

VARIETIES OF COOPERATIVES AVAILABLE TO THE POOR

All kinds of business enterprises can be organized on a cooperative basis. The variety of cooperatives being organized now in the South, for example, as an aftermath of the civil rights developments there, is extremely limited if compared with the varieties to be found around the world. There are cooperatives of shoemakers and garment makers in India or Mexico or Honduras. There are cooperatives of the blind and the handicapped, producing handicrafts and electronic components in Poland. There is a cooperative in Burma capturing and taming wildlife. There are fishermen's cooperatives on every ocean and sea and almost every coast around the world. This infinite variety of economic activity which can be undertaken by people who want to help themselves is a challenge to their legal advisors, a challenge to use imagination and to discover new things that can be done cooperatively.

The term consumer cooperative tends to restrict our imagination. We think in terms of the foodstore, the supermarket. In the urban poverty programs there are a good many things that are being done on a cooperative basis. Organizing a big supermarket that requires an investment of hundreds of thousands of dollars may be done as part of a large housing project. But small groups of poor people can organize buying clubs. They can go a step further and offer a "food fair," a sort of "exposition," a very small supermarket for one day. They can organize to get their drugs and medicines at substantial savings. They can organize to provide a business counseling service, showing members of the group how they can buy certain appliances, for example, at much reduced prices through buying at specific recommended places of business. This leads naturally to a sort of "bargaining association," and agreements with reputable businesses that want to aid the poor and are quite willing to aid them if the transactions are cash, avoiding the credit and collection problems which increase the cost of doing business so sharply. In short, a cooperative discount house for the poor. So all of these can be done and many other things, through multiservice buying centers or business advisory centers.

There are other services which can be provided at a saving. Insurance is one of these—the saving comes largely through group premiums. Burial service is another important service which can be obtained cooperatively at a lower cost, although it's pretty hard to get the extremely poor who are thinking about tomorrow's meals and paying for a radio, TV, or washing machine to think ahead to that inevitable day when they or their families will be faced with the heavy expense of a funeral service. And then there's credit, the most universal need next to food and housing. The answer is the credit union, the cooperative savings and loan association. This is the most fundamental of all cooperative organizations, the one that provides the most basic services to its members: encouraging thrift and savings, providing credit when needed, and developing financial independence and human dignity.

THE PROBLEMS OF THE POOR IN ORGANIZING COOPERATIVES

When considering the bewildering variety of possible cooperative enterprises, it is wise to go back to the definition of a cooperative: a business enterprise organized by a group of people on a self-help and user-owned basis. Look at each separate part of that definition and it becomes clear that those who organize cooperatives among the poor face difficulties that most businesses never face.

Self-Help

In the first place, *self-help* for the poor. There is some truth in the oft-repeated generalizations that the poor are poor by and large because they are uneducated, even illiterate, apathetic, or unambitious. In some quarters there is also an element of fear—fear of the loss of a job or fear of being evicted from a home. And finally there is a long dependence upon various forms of welfare and relief. No one of these handicaps applies to all of the poor; there are some among the poor who have none of these handicaps. But generally the poor do have handicaps in getting together for self-help. That means there has to be a well planned program, involving gradually increasing information and education—in the action sense of that word—and self-reliance, before any group of the poor is going to be able to organize on a self-help basis. They are the people least qualified to pull themselves up by their own boot straps, but that is essentially what a cooperative is—a group pulling themselves and each other up by their boot straps. If the enterprise is run by somebody else for the poor, then it may be welfare or charity but, certainly, it is not a cooperative.

User-Ownership

In the second place, *user-ownership*—that the people who use the business own it. By definition, the poor lack capital. Nevertheless, user-ownership is impossible without the investment by the prospective members of some risk capital—and the would-be cooperator must understand this.

No lawyer—nor any other counselor—should let anyone he advises join a cooperative under the assumption that he's going to get something for nothing. He is not going to get, but he is going to give. He's going to give his patronage, and pay for what he gets in food or appliances or medical services or whatever it is that he is acquiring through this cooperative. He is also going to make an investment—a capital investment. The poor today are going to have to do the same thing that the poor have always done when organizing cooperatives; they are going to have to put in a little money of their own. They are going to have to leave money in the business as they use it if it is to be a successful cooperative. This is true, even though the various agencies aiding may put in considerably more capital than the cooperators themselves initially. But still, the prospective cooperative member is going to have to gamble a little of his limited money. He must make the plunge of "going into business" if he is going to be a true cooperator. These two elements, investment and patronage, are necessary for a cooperative to succeed. The other side of the coin is that, in order to get off the ground, many kinds of cooperatives of the poor will need, in addition to the members' pennies or dollars, proportionately large amounts of capital investments from outside sources.

Group Enterprise

Third, a *group enterprise*. Now confidence and trust in each other are the very foundation for the ordinary business transactions in western society. If no man could trust another's word, his checks, his telephoned orders, his price quotations, where would our vaunted corporate business structure and our affluent society be? Confidence and trust in each other is even more significant in the democratic corporate structure of the cooperative—especially among the poor, who have so little to lose, and to whom that little means so much.

The poor weavers of Rochdale, who started the worldwide cooperative movement, saved their money, some of them only a penny a week, for a whole year and trusted those meager savings to one person who was their treasurer—a year before they could go into any business and expend any of their savings for even their first small stock of goods. The Raifeissen Credit Societies, organized among the poor farmers of Germany about the same time as the Rochdale pioneers, organized on a basis of unlimited liability. They saved their money in a society which could loan the money to any of their members who needed it. But if he didn't pay back, all the members of the society were liable —unlimited liability. That is the foundation of trust upon which cooperatives started in a day when they had no government aid. The poor in our cities have been conditioned to be wary, to be suspicious, to distrust the stranger, to distrust the businessman from outside the community who has a place of business in their immediate vicinity. These suspicions can be overcome only by dynamic, trustworthy leadership; patient, continuous education; and small steps, one at a time, in cooperative action.

Aided Self-Help Cooperative

There is a fourth factor in the definition of a cooperative organized among the poor under the provisions of the Economic Opportunity Act. It is not only a self-help, user-owned, group business enterprise. It is an *aided* self-help cooperative. There are many kinds of assistance available under the Economic Opportunity Act. There can be grants for developing an organizational base for cooperative pro-

grams. There can be grants for the conduct and administration of cooperative programs in their initial stages. There can be payment for advice and assistance of specialists, technicians, and consultants for various cooperative programs. There can be grants for training personnel needed in cooperative programs. There can be loans to cooperatives for furnishing essential services. This last is particularly true in the rural areas through the Farmers Home Administration. All these and other aids available are described in the book, *Moving Ahead With Cooperatives,* a manual prepared by the Cooperative League of the USA at the express request of and in cooperation with the Office of Economic Opportunity.

The very terms *aided* and *self-help* seem to be contradictory. They are not, they do go together. We have learned, I think all of us, that there is no such thing as a truly self-made man. We all get assistance from others in the development of our own characters, our own business enterprises, and our own careers, our own professional skills. So do cooperatives, even the most prosperous middle-class cooperatives.

The Hyde Park Cooperative Society in Chicago, which now does about $6,000,-000 worth of business a year and has the biggest food store within the confines of the City of Chicago, began as a little buying club meeting, doing business in one room of a private house. Individuals gave their time without pay to carry on the business in those depression years. Also, most of the now prosperous farmers cooperatives in the Middle West had in their initial stages persons and organizations giving time and energy without pay.

Today, it is even more true that most cooperatives among the poor will have to be aided self-help cooperatives. The trick is to get the aid at all, to get it at the right time, and to get enough to get the business going. At the same time, the help must not be too much. It must not be enough to kill the cooperators' own sense of self-achievement.

LEGAL STRUCTURE OF COOPERATIVES

Turning to the legal organizational structure of cooperatives, it is possible for a small cooperative to operate for a time without being incorporated. But it is wise for a group getting started to have a lawyer point out that this involves certain hazards. As long as a buying club is unincorporated, every person joining or placing an order to be delivered at a later date kisses his money good-by when he prepays that order. If the treasurer runs off before the next meeting he hasn't much recourse. But this experience with the unincorporated cooperative buying club or association does have the advantage of impressing upon all the members that they are dependent on each other, not upon Uncle Sam and not upon the lawyer. They must make it on their own and they must trust each other. Just to get that far with a cooperative group may be a matter of character building that will mean the difference between the members of that group staying in the disadvantaged class and being on their own.

But the time comes for most cooperatives when the business must be incorporated or abandoned. When this time comes, it is important to know the essential distinctive differences between a cooperative and an ordinary business corporation. There are four of these distinctive features which every member of a cooperative should understand.

First, the cooperative is organized under nonprofit corporate laws. The application charter should specifically state that the cooperative is organized not for profit.

The second feature is the implementation in a business enterprise of the not for profit restriction: the dividend, if any, paid on the shares of stock or the investment shall be strictly limited. In practice this means that the return on the investment in a cooperative is limited to an amount equivalent to a modest rate interest, or nothing at all on the investment.

If a cooperative is successful it does "make money" in the bookkeeping sense —it does have "profit." But there is a sharp distinction between "profit" in the bookkeeping sense and "profits" in the sense of the word used in defining a corporation as "nonprofit." That term, as used in defining both eleemosynary corporations and cooperatives, means that no one —(organizers of, officers in, contributors to, nor members of the organization) shall share in any moneys received from either its philanthropic or its business operations. The nonprofit definition as applied to a cooperative requires that the money that is made on the transactions shall not be distributed to the members as investors at a rate that is any higher than they could have gotten as interest if they had made a loan to the cooperative. That is the basic ethical principle. It is not legally stated quite that way in most laws but it is exceedingly important. This limitation on distribution of earnings or savings makes it possible for the cooperative earnings or savings to be returned to the members as *users* in proportion to their use of the business.

This, then, is the third and most distinctive feature of the cooperative—the patronage refund principle. This principle does not require that the members take their earnings out of the business. If they desire to devote their savings to social or community uses, such as a playground, they are perfectly free to do that under most cooperative laws. But if they do vote to "take their earnings out," it must be distributed in proportion to the volume of business done with the cooperative.

Finally, the fourth distinctive feature is the principle of democratic control. This requirement is often stated as "one member, one vote." This requirement is stated in all consumer cooperative laws. It is the direct antithesis of the ordinary or profit corporate business practice which gives each stockholder as many votes as he has shares. In cooperatives it is men not money that controls.

There are, of course, many other detailed requirements for incorporation under specific cooperative laws. Moreover, the laws vary from state to state. Some states have no laws for consumer cooperatives at all. Ohio, for example, has a detailed Cooperative Marketing Act for farmers' cooperatives, Ohio Revised Code, Chapter 1729, Sections 1729.01 to 1729.27, but only one section on consumers' cooperatives, Section 1729.28. In most states, it is advisable that cooperatives for low-income persons be incorporated under the District of Columbia Cooperative Association Act passed June 19, 1940, D.C. Code Sections 29-801 et seq.

The steps in organizing a cooperative are set out in detail in the manual, *Moving Ahead with Cooperatives.* It was prepared jointly by the Cooperative League of the USA and the Office of Economic Opportunity. It is written in simple language with the poor in mind, but it contains all the essential information found in more sophisticated publications.

A second source of information is a 32-page booklet entitled *A Model Consumer Action Program for Low Income Neighborhoods,* by Harry S. Shaden, Jr. This booklet was prepared expressly for neighborhood urban groups in the city of Chicago.

A third manual, entitled *Moving Ahead with Group Action,* details the step-by-step organization of a consumer buying club. In simple language and with numerous line drawings, it discusses the work members of buying clubs will have to perform for themselves, e.g., pooling their orders; ordering from the wholesaler, packaging, pricing, and handling the cash; and keeping the financial records. This manual also sets forth sample business forms and simple bylaws. In short, it is a complete guide to a simple but well-managed self-help consumer cooperative. This manual, like the other two mentioned above, can be obtained from the Cooperative League of the USA, 59 East Van Buren Street, Chicago, Illinois 60605.

THE LAWYER'S ROLE

The problem of organizing a consumer cooperative for the poor is not a problem of educating the poor until they are ready to start cooperative action and then incorporating. The most successful organizing procedure is to provide a little education, then a little action; another step in education, the corresponding action, and so on, with action and education reinforcing each other until the group has acquired sufficient experience to go into a larger business enterprise and has some capital to invest in that business. Then it is time to incorporate.

The lawyer has two functions in this educational process: first, to see that the group does not incorporate too soon before its members understand thoroughly what they are doing; and second, to see that they do not put off incorporation too long, and so unnecessarily jeopardize the capital —and the enthusiasm—they are accumulating.

The attorney for the organizing group can perform another valuable service during this organizational period. He can give some sound business advice under the guise of legal counsel. This includes, in part, the following:

1. He can point out the legal responsibility of the officers of the buying club to get the money in advance or when goods are delivered for their own protection and to prevent that most frequent cause of cooperative failure—uncontrolled credit.

2. Also, he can stress the legal and sound business necessity of recording every member transaction from the start. The allocation of patronage savings is impossible without such records. Unexpected liability for income tax may be incurred without records of all transactions between the cooperative and the individual member. It is not only the members of the cooperative who need this advice. The community action people who are going to finance the initial organizational expenses of a cooperative venture must stress that any cooperative which gets assistance from the taxpayers' money has to keep good records. Nothing creates more suspicion, doubt, and finally, hostility, than the failure to keep records that show where every penny of every member and every dollar of the government's investment, has gone. That means, in practice, a monthly operating statement and balance sheet.

3. The attorney should see that the adopted bylaws require bonding of all employees responsible for handling funds. If possible, he should check to see that the proper bonds are promptly obtained.

4. Finally, the attorney who by this time has established himself as the friend and protector of the cooperative can give this sound advice: "Get a good manager and pay him what he's worth." This advice may need to be given to the OEO officials as much as the poor themselves. If this means going outside of the immediate community, hiring somebody who isn't within the "poverty guidelines," insist on it as good business and sound legal advice. Some OEO officials may not be happy about such counsel, but the fact remains that the co-op manager and co-op board, or OEO officials who share in hiring him, are trustees handling other people's money. They must have someone who has had experience and whose reliability is beyond question.

The foregoing bits of advice may be beyond the strictly legal requirements of the law. But they are quite in keeping with the purposes of legal aid. For, in a very real sense, the cooperative's attorneys, like the cooperative's organizers, are also trustees—trustees of the spirit of a people attempting to lift themselves out of poverty.

14. Organization Building in Working-Class Communities

John L. Erlich

ORGANIZING DOMESTIC WORKERS

The media are no longer much interested in grass-roots social action. Gone are the heady days in which OEO-sponsored Community Action Programs seemed to spring up overnight, the campuses seethed with discontent over the war in Southeast Asia, and welfare mothers regularly confronted the administrators of public assistance programs. To all appearances, insurgent labor organizations are sharing a similarly diminished or beleaguered status. On the West Coast, for example, the United Farm Workers Union is locked in a struggle for survival with the Teamsters. Efforts to organize low-wage hospital workers are being met by strong resistance across the country. However, appearances can be misleading. Grassroots efforts for change and new forms of labor organization are very much alive. One such effort, and one which effectively combines many strategies and tactics of labor and grass-roots organizing, is the California Homemakers Association (CHA).

The CHA, a legally recognized labor association, is committed to securing the rights of workers, such as "domestics, attendant care workers, homemakers and workers in other areas of service work." The major effort over the year of CHA's existence has been toward organizing and gaining recognition as a bargaining agent for the 1,800 attendants and domestics who provide home care for an estimated

2,400 elderly, blind or disabled welfare recipients in Sacramento County. About 85 per cent are female. Many, perhaps a majority, are heads of households. By any standard, these domestic workers are severely underpaid. Hourly rates, which were in the $1 to $1.25 range fifteen or twenty years ago, had advanced to only $1.65 an hour as late as December 1973. At the moment, CHA claims a membership of 3,000, of whom almost 1,500 are attendant care workers. It is estimated that there are about 5,000 household workers of all kinds in the county, and the goal is to reach most of the 2.5 million workers nationally who provide such services.

The city of Sacramento has a population of 274,000, about 25 per cent of whom are racial and ethnic minorities—mainly black, Chicano, Asian and American Indian. There are roughly an equivalent number of whites in families headed by low-wage workers. The county which encompasses the city has about 670,000 residents, and includes "suburban" areas of both considerable affluence and obvious poverty.

Located at 3500 Stockton Boulevard in Sacramento, the main office of the association is part of a multinational, multiracial and multilingual working-class neighborhood. While the storefront office has, on occasion, held more than 100 people for a meeting, it is too cold in winter and too hot in summer. All of the furnishings and office equipment have been donated by friends of the organization. The enthusiastic members and spirited volunteer organizing staff—old and young, bilingual and multiracial—are surprisingly reminiscent of the early activists of the civil rights movement.

Like a number of grass-roots organizations, CHA had its beginnings in a meeting of a few deeply concerned individuals. Five people with broad experience in the problems of domestic and attendant care work and organizing launched the effort. The present ten full-time organizers are about equally divided between ex-attendants, other low-wage workers (some of whom have experience in welfare and civil rights organizing), and persons recruited from the community and labor-related social-change efforts across the country. They are currently assisted by four students from the School of Social Work, California State University, Sacramento, who are training to be organizers. Other student volunteers—from secondary schools, junior colleges, colleges and universities—are deeply involved in organizing activities. In addition, about 300 members serve regularly in some volunteer staff capacity, mostly in helping to maintain the two field offices (a new one has recently opened in an older community with the highest welfare and unemployment rates in the city), fund raising and in recruiting new members door-to-door. All the organizers receive room and board, and heads of households are given enough to help sustain their families, as the need arises. The fact that many members serve as organizers is regarded as a major reason why CHA is viable. The volunteer organizers and members are backed by a thirty-three-member organizing committee which, although consisting predominantly of low-wage workers, is broadly representative of the community; doctors, ministers, a university dean and students are included.

The financing for CHA, unlike many organizing efforts of the recent past, comes almost exclusively from the local community and that is another major reason for its viability. Although some funds have been solicited from sympathetic groups and individuals in the Sacramento area, the bulk of the money comes from members' dues and special benefits. Bucket drives are pretty much a daily activity carried out by two to ten people strategically placed in major shopping centers around the county. While upwards of $100 a week is regularly collected this way, the process also serves as a means to inform community people about the work of the organization. Indeed, not only supporters but a number of members have been initially contacted in this way. Two benefit dinners have added almost $1,000 to the association's coffers.

The CHA has gathered a mass of statistics to support its organizing effort. Nationally, it points out, there are some 3.5 million people who perform domestic and attendant care services, both in homes and institutions. In most areas, wages continue to average about $1.50 per hour, despite rapid inflation. The average annual income of the majority of domestics is less than $1,000. Only a few have steady, full-time employment. In many ways, attendants are at the bottom of the economic heap. On the basis of total hours worked, live-in attendant care workers average less than 30¢ an hour. While no norms have yet been established for the life expectancy of attendant care workers, the average for domestics is only 52 years.

In the year that the organization has been in existence, a substantial member-benefit program has been established. While it is extremely modest when compared with the benefits offered members of large, well-established unions, the program is remarkable for having been put together virtually without money. To most domestics and attendant care workers, the idea of fringe benefits is new and surprising. Even Social Security payments rarely are collected and sent in.

The benefits provided are job counseling, free legal services, free dental care, medical referral, emergency food, information and a newsletter. A volunteer staff of local attorneys is available to assist members with any legal problems related to their jobs, especially in regard to payment disputes and terminations. Because it is impossible to obtain free dental care locally, an arrangement has been made with cooperating dentists to offer emergency dental treatment. The same volunteer dentists offer many costly follow-up services that are recommended and these are either free or at a fee the patient can afford.

In the area of medical care, there are resources for obtaining such services as X-ray examination for TB, testing for sickle-cell anemia, determination of dietary deficiencies and the like. Because many members work in homes or institutions where people have serious illnesses, this benefit is particularly significant. An emergency "pantry" is always stocked with food for those in need. Staff people (members and organizers) also assist members in securing these services. A general information service catalogues programs which may be of interest to members—adult education classes, job training programs, emergency financial aid, courses in prenatal care and work-study programs. For the most part, these services are provided by "benefits workers" who are trained to serve their fellow members. Finally, the bi-monthly organizational newsletter, *The California Service Worker,* is mailed to every member.

Recruiting is done through door-to-door canvassing. The city has been divided into general target areas, and subdivided into those neighborhoods most likely to contain substantial numbers of low-wage workers: housing projects, older inner-city districts and other areas in which inexpensive housing predominates. Organizers (often joined by volunteer members who live in the area) generally work in teams of six to eight on a saturation basis: house by house, block by block and neighborhood by neighborhood. Wherever possible, follow-up house meetings are arranged for every few blocks. This serves not only as a device for sustaining membership but also as an opportunity for volunteer members to train side by side with organizers and then serve as organizers on their own.

General meetings are held monthly. For many members, their first meeting represents the first chance they have ever had to meet with other domestics and participate in an organization which is truly committed to serving their basic economic interests. A new awareness of what is going on in the community is part of becoming a CHA member. As one woman says, "You work hard all day, and when you get home you have no time for a newspaper and it's too late for the TV news." Where low morale had reached epidemic proportions for most domestic care workers in the Sacramento area, now there is beginning to be a glimmer of real hope.

The basic organizing sign-up device is a "Labor Authorization Form" which each prospective member is asked to sign. It indicates, "I fully understand the benefits of the Association and hereby authorize the Association or designated representative of the Association to act as my agent in any or all collective bargaining sessions authorized by the California Homemakers Association." A fee of 62¢ per month, or $7.50 a year, is charged to each participating member. Perhaps half the members are able to keep their dues payments up-to-date.

CHA won its first major victory last December. At that time, the Sacramento County Board of Supervisors agreed to increase the pay rate for attendant care workers to $2 per hour (from $1.65 per hour), four months before the new state minimum of $2 became law. William Redmond, county welfare director, indicated that he was "quite sympathetic to [the attendants'] demands for higher wages," but he declared that such increases would have to be taken from the budgets of other vital programs. Recently efforts have been made to support this tactic by suggesting (to local public welfare employees' unions) that were the salaries of attendants to be raised, the funds would have to come from the same moneys that would be used to increase the wages and improve working conditions of those employed by the Department of Welfare. This has been flatly denied by the Homemakers. Another strategy used by the Welfare Department in an effort to cripple the organization was to harass the attendants by asking them if they were members of CHA, and reducing or terminating the employment of selected members. A civil rights lawsuit and adverse media publicity temporarily terminated this practice before it had much effect.

One of the major issues of contention between the county, the local Welfare Department and the association is whether or not the attendants are county employees. At first, the county insisted that the domestic workers were employed by individual elderly or disabled recipients who paid them with funds that they received for that purpose from the Welfare Department. However, CHA countered that the funds for the program and conditions of employment were established by the county (through the Welfare Department) rather than by the individual recipient-employers. After numerous hearings and

confrontations with the county supervisors, the CHA scored a historic victory last March. For the first time, household workers won the right to bargain. In a noisy confrontation with the county supervisors attended by more than 400 domestic workers and their blind and disabled welfare recipient-employers, the members established their right to have the association represent them in negotiating individual service contracts with the county. However, the county neatly sidestepped the fundamental issue of whether the attendant care workers are actually its employees. In effect, the supervisors made it possible for the workers to bargain, while trying to withhold the opportunity to do it collectively. But the old system, which the Welfare Department controlled, and in which the recipients in need of care and the attendants who provided it played out a sham of labor democracy, is at an end. The county welfare director responded to this turn of events by noting that one of the results would be "upward pressure on wages." The attendants and their families are eagerly awaiting the fruits of this pressure. At this writing, CHA is engaged in a vigorous wage struggle and the attendants have filed a massive lawsuit to stop large-scale wage and hour reductions—a move taken by the county to halt the organizing effort.

Part of the Homemakers' success to date must be attributed to the quality of the organization's staff and active membership. With great pride members will tell you that more than fifty-five of their number have spoken before the Board of Supervisors. Ambrosine Campbell, 78, one of the early organizers, has done attendant care and domestic work for more than fifty years. At her "retirement" six months ago, she was working fourteen hours a day. She earned $197 a month, the most she had ever earned in her life. In recent years, her wages were as little as $30 a month. A moving speaker, she has addressed college audiences and a wide range of worker and community groups. Hazel Umblas, who was for many years a domestic, must now rely on attendant care herself because of a severe injury suffered while on the way to work. Despite her handicap, she comes regularly to CHA meetings and has developed into one of the association's best telephone liaison people. As she says herself:

If you don't fight these people, they'll keep on taking more and more from you. When friends have asked me why I would sign a lawsuit against the county, the same people who can cut off my aid, I tell them it doesn't matter. If I can't fight, I might as well be dead; you have to fight until there's not a breath left in you!

One of the five original organizers, Minnie Parker has done attendant care, domestic and other low-wage work for more than twenty years. The most she has ever earned is $230 a month, working an eight-hour day, five days a week in the home of an elderly, ill woman. Others heavily involved in the organizing effort include field director David Shapiro, a former Farm Worker organizer; Nelle Christensen, an ex-social worker, referred to by her fellow members as a "fiery" grandmother of five; and President Viola Mitchell who, along with her three children, devotes herself full time to the organizing struggle. In their adherence to the principle, "We must all be organizers," they have developed a collective strength of purpose and a self-confidence that has made them worthy adversaries of the County Board of Supervisors, other public officials and departmental administrators.

Both the association members and the organizers agree that the struggle will be long and mostly uphill. In this light, they take one of their slogans quite literally: "Here to Stay: Here to Win." CHA has announced that it will continue its efforts to bargain collectively for its members on the basis of the agreement reached in March. As Pearlie Alexander, a 62-year-old attendant care worker, recently put it to the County Board of Supervisors: "We'll be back. We'll stay with you until we get what we need, just like a yellow-jacket on a hound!"

EPILOGUE

More than two years have elapsed since this article was written. Although full collective bargaining rights have not yet been established, CHA now has expanded to five "entities" (active local organizations modeled after CHA) located from Orange County in Southern California to Southern Oregon. Although individual groups direct primary attention to pressing local issues, the core of each grass-roots organizing effort is made up of attendant care and other low wage workers. The dogged spirit of the participants—to hang in there and win—remains.

In considerable part, the success of this grass-roots organizing effort may be attributed to certain basic tactics which are reflected in this article and are currently being used in the new emerging groups.

1. Vigorous recruitment of full-time volunteer organizers (who receive compensation that is limited to room and board—except for special or emergency needs), especially college graduate and undergraduate students.
2. Vigorous and continuous recruitment of member-organizers (most of whom live with their families and are compensated on the basis of need and availability of funds). An important part of this is the ideological stance that all members can

—if they are willing to make the commitment—become organizers (who, in
turn, will help train other organizers).

3. The strong, but enormously time-
consuming, emphasis on fund-raising
from the local community. Within this
emphasis, the daily bucket drive—most
often in a shopping center or similar
commercial area—is a basic practice.
Benefit dinners, and other similar benefits are also a regular, if somewhat un-
predictable, source of support. The
basic dues structure ($.62 per month or
$7.50 a year) remains unchanged. And
the ability of members to maintain dues
payments up to date remains a problem
(recent economic improvements have
yet to reach the workers with whom
CHA and its new affiliates are working). Middle-class "friends" of the
groups are an important source for financial contributions.

4. The development of a good, responsive
member-benefits program is a priority
in each location.

5. The saturation door-knocking technique
used in carefully selected areas—by
teams of volunteer-organizers and
member-organizers—continues as an
essential ingredient of organization-
building.

6. In a time of widespread disillusionment,
a strenuous effort is directed at maintaining the commitment and guarded
optimism of the organizers and membership. It has been largely successful.
The sense of being part of a cause or
movement is contagiously present in
every office, and is steadily pushed and
supported by organizers.

7. As multi-racial groups organized
around social class issues (i.e. particularly economic), CHA and its affiliates
have a broad appeal in many communities that would not usually provide as
much support (financial, political, etc.)
to groups that included only a single racial or ethnic group.

15. Methods of Inducing Change

Gene Sharp

SOCIAL INTERVENTION

Methods which take the form of direct
intrusion in social behavior patterns, social

Reprinted with permission from *The Politics of
Nonviolent Action* by Gene Sharp. Hardcover edition: Boston, Porter Sargent Publisher, 1973, 928
pp., $24.95. Paperback edition in three volumes: Part
1 *Power and Struggle,* Part 2 *The Methods of Nonviolent Action,* Part 3 *The Dynamics of Nonviolent
Action,* Boston, Porter Sargent Publisher, 1974,
$2.95, $4.95, $5.95. Porter Sargent Publishers, Inc.,
11 Beacon Street, Boston, MA. 02108. Copyright by
Gene Sharp. All rights reserved.

occasions, and social institutions are
grouped as a subclass of nonviolent intervention. . . .

ESTABLISHING NEW SOCIAL PATTERNS

While social disobedience, a method of
social noncooperation, consists of the refusal to obey various social customs, rules,
regulations, practices, and behavior pat-

terns, another method of social intervention consists of new ways of behavior which may positively contribute to the establishment of new social patterns. These may be unplanned actions by individuals or a series of individuals or groups. Or they may be actions planned as organized opposition. A wide variety of social patterns may be involved. It is, however, easily illustrated with behavior which replaces social patterns of inequality, hatred, or avoidance with new relationships of equality and respect. In the 1830s American abolitionists, sometimes naturally and without deliberation, sometimes as a conscious act, associated with Negroes, who even in Northern cities were normally socially boycotted. Mabee reports that on the proposal of Sarah Grimke, a Quaker, the Antislavery Convention of American Women in 1838 adopted a resolution which stated: "It is . . . the duty of abolitionists to identify themselves with these oppressed Americans, by sitting with them in places of worship, by appearing with them in our streets, by giving them our countenance in steamboats and stages, by visiting with them at their homes and encouraging them to visit us, receiving them as we do our white fellow citizens." Some abolitionists did not approve of such practices, however, either because of a fear that they would provoke violence against abolitionists or against Negroes, or because of an opinion that the issues of slavery and racial prejudice should be kept separate. Among abolitionists the issue of public association with persons of another color was so sharp that there was fear in 1836 that the American Antislavery Society would split on it.

Various abolitionists in Boston, Philadelphia, New York City and elsewhere engaged in "walk-alongs" (as Mabee calls them), in which they simply walked in the streets with persons of the other color, and often the other sex, sometimes arm in arm. This often upset people; the mayor of Philadelphia in 1839 urged Lucretia Mott not to do this because it offended the white rabble at a time when an anti-Negro riot was expected. However, she persisted in walking publicly with people regardless of color. After a meeting the Boston physician Dr. Henry Bowditch invited Frederick Douglass to walk home down Washington Street with him to dinner; Dr. Bowditch was afraid he would encounter his friends but Douglass later said that it was the first time a white had treated him as a man. In 1849 Douglass wrote in his periodical, *North Star,* that the way for abolitionists to remove prejudice was "to act as though it didn't exist, and to associate with their fellow creatures irrespective of all complexional differences. We have marked out this path for ourselves, and we mean to pursue it at all hazards."

Mixed dining during the 1840 annual meeting in New York of the American Antislavery Society met with trouble from a mob, but by 1847 and 1858 similar events were not disturbed. Private individuals "interdined," i.e., ate together in violation of taboos against social equality between their groups. To cope with prejudiced Quakers during a Friends Yearly Meeting, the Quaker Isaac Hooper invited his Negro Quaker guests, Mr. and Mrs. David Mapes, to join him for dinner and told the other guests that if they objected to joining them, they could eat later when the first group had finished. None did. Various abolitionists entertained traveling abolitionists of a different color in their homes. However, in Pendleton, Indiana, a Quaker doctor who had been host to Frederick Douglass during his 1843 lecture tour was driven out of town by a mob. Social equality within abolition societies was not fully accepted; about 1835 the Unitarian preacher William Ellery

Channing, for example, advised against permitting Negroes to become members of such groups. That advice did not prevail, and Negroes held major offices in the national antislavery societies; but as late as the 1840s and 1850s Negroes sensed that they were not fully accepted. . . .

Another variation on this method has been the individual insistence on receiving equal treatment in public facilities, such as restaurants. For example, in 1837 Charles R. Ray and Philip Bell, the general agent and the proprietor of the *Colored American,* traveling up the Hudson on a steamer from New York City refused to have their tea in the kitchen, insisting on service in the dining cabin, even if they had to wait until the whites had been served. Ray and Bell insisted: " . . . we do not like to be the agents of our own degradation." Similarly, until threatened with physical removal, Frederick Douglass, also on a Hudson River steamer, insisted on taking dinner like the other passengers. In Cleveland in 1857, Susan B. Anthony, the woman suffrage leader, and other delegates to an abolitionist convention refused to enter the dining room until a black abolitionist, William Wells Brown, was permitted to join them; the hotel backed down and provided equal service for the remainder of their stay.

A number of these actions are almost identical with activities which have been undertaken in modern India for the eradication of untouchability and achieving communal unity. "Interdining" by people of various castes, untouchables and members of other religions has frequently occurred. Beginning in the 1930s Gora (born a Brahman), the prominent atheist Gandhian social revolutionary, organized intercaste and interreligious dining on a mass scale in India. Everyone brought his own provisions, and the cooking and dining were done without regard to caste or religious taboos, although intercaste dining was prohibited by orthodox Hindus. Special efforts were sometimes needed to overcome the hesitancy of lower-caste Hindus to eat with groups lower than themselves. Intermarriage has also been practiced and even encouraged as a means of ending untouchability. For example, Gora's children have been encouraged on that basis to marry outside the caste barriers, including with untouchables, and have done so.

OVERLOADING OF FACILITIES

Overloading facilities involves the deliberate increase of demands for services far beyond their capacity, so that the operation of the institution (government department, business, social service, and so on) is slowed down or paralyzed. Such overloading may be initiated by customers, the public, or employees of the institution. The objectives may vary and may include improved services, wage increases and political ends.

In 1965 at the Los Angeles County Hospital in California, for example, interns protesting pay policies initiated an overloading of facilities by admitting far more patients to the hospital than existing facilities could accommodate—even persons not needing hospitalization were admitted. This was called a heal-in. The interns' aim was to obtain a better bargaining position with the hospital administration. The hospital was filled with patients within four days, and the action cost the city around $250,000 in increased costs.

A similar case occurred in Massachusetts at the Boston City Hospital in 1967, where it was called an "around-the-clock heal-in." This action was begun by 450 residents and interns at Boston City Hospital on Tuesday, May 16, 1967. The purpose of the heal-in was to dramatize salary demands by doctors at Boston teaching hospitals; at that time the take-home salary of an intern was only sixty dollars per week. The doctors felt that it would be in violation of their oaths to go on strike, so they chose instead to practice "ultra-conservative medicine" in order to over-crowd the hospital. Dr. Philip Caper, President of the House Officers' Association, said: "Everyone gets the best of care," which was ensured by having all the interns and residents work twenty-four hours a day. "Every patient who might benefit from hospitalization will be admitted, and no one will be discharged until he is completely well."

The heal-in was patterned after the similar action at the Los Angeles County Hospital eighteen months previously. The Boston City Hospital doctors began their heal-in as an unannounced experiment on Saturday, with 874 patients in the hospital. On Sunday there were 890, on Monday 924, and on Tuesday at 7 A.M. (after the main action was begun) there were 982. An unidentified doctor stated: "With 1,200 or more patients in the hospital the laundry will not be able to keep up, the kitchens will have trouble getting the food out, the X-ray and laboratory departments will be swamped, and people will begin to listen to our demands . . ." By Wednesday morning there were over 1,000 patients, and 1,075 on Thursday. The heal-in was supported by private doctors and house officers at the other major Boston hospitals. Action was taken only at Boston City Hospital because house officers there had full responsibility for medical procedure, unlike the private hospitals.

Countermeasures by the administration began Tuesday afternoon with an announcement that there were no more beds for male patients, which was disproved that evening by the admission of two more patients. They next tried to influence the chiefs of services to overrride the admittances, which these doctors refused to do on the grounds that these patients were indeed getting the best of care. The administration's final effort was to deny their competence to make salary changes. On the evening of Thursday, May 18, they relented and promised to make salary adjustments. The doctors ended the heal-in voluntarily that night. Observers felt that it was a "safe, effective way of backing up demands for higher wages."

A student version of the method was applied in Japan in 1954. It was the practice in some private universities to admit more students than there were facilities, on the assumption that not all students would attend classes at the same time. The students organized a campaign of "united attendance" as a means of pressure against the university.

STALL-IN

The stall-in is a method that consists simply of conducting legitimate business as slowly as possible. This differs from stalling and obstruction, described in the chapter on political noncooperation, which is action by government employees to delay or prevent the implementation of some policy. The stall-in is undertaken by customers and clients for purposes which are likely to be social, but which may also include economic and political objectives. This method was applied in June 1964 by the Congress of Racial Equality against the Bank of America in San Diego, California, with C.O.R.E. customers taking thirty minutes to transact business normally done in about three. C.O.R.E. was seeking an end to discrimination in the bank's employment practices. In conjunction with the 1938 Harlem Negroes' "black-out boycott" movement, bill payers by the hundreds went to the electric utilities offices, each paying in nickels and pennies.

SPEAK-IN

A special form of nonviolent intervention occurs when actionists interrupt a meeting, church service, or other gathering for the purpose of expressing viewpoints on issues which may or may not be related directly to the occasion. Since the intervention is primarily interference with the social form of the meeting, this method can best be classed as one of social intervention, although it includes psychological and physical aspects also.

This form of action was often used by George Fox and other early Quakers. For example, in his *Journal* George Fox records how one Sunday (First-day) in 1649 he attended the Church of St. Mary in Nottingham, England, (a "steeplehouse," he called it, rather than a church) and was "moved" to speak during the regular service:

Now as I ... looked upon the town the greatest steeplehouse struck at my life ... , a great ... idolatrous temple. And the Lord said unto me, "Thou must go cry against yonder great idol, and against the worshippers therein," .... And when I came there, all the people looked like fallow land, and the priest, like a great lump of earth, stood in his pulpit above. He took for his text these words of Peter, "We have also a more sure word of prophecy, whereunto ye do well that ye take heed. . ." And he told the people that the Scriptures were the touchstone and judge by which they were to try all doctrines, religions, and opinions... Now the Lord's power was so mighty upon me ... that I ... was made to cry out and say, "Oh, no, it is not the Scriptures," ... But I told them it was ... the Holy Spirit, by which the holy men of God gave forth the Scriptures, whereby opinions, religions, and judgements were to be tried.... Now as I spoke thus amongst them, the officers came and took me away and put me into prison, a pitiful stinking place ...

In 1651 at Cranswick, in Yorkshire, one Sunday afternoon, a friend took Fox to meet the local priest, with whom he would talk after the service, which they attended. Fox records what happened:

And he took a text, which was, "Ho, everyone that thirsteth, let him come freely, without money and without price." And so I was moved of the Lord God to say unto him, "Come down, thou deceiver and hireling, for dost thou bid people come freely ... and yet thou takest three hundred pounds off them for preaching the Scriptures to them. Mayest thou not blush for shame?" .... And so the priest, like a man amazed, packed away: ... And so after the priest had left his flock, I had as much time as I could desire to speak to the people, and I directed them to the grace of God that would teach them and bring them salvation. . .

. . .

During the antislavery campaign in the United States, actionists at times interrupted church services in order to denounce the lack of effective opposition to slaveholding, and also the refusal of many churches to accommodate antislavery meetings. Thus Mabee reports:

One Sunday morning in 1841, a determined young Garrisonian, Stephen S. Foster, entered a Congregational Church in Concord, New Hampshire. In a lull in the service he rose and denounced the church for upholding slavery. The pastor asked Foster to stop speaking, but he continued until some of the congregation took him by the arms and led him out. In the afternoon Foster returned to another service and again spoke without permission. This time some of the congregation threw him down the stairs, and he was arrested for disturbing public worship.

. . .

GUERRILLA THEATER

Guerrilla theater, another method of social intervention, means a disruptive skit, dramatic presentation, or similar act. It came to be used in the United States in the late 1960s. The disruption may be of speeches, lectures, or normal proceedings of some group or institution. (The term guerrilla theater is also used for a spontaneous style of stage theater, usually with a political theme.)

Two examples are provided by Jerry Rubin, one of the more dramatic self-styled revolutionaries who emerged in the late 1960s. In late 1967 a conference of college newspaper editors in Washington, D.C., was debating whether or not to take a stand on the Vietnamese conflict:

Someone made a motion to table all resolutions and take no stand. The motion passed. Suddenly the lights went out and across the wall flashed scenes of World War II fighting, burning Vietnamese villages, crying Vietnamese women and napalmed children, image after image. The room echoed with hysterical screams, *"Stop it! Stop it!"*

A voice boomed over a bullhorn: "Attention. This is Sergeant Haggerty of the Washington Police. These films were smuggled illegally into the country from North Vietnam. We have confiscated them and arrested the people who are responsible. Now clear this room! Anyone still here in two minutes will be arrested!"

The editors fell over themselves rushing for the door. . . They believed they were going to be arrested for seeing a . . . film. They believe they live in a Nazi country. They accept it.

Earlier, in August of that year, Rubin and some others had used a similar device to denounce the American preoccupation with money. Rubin and his friends did this at the New York Stock Exchange:

The stock market comes to a complete standstill at our entrance to the top of the balcony. The thousands of brokers stop playing Monopoly and applaud us. What a crazy sight for them—longhaired hippies staring down at them.

We throw dollar bills over the ledge. Floating currency fills the air. Like wild animals, the stockbrokers climb over each other to grab the money.

"This is what it's all about, real live money. Real dollar bills! People are starving in Biafra!" we shout. . .

While throwing the money we spot the cops coming. The cops grab us and throw us off the ledge and into the elevators. The stockbrokers below loudly boo the pigs.

ALTERNATIVE SOCIAL INSTITUTIONS

One of the forms which nonviolent intervention may take is the building of new institutions. When their creation and growth produces a challenge to the previous institutions, the new ones constitute nonviolent intervention. These new institutions intervene in various ways, such as by becoming competitive rivals of the opponent's institutions, by replacing them partly or completely, by providing institutional implementation of the actionists' principles or program, or by increasing the effectiveness of other methods of nonviolent action being used in the struggle. In any of these cases the opponent's institutions will no longer have the field to themselves, and the actionists will have intervened by offering substitute institutions. Alternative economic and political institutions are discussed later in this chapter. The focus here is on social institutions, which of course include educational ones.

It may be useful, however, to note briefly some of the reasons why new institutions may be launched. For example, in a long-term nonviolent struggle a necessary counterpart to noncooperation with certain established institutions may be the building up of alternative institutions, social, economic and political. This is often necessary in order to make noncooperation with institutions controlled by the opponent effective and in order to develop or maintain an alternative social order. Sometimes also this is done in order to prevent "contamination" by the institutions which are opposed, or to fulfill needs neglected by established bodies.

In the nineteenth century, during their resistance to Austrian rule, the Hungarians developed both social and economic institutions to combat the "Austrianization" of Hungary. These included the National Academy of Sciences, the National Museum, and the National Theater, while economic bodies included the Agricultural Union, the National Protective Union, and the Company of Commerce. In 1905 in Ireland, Arthur Griffith developed a comparable Sinn Fein policy of building alternative educational, economic, political and diplomatic institutions for Ireland, built on the Hungarian pattern and designed to restore self-reliance and independence to the country. Gandhi, too, developed the theory of alternative institutions as a crucial part of his constructive program.

Sometimes, however, a resistance movement may select only a few institutions for parallel development. In the nineteenth century the American abolitionists and Negro churchmen, for example, protesting against segregation within the churches, withdrew from them and sometimes established new churches. This is how the African Methodist Episcopal Zion Church was established in 1821.

In addition to privately teaching slaves and free Negroes to read and write, abolitionists and others before the Civil War sometimes established new schools, usually for Negroes but occasionally for an integrated enrollment. In many states both such private instruction and schools were forbidden by law. In breaking up a school for slaves, a grand jury in Lexington, Kentucky, argued that the school would enlighten ". . . the minds of those whose happiness obviously depends on their ignorance." A Negro woman in Savannah, Georgia, taught a black school illegally for

over thirty years; in other cases the teacher went to private homes, as in Petersburg, Virginia. . . . After Quakers helped Myrtilla Miner to establish a normal school for Negroes in Washington in the early 1850s, boys on the street tormented the students, and a mob invaded the schoolroom. Miss Miner, however, "laughed them to shame; and when they threatened to burn her [school] house, she told them they could not stop her in that way, as another house, better than the old, would immediately rise from its ashes." A fire was set in 1860, but the building was nevertheless saved.

Schools seem to be one of the most common social institutions for parallel development, for the remaining two examples refer also to them, in very different circumstances. During the German occupation of their country Polish citizens set up an educational system independent of Nazi control. In 1942 in the Warsaw district alone more than 85,000 children were receiving education in small secret sessions in private homes. Over 1,700 had by that date been graduated from high school, receiving innocently worded cards which were after the war to be exchanged for official diplomas. . . .

ALTERNATIVE COMMUNICATION SYSTEM

Under political systems which have extensive control or monopoly over systems and media of communication, the creation by opposition groups of substitute systems of communication may constitute nonviolent intervention when they disrupt the regime's control or monopoly over the communication of information and ideas. This may involve newspapers, radio and even television. Systems for communication between individuals (as substitutes for the controlled postal or telephone system) may also be involved. Newspapers themselves, or radio broadcasts, . . . are classed as methods of protest and persuasion; but when these are developed as alternative systems of communication on a sufficient scale to challenge the controlled ones, the intervention of these new systems disrupts the opponents' control of these media. These new communication systems then become powerful tools of the nonviolent actionists; and, the opponents' control of communication of ideas and information having been broken, these systems in turn may enable the actionists in the future to resist and intervene in still other ways.

The underground newspaper systems . . . in certain Nazi-occupied countries were on a sufficient scale to constitute an alternative news communication system. This was clearly the case in the Netherlands. The very day after the German invasion the first hand-written underground bulletin appeared, and soon there were more handwritten or typewritten sheets or bulletins, called "snow-ball letters" (which readers were expected to copy and to pass on to friends). Major periodicals developed and grew to have very large circulations, especially considering the repressive conditions under which they were edited, published and distributed. *Vrij Nederland* with its local editions reached a circulation in September 1944 of one hundred thousand printed copies. *Het Parool* began as the first printed underground paper with six thousand copies, reaching a circulation of sixty thousand in 1944, and its daily news bulletins nearly reached a circulation of one hundred thousand. *Je Maintiendrai* grew from a small mimeographed sheet to a weekly which had a circulation of forty thousand in 1945. *Trouw* had a basic circulation of sixty thousand, but there were also about sixty local and regional editions; by January 1945 the total circulation of all its editions and news bulletins was about two million. In 1944 *De Waarheid,* a weekly printed in Amsterdam and Rotterdam, may have reached one hundred thousand copies. . . . With so extensive an alternative system of communication of political ideas, discussion of resistance tactics, and news, the illegal papers clearly rivaled the official ones and prevented the occupation forces from establishing a monopoly for the Nazi-controlled press and censored news reports.

Another type of alternative communication system is more specialized, involving the delivery of information and special messages to particular persons or groups, when the regular media for such communication, like the postal service, telephones and so on, are subject to interception or tapping.

The system of alternative radio broadcasting and television which operated in Czechoslovakia for a full two weeks, . . . is the most advanced development thus far of such an alternative broadcast system operating within an occupied country. It operated longer under those conditions than had been believed possible, but as yet there has been relatively little attention to the technical, organizational and other requirements which might enable such a rival broadcasting system to continue to operate periodically over months or years to assist a resistance movement.

CHAPTER IV

Exercising Influence

Introduction

There is nothing so frustrating as having a good idea that goes nowhere. Community practitioners—organizers, planners, and administrators—are rightly concerned with translating their ideas into action, exercising influence to achieve their objectives.

The context within which the practitioner must typically exercise influence is crucial. First, the decisions one tries to influence often are not subject to precise calculation of costs and benefits, particularly the latter. There is some ambiguity about the merits of one decision over another. Actors are faced with decision rules that leave them considerable room for choice. Second, practitioners who wish to influence decisions typically have no authority to make those decisions. That is, their preferences are not regarded as binding upon others, and they must rely on persuasion, inducements of various sorts, or other forms of influence.

The implications of these contextual features are that (1) decisions are basically in the hands of other people and (2) the practitioner cannot anticipate precisely what decisions other actors will make because decision rules are ambiguous or unstated. Thus, the practitioner who would influence decisions must try to understand the interests and preferences of those he or she hopes to influence. Further, he must seek concurrence with his plans at several independent decision points which he has no authority to control.

There are two basic strategies for exercising influence. One, based on social-psychological theory, endeavors to change behavior (or influence decisions) by affecting interpersonal attitudes. The idea is this: In the context of two or more groups with differing interests, the practitioner tries to deemphasize differences, build trust, increase communication and predictability of behavior, and so on. In the other strategy, derived from political science, influence is exercised through the mobilization and application of power, often by groups with a relative power disadvantage. The basic idea is to threaten one's opponent in a way that is credible. One may threaten others with harm, loss, inconvenience, or embarrassment through such tactics as unfavorable publicity, sit-ins, demonstrations, or work stoppages. In order for the power strategy to be effective, particularly in the hands of people who are at a relative power disadvantage, the group must skillfully manipulate uncertainty and ambiguity. That is, one's opponent must be made to believe that one is really able to carry out a threat, and one's precise objectives and priorities must be unclear to the opponent. Objectives are overstated, opponents are negatively stereotyped in order to maintain internal cohesion, threats are made, and so on.[1]

It is often desirable to combine strategies. For example, labor unions may use a power strategy during organizing and the early stages of bargaining, to be followed by friendlier tactics once they have obtained the concessions they want or in the administration of an agreement, such as the handling of grievances. Saul Alinsky's community organizing efforts often follow a similar pattern.[2]

Overcoming resistance to change is the principal task of the practitioner who would exercise influence. It is useful to look briefly at the means through which influence may be exercised. Banfield's summary is helpful:

(a) influence which rests upon a sense of obligation ("authority," "respect"); *(b)* influence which depends upon the wish of the influencee to gratify the influencer ("friendship," "benevolence"); *(c)* influence which works by improving the logic or the information of the influencee ("rational persuasion"); *(d)* influence which works by changing the influencee's perception of the behavior alternatives open to him or his evaluation of them, and which do so otherwise than by rational persuasion (e.g., "selling," "suggestion," "fraud," "deception"); and *(e)* influence which works by changing the behavior alternatives objectively open to the influencee, thus either absolutely precluding him from adopting an alternative unacceptable to the influencer ("coercion") or inducing him to select as his preferred (or least objectionable) alternative the one chosen for him by the influencer ("positive or negative inducement").[3]

One of the practitioner's primary tasks is selecting a means of influence which is likely to have the desired impact on the target and is also one which the practitioner has the necessary resources to utilize. Possible resources include (1) money and credit, (2) personal energy, (3) professional knowledge and expertise, (4) popularity, esteem, or charisma, (5) social standing, (6) political standing, (7) special position for receiving and controlling the flow of information, and (8) legitimacy or legality.[4]

It is clear that the impact of a means of influence will depend upon the nature of the target. For example, the executive director of a large organization is unlikely to be influenced in his capacity as an institutional leader by friendship or the desire to be helpful to others, but he is likely to take into account positive and negative inducements that affect his organization or career.

[1] Richard E. Walton, "Two Strategies of Social Change and Their Dilemmas" in *Strategies of Community Organization,* Fred M. Cox et al., eds., 2nd ed. (Itasca, Ill.: F. E. Peacock Publishers, 1974), pp. 365–371.

[2] Ibid., pp. 369–371.

[3] Edward C. Banfield, *Political Influence* (New York: Free Press, 1961), pp. 4–5.

[4] Robert Morris and Robert H. Binstock, *Feasible Planning for Social Change* (New York: Columbia University Press, 1966), pp. 118–119.

Also, practitioners will vary in the resources at their disposal. For example, the average practitioner may have considerable personal energy and professional knowledge, but very little in the way of money and credit or social standing. The practitioner who controls substantial public or private funds (e.g., grants) may use money as a resource, and the indigenous leader may have considerable charisma.

Finally, certain types of resources are appropriate (or inappropriate) to particular means of influence. For example, legitimacy may be used to obligate others to act but is hardly necessary in utilizing friendship; being in a position to control information may be important in persuasion or selling but superfluous in applying obligation or friendship.[5]

Although the selections included in this chapter illustrate both basic strategies—attitude change and power approaches to exercising influence—the emphasis is mainly on attitude change. This reflects the social atmosphere of the midseventies. However, a careful reading will reveal some examples of both basic strategies. For example, although Alan Connor and Jaime de la Isla use communication to change attitudes ("Migrant farm workers have the same health needs the rest of us have"), the information they develop and communicate to decision makers also serves as an embarrassment to the director of the local health department, whose resistance to change (the development of effective health services for migrant workers and their families) is neutralized thereby. John Tropman, Armand Lauffer, and William Lawrence, in their discussion of advocacy, include both "partisan" and "accommodative" approaches. Michael McCormick and Don Lau emphasize noncoercive approaches to fund raising in their discussion of their work in building support for "alternative services."

In general, these articles give considerable emphasis to the discussion of techniques that rely heavily on communication skills such as rational persuasion, selling, and to some extent, inducements. Little attention is given to means such as coercion, friendship, and authority. The reason is that practitioners have at their disposal resources which can most easily activate communicative methods of influence—that is, personal energy, professional knowledge and expertise, control over information, and, to a lesser extent, popularity and charisma, while they are generally short on money and credit, social and political standing, and a legal position to command assent.

The practitioner should keep in mind the full range of means and resources. Sometimes it is possible to mobilize a resource that is in short supply by using one that is more readily available, as when through persuasion or selling a practitioner obtains the support of someone with considerable social or political standing or gains control over a supply of funds.

Two particularly fine examples of guidelines for the use of communications skills are to be found in the articles taken from work done by the League of Women Voters. "Anatomy of A Hearing" gives detailed directions for being heard where decisions are being made, and "Elections '74–'76" makes sugges-

---

5. For a full discussion of these and related matters, see ibid.

tions for involving people in the political process, including the use of the mass media. Taken together, we believe these selections can be quite helpful to the practitioner looking for guidance in advocating on behalf of individuals or groups, being heard in the legislative and rule-making processes, raising funds, stimulating political participation, and using information to bring about change.

Fred M. Cox

16. Influencing Individuals and Groups

John E. Tropman, Armand Lauffer, and William Lawrence

A GUIDE TO ADVOCACY

The central question governing the behavior of an advocate in the human service field when negotiating on behalf of a constituent group is this: *Will the action I am inclined to take advance the welfare of my clients or constituency more than any other action I could take?* The question symbolizes what is central to the advocate's mission: that constituent interests are the controlling determinant of any action taken, and that the action taken must be the best possible action that can be taken in light of existing circumstances.

An advocate follows a circuitous route to answer this central question. He arrives at the answer by first asking himself a number of subsidiary questions, such as: *Have I considered all relevant information available to me? Am I predisposed toward an affirmative or negative answer because of extraneous, self-serving interests? Will my action produce a short-term gain but a long-term disadvantage for those whose interests I am promoting?*

The advocate may be motivated by an idealist's vision, but his behavior must be governed by a realist's considerations. He must make every effort to avoid entrapment in an arbitrary position, remaining constantly aware that conditions change. A decision that seems fully justified today may prove inappropriate tomorrow. New evidence is uncovered, or there is a significant shift in the circumstances promoting the decision.

Because of his awareness of the transitory nature of social interactions, the advocate rarely "goes for broke," but remains flexible in his interchanges with others. While he enters the situation with clearly formulated ideas about the housing or transportation program he would like to obtain for older people, he does not present these as "nonnegotiable issues." He knows that the assumption of an inflexible and adamant position runs contrary to the norms of conduct which society expects of those participating in community bargaining and decision-making.

ALLIANCES

When bargaining in the interest of older people, the experienced advocate is ever conscious of the fact of relative strength. Older people comprise a minority grouping. In most communities, they are relatively unorganized. Unless allied with other sectors of the community, they may have little capability for exerting political influence. Effecting such alliance assumes strategic importance for any advocate negotiating on behalf of the elderly. Establishment and maintenance of alliances, however, require that the advocate be flexible in his demands, adapting his ideas when necessary and appropriate to secure the support of needed others.

Experienced advocates know that this is no easy path to follow. Alliances sometimes take on lives of their own, putting their own demands on participants. The requirements of participation in an alli-

Source: Unpublished, John Tropman, Armand Lauffer and William Lawrence, "A Guide to Advocacy for Area Planners in Aging," 1974.

ance may subvert the advocate's original purpose for joining or forming it. Payoffs may be delayed or postponed. One of the greatest challenges an inexperienced advocate confronts is learning how to secure maximum support for the minimum in concessions.

Because of his need for alliances, the advocate is especially attentive to interests that fall within the concept of "the public (or community) interest." Because local perceptions of public or community interests will tend to place importance on certain issues or certain problems at a given point in time, the advocate must always take them into account in his negotiations. To challenge these interests can jeopardize his cause; aligning the interests he represents with the public interest can provide a desirable boost to his cause.

ASPECTS OF ADVOCACY

Four aspects of the advocate role warrant special attention. These include the advocate's: (1) objectives, (2) approach, (3) organizational position, and (4) style. Of the four, only organizational position is relatively fixed. The advocate, in agreement with others, is free to designate the objectives he will pursue, and determine the approach and style best suited for their pursuit.

Objectives

Objective is a conditioning factor, as we will demonstrate. It influences the choice of approach and style.

Area Agency staffs pursue two types of objectives: integrative and redistributive. Integrative objectives refer to efforts directed at securing those rights and services for clients that are mandated under existing law or policy but denied them in actual practice. Denial may stem from: (a) failure of a service provider to operate in con-

formance with the law or declared policy; (b) the ignorance, lack of skill, ill-will or inappropriate attitudes of service providers (i.e., unresponsiveness of service providers to the needs or desires of the aging or to specific segments of the aging population); and (c) unavailability, inaccessibility, or inappropriateness of services. These efforts are called *integrative* because they seek to integrate the needs of the elderly with the stated objectives of the providers of needed services.

The pursuit of *integrative objectives* is often problematic for Area Agencies. Development of means for relating older people to needed services depends on acquiring the cooperation of local service providers. Providers may be reluctant to give this cooperation if the Area Agency is viewed as being in conflict with a provider who is failing to comply with prevailing laws and policies.

Redistributive or partisan advocacy refers to efforts directed at expanding the service provisions available to older people or to segments of the older population with specific unmet needs. Following a redistributive strategy may involve: influencing decision-makers to channel resources they command into services for the aging instead of other competing interests; working with others in recruiting untapped resources for expanding existing services and developing new services for the aging; and assuring that the interests of the elderly are taken into account in the planning and administration of all relevant local services. These efforts are called *redistributive objectives* because they pertain to the redistribution of resources among competing interests. They are called *partisan* because they seek to promote only the interests of a particular population.

Approach

As indicated earlier, the experienced advocate varies his approach according to the objective pursued. At times, he takes a partisan approach, refusing to accommodate to others or modify his objectives at their behest. At other times, he is totally accommodative, seeking to achieve his aims through compromise and cooperation. The approach he takes depends on his and others' judgment of which approach is most likely, under the prevailing conditions, to advance the cause he is representing. The choice between following a conflict-oriented strategy or a cooperative one is dependent on the situation surrounding a particular issue.

When the social environment around an issue is already polarized and full of conflict, a conflict-oriented approach is often strategically sound. For example, in the face of strong opposition to a tax relief bill for older people, it makes little sense for the planner to try to cooperate with the opposition. When realtors organize to oppose zoning changes that would permit the construction of housing for the elderly, then attempts to reach a compromise may have little strategic impact. The point is to win, regardless of the opposition. The advocate must also know when to sit down and make a deal with the opposition, for the best possible tax bill or for the best housing development. In an all-out fight, older people could lose everything. The advocate must know when to use conflict for strategic purposes, and when to avoid it.

In many situations, cooperation is the best approach. When everyone in a community seems to agree that a new recreational facility for older residents is needed, conflict strategies are totally inappropriate. The mayor and the director of the city recreation department, for example, may both endorse the idea. A coordinating committee for the city's Golden Age Centers wants the project. Several social agencies have expressed an interest in providing "loaner" staff if a new facility can be built. Receptive as people are, however, no one in the community is actively pushing the idea. In this environment, the advocate should devise a cooperative strategy designed to bring the interested parties together to find funds, staff, a program, and get the project off the ground.

Organizational Position

Organizational position is a critical factor in shaping an advocate's performance. As a responsible staff member of an Area Agency on Aging, he must conform with the legal and administrative requirements assumed by such a position. Established policies and procedures are fundamental in determining the strategies and tactics he is free to use in promoting an objective. They represent basic considerations that must be taken into account in the choice of objective, approach, and style.

The area planner's normal organizational position is one of operating in the general community on behalf of older people; that is, he operates outside the population of older people he is working for. He is not chosen by old people to represent them. However, the area planner must sometimes work *within* the older population to sell himself and his ideas.

Two specific approaches to this often-neglected "internal" orientation are common: (1) "awareness building," and (2) "selling." Awareness building is oriented to increasing the general awareness by a specific population of those matters over which they should be concerned. This may require "consciousness raising," information sessions, and efforts to encourage older people to come to meetings, to join associations, to participate. Before the advocate planner can work for older people, he must engage in activities that assure their support.

Sometimes the advocate must "sell" his clients or constituents on some solution he has reached on their behalf. The planner may feel he has negotiated the best possible deal on a tax bill or housing project, but his constituents may not be convinced. When the deal is "no deal," it is time to renegotiate. A word of caution: once older people begin to see a planner as their advocate, they may expect him to accomplish miracles. Planners must take care to promise enough—but not too much and never too little.

Style

The vigor with which the advocate presses his case is important to the success of his effort. The planner can choose to come on strong or to be mild. Again, the choice should be a strategic one. For example, if the planner is pressing simultaneously on several issues, a mild approach to the newest matter may secure the best possible results. On the other hand, a robust approach may tell politicians and bureaucrats that the planner and his constituents want this particular goal very badly, and must be taken seriously. The choice between a mild or robust approach is often quite crucial. In the example given above, if the planner wants to get a number of already agreeable community forces behind a new recreational facility, he may choose a strong presentation as a way to galvanize somewhat indifferent people into action. His approach is still a cooperative one. However, the planner may function in a very different way if he is starting a battle with entrenched interests over a housing project. Here, he may decide to use a mild approach to reduce polarization in a conflict environment, if he assesses the impact of polarization to be detrimental to his objectives. A mild approach may be necessary in his appeal to other groups

for support. Once that support is assured, a more vigorous approach may be warranted.

In sum, the choices the area planner makes should always be strategic ones. He may use more than one approach on the same issue, or one approach for several issues. He may use several approaches within the same day, or several with the same people at different times during the day. Whatever the approach, they should always be selected with the view in mind of achieving a planning objective; not just to make a point. Planners should take care not to overuse a single style. Just as a carpenter would not hammer in the same way in putting in hardwood floors as in repairing an antique chair, an area planner must use different approaches and styles in different ways for different jobs. One style or approach, however useful in one circumstance, is never suitable for all circumstances.

SELECTING THE RIGHT APPROACH

The key to successful performance of the advocate role is the use of a variety of approaches to advance the constituents' interests. The experienced advocate will use only those approaches which will advance the interest of older people. The advocate planner cannot afford the luxury of simple-minded "knee-jerk" responses. Such behavior is unprofessional. Advocate behavior is professional only to the extent the advocate realizes he is an actor in a drama in which the finale has not yet been written. He must be resourceful and quick on his feet, able to shift among conflict and cooperation, vigor and mildness, from external to internal efforts, from an integrative to redistributive objective, and vice versa. Such versatility requires deliberation and judgment, but not indecision. At all times the advocate must attempt to maintain a posture of self-assurance and certainty. Such a posture should have its basis in being fully informed on the issues and sensitive to the circumstances of negotiation.

What then are the factors a planner should consider in selecting or shaping his approach to advocacy for older people? The following inventory may be used as a guide to factors to be considered:

1. The nature of the issue.
2. The planner's personal position.
3. The positions of others.
4. The positions of the planner and others on other pending issues.
5. How important or salient the particular issue is to clients in relation to other current and emerging issues.
6. The personalities of the advocates and other actors and how the community views them.
7. The advocate's organizational position and commitments on each issue.
8. The degree of political solidarity and influence of the client group.
9. The degree of public support the issue can get.
10. The extent to which this issue touches on other politically sensitive but tangential issues.

The Issue Itself

How emotional and controversial is the issue in the larger community? Is it highly politicized? Some issues, like tax reduction for older people, may be "hot." Others, like nutrition for the elderly, are not likely to be so emotionally charged. A hot issue usually calls for a milder approach. A cool issue often demands a robust and vigorous approach. Often, in fact, a robust approach can transform a cool issue into a hot one.

If major leaders in the community agree on both goals and the means to achieve them, the advocate should employ a cooperative strategy. If there is disagreement on means but agreement on the goal, the advocate should work to link disparate elements together. If there is not only disagreement on means but a conflict of goals, the advocate will most likely have to rely on a partisan stance and a conflict strategy. There are times, as experienced advocates have learned, when an issue is a subject of intense community conflict and taking no position on the issue is the best strategy.

The Planner's Position

Planners can get "typed." If they always take the same stance, they become predictable, and eventually less effective. Although the area planner must be consistent in his representation of the needs and interests of older people, he should be flexible in his position on any particular issue. He may give up on one issue in order to win on a bigger one. If he does, however, his constituents must understand that they are being wisely represented and not sold out. Never should the planner pursue an issue that can't be achieved, no matter what his personal position is. Changing one's objective or one's approach to reflect the circumstances does not reflect inconsistency. It is the way to be consistent. Consistency is best measured in terms of overall posture and overall success!

Positions of Others

No advocate planner can be successful without an appreciation of objectives. How do others stand on the particular issue at hand? Strongly in favor? Mildly so? Opposed? Indifferent? Are they preoccupied with other issues? Is this a strategic time to push a particular issue, or is it better to wait?

Other Issues

No single issue ever stands in isolation. In any planning and service area many issues are likely to exist simultaneously. Whatever the starting point, the planner may find that it may be better to drop one issue for another. Moreover, because a planner usually has several issues going at once, he may leave a meeting on housing to go to another meeting on transportation, only to find many of the same people involved. The planner must consider the interrelationships of such situations.

The advocate planner must be aware of the effect a particular strategic approach or pursuit of one issue has on other issues of concern to him, so that he can modify his approach when necessary. For example, he may want to adopt a conflict approach to get approval on a senior citizen housing project, and a cooperative approach for a retiree discount on public transportation. But since the city council must approve each issue, the planner may decide to be cooperative on both issues—in order to be sure of getting the discount. The key to his success may be to settle for the satisfactory solution to both issues rather than to pursue a maximal approach on one which may yield total defeat on another.

Importance of the Issue

Strategy and decisions do not rest only on the dispositions or predispositions of the relevant actors. They are also strongly affected by how important the issue is to people. A tax break or a housing project? Meals on Wheels or a discount bus fare? Such priority rankings are impossible to make accurately, largely because older people are seldom sufficiently organized or in total agreement. The advocate for the elderly works for a very diverse population. Nevertheless, choices must be made, and where possible, they should be made in reference to constituent preferences.

If the planner is able to make some sort of priority ranking based on preferences, this information should not be made public at the outset, if making that information public is not to his advantage. Labor negotiators do not start bargaining by telling employers what they will settle for. Nor do employers start by specifying the best package they can afford. Indeed, events as they develop may change the ranking itself. The planner may reserve the most vigorous presentations for the area of greatest salience to the aging. Or like a good negotiator, may feign with a vigorous presentation around a less salient issue so as to compromise on a better deal around a more salient one.

Personalities

Approaches to issues are often affected by the personalities of those involved. However, this seeming "truism" is often less true than thought. The fate of an advocacy effort may be affected by a host of other factors, more significant to the outcome of an intervention effort.

Nevertheless, the planner's personality can greatly affect strategy. For some planners, conflict is natural. Others are comfortable only with cooperative strategies. Some planners are better working within the client group, some at their best outside it. The advocate must know not only his own strengths but also the personal strengths and weaknesses of the others. In that way, he can make maximum use of himself, call upon his subordinates and collaborators when they can be most useful, and build a strategy that takes into account his own personality and the personalities of relevant others.

Organizational Auspices

Planners are rarely independent agents.

They work for and in organizations under various auspices, with different commitments. The planner's organizational auspice influences his advocate role in two important ways.

First, auspice affects his independence. An Area Agency on Aging that is not part of a larger administrative authority is usually able to operate more independently than an Area Agency located in a council of governments or a welfare council. A planner in the latter situation must, in effect, clear his actions with a larger authority before moving ahead.

Second, when an Area Agency is a unit of a larger authority, the administrative interests of that authority, not those of older people, may dictate how the Area Agency advocate must perform. This can lead to goal displacement, where the advocate mistakes victory within the organization as a victory for older people.

However, the situation is not entirely one-sided. There is inherent strength in functioning as a division of a larger administrative authority. It can contribute prestige and added political influence in support of the causes advocated by Area Agency staffs.

Political Power of Older People

Where it exists, or can be concerted, the political power of the community's older people can be a major factor in determining the advocate's strategy. In some places, older people seem able to wield a limited degree of political power on selected issues. Some local affiliates of politically sophisticated organizations such as the National Council of Senior Citizens, and some retiree groups of active labor unions such as the United Automobile Workers, have been able to lobby effectively and to deliver votes to candidates who support their positions. In these situa-

tions, older people's political power can be an important, even a determining factor in the advocate's strategy.

However, these situations are rare. In most communities, older people are not organized to any notable extent. Time after time, political scientists have concluded that a shared chronological age has insufficient force to bind older people together into an effective political coalition. While area planners should work to make the older population more aware of shared problems, they should be aware of the apparent limitations of this age group's political power. Older people seem most effective in the political arena when they can convince political parties, labor unions, and other organized interest groups to adopt their concerns as their own.

Public Support

Thus, the political power of older people is often largely a measure of their popularity and the popularity of their concerns in the eyes of the larger community. Advocates for older people may find powerful allies in the community. While the community is often indifferent to interests of the aging, few individuals and groups are actually organized *against* these interests; to the contrary, everyone is growing older, and most younger people have elderly parents and relatives. Potentially, the interests of the aging are the self-interests of all. The advocate should not hesitate to exploit this self-interest. Programs and benefits developed for today's older people will probably still exist for tomorrow's older people, those who are now young.

Of course, public support does not automatically follow perceptions of self-interest. Advocates must be on the prowl for incidents they can use to generate public support for issues. People who are generally neutral about issues affecting the aging may be moved by a fire in a nursing home, or by the publicity surrounding the plight of some particular older person. If the advocate is ready, he can build such incidents into support for older people in general, and for his program in particular.

Relationship to Other Issues

Any issue can easily become entangled with other issues. While other issues are often related to the planner's concerns, they should nonetheless be kept analytically separate. Frequently, for example, the question of better public transportation for older people becomes intertwined with the problem of public transportation in general. This may happen because the planner links his interest in transportation for older people with the interests of other groups more concerned for better transportation in general. Such an alliance can be effective and necessary, but it may be very costly if the planner is forced to shoulder the burdens and difficulties of the entire urban transportation system in order to help the aging.

CONCLUSION: THE COSTS AND BENEFITS OF ADVOCACY

The benefits of the advocate role are clearly evident. First, contrary to the impression this discussion may have given, an advocate position allows the planner to assume a relatively uncomplicated posture. He can keep choices within the context of that key question: "Will this particular action advance the interests of my clients or constituents relatively more than any other action?" From the advocate's viewpoint, the interests of others besides the aging are of only strategic concern. Other advocates will, or should, be looking out for those interests.

A second benefit of advocacy is in the increased ability to deliver for a particular population. When one's efforts are concentrated, the chances of success are often improved. Human service planners frequently achieve only limited success because they address diffuse issues and tend to be advocates in general rather than advocates for a particular group.

However, the costs in maintaining an advocate posture are considerable and should be well understood. An advocate usually works long days and long weeks. He must represent his clients whenever such representation is necessary, not just during the working day. This responsibility is even greater because timing is so highly important. Once an issue is moving, only the planner may be able to represent older people's positions at the meetings, the conferences, and in private sessions.

A second cost lies in the stress of advocacy. Successful advocacy involves more than pushing constituents' interests at the expense of others' interests. It also involves maintaining a calculating posture toward others. An advocate planner cannot easily relax. He must be ever vigilant, alert for momentary advantage.

Everyone likes to be liked. It is sometimes easier to compromise a client in order to avoid interpersonal stress in a meeting, wanting to be considered a "nice guy" rather than a "difficult person." Yet to be an advocaté requires being a "difficult person" at least some of the time, and perhaps much of the time. Being a "nice guy" to some may result in being a "sellout" to others. Advocates are not always liked, but good ones are respected. Each advocate must come to his own personal terms with this situation. Yet the pressures to modify one's advocate position are both insidious and invidious.

Area planners must be on constant alert against changing from a purposeful advocate into a bland "nice guy." The change too often occurs unconsciously. Planners may spend more time with other planners and human service agency administrators than with the old people themselves—particularly minority and poor elderly. This may be necessary, because agency administrators control the allocation of resources to the aging. However, the advocate is likely to gradually develop greater appreciation for administrators' problems than for the problems of old people.

At the worst, the advocate planner, removed from the pressing interests of his clients, may come to see himself as part of a communitywide human services elite, whose mission extends beyond the narrow partisanship of specific parochial interests. If this happens, his usefulness to old people is severely curtailed.

The possibility of succumbing to "bland boosterism" is perhaps greater among human service advocates than among attorneys. The legal profession, on which the advocate model is loosely based, provides its practitioners with three years of intensive training in advocacy methods. Partisan advocacy is central to the courtroom drama. It is rarely central to human service work. The lawyer is able to avoid taking attacks personally, realizing his oppo-

nent is just another lawyer pressing for advantage for his client. Human services workers have no such rigorous training in advocacy, and so are less well equipped personally for the role. In fact, the norms in many human service professions generally operate in the direction of cooperation rather than redistribution, toward communal, external views rather than internalized client-centered views. This reduces the range of strategic approaches available to many area planners.

For more information on advocacy, see these references:

"Advocacy and Pluralism in Planning," by Paul Davidoff, *AIP Journal,* November 1965.

"Advocacy and Urban Planning," by Marshall Kaplan, National Council on Social Welfare, University of Columbia Press, 1968.

Citizen Participation in Urban Development, vols. 1 and 2, by Hans B. Spiegal, Center for Community Affairs, NTL Institute for Applied Behavioral Sciences, 1507 M St., N.W., Washington, D.C. 20005

"Dilemmas of the Social Work Advocate," by Willard C. Richan, *Child Welfare,* vol. 52, No. 4 (April 1973).

Getting and Keeping People Together, by Alan McSurely, Southern Conference Education Fund, Louisville, Ky., 1967.

"Reflections on Advocacy Planning," by Lisa R. Peattie, *AIP Journal,* March 1968.

17.   Influencing Legislative Bodies: Lobbying

League of Women Voters Education Fund

ANATOMY OF A HEARING

Why vote? Things stay the same or get worse,
  no matter who wins.
If the trash isn't collected, I don't know where
  to complain.
You can't trust anyone in government any
  more.
Nobody cares about what I think or what I
  need.
Nobody listens.

People try in many ways to influence
government—to get someone to listen. Besides exercising their vote in choosing their
officials, they take part in party politics
. . . they vote to choose officials . . . they
write letters to them . . . organize and sign
petitions for changes they want . . . start,
or work with, pressure groups . . . stage
protest marches and parades . . . boycott
businesses or public services . . . even resort to violence.

The public hearing is yet another way to
influence public decisions. A hearing gives
a citizen or a group a chance for person-
to-person exchange. Because it is usually
geared to one issue or one area of concern,
the dialog can be sharply focused. Hearings are a viable and useful part of the
democratic process at every level of government—local, regional, state and national. Here, if anywhere, someone is listening.

WHY HOLD HEARINGS?

Government officials or advisory bodies

Reproduced by permission of the publisher,
League of Women Voters of the United States,
Washington, D.C. From *Anatomy of a Hearing*, ©
1972, pp. 3–15.

hold hearings for a good many different
reasons. Sometimes they really want to
hear from citizens; sometimes the law requires that they do so. Some witnesses are
asked to appear because they can supply
special knowledge, some because they represent a known point of view, some because of their status in the community. Individuals or groups that want to testify can
ask to be put on the agenda. In some cases,
anyone who wishes to be heard can simply
appear during a time set aside for citizen
comment. For example, in many open city
council meetings the presiding officer may
routinely ask if anyone present wants to
speak. Any citizen or group that responds
gets a hearing.

In General, To Communicate. In a
hearing, a citizen has a chance to take part
in a profitable face-to-face experience, if
the real purpose of the hearing is to communicate: to find out what citizens think,
to get expert analyses and data, to highlight the issue for better public understanding. The citizen can learn

What other citizens think and why
What the attitudes of officials are
What facts he has not considered or has not
  known
Where to get more information
What gaps there were in his own statement or
  viewpoint

To Rubber-Stamp. Officials may,
however, hold a hearing merely to substantiate a decision they have already
made. Then citizen opinion may get little
or no consideration. There are often clues
to indicate that the hearing panel is not se-

riously inviting citizens' views and that the real goal is to discourage citizen participation. When these symptoms exist, it's likely that the hearing is just an exercise:

Invited witnesses represent only one point of view.
Questions asked bring out only one kind of response.
Persons giving different points of view are passed over quickly, asked no questions or perfunctory ones.
Public notice of the meeting is short and announcements inconspicuous.
The hearing room is too small to accommodate all who want to attend.

To Inform and Educate. Governmental bodies may also hold hearings to inform the public about an issue. For example, the planning department may hold an open meeting to explain the master plan already approved by the city council. Or legislators may want to educate the public about an issue, so that, when laws are passed or proposals are put on the ballot, citizens will understand the problem and the chosen solutions. Questions and discussion may follow the explanation. Such a hearing, if it is well attended and if citizens have had a chance to study the plan beforehand, may bring about change even in an already approved plan.

To Learn. Some hearings are held to get help in drafting laws or ordinances, to find out whether or not a law is needed to solve a particular problem. City councils or legislative committees may want to find out:

What the dimensions of the problem to be solved are
What kind of law, if any, ought to be drafted
What it ought to contain
What effect a law to solve this problem would have on other areas of concern
How the law ought to be implemented; how it would or would not work

What the social and other costs will be, if there is legislation, and if there is not

Example. The Army Corps of Engineers often conducts public meetings around the country as it searches for solutions of specific problems, like improvements for flood control in certain areas, future water and land resource needs and problems of a river basin, etc. These hearings are open to all citizens. Sometimes the notices outline specific considerations and solicit surveys and reports that may have been made.

Example. A city commission is considering whether or not to change from electing the commission at large to electing from districts of equal population. It may have a committee to investigate. This committee may hold hearings to get citizen views.

To Test Alternatives. Besides hearings related to drafting laws (legislative hearings), some hearings are held to find out what people think about a proposed action that is already authorized by law (administrative hearings).

Example. A new highway is to be built through or around a community. Where should it go?

Example. The citizens have voted money in a bond issue for a new library. Where shall it be built? What kinds of services should it provide?

To Get Feedback. Officials may hold hearings to find out how well something is working, how the administration of a program is filling the need for which it was set up. Or a program is threatened with a reduction or a cut-off. And sometimes hearings are prompted by noisy dissatisfaction with procedures, an excessive number of complaints, or extensive publicity.

Example. A change in location is proposed for food stamp distribution. A clamor begins from those affected and sympathetic organizations. The newspaper runs a series of articles on the problems. The welfare department may respond by holding a hearing.

WHAT ARE THE RULES FOR HEARINGS?

Hearings that are required by law often must comply with certain specific rules: how much notice must be given; where and how notice is to be publicized.

Sometimes such regulations are ignored, but alert citizens can insist upon adequate notice, publicize failure to follow either requirements or traditions about hearings on important issues. Sometimes it is hard to find what the rules are, if any exist. An inquiry at the city or state attorney's office about hearing rules may produce results.

WHO TESTIFIES AT HEARINGS?

All citizens can and should use hearings to make their ideas known. An informal statement by a single citizen can be dramatic and effective. Sometimes the direct, forthright words of one person can begin the process of change.

However, testimony from an organization of like-minded citizens may carry more weight, simply because it represents the voices of many people. But "group" statements run the risk of being bland and general—although they should and need not be—because the spokesman is trying to reflect a broad, general agreement of his organization.

Suppose there is to be a hearing on converting some open space into a site for a city parking lot, and your group objects. What should your group do?

Should you testify? Some questions to consider are:

1. Would it be better to prepare joint testimony with another group with similar views?
2. Would separate but similar statements be stronger? Will yours supply a special emphasis?

3. Do you have an effective spokesman, especially good at answering questions?
4. Can you supply good substantiating data: the opinions of citizens who live nearby? locations and costs of other sites? comparison of open space and parks in your city with other nearby or comparable communities? effect of loss of this open space? who uses the open space area and for what?

Perhaps you may decide your group can be more useful by giving staff or technical assistance to the panel holding the hearing; by getting out a crowd; by publicizing the hearing. Or perhaps you could suggest a survey or sampling-of-opinion poll and offer help on designing and conducting it.

Should you involve others? Whether or not you testify, is the issue important enough to your group to warrant the time and effort necessary to encourage others? You probably know who your friends are on this issue. For most of them, a telephone call to be sure they know about the time and place and an expression that you hope they will appear is all you will need to do.

What if no hearings are scheduled? Let's say you hear about a decision to put a parking lot on an open space area, but no hearings have been held or scheduled. You and others can insist on a hearing so that both those supporting and those opposing can be heard. Approach the chairman of the council, the city planner, the park commission or director, the city manager. Ask that there be a hearing with adequate notice. Work with your media contacts. The news media will usually publicize the importance of a hearing, especially if enough people seem to want one.

You decide to testify. There are many pluses for testifying. It may result in the change you want. It may gain respect for you or your organization if you make an effective statement. The hearing, hopefully your testimony, can highlight the issues involved and thus educate citizens generally about them.

Make the most of the opportunity. Your statement is much more likely to make news if:

The issue is controversial, the testimony and questions lively
There is a sizable attendance, indicating wide interest
New points of view and/or new facts are uncovered

If you are really concerned, you will try to see that at least one of these newsworthy events takes place.

The hearing is a learning experience, not only for you but for the panel members as well. It lets them know what citizens think. An official may learn in some other way that there is opposition or support for a policy or proposal, but he has no way to assess or produce the visible political pressure that a hearing can generate.

HOW CAN YOU BE AN EFFECTIVE WITNESS?

You want to get the best possible mileage out of your effort. Even if you don't convince the panel, you can establish that you are a reliable and useful witness or that your point of view has merit.

Learn from watching and listening to this or other hearings before the same body: What seem to be good points to make? Which witnesses are listened to most attentively? Can you tell why? What kinds of questions are asked? What are the responses and attitudes of the panel members? You can pick up good pointers for now and for next time.

Steps To Follow

How to get on:
Schedule your appearance. Ask to be invited—simply telephoning your wish to testify often will do it.
For opportunities provided for informal statements in some city council or school board meetings, go early enough to get a seat near the front.

Rules:
Find out what the hearing rules are and follow them.

Who writes the statement?
Choose the best person to write the draft. You may need two people—a good writer and the one who knows most about the particular issue. Writing ability and depth in subject matter are sometimes, but not necessarily, found in the same person.

What to include in the draft:
Decide on what you want to include. A short, pithy statement, with attached facts and figures, is more effective than a long, rambling one. See that the attachments follow the pattern of the statement.
Select the most important and telling points. Consider both the issue and what you know about the panel members. Don't put in everything you know. Exercise restraint. You are trying not only to *inform* but also to *persuade.*

What not to include:
Know your panel's attitudes. If your group is part of a national organization and you are testifying on a local issue, you may turn the panel off by explaining the national position and its application to the local scene. Start right off on the local issue.
Avoid cliches and repetitive language.
Don't explain how your organization functions, how it comes to support or oppose issues. The *reasons* should be apparent from what you say—otherwise you are wasting your and the panel's time. Tell what you did: "We made a survey of the library facilities in the high school, the book collection, the uses to which the facilities are put. We interviewed teachers, students, librarians...We found that..." Then highlight the basic findings and what you therefore recommend.

Options for developing your arguments:
Begin with a clear statement of what you sup-

FIGURE 17.1

How to Put the Panel to Sleep

"The Junior Chamber *wishes to take this opportunity to express* its approval . ."
　　Go ahead. Express! "We approve . . ."

"We are concerned that periodically for some time problems involved in voter registration have come to the attention of this committee."
　　Meet it head on! "Over and over you have listened to problems citizens face in registering."

"*It was evident* from our interview with Mr . . ."
　　Better: "We learned from Mr . . ."
"*We would like to ask* how many . . ."
　　You don't need permission. Ask! "How many . . ." (Posing questions that ought to be answered is an effective technique.)
"*We want to go on record as in opposition to . . .*" or "*We want to express our stand in opposition to . . .*"
　　You want more than "to be on record" or to "express our stand." You want something to happen. "We do not approve . . . because . . ."
"*We wish to take this opportunity to thank you for . . .*"
　　Jargon again! "Thank you for . . ."
"The Neighbors for Denton Park Expansion *wish to express their interest in and approval of the city council's announcement of . . .*"
　　Needs pruning. "The Neighbors for Denton Park Expansion heartily favor . . ." and follow by stating simply what the Neighbors approve—surely not just the announcement!

---

port or oppose (avoid overuse of these two words); then offer your reasons. Or start with the reasons and then your proposal.

Make one point at a time with back-up data; or describe the problem as you see it, then how you see the way to solution.

If you oppose a proposal, specify why you think it won't work. For example, if the issue is improved coordination among environmental agencies, you may agree with that overall *goal* but think the *plan* is full of holes. Get off to a good positive start by agreeing with the goal. Then pick out a key sentence in the proposal: "Implementation of flood plain management would be the duty of local authorities." Point out the weakness: "How many local governments are there in the river basin that have the power to establish such zoning? Only four out of twenty (better to say than 20 per cent). How will they cooperate so that regulations will not vary substantially? How will duplication of effort or working at cross purposes be avoided?" The *questions* reveal the holes. If you can give examples of what might happen if Town A did thus and Town B so, so much the better.

If you agree with parts of a proposal but oppose others, begin with the positive. Example: "The legislature has, we believe, taken some important steps in improving its procedures." List them. Then get on to what else needs doing. "The average citizen knows and cares little about the state legislature; sometimes he does not even know who represents him there. Perhaps it needs to become more visible—by TV and radio coverage of floor sessions and of hearings; by . . ." For each suggestion, you might expand on how that particular change could increase visibility and citizen interest.

If you oppose the whole proposal, you still may agree that a *problem exists*. Then you might begin by describing the dimensions of that problem, giving the best data you have. Select carefully the facts and figures you use. Too many may give the panel indigestion. Be careful not to distort by your selection of statistics—your credibility and accuracy are important assets. You may want to draw on them in the future.

Point out consequences of inaction or "inadvisable" action. What has happened elsewhere is good evidence. Possible effects on other areas or on other problems are telling points. For example, a new library site is under discussion. *Where* the building is to go is important. Who used the old building? To whom was it accessible? Did the users live nearby? Are the proposed sites hard for them to get to—transportation? costs? traffic? Has a present-user survey been made? What effect will removal of the library have on the neighborhood?

Form of the statement:

The statement should have a heading that includes before whom you are testifying, the date, your name (and the organization you represent, if any):

TESTIMONY BEFORE
THE CITY COUNCIL
ON THE MASTER PLAN

By John E. Jones, President
Chamber of Commerce
April 10, 1972

Type double spaced, without errors, on one side of the paper. Leave even and adequate right- and left-hand margins. Make enough copies for all hearing panelists, press and media, and ten extra copies for other witnesses and interested observers. Sometimes rules require delivery of copies in advance—usually three or four days—to allow the panel members to read them before you appear. Find out what the rules are and follow them.

Check your statement:

The president, executive committee, or whoever is authorized checks statements made in the name of an organization. You as spokesman are thus protected from the wrath of members who misinterpret the organization's policy or what you said. There can be corrections in language that might be misunderstood or that does not reflect accurately the organization's position.

Informal testimony:

If you plan to speak without written testimony at a city commission or school board meeting, where opportunities for informal views are offered, make an outline of what you want to say. Your views will come off better if you do.

WHO SHALL TESTIFY?

Select the spokesman carefully. A hearing calls for persuasiveness, good delivery, public relations skills. A good voice, ability to think quickly, poise, a good sense of humor, unflappability are assets.

Choose the person early on. Include him in the writing—he should feel easy with the language and format. He may want to make changes to suit his own style. He does not need to be the most knowledgeable member in your organization on the subject matter; for that very reason, he may want to ask some questions.

Speakers develop skills with practice.

Bring in new witnesses. New leadership will not develop if the "old," experienced hands make all the appearances. For the first-time witness, practice before sympathetic critics is useful. The critics should remember that new approaches, individual and different styles of delivery, while they may not be the way "we've always done it," may be very effective. An organization can get in a rut.

FIGURE 17.2

Lively Testimony Makes News

An old ploy, but effective. A woman appeared before a city council to complain about the pollution of a stream that ran by her home. In her own words, without other facts or figures, she said the stream was dirty, and produced a quart of water dipped from it. She insisted that the stream be cleaned up!

Leading up to a climax. One organization, before testifying for public and nonprofit housing, conducted a tour of areas where such housing already existed, was being constructed and was proposed. Its members telephoned and paid for an ad in support of the most crucial site, giving the hearing time and place. They urged those who were to benefit to come. There was a crowd.

Just the facts. Another group, checking a local annual recreation budget, found that a sizable amount of money seemed to be missing between one bank account and another. It testified before the recreation board. The result of publicity over this newsworthy fact—a state audit and tighter bookkeeping procedures.

WHAT ABOUT THE QUESTIONS?

Be prepared to answer questions. You may want someone to appear with you to help you answer. Heads of agencies routinely are attended by staff. There is no reason why citizen groups should not use similar techniques.

Questions from the panel are often a compliment. Your input is important, or the panel wouldn't bother. Even if some questions seem hostile, at least you are important enought to elicit them. You will win points if you are cool and collected under fire.

On the other hand, no questions may mean that the panel agrees with you or finds your testimony compelling.

If you cannot answer the question, say so. Or say you will get the information for the panel, if you think it possible.

You might be asked, "Would your organization support *this* change in . . ." Here you must be careful. You may not be sure. If you are absolutely certain, yes or no, say so. If you are not sure or think the proposed change deserves careful weighing, say that your organization would want to consider it to see what the implications or effects might be.

WHAT CAN YOU LEARN FROM HEARINGS?

Observe as well as participate. What should you look for? The following list may help:

1. Which panel members are present? which absent? If you have been present for more than one day of hearings, are some consistent absentees? always present?
2. What kinds of questions does each panel member ask? Do they indicate special interests or concerns? Keep track.
3. Who or what organizations testify? on what issues? with what points of view? Are certain kinds of questions asked consistently of certain groups? If so, can you determine why? Are there variations in the reception given witnesses?
4. Who are your potential allies? on what issues? For those with opposing views,

can you determine why they differ? (You may already know, but you may get additional useful clues from careful observation.)
5. What kinds of issues draw a large audience? Why? Is the attendance because of wide-spread interest or strong emotional feeling? in response to efforts for a large number of bodies there?
6. Was the room chosen for the hearing big enough? Or was the interest in the issue a surprise to the panel? Who comes to listen? Does attendance differ according to the issue? status of witnesses? stature of the panel?
7. What indications do you see of effectiveness of hearings? (Keep notes.) What happens as a result? Nothing? A change? If a change, because of what aspect of the hearing—size and nature of the audience? status of witnesses? cogency and/or amount of testimony in favor of the change made? some dramatic incident? news coverage?

Consistent monitoring and reporting of hearings or meetings can provide useful data for either an individual or an organization. The data can be thermometers for timing action on an issue. They can indicate best possible points to make in subsequent testimony or campaigns and in selecting materials to highlight issues. They offer clues for approaches to individual officials and to those in the community who support or oppose your views. From both the hearings and media reporting, there are tips on what is newsworthy.

NEED BANDAIDS FOR EMERGENCY USE?

You want, of course, to put your organization's best foot forward. Unless you are a veteran spokesman, the approach to your first experience may be like a visit to the dentist—the worst part—the anticipation. Keep remembering that here is your chance for a face-to-face exchange, much more satisfying than writing or telephoning. Remember that you have a right to be heard.

As in any other venture, the unexpected can happen, and sometimes does. The panel chairman may suddenly notice that time is running out and announce abruptly, "The last three witnesses (you are one of those) will be limited to three minutes each." You were scheduled for 15 —so cut! You can present the full statement "for the record" or "for the committee's use." The reason for the lack of time may be that earlier witnesses took more than 15 minutes each—or the panel asked questions and got speeches instead of succinct answers. (Sometimes the first paragraph or two of a statement can be a short summary of the principal thrust you want to make. When the time is short, you can use just the opening.)

So you spill the glass of water at the witness table over your testimony. There are extra copies; don't panic. If not and you don't have a handy extra in your brief case, while you're mopping up the water, ask the panel if one of its members will lend you his "dry" copy.

Or the microphone you're to use doesn't work or stops in the middle of your remarks. Raise your voice! If you're sitting, stand up and proceed; your voice will carry better. Don't spend five minutes of your time fiddling with the equipment, unless you're an electronics expert.

The speaker just ahead of you makes a point in almost the same language of a paragraph in your testimony. Take advantage! When you get to that place in your statement, say, "Mr. Peters has already expressed very well that . . ." and abbreviate what he said. You will get points from the panel, and from Mr. Peters, for having listened.

One witness before local boards and commissions, becoming a veteran and liking the experience, had these comments to make:

On fringe benefits: "I was awarded a tuition-free two-year course in how to give public testimony."

On a particular hearing: "This hearing was the only one which had limits on speaking time, but unfortunately they didn't apply to the department's own witnesses."

On effectiveness: "It is very hard to gauge the effect of testifying. Sometimes there is an immediate vote, sometimes questions are asked, sometimes action is postponed. Sometimes the committee sits unmoving through a whole hearing. However, as far as I can tell, their eyes are usually open."

As a witness, you will learn from your experiences, too. You may see ways to improve the hearing process, to make it more accessible to citizens, to make committees and commissions and government more responsive to what citizens think. It is a vehicle for participation. It can be made a more responsible bridge than it is between people and their governments.

And remember . . . somebody may be listening!

18.   Influencing Financial Resources: Raising Funds

Michael McCormick and Donald Lau

LOCAL MOTION: RAISING FUNDS FOR ALTERNATIVE PROGRAMS

WHAT IS LOCAL MOTION?

Local Motion, Inc., located in Ann Arbor, Michigan, is a nonprofit cooperative organized to raise funds and advocate for community-based and alternative human services (i.e., services which are client and worker controlled, and which are less bureaucratic and more personalized than established human services). Its primary fund-raising method is a 2 percent voluntary community tax which is collected through sympathetic local businesses. Many of these businesses are patronized by those who benefit from the nonprofit services supported by Local Motion, or who agree ideologically with Local Motion. The types of businesses include food co-ops, natural food restaurants, and a variety of stores that sell products particularly appealing to young people and college students. The member organizations and beneficiaries of Local Motion are community based and alternative human services such as free health care clinics; child care centers; alternative counseling programs for young people, runaways, and drug abusers; women's services and publications; food co-ops; and legal services for low-income people.

These human service organizations comprise the bulk of Local Motion's membership. The remaining members consist of the collecting businesses and interested

individuals from the community. Criteria for membership include nonprofit status, a commitment to nonhierarchical structure, and a willingness to open the organization's financial records to Local Motion. These criteria apply only to human services: membership is granted to businesses and individuals on the basis of the desire to become involved.

The individuals who work with and support Local Motion, and those whose needs are met by the member organizations, consist primarily of young people in their twenties, many of whom have attended college. A large number of these individuals are low-income people, and the vast majority are struggling economically. Our support community also includes many children (from preschoolers to high school students), the aged, some third-world people, and people from the university community (i.e., students, professors, and other university employees). Most of the support Local Motion receives is given on the basis of ideological allegiance, which embraces people of all socioeconomic backgrounds, ages, races, and sexual preferences. While we recognize that community tax programs such as Local Motion initially attract mostly young, college-educated people, we are constantly striving to broaden our support to include all sectors of the community.

Local Motion and the community tax concept are not unique to Ann Arbor. Local Motion is modeled after similar organizations, including: the Philadelphia People's Fund; Sustaining Fund of Cham-

Source: Unpublished, Michael McCormick and Donald Lau, "Local Motion: Raising Funds for Alternative Programs," December 1975.

paign County, Illinois; Community Meeting and Sustaining Fund, Eugene, Oregon; Denver Sustaining Fund; Alternative Community Tax, Austin, Texas; and Common Sense, Washington, D.C.

Although the programs in these places are based on the same community tax idea, the specific structure and function in each location are geared to the needs of each community. For example, the Denver Sustaining Fund is responsive to the needs of Chicanos, as there is a large Chicano population in the area. In Ann Arbor, Local Motion is geared to the alternative services community. This is to say that all the issues faced by Local Motion are not common to all community tax programs.

WHY LOCAL MOTION?

The primary function of every government should be to serve the needs of its constituents: needs for decent housing, wholesome food, humane medical care, relevant education, loving child care, compassionate crisis intervention and counseling, free exchange of information about community and world affairs, and the nurturing of a full and varied cultural environment to enrich and fulfill the lives of its people.

These institutions should promote the vision of a community where services and a high standard of living are available to all without regard to race, sex, age, social class, or sexual preference. These institutions should be controlled by those who work within them, and by those whose needs they meet. People's needs should be met, fully and equally, without regard to profit potential.

Institutions which meet basic public needs but at present cannot be self-sustaining without undue hardship to staff members and clients should be supported by public funds through taxes. To date,

city, state, and federal governments have not recognized their responsibility in this critical area. This deplorable situation leaves but two options open to community institutions: they can fold, or they can develop alternative sources of funding independent of the shifting sands of established government.

Local Motion, Inc., is an attempt at establishing alternative funding for use in sustaining community institutions, fostering the development of needed institutions until such a time when they can gain access to government dollars. In this manner Local Motion is supporting the efforts of politically and socially deprived people to gain control over their lives. It is also a means of bringing community groups together to plan for their individual needs, and the needs of the broader community.

In this country, money is a rough equivalent of power. Local Motion is a step toward gaining both. As various groups work together to raise funds which are then used to strengthen member organizations and provide seed money to meet community needs, the scope and power of the allied organizations and their constituents grow. Further, when a wide spectrum of institutions with similar perspectives ally financially, raising and distributing funds as one, unity among them is built in practice, and in unity there is strength and power.

Local Motion is an advantageous development in many ways: (1) It can increase commerce and exchange among various groups, thus decreasing the political isolation that alternative and community-based services have faced. (2) It can reduce the divisive, competitive approach of human services in raising funds, as all member organization's books are opened to Local Motion. (3) As unity develops, members can better create strategies for pressuring the city and the county to devote a more significant proportion of their resources for meeting human needs.

Local Motion is a cooperative whose member organizations, businesses, and individuals participate in its activities in order to help improve the quality of community life. Local Motion is nonpartisan politically, with no direct links to existing political parties. However, Local Motion is opposed to the political concept of profiteering because of the human inequities inherent in our profit-motivated economy. The members of Local Motion agree that the needs met by community institutions, and the process of meeting them, are inextricably tied to our political and economic system. Local Motion is committed to action in any sector of the political arena it deems necessary to move our society closer to the collective vision its members share.

HOW IS THE COMMUNITY TAX COLLECTED?

The actual implementation of the Local Motion community tax program is still in its formative stages. Our Business Collective, which is responsible for the actual mechanics of the program, is still in the process of experimentation and is constantly looking for new and more efficient means to improve the process. The difficulty of gauging the success of our approach requires us to be open to whatever feedback we receive. Accordingly, we must be flexible in adopting alternative strategies.

When Local Motion was ready to start collecting the community tax in February, 1975, its Board of Directors gathered together a list of businesses in Ann Arbor which it felt would be sympathetic to the kinds of things Local Motion is attempting to do. Businesses considered included: food cooperatives; alternative product or "hip" businesses; natural food stores and res-

taurants; and businesses whose owners or managers are in sympathy with our ideas. This process continued through Local Motion's early months of operation. Local Motion initially had one collecting business (People's Food Co-op). As Local Motion's visibility in the community has grown over the past nine months we have found that various businesses are now approaching us to collect the tax. Presently, Local Motion has approximately fifty collecting businesses.

There are two major selling points Local Motion has used in enlisting the businesses to collect the tax. The first selling point is the idea behind Local Motion: the fact that the dollars collected would be disbursed to alternative human services in the local area which are in dire need of funds. This is an opportunity for local businesses to give something back to the community which supports their operation. The second selling point is Local Motion's advertising for businesses that collect the tax. Local Motion has run display ads in several local newspapers indicating which businesses collect the community tax. Display ads give the businesses and Local Motion exposure and the reader information on how to support Local Motion. The effectiveness of these display ads is uncertain. Local Motion also advertises its supporting businesses through community events.

The Local Motion community tax or "action pledge" is a 2 percent tax on the cost of the purchase. It is a voluntary tax which need not be paid by the customer. There are three systems through which the tax is collected. Usually a business employs the system which best fits its capacities. Local Motion has found some systems to be highly effective, though we are still seeking a system that provides high financial reward with less effort.

We presently use two systems of collecting the tax which we feel are effective. The first is to have cashiers ask customers if they support Local Motion and would like to contribute to the tax. People rarely give unless asked. This also personalizes the tax and allows the customer to ask about Local Motion if not familiar with the organization or give feedback which is vital to Local Motion's growth. This system produces the largest amount of revenue. The second is to have a separate line on the customer's invoice to list the tax. We have observed that people either do not notice the tax or do not bother asking about it. However, this system also allows for communication between the business and the customer if they choose. It must be made clear that the tax is voluntary even though it appears on the invoice. This method brings in our second largest amount of revenue.

The third system, and by far the least effective, is the cannister. Approximately 70 percent of our collecting businesses employ this method. It resembles the "March of Dimes" approach where a cannister is placed next to the cash register and customers drop in whatever amount they wish. This system is not effective because customers: (1) are not verbally or visually approached to contribute; and (2) may not notice the cannister depending on how prominent a place it occupies. The cannister approach may add visibility to Local Motion because they appear in a number of businesses and are identifiable by their orange color and the Local Motion logo. This system is popular among businesses because it involves the least work on their part. Eventually, we would like each business to have their cashiers ask each customer or have the tax appear on their invoices.

The process by which receipts are brought to the office has presented Local Motion with a number of problems. There

are basically two ways this is done. First, volunteers go to the individual businesses using cannisters and pick up the money. The problems with this system are: (1) we cannot get enough people to cover these businesses; (2) these collections are usually small and tend to discourage our collectors; (3) it is difficult to get people who are consistent in their collections; and (4) there is not enough communication between the businesses and the people who collect the tax for Local Motion. Second, approximately ten of our businesses send Local Motion a monthly check in the mail. This is by far the smoothest method and usually brings in the largest sum of money. The reason most businesses do not employ this method is that it involves extra work on their part. Eventually, we would like every business to employ the mailed check system.

DISBURSING THE TAX

It is important to note the process by which Local Motion recycles community funds. The idea of recycling reusable resources (i.e., money) is central to the philosophical base of the organization. Funds are collected via the community tax, as explained above, for the purpose of redirecting those monies back into the community at points of great social and financial need. To complete the recycling process, the disbursement of funds picks up where the collection of funds stops. This may seem elementary, but by ignoring this concept, established government fails to view tax collection and allocation as mechanisms for meeting the basic human needs of their constituents. Instead of returning the taxpayers' money to them in the form of badly needed services, governments too often take money from taxpayers and pass it on to corporations and other monied interests in the form of business district redevelopment projects, wider streets, land acquisition, and beefed-up government administrations. While it is true that such allocations result in some money trickling down to low-income people in the form of a few more poorly paid jobs, limited improvement in inadequate public services and increased availability of loans (for which many low-income people cannot qualify financially), the amount is much too small to meet the basic needs of such people. It is obvious that the greatest effect of such a system of allocation is not felt in the areas of greatest human need. Rather, the "haves" receive the bulk of the benefits, and the "have nots" get the residue. An effective way of meeting basic human needs is by greatly increasing direct allocations to services that meet the needs of low-income people. Local Motion's concept of recycling resources includes such direct allocations; whereas, the tax system maintained by established governments leaves obvious and painful gaps in the allocations to the community. A recycling system, if it is to justify its process, must redistribute resources at the points of greatest need. Therein lies the difference between Local Motion's recycling system and that of established governments.

The form used by those applying to Local Motion for funding was devised by a task collective within the organization. Volunteers for that collective were recruited from the general membership on the basis of individual interest in the task. Further ideas for creating the application form came from informal conversations among the members and written proposals and suggestions from individuals in Local Motion and from the community.

When the collective met to draw up the application form, the organization's constitution and policies were used as guidelines. Reaching decisions by consensus, the task collective completed a draft of the application form and it was taken to a board of director's meeting for review and approval. After consideration and approval by the Board, a final draft was printed and made available to all eligible organizations.

The form has two parts: a cover sheet and the application itself. The cover sheet delineates the funding regulations and criteria for funding. The most salient regulations are as follows:

1. All organizations applying for grants or loans must be Ann Arbor based and controlled.
2. Loans and grants are given by Local Motion with the understanding that the recipient organization will make every effort to achieve and maintain financial self-sufficiency.
3. A minimum of 30 percent of Local Motion allocation must be loans.
4. Decisions on funding will be made on the basis of comparative analysis of all the applications.
5. Organizational members in good standing can apply for grants or loans from Local Motion. An organizational member in good standing is any organization that has had an elected representative on the Board of Directors for at least six months and which has conscientiously fulfilled the responsibilities of membership. These responsibilities include:
   a. Having a representative attend at least every third Local Motion Board of Directors meeting.
   b. Having had a representative work for Local Motion an average of eight hours per month for the six months preceding the disbursement.
6. "Seed money" applicant organizations should be cooperative and community controlled or they must list steps taken to make the organization thus.

7. Every organization which submits an application for funding must endorse the Solidarity Clause. This is a statement that asks application organizations to recognize the financial inability of Local Motion to fund every organization that requests funds, and to pledge continued support of and participation in Local Motion regardless of the disposition of funding applications.

The criteria for funding can best be explained by the following:

Local Motion sets priorities in its disbursements along three dimensions: the kind of organization applying, the type of support requested, and the length of time for which support is requested. The following is the system of determining the priorities for funding applications. The lower the number, the higher the priority.

This system represents a general consensus of Local Motion members on the issues of life priorities and type and length of support. However, this system of priorities is subject to the widest possible interpretation based on an assessment of:

1. The type of constituency served, and its relative need based on its access to other means of support; the extent of oppression based on class, race, age, and sex; and the strategic placement of this constituency in the community, i.e., its ability to organize for and execute social change of the sort the Local Motion Board of Directors favors.

2. The extent to which the funds applied for would be used in a program that deals with the basic causes of social problems as opposed to the consequences or effects of the problem.

3. The extent to which the applicant organization:

a. Is comprised of members who face the problems directly rather than indirectly.

b. Has a system of constituent accountability and involvement in decision-making.

c. Attempts to reach out to the greater Ann Arbor community.

d. Encourages self-reliance among its constituents rather than fostering dependency on persons who have traditionally held positions of authority.

4. The merits of the specific proposal.

5. The past performance, if any, of the applying organization in assisting Local

Kind of Organization:

1	2	3
Food	Education	Culture
Health	Advocacy	Transportation
Mental health	Information	Entertainment
Child care		
Legal services		
Housing		

Type of Support:

1	2	3	4
Low-interest loan	No-interest loan	One-shot grant	On-going grant

Time:

1	2
Six months	Twelve months

Motion and other member organizations and the community.

6. The extent to which an organization has attempted to act upon previous recommendations given it by Local Motion.

7. The number of projects of a similar nature already funded by Local Motion.

8. The extent to which an organization provides essential assistance to its constituents in working for social change.

The funding application itself asks for identifying information, an explanation of the organization's goals and political philosophy, detailed responses to the funding criteria described above, a description of what is being requested and for what purposes, and complete budgetary information including a statement of other funding sources, both actual and potential. There are additional questions directed toward "seed money" applicants to determine, among other things, their financial and legal status and the need in the community for their proposed projects.

Through Local Motion media efforts, the people in the community are informed that all funding applications are available for inspection. Local Motion invites feedback on funding requests from all segments of the community before and during the actual disbursement.

Local Motion community tax dollars are released semi-annually to organizations which submit applications and receive approval of a grant or loan. All Local Motion policy and funding decisions are made by the Board of Directors at meetings open to everyone in the community. The Board includes individuals representing various sectors of the community. The percentage breakdown of the Board according to the constitution is as follows: 50 percent member organizations; 25 percent supporting businesses; and 25 percent individuals. The decision-making

process follows our philosophical ideals of community involvement and collectivity. It is vital to the success of Local Motion that business be conducted in the open, with everyone participating. Local Motion uses local media resources, its monthly newsletter, flyers, and word of mouth to insure that the community is aware of Board meetings, disbursement meetings, community events, and general information necessary for an educated community. With few exceptions, a three-fifths majority of a quorum is required for decisions although we strive for group consensus. The community tax, in theory, allows for taxation with maximum representation. There is no one group or person in control of the funding decision, but rather a collective spirit.

In order to get a better grasp of the actual mechanics of Local Motion's funding process it may help to analyze our initial disbursement meeting. In preparation for the meeting, the organization faced a number of problems. The first was assuring a quorum (three-fifths of the eligible voting members) so we could make decisions. Getting warm bodies to a meeting is tough!! Second, we had to make sure the meeting would run as smoothly as possible without inhibiting participation and the resolution of issues. We developed a handout of procedures laid out in the constitution and set by past Board decisions. We were prepared with documentation to answer any policy questions Board members might have to assure that procedural disputes did not get in the way of decision-making.

The meeting lasted approximately five hours. The Board reached a nearly unanimous decision on the final funding package. The meeting ran rather smoothly. Organizations were given an opportunity to clarify questions regarding their applications. The two people chairing the meeting had a detailed knowledge of the rules of procedure, but combined it with enough leniency to allow flexibility without disorder. Representatives from applicant organizations and Board members were objective, yet not impersonal. A major factor accounting for the smoothness of the meeting and the cooperation among those present was the fact that the amount of money Local Motion had to disburse was almost equal to the amount requested. There were only three applications for funds out of twenty-one eligible organizations. We cut one proposal by $50. Local Motion expects future disbursement meetings to be much more complex because of a greater number of member organizations submitting funding applications.

There were a number of problems during the disbursement meeting, although three major ones stand out. First, as Local Motion is basically a volunteer organization there is relatively high turnover among Board members. This creates a problem of continuity. Newer members were not familiar or in agreement with certain Local Motion policies. We found ourselves backtracking and trying to explain why certain rules were followed. This hampered the process considerably. Second, some applicant organizations are not skilled in writing proposals that are tight and self-explanatory. It was necessary for them to elaborate on many points, especially financial matters, because the information was not clear as written. One important result of this is that Local Motion recognized the need for workshops on grant writing and will set these up in the future. Third, the constitution worked against us. It was not sufficiently flexible. When constitutions are written they should be flexible enough to allow for changing situations. Constitutions should be written so the governing body has the power to make and interpret policy without overhauling the constitution.

Local Motion still has a lot to learn about its process for disbursing funds. With each disbursement the process will improve and eventually we will be able to live up to our ideals in recycling community funds.

CONCLUSION

Collectivism is at the core of our community tax program. In order to insure citizen participation in our decision-making process, we maintain a nonhierarchical structure within the organization. With the exception of a paid coordinator, the program is sustained and controlled by volunteers who represent the member organizations, some participating businesses, and the general community. Through this voluntary community input, we strive to realize the ideal of taxation *with* representation. We emphasize the fact that the community tax is voluntary, that people can choose whether or not they will cooperate to help support alternative and community-based human services. The tax program demonstrates how the community can decide, at the grass roots level, the way its tax dollars are spent.

The community tax also sets an example for channeling public funds in new directions. It stresses the necessity for new priorities in meeting community needs, away from commercial/industrial and toward basic human needs, especially those of low-income and other oppressed groups. It is hoped that the long-term effect of recycling funds back into the community through the tax program will be a shift in public priorities. The idea is to redirect the funds collected to those parts of the community with the greatest financial need. The recycling process can raise awareness of problems and thus help change government funding priorities.

Local Motion's fund-raising efforts do not occur in a vacuum. An equally important component of the program is community education. The community tax is used as a tool to educate the community about the basic needs of low-income people and other disenfranchised groups (i.e., women, gays, youth, third-world groups, etc.). Our community education work also involves calling attention to the funding needs of alternative and community-based human services, and acting as an advocate for those organizations before the government and various community groups. Furthermore, the mere existence of the community tax shows the community how its local government is failing to meet the basic needs of its constitutents.

Our educational efforts also include a push toward political unity. This can happen on two levels. On one level, the community tax program creates a united political front for those human service organizations that actively cooperate in the program. This becomes an interest group within the community which, by virtue of its strength in numbers and its shared control over information concerning human service needs, possesses a certain amount of political clout. On another level, the tax program draws support from diverse political factions in the community (i.e., from Republican City Council members to leftist students), and thus provides a point of agreement and a forum for communication on tax, human service, and other community issues. Both levels invite communitywide consideration of the total human needs of the community, and thus a more integrated, ecologically sound attitude toward the quality of community life.

19.   Influencing Elections

League of Women Voters Education Fund

ELECTIONS '74-'76

INTRODUCTION:
TURNING PEOPLE ON

Are Americans fed up with today's politics and politicians? The upcoming elections give citizens their big chance to act on their ideas and opinions—in the political campaigns, in support of candidates and issues, in the voting booths. In 1974, voters will go to the polls to choose one-third of the Senate, all the members of the House of Representatives and two-thirds

Reproduced by permission of the publisher, League of Women Voters of the United States, Washington, D.C. From League of Women Voters Education Fund, *Elections '74-'76 Community Guide,* © 1974, pp. 1–12.

of the governors, in addition to thousands of state and local officials. In 1976, the bicentennial year, voters will elect a President and Vice President and have another chance at the U.S. Senate and House, the state houses and city halls.

Will more voters turn out than in 1972? In that year, only 56% of voting age Americans actually cast ballots, a far lower percentage than in other democratic countries. In the last half century, the highest level of voting in a U.S. presidential election was only 64%. In non-presidential years, even fewer voters turn out for congressional and state elections. In local elections, the figures are lower still. Millions of citizens never even register to vote. The poor, the uneducated, the elderly, and minorities like blacks, Chicanos, and Indians— those citizens who might have the most to gain by change— register and vote in even smaller numbers than other groups.

Why don't they vote? Some think that their vote doesn't make any difference (though a few hundred votes have frequently made dramatic differences in American politics). Others find all the candidates equally unattractive or unacceptable. Many don't understand the issues involved. Some citizens don't care enough to take the trouble, or simply are not able to hurdle all the technical and administrative barriers to registration and voting. Others can't cope with the complexities of the ballot and don't even want to try.

But the problem runs even deeper than this recital suggests.

American citizens are turned off and tuned out. They no longer believe that their nation is run of, by and for the people. While disaffection with politics is nothing new in American life, the upheavals of the sixties, the events of "Watergate" and the problems of inflation and energy, appear to have deepened apathy into alienation. For too many citizens, disinterest in politics has become outright distrust of the political process, of politicians and of government officials.

Recent surveys of public attitudes have uncovered a "veritable floodtide of disenchantment" with government. Over half of those polled in a 1973 Harris study expressed feelings of alienation, cynicism and powerlessness; three-fourths believed that "special interests get more from government than the people do." In a nation-wide Gallup poll in the spring of 1974, only 25% approved of the way the President is handling his job and only 30% gave Congress a vote of approval.

As Americans' confidence in their government has declined, so has their participation in the political process. Citizens have opted out, forgetting that their aloofness from politics makes corrupt, secretive government possible and that their active, articulate participation is essential for open and responsive government.

What's to be done? The traditional methods of increasing citizen interest and getting out the vote simply won't work any more. In the current crisis of confidence, the same tired old techniques are not adequate to overcome the negativism, confusion and frustration among potential voters. Nor are they sufficient to counteract the influence of special interests inside and outside the parties. Citizens need to think not only that their votes count, but that their participation in the political life of the community can make a real difference.

This guide suggests some innovative and creative ways to inform, educate and turn on citizens, not just by motivating them but by identifying channels for getting involved. It provides specific examples—success stories—of what has been done recently to spark interest in the political process in many different communities by a variety of groups. Political action, if it is to be meaningful and effective, needs to be geared to the specific community in which it takes place. The first step, therefore, is to discover exactly what your community is like.

DRAW THE POLITICAL PROFILE OF YOUR COMMUNITY

A political profile is an analysis of the major community characteristics which affect political participation in general and voting in particular. You might start with a look at the census data for your area: population, age, income, education, etc. Then consider the economic base of the community: Is it urban or rural? What are the major industries and is it a one-industry town? What, if any, are the chief agricultural interests? Business interests?

Equally important but not always so easy to define: What is the life style of your community, its chief needs and concerns, its goals and interests? What are the areas of conflict, the issues and personalities involved?

Who are the opinion makers? You may find them in the media, from newspaper columnists and editorial writers to popular disc jockeys and news commentators. But likely as not, a member of the clergy, a prominent industrialist, union leader or even the local college president may be more effective in shaping community opinion.

Consider the political establishment. Who really wields the power and calls the shots? How do they do it —behind closed doors, on the floor of the legislature, in public forums? Is yours a one party town or district? How many Democrats, Republicans, independents or minor party members are there? Has the proportion been changing?

What are registration and voting patterns? Who votes and who doesn't? Are there significant differences in participation among various groups of citizens? Race? Ethnic groups? Sex? Age? Neighborhood? How many are young voters? How many are absentee voters? What is the voting status of college students in your community?

In getting the answers to these and other questions, touch base with a number of different sources in your community. Civic organizations, labor unions, political groups and parties, churches and commu-

nity centers, lobbies and the media may have compiled a lot of this material.

The Election Establishment

What about your board of elections? (It may go by another name in your area.) How is it chosen? Most city and even more county election boards are appointed, usually with some advice or consent from party leaders in the area. Many boards are required by law to reflect party divisions according to the last gubernatorial elections, for example. Some boards are elected. What role does the board play in facilitating citizen participation? How responsive is it to citizen needs?

Does your board, if appointed, reflect the major ethnic groups in your area? Are women represented? Blacks? Chicanos? Other minorities? If your board has been unresponsive, its composition may tell you why. If your board is appointed, who does the appointing? How many members are there? How long do they serve? How much authority does your board have? Is its ability to act subject to review by elected officials like County Commissioners or State Board of Elections? Does it have an adequate budget? Is it limited by restrictive election laws?

How easy is it to register in your community? Does your board of elections or registrar provide a variety of times and places of registration for prospective voters? Are there evening hours? Saturday or Sunday hours? Mobile registration? Registration by mail? Deputy registrars? A recent (1971) survey by the Election Systems Project (ESP) of the League of Women Voters Education Fund found that about 75% of the communities studied had no Saturday or evening registration during nonelection months. Even during the month before registration closed, about 40% offered no additional registration opportunities, such as mobile and temporary facilities. How does your community shape up on these points?

What do your election officials think of their own performance? Would they like to do more for the voter, or are they satisfied with things as they are? The ESP survey uncovered a striking difference between what election officials thought of registration procedures and what citizen groups thought. Most of the volunteer organizations who actively work in registration drives wanted less complex registration procedures, door-to-door registration, longer registration hours, more convenient registration places and mobile registration units. But many election officials did not think such practices should be adopted, nor did they realize that existing registration procedures were inconvenient for voters.

Maybe a frank discussion of the survey findings with your election board would give them food for thought and lead to improvements. Those officials who do want to improve their procedures are eager for information on how to do it. Almost all labor under inadequate budgets, however —something to remember when you call for large-scale reforms.

Encourage officials to use the full scope of their authority to help citizens register to vote. Invite your election officials to speak to your group to explain the problems from their point of view. Ask them again and again. Invite them to a press conference or an interview on TV or radio. If they fail to respond, advertise the fact in news releases and letters to the editor. Put the heat on!

Voter Information

Most citizens confess that they don't do their homework. Even those who want to can't easily find information on candidates and issues. Does your election board publish a voter information guide? Nine out of ten do not! Frequently volunteer groups such as the League of Women Voters have filled the gap. Check with other groups to see if they are working on guides. But urge officials themselves to provide such a guide, with your help. If you do some listening, you'll pick up leads to other bits and pieces of information that can flush out the profile you're building.

STIMULATE POLITICAL PARTICIPATION

As your community's political profile nears completion, it can help you decide what needs to be done and how best to do it. You may want to concentrate on encouraging registration, urging participation in political parties, or offering practical politics courses. Take an honest look at your own group, and the time and talent and resources your members can muster for a project. Know what *you* are good at, and what other groups might be better at. Tailor your efforts to match your own resources.

Encouraging Registration

Increased voter registration should, all things being equal, increase voter turnout. Many studies have shown that registration is the key, and that generally about 80% of those registered do vote. Your community political profile may have indicated two groups who need to be stimulated into political participation: (1) the middle class voter who usually wants to vote, but may have gotten sidetracked by moving to a new community or may not have been "turned on" enough by the campaign or the issues, and (2) the perennial *non*voter, often less well educated, and poorer, perhaps a member of a minority group.

Drumming up enthusiasm among middle class citizens can produce quick and gratifying results. This is where media campaigns, posters, public service announcements, and even card tables at the shopping center can make a difference. By providing information and recruiting your members to be deputy registrars, for example, you can expect a real payoff in increased participation from middle class groups.

Certainly taking registration to the people is bound to increase participation. Mobile units reach those who have difficulty getting downtown—factories, shopping centers, laundromats, gas stations and churches are good locations. Door-to-door registration by precinct committeemen may be even *more* effective.

The LWV of Cedar Rapids-Marion, Iowa registered in supermarkets, schools, and a hamburger drive-in.

The Jonesboro, Arkansas LWV had a booth at the Craighead County Fair. The County Clerk and 3 League deputy registrars ran the booth and registered over 300 voters.

The Urban League in Louisville, Kentucky enlisted the help of the Kentucky Colonels professional basketball team for their registration drive. People attending the Colonels' summer basketball clinics in the city parks could register to vote at the same time.

The Richmond, Kentucky LWV registered people as they went to the court house to get their auto tags.

Sometimes merely making information accessible is the clue.

Banks in Sherman, Texas enclose voters guides put out by the League of Women Voters along with the bank statements. Some industries enclose the guide with paychecks.

Many Leagues such as the National Capital Area have their guides and brochures printed by the newspapers as a public service.

The Oakland, California LWV sold public information boxes ($35/year) to businessmen to put into their waiting rooms. The boxes held citizen information materials that were updated periodically.

Reaching the Disconnected

These techniques may not work, however, in trying to reach the habitual nonvoter. This is the person who doesn't participate, either out of conviction, as in the case of alienated youth, or out of fear, disinterest, and distrust, as in the case of the inner-city or rural poor. Such people are particularly difficult to reach because they have no conviction that their vote affects their lives. And, indeed, in many cases they are more right than the moralistic do-gooders who exhort them to "plug into the system."

What, indeed, has the system done for them recently?

In the case of some nonparticipants, the "disconnected," the "shadow" government of the streets, the local numbers man and the loan shark affect their lives far more than their congressman.

When you find that blacks, or youth, or women, or Chicanos are not registered in proportion to their share of the community's voting age population, what, if anything, can you do? For one thing, you can talk to your election official about the possibility of more intensive registration efforts among these groups. Point out that many registration procedures unduly burden the prospective voter.

Often merely translating material into the language of the group you are trying to reach will make a big difference.

The LWV of Pawtucket, Rhode Island translated its material into Portugese for the large Portugese-speaking population.

The New York City League provided material on 900 school board candidates, printed by the election board in English, Spanish and, in two districts, Chinese.

In neighborhoods with large numbers of people who don't vote or who hesitate to register, your group might be more effective by cooperating with a trusted neighborhood organization. In working with traditional nonparticipants, as in any activity, you have to figure out whether what you want to do is possible, desirable, and whether you are the group to do it. Maybe you can provide the information and the other group can scout for potential voters. Deputy registrars, known in the neighborhood, may be very helpful in registering people who have an abiding distrust in a remote political process. Sometimes there is such suspicion of the "outsider" that all your efforts, however well intentioned, won't work. Tact, care and respect for special sensitivities are the key. And, most important, work with the *real* leaders of the community. They know their people.

Citizens Information Service of Illinois (a tax-deductible educational arm of the League of Women Voters of Illinois) has worked in voter education in inner-city neighborhoods since 1953. But CIS does not go into a neighborhood and single-handedly instruct potential voters; rather it works with local neighborhood organizations ranging from block clubs to school bilingual advisory councils, and then plans with them what topics they want covered in their workshops. Skill training and specific voter education materials are offered to neighborhood leaders who in turn work in their neighborhoods demonstrating, for example, how to use a voting machine. Neighborhood contacts come from a list of past pupils in leadership classes and from persons noted by full-time field workers. Paid field workers find out what aids the neighborhood people want and need. All CIS publications are in English and Spanish, and one field worker is Spanish-speaking.

In New Orleans, a coalition of the LWV, the Council of Jewish Women, and the Louisiana League of Good Government backed up a registration drive in neighborhood centers. The groups that actually worked in the neighborhoods included the NAACP Youth Council and the League of Latin American Citizens, among other local groups. In the ten weeks of the drive over 2000 citizens registered.

The National Urban League has launched its third round of voter registration and citizenship education efforts with a training conference on techniques designed to increase black political participation. Nine cities are targeted for the 1974 campaign: South Bend, Ind.; Buffalo and Yonkers, N.Y.; Akron, Canton and Massillon, Ohio; Tulsa, Okla; Milwaukee and Racine, Wisc.; with ongoing projects in Louisville, Ky.; Springfield, Mass.; Syracuse, N.Y.; and Tacoma, Wash.

In Fort Defiance/Window Rock, Arizona, members-at-large of the LWV have been involved in a variety of activities from financing a registration and information booth at the Navajo Tribal Fair to consulting with groups fighting a redistricting law suit to avoid gerrymandering of the reservation. The state League has advised the Leaguers, some of whom are Indian, on how to reach the Justice Department and they have considered entering an amicus curiae brief in the case. In another case, they have been successful in adding new voting precincts in the reservation.

The New York City League of Women Voters worked with 391 community groups to plan registration drives—working with Head Start groups, churches, schools, and welfare centers. The League trained 300 registrars, 55 speakers and 40 people to serve the Telephone Information Service. Materials were distributed throughout the city in English, Spanish and made available for translation into other languages. Braille materials and a program for the deaf were also developed.

The New York League pushed the "outreach" function even further. They brought voter registration and citizen education programs to narcotics addiction centers and detention centers as well as to senior citizen groups and hospitals.

Frontlash, a "youth project for political participation" concentrating on noncollege youth, has undertaken a number of successful registration drives and voter turnout drives and published information on how to lobby, etc. The group held its first Training Institute in Kelseyville, California in 1973 and another in Maryland in 1974 to increase the number of competent leaders. The institutes conducted intensive series of lectures and small group discussions designed to give organizers an understanding of Frontlash activity, the role of the labor movement, and strategies for change.

Open the Window in a Smoke-Filled Room

Encouraging voters to become involved in political party activities may be a neat trick in 1974 and 1976. Party strength and enthusiasm have been on the wane in recent years, but political parties are still the major channels for selecting and electing candidates. "Rising above party" may really be cutting off one's political nose to spite one's face. Parties *are* an integral part of the political process and will continue to be. One way a citizen can do something about integrity of party and government officials is by getting involved in party activities: indicating party preference when registering, attending local party meetings, joining a political club.

Since the majority of primaries are "closed," i.e., a person cannot vote unless registered with a party, the "independent" voter has no say in picking the candidate. In many states, political parties have precinct caucuses which are neighborhood meetings open to all eligible voters who identify themselves in some way with the party. The precinct caucus is the first step in the process that adopts the state party platform, selects party officers, endorses candidates for state and national offices and, in presidential election years, selects the party's delegates to the national convention.

Republicans and Democrats, and minor parties as well, are working to encourage greater participation, especially by women, blacks, youth, retired people and other groups not traditionally involved in party activity. The delegate selection process in the Democratic Party, for example, has in the last few years been the subject of intense self-study and evaluation by Democrats of all persuasions. The Rule 29 Committee of the Republican party is working to improve its convention and party rules and procedures.

Join party organizations even though you don't agree with every plank in the platform. If there is a "smoke filled room" go on in, even though you may not get an enthusiastic welcome at first. After you open the door, maybe you can open a window. If no one from the outside goes in, there certainly is no hope for change. Remember that at the precinct level your voice can be not only audible, but persuasive. Most voters feel that they are not heard in the upper reaches of the federal or even state and local governments and they are probably right. The precinct is the place where they can talk to candidates, to convention delegates and to the caucus which selects the candidate. It is also the place where they can work most effectively for party reform and for platform issues.

In Minnesota, the Republican and Democratic-Farmer-Labor parties joined forces with the League of Women Voters to promote precinct caucus participation. They sent a kit to 500 newspapers containing information about the state's political structure, caucus procedures and historical notes on the role of the caucus in this country's politics. Members of the coalition appeared on radio and TV interview shows. A telephone "hotline" directed callers to the location of their precinct's caucus.

In addition to encouraging members to attend their caucuses, the League of Women Voters drew up a list of suggested resolutions for them to introduce at their precinct caucuses. For those who were wary of attending a meeting for the first time, local Leagues held mock caucuses to introduce them to what typically goes on.

The LWV of Washington state published a lively and detailed guide on the how and why of party activity, *R.S.V.P. Your Political Party.* From the precinct caucus to state or national levels, the guide describes what goes on and the best ways to make your voice heard.

Practical Politics Courses

Uninformed citizens are uninvolved citizens. One reason that some people don't take part in the basic political process is that they don't know how it works and therefore don't know what one person can do. This lack of sophistication runs all the way from distrust of the voting machine to naivete about behind the scenes activities like lobbying.

A recent study of "Political Knowledge and Attitudes" by the National Assessment of Educational Progress, for example, found that of those people in the 26-to-35-year age bracket, two out of five didn't know how presidential candidates were selected and thirty-one per cent could not suggest a way to find out about a candidate's background. The 17-year-olds surveyed were in even worse shape.

Courses in practical politics are one effective way to inform citizens. There are as many varieties as there are sponsors and audiences. Practical politics has been "taught" in schools and colleges, or less formally in community groups, geared to all kinds of people from students to senior citizens, from residents of suburbia to the inner city.

More than 3,000 Baltimore high school students learned about how the system works from teams of teachers recruited from the Baltimore League of Women Voters. The teachers made every effort to avoid the I-talk-you-listen approach and to involve the students in discussion. And they left behind an extensive packet of materials which students could use at a later date.

The National 4-H Foundation sponsors a number of courses on government and the citizen's role within the system. Its Short Course, which lasts a week, runs all summer long in Chevy Chase, Md. attracting some 7,000 15-19-year-olds each year. Emphasis is on how the individual can make government work for him. One young woman was so "turned on" by the idea that, back in her home town in Iowa (population 300), she polled the citizens to find out what they needed. The result was that volunteers renovated an old building and landscaped the grounds. This 4-Her even became an unofficial advisor to the mayor. Another course

brings students to Washington for three days to learn about the legislative process, lobbying, what pressure groups do, and how a bill gets through Congress.

In Moline, Illinois, the LWV conducted practical politics courses at Black Hawk College for adult students who were working toward their high school diplomas. (Incidentally, the college provided day care and transportation facilities for the students.) Flexibility was the keynote. Each class was a mini-course in itself, with the topic generally picked by the students. Frequently, the "teachers" were outside experts and the students enjoyed and profited by this contact with people who actually affected their lives. For example, a health department nurse explained her work, a Vista volunteer explained how to get food stamps, a reporter talked about the news media, etc.

In 1974 the LWV of Ohio planned a practical politics course for senior citizens in conjunction with the State Commission on Aging, which suggested and funded the project. The League held a training session for leaders of senior citizens' groups, who would in turn train their own people. The training session helped these leaders define the needs of the elderly which can be met through political action and discussed effective ways to make their influence felt. A booklet prepared by the LWV and the Commission, *You and Your Government: Suggestions for Effective Advocacy for Ohio's Older Americans,* covering the political spectrum from registration and voting to parties and lobbying, was the basis for the workshop.

Citizens Information Service of Illinois has for many years successfully conducted practical politics courses as part of its voter education work. Pupils ranged from steel company executives to inner-city residents. In its publication, *Developing Community Leadership,* CIS points out that a practical politics course meets the needs of citizens frustrated by a lack of understanding of the political system "by supplying information about issues, imparting techniques of participation, and demonstrating that where politics is 'dirty,' apathy and indifference help make it so."

The New Jersey LWV ran a practical politics course in the spring of 1974 with experienced officials leading panels and workshops on how to get elected to New Jersey offices and how to be more effective once elected or appointed to office.

The third grade class of the Highland Park elementary school took practical politics to the Pennsylvania state legislature, petitioning to name the firefly as the state's official bug. The 26 students picked the issue themselves (after reading in their *Weekly Reader* that Maryland has a state insect) and, with the direction of their teacher, gathered 2100 signatures in a petition drive. They generated some 5,000 letters from other children in the state. Bills were introduced in the House and Senate, the children testified before the House Committee on state government, and Governor Shapp signed the bill six months later. "I cannot tell you how much these children learned. And I think they're all going to be politicians," said their teacher.

The Durham, North Carolina League held training sessions on local government for newcomers to the community, with names and addresses provided by the telephone or utilities companies.

Close-Up is a practical politics course for youth, funded by congressional appropriations, corporations and foundations. It attempts to reach high school students who would not normally have such an opportunity and brings them to Washington, D.C. for a week of seminars and workshops.

Start Running

The ultimate in practical politics is running for office. There is nothing automatic about being, or not being, political timber. And there is certainly nothing quite like being an office holder to influence policy. Many people start at a modest level, the local school board, for example, an area where the novice candidate feels at home.

Many organizations are specifically dedicated to encouraging and helping non-politicians turn into politicians. Women, for example, have traditionally shied away from running for office. When they have run, they have often lacked the political expertise and backing to wage successful campaigns. The National Women's Politi-cal Caucus' "Win with Women" campaign is trying to change that. They hope to double the number of women this year in statewide elective posts as well as increase their number in the U.S. Congress. Among the services offered are a how-to press kit, legal information, a directory of campaign resources and a strike force of politically experienced women to act as resource persons.

Women are becoming increasingly active in the political arena. More than 3,000 are expected to run for office in 1974, three times the number who ran in 1972. Most of these will be concentrated in local or state races, but even there, women have far to go; they currently hold only 7% of the state seats.

The National Urban League and the Voter Education Project have over a period of years encouraged and advised blacks to run for office with much success. Today there are over 1300 elected black officials in the South, 18 times the number in 1965. The Voter Education Project calls this increase a "quiet revolution now building in this region."

However, blacks still hold only about one-half of one percent of all elected offices in this country. The Voter Education Project is therefore planning on-going programs to "continue the momentum of black political progress."

The national Women's Education Fund runs regional "Campaign Training Technique Workshops" for current and potential women candidates and campaign workers.

In Wisconsin a number of local Leagues of Women Voters held workshops on "How to Run for Public Office," covering everything from election laws to campaign strategy and use of the media. One of the main purposes, of course, was to encourage qualified persons to run. Oshkosh concentrated on the office of county board supervisor. Oconomowoc invited social studies classes and their teachers from the local high schools to attend. Wisconsin Rapids recorded the workshop highlights on a tape cassette, available for borrowing at the public library.

The American Association of University

Women of New Hampshire and the League of Women Voters of New Hampshire compiled a detailed primer on *How to Run for Office.* The publication not only walks the potential candidate through the filing and campaigning and election process, but exhorts the neophyte onward. The Laconia-Gilford, New Hampshire League extended the state program to the local level, focusing on the Constitutional Convention. Within their jurisdiction, twenty-two people filed for the "Con-Con" delegate election.

Running for election is not the only route to policy-making office, since many influential positions are filled by appointment. In Cape Ann, Massachusetts a coalition of all major women's groups maintains a talent bank of qualified women willing to serve in local government.

Money and Politics

Scandal and daily headlines about illegalities and abuses in the financing of political campaigns have sparked intense interest and activity among citizen groups, and brought widespread demands for reforms and changes in the system.

Many people, although sick of dishonesty and secrecy and turned off by the influence that big money buys, don't know what, if anything, they can do about it personally. One way individuals can get involved in the political process is by giving small contributions to their favorite candidates. And small contributions can be mighty important to a candidate—witness the Wallace and McGovern campaigns! Fundraising parties are one way to stimulate small campaign contributions.

If more people knew that they could get a tax break by giving money to a campaign, they might be more likely to give. The tax incentives apply to contributions to candidates in any federal, state or local election, or to a political committee.

When an individual gives money to a party or a particular candidate, he can take a *tax credit* for one-half of his contribution. That is, he gets back $1 for every $2 given because the credit comes off his final tax bill. The maximum credit allowed is $25 for a joint return or $12.50 for a single return.

If he prefers, he can instead take a *tax deduction* in the same way he deducts a gift to a charity, church or other tax-exempt group. The current limits of $100 on a joint return and $50 on a single return may be doubled if legislation pending in Congress is passed.

And when income tax time rolls around, every taxpayer has the opportunity to check a box sending $1 of his tax money (or $2 in the case of a joint return) to the Presidential Election Campaign Fund for use in the 1976 general election. If a Senate bill now pending becomes law, the amount of the checkoff will be doubled and a negative check adopted: the taxpayer's money goes into the fund unless he checks "no."

Many states have already passed laws or are considering bills aimed at cleaning up and opening up the system of financing campaigns. Legislation is pending in Congress after months of hearings and debate marked by filibustering, delaying tactics and in-fighting between those for and those against public financing. A coalition of national organizations (including the League of Women Voters of the U.S., Nader's Congress Watch, ADA, ACLU, AAUW, Common Cause, church groups such as Friends Committee on National Legislation, United Presbyterian Church, United Methodists, UAHC, labor unions such as AFL-CIO, the National Farmers Union) has been lobbying for a combined system of public funding and small private contributions. The LWVUS undertook a 6-month study on campaign financing, then ran a nationwide petition drive in support of its threefold position: a mixed system of private and public financing, limits on contributions and expenditures, and effective enforcement by an independent body. Common Cause, through its monitoring project, has done an enormous job of analyzing and publicizing how much money was spent in the 1972 campaigns.

CURE—Coalition United to Reform Elections— spearheaded work for successful passage of campaign financing legislation in Maryland, testifying at committee meetings and lobbying members of the legislature. CURE brought the issues to public attention, worked with delegates on the bills and got action in the state legislature. Some participating groups: the League of Women Voters of Maryland, Common Cause, COPE (AFL-CIO), Maryland Citizens Lobby for Clean Politics, Maryland Society of Professional Engineers, National Organization of Women, and Legicuum, a church legislative group.

MONITOR THE ELECTORAL PROCESS

No matter how successful you may be in stimulating political participation, many potential voters and actual votes will be lost on election day because of problems with registration, absentee ballots, poorly trained election workers, malfunctioning voting machines, vote tabulation, etc. The importance of monitoring is obvious.

Monitoring is more than merely observing. It means keeping track systematically of the various steps in the election process. Pay particular attention to problem areas that concern you, for example, tabulating the vote or absentee balloting. You'll need to plan your project carefully. Get a plan-

ning committee together and dig into your state election law and election statistics. Find out as much as you can. You may discover, for example, that you need special permission to monitor. After you know how big a project you've tackled, ask other organizations to join you and recruit volunteers. Brief your monitoring volunteers with the material you've gathered.

Design questions to elicit the kind of information you want and distribute questionnaires to your monitors at the briefing session. These should cover very specifically what you are going to watch for. If you're monitoring registration, you need to check such things as whether the registration sites are accessible, whether the registrar uses the full extent of his/her authority to help and encourage registrants, whether extended hours and additional registration sites are offered.

If you're monitoring voting, you'll want to pay particular attention to procedures used at the opening and closing of the polls, the transportation of ballots to the counting center, the tabulation of write-in ballots and absentee ballots, and the actual counting procedures. Try to find out what causes lines and delays if these are a problem in your community. Do voters receive all the assistance they are entitled to? Are voters harrassed or intimidated in any way? Are all procedures done publicly in the presence of watchers? Are all legal safeguards used to protect the ballots? Do polling place workers seem well trained and competent? Are voting machines in good working order with sufficient maintenance personnel on hand? (For sample questionnaires see *Election Check-Up*, mentioned in "For your information.")

After your organization has monitored the registration and/or voting process, collect the questionnaires and have the planning committee analyze them. Tabulate responses to questions, and report the findings to your organization. Meet with your election official(s) and present your findings indicating your willingness to help the official correct any problems. Consider what happened in Tucson.

The Tucson LWV had long been trying to get the county recorder (registrar) to increase voter registration efforts, but could not prove the need. During the fall 1972 election period they collected information about the number of registered voters in relation to the voting age population on a precinct-by-precinct basis. They included a study of the model cities area and concluded with a list of registration priorities. Armed with charts and other visual aids documenting their investigations, they argued successfully before their county board of supervisors for an additional $30,000 to be spent on voter registration outreach activities.

A coalition of 15 organizations in the Pittsburgh area planned and carried out a community monitoring project in the 1973 municipal election period. They started planning early, first getting permission to monitor from election officials which turned out to be more complicated than expected. A training session for monitors was held the week before elections and an evaluation meeting two days after it was all over. Sixty-one persons monitored polls and 34 observed registration. Generally, observers found polling places smoothly run, but mechanical failures with machines and long waits for mechanics were problems. The question of what actually constitutes a "polling place" and how it should be marked was unclear—something to watch for.

In the 1973 Democratic primary in Albany, New York, two League members monitoring under the direction of the state attorney general's office and a nun pollwatching for a candidate questioned the election official's placement of polling place markers. The election official reacted by shoving the three women out of the polling place with the remark: "If I say it's a hundred feet, then it's a hundred feet." Later, the two League members were thrown out of the firehouse when vote tabulation got under way. Charges and countercharges ensued, the election official was indicted and then swore out arrest warrants for the two Leaguers—

who were not indicted. This was the first year that the attorney general's office had appointed monitors for a primary election, though they had worked in general elections before. The result of the confrontation was that the state attorney general's office became much more aware of what happens in primary elections, and party officials realized that their actions may be challenged by alert monitors.

Working at the Polls

How well do the polling place workers in your community perform? Perhaps they need more and better training. Ask your local election official how your group can help him improve his training session for polling place workers. Maybe he's never even offered any formal training before and would welcome some competent help. Provide volunteers as instructors (first making sure *they* are thoroughly familiar with procedures and with your state election law).

In Marietta-Cobb County, Georgia, members of the League of Women Voters are appointed by the local election official as an official board not only to train poll workers, but to order all supplies, oversee printing of the ballots—the whole bag—for which they are compensated.

Organize a small conference of community leaders and election officials from neighboring counties to talk about training election workers. Such an opportunity to exchange ideas and learn from each other is valuable to officials and community leaders alike. New ideas often emerge from these sessions. Press coverage may be a way of encouraging officials to participate.

At the request of the state director of elections, the Tennessee LWV contracted to assist in the preparation of a training manual to be used statewide (a first) in the training of election workers. Working with experts from the University of Tennessee, the Leaguers proofed the copy and supervised the preparation of diagrams to illustrate the points covered. Thus, the League was instrumental in moving Tennessee closer to the goal of uniform election administration and received a stipend to boot.

The West Virginia state legislature voted funds to make a training film for election day workers, after a two year lobbying effort by the state LWV. The film was made at the University of West Virginia with the Morgantown League supplying consultants and actresses to depict poll workers, watchers, voters, etc.

An example of another type of monitoring is provided by the LWV of Detroit, which conducted a survey on the school board election and filing procedure and obstacles to running for office. Questionnaires were mailed to 150 citizens who had requested petitions from the city clerk's office in order to file for school board candidates. The questionnaires drew about a 50% response and suggestions for simplifying or improving filing procedures.

STRESS THE REAL ISSUES

If citizens are to make informed and intelligent decisions in the voting booth, if they are to choose candidates to do what they want government to do, they need solid information on the candidates' background and they need to know how he or she stands on the issues.

The usual biographic material and a catalog of the candidates' most frequently touted opinions aren't adequate anymore. It doesn't really matter that Candidate A was class valedictorian, plays golf and is bullish about America. Voters want, and desperately need, substantive information, not just a TV image. Dig a little.

If the candidate has held elective office before, check on his or her actual voting record, a more reliable indication of ideas and attitudes than any speech or comment

he may make, and publicize it, over and over again!

Does the candidate belong to organizations? Some of them may indicate interests and leanings. Do look at major supporters—individuals as well as groups—and major memberships.

Has the candidate disclosed his financial status as well as the names of major contributors? If so, list them. If not, ask.

The Texas LWV asked the following question of congressional candidates for their primary election Voters Guide: "Using percentages, from what sources do you anticipate financing this campaign (e.g., contributions over $100, contributions under $100, party funds, etc.)?"

Press Candidates on the Issues

What are the best ways to get candidates to discuss openly the real issues of concern to the community?

Who identifies issues? Ask various segments of the community, the young, labor, business, academic, retired, etc., what bothers them and then see to it that candidates address the issues. Don't let the candidates make the issues and don't assume you know what they are. Ask others.

Identify the issue so that the candidate is forced to respond on the record. Get the real question before the candidate in such a way that it can't be evaded or disposed of with a simple I-believe-in-what's-good answer. In live sessions, allow time for follow-up questions so the citizen can follow the candidate's thinking wherever it leads. Dig under the rhetoric. Watch how good reporters question an official at a press conference and learn how good—and bad—questioning works. If there is a group of questioners who can band together, one can follow up the others if the candidate doesn't really answer the question.

Keep track of candidates on the issues. Do they say the same thing to different groups of people, or what they think each wants to hear? Assign members of your group to attend speeches given by a candidate to different groups. Note whether he or she vacillates on an issue or stands firm. Note discrepancies and evasions if they occur, consistency and outspokenness when they occur. Publicize any variances and call the candidate to task through press conferences, letters to the editor, etc.

Work with other community groups in organizing meetings at which critical questions for *that* particular group are surfaced. This strategy forces the candidate to respond to issues of importance to his constituents.

The Kent, Ohio League of Women Voters sponsored three well-attended and diverse pre-election meetings: at the first, a panel of press and radio people questioned candidates for mayor and council (one way to insure media coverage); in the second, a panel including a high school student, an elementary school teacher, a parent representing the PTA, and a journalism professor questioned school board candidates; the third meeting, requested by the local Services for the Aging, dealt with issues of special concern to them.

The Waukegan, Illinois League co-sponsored (with the American Association of University Women) two "Conferences for Candidates" in which representatives of the community and community officials outlined the scope of the job and the problems the winning candidates would face. This turnabout sharpened the inquiry and sidetracked the usual canned speeches. Instead, candidates listened to the people they would serve or work with. The first conference was for school board hopefuls, with community speakers representing taxpayers, parents, various ethnic groups, students and teachers. Before and after the meeting, candidates talked informally to voters and passed out literature from card tables. The turnout was four times the usual candidates' meeting.

Working with Kiwanis and the Jaycees, the New Bedford Area League (Mass.) used a voter poll on community issues to formulate questions for their Candidates' Night, which was aired on the local radio station. A panel of one Jaycee member, one LWV member, a newspaper man and a radio newscaster asked the questions, with the station providing the moderator and timing the candidates.

Occasionally there is one issue or community problem which needs to be discussed in depth. Perhaps your group should consider running a meeting, series of meetings or symposium on that one issue and all its ramifications.

The Evanston, Illinois League cosponsored a meeting with eight local community and church groups on a single topic: environmental quality. Candidates spoke to the issue, with a well-known local TV personality as moderator.

In 1974 the LWV of Pasadena, California held a "Community Conference on Education" to discuss the emotional issue of busing for school desegregation. It was set up not to provide answers but as a vehicle for people to express their concerns and to generate dialogue within the community. The format included a speech by a respected educator; a panel made up of a school board member, a teacher, a parent, a student, a president of the local teachers' college, etc.; and a series of workshops. Other organizations included announcements of the program in their newsletters. The local newspaper provided good coverage.

In cooperation with the local power company, the League of Women Voters of Madison, Indiana held an open forum about the nuclear power plant proposed for their county. The power company paid for the auditorium and ran spot announcements on the radio. Speakers included a vice president of the power company and a professor of nuclear engineering from Purdue University.

Keep in mind that a member of the U.S. Congress has to act on national as well as local issues, so question the candidate's stand on national issues. Does he have a grasp of the problems or is he bogged down in local battles? Challenge the candidate to look at national issues from the perspective of the country rather than concentrating solely on "What's in it for our state or district?"

Clarify Ballot Issues

Sometimes the voter has the chance to say yea or nay *directly* on an issue because it appears on the ballot. It may be a referendum, a bond issue, a proposition, a legislative initiative, etc. Frequently, however, voters don't vote on these ballot issues because they don't understand them. The wording is too obscure, complicated, or confusing.

Cluttering up the right side of the machine or the paper, these abstruse, convoluted paragraphs of gobbledygook would tax the talents of a secret service decoder, much less Jane and John Doe. Sometimes there is so much verbiage that even a speed reader couldn't possibly make it through in the time available.

Ask your election officials to write ballot issues that people can understand. The Connecticut League of Women Voters was successful in getting ballot issues clearly and simply worded. In Ohio, voters will decide on the creation of a Ballot Board to prepare the wording of ballot issues and explain their purpose and effect. According to the League of Women Voters of Ohio, this amendment gives voters a chance to express their preference for "simple understandable wording of all future ballot issues" rather than the confusing "vote-yes-if-you-mean-no" language of past issues. It would go a long way toward "helping voters better understand the choice they have when they enter the voting booth."

The 1974 *California Voters Pamphlet,*

put out by the state, features "one understandable explanation of every measure on the ballot." The new format was the result of legislation actively supported by the LWV.

When officials don't take the initiative, however, one useful public service a community group can perform is to translate the ballot issue into something the voter can understand, or at least be familiar with, *before* going to the polls. This is tricky, because you also need to make sure that you don't oversimplify a complex issue. A good, clear explanation of the legalese is the first step. Next, explain what the present situation is and what effect the ballot issue would have if passed. Name the sponsor of the measure, list supporters and opponents and provide a brief background or history of the issue when appropriate.

Simply stating pro and con arguments is frequently misleading, and even artificial —particularly if you have to strain to make the pros and cons come out even.

The League of Women Voters of the United States' *The ERA: What it Means to Men and Women,* approaches the Equal Rights Amendment in just this way. It explains in plain English what the amendment says and describes specifically how it would affect such areas as individual privacy, labor laws, social security benefits, states rights, etc. It answers some of the most frequently asked questions about ERA and lists organizations and national leaders supporting the amendment. Though not actually dealing with a ballot issue, this leaflet is a useful model for presenting information on any issue.

The city council of Portsmouth, N.H. asked the League of Women Voters to run a public hearing on a particularly controversial referendum question involving the adoption of a tax exemption for homeowners. Before the hearing, the League prepared an explanation of the question including an analysis of how different groups would be affected, which was printed in the *Portsmouth Herald.* All questions of ground rules, procedures, etc. were left to the League and the hearing was carried by the radio stations and cable TV.

PLAY THE MEDIA GAME

Publicity, public relations and public information are all parts of the same process: getting information from one person to the next. The techniques range from word of mouth—often the most effective —to major national TV and magazine campaigns. Each has its place.

In a campaign year, the airwaves and the newspapers are crowded with political information, and whatever important news your group wants to get across has to compete with all the rest. Somehow, you are going to have to get the attention of the media people and keep it—even with all the shouting in the background.

Most ways of getting attention are not relevant for a small community organization. You could get a lot of space and time if your story were so sensational you couldn't keep the reporters away, but most organizations are going to have trouble generating that kind of excitement—most often reserved for natural disasters and major trials. You can buy ads and TV spots if you have money, but most community organizations are nowhere near that budgetary stratosphere—although occasionally a coalition can get enough money together to consider the paid advertisement.

Most groups have to rely on their ingenuity and talents to get their points across. Like them, you will find that if what you have to say is well expressed, is genuinely interesting, if not breathtaking, and is conveyed to the right people at the right time in the right format, you will get space and time.

Sometimes it is possible to get coverage by digging out material the reporter can't or doesn't have time to research himself, e.g., answers to candidate questionnaires or statistical and other information on a current issue the reporter may be writing about.

Remember, above all, that the media want hard news. They are not in business just out of a sense of public duty; they are selling a product. Ask yourself what your story, announcement or tip will do *for them,* not just for you. What will attract the audience they—and you—want? It's really not too hard to see what will appeal if you back off a minute and ask, "Would I really want to watch—or read—that if I were not involved?" You can get regular coverage and even be sought out if your group takes a firm stand on tough issues. Don't be afraid to express frank opinions based on judgment and experience, or to ask devastating questions politely yet firmly.

Television

Figure out what your news resources are. To start with the most visible, what are the commercial TV stations, both network and independent? Is cable TV available? How about public television?

You may find that your best bet is to develop a regular program given to stimulating interest in political issues and citizen participation. Then as election time nears, you can slot in topics as appropriate.

A tri-state group of Leagues from Delaware, New Jersey and Pennsylvania has participated in a bi-weekly TV series, "The League Presents," aired over a commercial Philadelphia channel. Each League is responsible for one show about every three months. This is an interesting experiment because both the New Jersey and the Wilmington areas are dependent on Philadelphia's covering their events as they have no commercial TV station of their own.

You don't get on commercial TV without a little effort. Find out the name of the local news director or editor, the public service director who is in charge of the free time, and any reporters who show interest in your kind of material. Note any shows that you think your group might fit into and get the name of the producer, not just the on-camera personality.

Public Television

Since public television stations are committed to good informative programming, they are likely to be receptive to programming suggestions as well as to spot announcements.

The Pueblo, Colorado League of Women Voters and the Pikes Peak Region League did a 26-week series called "Voter" on the local PBS station. This was a 30-minute program in which interviews and some visuals were used to explore such topics as campaign financing, American Indians, recreation, land use and energy crisis.

The Seattle, Washington League produced eight one-hour shows, "Candidates and Issues," on the public television station. These shows, which were candidates' meetings in disguise, followed a "Meet the Press" format, with a panel of questioners made up of two reporters and one member of the League.

In Bryan, Texas the "Meet the Candidates" program produced by the League of Women Voters has become a regular pre-election feature on the public broadcasting station. When elections near, the station manager gets calls from voters anxious to make sure the show will appear. After the candidates give their background talks, phone lines are open for viewers to call in their questions and hear them answered on the air. Shows have gone on for 3½ hours without exhausting the supply of viewer questions.

Cable TV

Cable TV is a tremendously promising but still underdeveloped medium. In a few localities, wide-open public access channels allow a community group to borrow a camera and "do their own thing." In Reading, Pennsylvania, cable channel 5 has broadcast everyone from the fourth grade class to the marble champion to the Ku Klux Klan to the National Organization for Women and the League of Women Voters. To date, the audience for cable TV is quite limited: either there is no access or, where there is, not many viewers tune in.

Still, cable TV will join the major media sooner or later. So learn about it—courses are often offered at local colleges—and be ready.

And if you have access to cable, remember that even though it's free and there, that doesn't give you the right to bore your viewers. Spend as much time and energy as you would for commercial TV thinking up how you can present a candidate or an issue in an interesting way.

In Pittsfield, Massachusetts the League of Women Voters presented pre-primary programs on cable TV with the half dozen mayoral candidates appearing. The candidates made statements on prepared topics and then asked each other questions, after which viewers were invited to call in questions, with excellent response. Another forum including candidates for mayor, city council and school board was taped and aired before the general election.

The Cupertino-Sunnyvale, California League of Women Voters has a weekly program on the cable TV station in which League members interview public officials and other community leaders.

Radio

Radio is often a forgotten medium; we tend to think of it as somehow less important than TV. Yet radio tracks us from home to work to shop and back again.

Find out which stations do what—and don't just concentrate on the highbrow. If you've developed a good political profile for your community, you should be able to judge which stations and programs are most likely to draw the listeners you're after. It's not much good to get the college crowd if it's plant workers you want to reach. Make a list of the news directors, the public service directors and personalities whose shows might like your input. Contact the "morning person"— the disc jockey-newsman everyone listens to when they get up in the morning. Find out when call-in talk shows are on. Get a group to start a discussion on the airwaves.

In Bloomington, Ill. a radio station asked the LWV to help plan a new public service program. A question and answer format was decided on and the League president became the program coordinator for the once-a-week hour-long show. It deals mainly with consumer problems, with the League providing the answers to the phoned-in questions.

The League of Putnam County East in New York does a fifteen minute show—in the middle of a disc jockey program—on subjects of their choosing. It is generally informational, advising the community of the League's activities and discussing issues that affect the community.

The League of New Rochelle, New York has a weekly 15-minute radio show in which they interview one or more individuals who are experts in a subject area.

The Charleston, Illinois LWV presents a weekly 15- to 30-minute live radio show—on which they interview community leaders (e.g., director of the mental retardation program) and listeners call in questions.

The Lawrence, Kansas League has a 25-minute program twice monthly on a local radio station. They try to choose topics which are being discussed in other community meetings so that there is some community feedback. Many of the guests on the show come from the University of Kansas faculty.

Print

The print media, too, are frequently willing and able to work with community groups, to publish material about upcom-

ing meetings in a community calendar or to listen to ideas for editorials, stories, etc.

What are the major dailies in your area, not just your own town, but nearby? List the names of the city editor, the national editor, editorial page director and any reporters or columnists who have shown an interest in your kind of organization.

Don't stop at the dailies, however. Often a weekly newspaper is most interested in community material because it cannot attempt to compete with the dailies on national news. There are also special interest newspapers and underground papers. The ethnically oriented press is very active in English and foreign languages. Some cities have a local magazine. Some newspapers publish Sunday supplements of local interest. If your town has many visitors—either tourists or businessmen, there may be an "events of the week" publication that is put in hotels and motels.

The small publications are often one-man operations and they are happy to use material that is solid—and typed, so they can just send it down to the printer.

The League of Arlington, Virginia runs a regular column "The League Answers the Citizen," in the *Northern Virginia Sun,* a local, well-respected newspaper.

The public relations director of the Torrington, Connecticut League has written some thirty articles for the three daily newspapers read in that area: *The Torrington Register, The Waterbury Republican* and the *Hartford Courant.*

The League in Cambridge, Massachusetts has worked closely with the editor of the *Cambridge Chronicle* in compiling a voters guide —candidates information sheet—which the paper then published at its expense. As a final gesture, the paper gave the League city-wide distribution of the entire section.

Techniques for Reaching the Media

Once you know your news channels, how do you reach them? Nothing is as effective as a personal approach. The importance of personal relations between the press—broadcast and print—and the public information officers who give them news can hardly be overstated. But do remember that a city editor has more important things to do than just sit around chatting with every local PR person in his town. If you are invited to come in and get acquainted, do. Otherwise send a note saying who you are and that, as stories break, you will send them along and be available for anything the editors or reporters need. As your group proves that you can provide interesting material professionally and accurately, the news media will come to depend on you. They will seek you out because they need you.

Lunch meetings are one fine way to open up communications with media people; media workshops are another if media personnel take part.

The League of Women Voters of Wayland, Massachusetts had a lunch meeting with local reporters to identify and discuss community problems and find out how the press and the League could better help each other. One result was a weekly "Ask the Crier" column which answers questions on general government topics.
The San Diego, California League ran a workshop designed to cover 16 Leagues in southern California and co-sponsored by the local chapter of the National Academy of Television Arts and Sciences. In the morning, media experts discussed techniques—how to write public service announcements, how to put together a lively public affairs program and how to differentiate between public service and news, etc. In the afternoon, there was a discussion of how to act on camera, and participants were able to watch their own performances on tape play back.

After you have identified your news channels and know how to reach them, how do you use them?
Public Service. A public service message on the broadcast media simply announcing a meeting, rally or event is one of the easiest things to try. The broadcasters must, by law, provide some public service or lose their licenses. Many will want a whole script—20 seconds most likely—but others will rewrite from a press release. TV stations still sometimes help a group tape or film a public service announcement. Others want you to do it. As film and tape are expensive, a "voice over" with a few color stills of the size to fit a TV screen are more in line with most budgets. But when you contact the public service directors of the stations, find out just what *their* needs are, and try to fulfill them. Don't do a halfway job.

Many newspapers, too, have a "community calendar" and will accept press releases. A word about press releases. In this media-heavy world, most everyone knows how to put them together. But do keep them simple, with the most important facts at the top. Stay on one double spaced page if you *possibly* can and include release date and the phone number of someone who can answer questions. Hand deliver the releases if possible. If not, send more than one release just to be on the safe side, and follow up with a phone call. Don't bug people, but remember the squeaky wheel gets the grease.

Coverage. But suppose you are looking for *coverage* of the event, not just the announcement that you're having one. First, plan with an eye on the media. If you want photographic coverage, the event had better be photogenic. Meetings of four somber candidates discussing urban renewal at a long table are less likely to make the TV news than a walking tour of the slums. If urban renewal is a question, show rats, desolation and broken beer bottles.

In Pinellas County, Florida, the St. Petersburg and Clearwater Leagues are collaborating with the *St. Petersburg Times* in presenting a political fair with lots of hoopla and pizzaz. The newspaper is underwriting the cost of the fair—space rental, public address systems and entertainment. The idea is to present candidates, issues, parties, municipal agencies and the like to the potential voter in such a way that is both fun and informative. Not just candidate speeches, but marching bands, buttons, banners, etc.

Only registered voters, or those who will register right there at the door will be allowed in. The Leagues will ensure that all candidates have an equal chance, that booths, advertising and speeches are fair.

The newspaper will, of course, promote the fair extensively before it takes place. However, being lively and photogenic, the fair is assured of live broadcast media coverage as well.

Innovative ideas for meetings will attract the media.

Chicago, Illinois LWV held a candidates' meeting that got network TV coverage. At a beer-and-banjo nightclub, the League invited major and minor candidates both to speak and to mingle with the crowd. Lots of music was interspersed with politicking. By charging admission, the League even made a profit.

Timing. Try timing your material for a slack season. For example, even though a compaign year is pretty busy, there probably isn't too much doing in the dog days of August. Schedule a meeting in air conditioning if you can, or outdoors in the park.

Remember that Monday morning newspapers are short on solid political material and think of a way your group could fill the gap.

In other words, don't hope for coverage if you've scheduled a discussion of an irrelevant issue on the Fourth of July.

Remember that Sunday papers carry pages and pages of ads, and the editor needs some "can-use-anytime" material to slot around the white sales. This is the place for a good solid feature, written

either by one of your members, or by a sympathetic reporter.

Write letters to the editor. Even if reporters don't cover your meetings, this is one good way to break into print. Studies show that the letters column has a high readership rate.

Get It All Together. Most of all, try to coordinate both your own media output, and that of other organizations which you must work with. Try to make all your releases and information dovetail.

In Madison, Wisconsin, the League and the public television station, WHA-TV, worked together on an ambitious series of programs for presentation in over 30 hours of prime viewing time. (Too much public service programming is aired at a time when no one watches TV.) Candidates for mayor, city council and the board of education were presented along with ballot issues. A saturation multi-media advertising campaign preceded the shows, featuring a logo of Punch beating the drums. The League provided position papers and organized a telephone campaign to drum up viewers. In an election day survey, 76 percent of the voters completed a questionnaire about the series and over 50 percent of them said they had seen one or more of the programs.

If you are from a *tiny* community, which doesn't have its own newspaper or radio station, band together with groups in neighboring towns and pool your media efforts.

The Quick Break. Be alert for the few times when a natural media story comes your way. Be prepared so that you can call the right reporter at the right organization and be pretty certain that he or she will jump to cover the situation.

In Batavia, Illinois, the county clerk refused to allow a deputy registrar to go to the high school to register students, so the student council and the League of Women Voters hired a bus to get the students to a neighboring town to register. The story was plastered all over the local newspaper, much to the embarrassment of the county clerk.

From Shopping Bags to Network TV. There are as many techniques to use in getting publicity as there are people. If you can focus sharply on what you want to get across, and to whom, there is probably a medium that will publicize it. Leagues have had get-out-the-vote reminders printed just about everywhere, including supermarket bags.

In the sixties, the technique of dramatizing an issue by marching, demonstrating and sometimes throwing things became an "art form." Frequently it was counter-productive. But sometimes, the timing, the urgency of the issue and a good publicity campaign can get together to produce a real "happening."

In April 1970, hours and hours of network media coverage were devoted to a phenomenon called "Earth Day." Media personnel compared the ecology demonstration to the great marches and demonstrations of the sixties. In reality, according to its organizers, Earth Day was rather modest. But Earth Day got into the nation's consciousness by a combination of good timing—people were tired of violence, parents could agree with the need for trees, etc.—and very active promotion. In the grubby Washington, D.C. office where the group was based, young professionals (average age around 23) and a flock of volunteers flooded the media with stories, backgrounders, tips. They posed repeatedly for photographers and film crews. They courted the press and the press came close to smothering them. The media did their work for them.

EVALUATE AND PLAN AHEAD

Once the election activities—the registration and get-out-the-vote drives and the candidates' meetings, etc. —are over, you should take time to evaluate what you have done and how well you have done it.

The voter, too, should be encouraged to evaluate his own choices and figure out whether he picked a good long distance runner or a flashy sprinter.

"Accountability sessions" are a good way both to let the voter confront his choices and to keep up his interest between the election years.

In Crystal-New Hope, Minnesota, the local congressman asked the League to run a "Community Forum for Citizens" at which citizens could ask questions about congressional bills passed and proposed in the recent legislative session. The meeting was well publicized and held in a place accessible for wheelchairs. The result was a good turnout, particularly of handicapped young adults who were interested in welfare legislation which affected them.

In Oxford, Ohio, the League and a county civic improvement organization cosponsored a meeting for the governor and his constituents. It was an old-fashioned town meeting where citizens got to ask their questions straight and have them answered on the spot.

Organizations, too, need to see how they have performed in the election and ask themselves if they answered real needs in the community. Did you succeed in registering more people to vote—people who would otherwise not have registered? Good. If not, either you went about it the wrong way or you are the wrong group to try to do it. Who didn't vote who should have? Who did vote whom you didn't expect to? Can you figure out why? Did you get a good turnout at your meetings to discuss the issues of the campaign and did people really learn something? Good, then you can expand on this format. Maybe next election you can videotape the meeting and give the tapes to other groups.

people really learn something? Good, then you can expand on this format. Maybe next election you can videotape the meeting and give the tapes to other groups.

Build on what is good. Scrap what is bad. Politics is not a game for the nostalgic. Each experience, whether good or bad, can be a learning experience. What you do for citizens in the campaign of 1974 is a preparation for the campaign of 1976—the presidential election year as well as the nation's bicentennial. Upon your honest evaluation, you can base realistic, solid plans for the future.

20. Influencing through Communications

Alan N. Connor and Jaime de la Isla

INFORMATION: AN EFFECTIVE CHANGE TOOL

INTRODUCTION

Generally, information collected about a community or client system by a change agent is used to determine need, establish goals, inventory resources, and plan an action or change strategy. Such information can be used, sometimes, as a change tool or tactic[1] as well as a basis for deciding what tools to use and how to use them. Below we shall attempt to show how information was used as a tool for organizing a migrant labor health program in part of

one state in the North Central region. Four types of information will be discussed: (1) base-line statistical data describing the problem, (2) data regarding fiscal management, (3) history of previous attempts to solve the problem, and (4) political influence patterns.

The district office of United Migrants for Opportunity, Inc. (UMOI) is concerned with the health, working, and living conditions of migrant farm labor families in the area. Previous attempts to improve these conditions had not been successful. These attempts centered around monitoring health inspectors, providing funds for health services, and lobbying for more effective migrant health and safety legislation.

The Director of the Department of Public Health in one of the two counties in the area was thought to be a major obstacle to improvement of health care and services and environmental health conditions of migrant laborers. Delivery of health services to migrant families had diminished since 1970 as had state funding to support

---

Source: Unpublished, Alan N. Connor and Jaime de la Isla, "Information: An Effective Change Tool."

[1] Tactics are not defined in any of the community organization literature with which we are familiar. Erlich and Tropman discuss "strategies" definitively in Fred Cox et al., eds., *Strategies of Community Organization*, pp. 162–163. We define "tactic" as an action or phase of a strategy implemented to attain a limited objective which is instrumental to the attainment of a desired end state or goal. A "strategy" is a set of concomitant and/or sequential tactics.

Other pertinent discussions of tactics and strategies include: George Brager and Harry Specht, *Community Organizing*, Part IV. They do not distinguish between tactics and strategies, however; their tactics appear to be synonymous with Erlich and Tropman's strategies. Also see Ralph Kramer and Harry Specht, eds., *Readings in Community Organization Practice*, Parts C, D, E.

such services. It was believed that the reduction was due to reports of the Director to the State Department of Public Health indicating that need for such services had diminished. Staff at UMOI believed otherwise, but had no information or statistics to support their belief.

BASE-LINE INFORMATION

During the summer of 1973, UMOI organizers collected data about the county's migrant labor population. Data they sought included: incidence of disease among migrants, the number treated for various illnesses, where and by whom. Equally important was information on the costs of migrant health care, the benefits, the source of funds, the local administrative auspices, the amount allocated for migrant health care in the county in previous years, and the pattern of distribution of use of those funds.

Although much of the information was public, it was not easy to acquire. On the other hand, no systematic census of migrant laborers and their families had been kept. Any attempt at a head count was at best an estimate. Information regarding incidence of illness and treatment of members of migrant labor families was incomplete. The Director of the County Department of Public Health did not want to release the information which was available. An assistant who was sympathetic to the migrants' situation did provide what he could.

According to the County Department of Public Health, 1,161 migrant farm laborers and members of their families sojourned in the county in 1973 and 208 had received treatment for a variety of illnesses (Table 20.1). The Department of Social Services (DSS) which provided a number of migrant families with food stamps, emergency assistance, and certi-

TABLE 20.1

Migrant Labor Family Members Receiving Treatment by Age Group

Age Group	1972	1973
Under 1 year	6	7
1—4 years	20	23
5—14 years	33	47
15—44 years	91	108
45—64 years	20	19
65 and older	5	4
Total	175	208

Data from the County Department of Public Health, included in a report by Jaime de la Isla and Alphonso Ramirez, "Migrant Health Services: Monroe County, Michigan," *Innovator,* Vol. 5, No. 12, University of Michigan School of Education (April, 1974), pp. 3-6.

fied eligibility for Medicaid, estimated that 3,000 had stopped in or passed through the county in 1973, and thought its estimate was probably conservative. The DSS estimate for 1972 was also 3,000 people. The Health Department figure for 1972 was 1,000.

The number of migrants treated in 1972 was about 17.5 percent of the Health Department's migrant population estimate. In 1973 18.0 percent were treated. These percentages should not be regarded as reliable. The population estimates were guesses at best, and UMOI doubted that all persons treated or needing treatment were reported to the Health Department.

This information proves very little. Nevertheless, it did have an impact on the County Commission and the Comprehensive Health Planning Council. Most members of the Commission represented agricultural interests of the county. They and UMOI staff thought Department of Social Services migrant population estimates were more accurate than Department of Health estimates. Commissioners, UMOI staff, and health planning staff thought incidence of illness among migrant laborers

TABLE 20.2
Number and Types of Illnesses for Which
Migrants Were Treated by County Physicians

Diagnosis	1972	1973
Infectious Parasitic..................................	18	22
Neoplasms..	0	0
Endocrine, Nutritional, Metabolic..	11	29
Disease of Blood and Blood— forming Organisms.............................	9	6
Mental Disorders....................................	2	3
Nervous System.....................................	53	86
Circulatory System...............................	2	12
Respiratory System...............................	68	91
Genitourinary System............................	19	30
Digestive System....................................	48	26
Complications of Pregnancy, Childbirth, Puerperism.......................	1	0
Skin, and Subcutaneous Tissue.............	35	34
Musculoskeletal Tissue..........................	0	14
Symptoms, Ill-defined Conditions.........	19	24
Accidents, Poison, Violence...................	17	23
Total cases	302	400

Source: see Table 20:1.

and their families was higher than the data indicated, and that many were not receiving treatment. Their impression was that the data omitted more persons needing treatment than it included.

Data were acquired from the Health Department on the distribution of types of illnesses diagnosed and treated among migrants in 1972 and 1973 (Table 20.2).

While in this county, most migrants resided in the rural southern sector. Fifty-seven of the county's 64 physicians lived and practiced in the county seat, which is in the northern portion of the county. Only two physicians resided and practiced in the southern townships and one of those was practicing part-time only.[2] Most county physicians refused to treat migrants except on a cash basis. Many would not accept Medicare and Medicaid pa-

tients or vendor payments from the Department of Social Services as they had experienced delayed payment from this source.[3] Health services in the county were not easily accessible.

Political Import

Data regarding the cost of health services to migrants and the use of public funds allocated to provide such services in the county proved to be politically potent. Between 1961 and 1972, the Department of Public Health had received $152,305 in state and federal funds to provide health services to migrant laborers. Forty-two percent was never used. In 1973 the State Department of Public Health granted the local Department $16,750 for migrant health care (Table 20.3). Forty percent, $6,640, was allocated for patient care and 60 percent, $10,110, was to be used for administration, travel, and supplies.[4] Two members of the County Board of Health, the chairman and vice-chairman, were incensed that most of the funds had been allocated for administration and operations rather than patient care. They were disturbed further when they learned from the UMOI report that only half the patient care allocation but nearly 70 percent of the administrative funds had been spent. Any information that may be interpreted as mismanagement of public funds can be a political lever. This upsets politicians and taxpayers who elect them. The County Commissioners and the Board of Health were also disturbed to discover in the report that the average cost per migrant visit to a local doctor was about twice the average cost of a doctor's visit in the county.

---

[2] Regional Comprehensive Health Planning Council data in Jaime de la Isla and Alphonso Ramirez, "Migrant Health Services: Monroe County, Michigan."

[3] Verbal reports from UMOI staff.

[4] County Public Health Department data in de la Isla and Ramirez, op. cit.

TABLE 20.3
Monroe County Migrant Health Grants

Year	Source	Approved Budget	Expenditures	Estimated Migrant Population
1967................ DHEW		$29,847.00	$19,962.14	1,500
1968................ DHEW		39,592.00	10,298.05	1,200
1969................ DHEW		46,549.00	23,481.10	1,100
1970................ DHEW		18,017.00	14,259.94	1,000
1971................ DHEW		18,300.00	18,142.98	3,000*
1972................ MDPH–UMOI		12,903.23	12,901.38	3,000*
1973................ MDPH–UMOI		22,750.00	16,750.00	3,000

*Department of Social Services estimate

HISTORY OF PROBLEM-SOLVING ATTEMPTS

Chronology of Events

Another type of information which may have political import is the history and chronology of problem-solving attempts.[5] If such attempts can be documented with minutes, press clippings, official reports, witnesses, etc., so much the better. Reasons why such attempts were not carried out or were ineffective often can be deduced from such a history, and responsibility for the lack of implementation and ineffectiveness can be assigned.

On July 12, 1973, two UMOI organizers and the coordinator of the UMOI district office met with the County Public Health Director and one of his staff. The latter had been critical of the Department of Health's migrant health program. The purpose of the meeting was to discuss establishing a migrant health clinic in a village accessible to most of the migrant labor camps in the county. Both state and UMOI funds were available for this purpose as was a building in the village.

The director agreed that such a clinic should be established, and the funds available were sufficient to do so. He said it could be done in one week. All that was needed was County Commission approval which could be obtained at the next Commission meeting. As no county revenues were involved, approval would be no problem. Word that a clinic would be established at a specific location was circulated among the migrant families. However, it was not established, for it never was placed on the Commission's agenda.

Many migrant families sought medical care at the proposed clinic in vain. It would have been useful, strategically, for UMOI to have kept a record of the number of persons who sought such help, the personal consequences of not finding it, and subsequent treatment received, if any. The number of persons seeking but not receiving care would have been particularly important in documenting the need for a migrant health program. Nevertheless, the fact the meeting was held with the County Health Director and a decision made to establish a clinic was documented. That implementation of the decision was not carried out was embarrassing to both the Commission and the Board of Health. The County Director of Public Health was held responsible by both bodies.

---

[5] Fred Cox, "A Suggestive Schema for Community Problem Solving," in Cox et al., op. cit., pp. 425–444.

PATTERNS OF INFLUENCE

So far we have discussed three types of information: (1) statistical data, (2) financial data, and (3) historical data. In working to collect information in these three categories and in attempting to design a solution to the migrant labor health care problem, information on patterns of association and influence was discovered.

Critically influential organizations were: The County Commission, the Board of Health, the County Health Department, the State Health Department, the State Health Commission, the Regional Comprehensive Health Planning Council (CHPC), the County Medical Society, and local Catholic parishes and the Archdiocese.

Influential individuals include: the chairman of the County Commission, certain long-time members, the chairman and the vice-chairman of the Board of Health, the Director of the County Health Department, the State Representative from the county who is a member of the House Appropriations Committee and chairman of its Subcommittee on Health and Social Welfare and Retirement, the priest who provides oversight for county parishes, and a Spanish-speaking health planner employed by CHPC.

The County Commission makes local policy and allocates funds to implement that policy. The County Department of Public Health carries out health policy. The County Board of Health monitors the Department of Health, reports to the County Commission, and recommends policy. At the state level, the House Appropriations Committee and its Health, Social Welfare and Retirement Subcommittee recommend policies and allocations to the legislature. The State Department of Public Health executes the policies regarding health programs throughout the state and monitors county departments. The State Health Commission monitors the Department and reports back to the Governor.

The chairmen of these commissions, committees, and boards are in positions to wield influence which affects provision of health care at the local level. It is important to know how they respond to what kinds of input; what constraints limit them to what extent, and who influences whom.

The county's State Representative is a Democrat and a Catholic. He tends to support programs which benefit the poor, and is supportive of a migrant health care program in his county although he cannot take a public position on the issue. Many of his constituents would oppose assisting migrants. His recommendations to the State Health Commission and State Department of Public Health carry weight since his subcommittee recommends funding for these bodies. The State Representative also has influence with the Congressman for the district, a Republican who gets the majority of the vote in this Democratic county. If the State Representative asks him to support federal funding for migrant health care in the county, the Congressman is likely to do so.

The priest is politically active, but not overtly partisan. Parishioners are a majority of the county's voting population. It is believed that he can influence many voters. He is highly respected by the State Representative and many other officials throughout the county. He is also respected by the Archdiocese.

The County Public Health Director was authorized to interpret and execute public health policy in the county and had much discretion in doing so. He was seen by UMOI staff primarily as a representative of the County Medical Society. However, the report of the organizers and its subsequent discussion by the County Commission and Board of Health vitiated his influence.[6]

STRATEGY

The major concerns of the organizers were that: (1) primary health care programs for migrant laborers and their families be developed, (2) the program be independent of the County Department of Public Health and its Director, (3) migrants and local people who care about the welfare of migrants be members of the program's policy-making body, and (4) adequate funding for the program be provided.

Making the matter a political issue throughout the county was discussed as a possible strategy. This was eliminated because the majority of the county, Democrats and Catholics, had little contact with migrant laborers and most perceptions of migrants are not favorable. The majority of the county's population is white, rural, nonfarm, and blue-collar, employed in factories in adjacent counties. The prospects of mobilizing countywide support were poor and would require a sustained, long-term effort.

As federal funding is all that was available in the winter and spring of 1974, the strategy adopted was mobilizing support of key county and state government bodies and influential individuals. It was hoped that enough of that type of support would persuade the Department of Health, Education and Welfare to provide needed funds. Most of this influence would have to come from outside the county.[7] Approval of the County Commission and the County Board of Health and local influential individuals was needed to secure the support of state agencies.

The organizers' report, *Migrant Health Services in Monroe County*,[8] plus the Board of Health's negative evaluation of the Director of the County Health Department increased the probability that the County Commission would support a migrant health program which would be independent of the County Department of Public Health. The report was selectively circulated. Press coverage of the report and its discussion before the County Commission further increased that probability. The Commission found the adverse publicity embarrassing. After the newspapers published the story and radio stations broadcast it, the Commission publicly supported funding an independent migrant health agency.

The Regional Comprehensive Health Planning Council (CHPC) also supported the independent program concept. Although CHPC has no policy making or enforcement authority, its recommendations and advice are seriously considered by policy-making and legislative bodies and individuals because of its expertise in health planning, administration, and service delivery.[9] Local county officials were the exception.

Regional health planning staff wanted to develop some influence and credibility in the county and saw their involvement in the planning and development of a migrant health program as a possible entry. The organizers agreed to include CHPC in the planning process as a resource and ex-officio member of the eventual policy

---

[6] County Public Health Department data in de la Isla and Ramirez, op. cit.

[7] Roland Warren, in *The Community in America*, describes vertical and horizontal patterns of influence. The organizers were concerned with both in this case but recognized that the vertical was most critical.

[8] de la Isla and Ramirez, op. cit.

[9] See John R. P. French, and Bertram Raven, "The Bases of Social Power," in *Group Dynamics: Research and Theory*, Cartwright and Zander, eds., pp. 607–623. Expertise is one of five types of social power the authors define.

structure in exchange for its support of funding, independence and consumer participation in policy-making when advising the State Department of Public Health and the "Feds."

The priest joined the planning group, which subsequently became the Migrant Health Council.

Support was obtained for the program from all the necessary sources. One modification in the plan was that the adjacent county be included in the program. This meant quickly obtaining approval from that County Commission, Board of Health, Director of Public Health, and the regional CHPC which had jurisdiction. This proved to be no problem. The two county bodies and the Director saw establishment of the program as an opportunity to reduce county expenditure for migrant health. The second CHPC saw an opportunity to widen its influence.

Another modification was that the Migrant Health Council contract with a nonprofit health delivery corporation which had a proven record of accountability with HEW to administer the program. This was required by the federal regional staff.

Both modifications were accepted by the planning group, which had become incorporated as the Migrant Health Council with the aid of two University of Michigan law students.

Since the summer of 1974 the Migrant Health Council and the nonprofit health delivery corporation has operated a clinic in each county. The number of migrant family members treated at the clinic in the county with which this paper is primarily concerned was 667 in 1,278 visits during the first summer of operation,[10] quite an increase over the 208 migrant family members treated the previous year.

---

[10] Annual Report of the County Migrant Health Clinic, 1974.

CONCLUSION

In this paper we have described how information was used as an effective change tool in one community. Four types of information and their uses were discussed. They include: statistical data, financial data, history of problem-solving attempts, and patterns of influence and power relationships. The last type was used to design a strategy which included how and to whom the first three types of information would be disseminated. The second and third types were used to document neglect and misfeasance of local officials and the first type was used to provide evidence of need.

Admittedly, the strategy employed in this case did not consist solely of sharing information with influential government organizations and individuals. It was combined with bargaining—e.g., exchanging wider influence for plan support vis. the regional comprehensive health planning councils. Information sharing was the major tactic used to develop support in critical places and links with political resources.

In most community development or change projects information alone will not be a sufficient tool. But it should not be eschewed. In many cases it may be an effective change tool.

REFERENCES

Brager, George, and Specht, Harry. *Community Organizing.* New York: Columbia University Press, 1973.

Cox, Fred M., Erlich, John L., Rothman, Jack, and Tropman, John E., eds. *Strategies of Community Organization,* 2nd ed. Itasca, Ill.: F. E. Peacock Publishers, 1974.

de la Isla, Jaime, and Ramirez, Alfonso. "Migrant Health Services in Monroe County, Michigan." *Innovator,* University of Michigan, School of Education, Ann Arbor, Mich., Vol. 5, No. 12 (April 15, 1974), pp. 3–6.

Kramer, Ralph, and Specht, Harry, eds. *Readings in Community Organization Practice*. Englewood Cliffs, N.J.: Prentice-Hall, 1969.

French, John R. P., and Raven, Bertram. "The Bases of Social Power." In *Group Dynamics: Research and Theory*, 2nd ed., Dorwin Cartwright and Alvin Zander, eds. New York: Harper and Row, 1960, pp. 607–623.

Warren, Roland. *The Community in America*. Chicago: Rand-McNally, 1963.

———. *Studying Your Community*. New York: Free Press, 1965.

Hunter, Floyd. *Community Power Structure*. Chapel Hill, N.C., 1953.

Dahl, Robert A., and Lindblom, Charles E. *Politics, Economics and Welfare*. New York: Harper and Row, 1953.

CHAPTER V

Administering Programs

Introduction

The practitioner in community organization will often find himself or herself cast into an administrative role. Sometimes this results from a permanent job shift, and the practitioner must then seek (or perhaps has already sought) additional competency in a specific area. But often as not a small grant comes through, and a community organizer is placed in charge of it; a boss asks for some information in a personnel area; one is sitting at a committee meeting and finds that there is serious conflict among several of the constituencies with which one is working. Or, one is asked to develop a program plan and run that plan out into the future to test some of its implications. In such situations the community practitioner or policy planner is asked to perform certain administrative tasks and needs to know some of the techniques without necessarily becoming a full-fledged administrator. Indeed, our observation is that all community organization practitioners become somewhat involved in these roles.

What makes administration a relevant part of community organization? There is often no one else to perform the tasks, and thus it becomes a part of the job description of necessity. Many practitioners work in relatively small operations in which it is expected that they will perform a range of tasks. But even more importantly, the program is the vehicle through which the services often long sought by the practitioner are delivered. One cannot simply sit back and say that an administrator can take over. There is a continual interaction between the program and the community. Nothing makes this point more crisply than the piece by Elinor Bowles on developing a nonracist, nonsexist, child care program. For those who may have thought that planning such a program would be child's play, as it were, this piece will be instructive. It suggests a range of considerations the community organizer/administrator will want to keep in mind.

The matter of personnel is generally acknowledged as one of the most time-consuming and important in any organization. Community organizers are often involved in developing personnel policies for community groups or organizing against some set of policies in an oppressive organization. The guidelines developed by the YWCA which are included here represent a superb outline of the most salient considerations. Any community practitioner would be helped by keeping them generally in mind as he or she runs, or consults about, a program.

Situations often arise in which the practitioner needs some techniques to lay out a job into the future and thus test the implications of some particular schedule against time itself. Often one needs to work back from some specific date— *if* a proposal is due by June 1, *then* it must be at the printers by March 15, which in turn means that it must be to final typing by March 1, and so on. This approach is discussed by Joe R. Hoffer in his piece on PERT (Program Evaluation and Review Technique). The PERT scheme can become quite complex in a formal sense, and often practitioners shy away from it as something they cannot master; in reality it is a specification of a technique we use all the time, and Hoffer's discussion will be understandable to all.

Then there is the issue of meetings. Everyone knows how much time the community practitioner spends in meetings; we also know how few of them are productive! Antony Jay's piece on "How to Run a Meeting" is aimed at the practitioner; it lists a range of skills and techniques which can lead to more productive meetings. This goal alone, if it could be achieved, would be an important practitioner's aid. But the article does a little more than that. It suggests that meetings can become serious objects of attention rather than simply hours to be endured. It is a matter of attitude, as well as simple tactic and technique.

John E. Tropman

21. Staffing Meetings

Antony Jay

HOW TO RUN A MEETING

Why have a meeting anyway? Why indeed? A great many important matters are quite satisfactorily conducted by a single individual who consults nobody. A great many more are resolved by a letter, a memo, a phone call, or a simple conversation between two people. Sometimes five minutes spent with six people separately is more effective and productive than a half-hour meeting with them all together.

Certainly a great many meetings waste a great deal of everyone's time and seem to be held for historical rather than practical reasons; many long-established committees are little more than memorials to dead problems. It would probably save no end of managerial time if every committee had to discuss its own dissolution once a year, and put up a case if it felt it should continue for another twelve months. If this requirement did nothing else, it would at least refocus the minds of the committee members on their purposes and objectives.

But having said that, and granting that "referring the matter to a committee" can be a device for diluting authority, diffusing responsibility, and delaying decisions, I cannot deny that meetings fulfill a deep human need. Man is a social species. In every organization and every human culture of which we have record, people come together in small groups at regular and frequent intervals, and in larger "tribal" gatherings from time to time. If there are no meetings in the places where they work, people's attachment to the organizations

they work for will be small, and they will meet in regular formal or informal gatherings in associations, societies, teams, clubs, or pubs when work is over.

This need for meetings is clearly something more positive than just a legacy from our primitive hunting past. From time to time, some technomaniac or other comes up with a vision of the executive who never leaves his home, who controls his whole operation from an all-electronic, multichannel, microwave, fiber-optic video display dream console in his living room. But any manager who has ever had to make an organization work greets this vision with a smile that soon stretches into a yawn.

There is a world of science fiction, and a world of human reality; and those who live in the world of human reality know that it is held together by face-to-face meetings. A meeting still performs functions that will never be taken over by telephones, teleprinters, Xerox copiers, tape recorders, television monitors, or any other technological instruments of the information revolution.

FUNCTIONS OF A MEETING

At this point, it may help us understand the meaning of meetings if we look at the six main functions that meetings will always perform better than any of the more recent communication devices:

1. In the simplest and most basic way, a meeting defines the team, the group, or the unit. Those present belong to it; those absent do not. Everyone is able to look

around and perceive the whole group and sense the collective identity of which he or she forms a part. We all know who we are —whether we are on the board of Universal International, in the overseas sales department of Flexitube, Inc., a member of the school management committee, on the East Hampton football team, or in Section No. 2 of Platoon 4, Company B.

2. A meeting is the place where the group revises, updates, and adds to what it knows *as a group*. Every group creates its own pool of shared knowledge, experience, judgment, and folklore. But the pool consists only of what the individuals have experienced or discussed as a group—i.e., those things which every individual knows that all the others know, too. This pool not only helps all members to do their jobs more intelligently, but it also greatly increases the speed and efficiency of all communications among them. The group knows that all special nuances and wider implications in a brief statement will be immediately clear to its members. An enormous amount of material can be left unsaid that would have to be made explicit to an outsider.

But this pool needs constant refreshing and replenishing, and occasionally the removal of impurities. So the simple business of exchanging information and ideas that members have acquired separately or in smaller groups since the last meeting is an important contribution to the strength of the group. By questioning and commenting on new contributions, the group performs an important "digestive" process that extracts what's valuable and discards the rest.

Some ethologists call this capacity to share knowledge and experience among a group "the social mind," conceiving it as a single mind dispersed among a number of skulls. They recognize that this "social mind" has a special creative power, too. A group of people meeting together can often produce better ideas, plans, and decisions than can a single individual, or a number of individuals, each working alone. The meeting can of course also produce worse outputs or none at all, if it is a bad meeting.

However, when the combined experience, knowledge, judgment, authority, and imagination of a half dozen people are brought to bear on issues, a great many plans and decisions are improved and sometimes transformed. The original idea that one person might have come up with singly is tested, amplified, refined, and shaped by argument and discussion (which often acts on people as some sort of chemical stimulant to better performance), until it satisfies far more requirements and overcomes many more objections than it could in its original form.

3. A meeting helps every individual understand both the collective aim of the group and the way in which his own and everyone else's work can contribute to the group's success.

4. A meeting creates in all present a commitment to the decisions it makes and the objectives it pursues. Once something has been decided, even if you originally argued against it, your membership in the group entails an obligation to accept the decision. The alternative is to leave the group, but in practice this is very rarely a dilemma of significance. Real opposition to decisions within organizations usually consists of one part disagreement with the decision to nine parts resentment at not being consulted before the decision. For most people on most issues, it is enough to know that their views were heard and considered. They may regret that they were not followed, but they accept the outcome.

And just as the decision of any team is binding on all the members, so the decisions of a meeting of people higher up in an organization carry a greater authority than any decision by a single executive. It is much harder to challenge a decision of the board than the chief executive acting on his own. The decision-making authority of a meeting is of special importance for long-term policies and procedures.

5. In the world of management, a meeting is very often the only occasion where the team or group actually exists and works as a group, and the only time when the supervisor, manager, or executive is actually perceived as the leader of the team, rather than as the official to whom individuals report. In some jobs the leader does guide his team through his personal presence—not just the leader of a pit gang or construction team, but also the chef in the hotel kitchen and the máitre d'hôtel in the restaurant, or the supervisor in a department store. But in large administrative headquarters, the daily or weekly meeting is often the only time when the leader is ever perceived to be guiding a team rather than doing a job.

6. A meeting is a status arena. It is no good to pretend that people are not or should not be concerned with their status relative to the other members in a group. It is just another part of human nature that we have to live with. It is a not insignificant fact that the word *order* means (a) hierarchy or pecking order; (b) an instruction or command; and (c) stability and the way things ought to be, as in "put your affairs in order," or "law and order." All three definitions are aspects of the same idea, which is indivisible.

Since a meeting is so often the only time when members get the chance to find out their relative standing, the "arena" function is inevitable. When a group is new, has a new leader, or is composed of people like department heads who are in competition for promotion and who do not work in a single team outside the meeting, "arena

behavior" is likely to figure more largely, even to the point of dominating the proceedings. However, it will hardly signify with a long-established group that meets regularly.

Despite the fact that a meeting can perform all of the foregoing main functions, there is no guarantee that it will do so in any given situation. It is all too possible that any single meeting may be a waste of time, an irritant, or a barrier to the achievement of the organization's objectives.

WHAT SORT OF MEETING?

While my purpose in this article is to show the critical points at which most meetings go wrong, and to indicate ways of putting them right, I must first draw some important distinctions in the size and type of meetings that we are dealing with.

Meetings can be graded by *size* into three broad categories: (1) the assembly—100 or more people who are expected to do little more than listen to the main speaker or speakers; (2) the council—40 or 50 people who are basically there to listen to the main speaker or speakers but who can come in with questions or comments and who may be asked to contribute something on their own account; and (3) the committee—up to 10 (or at the most 12) people, all of whom more or less speak on an equal footing under the guidance and control of a chairman.

We are concerned in this article only with the "committee" meeting, though it may be described as a committee, a subcommittee, a study group, a project team, a working party, a board, or by any of dozens of other titles. It is by far the most common meeting all over the world, and can perhaps be traced back to the primitive hunting band through which our species evolved. Beyond doubt it constitutes the bulk of the 11 million meetings that—so it has been calculated—take place every day in the United States.

Apart from the distinction of size, there are certain considerations regarding the *type* of meeting that profoundly affect its nature. For instance:

Frequency. A daily meeting is different from a weekly one, and a weekly meeting from a monthly one. Irregular, ad hoc, quarterly, and annual meetings are different again. On the whole, the frequency of meetings defines—or perhaps even determines—the degree of unity of the group.

Composition. Do the members work together on the same project, such as the nursing and ancillary staff on the same ward of a hospital? Do they work on different but parallel tasks, like a meeting of the company's plant managers or regional sales managers? Or are they a diverse group—strangers to each other, perhaps—united only by the meeting itself and by a common interest in realizing its objectives?

Motivation. Do the members have a common objective in their work, like a football team? Or do they to some extent have a competitive working relationship, like managers of subsidiary companies at a meeting with the chief executive, or the heads of research, production, and marketing discussing finance allocation for the coming year? Or does the desire for success through the meeting itself unify them, like a neighborhood action group or a new product design committee?

Decision Process. How does the meeting group ultimately reach its decisions? By a general consensus, "the feeling of the meeting"? By a majority vote? Or are the decisions left entirely to the chairman himself, after he has listened to the facts, opinions, and discussions?

Kinds of Meetings

The experienced meeting-goer will recognize that, although there seem to be five quite different methods of analyzing a meeting, in practice there is a tendency for certain kinds of meetings to sort themselves out into one of three categories. Consider:

The *daily meeting,* where people work together on the same project with a common objective and reach decisions informally by general agreement.

The *weekly or monthly meeting,* where members work on different but parallel projects and where there is a certain competitive element and a greater likelihood that the chairman will make the final decision himself.

The *irregular, occasional, or "special project" meeting,* composed of people whose normal work does not bring them into contact and whose work has little or no relationship to the others'. They are united only by the project the meeting exists to promote and motivated by the desire that the project should succeed. Though actual voting is uncommon, every member effectively has a veto.

Of these three kinds of meeting, it is the first—the workface type—that is probably the most common. It is also, oddly enough, the one most likely to be successful. Operational imperatives usually ensure that it is brief, and the participants' experience of working side by side ensures that communication is good.

The other two types are a different matter. In these meetings all sorts of human crosscurrents can sweep the discussion off course, and errors of psychology and technique on the chairman's part can defeat its purposes. Moreover, these meetings are likely to bring together the more senior people and to produce decisions that profoundly affect the efficiency, prosperity, and even survival of the whole organization. It is, therefore, toward these higher-level meetings that the lessons of this article are primarily directed.

BEFORE THE MEETING

The most important question you should ask is: "What is this meeting intended to achieve?" You can ask it in different ways —"What would be the likely consequences of not holding it?" "When it is over, how shall I judge whether it was a success or a failure?"—but unless you have a very clear requirement from the meeting, there is a grave danger that it will be a waste of everyone's time.

Defining the Objective

You have already looked at the six main functions that all meetings perform, but if you are trying to use a meeting to achieve definite objectives, there are in practice only certain types of objectives it can really achieve. Every item on the agenda can be placed in one of the following four categories, or divided up into sections that fall into one or more of them:

1. *Informative-Digestive.* Obviously, it is a waste of time for the meeting to give out purely factual information that would be better circulated in a document. But if the information should be heard from a particular person, or if it needs some clarification and comment to make sense of it, or if it has deep implications for the members of the meeting, then it is perfectly proper to introduce an item onto the agenda that requires no conclusion, decision, or action from the meeting; it is enough, simply, that the meeting should receive and discuss a report.

The "informative-digestive" function includes progress reports—to keep the group up to date on the current status of projects it is responsible for or that affect its deliberations—and review of completed projects in order to come to a collective judgment and to see what can be learned from them for the next time.

2. *Constructive-Originative.* This "What shall we do?" function embraces all items that require something new to be devised, such as a new policy, a new strategy, a new sales target, a new product, a new marketing plan, a new procedure, and so forth. This sort of discussion asks people to contribute their knowledge, experience, judgment, and ideas. Obviously, the plan will probably be inadequate unless all relevant parties are present and pitching in.

3. *Executive Responsibilities.* This is the "How shall we do it?" function, which comes after it has been decided what the members are going to do; at this point, executive responsibilities for the different components of the task have to be distributed around the table. Whereas in the second function the contributors' importance is their knowledge and ideas, here their contribution is the responsibility for implementing the plan. The fact that they and their subordinates are affected by it makes their contribution especially significant.

It is of course possible to allocate these executive responsibilities without a meeting, by separate individual briefings, but several considerations often make a meeting desirable:

First, it enables the members as a group to find the best way of achieving the objectives.

Second, it enables each member to understand and influence the way in which his own job fits in with the jobs of the others and with the collective task.

Third, if the meeting is discussing the implementation of a decision taken at a higher level, securing the group's consent may be of prime importance. If so, the fact that the group has the opportunity to formulate the detailed action plan itself may be the decisive factor in securing its agreement, because in that case the final decision belongs, as it were, to the group. Everyone is committed to what the group decides and is collectively responsible for the final shape of the project, as well as individually answerable for his own part in it. Ideally, this sort of agenda item starts with a policy, and ends with an action plan.

4. *Legislative Framework.* Above and around all considerations of "What to do" and "How to do it," there is a framework—a departmental or divisional organization—and a system of rules, routines, and procedures within and through which all the activity takes place. Changing this framework and introducing a new organization or new procedures can be deeply disturbing to committee members and a threat to their status and long-term security. Yet leaving it unchanged can stop the organization from adapting to a changing world. At whatever level this change happens, it must have the support of all the perceived leaders whose groups are affected by it.

The key leaders for this legislative function must collectively make or confirm the decision; if there is any important dissent, it is very dangerous to close the discussion and make the decision by decree. The group leaders cannot expect quick decisions if they are seeking to change the organization framework and routines that people have grown up with. Thus they must be prepared to leave these items unresolved for further discussion and consultation. As Francis Bacon put it—and it has never been put better—"Counsels to which time hath not been called, time will not ratify."

Making Preparations

The four different functions just discussed may of course be performed by a single meeting, as the group proceeds through the agenda. Consequently, it may be a useful exercise for the chairman to go through the agenda, writing beside each item which function it is intended to fulfill. This exercise helps clarify what is expected from the discussion and helps focus on which people to bring in and what questions to ask them.

People. The value and success of a committee meeting are seriously threatened if too many people are present. Between 4 and 7 is generally ideal, 10 is tolerable, and 12 is the outside limit. So the chairman should do everything he can to keep numbers down, consistent with the need to invite everyone with an important contribution to make.

The leader may have to leave out people who expect to come or who have always come. For this job he may need tact; but since people generally preserve a fiction that they are overworked already and dislike serving on committees, it is not usually hard to secure their consent to stay away.

If the leader sees no way of getting the meeting down to a manageable size, he can try the following devices: (*a*) analyze the agenda to see whether everyone has to be present for every item (he may be able to structure the agenda so that some people can leave at half time and others can arrive); (*b*) ask himself whether he doesn't really need two separate, smaller meetings rather than one big one; and (*c*) determine whether one or two groups can be asked to thrash some of the topics out in advance so that only one of them needs to come in with its proposals.

Remember, too, that a few words with a member on the day before a meeting can increase the value of the meeting itself, either by ensuring that an important point is raised that comes better from the floor than from the chair or by preventing a time-wasting discussion of a subject that need not be touched on at all.

Papers. The agenda is by far the most important piece of paper. Properly drawn up, it has a power of speeding and clarifying a meeting that very few people understand or harness. The main fault is to make it unnecessarily brief and vague. For example, the phrase "development budget" tells nobody very much, whereas the longer explanation "To discuss the proposal for reduction of the 1976–1977 development budget now that the introduction of our new product has been postponed" helps all committee members to form some views or even just to look up facts and figures in advance.

Thus the leader should not be afraid of a long agenda, provided that the length is the result of his analyzing and defining each item more closely, rather than of his adding more items than the meeting can reasonably consider in the time allowed. He should try to include, very briefly, some indication of the reason for each topic to be discussed. If one item is of special interest to the group, it is often a good idea to single it out for special mention in a covering note.

The leader should also bear in mind the useful device of heading each item "For information," "For discussion," or "For decision" so that those at the meeting know where they are trying to get to.

And finally, the chairman should not circulate the agenda too far in advance, since the less organized members will forget it or lose it. Two or three days is about

right—unless the supporting papers are voluminous.

Other 'Paper' Considerations. The order of items on the agenda is important. Some aspects are obvious—the items that need urgent decision have to come before those that can wait till next time. Equally, the leader does not discuss the budget for the reequipment program before discussing whether to put the reequipment off until next year. But some aspects are not so obvious. Consider:

1. The early part of a meeting tends to be more lively and creative than the end of it, so if an item needs mental energy, bright ideas, and clear heads, it may be better to put it high up on the list. Equally, if there is one item of great interest and concern to everyone, it may be a good idea to hold it back for a while and get some other useful work done first. Then the star item can be introduced to carry the meeting over the attention lag that sets in after the first 15 to 20 minutes of the meeting.

2. Some items unite the meeting in a common front while others divide the members one from another. The leader may want to start with unity before entering into division, or he may prefer the other way around. The point is to be aware of the choice and to make it consciously, because it is apt to make a difference to the whole atmosphere of the meeting. It is almost always a good idea to find a unifying item with which to end the meeting.

3. A common fault is to dwell too long on trivial but urgent items, to the exclusion of subjects of fundamental importance whose significance is long-term rather than immediate. This can be remedied by putting on the agenda the time at which discussion of the important long-term issue will begin—and by sticking to it.

4. Very few business meetings achieve anything of value after two hours, and an

hour and a half is enough time to allocate for most purposes.

5. It is often a good idea to put the finishing time of a meeting on the agenda as well as the starting time.

6. If meetings have a tendency to go on too long, the chairman should arrange to start them one hour before lunch or one hour before the end of work. Generally, items that ought to be kept brief can be introduced ten minutes from a fixed end point.

7. The practice of circulating background or proposal papers along with the minutes is, in principle, a good one. It not only saves time, but it also helps in formulating useful questions and considerations in advance. But the whole idea is sabotaged once the papers get too long; they should be brief or provide a short summary. If they are circulated, obviously the chairman has to read them, or at least must not be caught not having read them. (One chairman, more noted for his cunning than his conscientiousness, is said to have spent 30 seconds before each meeting going through all the papers he had not read with a thick red pen, marking lines and question marks in the margins at random, and making sure these were accidentally made visible to the meeting while the subject was being discussed.)

8. If papers are produced at the meeting for discussion, they should obviously be brief and simple, since everyone has to read them. It is a supreme folly to bring a group of people together to read six pages of closely printed sheets to themselves. The exception is certain kinds of financial and statistical papers whose function is to support and illustrate verbal points as reference documents rather than to be swallowed whole: these are often better tabled at the meeting.

9. All items should be thought of and thought about in advance if they are to be usefully discussed. Listing "Any other business" on the agenda is an invitation to waste time. This does not absolutely preclude the chairman's announcing an extra agenda item at a meeting if something really urgent and unforeseen crops up or is suggested to him by a member, provided it is fairly simple and straightforward. Nor does it preclude his leaving time for general unstructured discussion after the close of the meeting.

10. The chairman, in going through the agenda items in advance, can usefully insert his own brief notes of points he wants to be sure are not omitted from the discussion. A brief marginal scribble of "How much notice?" or "Standby arrangements?" or whatever is all that is necessary.

THE CHAIRMAN'S JOB

Let's say that you have just been appointed chairman of the committee. You tell everyone that it is a bore or a chore. You also tell them that you have been appointed "for my sins." But the point is that you tell them. There is no getting away from it: some sort of honor or glory attaches to the chairman's role. Almost everyone is in some way pleased and proud to be made chairman of something. And that is three quarters of the trouble.

Master or Servant?

Their appointment as committee chairman takes people in different ways. Some seize the opportunity to impose their will on a group that they see themselves licensed to dominate. Their chairmanship is a harangue, interspersed with demands for group agreement.

Others are more like scoutmasters, for whom the collective activity of the group is satisfaction enough, with no need for achievement. Their chairmanship is more like the endless stoking and fueling of a campfire that is not cooking anything.

And there are the insecure or lazy chairmen who look to the meeting for reassurance and support in their ineffectiveness and inactivity, so that they can spread the responsibility for their indecisiveness among the whole group. They seize on every expression of disagreement or doubt as a justification for avoiding decision or action.

But even the large majority who do not go to those extremes still feel a certain pleasurable tumescence of the ego when they take their place at the head of the table for the first time. The feeling is no sin: the sin is to indulge it or to assume that the pleasure is shared by the other members of the meeting.

It is the chairman's self-indulgence that is the greatest single barrier to the success of a meeting. His first duty, then, is to be aware of the temptation and of the dangers of yielding to it. The clearest of the danger signals is hearing himself talking a lot during a discussion.

One of the best chairmen I have ever served under makes it a rule to restrict her interventions to a single sentence, or at most two. She forbids herself ever to contribute a paragraph to a meeting she is chairing. It is a harsh rule, but you would be hard put to find a regular attender of her meetings (or anyone else's) who thought it was a bad one.

There is, in fact, only one legitimate source of pleasure in chairmanship, and that is pleasure in the achievements of the meeting—and to be legitimate, it must be shared by those present. Meetings are *necessary* for all sorts of basic and primitive human reasons, but they are *useful* only if they are seen by all present to be getting somewhere—and somewhere they know they could not have gotten to individually.

If the chairman is to make sure that the meeting achieves valuable objectives, he will be more effective seeing himself as the servant of the group rather than as its master. His role then becomes that of assisting the group toward the best conclusion or decision in the most efficient manner possible: to interpret and clarify; to move the discussion forward; and to bring it to a resolution that everyone understands and accepts as being the will of the meeting, even if the individuals do not necessarily agree with it.

His true source of authority with the members is the strength of his perceived commitment to their combined objective and his skill and efficiency in helping and guiding them to its achievement. Control and discipline then become not the act of imposing his will on the group but of imposing the group's will on any individual who is in danger of diverting or delaying the progress of the discussion and so from realizing the objective.

Once the members realize that the leader is impelled by his commitment to their common objective, it does not take great force of personality for him to control the meeting. Indeed, a sense of urgency and a clear desire to reach the best conclusion as quickly as possible are a much more effective disciplinary instrument than a big gavel. The effective chairman can then hold the discussion to the point by indicating that there is no time to pursue a particular idea now, that there is no time for long speeches, that the group has to get through this item and on to the next one, rather than by resorting to pulling rank.

There are many polite ways the chairman can indicate a slight impatience even when someone else is speaking—by leaning forward, fixing his eyes on the speaker, tensing his muscles, raising his eyebrows, or nodding briefly to show the point is taken. And when replying or commenting, the chairman can indicate by the speed, brevity, and finality of his intonation that "we have to move on." Conversely, he can reward the sort of contribution he is seeking by the opposite expressions and intonations, showing that there is plenty of time for that sort of idea, and encouraging the speaker to develop the point.

After a few meetings, all present readily understand this nonverbal language of chairmanship. It is the chairman's chief instrument of educating the group into the general type of "meeting behavior" that he is looking for. He is still the servant of the group, but like a hired mountain guide, he is the one who knows the destination, the route, the weather signs, and the time the journey will take. So if he suggests that the members walk a bit faster, they take his advice.

This role of servant rather than master is often obscured in large organizations by the fact that the chairman is frequently the line manager of the members: this does not, however, change the reality of the role of chairman. The point is easier to see in, say, a neighborhood action group. The question in that case is, simply, "Through which person's chairmanship do we collectively have the best chance of getting the children's playground built?"

However, one special problem is posed by this definition of the chairman's role, and it has an extremely interesting answer. The question is: How can the chairman combine his role with the role of a member advocating one side of an argument?

The answer comes from some interesting studies by researchers who sat in on hundreds of meetings to find out how they work. Their consensus finding is that most of the effective discussions have, in fact, two leaders: one they call a "team," or "social," leader; the other a "task," or "project," leader.

Regardless of whether leadership is in fact a single or a dual function, for our purposes it is enough to say that the chairman's best role is that of social leader. If he wants a particular point to be strongly advocated, he ensures that it is someone else who leads off the task discussion, and he holds back until much later in the argument. He might indeed change or modify his view through hearing the discussion, but even if he does not it is much easier for him to show support for someone else's point later in the discussion, after listening to the arguments. Then, he can summarize in favor of the one he prefers.

The task advocate might regularly be the chairman's second-in-command, or a different person might advocate for different items on the agenda. On some subjects, the chairman might well be the task advocate himself, especially if they do not involve conflict within the group. The important point is that the chairman has to keep his "social leadership" even if it means sacrificing his "task leadership." However, if the designated task advocate persists in championing a cause through two or three meetings, he risks building up quite a head of antagonism to him among the other members. Even so, this antagonism harms the group less by being directed at the "task leader" than at the "social leader."

Structure of Discussion

It may seem that there is no right way or wrong way to structure a committee meeting discussion. A subject is raised, people say what they think, and finally a decision is reached, or the discussion is terminated. There is some truth in this. Moreover, it would be a mistake to try and tie every discussion of every item down to a single immutable format.

Nevertheless, there is a logical order to a group discussion, and while there can be reasons for not following it, there is no justification for not being aware of it. In practice, very few discussions are inhibited, and many are expedited, by a conscious adherence to the following stages, which follow exactly the same pattern as a visit to the doctor:

"What seems to be the trouble?" The reason for an item being on a meeting agenda is usually like the symptom we go to the doctor with: "I keep getting this pain in my back" is analogous to "Sales have risen in Germany but fallen in France." In both cases it is clear that something is wrong and that something ought to be done to put it right. But until the visit to the doctor, or the meeting of the European marketing committee, that is about all we really know.

"How long has this been going on?" The doctor will start with a case history of all the relevant background facts, and so will the committee discussion. A solid basis of shared and agreed-on facts is the best foundation to build any decision on, and a set of pertinent questions will help establish it. For example, when did French sales start to fall off? Have German sales risen exceptionally? Has France had delivery problems, or less sales effort, or weaker advertising? Have we lost market share, or are our competitors' sales falling too? If the answers to all these questions, and more, are not established at the start, a lot of discussion may be wasted later.

"Would you just lie down on the couch?" The doctor will then conduct a physical examination to find out how the patient is now. The committee, too, will want to know how things stand at this moment. Is action being taken? Do long-term orders show the same trend? What are the latest figures? What is the current stock position? How much money is left in the advertising budget?

"You seem to have slipped a disc." When the facts are established, you can move toward a diagnosis. A doctor may seem to do this quickly, but that is the result of experience and practice. He is, in fact, rapidly eliminating all the impossible or far-fetched explanations until he leaves himself with a short list. The committee, too, will hazard and eliminate a variety of diagnoses until it homes in on the most probable—for example, the company's recent energetic and highly successful advertising campaign in Germany plus new packaging by the market leader in France.

"Take this 'round to the druggist." Again, the doctor is likely to take a shortcut that a committee meeting may be wise to avoid. The doctor comes out with a single prescription, and the committee, too, may agree quickly on a single course of action.

But if the course is not so clear, it is better to take this step in two stages: (a) construct a series of options—do not, at first, reject any suggestions outright but try to select and combine the promising elements from all of them until a number of thought-out, coherent, and sensible suggestions are on the table; and (b) only when you have generated these options do you start to choose among them. Then you can discuss and decide whether to pick the course based on repackaging and point-of-sale promotion, or the one based on advertising and a price cut, or the one that bides its time and saves the money for heavier new-product promotion next year.

If the item is at all complex or especially significant, it is important for the chairman not only to have the proposed course of the discussion in his own head, but also to announce it so that everyone knows. A good idea is to write the headings on an easel pad with a felt pen. This saves much of the time wasting and confusion that result when people raise items in the wrong place because they were not privy to the chairman's secret that the right place was coming up later on in the discussion.

CONDUCTING THE MEETING

Just as the driver of a car has two tasks, to follow his route and to manage his vehicle, so the chairman's job can be divided into two corresponding tasks, dealing with the subject and dealing with the people.

Dealing with the Subject

The essence of this task is to follow the structure of discussion as just described in the previous section. This, in turn, entails listening carefully and keeping the meeting pointed toward the objective.

At the start of the discussion of any item, the chairman should make it clear where the meeting should try to get to by the end. Are the members hoping to make a clear decision or firm recommendation? Is it a preliminary deliberation to give the members something to go away with and think about? Are they looking for a variety of different lines to be pursued outside the meeting? Do they have to approve the proposal, or merely note it?

The chairman may give them a choice: "If we can agree on a course of action, that's fine. If not, we'll have to set up a working party to report and recommend before next month's meeting."

The chairman should make sure that all the members understand the issue and why they are discussing it. Often it will be obvious, or else they may have been through it before. If not, then he or someone he has briefed before the meeting should give a short introduction, with some indication of the reason the item is on the agenda; the story so far; the present position; what needs to be established, resolved, or proposed; and some indication of lines of inquiry or courses of action that have been suggested or explored, as well as arguments on both sides of the issue.

If the discussion is at all likely to be long or complex, the chairman should propose to the meeting a structure for it with headings (written up if necessary), as I stated at the end of the section on "Structure of discussion." He should listen carefully in case people jump too far ahead (e.g., start proposing a course of action before the meeting has agreed on the cause of the trouble), or go back over old ground, or start repeating points that have been made earlier. He has to head discussion off sterile or irrelevant areas very quickly (e.g., the rights and wrongs of past decisions that it is too late to change, or distant prospects that are too remote to affect present actions).

It is the chairman's responsibility to prevent misunderstanding and confusion. If he does not follow an argument or understand a reference, he should seek clarification from the speaker. If he thinks two people are using the same word with different meanings, he should intervene (e.g., one member using *promotion* to mean point-of-sale advertising only, and another also including media publicity).

He may also have to clarify by asking people for facts or experience that perhaps influence their view but are not known to others in the meeting. And he should be on the lookout for points where an interim summary would be helpful. This device frequently takes only a few seconds, and acts like a life belt to some of the members who are getting out of their depth.

Sometimes a meeting will have to discuss a draft document. If there are faults in it, the members should agree on what the faults are and the chairman should delegate someone to produce a new draft later. The group should never try to redraft around the table.

Perhaps one of the most common faults of chairmanship is the failure to terminate the discussion early enough. Sometimes chairmen do not realize that the meeting has effectively reached an agreement, and consequently they let the discussion go on for another few minutes, getting nowhere at all. Even more often, they are not quick enough to close a discussion *before* agreement has been reached.

A discussion should be closed once it has become clear that (a) more facts are required before further progress can be made, (b) discussion has revealed that the meeting needs the views of people not present, (c) members need more time to think about the subject and perhaps discuss it with colleagues, (d) events are changing and likely to alter or clarify the basis of the decision quite soon, (e) there is not going to be enough time at this meeting to go over the subject properly, or (f) it is becoming clear that two or three of the members can settle this outside the meeting without taking up the time of the rest. The fact that the decision is difficult, likely to be disputed, or going to be unwelcome to somebody, however, is not a reason for postponement.

At the end of the discussion of each agenda item, the chairman should give a brief and clear summary of what has been agreed on. This can act as the dictation of the actual minutes. It serves not merely to put the item on record, but also to help people realize that something worthwhile has been achieved. It also answers the question "Where did all that get us?" If the summary involves action by a member of the meeting, he should be asked to confirm his acceptance of the undertaking.

Dealing with the People

There is only one way to ensure that a meeting starts on time, and that is to start it on time. Latecomers who find that the meeting has begun without them soon learn the lesson. The alternative is that the prompt and punctual members will soon realize that a meeting never starts until ten minutes after the advertised time, and they will also learn the lesson.

Punctuality at future meetings can be wonderfully reinforced by the practice of listing late arrivals (and early departures) in the minutes. Its ostensible and perfectly proper purpose is to call the latecomer's attention to the fact that he was absent when a decision was reached. Its side effect, however, is to tell everyone on the circulation list that he was late, and people do not want that sort of information about themselves published too frequently.

There is a growing volume of work on the significance of seating positions and their effect on group behavior and relationships. Not all the findings are generally agreed on. What does seem true is that:

1. Having members sit face to face across a table facilitates opposition, conflict, and disagreement, though of course it does not turn allies into enemies. But it does suggest that the chairman should think about whom he seats opposite himself.

2. Sitting side by side makes disagreements and confrontation harder. This in turn suggests that the chairman can exploit the friendship-value of the seats next to him.

3. There is a "dead man's corner" on the chairman's right, especially if a number of people are seated in line along from him (it does not apply if he is alone at the head of the table).

4. As a general rule, proximity to the

chairman is a sign of honor and favor. This is most marked when he is at the head of a long, narrow table. The greater the distance, the lower the rank— just as the lower-status positions were "below the salt" at medieval refectories.

Control the Garrulous. In most meetings someone takes a long time to say very little. As chairman, your sense of urgency should help indicate to him the need for brevity. You can also suggest that if he is going to take a long time it might be better for him to write a paper. If it is urgent to stop him in full flight, there is a useful device of picking on a phrase (it really doesn't matter what phrase) as he utters it as an excuse for cutting in and offering it to someone else: "Inevitable decline— that's very interesting. George, do you agree that the decline is inevitable?"

Draw out the Silent. In any properly run meeting, as simple arithmetic will show, most of the people will be silent most of the time. Silence can indicate general agreement, or no important contribution to make, or the need to wait and hear more before saying anything, or too good a lunch, and none of these need worry you. But there are two kinds of silence you must break:

1. The silence of diffidence. Someone may have a valuable contribution to make but be sufficiently nervous about its possible reception to keep it to himself. It is important that when you draw out such a contribution, you should express interest and pleasure (though not necessarily agreement) to encourage further contributions of that sort.

2. The silence of hostility. This is not hostility to ideas, but to you as the chairman, to the meeting, and to the process by which decisions are being reached. This sort of total detachment from the whole proceedings is usually the symptom of some feeling of affront. If you probe it,

you will usually find that there is something bursting to come out, and that it is better out than in.

Protect the Weak. Junior members of the meeting may provoke the disagreement of their seniors, which is perfectly reasonable. But if the disagreement escalates to the point of suggesting that they have no right to contribute, the meeting is weakened. So you may have to take pains to commend their contribution for its usefulness, as a pre-emptive measure. You can reinforce this action by taking a written note of a point they make (always a plus for a member of a meeting) and by referring to it again later in the discussion (a double-plus).

Encourage the Clash of Ideas. But, at the same time, discourage the clash of personalities. A good meeting is not a series of dialogues between individual members and the chairman. Instead, it is a crossflow of discussion and debate, with the chairman occasionally guiding, mediating, probing, stimulating, and summarizing, but mostly letting the others thrash ideas out. However, the meeting must be a contention of *ideas,* not people.

If two people are starting to get heated, widen the discussion by asking a question of a neutral member of the meeting, preferably a question that requires a purely factual answer.

Watch Out for the Suggestion-Squashing Reflex. Students of meetings have reduced everything that can be said into questions, answers, positive reactions, and negative reactions. Questions can only seek, and answers only supply, three types of response: information, opinion, and suggestion.

In almost every modern organization, it is the suggestions that contain the seeds of future success. Although very few suggestions will ever lead to anything, almost all of them need to be given every chance.

The trouble is that suggestions are much easier to ridicule than facts or opinions. If people feel that making a suggestion will provoke the negative reaction of being laughed at or squashed they will soon stop. And if there is any status-jostling going on at the meeting, it is all too easy to use the occasion of someone's making a suggestion for the opportunity to take him down a peg. It is all too easy and a formula to ensure sterile meetings.

The answer is for you to take special notice and show special warmth when anyone makes a suggestion, and to discourage as sharply as you can the squashing-reflex. This can often be achieved by requiring the squasher to produce a better suggestion on the spot. Few suggestions can stand up to squashing in their pristine state: your reflex must be to pick out the best part of one and get the other committee members to help build it into something that might work.

Come to the Most Senior People Last. Obviously, this cannot be a rule, but once someone of high authority has pronounced on a topic, the less senior members are likely to be inhibited. If you work up the pecking order instead of down it, you are apt to get a wider spread of views and ideas. But the juniors who start it off should only be asked for contributions within their personal experience and competence. ("Peter, you were at the Frankfurt Exhibition—what reactions did you pick up there?")

Close on a Note of Achievement. Even if the final item is left unresolved, you can refer to an earlier item that was well resolved as you close the meeting and thank the group.

If the meeting is not a regular one, fix the time and place of the next one before dispersing. A little time spent with appointment diaries at the end, especially if it is a gathering of five or more members, can save hours of secretarial telephoning later.

Following the Meeting

Your secretary may take the minutes (or better still, one of the members), but the minutes are your responsibility. They can be very brief, but they should include these facts:

1. The time and date of the meeting, where it was held, and who chaired it.
2. Names of all present and apologies for absence.
3. All agenda items (and other items) discussed and all decisions reached. If action was agreed on, record (and underline) the name of the person responsible for the assignment.
4. The time at which the meeting ended (important, because it may be significant later to know whether the discussion lasted 15 minutes or 6 hours).
5. The date, time, and place of the next committee meeting.

22. Administering Personnel Policies

National Board of the Young Women's Christian Association of the United States

PERSONNEL POLICIES

PROVISIONS TO BE INCLUDED

Introduction

Since personnel policies cover staff who are employed to carry out the objectives and adopted program of the YWCA, policies should begin with a brief statement describing objectives and program. Pertinent excerpts from the Association's Affirmative Action Program and/or the Association's Policy of Nondiscrimination should be included.

Statement Re Purpose of Policies

This statement should:

• Give staff a clear understanding of conditions under which they are employed and work and to provide a positive work climate.
• Clarify the roles of persons responsible for personnel administration, including
    —Board of directors
    —Personnel committee
    —Executive director
    —Supervisory staff.

Conditions of Employment

Employment of staff shall be on the basis of ability to meet job requirements. Staff shall be willing to accept responsibility for implementing the Purpose, the

Reprinted with permission of National Board, YWCA, 600 Lexington Avenue, New York, N.Y., 10022.

Imperative and Program for Action as defined and accepted by the national convention and goals adopted by the employing Association's board of directors.

The executive director is required to become a member of the YWCA. Program and administrative staff should be encouraged to become members.

Letter of Employment

A letter of employment signed by both the staff member and executive director constitutes a formal employment agreement. Two copies are sent to the employee, who signs and returns one copy. In the case of the executive director the letter of employment is signed by the president.

This letter informs each employee of job title and job classification, beginning salary and salary range for the position and the beginning date. Provisions for payment of moving expenses for the executive director are usually included. A job description and a copy of the personnel policies are enclosed.

By signing the letter of employment and returning it the staff member signifies that there is mutuality of agreement; that she accepts responsibilities included in the job description and conditions of work as described in the personnel policies.

Professional Staff Development

In order that professional staff have optimum opportunity to grow on their jobs the Association provides a staff development program, including orientation, supervision and annual job performance appraisal as well as opportunities to participate in regional and national YWCA happenings and in community projects.

Promotional Opportunities

Current staff will be given the opportunity to make application as vacancies occur which provide for upgrading.

The Work Week and Hours of Work

Work week—usually 5 days and from 35 to 39 hours, not including the hour off daily for meals. For professional staff the work week schedule has to be flexible.

Hours of work include time for planning and preparation as well as the actual program; also included are staff meetings, supervisory conferences, training sessions and any other activity where a staff member represents the YWCA.

Staff should not be scheduled for more than two evenings a week or two periods in a weekend except in cases where more is spelled out in the job description and is a condition of employment. (A work period is a morning, afternoon or evening.)

Provision for 48 consecutive hours off each week—not necessarily Saturday and Sunday.

Overtime, that is work beyond the number of hours in the stated work week, is discouraged, but when necessary compensatory time off is granted but must be cleared with supervisor. The staff member is responsible for recording overtime and reporting it to her supervisor.

Overtime compensation for clerical and service employees must meet legal requirements—usually time and a half off or time and a half pay for over 40 hours.

Holidays

It is common practice to designate 11 holidays in each working year. Holidays should conform to local and national practice. They should be listed in the policies. Those usually included are:

New Year's Day	Independence Day
Martin Luther King's Birthday	Labor Day
Washington's or Lincoln's Birthday	Thanksgiving Day
Memorial Day	Christmas Day

Three additional holidays to be designated by the Association at the beginning of the program year. These are often related to the day after Thanksgiving or the day of the week upon which Christmas and New Year's fall.

Vacations

Provision should be made for paid earned vacations for all staff who work full time or half time or more. For all staff vacations are based on length of service within the program year, September 1 through August 31, or the fiscal year of the Association. For those on staff less than a year or part time, vacations are prorated.

Vacations are scheduled in consultation with the supervisor in relation to job responsibilities and approved by the executive director. Effort will be made to schedule vacation at the time desired by the staff member.

For professional staff: Historically the YWCA has allowed one month (22 working days) in the summer and one week (5 working days) in the winter. In recent years YWCAs have been flexible in scheduling 27 working days.

The purpose of vacation is rest and refreshment. To get greatest benefit it is recommended that if possible a major portion be taken consecutively. The remaining vacation time may be taken in days off.

Professional staff employed during a program year accrue vacation at the rate of 2¼ days for each completed month of service prior to September 1.

For clerical and service staff: Annual vacation is recommended as follows:

1 to 3 years of service: 12 working days
3 through 4 years of service: 16 working days
4 through 9 years of service: 18 working days
10 years and more of service: 22 working days

Clerical or service personnel employed during a program year accrue vacation at the rate of one day for each completed month of service prior to September 1.

Vacations are earned, and, if not taken prior to leaving the Association, compensation for unused vacation should be included in final paycheck. Salary for unearned vacation taken prior to termination will be deducted from final pay check.

Paid vacations are in addition to holidays, which may fall within a vacation period.

Vacation is not cumulative except in unusual cases and approved by the executive director. After a specified number of years of service, some Associations grant leave for professional staff in addition to vacation.

Leaves of Absence

Sick Leave for Personal Illness. Sick leave with pay usually accrues at the rate of 1½ days each month or 18 days per year to a total of 60 working days.

Provision should cover advancing sick leave to the 60-day limit if necessary, with the understanding that if the staff member leaves, salary for unearned sick leave used will be deducted from final salary.

Vacation and sick leave are not interchangeable. Special consideration may be recommended to the board in cases of protracted illness. A doctor's statement may be required in some instances—these should be spelled out in the policies.

The YWCAs which have had a policy of sick leave accrual have found that staff are more reluctant to use up sick leave annually. Staff recognize that accumulated leave is really "insurance" against a protracted illness.

Personal Leave. A limited number of days should be specified—usually 3 to 5—for family responsibilities, religious observances or other private matters. This leave is not cumulative and must be cleared with the executive director.

Leave for Study. Educational or study leave on pay is usually earned after 3 to 5 years of employment and is usually 1 month and can be used in conjunction with vacation or spread over a period of months if necessary. Continuing to work for the Association after leave is a usual requirement. The personnel committee will consider any staff member's request for time off or rearrangement of schedule to allow time to take a course relating to the job.

Leaves for Pregnancy and Childbirth. Provision should be made for such leaves. Unused sick leave, earned vacation, and disability benefits apply.

Maternity leave is usually limited. In states which have laws related to maternity leave, legal requirements must be taken into account.

Provision must be made for the staff member to return to a job of equal status when such a vacancy occurs, or to a lesser or part-time job when it occurs if the staff member prefers. Since the staff member's work will have to be covered during her absence, date of return must be left flexible.

Leave for Jury Duty. Time and salary are usually allowed. Such leave must be cleared with employee's supervisor.

Leave for Annual Military Duty. Ten

working days are usually allowed. Usually the staff member receives military compensation. If it is lower than the Association salary, the YWCA makes up the difference.

Time Off to Vote. Legal regulations must be met.

Health and Health Examinations

Annual health examinations are encouraged. Some Associations budget a minimum amount per staff member to be paid toward an annual checkup.

When in the judgment of the executive director the health condition is such as to justify it, a staff member may be requested to have a thorough examination. The staff member may select her physician. The expense of any such examination requested will be borne by the Association. Care must be taken that the employee's confidential relationship with her physician is not violated.

Economic and Fringe Benefits

Salaries. Salary ranges should be established for all job classifications and include an annual automatic increment. (Jobs are classified taking into account degree of responsibility for total program, level of academic or special training required, complexity of relationships, supervisory responsibility and necessity for exercising independent judgment.)

Salaries and salary scales with annual increments should reflect local and national trends. In developing salary ranges there should be some overlap with the next job classification.

Each employee is informed as to his or her job classification with the salary range and annual increment for the position.

Social Security. It is mandatory that all employees be covered by the Federal Social Security Act and its amendments.

Retirement Benefits. The Association participates in:

- YWCA Retirement Fund for the benefit of professional workers.
- The Savings and Security Plan for the benefit of clerical and service employees.

Persons in jobs classified as managerial or technical may choose which of the plans they wish to join.

Persons employed half time or more should be required to join one of the above plans.

Tax-Sheltered Annuities. Many Associations make tax-sheltered annuities available for purchase by full-time staff. Policies should include directions for making application.

Health Insurance. Hospital, medical and surgical insurance should be available at group rates. The Association may pay all or part of costs of such coverage for the employee—additional cost for extending coverage to family will be borne by the staff member.

Other Insurances. These may vary with state laws. For example:

- Workmen's compensation
- Unemployment compensation
- Disability coverage
- Blanket bond for staff handling money
- Additional insurance coverage for staff using own cars for Association business and program.

Payroll Deductions. Deductions may be made at the request of the staff member for any or all of the following:

- Additional payments to Pension Fund
- Contributions to YWCA, United Way

- U.S. Government Bonds
- Credit union
- Payroll savings
- Tax-sheltered annuities
- Union dues for any category of workers that is organized.

Job Expenses. Reimbursement for expenses incurred in carrying out job duties must be authorized in advance. They may include officially representing the YWCA in the community, attending YWCA meetings or conferences, conventions, etc. and may include travel, housing and meals, registration and tuition costs.

A mileage allowance should be set for staff using own cars on YWCA business or in carrying out job responsibility. This should be reviewed periodically in view of rising costs.

Staff member submits expenses in voucher form which must be approved by the supervisor.

Termination of Employment

Termination by Resignation. Staff members resigning have a responsibility to time resignations if possible so as to be least upsetting to the YWCA.

Minimum period of notice is usually:

Executive director:	3 months
Other professional staff:	1 month
Other staff:	2 weeks

Staff will be paid during period of notice and for any accrued vacation. Failure to give minimum notice means staff will forfeit earned vacation pay. (Check requirements of state law.)

Resignations should be submitted in writing to the executive director—in the case of the executive director, to the president.

Termination by the YWCA. Termination of employment may be initiated by

the YWCA for any of the following reasons:

- Unsatisfactory work performance including habitual tardiness, excessive absence or physical inability to carry the job. In such a case the staff member will be given the opportunity to resign.
- Discharge for cause (conduct inconsistent with the principles of the YWCA or malfeasance).
- Elimination of a position due to reorganization or retrenchment.

Notice of termination. Except in cases of discharge for cause, the YWCA will give notice of termination or pay a severance allowance as follows:

Executive director:	3 months minimum
Other professional staff:	1 month minimum
Other staff	
Less than 1 year service:	1 week minimum
More than 1 year service:	2 weeks minimum

In cases of termination due to reorganization or retrenchment the YWCA will give notice:

To professional staff:	3 months minimum
To nonprofessional staff:	1 month minimum

Termination Payments. Except in cases of discharge for cause, staff members terminated will be paid for unused earned vacation to which they are eligible. In cases of termination where job is eliminated, special severance pay is usually provided—based on each completed year of service. In any termination payments, pay for unused sick leave is not included.

Appeals

A staff member having a complaint should first try to settle it with the immediate supervisor. If this fails, the next step is to discuss the matter with the executive director. If settlement cannot be reached with the help of the executive director, the staff member may request in writing a hearing with the appeals committee.

The appeals committee is composed of the personnel chairperson, president, committee chairperson or persons most closely related to work of the staff member. (In a branch the last mentioned would be a member of the branch committee on administration.) The appeals committee must hold the hearing promptly, usually within 2 weeks. Its decision is binding.

Since this process is in no sense a legal hearing, the employee may be accompanied by one person who may be a member of her committee or other person familiar with the circumstances, excluding staff members and attorneys.

The committee to hear appeals of the executive director is composed of the personnel chairperson who presides, president, and one or more board members.

Retirement Policy

Age 65 is the normal retirement age. The Association notifies the employee of the date of retirement three months in advance. If the employee is continued after age 65 it should be on a year-to-year basis.

Personnel Records

Personnel records are kept for all staff members. This is the responsibility of the executive director. These records are confidential and available only to the personnel chairperson, the president and the executive director.

Personnel records include:
- Application and references
- Letter of employment
- Job description
- Salary
- Medical information
- Personal leave record
- Vacation record
- Record of sick leave
- Record of compensatory time
- Training activities
- Annual job performance appraisal
- Summary of job performance appraisal
- Any other confidential materials relating to the job
- Record of termination interview also
- Home address and telephone number
- Person to be notified in case of an emergency

EMPLOYMENT PROCEDURES FOR PROFESSIONAL STAFF

Executive Director

When it is necessary to fill the position for executive director, the president, the personnel chairperson and three other board members shall comprise a special search committee to work on the vacancy. This committee shall outline needed qualifications and prepare the vacancy registration form for registering the position with the national Membership-Leadership Development Unit. It shall review applications of candidates secured from the national office and/or other sources, arrange candidate interviews with members of the search committee and recommend the candidate of the committee's choice to the board of directors.

Immediately after affirmative board action, the president will notify the candidate of her appointment and send her a letter of employment stating the terms of employment, a copy of the personnel policies and a job description. The Association will cover moving expenses for the executive director.

Other Professional Staff

The executive director, acting on behalf of the board, has authority to fill other staff positions. She consults with the appropriate volunteers and staff related to the job in preparing the vacancy registration form for registering the position with the national Membership-Leadership Development Unit. She may review applications of candidates with the personnel chairperson and appropriate chairperson and arranges for interviews. The executive director, committee chairperson, personnel chairperson and related staff may be included in the schedule of interviews, if possible.

When the interviewers, after consultation, have decided on the candidate of their choice, the appointee is notified by the executive director immediately and is sent a letter of employment stating the terms of employment, a copy of personnel policies and a job description.

All Employed Staff

Employed staff must be willing to accept responsibility to further the achievement of the Purpose in the life of the Association.

It is a condition of employment that a new staff member request her physician to submit to the personnel chairperson or executive director a statement to the effect that she is physically able to perform the duties of the position for which she is being considered. The cost of consultation up to $15.00 to enable her physician to provide a health statement will be borne by the Association.

Expenses for personal interviews are borne by the employing Association.

STAFF DEVELOPMENT PROGRAM

In order that professional staff have an optimum opportunity to grow on their jobs provision is made for:

1. Orientation of new staff. The executive director works with appropriate board and committee members in making a plan to introduce a new staff member to the community and the Association. In the case of a new executive director, the president and the personnel chairperson are responsible. The National YWCA offers orientation institutes and basic training each year for staff who have been on the job for two years or less.

2. Supervision—a continuous process. It will begin with orientation as a new staff member is helped to become acquainted with the Association and the job. The supervisory person related to each staff member is indicated on the job description. Regular supervisory conferences are planned for in the time schedule. These conferences provide an opportunity for expediting the work of the Association and for teaching and learning as problems are tackled. They can be stimulating and rewarding as both persons feel the program is moving ahead.

3. Staff meetings help all staff to see the program as a whole and to understand their various roles. They provide, too, the points to be followed up in supervisory conferences and are the place where problems from the supervisory conference relating to a whole staff are worked on further.

4. An annual job performance appraisal is a formalized part of the whole supervisory process—a time of stocktaking and deciding where emphasis shall be put. Both supervisor and supervisee will prepare for this conference constructively by pointing up progress or lack of it. The supervisor is responsible for conferring, prior to the evaluating confer-

ence, with those persons who are officially related to the staff member's work. The appraisal will be written by the supervisor after the conference and shared with the staff member in written form. It becomes a part of the confidential personnel file. If there is a difference in point of view which cannot be reconciled, both opinions should be filed with the personnel record.

A summary of the annual job performance appraisal is prepared by the supervisor, shared with the staff member and the executive director and is signed by all three. A copy of the summary is sent to the Membership-Leadership Development Unit, National Board.

The procedure for the annual job performance appraisal of the executive director differs from that for other staff in one respect only. Since she has no supervisor, the appraisal is done by a special committee chaired by the personnel chairperson. She, the president and two other board members participate. The two board members are selected by the president and the executive director. They will be persons with whom she has worked on special projects or with whom she has worked closely on specific day-by-day responsibilities.

The basis for the appraisal, as for other staff, will be the job description and work plans which have been developed with the particular board members as they have worked together.

A summary of the annual job performance appraisal is prepared by the personnel chairperson, shared with the executive director and signed by both. A copy is sent to the Membership-Leadership Development Unit, national headquarters.

5. Opportunities for staff to participate in

and carry leadership responsibilities in YWCA conventions, conferences, institutes and workshops and to be a part of round-table groups are allowed for in time schedules of staff members.

6. Educational or study leave on pay is usually earned after 3 to 5 years of employment and is usually 1 month and can be used in conjunction with vacation or spread over a period of months if necessary. Continuing to work for the Association after leave is a usual requirement. The personnel committee will consider any staff member's request for time off or rearrangement of schedule to allow time to take a course relating to the job.

7. Special training for experienced administrative and/or program staff offered by the National YWCA provides opportunities for staff development and help in coping with problems the YWCA faces currently. The Association budgets for such training.

RETIREMENT FUND AND SAVINGS AND SECURITY PLAN

Suggested Statement re Participation in the Retirement Fund

All new full-time professional staff members, under age 65, shall be required to join the YWCA Retirement Fund after one year of employment. All such eligible staff members, as well as those employed at least half time, shall be permitted and urged to join immediately upon employment or during the first year.

Staff members whose positions are classified as managerial or technical shall be permitted to choose between participation in the Fund or The Savings and Security Plan of the YWCA, but they must join one.

If a new professional staff member, at the time of her employment, is participating in a retirement system which provides benefits substantially the same as those of the Fund, she shall be permitted to continue in that system (provided the system allows such continued participation) and need not join the Fund, and the Association will make the employer payment to that system. This provision applies to such retirement systems as YWCA, TIAA and various church plans but does not apply to personal insurance programs to which the employer makes no contribution.

The annual budget shall include an item to cover the Association contribution for each eligible staff member.

Important to Note. Staff members who join the Retirement Fund must now participate at least 5 years as well as be age 55 or over when they terminate YWCA employment in order to qualify for a service retirement allowance. Those who are age 60 or over when they join will qualify for service retirement if they remain in the YWCA until after age 65 (the normal retirement age), regardless of the number of years of participation.

It is recommended that new staff members over age 60 take advantage of membership in the Fund, for they would have the protection of a death benefit while employed and the privilege of a refund of their own payments, plus interest and dividends. But more important, they could qualify for a service retirement allowance if they continue in the YWCA until after their 65th birthday. While their annuities would be small, they would provide some retirement income which they would not otherwise receive.

Suggested Statement re Participation in Savings and Security Plan

The _____ Association participates in The Savings and Security Plan of the YWCA for the benefit of its clerical, maintenance and food service employees. The Plan provides retirement benefits, death and disability protection. Membership in the Plan is a condition of employment for all new eligible employees after the successful completion of _____ months' employment.

Eligible employees are all those under age 65, working at least half time in positions classified by the Association as clerical, maintenance and food service. The annual budget shall include an item to cover the Association contribution for each eligible employee.

Note: So far as the Plan is concerned, participation may begin immediately upon employment. However, the Association has the right to determine whether a specified waiting period shall elapse before new eligible employees are required to join. The majority of YWCAs specify either three or six months.

PROCEDURES IN TERMINATIONS INITIATED BY THE YWCA

Procedures initiated by the YWCA shall be only for these reasons:

- Unsatisfactory work performance or physical inability to meet job requirements
- Conduct inconsistent with the principles of the YWCA, and/or malfeasance
- Reorganization and/or retrenchment

Unsatisfactory Work Performance. In all cases where work performance is questioned there shall be a written appraisal pointing up strengths and weaknesses. This will be shared with the staff member, and a period of time in which to show improvement will be mutually agreed upon.

If at the end of this period performance is still considered unsatisfactory by those participating in the evaluation, the staff member will be so informed by the executive director or the supervisor. The staff member will be given an opportunity to resign.

At any point during the process a staff member, after first discussing her problem with her immediate supervisor may, if she desires, confer also with the executive director. If she feels unsatisfied with this conference, she may discuss her situation with the personnel chairperson or the president. The executive director reports any termination to the board.

In the case of a staff member other than the executive director, the group participating in making judgment about unsatisfactory work performance will be the executive director and/or the supervisor if other than the executive director, related chairperson and the personnel chairperson. Judgments will be based on the cumulative job performance appraisal. If a staff member wishes, appeals procedure can be used.

In the case of the executive director, there shall be an appraisal pointing up strengths and weakness. (This appraisal will be made by a committee chaired by the personnel chairperson and composed of one or more board members agreed upon by the president and the executive director. These board members will be persons with whom the executive director has worked closely on a day-by-day basis.) After the appraisal the executive director will be given a probation of at least three months. If at the end of this period the appraisal committee still feels that her work is unsatisfactory, she will be terminated.

Conduct and/or Malfeasance

Executive Director: If, in the judgment of the president, other officers and the personnel chairperson, the conduct of the executive director should be such as to bring discredit upon the Association or in any way jeopardize its positon in the community or she is guilty of malfeasance, the executive director is so advised by the president and/or the personnel chairperson and given an opportunity to resign. In such cases immediate termination of employment may be advisable; the executive director may or may not be paid for the usual notification period and may or may not forfeit all other benefits. The personnel chairperson reports termination to the board of directors for action. (Check requirements of state law.)

Other professional staff: Whenever in the judgment of the supervisor, related chairperson, executive director and personnel chairperson a staff member's conduct is such as to bring discredit upon the Association or in any way jeopardize its position in the community or she is guilty of malfeasance, she shall be so advised by her direct supervisor and given an opportunity to resign. The executive director reports the termination to the board of directors. In such cases immediate termination of employment may be advisable; the employee may or may not be paid for the usual notification period and may or may not forfeit all other benefits.

Reorganization and/or retrenchment. In cases of reorganization and/or retrenchment the Association notifies the staff member as early as possible—for professional staff no less than 3 months in advance of the termination date. The formula for special severance pay is usually one week's pay for each year of service.

Elinor Bowles

NONRACIST, NONSEXIST GUIDELINES FOR CHILD CARE PROGRAMS

For minority ethnic groups in America, early childhood education programs are not primarily a means for allowing mothers time to pursue their individual interests. Nor are they a means for creating new family patterns. Rather, apart from the obvious and central goal—the education and development of young children—child care centers in minority communities are viewed as vehicles for strengthening the family by strengthening the relationships between parents and children and between families and the community. The goals of child development programs, therefore, must be (1) child development, (2) parent and family development, and (3) community development. These programs should consider their role as educative, supportive, facilitative, and coordinating. An important function of day care programs is to stimulate parents and community toward a greater awareness of how these three forces—children, family and community—interact with one another. We cannot have healthy, self-fulfilling children without healthy, stable families and communities.

I would like to thank all those individuals who so generously gave their valuable time and their thoughts on the issue of non-racist, non-sexist early childhood education.* They were persons engaged in all

levels of early childhood education, including staff of national and local organizations, day care directors, parents, architects, educators, and psychologists. The following set of guidelines is a synthesis of their views.

ROLE OF THE YWCA

Many YWCAs throughout the country are engaged in providing child care, and others are interested in doing so. These programs, existing and planned, must reflect the YWCA's one imperative, "The Elimination of Racism," and its commitment to the elimination of sexism. The role and functions of the YWCA must be carefully examined and understood so that branches may use their resources wisely and in the best interests of the community.

YWCAs can choose between two viable alternatives when considering their role in the provision of early childhood education. The first is as an organizer of child care programs that will ultimately be turned over to the *complete* control of the parents and the community. The second is to maintain *shared* responsibility and control. While the consensus of those interviewed during the preparation of these guidelines is that the best solution is complete parent/community control, local conditions and the policies of the YWCA may dictate the second alternative. If this second option is chosen, it should be understood that parents must at all times represent a majority on policy-making boards and committees.

Reprinted with permission of National Board, YWCA, 600 Lexington Avenue, New York, N.Y., 10022.

* The YWCA identifies racism as any attitude, action, or institutional structure which subordinates a person or group because of color. It defines sexism as the subordination of women because males have traditionally been those in power.

1. The YWCA should consider itself a catalytic agent.
2. Its main functions should be (a) to help organize the community around its day care needs, (b) to serve as a vehicle for funding, (c) to help organize the program, (d) to provide technical assistance and consultation, (e) to provide training in the skills necessary for the community to run the program, i.e. organizational development, program planning and development, management, staff utilization and development, communication and sensitivity, program evaluation, and (f) to help monitor the program.
3. From the beginning a clear distinction must be made between the role of the YWCA and the role of parents and the community. This does not mean a hierarchy of power, but rather a partnership. The YWCA must continuously examine its role and functioning to ensure that it is sensitive and responsive to community needs and aspirations.

PARENT/COMMUNITY CONTROL

In order for child care programs to be truly non-racist their program and policy must be determined by parents and the community and reflect their needs and concerns. Parent/community control requires more than a declaration of intent. It requires commitment to the idea that productive early childhood education must incorporate in policy-making roles the most important individuals in a child's life— his/her parents and his/her community.

1. Parents as well as interested individuals and institutions in the community must be included in the planning from the beginning and should help develop the proposal for child care funding.
2. Ultimately the parents and the commu-

nity must have responsibility for operating the program. If complete parent/community control is the goal, the proposal should include clearly stated mechanisms and a time plan for this to occur.
3. Child care centers must primarily be concerned with the needs of the children and families they serve and must avoid being used as power building mechanisms for groups and individuals with vested interests unrelated to healthy child development.

PARENT PARTICIPATION AND ACTIVITIES

Many child care programs that have been designated "parent/community controlled" are still grappling with the problem of developing programs and techniques that will make the label a reality. How do we effectively engage parents in policy making, program development and parent activities? This is a question for which there are no readily available answers. Parent involvement in child care programs can be viewed as existing on two levels, which are somewhat arbitrarily distinguished and which in actuality represent a continuum: (1) those programs designed to involve parents in the operation of the school, and (2) those programs geared to the individual and group needs of parents. Parents must regard the center as theirs and recognize that its success or failure depends on them. They must also have reinforcements of their awareness that they are the most important people in their children's lives.

Cultural variations in institutional participation must be taken into consideration. Many minority and lower socioeconomic parents are not accustomed to participating in the institutions that affect their lives (i.e., feelings of powerlessness) and are therefore inclined to defer to those groups they consider to have more experience and expertise. They often have a handicapping sense of awe when confronted with those areas they have traditionally associated with professionalism, e.g., education. Consequently, many parents must first be convinced of their self-worth and the fact that they indeed have something to contribute. Culturally determined sex role values also may affect the type and degree of participation of mothers and fathers.

1. A wide range of activities relevant to various abilities, experience, interests, needs, and goals must be provided. They should include educational, recreational, and social events.
2. Techniques and programs for recruiting parents into active involvement in the center must be sensitive to their life circumstances, e.g., available time, money, energy. Meetings should be scheduled at appropriate times; baby sitting services should be provided by the center. In some instances it may be necessary to provide taxi fares or other means of transportation for parents to attend meetings held in the evenings.
3. Leaders among the parents must be identified and their abilities and enthusiasm utilized to stimulate others.
4. Parents should be guided into a stronger awareness of the value to their children of parent participation in the program. They should participate in the total educational process—the classroom, field trips, special events. Special talents, e.g., music, art, storytelling, should be utilized.
5. There should be a staff member whose only or major responsibility is to work with parents. Such a person should have social work, group work, or adult education skills. A committee of parents

also should be actively engaged in developing parent and community activities.
6. Fathers should be encouraged to participate in all facets of the program and activities developed that will appeal to male interests.
7. An issue to consider is whether parents should be required to participate in the center in some way related to their availability and skills. While there are positive aspects to this policy, it can have negative repercussions.
8. A valuable tool in involving parents is a center newsletter that contains information on the children's educational activities, policy and operational concerns of the center, parent activities, local and national issues related to child care, other social and political issues.

COMMUNITY INVOLVEMENT AND DEVELOPMENT

There are many individuals and institutions in the community whose concerns and activities are directly related to those of the child care center and who can be mobilized to enhance its program and contribute to the well being of the children and families. Where possible they should be directly involved in the life of the center and share in the responsibility for its success or failure.

1. If possible, a full-time staff person with responsibility for community development should be employed. This same individual might also have responsibility for parent programs.
2. Individuals from the community should be involved in all aspects of the center's program—policy making, training, supportive services, classroom activities, field trips, parent programs.
3. Working relationships and alliances

with community organizations and institutions should be established.

4. Commercial institutions should be solicited to donate goods and services.

5. Where possible and necessary, the facilities of the center should be available to other community groups.

6. Parents should be kept informed about the political and social issues of the community (health services, social welfare, education, sanitation, housing, consumer affairs) and helped to recognize how all of them affect their individual lives.

7. Parents should be organized and encouraged to participate in community affairs.

STAFF

In providing non-racist, non-sexist early childhood education, the most crucial factors are attitudes and sensitivity. Knowledge of administrative skills, educational methods and materials, and child development are meaningless unless all those involved bring to their task an awareness of their own feelings and an openness to the feelings and needs of others. The most beautifully conceived program will be a failure unless those responsible for its implementation are sincerely committed to the children, families, and community the program serves.

1. As far as possible, staff should be composed of community residents.

2. The staff must reflect the ethnic and language groups in the program.

3. Males should be included in both child caring and other facets of the program.

4. Staff must be aware of the child's total environment—family, community, and influencing social and political conditions—and the role of each in the child's intellectual and emotional growth.

5. Staff must be well informed regarding the history and culture, past and present, of the minority ethnic groups in the program, with some coherent philosophy about the future.

6. Staff should represent reliable, trustworthy, nurturing adults who reflect in their attitudes and behavior the philosophy of the program.

7. Staff must be committed in attitudes and behavior, not merely in theory, to the importance of parent/community control. They must recognize its value to the healthy development of children. They must expose, examine, and work through any negative feelings they may have toward parents and other lay people (non-educators) in authority positions.

8. Continuous in-service training for staff, both professional and paraprofessional, must be provided.

9. In-service training should include staff exploration of attitudes toward themselves, other ethnic groups, male and female roles and relationships, poverty, social and political issues.

10. Resource persons representing various ethnic groups from the community should be used in in-service training.

11. The relationship, functions, and responsibilities of professionals and paraprofessionals should be clearly defined, yet flexible, and involve a mutuality of respect for the skills, experience, and expertise of each. Criteria for the selection of paraprofessionals should be carefully determined, and there should be collaboration with colleges and universities in the development of educational and training programs. Avenues for professional mobility should be provided.

12. Parents should share responsibility for

determining criteria, screening, hiring, and dismissing staff.

CURRICULUM

While many early childhood education centers are developing curricula designed to develop cognitive skills, emotional strengths, and cultural pride among minority ethnic group children, there has been little formalization to date of such curricula. The efforts range from adapting widely accepted approaches to creating new ones based on the individual program's population, philosophy, and goals.

1. All areas of the curriculum must be concerned with the development of the individual child, assuring self-worth and potential for growth and helping develop a respect for learning and a positive concept of oneself as a learner.
2. Standardized I.Q. tests should be used with care, if at all, for they often do not adequately measure the minority group child's true abilities.
3. Each child's individual style of communication must be appreciated and responded to sensitively. Attention should be paid to "what" is being said rather than "how". The use of ethnic speech patterns by the child should not be deprecated. This does not mean, however, that the child will not eventually learn what is termed "standard English." (There is presently a great deal of discussion and controversy among educators regarding the use of Black vernacular English in books for children, with some educators feeling that it can enhance the child's self-image and need not interfere with the learning of standard English. Others take an opposite position and feel that the use of Black vernacular handicaps the child. This is an area that must be

approached with caution and sensitivity and include the thinking of parents.)

4. Cognitive skill development must be a basic ingredient of the curriculum.
5. Coping skills—helping the child learn how to live in this world—must be developed.
6. The curriculum must create in the child an appreciation for his/her ethnic history and culture, i.e., ethnic pride. Books and audio-visual materials, as well as playthings, must be carefully selected to reflect a positive ethnic self-image. Ethnic materials can be integrated into all phases of the child's learning: cognitive, emotional and physical development. Food can be an effective tool for learning about cultural traditions and should include ethnic dishes.
7. The curriculum must also develop an appreciation and understanding of the ethnic backgrounds of all children whether or not represented in a particular child care center.
8. Special celebrations should be provided to commemorate important events and individuals in ethnic history.
9. A creative plan should be evolved to integrate parents into the learning process. Apart from classroom participation, they should be given, or allowed to borrow, books and other materials for use at home. Workshops and lectures on child development should be offered.
10. The curriculum should be subject to continuous assessment and evaluation. On the other hand, criteria for formal research should be carefully established. No research should be conducted by the center of an outside institution without the approval of the parents. It is extremely important that

all research be relevant and meaningful to the community and carefully screened to ensure against a negative bias. Parents and community must have access to the results.

SUPPORTIVE SERVICES

The role and importance of the whole person in the educational process must be kept in mind at all times. Supportive services provided by child care programs must be addressed to the total needs of the children and their families: social, emotional, health, legal, economic, educational; and they must reflect community needs.

1. A survey should be made of existing services in the community in order to determine the gap between need and availability.
2. A decision must be made regarding which services can, and should, be supplied directly by the center; which existing institutions should be stimulated to strengthen or broaden their services; and where it is necessary to develop, in cooperation with existing organizations and institutions, new institutional providers.
3. Staff must be knowledgeable about existing services in order to make appropriate referrals.
4. The center should coordinate the services being received by each family. Families should view the center as a place where they can come with all their problems and know that they will get appropriate service or referral.
5. The staff should be large enough to provide the services which fall within their province; innovative techniques must be developed for service delivery. In the provision of services, staff must view themselves as complementary to the family rather than substitutes for them.

6. Creative and meaningful use should be made of paraprofessionals.

SEXISM

Sexism means different things to different individuals and to different social and ethnic groups—and to some it might mean nothing. While certain groups in our society have become highly sensitized to what they consider sexist values in our culture, others are indifferent or even hostile to the renewed thrust for female emancipation. (Some issues related to sexism have been dealt with in earlier sections.)

1. Staff should recognize and appreciate the sex role values of different individuals and ethnic groups and not attempt to impose their own values.
2. At the same time, however, staff must help parents to allow their children to develop according to their individual capabilities and not be unduly restricted by culturally determined sex role stereotypes.
3. Staff should become sensitized to their own sex role values and encouraged to examine their own conflicts and ambiguities.
4. Books and audio-visual materials must be carefully selected to eliminate portrayal of negative and restrictive sex roles.
5. Children should be allowed to participate in activities that interest them, not being discouraged from participation in activities because they may have been culturally designated as male or female.

DESIGN OF FACILITIES

Design has been called one of the three crucial interacting components of child development programs (the other two are philosophy and staff). All must be in harmony in order to have a successful program.

1. Space requirements must be realistic in terms of (a) the educational and social needs of the population and (b) the types of space available in the community. If child care licensing requirements do not reflect these realities, centers must organize to make licensing agencies responsive to their needs.
2. Design should take into consideration the developmental needs of children of different stages of development.
3. While space and design should permit freedom and the possibility for creative play, they should be organized in an orderly fashion so that children know where to go for what and do not feel surrounded by chaos and confusion.
4. Centers should have a warm, homelike atmosphere, with rugs on some spaces, a comfortable chair or two, pleasant lighting, and other homey touches, including places where children can go to be alone and where teachers can take individual children for comforting or a private chat.
5. Outdoor areas should be creative, attractive and, especially, safe, and should provide enough open space for running, riding vehicles, and feeling free.

CONCLUSION

Two of the most crucial questions facing providers of early childhood education are (1) how to effectively engage parents in the operation of the program and (2) how to constructively include ethnic material in the curriculum. There are presently no easy answers to these problems. Parent/ community controlled non-racist, non-sexist, child care centers make great demands on all concerned. Some staff may find it difficult to relinquish authority and some parents may be unclear about their role in the concept of parent/ community control. However, as day care staff and parents grow in openness and sensitivity and as innovative programs reflecting community needs are developed, more learning and clarity will emerge. The YWCA can play an important role in creating quality, non-racist, non-sexist early childhood education by providing opportunities for sharing insights and experiences through publications, conferences, workshops, and training programs.

These guidelines are intended to focus on those issues that are most pertinent to non-racist, non-sexist early childhood education. Consequently many issues that must be considered for all child care programs have not been discussed but must be kept constantly in mind, since non-racist, non-sexist child care is first and finally quality child care.

24. Administering Programs

Joe R. Hoffer

PERT: A TOOL FOR MANAGERS OF HUMAN SERVICE PROGRAMS

INTRODUCTION

With rare exceptions, no period engenders a greater sense of urgency and uncertainty among directors of newly instituted Area Agencies on Aging than the "start-up" phase. At this initial point, the director is faced with a nearly overwhelming array of projects that must be undertaken and completed before the Agency can concentrate upon its primary service planning and development mission. Facilities must be located, acquired, and properly equipped if staff are to perform competently. Staff must be recruited, screened, hired, and oriented. Effective working relationships with state and local organizations must be established, and a well-conceived public relations program begun to enhance the general understanding, acceptance, and legitimation of the Area Agency's prescribed role within local areas. Further, it is imperative to begin work on the plan that will comply with state requirements and attain state acceptance.

This is only a partial and suggestive listing of the projects confronting a director at the inception of an AAA. It is far from inclusive. The director's anxiety is aroused by the fact all the projects seemingly demand equal and immediate attention, a condition obviously beyond his ability to meet. If he is to minimize uncertainty and a loss of productivity, his best alternative

is to order impending work requirements and arrange them in a priority sequence.

Once sequentially ordered, the director should estimate the time and manpower demands of each project, as well as the sum total of projects. Such an estimate will provide him with a control mechanism of inestimable value.

This article introduces such a mechanism. It is called PERT (Program Evaluation and Review Technique). It is a management technique especially designed to enhance administrative control over the use of time and staff. When properly applied, it provides the director with fresh information about the expected and actual progress made in the conduct of a project. It can also identify areas where shifts in manpower can lead to better use of staff.

I. WHAT IS PERT?

If you are going to write a book, you make an outline before you start. If you are going to make a report of the financial status of an agency, you put figures down in an accounting arrangement. Similarly, if you are going to make a plan to implement a program for older people, you should—among other things—define the objectives; identify the services; prepare graphic charts; describe the plan in narrative detail; or construct an activity network.

PERT is one of the important tools developed in recent years as part of the modern management-information systems ap-

Source: Unpublished, Joe Hoffer, "PERT: A Tool for Managers of Human Service Programs," Guide to PERT for Area Planners in Aging, 1974, by Project TAP.

proach to executive decision-making. It provides a logic chart or flow diagram which is much more comprehensible than the same material in narrative form. More important, it enforces a certain discipline that will help you to avoid gaps in the overall logic of your system. A network produces a clear outline of the Activities that must be undertaken and of the Events that must occur before an end objective is reached. It provides a simple, clear, and readily understandable description of the program undertaken.

In other words, it will provide a true means for identifying the exceptions so that you can manage by this method. Many managers claim they manage by exception, but they have no logical way of identifying the exceptions.

Besides being a convenient shorthand for you, the manager, the network is like a map and it is an ideal communication medium. Even in a relatively small program, the operation being planned will generally affect several groups, paid staff, and volunteers. Without some easily understood physical picture of the whole plan, misunderstandings will often occur. The various people involved will plan elements of what they think is an integrated whole but what is, in fact, fragmentary and disassociated. The advantages of having all concerned discuss and argue out details of relationships, inclusion of significant events, estimated times and the like—with a network plan before them while they are doing it—cannot be overemphasized. The clarity in a network leaves little room for confusion or doubt.

The interrelatedness of activities also needs more interpretation. Office production schedules once considered too technical by those not directly concerned require more interrelation among staff divisions and between volunteers and staff. Some departments will accuse others of delaying

projects. Actual schedules and budgets are established only to find time targets missed because of some unorganized and random activity.

Obviously, some of these experiences are caused by insufficient planning and lagging leadership. In most cases, however, they are symptoms of a need for still better planning and organization. Discussions with administrators have disclosed that a major source of their frustration is concerned about getting people through their complex organizational mazes.

You may have seen various types of systems charts used to describe complicated operations and projects. Our purpose is to suggest one of them, an application of PERT, which will help you administer a local or regional program for human services. If you are interested in using this method fully, consult the References given at the end of this chapter.

Conventional Methods

Conventional methods of administering a broad-scale program have produced notable successes. These methods include orientation of key staff and volunteers through written instructions, audio-visual methods and conferences about the necessary procedures, problems, research, and recommendations from earlier programs. Then a plan for a program is drawn. Such "blueprints" may comprise organization, time and activity charts; job description manuals; monthly schedules for staff and volunteers and similar guides. (Simultaneously, related production and control schedules for the professional and clerical use are developed which most workers considered too technical for their participation.) Of course, revisions are made in all these items in light of past experience.

This procedure is carried through the second echelon of program leadership.

Below this level, workers may receive very simple schedules of expectations in their kits at training meetings. Before these meetings the only other information they received was presented through progress meetings called by the executive or chairman—or by mail or telephone.

Even though these traditional methods contributed toward success, they are often insufficient. Far too often, as the program grows bigger and more complex in our rapidly changing society, planning and scheduling procedures do not create a sufficient sense of urgency with staff and volunteer leaders. This happens because plans are reviewed too hastily. Busy men and women are increasingly learning to skim words. Procedures and schedules, because they are printed words, become too time-consuming to comprehend and don't convey enough meaning until it is too late.

Also, plans don't induce necessary action "on schedule." There is a tendency toward self-determination and delay with whatever seems unimportant. In some cases the walls get built before the foundation.

Characteristics of PERT

PERT is defined as:

A Manager's Tool . . . for defining and coordinating what must be done to successfully accomplish the objectives of a project on time.

A Technique . . . that aids the decision-maker but does not make decisions for him.

A Technique . . . that can present statistical information regarding the uncertainties faced in completing the many activities associated with a project.

A Method . . . for focusing managerial attention on: (1) latent problems that require decisions; (2) procedures and adjustments regarding time, resources, or performance, which may improve the capability of meeting target dates.

There are simple elements in PERT:

1. An *Event*—The start or completion of a task, e.g., Report mailed; Meeting held; Charts started; Legislative project completed. It is important to remember that an event is not the actual performance of a task. Events may be called certain significant keypoints or milestones that must be encountered but which do not consume time or resources.

2. An *Activity*—The actual performance of a series of tasks is an Activity. An Activity must link two consecutive Events in a PERT network. Activities represent time; time is work; therefore, Activities require manpower, material, space, facilities, or other resources. It is suggested that the minimum time for an activity be one week.

3. *Task(s)*—Specific work required to accomplish objectives of each Activity. It is suggested that the time element be a minimum of one hour.

4. *Successor Events*—Events are connected by Activities to form a PERT network. The Event or Events that immediately follow another PERT without any intervening Events are called *successor* Events.

5. *Predecessor Events*—The Event or Events that immediately come before another Event without an intervening Event is called *predecessor* Events to that Event.

6. A *Network*—A diagram showing the Events and Activities in logical sequential order and that no Activity can be started until the Event prior to it is complete.

This is a simple PERT network:

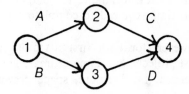

The Events have been numbered 1 through 4; the Activities are designated A through D. Events are typically represented by numbers and activities by letters. *Event* 4 cannot take place until both *Activities* C and D prior to the Event have been completed. *Activity* D cannot be completed until *Event* 3 has taken place.

Each Activity lies between two Events. In the case of Activity B, Event 1 is the initiating Event, and Event 3 is the terminating Event. An Activity cannot be completed until its initiating Event has taken place. An Event is not considered as having taken place until all Activities leading to the Event have been accomplished.

7. *Estimated Performance Time*—After the PERT network has been firmly established and put on paper, it is necessary to obtain estimates on the "performance times" for each Activity.

Finding Time

Any project director knows that as a deadline approaches, more *time* is usually required for job completion. "If we only had an extra week" is the remark often heard during such situations. PERT will help you to avoid this predicament, by foreseeing any possible time shortages and by predicting them long before the required or scheduled target date arrives.

If we are to follow PERT, we would secure three time estimates for each Activity from someone who is very familiar with that particular Activity: Optimistic Time, Most Likely Time, and Pessimistic Time. These estimates should be stated in hours, days, weeks, or months and will then be used in PERT technique to compute the *overall* time required to complete a project.

However, for both first attempts and modest projects, one Time estimate is recommended. Furthermore, space prevents

us from demonstrating the method of determining the *overall* time and the use of variance and probability of success. The Project Manager has the right to revise his time estimates if there is a definite change in the scope of the original program plans.

After we have established our PERT network, showing the interrelationships between the Events and Activities, we obtain the time estimate for each Activity and enter their value on the PERT network above the Activity line that they represent. Here is an example of what we mean:

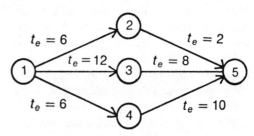

Note: All the t_e's in this particular network are in weeks. In this network Event 2 is the successor and Event 1 is the predecessor of the Activity connecting the two. This Activity has a t_e (expected time for completion) of 6 weeks.

Using the above network as a guide, the following chart can be drawn:

	Predecessor Event	Successor Event	t_e (weeks)
Begin planning for legislative hearing......	1	2	6
Meeting of Legislative Committee held............	1	3	12
Begin organization of Coalition.............	1	4	6
Final meeting of Legislative Committee held.............	2	5	2
Begin arrangements for presentation to legislators.................	3	5	8
Hearing in State Capitol held.............	4	5	10

The next step in the completion of a PERT network is to establish the times you can expect to reach the Events in the network. These expected times are represented by the symbol t_e and appear above the Events on the PERT network.

The t_e of an Event represents the earliest possible time that the Event can be reached. The t_e is computed by adding the t_e's of the Activity paths leading to the Event.

Take a look at the following network:

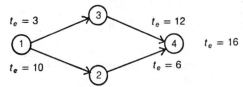

$t_e = 3$ $t_e = 12$ $t_e = 16$ $t_e = 10$ $t_e = 6$

1. The time you can expect to reach Event 1 is zero time. No Activity precedes the Event and therefore no time can be consumed in reaching it. The t_e for Event 1 is zero. This Event starts the project rolling.
2. The Activity that connects Event 1 with Event 2 has a t_e of 10 weeks. Therefore, the time we can expect to reach Event 2 is 10 weeks after the start of the project. Event 2 has a t_e of 10 weeks.
3. The Activity that connects Event 1 with Event 3 has a t_e of 3 weeks. Therefore, the time you can expect to reach Event 3 is 3 weeks after the start of the project. Event 3 has a t_e of 3 weeks.
4. According to our network, all Activities must be completed before Event 4 can be reached. Since there are two paths leading to Event 4, the largest time-consuming path represents the earliest possible time you can expect to reach Event 4.

The next step in the completion of our PERT network is to determine the latest allowable completion time for each Event. t_L is the symbol for the "latest allowable completion time." By definition t_L is the latest time by which an event must be completed to keep the project on schedule. These times are derived from a previously established completion time or contractual obligation date. The completion or contractual obligation date is given the symbol t_S.

The values of the t_L's are computed for each Event and inserted below the Events on the PERT network. The t_L's are computed in exactly the opposite manner from that in which the t_e's were computed.

1. You start from the last Event and work back toward the first one.
2. To compute the t_L for an Event, you must subtract the value of the t_e from the value of the t_L for the successor Event.
3. If more than one value of t_L is obtained, the smallest value is selected.

Follow through the following PERT network:

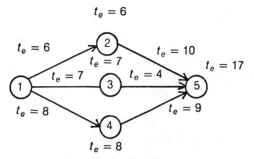

$t_e = 6$ $t_e = 6$ $t_e = 10$ $t_e = 17$ $t_e = 7$ $t_e = 7$ $t_e = 4$ $t_e = 8$ $t_e = 9$ $t_e = 8$

1. The t_e for the Activity connecting Event 5 and Event 2 (Activity 2–5) is 10 weeks. Subtracting 10 weeks from the t_L of 17 weeks for Event 5 gives a t_L for Event 2 of 7 weeks.
2. The t_e for Activity 3–5 is 4 weeks. Subtracting 4 weeks from the t_L of 17 weeks for Event 5 gives a t_L for Event 3 of 13 weeks.
3. The t_e for Activity 4–5 is given 9 weeks. Subtracting 9 weeks for the t_L of 17

weeks for Event 5 gives a t_L for Event 4 of 8 weeks.

4. In a similar manner, the t_L for Event 1 is computed for three different paths:

a. From Event 1 to Event 2, $t_L = 1$ week
b. From Event 1 to Event 3, $t_L = 6$ weeks
c. From Event 1 to Event 4, $t_L = 0$ weeks

5. The smallest value of 0 weeks is selected as the t_L for Event 1. Our final PERT network looks like this:

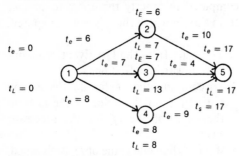

The definition of t_L is the latest allowable time we have to complete an Event so that the entire project can be kept on schedule.

Suppose you needed an award plaque that will be presented five weeks from today. Also, you discovered today that it would take a commercial concern five weeks to prepare the plaque. When do you think you would need to prepare the design for reproduction? Today, naturally! In other words, the t_e for the event "reproduction of the plaque design" is zero and it must be completed immediately.

Now you know how to derive the latest allowable time (t_L) and expected time (t_e) for each event. From these two values, it is possible to calculate the slack of an Event. The slack of an event is $t_L - t_e$. In other words, if you are allowed 25 weeks to complete a project and you can, in fact, perform it in 20 weeks, you have a 5-week period of grace. In the PERT method, this given period is called slack and is very significant in analyzing the complete project.

The value of slack can be either positive, negative, or zero, depending upon the relationship between t_L and t_e.

One must remember the definition of slack. Slack is the difference between latest allowable time and expected time $(t_L - t_e)$. If these two figures are exactly the same (zero slack), you do not have a margin of safety. You do not have any excess time or money to spend on the task. Any events that have zero or minimum slack form the most critical path.

Finding the Critical Path

The critical path is the heart of PERT. As a manager, it can be of most help to you. The critical path will tell you which project requires the most time to get from the initial event to the final event. In other words, any event on the critical path that slips in time will cause the final Events to slip by the same amount.

There are two schools of thought in management planning. The question of whether to plan forward or backward is still open and depends, in the final analysis, on the objective and whether or not a fixed date is established, e.g., Annual Meeting, Legislative session, etc. In some complex situations, one might combine both. An example of the latter is illustrated below.

It is always difficult to produce order from disorder. The network planner can simplify his task and get better results if he follows certain simple rules. The following series of steps will fit the average case:

1. Define the end objective precisely. This is frequently difficult, but close definition is fundamental to a complete plan.

Event 1
Completion of network
End Objective

2. Define all significant Events that are precedent to the end objective. Do not start on any "chain" until this is done. The purpose is, of course, to make sure that no elements are left out inadvertently.

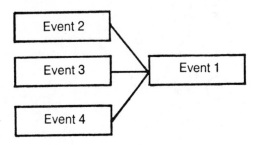

3. Define all significant Events precedent to Event 2. This is a continuation of the strategy in the second step. Again, the purpose is to assure that nothing significant in the whole plan is left out.

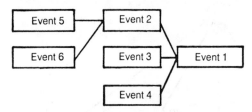

4. Define all significant Events precedent to Event 3. If it is found that some Event already shown is precedent to the Event being worked on, interconnecting lines must be drawn (see asterisks).

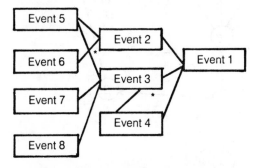

5. Continue in a similar manner with other Events. Work back at a level at a time, making sure that all significant precedent Events are established.

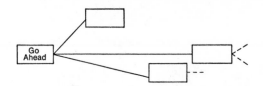

6. Make sure that all Events except the beginning and ending ones have at least one connection at each end. Recheck for any important Events left out. If there are any, there has been a serious error somewhere. If the omitted Event is really important, find out whether it is covered by the scope of the work or related to it.

In developing the network, it is important to discard irrelevant matters from consideration. There is a tendency to over-elaborate a chart by including minor events which have little or no time implications. Although these Events may be written down somewhere for reference and follow-up, they should be kept out of the network. The network should include only those Events with time significance.

II. AN EXAMPLE

The following is an example of how the PERT approach would be applied to a protective services program for the aging (Figure 24.1) The final event is an operational extension policy approved by the Board of Directors of Council on Aging.

III. COMPARISON WITH OTHER TECHNIQUES

Gantt Scheduling

Henry Gantt developed the Gantt scheduling technique over 50 years ago. It basically involves the use of bar charts to reflect activities within a job. Horizontal

FIGURE 24.1
PERT/Time Network—Coordinated Approach to
Protective Services to Aged

EXHIBIT 6

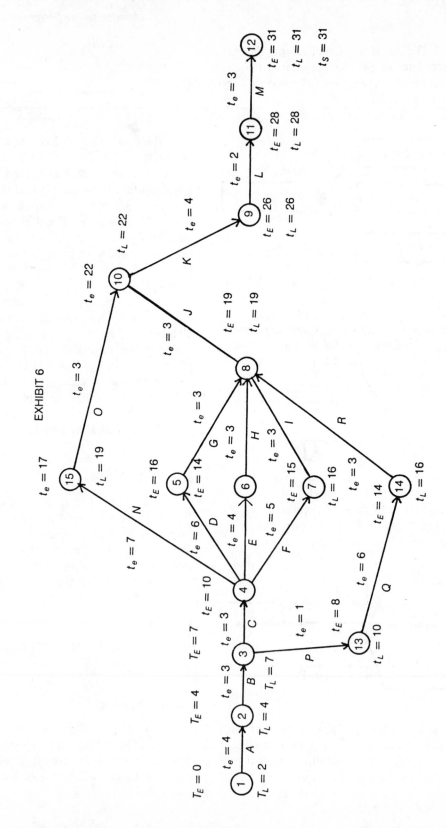

Ref. No. and Event	Predecessor Event
1. Board member requests consideration of special program for aged	0
2. Tests completed regarding validity of request	1
3. Authorization given by Board of Directors to conduct broad community survey	2
4. Survey Committee appointed	3
5. Report presented to Survey Committee of existing services in community	4
6. Report presented to Survey Committee regarding similar studies in the U.S.	4
7. Report presented to Survey Committee on other needs of older citizens	4
8. Priorities determined regarding kind of services	5, 6, 7, 14
9. Method of financing services determined	10
10. Method of implementing services determined	8, 15
11. Extension policy draft approved by Committee	9
12. Extension policy accepted by Board of Directors (Final Event)	11
13. Cooperating agencies and individuals (governmental and voluntary) notified	3
14. Reactions received from other agencies	13
15. Facilities available for use in new program determined	6

Between Events		Activity	t_e (weeks)
1 and 2	A.	*Ad hoc* Committee of Board and Staff appointed to examine request	4
2 and 3	B.	Recommendations sent to Board and Staff	3
3 and 4	C.	Resource people and community representatives recruited for Committee Staff assigned to Committee.	3
4 and 5	D.	Staff prepares report of existing programs. Secure cooperation between the agencies offering special services. Determine types of services available.	4
4 and 6	E.	National agencies, e.g., Institute of Gerontology written for similar studies. Follow-up on local communities indicated by several national agencies.	4
4 and 7	F.	Study of needs by resource people and representatives of community. Locate and identify those needing protective services.	4
5 and 8	G.	Report studies and integrated with others.	3
6 and 8	H.	Report studies and integrated with others.	3
7 and 8	I.	Report studies and integrated with others.	3
8 and 10	J.	Best methods for meeting needs reviewed.	3
10 and 9	K.	Financial resources explored.	4
9 and 11	L	Decisions to date collated. Draft policy written and sent to Committee.	2
11 and 12	M.	Draft policy distributed to Board of Directors. Special meeting of Board called.	3
4 and 15	N.	Agencies and others contacted. Workers in selected social agencies trained in services of other agencies.	7
15 and 10	O.	Schedules and kinds of use discussed.	3
3 and 13	P.	Letters sent to national agencies	1
13 and 14	Q.	Nonrespondents contacted by phone.	6
14 and 8	R.	Priorities from others rank ordered.	3

Gantt Schedule

Activity	July 6 13 20 27	August 3 10 17 24 31	September 7 14 21 28	October 5 12 19 26 29
A.	------------------------- .			
B.	----------------------------------- .			
C.	----------------------------- .			
D.		--- .		
E.			--- .	
F.			----------------------------- .	
G.		--- .		
H.		----------------------------- .		
I.				----------------------------- .

lines are drawn whose lengths are proportional to the duration of the activity. Progress on activities is monitored with parallel lines drawn adjacent to the activity lines. The technique has been used in all types of programs and projects. A sample schedule of a hypothetical project is illustrated in a Gantt schedule which appears above.

The illustration of the Gantt schedule basically indicates activities, and not Events and Activities as in the PERT network. The Activities are labeled in the first column on the left. Using the Gantt technique in the "forward direction" we work from left to right, plotting activities as they must occur in time relation to other activities, and establishing a completion date for the job.

There are several weaknesses in the Gantt technique. It is nearly impossible to reflect a particular slack into the other activities. Interrelationships among Activities are not indicated in the Gantt technique, as they are with the PERT. Furthermore, coordinate Functions and precedent relationships are not shown.

Sched-U-Graph

The Sched-U-Graph is a Remington Rand product and is a simple and useful beginning tool for scheduling activities and projects. The instrument is a chart (24" x 42") containing pockets into which 3 x 5 cards can be inserted. The functions of the organization are labeled and inserted vertically into the Sched-U-Graph. The horizontal portion of the chart is labeled by months. The specific activities or tasks are typed on 3 x 5 cards and inserted in the appropriate slots. For example, if we were preparing our budget for presentation to the Board of Directors in November, we would make calculations regarding the various activities or duties and the approximate time to begin and complete them. See example below.

Here again, there are some weaknesses. It is difficult to determine the time needed to complete the tasks and we schedule more tasks than can be accomplished during any one particular month. Furthermore, it is impossible to show any relationship among the various Activities and tasks.

July	August	September	October	November
Budget Sheets Duplicated	Preliminary by staff completed	Tentative Budget completed, Mail budget to treasurer	Final Draft approved by Treasurer, Mail to Board of Directors	Approval by Board of Directors

We have examined some of the advantages and disadvantages of PERT and made some practical observations. PERT cannot eliminate negative slack but helps considerably in avoiding it. As an analytical tool, PERT leaves much to be desired, although it does have some practical value. On the other hand, we found that it can play an important role in the communication and reporting functions, and that it provides a better estimate of a job schedule than any other planning schedule yet available.

IV. CONCLUSION

We have simplified the PERT for use by managers of human service programs. We believe that it will serve your purposes well and that it will not be too difficult or complicated to use. Most of the calculations can be done manually or with a conventional office machine. A computer is not required until you have more than 100 Activities.

We would suggest, however, that you consult one or more references on PERT and consider seriously several other elements which will increase the effectiveness of the system.

Two elements which require some elementary mathematics are "the three-time estimates" and the introduction of "probability of success" into the PERT network. Probability enters the network only as a tool for judging the accuracy of the "completion date." It cannot be construed as an analytical tool in the sense that the "network slack analysis" is for controlling job progress. It is a scheduling device. If PERT were used as an analytical tool only and not for scheduling, the "three-time" estimate and probability coefficient associated within would be of no value.

Another valuable element of the PERT system is PERT/Cost—an extension of the PERT technique. Its objective is to develop a plan of action for cost expenditures by applying the necessary cost-estimating techniques and to act as a monitor in determining variances—that is, where actual costs are different from planned cost.

Finally, we should recognize that there are some weaknesses and limitations in planning and management techniques, especially in the delivery of human services. Therefore, we wish to emphasize that people—paid and volunteer—still play an important role in the planning process, one that is more important than any technique yet devised.

EXERCISE

The following exercise provides an experience in the utilization of PERT. It focuses on the objective of assessing transportation needs of the elderly within an area. These are some possible events which would occur in an assessment of transportation needs:

1. Staff allocated to needs assessment project.
2. Data or information requirements determined.
3. Survey instrument designed.
4. Survey population selected.
5. Survey workers hired.
6. Survey workers trained.
7. Begin data collection.
8. Data collection completed.
9. Data compiled.
10. Data analyzed and interpreted.
11. Summary report written.

Using the Hoffer reading as a reference, do the following:

1. Examine the list of events for completeness. Are there others you would add?
2. The list is in a reasonable chronological order. Determine the predecessor events for each event.

3. Beginning with the last event, place its immediate predecessor events before it. Follow this procedure until you have reached the first event.
4. Now chain the events together with lines showing the relationship of each event to its predecessor. (Consult sketches in Hoffer's article for examples of a "network.")
5. Determine the time needed to move be-

tween each of the events and note this along each line.
6. Now determine the critical path by adding the times required to move from the first to last event along each conceivable path. The longest time illustrates the critical path. Any delay along this path will delay the completion of the needs assessment.

Possible PERT Chart of Events 1-11 in Excercise (time in weeks)

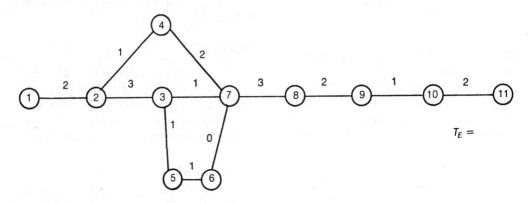

T for Path 1 - 2 - 4 - 7 - 8 - 9 - 10 - 11 is 13
T for Path 1 - 2 - 3 - 7 - 8 - 9 - 10 - 11 is 14
T for Path 1 - 2 - 3 - 5 - 6 - 7 - 8 - 9 - 10 - 11 is 15

For more information about PERT, see these references:

Critical Path Scheduling—A Practical Appraisal of PERT, by James P. Fourre, American Management Association, New York, 1968 (16 pp.).

PERT for CAA Planning: A Programmed Course of Instruction in PERT, prepared for OEO, Community Action Program, by Policy Management Systems, Inc.

"PERT and Its Possible Uses in Planning Y.M.C.A. Programs," by Clair A. Buckley, *Forum,* April 1970, National Council Y.M.C.A., New York, pp. 11–14.

PERT: A New Management Planning and Control Technique, J. W. Blood (ed.), American Management Association, New York, 1962 (192 pp.).

A Programmed Introduction to PERT— Program Evaluation and Review Technique for Planning Large Projects in Social Welfare, by Joe R. Hoffer. Available from National Conference on Social Welfare, 22 West Gay St., Columbus, Ohio 43215 ($6.00).

25. Managing the Finances

William Lawrence with Bernard W. Klein

FINANCIAL MANAGEMENT

Financial management and control is unquestionably one of the most critical challenges in the operation of social programs. Properly instituted, it is a valuable tool for achieving program goals and enhancing program performance. A competently developed fiscal management structure provides service administration and staff with a vital planning aid, impelling awareness of a program's totality and the interrelationships among its parts. It makes personnel aware that undisciplined expenditures in one area of activity reduces essential financial support for another area.

Fiscal control also functions as an evaluation and monitoring instrument, producing information that can reveal errors in program design and faulty patterns of service practice. No responsibly conducted service program can exist without this information, and the greater its accuracy, the greater are the chances for the program's success.

The administrator and his staff must also be alert to the very real possibility that instances of inept fiscal management will be exploited to discredit their program. While improper accounting is not indicative of a poor program, critics are not necessarily constrained by the niceties of logic. Those opposed to a program will not hesitate to use accounting deficiencies to generate public doubt about the validity of the program concept and performance. When subjected to such an attack, an ad-

ministrator is hard pressed to defend the value of his program. The public is extremely sensitive about the handling of public funds and quick to presume that faulty accounting is uncontestable evidence of general administrative incompetence.

In the area of grant funds, preoccupation with fiscal control has intensified in recent years. Mounting concern is justifiably evidenced not only by funders but by the public at large. Too many social programs have fallen into disrepute because of apparent administrative indifference to competent fiscal accounting.

FISCAL CONTROL PROCEDURES

Competent fiscal management consists of a set of related functions. For purposes of discussion, we will separate these into two groups: basic functions, and additional procedures.

I. BASIC FUNCTIONS

Four interdependent functions make up the basic fiscal process: budgeting, accounting, receipt and disbursement or custodianship, and auditing. Properly integrated, the combination provides administration with a series of checks and balances for controlling the allocation and use of funds.

The process is structured differently from setting to setting, with the differences largely determined by organizational size. In very large settings where a sizeable number of fiscal transactions occur daily, each function may be the responsibility of a separate management

Source: Unpublished, William Lawrence with Bernard W. Klein, "Financial Management and the Area Agency," 1974.

unit, with segregated lines of accountability directly to the administrator or a deputy administrator. In many instances, especially in the governmental arena, the custodial function may be invested in another agency, such as the city comptroller's office.

In small organizations with a very limited fiscal flow, the natural tendency is toward the consolidation of functions in a single management unit. Even in these instances, some division of function is usually instituted to insure a proper and responsible administration of funds. For example, the director of an agency may keep the books while a fiscally experienced member of the board serves as the agency's treasurer, with the power to issue checks.

The Budgeting Process

The budgeting process possesses a mystique for many service personnel. Actually, there is nothing mysterious about a budget. It is a product of human analysis and judgment, and once formulated inherits no self-contained and impelling authority. Its value will be no greater than the thoughtfulness and care put into its construction and the intelligence and skill invested in its use.

An administration must avoid at all costs assuming or conveying the notion that a prepared budget is immutable. Not to adapt a budget to changing circumstances is as irresponsible as to ignore the document altogether. If correctly managed, the budget is subject to constant review and adjustment as new and anticipated events arise during the fiscal year. Otherwise, it would fail to serve its purposes of facilitating administrative decisions, guiding expenditures, and providing an accurate record that can be used for planning funding allocations in subsequent years.

Reduced to its simplest terms, a budget is an estimate of how anticipated income during a designated period of time will be distributed among competing forms of agency activity. It relates costs to categorically itemized sets of inputs or resources required in performing an activity, to the programs or services the agency provides, or to the objectives or outcomes these services are expected to accomplish. The itemization used depends on the uses of the budget and the type of information it is intended to transmit to the various organizational audiences.

When the objective is to specify the level of investment allocated to various operational divisions of an organization, a *resource budget* is prepared. When it is to define the proportion of total operational income allocated to each of the discrete programs of an agency, a *program budget* is relied upon. And when the objective is to relate cost to production or outcome of service, a *Program Planning and Budgeting System* (PPBS) is used.

The PPBS is the most sophisticated form of budgeting and is coming into increasing prominence in the social service field. Its value lies in focusing administrative attention on the crucial issue of an organization, i.e., the relationship between expenditure and what that expenditure buys in the form of benefits to clients and actual agency accomplishments.

When PPBS is properly implemented, the budget structure or categories will be stated in terms of major goals of the organization. Each goal, in turn, will be interpreted in the form of an objective or objectives, and the objectives to the extent possible translated into measurable quantities.

For example: If one goal of an Area Agency on Aging is to enrich the nutritional diet of a population of older people, an associated program may be the provision of communal eating experiences. One aspect of such a program would be the serving of congregate meals. The objective would and should be expressed in quantifiable terms: the number of meals to be provided and the number of people to be served over a definitive period of time. Other objectives of the program may not readily lend themselves to rigorous quantification, since they refer to subjective qualities such as personal satisfaction. This type of objective is translated into some approximate measure, such as the attendees' personal assessments of the program.

Implementation of PPBS has distinct implications for agency structure. It can be effectively performed only if the organization includes ongoing and integrated planning, budgeting, and evaluation functions. Through this integration the organization engages in a constant process of research and assessment directed to identifying the most cost-effective alternative means of accomplishing objectives. Cost-effectiveness pertains to the means that provide the greatest benefit per unit of expenditure.

PPBS is a highly complex process and still in a formative stage with many uncertainties, especially as applied to the social service field. Area Agency on Aging personnel are encouraged, however, to become familiar with the process as it is developed. PPBS will undoubtedly play an increasingly influential role in federal and state funding decisions.

Another type of budgeting with which personnel should become acquainted is *performance budgeting*. It is a less complicated procedure than PPBS, but retains some of the latter's advantages. Unlike PPBS, performance budgeting presents no information about accomplishments, but it does focus administrative attention on the relationship of expenditures to a program

or distinct agency service. The budget structure consists of categories identified by separate areas of service: *information and referral, nutrition, home health care,* etc. In this way, as with the PPBS budget, administration can see the total costs allocated to one organization service and compare that cost with expenditures assigned to other priority services. Its value lies in ignoring the functional divisions of labor that characterize an organization, and relating every cost of a program to a specific service, regardless of the division performing it.

Every program budget eventually must be converted into a *line budget* which relates expenditure to personnel functions and activity supports. This conversion is termed a "crosswalk." In most situations, the line budget stands alone for guiding agency administrative decisions and allocations.

The reason the line budget assumes such a common and prominent position is that it is especially constructed to serve as a fiscal control document. It tells the administrator exactly what proportions of income are allocated to the various functional units or divisions comprising the organization, and tells the unit managers the cost parameters within which they must be prepared to perform. In addition, it provides accounting staff with an instrument for assessing rates of expenditure, determining which units are under- or overspending assigned allocations, and informing the administration when corrective action in relation to appropriations is required.

The line budget is familiar to most personnel. It is the form used by both public and private funding sources for grant requests, and simply stipulates how a requested amount of financial support will be invested in resources to accomplish the objectives and activities described in the narrative of the grant proposal.

The budget structure is characterized by such designations as *personnel, equipment, facilities* (rental, leases, etc.), *supplies, travel,* and other types of costs. A completed agency line budget consists of a series of subbudgets and a master budget. Each subbudget indicates the amount of income allocated to a single agency unit—the administrative staff, accounting office, information and referral unit, counseling staff, etc.—and how the money will be used. The master budget provides the representation of how total income is to be distributed among these interrelated organizational divisions.

In preparing a line budget or any other type of budget, competence is exemplified by the inclusion of all relevant detail about a category of expenditure. Under *personnel,* for instance, it is not sufficient simply to present the amount to be expended for this category. The budget should show such things as the number of persons to be paid from the allocated funds, their classification if a classification system is in effect, rates of pay, and percentage of working time each employee is to contribute to the unit. In most instances, basic information is presented on the budget sheet and an explanation and elaboration of the presentation follows on attached sheets headed "Budget Justification."

When an agency has operated for a year or more, the budget should present comparisons of the current year with past ones, providing explanation and justification for any changes. These justifications should be brief and to the point, providing administration with only the salient information needed to decide whether the change is merited and feasible in light of other budgetary demands.

Skill in budget preparation is attained only through experience. With time, those contributing to the preparation learn what

to report and how much to report. They learn to avoid not only underreporting, a common error, but the even more pervasive error of overreporting. The latter error tends to occur if (a) the budget process limits communication between unit representatives in regard to the prepared budget, and does not allow for subsequent discussion of the document between administration and unit personnel, or (b) unit personnel fail to understand that they will have opportunity in a review to elaborate on information contained in their budget submission. Overreporting can be as deadly for the administrator as underreporting. It drowns him in information, often leaves him confused, and absorbs time that he could put to better purpose.

A well prepared budget submission will contain only:

1. Whatever detailed information the administrator needs to understand how requested funds will be used and how their use is expected to contribute to agency interests;
2. The information the accountants need to assess whether or not funds are being expended as mandated.

Additional clarification should be retained for presentation during review if requested.

The above discussions have touched on what are known as operating budgets. Still another type of budget is called a *capital budget.* This budget is prepared by organizations to cover long-term capital investments (buildings, expensive equipment, etc.) which are financed over many years. It is highly unlikely that area planners in aging will be directly concerned with this type of budgeting, but they should be aware of it since many of the organizations with which they deal will be involved with capital financing.

The Accounting Function

Accounting is the day-to-day control function of the fiscal management process and involves the maintenance of continuously updated and accurate records of the flow and relationship of income and expenditure as prescribed by the budget. Its purpose is not only to ensure that funds are spent as prescribed and that expenditures do not exceed expected or available income, but that the rate of expenditure is appropriate.

Too often the accounting procedure is misperceived; it is seen as simply a process for determining whether or not current expenditure overreaches currently available income. Competent accounting is a much more complex procedure. It entails looking ahead from any given time within the fiscal year and determining with relative assurance that expenditures and ascertained operating income will be closely in balance at the close of the year. Such forecasts are difficult because many units of an organization do not expend monies at a constant rate. The nature of their function necessitates varying levels of expenses throughout the year.

A helpful way to visualize this differential rate problem is to think of a year-round camping program organized to serve older people during the holiday seasons. During the summer months costs will maximize, with the organization carrying a full complement of staff and expending funds for actual operation. Once school opens, cost will reduce to a low point with only a small staff and their maintenance placing a demand on income. Costs will again approach maximum during the Christmas season, then drop off until they mount again during the Easter holidays.

Because of such fluctuations, an accountant simply cannot relax when expenditures are in a low trough. He must be constantly assessing the rate of low expenditure to determine whether it is draining off income that will be required to cover the committed level of efforts at a high point of expenditure.

Actually our example oversimplifies the forecasting task. It implies that concern is restricted to the fluctuation of aggregate expenditures for the total organization. This, however, is seldom the case. The Area Agency on Aging, like most agencies, will be administering a number of accounts reflecting the correlation of expenses and allocated income for multiple operating units. The ups and downs of the expense curves for each of these accounts will be different. Consequently, the accountant must be making multiple forecasts to ensure that the income-expenditure relationship is in alignment for each unit of an organization.

Fluctuating expenditure rates are not the only complicating factor for accounting. Income can present analogous problems, especially when agency funding is based on governmental appropriations and public and private grants.

Few social service organizations today have the luxury of depending on a single funding source. Instead they obtain their operating income from a range of governmental agencies and private grantors, from which funds are received at different points throughout the fiscal year. On occasion, expected funds are late in arrival because of delayed actions by public and private funders, and the amount received may vary from the amount anticipated. All these factors create budgeting and accounting headaches.

The budget is generally based not on money in hand but on receipts expected during the fiscal year. Invariably a degree of risk is involved in estimating income. How much risk there is will depend on administrative judgment, but the general rule is not to plan on other than reasonably certain income and to revise the budget should "possible" income materialize at a later date. A more speculative approach to budgeting can be disastrously misleading. Those responsible for accounting can become lulled into the impression that income estimates are reasonably definite, and reflect this in the allowed rates of expenditure. The error of their ways is not brought home until possible income included in the budget fails to materialize, and then a fiscal crisis occurs.

There is no easy way to handle the differential flow of income over the fiscal year. Accounting is usually denied the benefit of pooling, or *co-mingling*, funds received from different sources in order to pay bills from a central pool without regard to what agency unit contracted them. Each funding source usually sets constraints on how its funds may be used. Because of these constraints, accounting is impelled to set up and control multiple accounts and forecast the income flow for a specific account against legitimate expenditures from that account.

This structure of separate accounting for differing aspects of agency activity does not pose total inflexibility in making money transfers as conditions dictate. Government as well as many private funders recognize that agencies can be caught in fiscal binds. Income for a particular activity can be late in arrival, or a peak in expenditure can deplete income before the scheduled date of replenishment. Unless accounting can borrow from another account where funds are in adequate supply, the activity will be placed in jeopardy or terminated. Funders of the other account will usually permit this borrowing if the agency follow the funder's procedures and correctly requests permission to make a temporary transfer.

Sometimes the transfer is not between accounts but between categories within a given account, as when one category of expense has exceeded the predicted while another is running under the anticipated amount. Here again, accounting must not act without proper clearance with the funder. In all instances when requesting transfer of funds, the agency should insist on receiving permission in writing in order to avoid later misunderstandings when accounts are subjected to an outside audit.

Sometimes when an agency is short of funds in an account but in good fiscal standing, it elects to cover a momentary deficit through a bank loan against the impending receipt of income. This option should only be used when other alternatives are foreclosed, and the agency has the funder's concurrence. In most instances of this kind, the funder will not agree to paying accrued interest on the loan.

To effectively forecast and maintain fiscal control, the accountant should command information on encumbrances. Too often he does not learn of an expenditure until he receives the bill from the supplier —a month or more after the actual commitment to purchase, or the encumbrance of funds. The encumbrance of large sums without accounting's knowledge can be extremely misleading. The accountant is led to believe the unit is operating within its spending limits, only to learn after the fact that the unit has overspent. Only if informed immediately whenever an encumbrance is made can accounting provide effective fiscal control and engage in competent forecasting.

Because his function centers on control, it is evident why the accountant's role is often a source of conflict and he is seen by practitioners as an irritant if not an obstacle to service. His day-to-day interactions with other staff tend to deemphasize the values his function can contribute to organizational welfare by preventing fiscal crises and providing information and guidance for more efficient and effective provision of service.

The potential for conflict can be significantly reduced, if not eliminated, if organizations refrain from isolating the fiscal control function and concentrating it in the accounting unit. In a properly structured situation, control is a shared responsibility, with the accounting office providing only leadership and support to other units. It is incumbent on the staff of each unit to participate actively in each phase of the fiscal management process and remain in continuous communication with the accounting office. Such arrangements can dissipate the myth that service and fiscal management are disassociated functions.

Fund Custodianship

Custodianship is a minor concern for most service organizations, since their administration rarely touches cash. In the case of federal appropriations and grants, a letter of credit is usually deposited with a local bank and the agency draws on this credit through a voucher system. These vouchers are an integral part of the accounting system and serve as back-up documentation when agency accounts are audited. Many administrators countersign each voucher, though this authority may also be vested in subordinates, because they believe the procedure adds to control and keeps them appropriately informed about the organization's fiscal activities.

Custodial procedures will of course differ with funding sources. Those mandated by federal authority are not necessarily the same for state, county, or city government, and the agency must adapt

its fiscal management to conform to these variations.

While the agency is unlikely to handle large sums of money, it probably will have petty cash funds in its direct care. It is important that these funds also be subjected to accurate accounting, and petty cash expenditures periodically integrated into the appropriate program accounts.

Equally important is the administration of petty cash. Preferably it should be administered by one person, never scattered around among units or kept in easily accessible places. It should never be allowed to exceed one hundred dollars.

The Auditing Procedure

Audits take place at intervals and involve the examination of fiscal records to determine whether expenditures have been made in conformance with appropriation regulations, are in the proper amounts, and have been properly documented. The procedure can be either an internal audit (done by the agency's accounting staff) or an external audit (done by a governmental or other outside accounting group).

Traditionally, auditing is conceived as fiscal review instituted to ascertain whether any irregularities have occurred in the handling of funds. In recent years, however, the concept of *performance audit* has been introduced. Performance audit is an evaluation process designed to assess the relationship of expenditure to the conduct of a program and the achievement of its goals. The process is obviously not as precise as financial auditing, since it entails qualitative judgments and the use of operational standards that cannot be as exact as monetary measures. Nevertheless, the process is being used more and more by federal and state funders, and administrators should be aware of the trend. It provides an additional reason why administrators must be able to effectively relate service activity and the expenditure categories discussed earlier.

II. ADDITIONAL PROCEDURES

Purchasing

In the course of administering a program there will be many occasions when small or large purchases must be made. Ordinarily a dollar amount is set above which purchases must be done through competitive bidding. When an item to be purchased is in this category, at least three estimates should be obtained from different vendors. All other factors being equal, the item should then be purchased at the lowest price. At times there may be reasons (better service, reputation, etc.) to purchase from a vendor whose price is not lowest, but these decisions should be carefully documented in case they are ever questioned by auditors.

Most items to be purchased fall below the price range where competitive bidding is required, but in many of these cases it is still desirable to shop around for the lowest price. If the operations of the program are located in a community where there are several competing vendors of certain items, it is advisable to alternate the choice of vendors so that no charges of favoritism can be justified.

The administrator of a program should also set internal limits as to the level of purchases made by subordinates at their own discretion. Certainly the purchase of any major items should be approved by the administrator and handled by voucher so that adequate records are kept. Where items are delivered there should always be someone able to verify the accuracy of the items against the invoice accompanying them. No items should be received C.O.D. without such verification, and certainly no

vouchers should be issued for payment without verification.

A matter to bear in mind is that all purchases made by governmental bodies (federal, state, or local) are free of federal taxes. A form indicating the tax-exempt status of the organization should accompany all purchases where federal taxes are being waived.

Supply Management and Inventory Control

Periodic inventory of major items in the possession of the program is important. Equipment such as furniture, typewriters, calculators, movie projectors, etc., should have tags affixed that are difficult to remove. Each tag should contain at least the initials of the agency and a series number for identification of the item of equipment. The list of serial numbers and descriptions of the items they identify should be checked and updated at regular intervals of perhaps six months or a year. Where items are borrowed or taken off the premises for use at another location, they should be signed out so that the location of all items of major equipment can be ascertained at any time.

In the control of ordinary supplies a good administrator should steer a middle course between petty possessiveness and frivolous waste. Ordinary items such as paper, pencils, staples, clips, ribbons, etc., should be readily available for the use of staff. Records of available supplies on hand are as much a guide for replenishing dwindling supplies as an indicator of the extent of use of these items.

Property Management

Occasions will arise when administrators of programs will need to go out and rent or lease space for their activities. Much care should be exercised in finding out the going rate per square foot in the area, the types of facilities available, and what services are included in the rental. Locations should be looked at in terms of easy accessibility, availability of parking facilities, closeness to other offices, restaurants, bus lines, etc. In deciding where to rent space, the procedure should be similar to that for the purchase of major equipment; that is, proof must be shown of comparison shopping, and where a place other than the lowest priced one is chosen, adequate rationale must be provided for the selection. Obviously the costs of renting space should not exceed the amount budgeted for that purpose.

In negotiating with the property owner or manager, both sides should make clear in writing the understanding reached regarding any alterations to be undertaken and who is to pay for them. Understanding should also be reached as to who is responsible for custodial and maintenance services. The longer the lease the program is able to commit itself to, the better the terms that can be negotiated. Therefore, the administrator of the program should find out from the central administrators for how long a term he is legally able to lease facilities. In no case would it be for a period of less than a year.

Phone Service

Associated with the choice of facilities is telephone service. Adequacy of service of course depends on the number of people using it, the availability of incoming lines for people who call the agency, and the ease with which personnel can make or receive calls. These are matters that can be negotiated with the phone company and should not present much of a problem. What is of somewhat greater concern is the control over toll or long-distance calls. Careful records should be kept and turned

in monthly by all persons authorized to make such calls, and these should be checked against the itemized charges made by the phone company. There may be times when greater use is unavoidable (prior to conferences and other long-distance matters), but adjustments must then be made on an annual basis so the totals do not exceed the budgeted amounts.

One item of caution regards keeping phones locked when facilities are being used by public or clientele groups without staff members present. Failure to do this has resulted in abuse and lack of control of phone service—a favorite target of outside auditors.

Travel

Personnel of the program will on occasion travel in the conduct of their assignments or to professional meetings and other types of conferences. Allowable costs for travel in mileage allowance, air fare, lodging, meals, etc., are carefully set forth by the federal government and are altered from time to time. Where federal monies are involved, current regulations should always be followed as closely as possible. Aside from normal travel in carrying out routine duties, subordinates should never engage in trips unless they have the prior approval of the person in the program authorized to grant such approvals. And, as with all other expenditures, the amount spent for travel by personnel of the program should never exceed the amount set aside in the budget for that purpose.

Payroll

Records should be kept of hours worked by all personnel, absences, sick leave, vacation time accumulated, etc. No payroll should be approved without the necessary documentation to back it up. Where paychecks are not mailed directly to individual recipients, but sent to the agency for disbursement, each employee should sign his name next to the appropriate date on a listing as he picks up his check.

Record Keeping

From the start a filing system should be developed in which all receipts and other fiscal records are kept. Duplicates of all receipts given for money from individuals or groups should be available for auditing purposes, as should duplicates of all invoices, vouchers, and other records of transactions and activities of the agency.

If one must err, it should be on the side of being overmeticulous in the maintenance of good financial records. These records can be of great assistance to the Area Agency administrator in planning and evaluation, as well as providing the necessary documentation for auditing purposes.

SUMMARY AND CONCLUSIONS

The skills involved in proper financial management are not inborn, but rather must be cultivated and nurtured. When questions arise regarding fiscal matters, an administrator should not hesitate to seek assistance and guidance.

Specific guidelines for proper financial management will be provided by fiscal officials, and an administrator should become thoroughly acquainted with them. However, if one were to extract rules of behavior for proper financial management they would be as follows:

1. Always attempt to relate financial facts and figures to the program being carried out: What has been served? What activities did the money provide? What level of services?
2. Never transfer funds from one account to another or from one budget category to another without written approval by a top fiscal official of the agency.
3. Be a stickler for adequate documentation of all financial activities—purchases, leases, payroll, travel, account transfers, budget transfers, phone usage, postage, and all other activities involving finance.

While specific details of management may differ from one organization to the other, the basic principles are fairly similar. It is the basic approach in terms of the aforementioned suggestions that an administrator should cultivate.

It is to be hoped that the time will come when programs will be judged and funded on their own merits, but in the meantime much is riding on the attention—or lack of it—paid to the more mundane aspects of financial management in the carrying out of all public programs.

CHAPTER VI

Evaluating Programs

Introduction

At best the impact and effectiveness of community practice programs are hard to demonstrate. Probably no other area of social work presents as many difficulties for evaluators, administration, staff, and client populations. But the need for more precise measurement is clear and growing. Today practitioners must be prepared to be accountable for their work. At the same time, most programs can benefit greatly by better specification of the relationship between our efforts and the goals to which they are directed. To try to remain aloof from more rigorous scrutiny of our work will increasingly deny important resources to community programs and eventually jeopardize their existence. If practitioners do not soon become more amenable to joining in the process of evaluation, they are likely to find influence over its terms and conditions beyond their grasp. The potential for improving social programs is enormous. However, the state of evaluation (science and art) suggests that skepticism as well as support is healthy.

How should evaluation be defined? One definition which we like because it is broad and emphasizes the relationship between aspects of decision making and evaluation is:

The process of determining the significance or amount of success a particular intervention has had in terms of costs and benefits and goal attainment. It is also concerned with assessing adequacy of performance, appropriateness of the stated goal, the feasibility of attaining it, as well as the value or impact of unintended outcomes.[1]

This perspective on evaluation seems particularly useful for those who must decide whether programs are to be continued, modified, drastically altered, or ended. Seeing evaluation as a process rather than a product also leads in the direction of policy-maker, administrator, staff, and client involvement.

What basic criteria might be used to judge the success or failure of a given program? Suchman provides us with the following:[2]

---

[1] Robert Washington, draft manuscript on Program Evaluation, 1975, p. 4.
[2] Edward Suchman, *Evaluative Research* (New York: Russell Sage Foundation, 1967).

1. *Effort*—What goes into the program (without regard to what comes out).
2. *Performance*—What comes out of the program (without regard to effort).
3. *Adequacy of Performance*—The relationship of the performance to total need (among the population addressed by the program).
4. *Efficiency*—The relationship of effort to outcome or impact in terms of costs, as compared with alternative approaches.
5. *Process*—How did the program get where it went (including unintended consequences, desirable and undesirable).

The commonsense quality of these criteria lends credence to the possibility that they be used to differentiate stronger and weaker program aspects and thus contribute to the improvement of social programs.

Another key perspective on the process of evaluation has been suggested by Tripodi, Fellin, and Epstein.[3] This involves looking carefully at the stages through which all social programs must go (at least those that manage to get underway). The first is Program Initiation, the stage at which ideas are translated into a basic strategy or plan of action and the necessary resources secured. The second stage is Program Contact, in which the program staff attempt to become actively involved with the target client group (and address both limiting and facilitating conditions in the physical and psychological environments). Finally, there is the Program Implementation stage, during which the intervention modes of the program are applied and services are delivered. These stages are important because often they must be considered separately, and judged on their individual merits. Thus, for example, the services provided during implementation may be hampered by an inadequacy in the mobilization of needed resources during program initiation rather than because of any deficiency in the service delivery system established. Each stage may be appraised in terms of specific subgoals or incremental goals instead of overarching program objectives. In general, the viewpoint of "differential evaluation"—assessment in terms of different program aspects—seems a modest but sound stance for the practitioner involved in program evaluation.

The authors selected for this section do not represent a single theory of, or orientation toward, evaluation. Rather they offer perspectives on the strategy, tactics, and techniques of evaluation that can be helpful to the practitioner whose program is being evaluated and to the practitioner-evaluator.

Carol Weiss's article is particularly appropriate because it addresses the tensions, controversies, confusions, and "politics" of the evaluation process. Clear and specific suggestions are made for how these may be lessened, including an appraisal of how practitioners can be contributing partners in the evaluation process.

While the context of Darwin Solomon's article is the small communities of Saskatchewan, the suggestions he develops seem applicable to program evaluation in large cities, even in the largest metropolitan areas. The reasons for evaluation, who should do the evaluation, steps in evaluation, and practical problems in evaluation are explored in turn. Taking a step backward for a

---

[3] Tony Tripodi, Phillip Fellin, Irwin Epstein, *Social Program Evaluation* (Itasca, Ill.: F. E. Peacock, 1971).

broader perspective, Robert Washington's article presents four basic frameworks in which program evaluation can take place—the systems model, the goal attainment model, the impact model, and the behavioral model. The strengths and limitations of each approach are explored and assessed.

The article on utilization of data by Richard Douglass is an original attempt to lay out some basic ways of quantifying and depicting data. It is addressed to practitioners and the kind of community information with which they are very often confronted. Finally, John Gottman and Robert Clasen's "Troubleshooting Guide" is a handy index of basic evaluation concepts and offers illustrations of the ways in which they may be applied in action situations.

Taken together, we believe that these articles represent an important set of perspectives on the process of evaluation and provide many tools, both for those whose programs are being evaluated and those who are going to be doing the evaluating.

John L. Erlich

26. Overcoming Obstacles to Evaluation: The Politics of Evaluation

Carol H. Weiss

THE TURBULENT SETTING OF THE ACTION PROGRAM

A characteristic of evaluation research that differentiates it from most other kinds of research is that it takes place in an action setting. Something else besides research is going on; there is a program serving people. In fact, the service program is the more important element on the scene. The research is an appendage, an also-present, a matter of secondary priority. Researchers frequently propose changing the order of priority, and with some justification. If we do not find out whether the program is really doing what it is supposed to be doing, how do we know whether it is worth having at all? But whatever the cogency of the argument in any universally remains the first order of business. The evaluation has to adapt itself to the program environment and disrupt operations as little as possible.

Obviously, some interference will take place. For one thing, data have to be collected. Staff members and program participants will be asked questions, observed, asked to fill out forms. Certain research requirements are uncompromisable. But all too often, evaluators ask for more information than they need or will ever use. With a clear focus for the study and some self-restraint, they can lower their demands and lessen their intrusion. But however cooperative and congenial the evaluator may be, there are some features of an action setting that can create serious

Carol H. Weiss, *Evaluation Research: Methods for Assessing Program Effectiveness,* © 1972, pp. 92–109. Reprinted by permission of Prentice-Hall, Inc., Englewood Cliffs, New Jersey.

research problems. We will discuss three in this chapter: (1) the tendency of the program to change while it is being evaluated, (2) the relationships between evaluators and program personnel, and (3) the fact that the program is embedded in an organizational system and that the nature of the system will have consequences for outcomes.

THE SHIFTING PROGRAM

In an earlier chapter [not reproduced here] we anguished over the complexity of social programs and recommended serious attention to monitoring, describing, and classifying program characteristics. The conscientious evaluator, heeding this advice, completes his specification of the program and files it away. Then in midstream, while the evaluation is still going on, the program slithers out of his carefully constructed categories. Conditions change and the program changes.

It may change little by little, as practitioners see that present methods are not working and conscientiously innovate until they find satisfactory arrangements. Perhaps changes in clientele or in community conditions lead to subtle changes in activities and principles. Or the program may change quite suddenly. More money becomes available—or less. Staff members resign, and staff with different viewpoints or qualifications are hired. The political winds shift, and old relationships are shut off. A decision is made in Washington or the state capitol to discontinue certain styles of operation and adopt others. Such factors affect even programs set up as "demonstrations," "models," or "social experiments." The longer and more complex the program, the more likely it is to experience change. For the evaluator even to know that the program is changing requires periodic stock-taking. He has to be in close enough touch to talk to directors and staff, examine records, perhaps attend meetings or observe the program in session. One signal that should alert him to turn up on the scene is a change in top program management.

If the program has altered course, what does the evaluator do? If he goes ahead as if he were studying the same program, he will never know what it was that led to observed effects or the lack of them—the old program, the new one, the transition, or some combination of everything going on. If he drops the original evaluation and tries to start over again under the changed circumstances, he may lack appropriate baseline data. He may not have measures relevant to the new goals and program procedures.[1] Further, he has no guarantee that the same kind of shift will not occur again.

One thing he can do is update his original specification of the program through continuing observation and definition. He can develop a dynamic rather than a static model of the program to categorize it in terms of its movement as well as its conceptual location. This makes for a more complex description of what the program is, but one more in touch with reality.[2] That, you may think, is all very nice; we

are certainly for program descriptions that are dynamic and accurate over those that are static and wrong. But in evaluation, we usually want to learn which component, which strategy, of the program is associated with success. How does even an accurate dynamic description help us here?

The Issue for the Evaluator

The way that the issue is frequently posed: How can we hold the program steady? The assumption is that when things are changing, there is no way of separating out the useful components from those that are neutral or counterproductive. Continuity of input seems essential for any fair test of what the effects of that input are likely to be. Observers have proposed a variety of solutions. Some authors, and Fairweather is a good example,[3] recommend that when innovative programs are being tested, the researcher should be in control of the entire operation. Then the program will be conducted with evaluation requirements in the forefront and random changes will be fended off. Even when the researcher is not in control, he can still play the role of advocate for program maintenance. Freeman and Sherwood suggest that the evaluator has the responsibility to hold the program to its original concepts and principles. He should stand over it "like a snarling watchdog" to prevent program practitioners from altering its operations.[4]

Mann, after reviewing several hundred evaluations, found that programs are too complex and variable in operation to provide fair tests of program principles. For

[1]Sidney H. Aronson and Clarence C. Sherwood, "Researcher Versus Practitioner: Problems in Social Action Research," *Social Work*, Vol. XII, No. 4 (1967), pp. 89–96.

[2]See Alfred P. Parsell, "Dynamic Evaluation: The Systems Approach to Action Research," SP–2423 (Santa Monica, Calif.: Systems Development Corporation, 1966).

[3]George W. Fairweather, *Methods for Experimental Social Innovation* (New York: John Wiley, 1967), pp. 24–36.

[4]Howard E. Freeman and Clarence C. Sherwood, "Research in Large-scale Intervention Programs," *Journal of Social Issues*, Vol. XXI, No. 1 (1965), pp.11–28.

drawing conclusions about the relative merits of different approaches, he gives up on action settings and recommends taking programs back to the laboratory. There small segments of program can be studied rigorously, and successful practices can be identified for given conditions. Once this type of basic knowledge is obtained, the individual components can be built back up into operable programs.[5] Weiss and Rein have looked at large-scale programs that are exploratory and unclear in orientation, that inevitably cast about for new directions and methods. In cases such as community-action or model-cities programs, they believe that it is better to discard the investigation of goal achievement altogether. The researcher will learn more from careful analysis of what is actually going on. He can investigate such pressing issues as why and how programs change, how agencies absorb new inputs of money and direction and emerge relatively unscathed, how adaptations are worked out between innovative programs and resistant systems.[6]

Perhaps it is possible to redefine the controversy. Holding the program steady, let alone controlling it, is beyond the authority of most evaluators in most settings I have seen. There *are* programs that remain clear, coherent, and intact by themselves without the evaluator's cajolery or imprecations. But if they are under strong pressures to change, there is a limit to what he can do to hold back the tide. On the other hand, surrender to complexity and retreat to the laboratory look like a cop-out. It is true that many

programs are rushed into the field prematurely without the painstaking developmental work required for effective service. We are in a hurry for solutions; we want to serve thousands of people right away. Although the program may be inadequately conceptualized, we hope that the whole thing will somehow work and that at our leisure, we can sort out the features responsible for the success. It is worth heeding Mann's advice that more research should be directed toward the careful development and testing of program components. Furthermore, for the accumulation of a body of tested knowledge about the relative effectiveness of strategies, a grab-bag collection of disparate evaluations is hardly the ideal basis.

But the laboratory is not the real world. In the artificiality of the laboratory, all manner of things seem to work that do not survive their brush with operating conditions. Even optimum program components will get contaminated when they emerge, and further research will have to be done under an almost limitless set of circumstances to define the "best" components for each contaminated condition.

Some Practical Approaches

To cope with such problems, Suchman has proposed a four-stage developmental process.[7] He differentiates a pilot phase, when program development proceeds on a trial-and-error basis; a model phase, when a defined program strategy is run under controlled conditions; a prototype phase, when the model program is subjected to realistic operating conditions; and an institutionalized phase, when the program is an ongoing part of the organization. It is

---

[5]John Mann, "The Outcome of Evaluative Research," in *Changing Human Behavior* (New York: Charles Scribner's Sons, 1965), pp. 191–214.

[6]Robert S. Weiss and Martin Rein, "The Evaluation of Broad-Aim Programs: A Cautionary Case and a Moral," *Annals of the American Academy of Political and Social Science,* Vol. 385 (September, 1969), pp. 118–32.

[7]Edward A. Suchman, "Action for What? A Critique of Evaluative Research," in *The Organization, Management, and Tactics of Social Research,* ed. Richard O'Toole (Cambridge, Mass.: Schenkman Publishing Co., 1970).

only in the model phase that the program must be held stable for experimental evaluation. At other stages, less rigorous study suffices, and variation in input is not only tolerated but expected. If an agency were committed to such a rational course of development (and maintained it!), it would effectively resolve the issue of program shifts. The evaluator may find it rewarding to encourage the agency to move toward such clear demarcation of program phases, with appropriate evaluation at each step.

The approach that Weiss and Rein propose is, I think, refreshingly relevant for programs of the scale and ambiguity that they discuss, although they give only fragmentary clues to the methods by which such complex processes can be analyzed. What they recommend is basically a study of the implementation process, rather than evaluation. We know that implementation is a critical juncture between the best-laid plans of program developers and the "gang aft agley" of operation.[8] The differences in perspective between planners and operators, the pressures that beset the local program, the responses necessary for survival and support all alter and reshape the original concept. Understanding what

happens in the political and social complexities of broad-aim intervention programs may well be a priority order of business if we are to learn how to develop programs more realistically, to reduce the slippage between intent and action, and to address social problems with greater effect. Present inattention to this facet of program life is difficult to understand or condone.

Nevertheless, study of implementation does not supplant evaluation of outcomes. Critical as it is to learn more about the dynamics of operation, it remains important to find out the effects of the resulting programs on people and institutions. The two research efforts should be complementary. As we learn more about implementation, we can begin to identify vital elements in the operating systems and move toward description and measurement of them. In time, we can combine the study of program process with the study of outcomes. In the interim, it is not unimportant to know how the intended beneficiaries of the program are faring.

Evaluators used to yell and pound on the table that program staff should not wait to call them in until the program was in operation. They wanted not only to be in on the ground floor when the program was being planned; they wanted to "help dig the foundation."[9] Many program people have learned the lesson; evaluators are often in from the start. Now, however, it becomes clear that there is such a thing as premature evaluation.[10] Evaluations begin before the program has found its goals, its functions, or generally accepted

---

[8]In defining the career of social problems, Herbert Blumer lists five stages, the fifth of which is "the transformation of the official plan in its empirical implementation." He goes on to say, "Invariably to some degree, the plan as put into practice is modified, twisted and reshaped, and takes on unforeseen accretions." "Social Problems as Collective Behavior," *Social Problems,* Vol. XVIII, No. 3 (1971), pp. 301, 304–5. For a description of federal planners' "naiveté" about the complexity of translating official plans into operating programs, see Walter Williams, "Developing an Evaluation Strategy for a Social Action Agency," *Journal of Human Resources,* Vol. IV, No. 4 (1969), pp. 451–65. He notes three aspects that impinge on implementation: How well articulated the plan is, how administratively capable the local staff is, how much authority the federal agency has to force compliance (or obversely, how much political insulation the local agency has to resist change).

[9]Elizabeth Herzog, *Some Guide Lines for Evaluative Research* (Washington, D.C.: U.S. Department of Health, Education and Welfare, 1959), p. 84.

[10]Nelson Aldrich, ed., "The Controversy over the More Effective Schools: A Special Supplement," *Urban Review,* Vol. II, No. 6 (1968), pp. 15–34. The evaluator himself believed that the study was premature.

ways of work. An analysis of the system can help program developers as they seek direction. It is a rewarding research activity, but it is not evaluation. Evaluation comes later, when there is an entity, however complex and interrelated, that can be defined, tested, and replicated. In the interests of social policy, we cannot postpone this part of the study too long.

If there is some recognizable set of principles and procedures that can be called a program, I am not sure that it is necessary to hold it steady in the arbitrary and argumentative way in which most raisers-of-the-issue propose. Programs almost inevitably drift. If the program and the drift are classified and analyzed, it seems possible to attribute the ensuing effects to the program in terms of how it worked and will often work in this disorderly world. Here are some suggestions that may be workable:

1. Take frequent periodic measures of program effect (for example, monthly assessments in programs of education, training, therapy), rather than limiting collection of outcome data to one point in time.[11]
2. Encourage a clear transition from one program approach to another. If changes are going to be made, try to see that A is done for a set period, then B, then C.
3. Clarify the assumptions and procedures of each phase and classify them systematically.
4. Keep careful records of the persons who participated in each phase. Rather than lumping all participants together, analyze outcomes in terms of the phase(s) of program in which each person participated.

5. Press for a recycling of earlier program phases. Sometimes this happens naturally; on occasion, it can be engineered. If it is possible, it provides a way to check on earlier conclusions.
6. Seek to set aside funds and get approval for smaller-scale evaluation of (at least) one program phase or component that will remain stable for a given period.[12] For this venture, experimental procedures can be applied, even though less rigorous and more flexible methods may be sufficient in other program areas.
7. If nothing works and the program continues to meander (chaos would be the proper word in some contexts), consider jettisoning the evaluation framework in favor of meticulous analysis of the what, how, and why of events.

RELATIONSHIPS WITH PROGRAM PERSONNEL

The evaluator works on the turf of another profession. His relationships with the program professionals (teachers, recreation workers, trainers, correction officers) can range from friendly and cooperative to extremes of hostility. Occasionally, an evaluation closes down before completion because of the effective resistance of operating program personnel. The more usual situation, however, is wary coexistence.

Sources of Friction

What causes friction? There are many contributing factors.

[11] For example, Nathan Caplan, "Treatment Intervention and Reciprocal Interaction Effects," *Journal of Social Issues,* Vol. XXIV, No. 1 (1968), pp. 63–88.

[12] For further discussion see Edward L. McDill, Mary S. McDill, and J. Timothy Sprehe, *Strategies for Success in Compensatory Education: An Appraisai of Evaluation Research* (Baltimore, Md.: The Johns Hopkins Press, 1969), pp. 66–71.

Personality Differences. Some observers cite the personality differences between people who go into program practice and those who go into research. The researcher is likely to be a detached individual, interested in ideas and abstractions. He thinks in terms of generalizations and analytical categories. His interest is in the long-term acquisition of knowledge, rather than the day-to-day issues of program operation. He seems cool, uncommitted to any program philosophy or position, without personal loyalties to the program or the organization. As Leonard Duhl has said, the researcher is a "marginal man."

The practitioner, on the other hand, is likely to be a warm, outgoing personality. (This at least is the common expectation in such service professions as teaching, therapy, health care, social work, and occupational counseling, although it is clearly not true of everyone and may not even be the norm in some occupations.) The practitioner generally is intensely concerned about people, specifics, the here and now. He is committed to action. He finds the researcher's skepticism uncongenial, and he finds it difficult to warm up to him as a human being.

Differences In Role. Other observers believe that differences in role are more significant than any underlying personality variables. Basically, a practitioner has to believe in what he is doing; a researcher has to question it. This difference in perspective creates inevitable tensions.[13]

Whatever their initial personal or value characteristics, once they go about their divergent tasks, they are almost bound to see things differently. Paula Kleinman tells a story about her experience as a graduate student working on a "training-and-evaluation" project. The project had a staff of four. At first they were assigned interchangeably to training and to evaluation tasks. Everyone got along very well, but there was concern that their commitment to the training program might "contaminate" the evaluation data. In the interest of objectivity, the group was divided in half, two people assuming training roles and the other two assigned to evaluation. Almost immediately, the comradely relationships deteriorated and dissension developed. The main issue was that the training group wanted to use the data from the preprogram questionnaires in later training sessions in order to enrich the training; the evaluators opposed the release of the data on grounds that trainees' knowledge of Time 1 answers might artificially alter Time 2 responses. Differences in role and responsibility had introduced frictions.

Lack of Clear Role Definition. Evaluation often requires practitioners to take on new roles, such as referring people to the "experimental" program, adhering to the specific program approaches (curriculums, treatment modalities) being tested, collecting data, collaborating with the evaluator. The new roles may not be clearly defined in advance and become apparent only after a series of disputes with the evaluators. Even when roles are not new, the division of roles between practitioner and evaluator may be murky. Tensions can arise over differences in inter-

[13]See Hyman Rodman and Ralph L. Kolodny, "Organizational Strains in the Researcher-Practitioner Relationship," in *Applied Sociology: Opportunities and Problems,* ed. Alvin Gouldner and S.M. Miller (New York: The Free Press, 1965), pp. 93–113. For further discussion, see W. L. Slocum, "Sociological Research for Action Agencies: Some Guides and Hazards," *Rural Sociology,* Vol. XXI, No. 2 (1956), pp. 196–99; Joel Smith, Francis M. Sim, and Robert C. Bealer, "Client Structure and the Research Process," in *Human Organization Re-*

search, ed. R. N. Adams and J. J. Preiss (Homewood, Ill.: Dorsey Press, 1960), Chap. 4; William F. Whyte and Edith Hamilton, *Action Research for Management* (Homewood, Ill.: Dorsey Press, 1964), pp. 209–21.

pretation about who has responsibility for which functions. Particularly frustrating are uncertainties about the authority structure; it is often unclear who has authority to resolve the differences that arise.[14]

Conflicting Goals, Values, Interests, Frames of Reference. The practitioner is concerned with service. He sees evaluation as a diversion and possibly even a threat. It seems to take things away from the program—money, time, administrators' attention—and promises the dubious return of a "report card." The evaluator, after all, is judging the value of his work, and by extension, his professional competence and *him*. The ultimate result of the evaluation, if it is used in decision making, will affect the future of his particular project and perhaps his own job. It may be perfectly true that the purpose of the evaluation is to add to knowledge and to rationalize social policy making, but it is he and his project who will bear the consequences if the results show project failure.

Sometimes practitioners see the evaluation as part and parcel of an innovation in programming that violates cherished concepts of service and tradition. They visit their dislike on both the program and its evaluation component. If the program runs counter to traditional agency values (for example, if it stresses social factors in the rehabilitation of mental patients when the accepted emphasis has been on psychological factors), they may actively or passively undermine the program and—as a consequence—the evaluation.

The practitioner sometimes questions the worth of the evaluator's research tools. He sees the measuring instruments as crude, good enough only to pick up gross changes. He doubts their ability to detect

the subtle effects—such as growth in a person's self-confidence—that are vital effects of the program. The program practitioner on the spot sees growth and achievement that the evaluator, with his "insensitive measuring devices," misses.

On the other hand, of course, the practitioner is an interested party, and he may be seeing changes that are not actually there. While the practitioner levels charges of "insensitive indicators," the evaluator counter-charges with "self-serving observation." There may be some element of truth on both sides, but the implications for the evaluator are clear. First, if he is to win the support of practitioners, he has to develop instruments that measure the factors that practitioners believe are the key effects of the program. They may believe that they deal in attitudes and values, perceptions and beliefs; if these are important program effects, he should find effective ways to measure them. Second, he may seek to convince practitioners that programs are almost always behavioral in intent. They aim to change what people *do*. His measuring tools will be designed to detect the vital effect—the change in behavior.

There is another aspect to this general resistance. In human service professions, practitioners deal with individuals. They are very much aware of individual differences, and they gain esteem and professional recognition from their sensitivity to the facets that differentiate one human being from another and their ability to tailor service to individual needs. The evaluator, on the other hand, deals in statistics—means, percentages, correlation coefficients—gross measures that lump people together. (He may, of course, break out the data by sex, age, race, length of program experience, and other factors, but that does not vitiate the practitioners' pervasive sense of mass data.) In confronting

[14] Carol H. Weiss, *Organizational Constraints on Evaluation Research* (New York: Bureau of Applied Social Research, 1971).

the evaluation data, the practitioner seldom sees that the conclusions are relevant to the specific people with whom he is working. It may be true, for example, that long periods of incarceration are associated with poor postprison adjustment, but the correctional officer cannot really believe that this datum deserves much weight when he has all his knowledge and experience and Johnny Jones standing in front of him.[15]

Institutional Characteristics. When an agency has a history of internal conflict, evaluation may be viewed with particular suspicion. Staff are apt to see the evaluators as management hatchet men—or as the agents of one faction out to do in another. Evaluators' secrecy—their refusal to share data prematurely, their insistence on the confidentiality of individual records—may look threatening in a troubled organization. In fact, the staff of any agency where grievances are strong and satisfaction low may resent the evaluation as another cross to bear.

Other aspects of the institutional setting have consequences as well. Evaluator-practitioner relationships are affected by such aspects of the agency as the administrative structure, the fiscal and bookkeeping arrangements for the evaluation, supervisory practices, openness of communication channels, and the state of relationships with cooperating agencies who refer participants, receive referrals, or offer complementary services.[16] Where ambiguity and fragmented authority flourish, the evaluation is apt to suffer the strains of misperception, conflicting goals, and inadequate support.

Issues That Lead to Friction

What are the issues that provoke conflict?

Data Collection. The request that practitioners administer questionnaires, interviews, and tests to clients is a frequent source of trouble. Often, the evaluator wants the practitioner too to fill out forms or submit to interviews and observation. The practitioner is trying to get a job done. He finds the intrusion time-consuming and disruptive.[17] Since he sees no obvious payoff to the program from the information collected (much of it looks like pretty abstruse and irrelevant stuff), he boggles at the amount of time away from the task at hand. Even when the evaluator has his own staff to collect the information, there are occasional conflicts over access to people, annoyance, and scheduling.

Changes in Record-Keeping Procedures. If the evaluator seeks to collect information from the agency records, another set of squabbles may arise. The records are almost never complete enough and well enough kept for his purposes. (This appears to be a good generalization no matter what the type of agency.) Once he starts asking that practitioners get the records up to date and fill in the missing information, he encounters resistance. If in addition, he has the temerity to ask that the records be kept in a different form, with information items coded to suit the purposes of the evaluation, the disruption

---

[15] See Francis G. Caro, "Approaches to Evaluative Research: A Review," *Human Organization,* Vol. XXVIII, No. 2 (1969), pp. 87–99.

[16] Conflicts over these issues and others are discussed in Gwen Andrew, "Some Observations on Management Problems in Applied Social Research," *The American Sociologist,* Vol. II, No. 2 (1967), pp. 84–89, 92.

[17] A frustrating attempt to add the job of research interviewer to that of social caseworker is discussed in Michael A. LaSorte, "The Caseworker as Research Interviewer," *The American Sociologist,* Vol. III, No. 3 (1968), pp. 222–25.

of established ways of work can create further friction.

Selection of Program Participants. The evaluator usually wants a say in how participants are selected for the program. He is likely to opt for some kind of random procedure. Practitioners, on the other hand, usually want to choose participants on the basis of their amenability to help, the seriousness of their need, or other obvious or subtle characteristics. Random procedures negate their professional skills of diagnosis and service planning. But what the practitioner sees as responsible individual selection makes the participant group "special" in unspecified ways, and thus makes comparison between participants and controls useless as an indication of program effect. Further, the evaluator does not know to what other populations the results are generalizable. Selection, then, is a common bone of contention.

Control Groups. Another problem is control groups. Evaluators want them for the obvious purpose of ruling out rival explanations for the effects observed. Practitioners frequently regard them as a denial of service to needy people that violates all the ethical imperatives of service professions. Only when there are more applicants than available program slots are they likely to accept the researcher's requirements for controls. And when participants drop out of the program, it is not unknown for practitioners to raid the control group for new clients. Or they can upgrade services to controls who are supposedly receiving routine treatment in a competitive effort to "look good." It is difficult enough for evaluators to maintain contact and cooperation with controls who are not receiving the new showcase program, but when practitioners regard this as a "silly frill," they can further sabotage the effort.

Feedback of Information into the Program. Feedback—the communication of early evaluation information to affect later stages of the program—is another issue. Practitioners want to see the program improved by whatever means. If evaluation data can show them ways to increase effectiveness, they do not see why evaluators should object. (Isn't the purpose of evaluation to improve the program?) Of course, that may or may not be the purpose of a particular evaluation. When the purpose is longer range—for example, to decide on the worth of a particular program theory and approach—the evaluator wants the basic program model to remain stable for a long enough time to study its effects. He doesn't want his data to be used to shake things up drastically. But refusal to help is viewed as lack of commitment to the organization. The evaluator is refusing to come to grips with practical problems; he is not accepting any share of the responsibility for the program. (In the longer run, of course, when he has findings to report, he may play an active role. But in the interim, staff members see him as aloof and uncommitted.)

Status Rivalry. Practitioners on occasion resent what they see as the higher status accorded researchers. They slave away and do the day-to-day drudgery, while the evaluator observes, measures, writes a report, and collects all the kudos—programmatic, academic, and sometimes financial as well.[18] As they see it, the evaluator asks them to make all the sacrifices while he collects all the rewards, through publication and professional recognition. They are likely to be particularly resentful when the evaluator produces the report, turns it in, and goes away without acknowledging any further obligation to the program. He appears to be milking the program of opportunities to further his

---

[18] For further discussion, see Rodman and Kolodny, *op. cit.*

own career without giving much in return.

Of course, should the evaluator try to get a hearing for his report in decision-making councils, some practitioners will not be happy, either. For them, the report usually means some kind of impending change. No evaluation report finds *everything* in perfect shape.[19] They may or may not agree with the cogency of the findings, but the almost inevitable implication is that they should change their ideas and procedures and perhaps learn new skills as well. Change is hard, and the evaluator who suggests it wins no popularity contest. If the evaluation is less than convincing, then they see little reason to depart from ways of work that have long stood them well.

Lessening the Friction

This is an imposing catalog of sources of conflict, and it may seem that evaluators and practitioners are inevitably at odds. This is not necessarily so. With good communication and careful planning, most evaluations can proceed in a calm and cooperative atmosphere. If practitioners and evaluators rarely become close chums, they can usually settle their disputes in amicable fashion under appropriate conditions. When it comes time to put the results of evaluation into practice, differences may crop up again. . . . Here we will talk about ways of assuaging potential frictions.

Very little empirical research has been done on arrangements and methods that lessen tension in applied research projects. We therefore have to depend for guidance on the "received wisdom," the generally accepted lessons of experience. Six main conditions appear to be most successful in

enabling people to function together comfortably.

Support from Administrators. As previously mentioned, it is essential to involve project administrators and managers in planning an evaluation. Through dialog with them, the evaluator develops insight and focus, and the administrators gain commitment to the study and to its eventual use in decision making. The support of top administrators is also crucial to getting and maintaining the cooperation of the program staff. They provide incentive, recognition, and reward for staff members who help, rather than hinder, the evaluation enterprise.

Involvement of Practitioners in the Evaluation. Involving the practitioners in planning the evaluation has further payoffs. A first benefit of bringing them in is that they gain understanding of what evaluation is all about. They learn what it is for and how it proceeds. This knowledge dispels some of the sense of threat (Why are they investigating what I'm doing?) and some of the suspicion generated by the presence of alien characters asking questions. Second, they have information and ideas to contribute. They can teach the norms of the project, the realities of its operation, and its jargon. Their contributions often enrich the evaluator's understanding and the sophistication of his study and make the evaluation more relevant to the needs of the agency. They can also keep him from making *faux pas* or unacceptable requests. Early consultation often forestalls later explosions. Further, they are more likely to be cooperative about new procedures and extra work when they see the sense of the requests. They are particularly likely to cooperate if they have had a chance to *contribute* to the development of the new procedures. When group meetings have been held and each member has seen group consensus

---

[19] In fact, the tendency to negative findings is a common feature of evaluations to which we will return in the next chapter.

develop on acceptance of the evaluator's requests, support for the study solidifies.

Although involvement in the early phases of the evaluation is important, it is equally necessary to continue communication through the life of the project. Each person whose work is affected by the evaluation should be kept informed and be given a chance to express his ideas and concerns. Whatever part the program staff plays during the course of the evaluation, the end of the study signals another opportunity for involvement. The evaluator has a responsibility to present his findings to the staff. He may find it stimulating, too, to ask for their help in interpreting the results and drawing conclusions for future action. He is not bound to accept their interpretations, but more than one investigator has found that they have interesting insights. Once they overcome their defensiveness, they can be useful colleagues in understanding the causes of past successes and failures, the process by which the program got where it is, what should be done in the future, and how to make future directions palatable to interested parties.[20]

Minimizing Disruptions. Another tension reliever is adherence to the rules of the road. If evaluators have the good manners to recognize program priorities and limit their demands to indispensable issues, practitioners are likely to follow suit. The trick is to know which issues cannot be compromised and which are susceptible to negotiation. Far too often, evaluators impose heavier demands than their needs warrant. They ask eighty questions instead of twenty; they administer twelve batteries of tests when four would suffice. The reason is usually that they are not clear about what they are looking for, and they take all possible precautions not to miss any-

thing that may turn out to be important. Better focus of the study at the outset—including clearer definition of the theory and expected process of the program— would lessen the zeal to cast a wide and undiscriminating net. Evaluators can become less of a nuisance as they become better informed.

Hiring research assistants to collect evaluation data, rather than asking already-burdened program staff to take on extra duties, is a good investment. Not only do they have more time and knowledge of research requirements, but their allegiance is not divided. Their commitment is to the quality of the data, not to the client or the program. When there is a separate research staff, however, the demarcation of duties should be clear to everyone. The researchers should not be suspected of invading the practitioners' domain or duplicating their work.

Emphasis on Theory. Almost every evaluation is out to discover more than whether this particular program works in this particular time and place with this staff and these participants. Even the most practical manager wants to know whether it will work next year with different participants and some changes in staff and emphasis. It is important to be able to generalize about the basic approach that underlies the program. Is an educational film *as a technique* useful in changing people's use of medical services? Are small-group discussions more effective in changing attitudes on discrimination than lectures?

There is some kind of theory implicit in almost every program. If the evaluator can draw it to the surface and make it the central focus of the evaluation effort, he is on the way to alleviating the very real uneasiness that practitioners feel about being judged and having their performances critically rated. It is nice to think that if it

[20] See M.A. Steward, "The Role and Function of Educational Research—I," *Educational Research,* IX, No. 1 (1966), 3–6.

is the *theory* of the program that is being judged, the practitioners can become eager partners in the investigation. This strikes me as overoptimistic. Practitioners realize that the evaluation, however theoretical in concept, is concerned with real events and can have real (and possibly baleful) consequences for the future of the program.[21] But an emphasis on theory can widen the perspective.

The Feedback of Useful Information. If the evaluator can provide information that managers and practitioners need, he gains their support, even for some of his more bothersome and esoteric enterprises. Sometimes he can happily provide the information with no unpleasant side effects. But sometimes feedback, by changing subsequent program inputs or by contaminating later responses, would jeopardize his study. In that event, the best solution may be a separate data collection effort, apart from the evaluation, to satisfy program needs. In-house evaluation departments can do this more easily, both psychologically and financially, than outside research organizations, and they are more amenable to churning out the required data (and maybe even a speech or two for program people to give). This kind of practical side benefit can serve as an illustration of the utility of research data and increase practitioners' regard for the usefulness of the evaluator and his skills.

Clear Role Definitions and Authority Structure. People should know what is expected of them and of others. There should be clear understanding of the scope and limits of their roles. If practitioners perceive some of their obligations to be incompatible (for example, teaching to the best of their ability *and* using only the one instructional method being evaluated), ways should be found to communicate, interpret, and—if necessary—change role

prescriptions in *advance* of the onset of the program.

When differences arise between program and evaluation personnel that cannot be reconciled by negotiation, the lines of authority should be clear.[22] Everyone should understand the channels of appeal and the person or groups of persons who will make decisions. If interagency relations are involved, the situation may be complex but it is even more vital to establish clear lines of jurisdictional authority.[23]

THE SOCIAL CONTEXT OF THE PROGRAM

Every program takes place in a setting that has consequences for its effectiveness. The primary context is the organization that sponsors and conducts the program. Even if the programs themselves are highly similar, one would expect differences between the outcomes of a community organization program run by the Chamber of Commerce and one run by a radical student group, or between a foreign technical assistance program supported by the U.S. Department of Defense and one supported by UNESCO. Programs in turn have effects on the organizations that run them. The effects may be favorable (raising the prestige of the agency), competitive and draining (drawing the most competent and committed staff from the regular run of programs into the "special" program), destructive (diverting the organization from the mission at which it is skilled and enmeshing it

---

[21] Aronson and Sherwood, op. cit.

[22] For a case where the structure was unclear, see Hans Nagpaul, "The Development of Social Research in an Ad Hoc Community Welfare Organization," *Journal of Human Relations*, Vol. XIV, No. 4 (1966), pp. 620–33.

[23] A first-rate analysis of this and related issues is given in D. B. Kandel and R. H. Williams, *Psychiatric Rehabilitation: Some Problems of Research* (New York: Atherton Press, 1964).

in programs and conflicts it is poorly equipped to handle).

The larger social frameworks of neighborhood and community also affect programs and their consequences. So, too, do national systems of values, laws, and sensitivities. Family planning programs will be welcomed in one country and boycotted in another. Local mores even determine what can be studied and what cannot. Thus, new nations or those engaged in modernization may be extremely sensitive to studies revealing the extent of poverty or maldistribution of wealth.[24] In the United States, drug use is defined as a criminal activity. Programs for addicts have therefore been under pressure to regard abstinence from drug use as the only possible goal. Meyer and Bigman report that until recently, it was almost impossible for a program to aim for anything less than abstinence, or for evaluators to study program results in terms of improved social functioning without regard to whether the patient was on or off drugs.[25] Hardy souls have now raised questions about alternative goals and criteria of program success.

Just as the program is embedded in a social context, so too is the person who participates. He does not come to the program empty, unattached, or unanchored. He has beliefs and values, he has friends and relatives, habits, patterns of behavior, and ideas. Often the pull of his existing social arrangements works against the efforts of the program to bring about change. This may mean that program efforts are inundated by the flood of other influences which are part of his everyday

routine. One implication for evaluation may be the value of exploring the supportive and inhibiting features of the interpersonal context. It might investigate the attitudes and behaviors of key people in the participant's environment (family, coworkers, teachers) during the time the program is trying to instill new patterns of behavior. For example, for in-service training programs that teach new styles of work, the responses of supervisors back on the job may be crucial for the retention or fade-out of the lessons taught. Brim found that among mothers urged to adopt new feeding practices, husbands' reactions—although they did not influence the probability of trying the advised procedures—were influential in continuation of the trials and eventual adoption of the new practices.[26] Unless participants receive support from their social environment, or are at least freed from some of its binds, program efforts may founder. The evaluator who locates the operative sources of support or obstruction can help program planners direct the attention to reaching and affecting these groups and thereby strengthen program impact.

Agencies are similarly affected by the pull of existing arrangements. Their efforts to run novel programs may run afoul of obligations to established constituencies, public reactions, or countervailing pressures. On the other hand, their most potent effects may be the rearrangement of traditional patterns of thought and behavior in other agencies. Legal service programs for the poor, for example, may have greater impact on the practices of public agencies that deal with poor people than their direct benefits to the clients themselves. Evaluation can find this out.

Evaluation need not be limited to local

---

[24] Ralph L. Beals, *Politics of Social Research* (Chicago: Aldine-Atherton, 1969), p. 27.

[25] Alan S. Meyer and Stanley K. Bigman, "Contextual Considerations in Evaluating Narcotic Addiction Control Programs," *Proceedings of the Social Statistics Section* (Washington, D.C.: American Statistical Association, 1968), pp. 175–80.

[26] Orville G. Brim, Jr., "The Acceptance of New Behavior in Child Rearing," *Human Relations,* Vol. VII (1954), pp. 473–91.

effects or low horizons. Sometimes the most important influences on a program's success lie outside the program's immediate purview. Sometimes the most important consequences of a program are not the effects on participants directly but on other people, agencies, or community institutions. The lesson for the evaluator is: Be alert. The studies that are ultimately most practical and useful are often those that open our eyes to new elements on the scene.

27. Conducting an Evaluation

Darwin D. Solomon

EVALUATING COMMUNITY PROGRAMS

WHY EVALUATE PROGRAMS?

The question—*Why evaluate programs*—may seem unnecessary. Do we not constantly ask ourselves whether a program was worth the effort? Did we like it? Were our clients satisfied? Was it what we (or they) expected?—Less frequently, we may ask what was learned from it.

We Evaluate to Economize on Effort

In one typical Saskatchewan community, it was found that eighteen individuals were devoting an average of forty-four hours per week to meetings and community activities of various kinds. Often only a few citizens are deeply involved in programs designed to meet individual and group needs. Most leaders are constantly looking for ways to improve these efforts: They would like to see their investment of time and energy pay better dividends. Accurate evaluations of past efforts, applied to the planning of future programs, can help them achieve this.

We Evaluate to Improve Programs

In one community the recreation board had been sponsoring a number of recreation projects for two years. There were a Little League Ball Club, hockey and baseball programs for older boys, a swimming pool; a start had been made on beautifying the park. Then, as a basis for further planning, the board, with the help of the community council, decided to make a study of the utilization of recreational facilities. A sample of citizens was asked how they spent their spare time, whether they participated in available activities, what they liked and disliked about them, and what changes and additions they would suggest.

As a result of the survey, a number of important changes were made. Special committees were set up to develop recreational opportunities for girls, young adults, and the elderly. A half-day workshop on leisure-time use in the community was to be held every other year in connection

Reproduced by permission of the publisher, Center for Community Studies, University of Saskatchewan, Saskatoon, Saskatchewan, Canada. From Darwin D. Solomon, as one in the *Key to Community Series* of pamphlets which is still being distributed, © 1963, pp. 3–22.

with the annual sports field-day, in order to enable leaders to review recreational programs and make needed adjustments. In working out these plans, the board and its committees used the resources and advice of the Fitness and Recreation Office of the Department of Education, Arts Board, Adult Education Division, and social scientists from the Center for Community Studies.

In this instance, the focus of the survey was on program improvement. Evaluation led to the realization that flexibility was required to meet the varying needs of the community. Opportunity was provided for citizen participation in future evaluation and planning. The community was learning to improve, rather than trying to prove what a good job it had done.

We Evaluate to Get Support for Programs

Citizens need to know what the effects of a program are if they are to give it their continued support.

The Loamville community council kept the public informed about its activities through news media and annual community meetings. Every year the council held an evaluation meeting to review accomplishments and weaknesses. This was followed by a session to plan the next year's program. Both events were well publicized. At the end of the second year, a public meeting had been held so as to involve a wider segment of the community in evaluation and planning and in setting priorities. By the third year, the council was well-known and widely supported. This was largely due to the following factors:

1. The council was able to prove that it had assisted in important projects and contributed to the progress of the community. Each member organiza-

tion was given credit for the part it had played.
2. A degree of objectivity was ensured by wide participation in the evaluation process. Distortions of fact, often due to a desire to prove success, cannot remain hidden for long and, if allowed to persist, are self-defeating in the long run.
3. Thanks to periodic evaluation, the council was able to work on weak points and present a stronger program every year. Thus its public image became associated with worthwhile improvements.
4. The people saw the council as *their* organization: They felt responsible for it.

We Evaluate to Determine Change in Conditions or Behaviour

Community progress is usually measured in terms of physical things produced, such as the number of street lights installed, city blocks paved, or buildings erected. Sometimes the activities resulting from programs are listed; but rarely are changes in people or the quality of the relationship among citizens seen as measures of progress.

To build its community hall, Westend had to co-ordinate the efforts of a large number of organizations and resource agencies. To maintain the hall and regulate its use by various groups, a continuation of these co-ordinative relationships was necessary. Leaders and citizens could not go back to their old ways of thinking and acting.

In another Saskatchewan community, the council's stated objectives were:

1. To co-ordinate suggestions presented by various community groups;
2. To create leadership;

3. To encourage citizens to examine their community.

But when they took stock of accomplishments, did they mention these purposes? No, they reported:

1. A recreation program and a recreation board set up;
2. Water and sewage-disposal systems installed;
3. A community hall built and operated by one organization.

They did not talk about the increased effectiveness of their leadership, better communications among groups, greater awareness of community problems and world affairs, and improvements in organizational participation by citizens.

A complete evaluation requires that:

1. Before the program is started, a decision be reached on the evidence of change to be used, and on the ways and means of obtaining it;
2. The evidence be gathered systematically and submitted to those who are to evaluate the program;
3. Sufficient time be allowed for hoped-for changes to take place before an attempt is made to evaluate them.

We Evaluate to Provide Personal Satisfaction and Security

Where the object of evaluation is personal satisfaction and assurance that one's efforts have been worthwhile, the following conditions must be met:

1. Tangible signs of progress are needed, especially in the early stages of a new program or organization. Goals should be stated and programs planned in such a way that solid ac-

complishment can be shown. Short-term goals should be seen as steps toward long-range ones.
2. Unflinching commitment and support by key persons and decision-makers is needed for effective evaluation. Uncertainty or doubt expressed by leaders may hinder community participation and prevent utilization of the findings in subsequent program planning.
3. Evaluation should be seen, and provided for, as an ongoing function of program planning. Trouble spots pointed out can lead to ultimate satisfaction only if ways are found to overcome them; otherwise, frequent evaluations may cause unhappiness and anxiety and destroy confidence.
4. If necessary, the planner must be willing to revise goals and set more realistic standards of accomplishment. The more certain citizens are of progress toward their objectives, the more satisfaction they feel and the harder they will work.

INFORMATION NEEDED FOR EVALUATION

Programs of development start with two important points of reference: (a) the present situation or condition, and (b) the situation or condition (goal) to be reached. The program or project is the means used to get from one to the other.

To find out how we are doing, either at some mid-point or at the end of a project or program, a number of key questions must be answered: How far are we from where we started? How close are we to our goal? Did anything unforeseen happen? What methods did we use, and how effective were they? What, besides the things we did, influenced the results? What difficulties did we have?—In short, we ask ourselves whether the program has helped us to reach our objectives and if so, in what way.

When the goals are physical facilities, such as new sidewalks or a community hall, the answer will be easy. But we may also want to know whether, as a result of our program, the community has become a better place to live; whether the people, and in particular, the leaders, have come to know more about themselves, their community, the world; whether they have learned to work together more effectively. Just what information is needed to answer questions like these?

What Difference Did the Program Make?

There are many aspects of a program that can be evaluated. However, the crucial question is whether it has brought about any changes. To answer this question, we must know the point from which we started and the situation that resulted. We need evidence that can be seen, understood, and accepted by all.

The Benchmark. Our starting point is indicated by a *benchmark*. This is not a complete description of the situation. For the sake of economy, only certain key aspects or *indicators* are selected. For example, if the object of a program is to combat delinquency, we may use police and court records as indicators. Similarly, numbers and values of businesses are indicators of the economic level of a community; years of schooling received indicate levels of education; member participation in programs provides a measure of the effectiveness of an organization; and so forth.

Without a careful record of such benchmarks, we would have to rely on subjective judgments and memory; evaluation would be affected by the hazards of forgetting and of changing opinions. It would, at

best, be like navigating by floating icebergs. Only if we have objective indicators can we stop and "take a fix" on the permanent landmark, i.e., our starting point.

The Changes. After the program has been in operation for some time, we take another look at the indicators. For example, if a survey was used to establish our benchmark, we return to the same kinds of persons or records with the same questions as those used in the original survey. Differences in the findings obtained by the two surveys indicate the changes brought about by the program. If the indicators have not changed, it is reasonable to assume that we are not moving towards our goals—or that we have used the wrong indicators.

In the course of its development, a community will change in the following five areas:

1. Citizens' Knowledge and Skills. What experience have citizens gained in relation to community problems? How competent are they in organizing and planning? Do they know where to look for help? What things, besides their regular occupations, are they able to do and like to do?

Economic and physical assets are important, but the most valuable resources are skills and knowledge that are shared with others and used for the benefit of the community.

2. Community Organization. What groups are there in the community? What do they do, as individual organizations and in collaboration with other groups? What informal cliques are there? What kinds of businesses and services does the community have? Who are the leaders, and how is leadership distributed or concentrated? Who is expected to do what? Where is there co-operation? conflict? compromise?

Understanding the nature of the relationships in a community—i.e., between organization leaders and members, businessmen and customers, officials and citizens—is as important as knowing that such relationships exist.

3. Community Feelings and Attitudes. How does the community feel about the sponsors of a program? About resource agencies and advisors from the outside? Has the program brought about changes in the way citizens look upon their community?

People's feelings about an activity and its sponsors will determine whether they are going to participate, how much they are likely to learn, and what resources they will use.

4. Outside Agencies. What do outside agencies and their workers know about the community? How effective are they in working with and serving the needs of the citizens? What have they learned as a result of programs in which they had a part? How influential are they?

An awareness of these aspects of the community-agency relationship is of value to both the community leader and the agency representative as they plan and work together.

5. Physical Aspects. How is the community laid out? How do its surroundings affect its shape, size, and other characteristics? How many homes and other buildings and facilities are there, and what is their condition? What physical resources does the community possess?

Physical factors may, on the one hand, aid or limit a community's development in specific ways; on the other, they are often indicators of past accomplishments.

Who Was Affected by the Change?

Community and agency leaders need to know who is being affected by a program and who is not. For instance, how many

and what types of farmers have adopted a new variety of wheat? What kinds of leaders and organizations are using planning and meeting methods that were recommended in a leadership training program? Projects benefiting businessmen may actually bring hardship to persons dependent on fixed incomes or to the unemployed. A different approach may be needed for, say, low-income groups than for skilled workers.

Why Did It Happen This Way?

In one town, the community council gave high priority to rebuilding the hospital. Some funds were made available through a government agency. Then it was discovered that the town's resources were inadequate and its population too small to maintain the projected hospital. In order to qualify for provincial assistance, the community would have to co-operate with neighbouring municipalities. At this point the project died. Full information on why this happened is not available.

Frequently, when a project is in trouble, valuable energy is spent in complaining or blaming others. Knowledge of the causes underlying the problem might guide action into more constructive effort. It may be a matter of poor timing, or miscalculation of resources needed. Often, the difficulty arises from ignorance and lack of appropriate involvement on part of the public: For example, in one town, a check on negative votes on fluoridation of water supplies revealed that the citizens did not know much about the issue. An information campaign was launched by the community council. This resulted in a positive vote by a wide margin and a better understanding by all of the purposes and problems of the whole community.

We are often members of several groups at once, each with its own standards and goals. We are influenced by these groups in different ways at different times. We may be torn by conflicting pressures. Knowledge of these ties and influences is crucial in understanding why things happen as they do.

How Consistent and Widespread Is the Change?

In order to judge the effectiveness of a program, it is not enough to ask who or what has changed. We also need to know how permanent and how widespread the change is. Some physical improvements—e.g., sewer and water installations—are once-in-a-lifetime propositions. However, others, such as a clean-up campaign, are relatively impermanent unless they are accompanied by changes in the citizens' thinking and habits.

This is a particularly important consideration in the case of leadership training projects. Questionnaires filled out at the end of a leadership institute may show that a certain number of people have "learned" (in words) what the instructors were talking about. Yet a survey made six months or a year later to find out whether, and how consistently, leaders are applying their new knowledge may reveal that the learning was merely transitory and produced no observable lasting effects.

Were There Any Unforeseen Side-Effects?

Some Community Members May Suffer. Programs often produce *side-effects* that were neither planned nor anticipated. For instance, one seldom thinks of a sewer and water system as a hardship for anyone in the community. However, the increase in property taxes may further impoverish pensioners and others on low incomes. Obviously such an effect would not have been deliberately planned.

Conflicts and Divisions May Develop. Riverton had been trying for years to get a community skating rink. A local service club had started raising funds. The club's representative welcomed help from the community council, which sponsored two community meetings. At the first meeting, a fund-raising committee was set up. At the second meeting, this committee submitted a progress report. It was decided that the funds it had collected should be turned over to the service club, and that the latter should build the rink.

One unexpected result of the community council's involvement was the withdrawal of the service club from the council. Although the club's representative had invited help, and although the club was, in the end, entrusted with the construction of the rink, some members resented the "interference" of the council and the fund-raising committee: they wanted the rink to be seen as *their* project. The fact that the leadership of the council and that of the club held opposing political views may have contributed to the split. Moreover, the club's and council's respective roles were never clarified. It is possible that the success of the fund-raising committee was seen as a threat to the club's prestige in the community.

Leadership May Shift. Effective programs are likely to bring forth new leadership, especially if they are concerned with the development of the human as well as the physical aspects of the community.

When a large industry moved to Parkville, the town's new needs and interests led to a change of mayors. The program initiated by the community council gave several hitherto inactive citizens a chance to demonstrate their leadership abilities. Thus, community progress may be expected to result in the advancement of some leaders and in the replacement of others. Such shifts can easily create conflict and friction.

Precedents Are Set. Any organization creates expectations through its programs. In one community, the council sponsored a fund-raising drive for an outside agency. Soon it began to receive requests to sponsor similar drives for other groups.

In another community, the council had no function other than channelling requests for action to its constituent organizations. Before long, the council's importance had declined to a point where it no longer rated the support of the citizens.

The expectations and precedents an organization sets early in its life can be decisive in determining its influence and effectiveness in the community.

New Obstacles May Defeat Long-Range Goals. The leaders of one community wanted to join a larger school unit. However, they were fearful that the high school might be located in another town. To improve their bargaining position, they decided to develop their school and expand the attendance area as much as possible. They increased taxes, issued bonds, constructed new buildings. These moves produced some unforeseen and unwanted results: (a) Local ratepayers in effect were subsidizing students from surrounding low-tax areas who had moved to the town for the duration of their high school attendance. (b) It became difficult to negotiate consolidation with surrounding low-tax areas unwilling to raise their taxes to assist with the retirement of the school bond debt. (c) Any increase in tuition rates for those commuting or residing in town only during the winter would have resulted in a loss of students and support to neighbouring units. The town kept its school, but at the cost of high rates and new obstacles to consolidation.

In evaluating programs, we should be alert to side-effects which might jeopardize our ultimate objectives.

WHO SHOULD EVALUATE?

Facts do not speak for themselves. Someone has to interpret them, to decide what they mean. Who, then, should help the facts to speak?

The town of Lost Lake, concerned about juvenile delinquency, had for a number of years employed a recreation specialist to keep young people occupied during the summer months. Although most citizens agreed that the program had produced some benefit, many were questioning the continued value of the expenditure involved. The recreation board therefore decided to have the program assessed. They asked the community consultants at a nearby university for help. A staff member was assigned to the task.

A brief survey of existing recreation facilities and needs had been made at the beginning of the program. This, together with police, welfare, and school records, provided the benchmark—i.e., a measure of where the community had stood before the program started.

At a community-wide meeting called by the recreation board, the consultant proposed the appointment of a steering committee, representing interested agencies, to direct the evaluation study. This suggestion was readily accepted. The committee's job, as defined at the meeting, was to determine *(a)* what the original objectives of the program had been; *(b)* to what an extent the program had succeeded in meeting these objectives; and *(c)* whether the public considered such objectives adequate for a community recreation program.

Through informal talks with the recreation board and other community leaders, the steering committee established that the program's major purpose had been to keep young people out of trouble by providing constructive leisure-time activities for them. To assess its effectiveness in accomplishing this purpose, a sub-committee was set up to check agency and community records for any changes that might be due to the program. Another sub-committee was to plan and conduct an opinion poll to find out *(a)* what citizens had originally expected of the program, and what they thought of it now; *(b)* how they were using their leisure time; *(c)* what new or expanded facilities and opportunities they would like to have; and *(d)* whether they would be willing to pay for such facilities and opportunities.

In planning and carrying out its assignment, the poll sub-committee secured the help and advice of both the provincial recreation specialist and the community consultant. Volunteers, recruited through personal contacts and appeals to community organizations, conducted the interviews, tabulated the results, and, with the help of the two specialists, interpreted the responses. The steering committee and recreation board, meeting in small groups for several evenings, prepared a report on the findings of the study and made recommendations for further programming. An editing committee was put in charge of the final drafting and reproduction of the report which was issued jointly by the steering committee and the recreation board. Every household in the community received a copy.

A week later, a second public meeting was called to discuss the report, question the findings, revise recommendations, and approve proposals for continuing and new programs.

To sum up: The recreation program was evaluated by the *whole community*. Citizens not only had a chance to express and compare opinions; they also took responsibility for collecting and interpreting new facts and for deciding on future action. They used *specialists'* broader experience to (a) help check the accuracy and completeness of their information, (b) locate resources they might not have thought of themselves, (c) select suitable yardsticks for evaluation, and (d) provide guidance for effective procedure.

Frequently specialists are hired, not as consultants (as in the Lost Lake case), but to assume responsibility for the entire evaluation process and its product. However, unless such assessments are fully understood and accepted by the community as their own, the motivation to further action may be lacking. The subjective judgments of citizens, in the final analysis, provide the motive power for community action. More objective viewpoints, introduced from outside, may be more accurate but cannot replace citizen evaluations in the planning of community-based programs.[1]

STEPS IN EVALUATION

We can look at evaluation as a series of steps whereby groups reach some common judgment of what they have accomplished. Whatever the procedure, certain principles should be observed. The case of one community may serve to illustrate those principles.

Arden Evaluates Its Recreation Project

In Arden (pop. 3000), the building of a community recreation center had been proposed. The town was located about sixty miles from the nearest city. The arguments for and

---

[1] This does not deny the value of more systematic program evaluation by outside experts in determining government policies. It is especially important when deciding whether to continue or discontinue a policy or a program.

against the center were many and varied.

Some were concerned over an increase in juvenile delinquency. Others thought that a home-grown program and good facilities would slow down the trend for youth and whole families to seek recreation in, and hence take business to, the city. Better recreational opportunities for all age groups might increase loyalty to and pride in the community and strengthen family life.

On the other hand, many felt that too much emphasis on recreation might lead to distraction from school and home life. Then there was the question of costs. Was there a real need for a new building? Taxes were already high: Who would pay for the proposed structure? If outdoor sports facilities were to be added, the cost would be even higher. Moreover, a number of other community projects were competing for funds and leadership.

The citizens finally agreed to set up a two-year experimental recreation project making use of existing facilities. At the end of this period, the question of new buildings would again be approached.

A temporary recreation board was set up to co-ordinate the various parts of the project and the survey that was to accompany it. Areas that might be affected by a recreation program included school, home life, business, attitudes toward the community, and trends in responsibility and delinquency among youth and adults. The indicators that were to measure changes in these areas were decided upon. The Home and School Association, in co-operation with the school administration, agreed to sponsor a study of student grades, study habits, and classroom problems. The Board of Trade was to collect facts about business volume and trading patterns during the same one-month period in two consecutive years. A survey of a 50 percent sample of all local households was made to determine how family members spent their free time, what shopping and service centers they used, what their recreational preferences were, and how they felt about the community.

Facts were to be collected before the program started and again two years later. The results of the study would determine whether the proposed recreation center should be built. Thus from the beginning evaluation was seen as one of the objectives of the program.

What were the most important steps in evaluation in this case?

Build Evaluation into Planning

Program evaluation cannot be considered apart from program planning.[2] In Arden, arrangements had been made for the gathering of information before, during, and after the project; results would be weighed in relation to the community's goals and expectations. In Lost Lake, evaluation was related to past objectives so as to provide a basis for future plans. In both cases, it became a part of programming and action. Both communities utilized an assessment of the success of one phase in their planning for the next phase.

Set Clear Program Objectives

General purposes of agency programs are often statements of lofty social values, irreproachable, all-inclusive umbrellas like the following: "To create a healthy society"; "to meet people's needs"; or "to provide a medium through which desirable ... environments are brought into existence whereby rural people may help themselves or obtain help in meeting their needs ... solving problems, and accomplishing their desires and goals."[3] Similarly, the purposes of community programs are often stated in very general terms. Where objectives are as vague as these, it becomes impossible to measure progress.

In Arden, one early short-term objective was to get complete and reliable information on the effects of a recreation program on various areas of community life. In

---

[2] For further discussion of this point, see also Key to Community No. 2, "Community Program Planning," by H. R. Baker.

[3] Quoted from objectives of field service divisions of departments of the Saskatchewan Provincial Government as reported in *A Self-Survey of Agency Resources,* coordinated by the Center for Community Studies, 1961.

their long-term goals, the townspeople went beyond the mere provision of facilities in seeking to improve their community generally by stimulating local business, reducing delinquency, encouraging positive attitudes and community responsibility among citizens, etc. Their procedure allowed them to become increasingly specific in their objectives as their planning progressed.

Decide on Indicators of Progress

Indicators are the means by which we gauge, estimate, or measure progress toward goals. For example, if we are building a recreation center, evidence of completed or partially completed facilities will be an important indicator of progress. If, however, the goal is to strengthen community and family life or to reduce delinquency, recreation being seen merely as a means to that end, then the choice of indicators becomes more difficult.

The following indicators were used in the Arden study: *(a)* The Board of Trade's figures on *volume of trade* during the same month in two consecutive years were compared to assess the effect of the program on business activity. *(b)* A comparison of *students' scholastic records* for the year immediately preceding the experiment and the first year of the study showed whether the program had affected scholarship. *(c)* Each year, students in the junior class were asked to keep a record of their *leisure-time activities* during three designated one-week periods. *(d)* To measure the effect of the program on home life, *records of activities of the members of a sample of households* for the same ten-day period in each of the two years were compared. *(e)* *Opinions* of heads of families about the program were obtained through interviews.

Select, and Plan for Appropriate Use of, Procedures and Tools

To ensure valid evaluations, we need a reasonably complete and accurate picture of how things have gone.

Two types of information may be sought: One reflects people's feelings about the program—whether they think it was good, useful, effective, etc. The other deals with the specific ways in which the program has been good, useful, effective; whether, for example, it has increased business activity, reduced delinquency, strengthened family or community ties, and so forth. Arden tried systematically to obtain both kinds of information.

Facts can be secured in several ways: *(a)* by asking others; *(b)* by observing for ourselves; and *(c)* by studying records and documents. Procedures range from informal talks with neighbours to surveys conducted by means of questionnaires; from simple interviews to formal tests and scales; from consultations with groups of officers and leaders of organizations to the study of agency records or newspaper files; from the efforts of community volunteers to the employment of specially trained observers. Different methods usually produce different kinds of information.[4]

In selecting procedures and tools for assessing the effects of a program, the following pointers may be helpful:

1. If possible, get some experienced help and advice. Such advice might come from social science departments of universities, social science research workers in government departments, commercial polling agencies, organizations like the Center for Commu-

---

[4]For further discussion of community fact-finding procedures see Key to Community No. 3, "The Self-Survey in Saskatchewan Communities," by V. W. Larson.

nity Studies, and extension and social agency field workers with some previous experience.

2. Plan for collection of the information needed for evaluation during every phase of the program.
3. Keep records of important aspects of the program as it develops.
4. Use procedures that are "reliable", i.e., that produce the same results regardless of who uses them (provided the information-gatherer has received a minimum of instruction).
5. Procedures should fit the type of information sought as well as the conditions under which the facts will have to be collected.
6. Procedures should come within the limits of available resources. Thus it is important to know what a given procedure requires in terms of skills, money, equipment, and time.

Decide What It All Means

Findings need interpretation. This should be done by those most directly concerned, i.e., the leaders of groups affected by the program. Too frequently, citizens are unwilling to spend the time necessary to discover the meaning of the information they have gathered. Or, they may feel that the expert should do this for them.

Expert opinions are most useful for *added* insights and more general testing of local judgments. When the findings of the Lost Lake survey had been summarized, the consultant was asked to explain their meaning. He, however, insisted that the citizens put forward their own interpretations; he challenged their thinking by raising more questions than he answered in the discussions that followed. The resulting conclusions and recommendations were validated by the whole community at a public meeting.

The following guides will help groups to make the most of their data:

1. Add up all the facts and arrange them in logical order. It is easy to jump to unwarranted conclusions on the basis of incomplete information.
2. Raise as many questions as possible about relationships among the various findings and between these findings and other known facts. For example, let us suppose that in community X, (i) many of the elderly say they are lonely or do not know what to do with themselves; (ii) little organized activity exists for such persons. We might then ask ourselves whether it is hobbies they want, or opportunities to get together and talk, or a chance to do something useful for others, etc.
3. List interpretations and try to reach agreement on them. Test them against known facts and past experience.
4. In attempting to make recommendations, list as many courses of action as possible. Examine each for strengths and weaknesses. Let each member of the group have his say. Probe for the causes underlying disagreements.
5. Involve those responsible for action in the drawing up of recommendations. As suggested earlier, the facts have meaning not only for what has already happened but, more significantly, for what is to be done in the future. If groups and individuals responsible for next steps are a party to the recommendations, the likelihood of action is greater.

PRACTICAL PROBLEMS

For most of us, evaluation is an automatic part of our thinking. To improve it, we must become aware of the blocks that often hinder effective evaluation.

Failure to Build Evaluation into Program Planning

As indicated above, it is difficult to do a good job of evaluation if it is not built into the original program plan. Evaluation takes the fuzziness out of planning; good plans take the fuzziness out of evaluation.

Adequate Procedures Cost Time and Resources

Most people are far more interested in getting things done than in *post-mortems*. If each project is seen as an end in itself, unrelated to the next step, there seems to be no point in reviewing methods and results: Once the job is finished, we lose interest.

However, where, as in the case of Arden, a project is perceived as merely one phase in a program leading to increasingly effective leadership and action in succeeding stages, citizens are willing to invest time and resources in evaluating their efforts.

Changes in Adults Come Slowly

It may take years before changes become measurable. Persons who change quickly are usually not highly regarded by their fellows: they are considered "undependable". Studies show that ten or more years are required before a majority of farmers will adopt even simple new farm practices.

The individual who has learned how to do things better may have to wait for the group to catch up. Nowhere is this more evident than in leadership methods. Organizations and communities, accustomed to operating in a particular manner, cling to the ways that are familiar to them. They will not accept and effectively use a new method, no matter how good, until they have practised it for some time and become comfortable with it. The group puts pressure on its leaders not to change too rapidly if they value their position.

Some Changes Do Not Last

In the leadership clinics held in several communities, participants' knowledge and attitudes toward leadership and methods of problem-solving had changed measurably. However, a subsequent survey showed that, a year later, these leaders had reverted to the attitudes and views held before the clinics. Perhaps they had been retaught by their communities; or they may not have been confident enough in their new learning to apply it, so that they lost it through disuse.

It Is Often Difficult to Distinguish Between Cause and Effect

Even if we can show that changes have occurred, it is not always easy to prove that they were the result of our program. They might have happened anyway. Simple cause-and-effect relationships are rare; and there are always unexpected side-effects. In evaluating programs, it is useful to look for explanations of change other than the apparent ones.

Conflict Between Professional Standards and "Do-It-Yourself" Attitudes

There is a tendency to separate the things people can do for themselves from those that should be done by experts. Anything requiring special skill or knowledge usually is in the latter category.

The professional working with a community should learn to bridge this gap; he should meet leaders where they are and offer them his help. One agency representative failed to do this. He spent an evening telling local leaders what he thought they ought to do. As a result, they became angry and did nothing. Similarly, a research technician may be too much of a perfectionist to help a community improve its fact-finding procedures. On the other hand, citizens often do not know how to use the expert. They seldom ask for assistance in improving on the methods they have been using. Rather than seeing him as a resource, they ask for a judgment which they can either wholly accept or reject.

Some of Our Motives Get in the Way

Often unconscious wishes and attitudes distort our perception. Wishful thinking may get in the way of objective evaluation. An awareness of motives such as the following can help us to deal with them:

1. Fear of evaluation may be due to uncertainty about our objectives.
2. Positions of leadership are sometimes used for personal ends rather than for the benefit of the group or community being served. Although this is always the case to some extent, we find it difficult to admit publicly.
3. We tend to place all responsibility for the actions of our organizations on the elected officers, and to criticize or desert them if they have failed. A more democratic philosophy, and one leading to stronger organizations in the long run, sees two centers of authority—namely, the membership *and* the officers. The latter are elected for specific functions, but not for *all* functions. Final responsibility should rest with the membership.
4. Where evaluation is seen as personal criticism, it is often considered a sign of distrust of leaders and hence, reprehensible. If programs are a group re-

sponsibility, evaluation is less likely to carry such implications.

5. Judgments of goodness, rightness, and even effectiveness are often based on feelings or habit; we may resist having such judgments challenged by provable and demonstrable facts. The opposition to water fluoridation is a case in point.
6. Some things are honoured by tradition and custom. They were, it seems, evaluated long ago and once and for all; they are above questioning. This is true of many religious and patriotic matters, education and school routines, and, to some extent, of the recognized rights and privileges of various groups.
7. An all-or-none attitude sometimes prevents us from taking small steps to refine our present procedures and habits. If we cannot run, we are not going to walk. Because our present approaches to evaluation are so far from the ideal, we may hesitate to attempt improvements of the planning procedures and the collection and use of information that make measurement of progress easier.

SUMMARY OF PRINCIPLES OF PROGRAM EVALUATION

From the foregoing discussion, some general principles can be drawn which may be helpful in other community situations.

1. All program planning and action should include some systematic evaluation. This will enable us to understand why we have reached, or failed to reach, our objectives. In community programs, we want to know whether, and in what ways, the

community has changed, and what procedures were most effective.

2. Start in simple ways, by using easily available and observable indicators at first, but seek increasingly accurate and dependable means of measuring progress toward planned changes.

3. Plan to evaluate the effectiveness of your program in relation to short-term, tangible goals as well as to learning and human-relations objectives. The former include such things as physical facilities, community calendars, or numbers of meetings held. The latter have to do with ways of working together, with relationships among organizations, with techniques and procedures. Both kinds of objectives are essential to community change: While one gives citizens a feeling of accomplishment, the other is important to human development.

4. Provide enough resources to carry out the evaluation you have planned. The minimum required is the time of volunteer workers and some knowledge of procedures. As more accurate data are desired, specialists, trained interviewers, and facilities for tabulating and analyzing findings will be needed.

5. Involve as many people as possible and appropriate—resource persons, officials, leaders, and all those who play a part in the program. When analyzing information about planned changes and unplanned side-effects it is particularly helpful to have a wide variety of views; this will ensure interest in and support for the next steps.

6. Do not attempt an evaluation unless you are prepared to face some hard facts. The sweepings under the rug

may be found. New and unexpected problems may appear.

7. Divide the program into manageable units for evaluation. Rather than attempting to assess the whole program at once, select one project at a time, or focus on changes in key aspects of the community, such as organization, distribution of leadership, levels of income and standards of living, or morale. Then study the relationship of these changes to the various parts of the program. By adding up such partial assessments you will obtain your total evaluation.

By making it possible to analyze the weak points of a generally successful program, or the bright spots in an unsuccessful one, this bit-by-bit approach will yield information more useful for further planning than overall judgments of accomplishment.

8. Evaluate the psychological conditions, or climate, of change. Citizens' attitudes towards leaders, resources, or agencies are important in determining the success or failure of a program. In a favourable climate of feeling, a relatively ineffective program, especially if traditional in character, may continue almost indefinitely. On the other hand, little will be accomplished if attitudes toward a program or its sponsors are negative. Without participation and support, the best-laid plans will lack the motive power necessary to translate them into action.

9. Do not be afraid to try different procedures for gathering or evaluating information. This will encourage an experimental and enterprising attitude among leaders and members of a community.

10. Before launching a program, consult

social scientists and others experienced in planning and collecting social information. Consultation does not commit you to any particular line of action, but it may provide valuable ideas and help to prevent unnecessary mistakes.

11. Begin where people are, and do not expect too much too soon. We are all in the habit of judging actions, people, and things—usually on the basis of very limited impressions or chance observations. Similarly, communities have their own built-in evaluate processes: Some rely heavily on the judgment of one or two persons; others depend on informal exchange of opinions, on the chance encounter, back-fence conferences, barbershop discussions, or after-church comments. Most communities use methods developed in an age of simple face-to-face interaction. We now need more reliable procedures for gathering information from and about events and persons we seldom see. As changes in individuals and groups take time, patience, and planning, so does the development of effective evaluation skills and habits and, above all, of the ability to suspend judgment until all relevant facts have been collected and analyzed.

Community programs are becoming big business; mistakes and poorly laid plans may be costly in terms of money, effort, and time. To an increasing degree, community decision-making must be based on facts evaluated in an objective and reliable fashion.

28. Choosing an Evaluation Method

Robert Washington

ALTERNATIVE FRAMEWORKS FOR PROGRAM EVALUATION

There are at least four conceptual models which are generally accepted as analytical frameworks within which to conduct evaluative research.

The term, "conceptual model" is used here to refer to an explanatory frame of reference within which certain social and behavioral science concepts are used as tools for circumscribing evaluative behavior. This explanatory system offers the evaluator a way of thinking which defines the means to be employed as well as the ends to be served in evaluative research. The term also suggests that there are precisely formulated concepts drawn from business and public administration which provide us with clues as to what it is about human service delivery systems that should be studied and evaluated. In other words, a conceptual model provides us with a "change" or "intervention" theory

---

[1]Source: Unpublished, Bob Washington, "Alternative Frameworks for Program Evaluation," 1975.

which forms the analytical framework within which the evaluation will be conducted.

Since outcomes from most services imply directed social change, it is useful to have a "change" or "intervention" theory. Such a theory tends to identify what constitutes the desired change to be measured as well as to provide clues as to how the change should be measured. Usually, the change or intervention theory developed by the evaluator will be couched in a particular discipline. For example, some evaluators use organizational theory as their analytical framework. Organizational theory uses the rigorous methods of economic analysis, but also incorporates findings of behavioral science research. Using organizational theory then, the evaluator is likely to conceive of a human services program as a complex social system. This framework, for example, provides the foundation for the *systems* model of evaluation.

THE SYSTEMS MODEL

The systems model of evaluation is based upon efficiency and relates to questions of resource-allocations to produce certain outputs.

The systems model assumes that certain resources must be devoted to essential non-goal activities such as maintenance and preservation of the system. From this viewpoint, the central question in an evaluation of the effectiveness of an intervention should be: How close does the organization's allocation of resources approach an optimum distribution? Etzioni (1969), a central proponent of this model, suggests that what really is important is whether there exists a balanced distribution of resources among all organizational needs rather than the maximal satisfaction of any single organizational requirement.

The systems model of evaluation assumes that the evaluator must answer at least four questions: (1) how effective is the coordination of organizational subunits? (2) how adequate are the resources? (3) how adaptive is the organization to environmental and internal demands? and (4) were the goals and subgoals met?

While the measurement of general organizational goals is central to the systems model, proponents of the systems model tend to minimize the need to measure how well a *specific* organizational goal is achieved. They contend that such a strategy is unproductive and often misleading since an organization constantly functions at a variety of levels with a variety of goals which are sometimes conflicting. Moreover, they contend, over-attention to a specific goal will lead to under-concern for other programmatic functions. The fact that an organization can become less effective by allocating excessive means to achieve a particular goal is viewed by systems protagonists as just as detrimental as withholding such resources.

The systems model of evaluation tends to be more productive in decision-making among organizations which employ program budgeting. The general idea of program budgeting is that budgetary decisions should be made by focusing upon overall goals. In other words, program budgeting is a goal-oriented program structure which presents data on all of the operations and activities of the program in categories which reflect the program's goals. Inputs, such as personnel, equipment, and maintenance are considered only in relationship to program outcomes. Program budgeting then, lays heavy emphasis upon relating costs to accomplishing the overall goal.

Program budgeting has two essential characteristics: (1) the budget is organized by programs rather than by objects-of expenditures and (2) the program shows not only current needs but also future needs for resources, as well as the financial implications of the programmed outputs.

From the perspective of the evaluator, program budgeting contains two important pieces of information. First is the organizational goals and objectives. The second piece of information needed is a statement of the financial resources required to achieve the goals and objectives.

Drawing from program budgeting procedures, the two most frequently used evaluation strategies employed in the systems model are cost-effectiveness and cost-benefit analysis.

Cost-Effectiveness Analysis

There are many and varied reasons why it may be of limited value to apply cost-benefit techniques to a particular human services program. However, such a program may be effectively evaluated with a slightly modified version of cost-benefit analysis known as cost-effectiveness analysis. Unlike cost-benefit analysis, which attempts to quantify benefits of a program in money terms, cost-effectiveness analysis utilizes output variables in non-monetary forms to serve as indices for benefits of specific programs. The output variables are specified by various goals of a specific program, such as number of persons trained in a given skill, employment, or level of proficiency on a standardized test.

Cost-Benefit Analysis

Cost-benefit analysis involves the use of economic theories and concepts. It is designed to tell us why a program or one of its components works in addition to how well it works. The concept of "cost-benefit" defines the relationship between the resources required (the cost) to attain certain goals and the benefits derived. One of its basic premises is that many decisions involving the allocation of limited resources are often made on the basis of how those resources can be most optimally used, avoiding waste, duplication and inefficiency. Cost-benefit analysis is a tool for decision-makers who need to make choices among viable competing programs designed to achieve certain goals. It is not designed to favor the "cheapest" nor the "costliest" program, but rather the optimal program in terms of the available resources and the explicit goals.

Usually cost as well as benefits are given a dollar value over time, and benefit over cost ratios are computed. A ratio in excess of one indicates worthwhileness from an investment point of view. The higher the ratio, the greater the value and worth.

The cost-benefit calculus is not a wholly satisfactory tool for evaluating human services programs, because of its incapability to measure "psychic" or "social" benefits. Psychic and social benefits are defined here to refer to the state, or well-being of the recipient or the changes that take place in attitude and behavior as outcomes. Weisbrod (1969) argues that an evaluation design built around cost-benefit analysis is likely to reach negative conclusions about the effectiveness of any human services program since only "economic" benefits and costs are taken into account. (Remember, an evaluation design built upon the systems model is concerned primarily with "allocative efficiency.")

One of the precautions in interpreting cost-benefit data relates to the fact that, while a particular human services program may be judged inefficient, it may not necessarily be considered undesirable. It may, for example, have certain favorable income redistributional consequences that are socially preferable to other benefits.

In applying cost-benefit analysis to evaluation of compensatory educational programs, Thomas Riblich (1968) in his study argued that the kinds of educational changes put into effect through the use of Title 1 ESEA funds, is not the kind of impact or change measured by the "payoff-rate" concept. He concluded: "New measurements are needed that have a more direct bearing upon current policy." Thomas (1967) supporting this point of view noted:

. . . the social benefits of education, whose value is almost impossible to express in quantitative terms, are a major portion of education's output. Examples of these nonquantifiable benefits are reduction of civil strife, greater social harmony between persons of diverse ethnic and social backgrounds, less capacity for the political process to be seriously influenced by extremist groups, etc. The problem for the evaluator is that such benefits, while impossible to quantify, are nonetheless of crucial importance relative to the basic justification of a particular program.

There is general agreement that the utility of a cost-benefit model as an evaluative tool lies in its emphasis on a systematic examination of alternative courses of action and their implications. But it is important to note that data from such a model should be only one piece of evidence in the appraisal process; and, from the vantage point of the evaluator who is concerned more with "social" than economic benefits, such data may not be the most significant piece of evidence. When programs have goals that go beyond simply maximizing the return on public investments irrespective of who receives the benefits, a simple cost-benefit ratio is an insufficient indicator of program effectiveness.

THE GOAL-ATTAINMENT MODEL

Of the models to be presented, the goal-attainment model of evaluation is the most commonly used. This model, given prominence by Sherwood (1964) and expanded upon by Levinson (1966) stems from a conception of evaluation as the measurement of the degree of success or failure encountered by a program in reaching predetermined goals.

The goal-attainment model of evaluation relies heavily upon strategies which measure the degree of success in achieving specified goals. It assumes that specific goals can be assessed in isolation from other goals being sought by the program. The goal-attainment model is derived from theories of motivation (forces which energize and direct behavior) and Lewinian field theory. This model is very useful in measuring abstract goals and functions "to define the indefinable and to tangibilitate the intangible" (Mager, 1972). A basic premise of the goal-attainment model of evaluation is that if the ultimate goal is met, then a series of prior accomplishments were fulfilled. This model emphasizes the measurement of outcomes rather than inputs, assuming that if the goal is met, then the appropriate combination of inputs was made.

The evaluator does not measure the phenomena he is studying directly. Rather, he observes and measures empirical manifestations or indices of these phenomena. It is not criteria themselves which are measured, but their equivalents—indicators. For all practical purposes, the goal-attainment model employs the ex-post facto research design. Since the fundamental question asked by the model is: *was the goal met?*, empirical inquiry can take place only after manifestations of the independent variables have already occurred. Therefore, the focus of the model is upon the clarification of goals and program objectives, and the evaluation of their accomplishment. The evaluation of accomplishment is intended to test the hypothesis that a certain form of intervention has a beneficial outcome.

Goal-Attainment Analysis

Analytically, measuring goal-attainment involves five steps. They are as follows:

1. *Specification of the goal to be measured.*

In using the goal-attainment model, the evaluator must make clear distinctions between goals and objectives. A goal for our purpose is a statement which represents in general terms an end to which a planned course of action is directed. A goal statement should also state, explicitly or otherwise, the outcome behavior of the consumer and/or a desired state or condition once the planned course of action is completed.

2. *Specification of the sequential set of performances that, if observed, would indicate that the goal has been achieved.*

A level of performance achieved within some temporal context which represents an approximation toward the goal is defined as an objective. An objective is operationally defined in terms of a beginning and an end point, so that either the existence or nonexistence of a desired state or the degree of achievement of that state can be established. It may be *qualitatively* or *quantitatively* defined. A qualitatively-defined objective is one that is either obtained or not in terms of empirical observation. A quantitatively-defined objective is one that is obtained and can be measured in terms of degrees.

For purposes of evaluation, then, goals should as far as possible be defined operationally. That is, they should be expressed as discrete objectives. In this way, the degree of achievement of the various objec-

tives or level of performance of the target for change can be a direct measure of goal-attainment. Conceived in this way, goal-attainment can be measured in terms of achieving certain objectives. Therefore, the achievement of all of the objectives should represent 100% goal-attainment.

3. *Identify which performances are critical to the achievement of the goal.*

An evaluation process must identify proper criteria to be used in measuring program success. In the goal-attainment model, success criteria are stated in terms of benchmarks. The use of benchmarks presumes that certain levels of performances are more critical to goal-attainment than others. These are treated as criterion tasks in that they constitute specific necessary conditions of goal-attainment. Precise measures of achievement are set up, and data on them are collected systematically. Since achievement of performance is expected to occur in a time sequence, achievement of data should be expressed in terms of changes.

One of the major characteristics of the goal-attainment model of evaluation is that it does not require that input factors be individually defined. For example, if one were evaluating a counseling program, one need not be concerned about the number of counseling sessions; the amount of money spent for counseling; the amount of effort the counseling staff exerts toward the achievement of counseling goals; the nature and demands of the counseling component in relationship to other program components; the characteristics inherent in staff members which affect their ability to carry out the goals or the debilitating and facilitating features of the counseling environment. As already pointed out, the basic question is: was the goal met? Consequently, the evaluator can identify what goals were achieved, but he may or may not be able to explain why they were achieved or why others were not.

4. *Describe what is the "indicator behavior" of each performance episode.*

For the most part, indications of goal-attainment will be observed as measures of changes in performance, using some normative criteria. Moreover, since achievement of objectives is defined in terms of beginning and end points, the achievement of an objective may represent the conclusion of a "performance episode." Therefore, the "indicator behavior" of a performance episode is some measurable behavior which can be observed in kind or amount within some time frame. For example, let's say that the goal is to improve morale among workers. The "indicator behavior" may be characterized as absenteeism. Measures of absenteeism are selected as *frequency* and *length*. In this case, the objective may be to reduce absenteeism each month more than it was the previous month over a six month period. Benchmarks for measurement may be established as a reduction of at least one absence per month over the previous one.

5. *Test collectively whether each "indicator behavior" is associated with each other.*

In most cases, the indicator behavior should be the same for each performance episode. This facilitates standardization of measurement and makes it easier for outcomes to be compared from one episode to the other. Different evaluators studying the same phenomena may report different outcomes. Without standardization, there is a problem of determining whether the differences are in fact actual differences or differences in measures. When measures are standardized, one source of the differences—the measures used—is controlled and the likelihood is then increased that the differences observed reflect differences in the phenomena.

In some situations, the nature of the change being measured will dictate different indicator behaviors from one performance episode to the other. The evaluator, therefore, must be sure that he adheres to proper research methodology to ensure this; multiple measures are preferred because they yield higher validity than single measures.

Measurements of goal-attainment yield, principally, information about outcomes. For program planning, the human services worker may also need a more detailed description of the social environment that produced outcomes. More often than not, program administrators need information on what were the specific levels of input, what resources they require and how these levels of input relate to outcomes. In other words, did a particular level of input make a difference?

Strengths and Limitations of the Goal-Attainment Model

One of the major limitations of the goal-attainment model is that as an ex-post facto study, the evaluator cannot always attribute goal-attainment to a specific set of input variables. Also, goal-attainment may be the result of environment factors over which the human services worker has no control; or there may be factors which the worker nor the evaluator can account for.

A third limitation of the goal-attainment model centers around the fact that evaluators often ignore the distinction between ends and means, or output and input. As Terleckyj (1970) suggests, the mere expenditure of funds for a certain goal is often equated with the intended achievement.

A fourth limitation of this model is that it may be too narrow in its evaluation methodology and too formal in its consideration of goals. Also, it may not take into account sufficiently the informal goals that emerge or the unanticipated events that produce new goals and activity.

A strength of the model is that it assumes that individual goals in a program can be evaluated in isolation from other program goals. Another strength is that the model is considered an objective and reliable analytical tool because it omits the values of the evaluator in that he is not required to make any judgments about the appropriateness of the program goals.

A third and important use of the model is its capacity to measure abstract goals by operationalizing the goal into discrete measurable objectives. Finally, perhaps, one of the major strengths of the model is that the measurement of goal-attainment need not be rigidly quantitative. For example, the achievement of an objective signifies that the goal has been met to some degree in terms of some defined event. When all the objectives have been achieved, the goal is said to have been met. This argument is based upon the assumption that the goal is met if a series of prior accomplishments are fulfilled.

When to Use Goal-Attainment Model

Evaluations may be classified in a number of ways. They may be classified by *what* is being evaluated, by *who* conducts the evaluation, by the *decision* that is to be affected by the evaluation, and by the *method* used. The appropriate classification used depends upon the purpose of the evaluation.

Evaluations may also be classified in terms of their purpose. They may be conducted in order to make decisions about resources allocation, program changes, capacity building and for measuring accountability.

The goal-attainment model of evaluation seems to be best suited for capacity building. In other words, it serves the purpose of developing a data base, improving in-house capacity to collect and assemble relevant outcome data and measures, and provides rapid feedback on problems requiring technical assistance.

The goal-attainment model of evaluation is relatively easy to carry out but the conclusions that may be drawn are necessarily limited. Therefore, this evaluation strategy can be justified only when the relationship between inputs (as independent variables) and goals (as dependent variables) has already been demonstrated or will be tested in subsequent studies.

THE IMPACT MODEL

The next model of evaluation to be discussed is the *Impact* model which involves the formulation of hypotheses that are to be tested. It employs experimental designs in which hypotheses are stated in terms of the comparative effectiveness of certain program inputs. It begins with the premise that since human services programs are designed to improve the social position of recipients, the experimental hypotheses should be stated in a manner which predicts that the intervention will be more beneficial to the recipient than the usual social practice (control condition). As implied from the foregoing, an essential difference in the application of the impact model and the goal-attainment model is in the assumptions made in the use of the impact model. One assumption is that in order for the evaluator to estimate the effects of a particular human services program, it is necessary to compare the experiences of the recipients of services with those of some reference group. Comparisons of the outcomes of the reference group represent what would have happened to the consumers in the absence of the program or intervention.

A second assumption is that the impact model is predicted upon the notion of cause and effect. It consists of (1) a set of theoretical concepts or ideas which trace the dynamics of how it is expected that the program will have the desired effects, and, (2) a theory which logically interrelates a set of principles and procedures, which imply that certain decisions rather than others be made with respect to day-to-day program situations.

Since most program outcomes are influenced by multiple causal factors, a search for cause-effect relationships becomes largely one of testing for associations between some arbitrarily selected causes and the hypothesized effect. The question raised by the impact model is: *"What difference does the intervention make?"* In this sense, the impact model is more rigorous than the goal-attainment model. It assumes that in order to determine what differences the intervention makes, it is necessary to measure the relationships between the program goals (the dependent variables) and a variety of independent variables, including the personal characteristics of participants, the program components, and the conditions under which the program operates. The notion that most of the dependent variables with which the evaluator deals are functions of more than one independent variable is essential to the model. Therefore, the analysis should treat simultaneously all of the independent variables which are believed to be relevant. To omit some variables in the analysis may lead to distorted conclusions due to correlation or interaction among these variables and those independent variables which are included in the analysis.

This line of reasoning calls for the use of multivariate techniques. Proponents of the impact model often complain that the weakness in the goal-attainment model is that few investigators use regression analysis, for example, as a means of controlling for the effects of population in determining differences between programs.

To maximize the use of experimental techniques, Freeman and Sherwood (1970) suggest that the impact model should incorporate three kinds of hypotheses: (1) *Causal Hypothesis*—A statement concerning relationship between the input and the outcome. "A statement about the influence of one or more characteristics or processes on the condition which is the object of the program. The hypothesis assumes a causal relationship between a phenomenon and the condition or behavior in which change is sought." (2) *Intervention Hypothesis*—A statement about what changes the input will produce. "A statement which specifies the relationship between the program (what is going to be done) and the phenomenon regarded, in the causal hypothesis, as associated with the behavior or condition to be ameliorated or changed." (3) *Action Hypothesis* —A statement about how that change will affect the behavior or condition the worker is seeking to modify. The action hypothesis is necessary in order to assess whether the intervention, even if it results in a desired change in the causal variable, is necessarily linked to the outcome variable, that is the behavioral condition that one is actually seeking to modify. This hypothesis is also necessary because although the chain of events may be true in a real life situation, it may not necessarily hold true when it is brought about by intervention.

Impact evaluations should provide five essential sets of information. They should provide all of the data necessary: (1) to determine if a particular program should be continued; (2) to determine which of alternative programs achieve the greatest gains for a given cost; (3) to present information on the components of each program and the mixes of components which are most effective for a given expenditure so that maximum operating efficiency can be achieved; (4) to provide relevant information for determining which programs best serve individuals with particular demographic characteristics; and (5) to suggest new program thrusts.

The impact model is essentially an experimental design. Therefore, it insists upon random assignment of subjects to the experimental and comparison groups. Herein lies the limitation of the model. Developing designs based upon controlled experimentation in evaluative research has always been troublesome. While it is always desirable, it is not always essential nor possible.

One of the basic principles of controlled experimentation in evaluating human services programs is that treatment and control conditions must be held constant throughout the period of intervention. Under these circumstances, experimental designs prevent rather than promote changes in the intervention, because interventions cannot be altered once the program is in process if the data about differences engendered by intervention are to be unequivocal. In this sense, the application of experimental designs to evaluation conflicts with the concept that evaluation should facilitate the continual improvement of the program. Dyer (1966) makes the following observation:

We evaluate, as best we can, each step of the program as we go along so that we can make needed changes if things are not turning out well. This view of evaluation may make some of the experimental design people uneasy because it seems to interfere with the textbook rules for running a controlled experiment . . . There is one kind of evaluation to be used when you are developing an educational procedure . . . I would call *concurrent* evalua-

tion. And, there is a second kind of evaluation . . . I would call *ex-post facto* evaluation; it is what the experimental design people are usually talking about when they use the word evaluation.

The objective of the impact evaluations is to be able to say definitively that a particular intervention has led to a particular outcome that would not have occurred otherwise. In the absence of experimentation, this is not wholly possible. But the larger problem in conducting an experimental evaluation in the human services field is related to the ethical problem of denying services in order to have a truly experimental model.

In a true experimental study, random assignment of subjects is based upon the probability theory that each subject has an equal chance of being assigned either to the control or treatment group. In the regular course of service, consumers are almost never assigned to programs on this basis.

THE BEHAVIORAL MODEL

The newest model is derived from behavioral constructs. It places a heavy emphasis upon measuring goal-attainment, but regards goal statements as statements which define the dependent variable only in terms of behavior(s) the consumer should be able to demonstrate at the end of the service intervention. It differs from the impact model in that it places little importance upon controlled experimentation on the ground that the selection of comparison groups which match up in all respects except for the intervention is rarely if ever possible.[1] The basic strategy of the

[1]More often than not, evaluations are conducted as ex-post facto research. Therefore, the investigator cannot achieve random assignment of subjects to groups or experimental manipulation of independent variables. On the other hand, if subjects are randomly preassigned to groups or treatment for the sake of evaluation, program administrators are confronted with a moral dilemma.

behavioral model of evaluation (BME) is to use the "treatment" group as its own control by employing pre and post treatment measurement. In using this procedure, the assumption is that each subject is his own control and that the behavior of the group before the program intervention is a measure of performance that would have occurred if there had been no program service.

The BME places far less importance upon allocative efficiency than the systems model; however, one may apply cost-benefit analysis to program outcomes not defined as "psychic" benefits. The BME also uses process data for identifying independent and intervening variables.

The BME begins from the premise that the effectiveness of human services should be measured in terms of the extent to which desired changes in the behavior of consumers take place. This model is grounded in three important behavioral science concepts which argue that: (1) the phenomenon with which the evaluator deals is behavior (dependent variable) and the independent variables which control behavior are elements of the environment; (2) since behavior is a function of an environmental stimulus, then, the most effective way to change behavior is to change the environmental circumstances which influence it; and (3) since behavior is a function of the environment, the social function of human services programs is to provide the individual with the skills to cope with the environment.

The primary question raised by the behavioral model of evaluation (BME) is: *To what extent has the program intervention improved the consumer's ability to gain mastery over his environment?*

The BME appears to conform to a formative evaluation design, in which program administrators are looking for information on a feedback basis for strengthening program administrative patterns and service delivery. Therefore, the initial concern of the evaluator should be goal clarification.

SPECIFICATION OF GOALS

Goal clarification is an essential feature of the BME because the evaluator is concerned, not only with goal-attainment, but also with the appropriateness of the goal and the feasibility of attaining it, both in terms of costs of resources and effort and in aiding the consumer to gain mastery over his environment.

For purpose of analysis, a program is regarded as consisting of three subsystems: (1) *donor*, the group that allocates the funds and develops the policy, guidelines and mandate by which the program operates; (2) *the service delivery*, the program staff who are responsible for service delivery; and (3) *the consumers*, the persons who receive the services.

Program goals, then, should reflect the value orientations of all three subsystems. Very often, if evaluation takes place during early program development, the most significant contribution the evaluator makes to the program may be the clarification and reconciliation of the perceived goals of members of the three subsystems.

It becomes clear then that there is a distinct advantage, when using the BME, to have the evaluator on board at the time of goal-setting. One of the initial ways in which the evaluator provides valuable technical assistance to the program administrator is by helping him to: (1) Clearly define goals in terms of behavioral outcomes; (2) specify quantitative measures and criterion conditions accepted as standards of program success, and; (3) set up a data collection system for collecting the kinds of evidence needed to measure program success.

Since the BME calls for the evaluator to be an integral part of the organization from the outset, he can provide ongoing feedback about whether program development is consistent with the predetermined goals.

Specification of Indicators of Goal-Attainment

Specifying goals as discussed in the preceding section is as much a planning and program development process as it is an evaluation task. On the other hand, formulating indicators of goal-attainment is regarded solely as a part of the evaluation strategy. This is so principally because such indicators must be both observable and measurable.

Indicators of goal-attainment infer a state-change relationship. That is, the evaluator collects as evidence of goal-attainment, data which illustrate a change in the state of the consumer on some baseline measurement. The context within which change (dependent variable) is defined is couched in the behavioral construct (man vis-a-vis his environment) and should represent mastery over the environment. Indices of mastery over the environment are measures of changes from one level of dependency to a higher level of independence or evidence of improved life chances.

Gil (1970) defined these as ". . . changes in the quality of life or the level of well-being of society's members, as observed on demographic, biological, psychological, social, economic, political, cultural and ecological indicators." He categorized indices of mastery over the environment as:

1. Changes in the development of life-sustaining and life-enhancing resources, goods and services.

2. Changes in the allocation of individuals and social units of specific statuses.
3. Changes in the distribution to individuals and social units of rights and rights equivalents.
4. Changes in rewards, entitlements, and constraints, and in the proportion of rights distributed as rewards and entitlements.
5. Changes in the quality and quantity of real and symbolic resources, goods and services distributed.
6. Changes in the proportion of rights throughout society and in the degree of structural inequality of rights among individual members and social units.
7. Changes in the extent of coverage of a defined level of minimum rights for all members of society.
8. Changes in the extent to which the distribution of rights is linked to allocation of statuses.

Data Collection

Once the evaluator has specified the dependent variables against which to measure program effectiveness and goal attainment, he can begin to collect evidence. The behaviorally oriented evaluator relies heavily upon the use of questionnaires, observation, attitude scales, idiographic data and interviews as the primary bases of data collection.

Data Analysis

The basic design used by the evaluator is the pretest-posttest design; then applying an appropriate statistical test to determine whether the difference is significant.

As pointed out earlier, the analytical framework of the B.M.E. is the measurement of program effectiveness in terms of the extent to which the intervention helps consumers to gain mastery over their respective environment. However, the evaluator is also concerned with accountability of service delivery which is measured in terms of responsiveness to consumer needs.

Feedback

As already described, the B.M.E. emphasizes a formative strategy. That is, it is designed to provide feedback information to the program administrator and the staff at any time during program implementation. Feedback data are used to modify program operations and to make any changes which seem to foster the achievement of program outcomes.

Since the evaluator is an integral member of the project staff, he can provide client satisfaction information to members of the staff shortly after the completion of each episode of service. Inasmuch as client satisfaction is measured in terms of satisfaction with the process as well as with outcomes, the evaluator can also provide information to members of the entire delivery system about assessibility and continuity. Furthermore, since the evaluator usually has the responsibility for providing needs assessment data and determining whether goals and priorities conform to needs data, he can also provide authoritative data for program modification.

One advantage of the B.M.E. is that certain program inputs can be modified after each episode of service. In this way, the outcome data from one set of service delivery activities become the baseline data for the set of modified activities. This cybernetic approach in which outcome data are treated as input within some temporal dimension is a key element of the feedback process. In this way, the feedback process serves as the nexus between service delivery and accountability.

Another feature of the B.M.E. is that it consciously treats values, attitudes, program priorities, environmental and managerial constraints as input variables. The B.M.E. probably falls into Kogan and Shyne's (1965) category of a tenderminded approach to evaluative research.

However, Weiss and Rein remind us that the "tough-minded" approach often results in technical and administrative problems which minimize the utility of the evaluation data.

Perhaps, the feature that distinguishes most the B.M.E. from other models of evaluation is its theoretical base, the independent variables it espouses and its definition of dependent variables. For example, the B.M.E. begins from the premise that behavior is a function of the environment and the individual's perception of the environment. Therefore, one of the ways to change the behavior of the consumer is to change the environmental circumstances that impinge upon his behavior. Relating this to human services programs, the B.M.E. presumes that program effectiveness is measured in terms of the extent to which these programs aid in the reduction and elimination of social and economic inequalities through the redistribution of resources and social and economic opportunities. In this context, the dependent variable is always couched in terms of gaining mastery over the environment and the independent variable in terms of facilitating mastery over the environment.

The major limitation of the B.M.E. is that it is most effective only when the evaluator is on board at the outset of program planning. Since most evaluations are conducted in retrospect, essential features of the model are lost.

The absence of a control or comparison group often creates problems of internal validity. This is another limitation of the model.

CONCLUSION

This article set out to present four conceptual models of human service program evaluation. An underlying premise is certain human services programs lend themselves to particular research designs and, in turn, particular statistical and analytical procedures. Another point presented in this paper is that each conceptual model represents a particular way of thinking which defines what evaluation questions should be asked. Each model also provides the evaluator with clues about what to measure and why.

The goal attainment model asks the question: *Was the goal met?* It usually employs the ex-post facto research design, relying principally upon descriptive-inductive analysis. The impact model employs the experimental design. However, such a "tough-minded" approach to human services program evaluation often results in both technical difficulties and intraorganizational friction. It responds to the question: *What difference does the intervention make?* Since most program outcomes are influenced by multiple causal factors, such a design also calls for the use of multivariate techniques.

The systems model asks the question: *How close does the organization's allocation of resources approach an optimum distribution?* It presumes that certain organizational goals are nonconsumer related; and that certain resources must be devoted to system maintenance. The most popular analytical tool used by systems evaluators is the cost-benefit calculus. The lesson to be learned is that while cost-benefit analysis represents a major step toward rigor, program evaluation should not rest solely on cost-benefit analysis.

The behavioral model of evaluation (B.M.E.) is the newest model. It defines goals in terms of service intervention. The B.M.E. asks: *To what extent has the program intervention improved the consumer's ability to have mastery over his environment?* It employs the pretest-posttest design on the assumption that each subject

is his own control and that the behavior of the group before the program intervention is a measure of performance that would have happened if there had been no program service.

A major strength of the B.M.E. is that it requires the evaluator to consider the value orientations of the consumer as important as those of the service provider and the donor. Another strength of the model is its assumption that the reduction and eventual elimination of social and economic inequalities through redistribution of resources and economic and social opportunities is a core function of human services program.

The limitation of the model is that it is only effective when the evaluator is on board at the outset of program planning.

The very nature and variety of human service programs require different evaluation strategies. No single model accommodates the evaluation requirements of most programs. In most situations, the evaluator will need to select elements of several models in order to achieve a comprehensive evaluation strategy.

REFERENCES

1. Dyer, Henry S. "Overview of the Evaluation Process," *On Evaluating Title I Programs.* Princeton, N.J.: Educational Testing Service, 1966, p. 18.
2. Etzioni, Amitai. "Two Approaches to Organizational Analysis: A Critique and a Suggestion," in Schulberg *et. al.* (Eds.).
3. Freeman, Howard E., and Sherwood, Clarence C. *Social Research and Social Policy.* Englewood Cliffs, N.J.: Prentice-Hall, 1970.
4. Gil, David G. "A Systematic Approach to Social Policy Analysis." *The Social Service Review.* Vol. 44. No. 4 (December, 1970).
5. Kogan, Leonard S., and Shyne, Ann W. "Tender-Minded and Tough-Minded Approaches in Evaluative Research."

Paper presented at the National Conference on Social Welfare, 1965.

6. Levinson, Perry. "Evaluation of Social Welfare Program." Welfare Review 4 (December, 1966), pp. 5–12.

7. See Robert F. Mager. *Goal Analysis.* Belmont, Calif.: Fearon Publishers, 1972, p. 10.

8. Ribich, Thomas I. *Education and Poverty.* Washington, D. C.: The Brookings Institution, 1968.

9. Sherwood, Clarence C. "Methodological measurement and social action considerations related to the assessment of large-scale demonstration programs." Paper presented at the 124th Annual Meeting of the American Statistical Association. Chicago: the Association, 1964.

10. Terleckyj, Nestor E. "Measuring Possibilities of Social Change." *Looking Ahead.* National Planning Association. Vol. 18. No. 6 (August, 1970).

11. Thomas, Alan J. "Efficiency Criteria in the Urban School System." Paper presented to the AERA, New York City, February 18, 1967. Mimeographed.

12. Weisbrod, Burton A. *Benefits of Manpower Programs: Theoretical and Methodological Issues in Somers and Wood. Cost Benefit Analysis of Manpower Programs.* Kingston, Ontario: Queen's University, 1969.

13. *Program Evaluation in the Health Fields.* New York: Behavioral Publications, 1969.

29. Describing the Findings

Richard L. Douglass

HOW TO USE AND PRESENT COMMUNITY DATA

The demand for quantitative demonstrations of service needs, program effectiveness, and other aspects of accountability being made on community service providers increases each year. Federal, state, and local governments, private foundations, and other sources of philanthropic support are demanding that service providers give an accounting, in quantitative terms, of their activities. A long-felt trend toward increasingly quantitative planning and decision-making in other sectors of society including industry, business, medicine, and public health now has reached the service community. It is timely for human service professionals to accept the probability that the future of human services will be characterized by more, rather than less, emphasis on measurement of activities, services, and outcomes and the quantitative analysis of such measurements.

REASONS FOR INCREASING EMPHASIS ON QUANTIFICATION

The reasons for the trend toward more emphasis on measurement in the planning, managing, and evaluation of service programs are numerous. During the last several years the resources available for human service provision have been alternately abundant and scarce. Today, however, and in the foreseeable future, scarcity of fiscal and human resources appears to be an enduring problem. During the same period the number of units compet-

Source: Unpublished, Richard L. Douglass, "How to Use and Present Community Data."

ing for those scarce resources has greatly enlarged, often including organizations with considerable sophistication in quantitative methods. The net effect has been an upgrading of quantitative sophistication among competing units bidding for resources and, more important, a greater expectation of quantitative information among governmental departments responsible for the distribution of resources. Thus, at the same time that the market for resources has become more crowded, demands for sophistication in measurement and analysis have increased. Success in this environment will depend increasingly upon the ability of the competitors to generate and use quantitative information.

Another social force that has increased the emphasis on quantification is the apparent failure of the many new programs aimed at solving social problems. The alarming expenditure of resources for poorly documented problems, the inadequate assessment of need, evaluation of outcome, and determination of the efficiency of procedure has triggered a cry for accountability, expecially from the governmental units responsible for distributing resources.

An immediate by-product of the interest in quantification of service needs and program activities and outcomes is that successful human service administrators discovered that improved information helps them plan and provide better services. Thus, the external demand for increased quantification generated a demand within the service delivery system itself for more precise and adequate measurement.

Underlying all of these trends has been a virtual explosion of new technologies to perform inexpensive measurement. Time-efficient systems, generally computerized, are prevalent and may soon be universal among the major service delivery organizations. Community data sources, and local, state, and national statistical information are more accurate, current, and available for use at the local level. Professional boundaries are becoming less rigid and a broader range of disciplines are providing manpower for the human services. Frequently these new sources of manpower have introduced new quantitative skills to service systems with little quantitative tradition.

To summarize, the competition among human services for scarce resources, the demand for accountability, professional recognition of the value of accurate measurement for planning and administering services, and an influx of quantitatively skilled personnel and technologies have interacted to produce an emphasis on quantification in the human services. This trend has been long in coming. Most other fields have developed quantitative methods earlier. However, many human service professionals have misgivings about translating the human condition into numerical abstractions and often are quite threatened by the trend toward quantification. Hopefully the information presented here will serve to reduce that anxiety.

WHAT ARE COMMUNITY DATA?

Practitioners frequently are unaware of many useful data sources bearing on community dynamics, population movements and changes, economic conditions, housing characteristics, etc. It is perhaps true that such collections of community data are not recognized because of a hesitation to use them. Community data are compilations of periodic measures of the status of the community, activities of specific organizations and services, and other descriptive information including health, vital statistics, housing, and economic conditions. Community data consist of records, often collected routinely for purposes of documentation. Any specific analysis of such information with the intent of identifying changes or trends, or of making inferences about social conditions is secondary to the purposes for which the data are collected. Thus, they are called "secondary data." In contrast, measurements specifically intended to be used for a particular analysis are referred to as "primary data." The utility of primary and secondary data for the community practitioner is largely determined by their characteristics. These will be discussed below.

PRIMARY AND SECONDARY DATA

Primary data are those sets of measurements collected by investigators for a specific purpose. Primary data include specially designed surveys of community residents, organization representatives, or service recipients. Primary data can take the form of special data collected during intake, termination, or follow-up interviews with the clients of social services. However, the overriding distinction between primary and secondary data is that primary data are defined and collected only for the specific analytic purpose at hand, while secondary data are routinely collected for various purposes including documentation and subsequent use by others. [1]

Primary data, unlike case records, are not prepared routinely by community ser-

vice organizations. Special-purpose measurements, however, frequently are routinized. The difference between routine and routinized is subtle, but significant. Routinely collected data, such as client records, often are characterized by considerable missing information, less than optimum quality controls, and little or no understanding on the part of the personnel recording the measurements of why the data are being collected. Frequently, there is no perceived need for the data and the recording process is a burden to staff members.

Routinized data collection procedures are most common to primary data. The value and immediate utility of the measurements are usually well understood by the personnel involved in data collection. For these reasons, primary data tend to be specific and precise. Secondary data collection can be well supervised and the recording process routinized with adequate quality control. However, with the exception of secondary data collected by the Bureau of the Census and other highly skilled organizations, it would be folly to assume that secondary data generally approach the level of standardization and accuracy achieved in primary data collection.

Operational consistency of the data is the primary issue raised in routinizing or changing data collection methods. Operational consistency is defined as the comparability of measurements of a variable between groups or jurisdictions, or for single groups or jurisdictions over a period of time. Data collection is often poorly controlled. Routine data frequently have errors of recording, missing measurements, inconsistently defined meanings, and other shortcomings. Such negative characteristics reduce their utility for human service professionals. With the exceptions noted, primary data are more likely to be opera-

---

[1] It should be noted that data collected for a specific purpose may subsequently be used for other purposes, taking on the character of "secondary data." The principal examples are survey data collected by universities and private polling organizations which are stored in libraries and made available to investigators for purposes other than those for which they were originally collected.

tionally consistent than are secondary data.

However, primary data are expensive to gather. Because the measurements are uniquely defined, designed, and collected, primary data collection requires the allocation of resources far beyond the requirements of acquiring secondary data.

In addition to being expensive, primary data cannot be collected to measure factors in the past. Furthermore, the collection of primary data may present problems of confidentiality and practicality. Thus, secondary data are often the only realistic source of community information. The likelihood of errors and operational inconsistencies in secondary data must be identified and understood before a reasoned analysis can be made.

Secondary data are available to community services from a variety of sources, discussed below. These and other sources of secondary data contain a wealth of information that is potentially useful for those who plan, manage, and offer services and evaluate community programs.

Major uses of secondary data in human service programs are: (1) to describe a community statistically, (2) to identify human service needs in the community, and (3) to test hypotheses of change in a social condition after a change in services or the introduction of a new program.

Accurate and useful description of change depends upon the operational consistency (or reliability) and the correspondence of the measurement used to the concept or idea being measured (or validity). While primary data often are more valid and reliable, secondary data may well be the only practical source of data because of constraints on staff, time, and budget. Fortunately, a careful search for secondary data often results in data adequate for the needs of the investigator at a minimal cost.

SOURCES OF COMMUNITY DATA

A practitioner should undertake a thorough search to identify sources of information available locally and their usefulness before considering the collection of primary data. Because special-purpose investigations are often costly, there is a considerable payoff if existing data are uncovered.[2]

Possible sources of information include:

1. Federal and state government agencies, e.g., the Departments of Labor, Commerce and its Bureau of the Census, Housing and Urban Development, Health, Education, and Welfare, and comparable state agencies.
2. City and county planning departments and regional councils of governments.
3. State and local health departments and specialized units such as the Public Health Service Center for Disease Control and the National Center for Health Statistics.
4. Federations of social, health, and recreation agencies such as community welfare councils and united community services.
5. Comprehensive regional health planning councils.
6. Mental health associations and community mental health agencies.
7. Funding agencies, both public (see 1 and 3 above) and private such as "the United Way," united funds, and community chests.
8. Clearinghouses in many problem areas; e.g., the National Institute of Mental Health maintains clearinghouses which administer data banks and publish summary data on drug abuse, alcohol abuse, and mental

---

[2] In Chapter 1 above, Anne K. Beaubien provides a detailed discussion of data sources available in many libraries. See Reading 5.

health; its Biometry Branch publishes a useful "Statistical Note" series.

9. Universities, including departments, schools, libraries, research institutes, and individual faculty members with relevant research interests.

10. Libraries and local newspaper archives.

PRESENTATION OF COMMUNITY DATA

The statistical analysis of community data is beyond the scope of this article. However, the utilization of data eventually depends upon the clarity and accuracy of printed presentation. By this I mean the tables, charts, graphs, and other displays of numerical information that any data analysis ultimately requires. This section will describe the construction and variety of ways that numerical information can be presented.

Tables: Numbers, Titles, Rows, Columns, and Cells

A table is an orderly arrangement of numerical information in columns and rows. There are few hard and fast rules for table construction. Perhaps the wisest are those given by a former director of the Bureau of the Census who wrote in the foreword of a manual on tabular presentation,

In the final analysis, there are only two rules in tabular presentation that should be applied rigidly: first, the use of common sense when planning a table, and second, the viewing of the proposed table from the standpoint of the user. The details of mechanical arrangement must be governed by a single objective; that is, to make the statistical table as easy to read and to understand as the nature of the material will permit.[3]

---

[3] U.S. Bureau of the Census, *Bureau of the Census Manual of Tabular Presentation*, by Bruce L. Jenkinson (Washington, D.C.: U.S. Government Printing Office, 1949), p. iii.

Numbers. If more than one table is used in a report, each table should be numbered to indicate its place in the series. It is also easier to refer in the text to a specific table by use of its number.

Titles. Each table should have a title to indicate the what, where, and when of the contents of the table. Table 29.1 is used to illustrate these points. *What* the table contains indicates whether absolute numbers, computed numbers or both are used; the title indicates how the contents of the table have been defined. For example, the title for Table 29.1 states that both the number of deaths and death rates are classified by age and sex. The *where* indicates the geographic area to which the information applies, as the "United States" in Table 29.1. The *when* is the time for which the data apply; in Table 29.1, this is 1963.

The title should be as brief as possible; however, the content of the table should be absolutely clear from reading the title. Titles of more than two lines are usually avoided. Further information needed for the understanding of the contents of the table can be placed in a *headnote*. The headnote follows the title and may be printed in smaller type and enclosed in brackets or parentheses. The information in the headnote should apply to many if not all items in the table. Such information may also be given in a note to the table, as in Table 29.2.

In Table 29.1 the headnote indicates that the deaths included in that table are those occurring within the country, and deaths of U.S. citizens taking place outside the boundaries of the nation are not included. It also indicates that no fetal deaths are included in the numbers.

Columns. Each column has a caption to state what is referred to in that column. Sometimes several columns will be bracketed together and the *spanner head,* the

TABLE 29.1

Number of Deaths and Death Rates by Age and Sex, United States, 1963
(only deaths occurring within the United States; exclusive of fetal deaths)

Age	Number			Rate per 1,000 population		
	Total	Male	Female	Total	Male	Female
Total	1,813,549	1,027,686	785,863	9.6	11.1	8.2
1	103,390	59,734	43,656	25.4	28.7	21.9
1 4	16,571	9,140	7,431	1.0	1.1	0.9
5 14	16,524	9,955	6,569	0.4	0.5	0.4
15–24	29,321	20,680	8,641	1.1	1.5	0.6
25–34	32,879	20,841	12,038	1.5	1.9	1.1
35–44	74,277	45,053	29,224	3.0	3.8	2.3
45–54	160,429	102,905	57,524	7.5	9.8	5.2
55–64	282,960	183,050	99,910	17.3	23.2	11.8
65–74	440,362	263,231	177,131	38.9	51.1	28.6
75–84	445,667	226,255	219,412	85.2	100.9	73.4
85+	210,541	86,472	124,069	210.1	224.6	201.1
Not Stated	628	370	258	—	—	—

Source: Public Health Service, National Center for Health Statistics, *Vital Statistics of the United States, 1963*, Volume II, Part A. Government Printing Office, Washington, D.C., 1965.

caption for this bracket, will apply to all columns under the bracket. In Table 29.1, two spanner heads are used, one with the caption "Number," indicating that the contents of all three columns under the bracket will be numbers of deaths for both sexes, for males, and for females in the separate columns. The second spanner head, "Rate per 1,000 Population," indicates that the numbers in the three columns under that bracket are rates.

In column captions and spanner headings, only the initial word and proper nouns may be capitalized. (In published tables, this depends on the style of the publisher.) In order to save space, there is a temptation to use abbreviations. These should be avoided unless the abbreviations will be readily understood, as those for the names of states, or days of the week. (In published tables, vertical rules dividing columns are usually omitted in the interests of economy. In this case, period leaders go from the stub to the first column.)

Rows. The first column of the table is called the *stub column;* it contains *row headings,* which serve the same purpose as column captions, indicating what is contained in a particular row. The caption of the stub column indicates the variable that is classified in the row headings.

If data are stratified by more than one variable, for example, by age and sex, ethnicity, or cause of death, the variable which is stratified, or classified, in the stub column is mentioned first in the title of the table. In Table 29.1 the stub column contains the various strata of age, so age is mentioned before sex in the table title. Like column captions, only the initial words and proper nouns are capitalized in the row headings, and abbreviations are used only when they are readily understood.

If stratification of items in a table is by two variables, common sense suggests that

the one which will have the greater number of categories will appear in the stub column. If classification is by age and sex or age and ethnicity, there will be more age groups than categories for sex and ethnicity, so that the age groups will appear as row headings in the stub column. If deaths are stratified by age and by all causes of death (as in a table appearing in an annual report of a health department), there would be many more causes of death than age groups, so that the causes of death would appear as row headings in the stub column while the age groups would be used for column captions.

The order in which row headings or column captions are arranged depends largely on whether or not there is progression. In a table presenting an age distribution, the youngest age group would appear as the first row heading followed by the other age groups in ascending order of magnitude. If the information in the table represents a time series, that is, information for different years, months, or days, the proper chronological order would be followed in the stub column or in the column captions.

If there is no progression from one group or another, as is usually the case with qualitative information, the order in presentation of row headings (or column captions) is determined by the size of the frequencies to which they apply. The category with the largest numbers should appear first, followed by other categories in descending order of magnitude of their frequencies. In Table 29.2, showing orphans of three types, it is shown that most orphans have lost only the father, which is the first type-specific column. Maternal orphans, in which only the mother died, follows the paternal column, and full orphans, with both parents deceased, is the third column under each spanner head.

Cells. Below the column captions, to

TABLE 29.2

Orphans, by Type: 1940 to 1972

	Number (1,000)				Percent of Child Population			
	Total	Paternal	Maternal	Full	Total	Paternal	Maternal	Full
1940, October..........	2,930	1,890	960	80	6.1	3.9	2.0	0.2
1955, July	2,710	1,830	820	60	4.8	3.2	1.5	0.1
1960, January	2,955	2,055	840	60	4.5	3.1	1.3	0.1
1965, January	3,290	2,330	890	70	4.7	3.3	1.3	0.1
1970, July	3,260	2,300	890	70	4.6	3.2	1.3	0.1
1972, July	3,074	2,166	838	70	4.4	3.1	1.2	0.1

Note: Beginning 1960, data include Puerto Rico and Virgin Islands. Covers children under age 18 who have been orphaned at any time. Paternal orphan refers to loss of father, maternal orphan to loss of mother, full orphan to loss of both parents. Percentage of child population based on Bureau of the Census estimated population of children under 18, as of July 1. Data not exactly comparable for all years because of changes in methodology.

Source: U.S. Social Security Administration. Data appear irregularly in *Social Security Bulletin, Statistical Abstract of the United States, 1973*, p. 313.

the right of the row headings in the stub column, is the so-called *"field"* of the table, made up of *cells*. A cell is a space representing an interaction of a column and a row and containing a number or a symbol. The number may be an absolute number (as the number of paternal orphans) or it may be a relative number (a percentage of the child population in Table 29.2).

If the table contains computed values, such as percentages or rates, they should all be expressed with the same number of decimal places. One would not record such values as:

25.485	but as	25.5
12		12.0
3.61		3.6
.7149		0.7
11.6		11.6

Percentages and rates are usually expressed with one decimal place to show that they are computed values, not absolute numbers. If rounding to the nearest tenth gives a whole number, this is written with a 0 in the tenths position, as the 12.0 above. If the value is less than 1, this is written with a 0 in the units position, as 0.7.

If computed values are included in the table, the reader should be informed as to what they represent. If they are rates, are they rates per 100, per 1,000, or per 100,-000? If the computed values are rates per 1,000 this information may sometimes be included in the title, in a headnote, in a column caption, or in a spanner caption. Occasionally, the information may be given in a footnote.

In some tables both column and row totals will be given (Table 29.1). In others only one set of totals will be given, as Table 29.2 which includes only row totals. Occasionally, no totals will be given in a table, as one which might give the number of births and deaths in Michigan for each year from 1900 to 1976. In such a table, neither row nor column totals would have any meaning.

If the totals are considered to be important, of more importance than individual items in the table, column totals will appear at the top of the columns and row totals will appear on the left, in the first column following the stub column. If the totals are of less importance than other items in the table, however, the column totals will appear at the bottom of the columns and the row totals in the column on the extreme right.

Graphs: Bar Chart, Histogram, Polygon, Time Series

A graph presents numerical information in pictorial visual form. The graph does not present the information more accurately than does a table, but presents it in such a form so that contrasts and comparisons are more readily seen than in a table. Graphs are most meaningfully used in combination with tabular presentations of the same information.

Bar Chart. Such a chart or graph consists of a series of rectangles, equal in width, equally spaced, but varying in length, the length of each rectangle or bar being dependent upon the amount that it represents.

Bar charts are usually used with qualitative variables (such as type of housing, type of treatment) with quantitative variables when measurements have been grouped into categories (such as age groups divided into under 15 years, 15–64, and 65 years and over), for comparison of geographic areas, or for chronological data when there is a wide gap between years, such as 1920, 1960, and 1970.

The bars may be horizontal or they may be vertical. While it is by no means a rule, there is a tendency to use vertical rather than horizontal bars when the information is for time periods.

To construct a bar chart, a scale is first drawn. If bars are to be horizontal, the scale appears at the top of the graph; if vertical bars are to be used, the scale will appear at the left. The scale must start at 0 and extend to some value beyond the highest amount represented by any of the bars. The scale is divided into equal intervals, with the intervals usually being 2, 5,

10, 25, 100, etc., depending upon the quantities represented by the bars. If the scale is to be a part of the completed graph, the scale should have a caption indicating what the numbers represent— population in thousands, rate per 100,000 population, etc. If the scale is eliminated in the final graph, this information must be conveyed to the reader in the title or in a footnote.

All bars are equal in width and equally spaced, the space between bars usually being approximately one-half the width of the bars and the first bar being placed this same distance from the scales. The length of each bar is determined by the scale, although it is often necessary to approximate its length.

If there is progression, bars would be arranged in order of that progression. In Figure 29.1, each age group, 18, 19, 20, 21, 22, and 23 years of age, appears in order, regardless of the bar lengths. With

FIGURE 29.1
Vermont Late Night, Single-Vehicle Accidents with Male Drivers, by Age of Driver, 1971

Source: Highway Safety Research Institute, University of Michigan.

most qualitative variables there is no such progression, and bars are arranged in order of length, with the longest horizontal bar appearing at the top or, if vertical bars are used, at the left.

Each bar should be labeled to indicate *what* and *how much* it represents. If all bars are quite long and if the labels are short the information may appear on the bar itself. It is also possible to label the bars on the right, but a better practice is to put the part of the label indicating *what* the bar represents on the left, the amount on the bar itself.

In order to show more contrast the bars should be colored or cross-hatched. Generally the same color or the same cross-hatching pattern will be used rather than using a different color or a different pattern for each bar.

Like a table, a graph should have a title telling the what, where, and when of the information portrayed. If the graph is for display purposes only, the title may appear at either the top of the graph or below it. For graphs included in reports or publications, it is common to find the title below the graph. If more than one graph appears in the series, they are numbered and are referred to as Figure 1, Figure 2, and so on. (In publications, double numbers such as 29.1 indicate the chapter or reading number, plus the table number.)

Histogram. This form of graph is used to show a frequency distribution, preferably a distribution with groups of equal intervals. A histogram has two scales, one on the vertical axis, and one on the horizontal axis. The vertical scale usually presents the frequency (size) of the concept or variable. The horizontal scale is used for some set of characteristics of the population or subject of the graph. These conventions are clearly shown in Figure 29.2.

The scale on the vertical axis should always start at 0, as the picture will be distorted if the scale starts at some value other than 0. The scale on the vertical axis would be divided into equal intervals, the intervals being 2, 5, 10, 25, 100, or even higher values, depending upon the highest frequency in the distribution. If the highest frequency were 79 the scale would be

set up in intervals of 10, going up to 80; if the highest frequency were 790 the scale would be set up in intervals of 100, going up to 800.

The horizontal scale starts at the lower

FIGURE 29.2

Washtenaw County, Michigan, Late-Night, Single-Vehicle Accidents with Male Drivers 18-to 20 Years Old, 1968–1973, in Six-Month Intervals

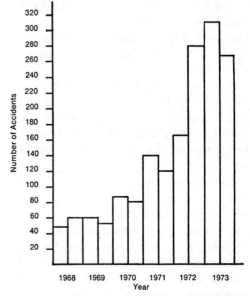

Source: Highway Safety Research Institute, The University of Michigan.

boundary of the lowest measurement group. For example, if the ages of all persons in the United States were of interest, the scale would start at zero. However, if only those who were eligible for Medicare were of interest the scale would start at 65.

Each scale should have a caption, indicating what the measurement is (on the horizontal scale) and what the frequency represents (on the vertical scale). When very large frequencies are involved, the scale on the vertical axis might have a caption "Number in thousands" or "Number in millions," thus reducing the number of figures used on the scale itself.

In Figure 29.2, for the first measurement group, the first half of 1968, a line is drawn parallel to the horizontal axis from the lower boundary (the first part of 1968) to the upper boundary (the end of 1968) of the group at a height determined by the number of accidents in first half of 1968. Vertical lines then connect this line to the horizontal axis forming a rectangle. The procedure is repeated for each measurement group so that the resulting graph consists of a series of rectangles, similar in appearance to the bar chart in Figure 29.1, but differing from it in that there is no space between the rectangles.

Frequency Polygon. The same information that was used for the histogram could also have been used for making one form of *line graph* known as the frequency polygon (Figure 29.3). The scales on the

FIGURE 29.3
Washtenaw County, Michigan, Late-Night, Single-Vehicle Accidents with Male Drivers 18 to 20 Years Old, 1968–1973, in Six-Month Intervals

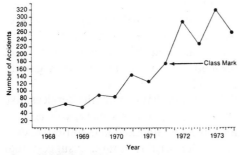

Source: Highway Safety Research Institute, University of Michigan.

horizontal and vertical axes would be set up in the same way as for the histogram.

Instead of drawing a line between the upper and lower boundaries of a measurement group, a point is plotted at the height determined by the frequency of the group, at the midpoint *class mark* of the measurement group. The class mark is the aver-

age frequency for the group, as defined by units of the horizontal axis. When the frequencies for each measurement group have been plotted, the points are joined by straight lines. The frequency polygon has an advantage over the histogram in that more than one frequency distribution can be shown on the same graph. A special purpose frequency polygon is a time series.

Time series. If a graph is to illustrate a time series, points are plotted at a height, according to the scale on the vertical axis, corresponding to the amount that is represented. If the quantity to be plotted is an average, the point is plotted midway between two points on the scale on the horizontal (time) axis. If the frequency being plotted represents totals, such as the accidents in an area with monthly totals for the time period 1968–1973, the series is graphed as in Figure 29.4 [Page 364].

With respect to changes taking place over time, there are two techniques to be considered related to the *amount* of change that has taken place and the *rate* at which change has taken place. For example, we might wish to draw a graph to show the changes in the new-home purchase rate from 1960 to 1970. If we were interested in the amount of change, the graph would be drawn with the scale on the vertical axis being an arithmetic scale; if we were concerned with the rate of change, then the scale on the vertical axis would be a logarithmic one (as shown below).

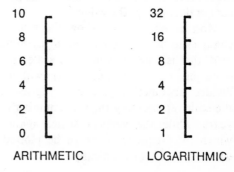

FIGURE 29.4

Total Washtenaw County, Michigan, Accidents, 1968–1973 (August)

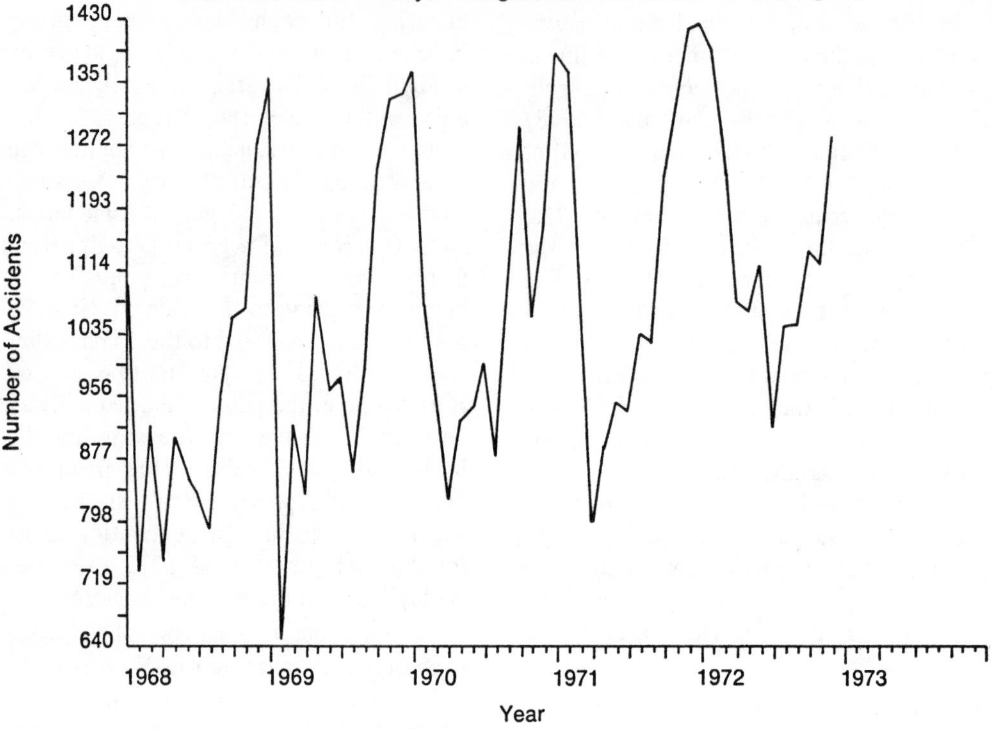

Source: Highway Safety Research Institute, University of Michigan.

Note that in the scale on the left [see scales in right-hand column on page 363], equal distances on the scale represent the same *amount* of increase, in this instance, an increase of 2. On the scale on the right, equal distances do not represent the same amount of increase but they do indicate the same *rate* of increase, with each increment representing an increase of 100 percent or doubling of the value.

Most graphs used to show the rate of change will be made on a *semilogarithmic grid;* that is, one on which one scale (the scale on the horizontal axis) will be divided arithmetically, equal lengths of the scale representing the same number of years, while the vertical scale, against which the frequencies are to be plotted, will be scaled logarithmically.

SUMMING UP

I have attempted to suggest ways of thinking about community data, finding such numerical information and ways of presenting such data in tabular or graphical display.

It appears that community services, like other systems in our society, will become increasingly interested in quantitative data in the foreseeable future. I suggest that this trend represents a challenge and an opportunity. If we accept the challenge and become more quantitatively oriented, it is likely that better planning, management, and evaluation of human services will be a visible consequence. Then we will have an opportunity to rationally change, to innovate and improve our community services.

30. Identifying Appropriate Evaluative Techniques

John Gottman and Robert Clasen

TROUBLESHOOTING GUIDE FOR RESEARCH AND EVALUATION

WHY A TROUBLESHOOTING GUIDE?

The idea of this guide is to give you an intuitive feel for what kinds of techniques are available for research and evaluation so that you can be an intelligent seeker of these tools.

INDEX TO THE TROUBLESHOOTING GUIDE

I. DESCRIPTIVE STATISTICS

Purpose:

To describe a population from a variable by describing the distribution of that variable in the population.

Example:

Distribution of Income per Month in the Pokohaches Swamp School District. It presents a table of incomes and the percent of the population earning that income.

Useful Concepts:

The *"Mean"* is a measure of central tendency of the distribution (the arithmetic average).

The *"Standard Deviation"* is a measure of the amount of variability of a given variable around the average. If most people have values of the variable close to the average, the standard deviation will be small.

"Probability." It is the likelihood of an event's occurrence, or the relative frequency of a value or set of values of the variable. For example if 80% of the people earn between 4 and 6 thousand dollars a year, the probability is 0.80 that an individual chosen at random from the population will earn between 4 and 6 thousand.

II. INFERENTIAL STATISTICS

Purpose:

To make inferences about a population from knowledge about a random sample or random samples from that population.

Example:

Gallup Poll of opinions.

Useful Concepts:

"Random Sampling." This is a procedure for selecting a group to study which insures that each member of the population will have an equal chance of being selected to be in the sample.

"The Central Limit Theorem" establishes the importance of the normal distribution because the distribution of all sample means of a certain size is normally distributed regardless of the original distribution's shape.

"Statistical Significance" gives the maximum risk of generalizing from a sample to the population. Risk is the probability of error. *"Statistically significant at p 0.05"* means that there is less than a 5% risk in generalizing from sample to population.

The *"Null Hypothesis"* is a hypothesis that the population mean equals a fixed constant $\mu = \mu_0$, or that two samples come from the same population $\mu_1 = \mu_2$.

"A Statistically Significant Result at the 0.05 level" means that there is less than a 5% risk in rejecting the null hypothesis that $\mu = \mu_0$ (or that $\mu_1 = \mu_2$).

The *"Variance Accounted for"* is an index of co-relation between two variables. If you account for variance in weight by the variable height, it means that height and weight are correlated. (The square root of the variance accounted for is the correlation coefficient, e.g., 49% variance accounted for is equivalent to a correlation coefficient of 0.70.)

"t-Tests" are tests for comparing the means of two samples to test the hypothesis that they really came from the same

population and the observed difference is not larger than sampling error.

The *"Chi-Square Test"* is a test for comparing two samples when the measurement operation is counting. This test compares observed to expected frequencies. In the table below, we can see that in the sample in question, the males were predominantly brown-eyed and the females blue-eyed whereas we would have expected the color of eyes not to be sex-linked.

	Males	Females
Brown Eyes	15	6
Blue Eyes	7	16

III. EXPERIMENTAL DESIGN

Purpose:

To eliminate plausible rival hypotheses that account for observed differences.

Example:

We know that the tested reading comprehension of girls is better than that of boys. One hypothesis is that the observed difference is due to the interest of the material read in school. A design is the detailing of the strategy to be employed in eliminating the rival hypotheses. Designs depend upon many factors including sample size, observation intervals, number of variables, and kind of data.

	Fashion Story	Baseball Story	Total
Boys	25	43	68
Girls	55	20	75
Totals	80	63	

Note that the number in the top, left-hand box is the average score of boys on the fashion story (25). Here we can see that overall girls read better (75 as opposed to 68) but that boys do better on the baseball story than girls.

Someone suggests a plausible rival hypothesis: "How do you know boys don't do better on the baseball story just because they have previous knowledge on the subject and the girls don't? It may not be interest at all." We would then have to control for that variable in our design.

Useful Concepts

Dependent Variable—This is the variable we are studying. For our example, it's reading comprehension.

Independent Variable—This is the variable we're trying to use to explain the observed variation in the dependent variable. For example, we might hope to explain differences in reading comprehension by the variable of the masculinity or femininity of the story.

Partitioning Variance—The central idea of this procedure is to partition the total variance into independent parts, each of which represents a different variable's effect.

Total Variance in Reading Comprehension = Variance due to Sex Differences + Variance due to Interest Differences in Story Material + An Interaction of Sex and Material + Sampling Error.

F-Test—This test may be used to compare variances after the total variance is partitioned. For example, does the variance due to sex seem large in relation to sampling error?

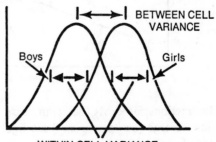

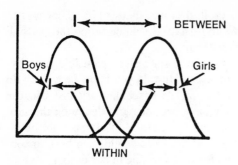

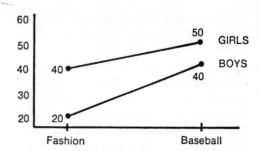

The *F*-test is mainly a ratio of between-cell variance to within-cell variance. In the curves on the left, the within cell variance is large compared to the between cell variance. In the figure on the right, the within cell variance is small compared to the between cell variance.

Interaction—In the design given in the example above, we can plot the cell means.

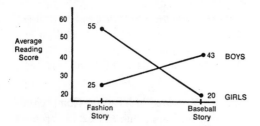

This is an example of interaction. Interaction is zero if the lines are parallel. In this case an interaction of zero would mean that boys (or girls) read better on all stories.

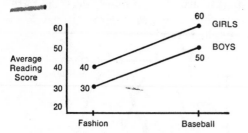

Interactions can cross (be "transverse") or just diverge (be "divergent," see figure at top of next column).

In this case, while girls are still reading better than boys, the difference is reduced in the baseball story.

Analysis of Variance—The analysis of variance is an experimental design for studying differences between cell means or combinations of cell means. The means are compared with respect to a common variance unit.

Blocking—Sometimes we want to split our design by blocking on a variable. For example, we may want to look at that reading data for high and low socioeconomic status children. Then our design would be

		Fashion Story	Baseball Story
B O Y S	High Socio-Economic Status		
	Low Socio-Economic Status		
G I R L S	High Socio-Economic Status		
	Low Socio-Economic Status		

We do this hoping to reduce the within-cell variability by introducing a new variable. We also may wish to contend with the plausible rival hypothesis that we have not accounted for socioeconomic status and that perhaps that variable would explain our results.

Analysis of Covariance is a way of trying to control statistically for a variable which we are not able to control experimentally.

For example, two groups may differ in IQ. We could block by IQ (see Blocking), or we could use an analysis of covariance.

Here's how an analysis of covariance works. The dependent variable is related to a *covariate*. (Reading is related to IQ). We use this relationship to try to predict reading score from IQ. Then we subtract the predicted score from the actual score and analyze the residual. We still hope to reduce the within-cell variability.

[Generally analysis of covariance is inferior to blocking unless the correlation between dependent variable and covariate is greater than 0.60 (Meyers, 1967).]

Internal and External Validity— Campbell and Stanley (1963) list sources of plausible rival hypotheses which may jeopardize the conclusions of any experimental design. Please read their excellent article for an elaboration of these and examples of commonly used designs compared on these factors.

Internal Validity—factors representing extraneous variables which will confound the experimental variable if not controlled.

1. *History*—specific events occurring between the first and second measurement in addition to the experimental variable.
2. *Maturation*—processes within the subjects operating as a function of the passage of time, per se (growing older, hungrier, fatigued, or less attentive).
3. *Testing*—the effects of testing upon the scores of a subsequent testing.
4. *Instrumentation*—changes in obtained measurement due to changes in instrument calibration or changes in the observers or judges.
5. *Statistical Regression*—a phenomenon occurring when groups have been selected on the basis of extreme scores.
6. *Selection*—biases resulting from the differential selection of subjects for the comparison groups.

7. *Experimental Mortality*—the differential loss of subjects from the comparison groups.
8. *Selection-Maturation Interaction, Etc.* —interaction effects between the aforementioned variables which can be mistaken for the effects of the experimental variable.

External Validity—factors which jeopardize the representativenesss or one's ability to generalize.

1. *Interaction effects* of Selection biases and the experimental variable.
2. *Reactive or Interaction effect of Pretesting*—The pretesting modifies the subject in such a way that he responds to the experimental treatment differently than will unpretested persons in the same population.
3. *Reactive effects of experimental procedures*—effects arising from the experimental setting which will not occur in nonexperimental settings.
4. *Multiple-Treatment Interference*—effects due to multiple treatments applied to the same subjects where prior treatments influence subsequent treatments in the series because their effects are not erasable.

Samples of Common Designs

1. One-Shot Case Study (lousy design)

X	T_2
Intervention	Posttest

2. One Group Pretest-Posttest

T_1	X	T_2
Pretest	Int.	Posttest

3. Randomized Control Group

	Pretest	Int.	Posttest
Group 1 (R)	T_1	X	T_2
Group 2 (R)	T_1		T_2

(R)=Subjects are randomly assigned to groups. Group 2 gets everything but the intervention, *X*.

4. Posttest-Only Design

	Int.	Posttest
Group 1 (R)	X	T_2
Group 2 (R)		T_2

Group 2 gets the posttest only.

5. Solomon Four-Group Design

	Pretest	Int.	Posttest
Group 1 (R)	T_1	X	T_2
Group 2 (R)	T_1		T_2
Group 3 (R)		X	T_2
Group 4 (R)			T_2

This design is equivalent to a two by two (2 x 2) *factorial design.*

	Pretest	No Pretest
Intervention	Group 1	Group 3
No Intervention	Group 2	Group 4

(Every group gets a posttest)

This design is recommended as a good experimental design by Campbell and Stanley (1963).

6. Interrupted Time-Series Design

$$T_1\ T_2\ ---\ T_N\ X\ T_{N+1}\ T_{N+2}\ ---\ T_{N+M}$$

7. Time-Lagged Time-Series Design

Group 1	$T_1\ T_2\ ---\ T_N\ X\ T_{N+1}\ T_{N+2}\ ---\ T_{N+M}\ \ T_{N+M+1}\ ---$
Group 2	$T_1\ T_2\ ---\ T_N\ \ T_{N+1}\ T_{N+2}\ ---\ T_{N+M}\ X\ T_{N+M+1}\ ---$

8. Time-Series Flip-Flop Design

Group 1	$T_1\ T_2\ ---\ T_N\ X_A\ T_{N+1}\ ---\ T_{N+M}\ X_B\ T_{N+M+1}\ ---$
Group 2	$T_1\ T_2\ ---\ T_N\ X_B\ T_{N+1}\ ---\ T_{N+M}\ X_A\ T_{N+M+1}\ ---$

The time-series designs are recommended by this book as excellent quasiexperimental designs. They can also be used to monitor and assess change in one person (doesn't have to be groups).

IV. MEASUREMENT

Purpose:

We often wish to make the assumption that we are measuring one variable on one continuum. Some techniques in measurement design allow us to test these assumptions.

Example:

Designing an opinionnaire to measure students' attitudes toward school, peers, teachers, studies and teaching methods. A student is asked to register the extent of his agreement with statements such as

	Disagree		Neutral		Agree	
School is fun.	1	2	3	4	5	6	7

by circling the number which best represents his opinion. Certain items are clustered as belonging to one scale or another.

Useful Concepts

Reliability—the extent to which the measurement procedure gives similar results under similar conditions. Methods of assessing:

1. *Stability (test–retest)* correlation between two successive measurements with the same test or inventory must assume times of testing are "similar conditions."

2. *Alternate forms*—two forms are constructed by randomly sampling items from a domain and a correlation is computed between "equivalent forms."

3. *Split-half*—a procedure used in place of

alternate forms by dividing the items in half, hopefully into "equivalent halves."

4. *KR-20 and KR-21* are formulas used to assess an alternate form reliability. Formula 21 is given here (less accurate than formula 20, but easier to compute)

$$r = \frac{K}{K-1} \left(1 - \frac{M(K-M)}{KS^2} \right)$$

where the items are scored 1 if "right," 0 if "wrong," K is number of items, S is standard deviation, and M is the mean of the scale.

Validity is the extent to which a measurement procedure measures what it claims to measure. Methods of assessing:

1. *Content Validity* (snapshot). How well does the individual's performance in this situation correlate with his performance in other similar situations?
2. *Criterion-Related Validity* (motion picture). How well does this individual's performance on this measurement predict his performance in future related situations (how well do achievement test scores predict grades in college?).
3. *Construct Validity.* Does the measurement procedure make sense as measuring what it claims to? Do the items which are supposed to be on one scale "hang together"? This can be assessed empirically by relating the extent to which presumably related construct explain variation on the instrument in question. Here is an example where this kind of validity is crucial. Suppose you show that 92% of all high school seniors cannot read election ballots with comprehension. The instrument is *face valid*. It has construct validity and you don't need to show content or criterion validity.

Convergent Operations. Different measurement procedures have different weak-nesses. More confidence is obtained in a result when several different measurement procedures point to (or converge to) the same result.

Scales are attempts at quantifying a construct and converting it into a continuum.

1. *Likert Scale.* A scale composed of items each of which the subject rates on a scale. Examples:

a. School is fun. *SA A N D SD* (*SA* = strongly agree, *A* = agree, *N* = neutral, *D* = disagree, *SD* = strongly disagree)
b. School is (check the blank):
Fun: — : — : — : — : — : — : — : Dull

Item *b* is sometimes called a *semantic differential* item. In this kind of item we can put any two words on either side of the line, for example,

strong: — : — : — : — : — : — : — : weak

2. *Thurstone type* or *equal-appearing interval scales.* These scales scale the items themselves. Items are first sorted by judges into three categories, then each category broken down into three others along a continuum (hostility, favorableness, disruptiveness, assertiveness). Items are eliminated if there is large disagreement between judges. Items are selected to have mean values (across judges) spread across the continuum from 1 to 9, preferably equally spaced. The individual taking the inventory checks those items with which he agrees (or finds hostile or disruptive). He is given the score which is the sum of the mean judges ratings for items checked. We might scale situations for the degree of assertiveness required and ask the subject to check the situations which are problems for him. The items not checked could be used to give an assertiveness score for him by adding the average of judged ratings. This places the individual along an assertiveness continuum.

3. *Guttman-Type* scales have items which vary along an attribute. Items can be ordered in difficulty, complexity, or value-loading so that answers to the last item will imply success or approval to all those preceding. Examples:

Difficulty:

> I can add two numbers.
> I can multiply two numbers.
> I can divide two numbers.
> I can compute a mean.
> I can compute the standard deviation.

Favorableness:

> 1. Would you object to a retarded person living in your community?
> 2. Would you object to a retarded person working where you work?
> 3. Would you object to having lunch with a retarded person at work?
> 4. Would you object to a retarded person coming to your home for dinner?
> 5. Would you object to a retarded person marrying a member of your family?

Item Analysis is a procedure for selecting only items which discriminate in the same way the overall instrument is intended to discriminate.

A correlation is computed between each item and the total score on the instrument. For *dichotomous items* (yes, no; pass, fail) a two by two chi-square table is constructed.

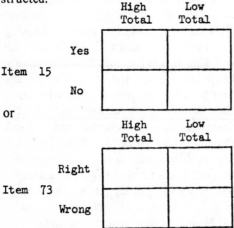

For a multiple-choice test we wish there to be a strong relationship between choosing the correct alternative and high total score; also we want there to be a weak relationship between choosing distractors and high total score.

Factor Analysis in Measurement Design is a method for analyzing the extent to which items cluster by studying their intercorrelations. We have confidence in the conclusion that our test has four independent scales if the items within scales correlate highly but items across scales do not correlate very highly (see analysis of data).

V. ANALYSIS OF DATA

Purpose:

To study the nature of relationships between variables.

Example:

We wish to determine which variables will predict whether a citizen will vote Republican (or Democrat) in the forthcoming election.

Useful Concepts

Correlation measures the degree of relationship between two variables. Usually a scatter diagram will provide an index for the eyeball.

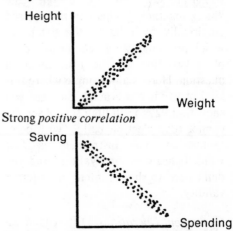

Strong *positive correlation*

Strong *negative correlation*

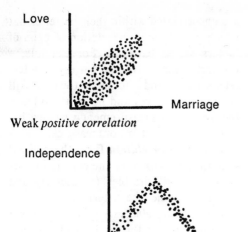

Weak *positive correlation*

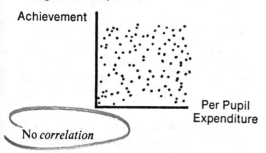

Curvilinear correlation (*positive* sometimes, *negative* others)

No *correlation*

The *Correlation Coefficient* gives an index of the degree of association (linear). 0 is no correlation, -1 is strongest negative, +1 is strongest positive correlation.

Partial Correlations involve calculating the correlation coefficient between two variables while statistically holding another variable constant. For example, ice cream sales may correlate with crime rates but not if the average daily temperature were controlled. Since we cannot control average daily temperature experimentally, we do it statistically. The correlation between ice cream sales and crime rate may be high but the partial correlation, controlling average daily temperature, may be quite low. Blalock uses this technique to argue from correlation to causation.

Regression is a statistical procedure which is like a recipe for converting from one variable to another using the best (least-squares) equation.

Multiple Regression is a statistical procedure like a recipe relating one variable to a set of other variables. For example, if we relate high school dropout rates to school expenditure, teacher experience, and the average number of library books in the classroom, we will have a recipe that says, "our best guess from the multiple regression is that if we spend $3 more per pupil, dropout rates may decline by 2%. We could spend $1 per pupil by buying some books, and the other $2 by hiring more experienced teachers."

The multiple regression gives you a mathematical equation of the relationships between one variable and a set of variables.

It's like a recipe in the sense that how good a cake turns out is related to a host of variables (how much sugar, salt, flour, etc., you add). It differs from a recipe in that you can improve the product by adding more of anything, except that some variables are more important than others.

Factor Analysis is a technique for data reduction. It analyzes the statistical dependencies between a set of variables by looking at the way variables correlate. For example, it may reduce a set of 50 variables into 3 basic variables. Each of the three will be statistically independent (zero correlation if the variables are normally distributed) of the other two. Each of the three will be linear combinations of the original set of fifty. Some of the fifty will "load" more highly on one factor, others will load on other factors. Each factor is a weighted sum of the original fifty.

The three factors should try to account for as much of the variance in the original fifty as possible.

Problem comes in *naming* the factors, i.e., giving them some physical interpretation in the real world. This is where the procedure becomes subjective.

No one has really derived the sampling distributions of factor loading coefficients, so its not clear how *stable* factors are. (See Principal Components Analysis.)

Principal Components Analysis tries to reduce data by a geometrical transformation of the original variables. An example is a scatterplot in three dimensions which gives a swarm of points in the shape of a football.

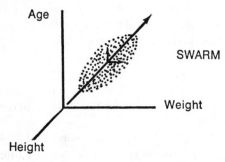

The new axes are those emanating from the swarm. The principal component is the main axis of the football. If most variance in the swarm is along one principal component (which will be a combination of the first three variables) we have reduced our data from three variables (which were correlated) to one variable. In general, we will reduce a large set of variables into a smaller set. Each variable in the smaller set is a linear combination (a weighted sum) of the original variables, and the new smaller set of variables are independent of one another.

The problem comes with interpretations —it's usually worse with principal components than factor analysis although the geometrical meaning is clearer.

Canonical Correlations are a procedure for factor analyzing two batteries of tests simultaneously to extract factors which are uncorrelated within their batteries but which provide high correlation of pairs of factors across batteries. For example, a researcher may have one battery of interest measures and another battery of skill or ability measures and he wants to know the overlap in measurement variance between the two systems of measures.

Multiple Correlation finds the optimal weighting to maximize the correlation between several variables (predictors) and another variable (the criterion).

Multivariate Analysis of Variance is a generalization of the analysis of variance (see section on Research Designs) to the situation where several variables are measured and these variables are statistically related.

The research issue behind the generalized tests is whether two or more sample groups should be thought of as arising from a single multivariate population or from two or more multivariate populations.

Discriminant Function Analysis is a procedure for predicting group membership of an individual on the basis of a set of other variables.

For example, if we can take medical measurements of various kinds can we find the best way to combine these (weight them) to predict whether or not a person has cancer?

Discriminant function analysis is used extensively in theory construction finding *which* variables in *what* combination predict political party membership or any other group membership.

Time-Series Analysis is a procedure for analyzing observations over time for predicting trends, understanding the basis for fluctuations, and assessing the effects of interventions.

CHAPTER VII

Work Guides

Introduction

Our search for materials turned up articles and other performance guides that seemed particularly useful and timely, but which did not fit neatly into one of the chapters. In many cases, the pieces were judged to have application in all or most areas, and often had been overlooked in the literature. In every instance, the editors agreed that the information provided had direct application to one or more field situations in which they were currently involved. The range is from the often discussed but long neglected subject of professional writing to an illustrative format for financial statements to a "things to remember" checklist for meeting-makers.

The article by John Tropman and Ann Alvarez on professional writing provides guidelines for practitioners and students, whatever their practice arena. Whether you are preparing a community assessment, a plan for action, newsletters and press releases, correspondence, persuasive documents designed to influence decisions, job descriptions, personnel assessments, or program evaluations, their suggestions may support your efforts. Closely related is the Junior League's checklist of questions for rating a newsletter which gives those who must make judgments about this popular form of communication some guidance.

Milan Dluhy's study of a homeowner's association provides insights into the factors that make for their successful operation. It may help practitioners who want to have influence on city councils or county boards of supervisors consider what they must do to improve their chances. The suburban context makes this article especially timely.

The preparation and interpretation of financial documents is a pervasive and increasingly critical problem. A format recommended by three major national health and welfare agencies is presented here.

Staff selection requires careful procedures. Richard Kaplowitz has prepared a useful chart showing the steps followed in selecting academic administrators; we believe it has application for community practice.

John Ingalls's checklist of items to consider in arranging a meeting can help the practitioner avoid overlooking some of the key components, both large and small, that help to make a meeting go. Finally, the League of Women Voters' condensation of parliamentary procedures should be helpful to those who conduct meetings or who must assist in resolving the conflicts that may arise over the procedures followed by a chairperson.

Fred M. Cox

31. Work Guides

John E. Tropman and Ann Rosegrant Alvarez

WRITING FOR EFFECT: CORRESPONDENCE, RECORDS, AND DOCUMENTS

INTRODUCTION

The community practitioner in policy, planning, organizing, administration, and evaluation needs some specific skills in written communication. Social work, like some of the other helping professions, tends to have an "oral history," and social workers generally are not trained well in the practice of written communication. Additionally, our profession shares with many other groups in society a general hesitancy to "put it in writing." Nevertheless, many important types of communication are written. Memos, minutes, and letters are some of the most common forms of written communication the social worker will use; others are reports, studies, summaries, and press releases. What is important to the practitioner is not "style," in the most highly developed sense of that concept, but rather simple, declarative sentences, informed by correct grammar and punctuation. Although the proper use of language and application of the rules governing it are important, it is also necessary that the worker-writer keep in mind two crucial elements: readership and format.

In all writing, it is important to remember who, and what groups, will be reading the piece produced. It is of the utmost importance to have some anticipation of who the readership will be and the constraints upon and desires of the readership group, so the text can be adjusted to accommodate the group. Most community organization practitioners who come from college undergraduate and graduate programs, for example, learn to write for academic purposes, where the sole readership is the professor who made the assignment. In actual practice, audiences are different. They tend to be less theory oriented and to seek the direct, pointed conclusions of a piece first, with the supportive evidence coming later. We will be discussing some of the readership issues and their implications.

Issues of format are also very important. People who think that there is only one way to write a letter or a memo, or that the format of a report does not make much difference, could not be more mistaken. There are many ways to put a written document together, from using different type faces and spatial arrangement on a page, to the more complex interleafing of parts and pages, recommendations and appendixes of a major report. Format is important in all written communication, but it becomes especially crucial in documents of some length. Then it is absolutely necessary to have summaries and references so arranged that the reader can find the material of interest quickly and can proceed into the more complex material in stages.

We should note that none of these points is very startling, nor will anything said in subsequent sections be very new.

Source: Unpublished, John E. Tropman and Ann Rosegrant Alvarez, "Professional Writing."

Rather, we are reviewing some of the most common areas of writing from the perspective of the practicing community organizer.

WRITING FOR COMMUNICATION

Written communication should be clear and direct. The language used should be varied and fresh. Repeating the same word over and over should be avoided; the use of a thesaurus—a reference which supplies synonyms and words of related meanings for a key word—may be invaluable in this regard. (Inexpensive paperback editions are available.) You should never use "you" as a generalized subject, in the sense we used it to begin this sentence; the word "one" can be substituted. The word "this" is not a noun, and so can never serve as the subject of a sentence. It is quite common to see sentences beginning, "This is a key point. . . ." Since "this" is an adjective, however, whatever it modifies should be present as the subject of the sentence. Something else to keep in mind is that a preposition is a bad word to end a sentence with. Rather, one should say that a preposition is a bad word with which to end a sentence.

These points are among the most common errors we have seen in professional writing—not including, of course, errors in grammar. Beyond specific hints and suggestions, there is a flow to a paragraph which the writer should keep in mind. Each paragraph needs an introductory sentence or two which orients the reader to what is coming in the remainder. The middle sentences of the paragraph convey the main content. The last sentence or two can serve as a summary and transition to the next paragraph. This basic model—introduction, content, and recapitulation—is a highly general one which serves, in extended form, for paragraphs in an essay, chapters in a book, and so on. While there is no general rule for the length of paragraphs and their content, we recommend the inclusion of only one or two ideas per paragraph. The writer should not overload a paragraph but should instead use briefer, more numerous paragraphs. In general, the standard page with standard type contains about 250–300 words (based on 25–30 lines of 10 words each). This estimate means that one should think in terms of about three paragraphs of 100 words each per page, a limit which we have found sensible.

There is one point which relates to the factual content of the written piece which is always important, regardless of the audience: accuracy. Accuracy involves checking, and perhaps double checking, the facts one presents. Phrases such as "research shows," "people think," or "it seems" abound in writing, and many writers seem to think that such statements in themselves constitute verification. If "research shows" it, cite the research; if "people think" it, name the people; if "it seems" means "I think that," say the latter. We are not saying that all the verification must be in the text or in that very spot. For example, a footnote may suffice. But it is extremely important (1) to have the verification and (2) to list it somewhere in the text. The listing serves a triple purpose. First, it serves as additional proof for the reader. Second, it serves as an additional and final check for the writer; having to cite the actual source often reveals errors in the rendering that would otherwise have been missed. Finally, listing the source serves to place on record the location of information which might otherwise be lost. Practitioners will recognize the seeming inevitability that the crucial references to significant minutes, the most important letters, and so on are those one is never able to find unless their location is clearly noted.

The listing of information, and the way in which the information is recorded, can be worked out as the writer moves through several drafts. The concept of writing and rewriting seems difficult to many people—especially those who find putting things on paper hard in the first place. Of course, judgment must be used with respect to the type of writing under consideration. Yet we have found that nothing—not even the simplest letter—can be done in a single draft. More complex pieces, those where space is at an absolute premium (such as a press release), items of any sort which might be of special importance, or items which one suspects might be reprinted for a wider public deserve special care. From our perspective, "special care" often means at least three drafts, and perhaps more than that.

The potential of any written document "going public" is something that a community practitioner might well keep in mind. One rule of thumb is to put nothing on paper which would not be acceptable on the front page of the public press. It would, of course, be rare for such a thing to happen. Nonetheless, "confidential" documents do occasionally become public, and many practitioners have wished that an unfortunate speculation, comment, or proposal had been omitted from a supposedly confidential draft.[1]

Doing several drafts requires at least a primitive set of records to make sure that drafts and pages do not become confused; such confusion often leads to chaos. A good technique is to date each page, and

after the date put the draft number (D-1, for example). Planners, especially, are very likely to circulate first, second, third, and further drafts of papers and reports to community constituencies, and it is particularly important when external or quasi-external groups are involved to keep oneself and the group informed of exactly which draft is being circulated. When new language is being substituted for old, *the new phrases are underlined* (and the old ones placed in parentheses).

Early drafts should be done with triple or quadruple spacing between the lines and with ample margins on one side of the page. This procedure facilitates the reworking of the draft, since it leaves plenty of space for changes, corrections, and additions and for cutting and pasting. Being able to cut up a draft and rearrange it is a great help and can eliminate much needless retyping. Final drafts—or close-to-final drafts—can be reduced to double or single spacing in order to test for total length and format style.

Finally, one should, if possible, allow a period of time to elapse between an initial draft and a rewrite. The written word has a tendency to express concretely, and in single-message form, what orally may be qualified and expressed in double- or triple-message format. For example, an "agreement" made in a sarcastic tone can actually express disagreement in the oral mode; tone is less important in writing, and statements must be qualified or expressed tentatively solely through the use of words, rather than actions, glances, and so on Partly because of this, it is prudent to let some time elapse between the initial writing and the final production or release of a piece, since in looking at a statement 12 hours after writing it, one may well see things which were less than clear in the heat of the actual writing. Flights of fancy, which may have taken on the ap-

---

[1]Moynihan's piece on the black family is perhaps the most widely known example of this phenomenon, and it is certainly a striking one. For a detailed analysis of both the original document and the sequelae, see Lee Rainwater and W. Yancy, *The Moynihan Report and the Politics of Controversy* (Cambridge: The M.I.T. Press, 1967).

pearance of concrete proposals and commitments in the written format, can be caught before they go out. In addition, allowing for a short time lapse permits practitioners to share preliminary drafts and to ask others to read and comment on them. We recommend the use of others as readers and reactors, especially in the case of major documents.

To ensure maximum accuracy, the major writer of a draft should keep one master copy and enter all corrections on it. Often people will phone in with comments, and unless there is some way to record them, other than by making notations on miscellaneous pieces of paper, the comments may never reach the major text. As draft copies come back, they can be divided into separate piles by individual pages. (It is for this reason that the initials of every reader should be on each page of his or her copy.) This procedure is important because one not only wishes to secure comments from others but to compare them as well.[2]

Fortunately, mechanical means have been developed which can aid the practitioner-writer in the process of preparing these several drafts and incorporating comments from a variety of sources. The memory typewriter, which places a letter or a page on a card or tape and then operates the typewriter electronically, is of primary assistance. Since the changes on drafts tend to become progressively less drastic, more and more of the previous draft is retained. This machine will simply retype the text to the point of change; the

changed word, paragraph, or whatever can be entered; and then the machine automatically rearranges the remainder of the text.

SPECIFIC TYPES OF WRITTEN WORK

The general discussion above applies, broadly, to all types of written work. It represents a set of considerations which is, however, modified and augmented as applied to specific types of written communication. We have divided the basic types of written communication of interest to the community practitioner into four broad categories. Perhaps most frequently used is *correspondence;* in this category we stress the letter and the memo, which are very common. *Program records* are a second type of writing. Under this heading, we consider minutes and other types of administrative documents which aid in assessing a program's progress and recording its history. These two forms of writing focus on relatively specific and known audiences, so the writer can make some reasonable assumptions about what the reader may know. In the other two cases, readership is less specified or completely general. The third category, *publicity documents,* consists of writing aimed exclusively at the general public or some segment of it. Such items as flyers, brochures, and newsletters belong in this category. Finally there are *substantive documents,* a category comprised of longer, more content-oriented reports, studies, research summaries, and the like. The main purpose of documents of this type is to bring new knowledge to bear in some situation.

CORRESPONDENCE

For the community practitioner, an important part of every day is spent in read-

---

[2]It is not the intent here to consider the broader implications for community organization, policy, and administrative practice of the "clearing" process. To some extent, this aspect is covered in Chapter IV by Connor and de la Isla (Reading 20). However, we do want to say that the securing of comments on proposed documents serves important participatory goals, as well as improving the style and clarity of the document

ing and writing letters and memos. Indeed, this activity seems so much a usual part of the workday that often no systematic attention is given to some of the problems and difficulties associated with it and some of the guidelines which can simplify and improve the process. We suggest, as a general rule, that a specified portion of the day be set aside for this activity. During this time one can read incoming mail and answer it, as well as mail and correspondence from previous days. It is all too easy to let correspondence pile up. Time and again, people claim they did not get notices of meetings, or were unaware of this or that proposal, when the true situation (which they will not admit, or of which they may not even be aware) is that the material is still resting in the "In" box. It is perhaps obvious that an important skill in connection with writing is *reading* —not only because reading gives one examples of a variety of styles and approaches to written expression, but also because one is often writing a reply or comment to something someone else has written; a complete understanding of the original document thus is essential.

Letters

We start from the premise that all letters should be answered. This principle applies to letters of congratulation, comments, requests, and so on. Sometimes the reply may be very brief, a simple thank you. Other times the reply may be negative, as when someone is notified that requested information is not available, or the reply may be quite extensive. In any case, the practitioner should get into the habit of answering mail. Although our "oral tradition" may not emphasize it, written communication is one very effective way in which relationships are built and maintained.

There are many good guides, often designated for "secretaries," on writing business letters. The practitioner would do well to consult one of these as regards format and stylistic conventions. It is not the specific format we are concerned with here, but rather the occasions for use and type of content which might be included.

Thank You Notes. The practitioner should develop the habit of expressing appreciation and thanks where appropriate. All too often it is assumed that people "know" their efforts are appreciated. A useful practice is to consider sending a note not only to the individual but also to his or her superior or boss as well. This way the person's superior knows that you think well of his or her staff. The little touch makes the reply much more meaningful for the subject. In such a note, it is also important to avoid generalizations and to be specific about what is appreciated.

Letters of Agreement. Practitioners meet and discuss many possible courses of action with many persons in the organization and the community. When such a discussion is completed, it is often very useful for the practitioner to write a letter to the person(s) with whom the meeting was held and outline the agreements the practitioner understood to have been reached. This procedure is especially important if matters of finances, space, or any kind of concrete resource allocations are discussed. It is then up to the recipient of the letter to agree or disagree with the written presentation, and substitute his or her own version, when appropriate. In this way, agreements can be captured on paper which would otherwise have remained vague and unclear, or "clear" but contradictory in the minds of individual participants.

Memos

For memos, aspects of format and content are more important than type in designating subdivisions of the category.

Brevity. A memo should be brief. Our experience is that a single page, or at most a two-page memo, is the optimal length. This judgment is based on common sense and practical politics—a message written on one page, or on both sides of one sheet of paper, is usually more likely to be read than longer efforts. Practitioners and students often complain that content cannot be reduced to a page or two, but we judge this reasoning to be false in most cases. Rather, it is a question of taking time, and developing the ability to achieve economy in redrafting. T. S. Eliot once excused verbosity by explaining, "I did not have time to write it briefly," and this reason often explains why so many people cannot (or claim they cannot) write crisply. They do not take the time.

Arrangement of Content. The specific substance of the memo will be a factor in its arrangement. However, there are some overall steps that one can use as a guide.

1. State the problem or the issue which occasions the note; refer to other relevant documents as appropriate.
2. State what information this memo has to offer with respect to (1) above; *do not* put "report level" detail here, but refer to attachments or offer to produce them, if needed.
3. Offer any conclusions suggested by (2); be sure to differentiate between *your personal* conclusions and factual ones stemming directly from the data.
4. If it seems appropriate, conclude by offering to meet and discuss or do further work.

It is our judgment that almost everything with respect to a content area can be placed into these categories.

Use of Attachments. Since we define a memo as being brief, it typically cannot, and should not, contain the specific substantive content which leads to a conclusion. Rather, it is a summary of that content, which can be presented in full detail in a report. The relationship between a memo and a report is one of "attachment" —that is, where appropriate, the report is attached to a memo. Other material, such as relevant letters, other memos, and the like, can similarly be attached to a memo. Then the memo reader has the substance of the point in a short document, with additional documentation attached for perusal by those who want more detailed information. The advantage of this arrangement lies in the fact that one can be crisp in the memo and more thorough in the report. Many persons make the mistake of attempting to combine the memo and the report, thus producing a document which is too short to be informative as a report, but too long to be a concise and effective memo.

Salutations and "Carbon Copy" (cc:) Procedure. Practitioners often ignore the fact that the salutation, that part that says, "Memo To:_____", conveys a message. Care should be taken to use the appropriate title of the person, or persons, receiving the note. Similarly, the order of names needs careful attention. If there is an organizational hierarchy, protocol demands that the highest ranking person be listed first, followed by the next highest ranking, and so on. When this procedure is followed, the titles of the persons follow their names, and the first person on the list gets the ribbon copy. If titles are not used, the names should be placed in alphabetical order, or the readers will assume that the order of names reflects some loose level of organizational prestige. Similarly, care should be taken with respect to the "cc:"

notation, since it is not always clear who should get copies, and why. Although there are no rules here, the practitioner should be sensitive to the implications of sending copies around. If, for example, a memo is sent not only to Practitioner X but also to his or her employer or supervisor, the notation serves as a prod (welcome or unwelcome) to X. Letting someone know that his or her superior has been informed of a situation will have an effect, and the possible results must be taken into careful consideration.

PROGRAM RECORDS

Program records are any and all documents which relate to an identifiable "program," function, or task with which a practitioner is associated. If, for example, the practitioner is working on a block club development, all materials, reports, correspondence, and minutes of meetings should be kept and filed under the record for that program.[3] Thus, many types of written communication can be included in the program records. However, there are three types which fall specifically within the category of program records—logs, minutes, and annual reports.

Logs

Logs are primarily for the practitioner's own use, although they may also serve as bases for discussions with supervisors and superiors. A log is helpful in keeping the worker on the track and is also useful when the worker is making periodic reports. Basically, a log consists of a daily

---

[3]Implicit here, of course, is the fact that there may be more than one copy of letters and memos "for the file," and duplicate materials may be simultaneously filed under several separate headings. We do not wish to discuss filing systems themselves but only to note that any system which has full information by assignment or program is acceptable.

record of activities and could include calls made, letters written, and so on. Logs fall into two types: process and substantive.

Process Logs. The process log details how all the time during the day is spent by the practitioner. Included are not only the specific actions but also the practitioner's observations about, interpretation of, and reaction to what occurred. Generally, these logs are more useful to beginning practitioners than to more experienced ones.

Substantive Logs. The substantive log is a recording of the key elements of the content of what happened during some specified period of time. All of the detailed and inclusive recounting of particular instances is eliminated from the substantive log, and only the essential conclusions, or elements, are recorded. This approach to recording is especially helpful in noting those decisions and actions which have implications for the future. It may help to eliminate the tendency for something one must do in the future to become lost in a welter of detail.

Minutes

Minutes of meetings are the most common forms of writing that the practitioner undertakes. Minutes of meetings are critically important as a part of the formal record of a committee or group and serve as a guide to "what happened" at a meeting. Minutes can be written in different ways, which, in essence, correspond to the styles described for process logs and substantive logs. Process-oriented minutes reflect everything said by everyone, and are as close to a verbatim transcript as can be achieved. Substantive minutes, on the other hand, tend to reflect the main points of view and main decisions made, without recording every word. Substantive minutes demand great judgment on the part of the practitioner, because he or she must reflect what happened in such a way as to be accurate and fair to all points of view, while omitting unnecessary details.

The style of minute-taking is not entirely up to the group and the practitioner, however. There may be rules and bylaws or traditions which govern the form in which the minutes must be taken; there may be, in certain situations, laws governing the content of records. It is the task of the practitioner to find out what, if any, these restrictions are.

Annual Reports

We believe it to be sound practice for the practitioner to file an annual report when he or she has completed a year with a project. Many practitioners think of annual reports as something put out only by corporations. The annual report, however, is appropriate for every project the worker undertakes. Community organizers frequently work on such diverse assignments that, unless they take the time to compose some sort of a formal report, they cannot provide information on the status of any given project. The annual report thus provides an occasion for the worker to determine and clarify his or her own assessment of progress on each project or program. Additionally, the status of the project is communicated to all other interested persons or parties, including those involved in funding decisions. The annual report (see Figure A.1) thus becomes a vehicle which encourages both accountability and proper evaluation.

The fact that practitioners are being asked increasingly often to evaluate their work, or to have it evaluated, means that annual reports are going to become more common. Some kind of ongoing log may well be kept even by more experienced practitioners, as the basis of the annual

FIGURE A.1
Outline of Suggested Content
for Annual Reports

1. General introduction and overview; plans for coming year.
2. General summary of results obtained during the past year.
3. Specification of mandate, listing of formal changes, etc.
4. Specification of main activities leading toward the accomplishment of the mandate.
5. Specification of any problems of a special nature encountered during the year.
6. Specification of personnel involved; time spent by each.
7. Specification of financial information—costs of supplies, equipment, etc.
8. Specification in more detail (than in No. 1) of plans for coming year.
9. Summary and conclusion.

APPENDIX

Attachment of budgets, reports, publicity, etc., which substantiate or relate to sections of the main body of the text.

If final report, follow Nos. 1 through 9 and insert before Appendix:

10. Evaluative overview, problems and prospects, comparison with other projects; recommendations, if any.

Note: The order of items is not crucial; the list represents the main topics we have found to be generally useful in pulling together an annual document. It is important that the initial section present a true overview, so that the casual reader can get the gist of the report without reading through all the details.

compilation. The importance of ongoing records, as well as annual ones, is further increased because of the possibility that the worker may be transferred to another assignment, and a new worker may enter the picture. This new professional needs to have complete records available in order to begin work. The log is thus analogous to the medical record a physician keeps on a patient; it is needed so new and different physicians can become involved.

Interim Reports. Logs and annual reports represent the two ends of the spectrum with respect to time covered by records of program activity. It thus is sometimes difficult to work directly from daily or weekly logs to produce an annual summation. Recognizing this fact, people who work with finances insist upon the production of periodic reports. We believe this practice is a sound one and should be adopted by practitioners for their own work in community organization. This practice can be especially important if the program is in trouble or beleaguered in some way. Interim reports can also serve as a kind of newsletter of activity and let the community of interest know what is going on.

Final Reports. Whenever a project is completed, a final report should be prepared. This rule obtains no matter how short a time has elapsed between the last annual report and the termination of the project. If it appears that those dates are going to be close together, they can sometimes be made coterminous, and the last annual report can be the final report.[4] Sometimes, of course, a short program ends before there is an opportunity to have an annual report, in which case only a final report would be submitted. The final report should contain, in addition to the general content of an annual report, some explicit attempt to assess the success of the project in achieving the goals set out for it, and some assessment of the reasons that these goals were or were not accomplished.

PUBLICITY DOCUMENTS

The practitioner often needs to write documents for purposes of public information. Press releases, newsletters, flyers, and brochures are among the most common examples of these. Perhaps the two key concepts which inform all writing of this sort are (1) brevity and (2) factual ac-

curacy and completeness. Space is always at a premium in this kind of writing, usually because of either costs or competition. The standard rule of journalism—that information on "who, what, where, why, and when" should be provided in the opening paragraph—supplies the razor a practitioner can use to cut his or her copy to the very bone.

Press Releases

The use of the press to make an announcement is a time-honored technique of all those dealing with the "community" and may be used as a sort of official recognition of "what's happening." There are often special formats to be used in preparing copy for the press; one should check with the local papers to find out if there are any particular local requirements of deadlines which apply.

The practitioner should remember that newspapers cut material from the bottom, or end of an article, up toward the beginning. Thus, all of the information provided by the "five W's" should be in the initial paragraph, with elaboration and specification following in later paragraphs. Then, if the paper cannot use the whole release (which is likely), at least the essential information will be printed.

Although many practitioners seem to think that press releases are prepared mostly for routine announcements or crises, nothing could be further from the truth. Any notable activity of the agency or program can be the subject of a press release. For example, when the annual report is completed, a one-page summary of the entire document can be provided to the press. Promotions of staff, changes of the directorship, election of new members of the board, or the completion of a significant report—these and many other activities can be used as the basis for a press re-

---

[4]It should be noted that annual reports can be due on any date, because they come at the anniversary of the beginning of the project, rather than coinciding with the dates of the beginning or end of the fiscal or calendar year.

lease. One should not think that such releases serve only the interests of the agency, either; they serve the broader community by informing it of the activities of the agency, program, or specific local group.

Practitioners often seek out the press; however, there is one generalized type of instance in which the press seeks out the practitioner: when there is trouble or controversy of some sort. This type of situation is the one in which practitioners are most often unprepared. When the phone rings and it is the local newspaper or TV or radio station asking for a statement on a recent firing, on the conditions of facilities under investigation by a community group, as likely as not the practitioner will not be prepared with a statement. Thus, our suggestion is that when an issue develops that seems as if it might be "hot," or controversial, the practitioner should prepare press releases in advance. In many cases, one may not wish to volunteer these statements to the paper; however, if the press calls there will be something coherent and accurate to say. Those who have had experience in this area know that it is very difficult to think as clearly as one would like and to secure the proper clearances for a public statement when someone is on the phone or at the door waiting for a response. If, however, advance preparation is made a routine matter of business, these kinds of problems can be minimized or avoided.[5]

_____
[5]Although beyond the scope of this article, it should be noted that the mass media may be used for tactical purposes. Familiar to those who are abreast of political strategy, particularly at high levels, is the "news leak," press briefings that are given with the understanding that the source will not be identified in the press. These are used to test public reaction before decisions are taken. Another tactic is to create a media event that cannot be ignored by the press, designed to bring attention and favorable public response to some program or event. A third tactic, used by Saul Alinsky and those inspired by his work, in-

Flyers and Brochures

The flyer or brochure usually has one overriding purpose—to inform people about the essence of an issue in such a way as to interest them in getting more information. Sometimes this information is distributed to those who write for more detailed accounts (as is the case with a brochure on agency objectives and practices); sometimes it is passed out to those who come to a public meeting or a mass rally, etc. From a communications point of view, a flyer is most effective when people are already aware of some aspect of an issue, and their awareness is being expanded in some important way. Thus, in the case of a practitioner's putting out an election flyer for a candidate, although the recipients might or might not be oriented to the content of the flyer, they would probably be oriented to the fact that there is an election coming up. Alternatively, a community group may be waiting for information on an issue, and the flyer may be the most efficient and effective way to provide it. The flyer may thus reach an entirely uninformed readership, so it must be carefully designed and worded.

Because flyers are intended to convey initial information on one page which can be left on doorsteps or posted on bulletin boards, maximum information should be presented in simple form, similar to—but even more abbreviated than—that of a press release. Attention to graphics is important here and in brochures; a picture, a boldly lettered word, or any other device which will catch the attention of the

_____
volves the discussion of actions to be taken by a community organization that can be highly embarrassing or disruptive to the target of the action. The discussion is arranged so that it takes place before persons who relay the plans to leaders or officials in the target organization. The intention is to bring the target group into a bargaining relationship with those planning the action without actually having to carry out the proposed action.

reader visually can be useful. The initial eye-catching design will usually be accompanied by a brief text outlining the specific factual information. Be sure to include *all* the pertinent information. For example, when a meeting is being announced, information as to time, date, place, purpose, sponsoring group, fee (if any), and contact person should be given. It is surprising—and frustrating—how frequently one or more of these crucial ingredients is neglected by even the experienced practitioner.

A brochure follows the same principles as a flyer, except that there is an intent to convey more information about a topic. Normally, while a flyer reaches people who may know either a great deal about a topic, or nothing at all, a brochure reaches people in the middle range of this continuum. That is, they are likely to have moderate but limited knowledge of and/or interest in the subject. The information presented thus may be fairly complete, but must be very basic. Things which the practitioner might take for granted must be explained in a brochure, since it must be assumed that the reader is a novice in the area.

Newsletters

Unlike the flyer or brochure, the newsletter is a regular publication aimed at a wide readership of both the informed and the uninformed, friends and those not so friendly. Its purposes may be informational, public relational, intellectual, and personal, among others. A newsletter may carry pieces on times, places, and dates of meetings; columns encouraging a large turnout at an upcoming event; a feature piece discussing in depth some issue in the agency or program; a list of persons who have been honored recently in the commu-

nity or agency; advertising; and so on. It is this mixture of purposes which is the ultimate downfall of most newsletters. In trying to do too much and to be all things to all persons, they may end up serving no real purpose and having no consistent audience.

Thus, the first task of the practitioner putting out a newsletter is the editorial one of deciding upon the primary and subsidiary missions and purposes of the newsletter. Once these decisions are made, the practitioner can order and arrange the newsletter in a way that makes internal sense. Indeed, the practitioner is likely to be as much an editor as an author, although in the case of smaller newsletters the worker may do as much writing as editing.

In any case, the worker should be aware of some editorial guidelines. As an editor, one is involved in cutting and shaping the work of others. Regardless of the source of the material, it is important, as we have indicated before, to keep in mind what the readership is likely to be and what type of service the newsletter is assumed to provide for them. While it can be hoped that writers will be sensitive to the needs of the newsletter's readers, many will not be. Their work will have to be reshaped to fit the purpose and space of the particular newsletter. Good initial information from the editor on the specific requirements of the newsletter can help avoid a situation which might later be the cause of bad feelings. It must also be remembered that, depending upon the purpose of the newsletter, "good writing" may not be all that important. In a community setting, for example, it might be most important that community members express themselves in writing within the local context; extensive editing for editorial reasons could be offensive. Indeed, sometimes the fun of putting out a newsletter can overshadow the purpose—which should remain in the forefront of the editor's mind.

Special attention needs to be given to the overall format, the use of graphics, and the layout of the individual pages of the newsletter. The format and style used for different newsletters varies considerably according to the newsletter's purpose, the readership, the funds available for production and distribution, and the philosophy, skills, and inclinations of those who are producing it. The newsletter may thus be anything from a sophisticated, professional, organizational bulletin, to a handdone, "down-home" chronicle of community events. As it is likely to be somewhat longer than other pieces of writing geared for public distribution, special care must be taken to make the newsletter visually appealing and interesting. A sample front page of a newsletter is given in Figure A.2. Such a simple two-column format can be quite attractive and effective. Note the inclusion of volume and issue numbers, as well as dates, to establish the unique identity of each issue. The use of space and headings can be important and should not be dismissed as trivial. Graphic aids such as "press-type" should be investigated; many of them are inexpensive and easy to use, and they can add drama and interest to relieve the monotony of a series of uniformly typed pages.

Above all, it is important to remember that the newsletter must be read in order for any of its purposes to be accomplished. Because of this, anything that makes it more readable should be encouraged, and anything that makes it less readable should be avoided or discontinued.

FIGURE A.2
Sample Newsletter

THE COMMUNITY COURIER

| Volume 2, Number 4 | *Donations Welcome* | August 19— |

From the Editor

In this hot weather, if you can't keep cool you can at least take your mind off the heat by keeping busy. One good way to keep busy is to help put out the *Community Courier!* We need more volunteers and invite you to join your hands with ours to get the news out!

Contributions are also welcome, so if you have a news item, a poem, or an announcement for us, please let us know.

This issue features a list of exciting "Coming Events," news on nutrition and the newborn baby, the first in a cartoon series by our own Jackie Porter, some tips on landlord-tenant relations, and some price comparison between name brands sold at local grocery stores.   (Cont'd. on page 3)

!! COMING EVENTS !!

— Playground activities continue this month at Cedar Park. Call for schedule information.

— Don't forget to vote on local issues in the August 23 special elections. Your voice can count, so come out and be heard!

— The Third Annual Community Health Fair will be held in mid-September. Call Mrs. Green at the Center if you have suggestions or if you can volunteer some time to help out.

— A new shopping service especially for senior citizens will begin this month. Call the Salvation Army for details.

(OVER)

West Side Community Center
401 West Locust Street
Bigtown, Anystate USA 49106
Phone: (313) 343-9216

SUBSTANTIVE DOCUMENTS

The longest and most complicated pieces of writing that the practitioner will undertake come under the category of substantive documents. These documents include proposals for grants, reports on results of original research or community studies, reports on library research, and the like. In one sense, the practitioner may have an advantage in this type of writing, because these documents are the ones which most closely resemble those he or she may have written in school. On the other hand, the format and style of presentation as well as the purpose of these documents are quite different.

Generally, the purpose of substantive documents is to convey a detailed—often extensive—array of information, based usually on research and scholarship. Thus it is important to cover methodology as well as substance, since some of the confidence readers have in the findings will depend upon the degree of satisfaction they have with the method. As with the newsletter, however, the practitioner should seek to determine the key readership and purpose of the document *before* writing begins. In that way the document can be directed, even in its early drafts, toward serving the intended goal.

A second point of importance is to construct an outline. Substantive documents contain relatively large amounts of material. In the writing, it is likely that some of this material might be mislaid, forgotten, or otherwise unintentionally omitted. The outline ensures that questions of *content* can be answered independently of questions of style of presentation. Since the first problem of the document is the presentation of content, such a helpful technique should not be ignored. One of the greatest problems many practitioners (and students) have in writing is their failure to use the outline method. They often begin directly with the first sentence and have only the most crude idea of the overall structure to follow. Naturally, the anxiety of the whole enterprise falls heavily upon that one sentence. Use of an outline gives confidence that all matters will be discussed in turn, and each will be given its appropriate share of attention.

We suggest that the writer use the page-per-time technique when working to meet deadlines. After an outline has been completed, it may be helpful for the writer to establish a set number of pages per hour which are to be produced. We have found between three and six pages an hour—or about 750–1,800 words—is reasonable for a rough draft. We use the words "rough draft" literally, believing that it is often much easier to revise, to cut and paste, and to reconstruct once something is on paper. Thus, we urge the practitioner to write, write, write! Pay no attention to misspellings or awkwardness, but get the thoughts down. There will be time to polish them later. As one uses this technique, it is likely that each subsequent draft will improve. Of course, this style can be used to varying degrees. Some people prefer to write as closely as possible to the final version, leaving only the finer points to be checked and reworked. Others may prefer to work very quickly and depend upon later, major revisions to smooth and tighten the original rough version. The latter approach is suggested for those who have difficulty getting started.

The format of a report is extremely important. If it is very long, a table of contents is useful. Throughout, the use of side and center headings (as we have used in this article) helps the reader to move through the piece logically and smoothly. Unlike the scholarly document, in which the reader is led from the problem through the evidence to the conclusion, the format in this case should begin with a brief statement of the problem or mission, then a statement of the findings, followed by details of the evidence. As with memos, the most important element is to get the key findings immediately before the reader, with the support for those findings following.

The practitioner should be aware that there are texts available which can serve as guides to various forms of substantive writing. Proposal writing, in particular, has been covered in a number of publications, and there are also excellent workshops and courses on the subject in many areas. These may be quite useful to the worker in learning how to interpret and fulfill the requirements of grant requests, which are often quite confusing. Regardless of the degree of complexity of the document, the practitioner will do well to keep in mind our previous reminders: direct the writing toward its purpose and readership, work from an outline, choose a format for its simplicity and clarity, and write boldly and quickly, allowing for subsequent revision.

CONCLUSION

In this article we have stressed the importance of written communication to the practitioner in community organization. We have presented some basic concepts and suggestions which should be helpful as "refreshers" for the experienced practitioner-writer and may provide the beginner with some elementary guidelines.

We have categorized the most typical kinds of writing with which the worker might be involved under four major headings: correspondence, program records, publicity documents, and substantive documents. Within each category, we have reviewed some of the most salient characteristics and requirements of the various types of writing, including letters, memos, logs, minutes, annual reports, press re-

leases, flyers and brochures, newsletters, grant proposals, and scholarly reports.

Although each specific type of writing has its own peculiarities, we believe there are some generalizations which can be adapted and applied to all, with modifications when necessary:

1. Be sure to proofread carefully and repeatedly, to check for ordinary errors in spelling, grammar, punctuation, and typing or reproduction.

2. Be aware of the power of the written word to solidify and rigidify positions and concepts. Make sure that whatever is written conveys precisely what is intended.

3. Be accurate. Always verify names, dates, monetary amounts, quotes, etc. Even a very valid position or statement is easily weakened if it can be demonstrated to be based on false or inaccurate information.

4. Write simply and clearly. Most readers truly appreciate economy and directness of language much more than elegance of style or use of jargon. Because of this, one's efforts are much more likely to be read if they are expressed concisely and straightforwardly.

5. Plunge fearlessly into a writing task. Once something is on paper, it can and should be revised several times. When time permits, the draft should be submitted to others for suggestions, which can then be incorporated into the final manuscript. Initial production, however, is obviously essential and should not be needlessly delayed because of hesitancy to make the attempt.

6. Remember to keep in mind the purpose and the expected readership of whatever is written. The style, format, and content are dependent on these factors, since any piece will be effective only to the extent that it accomplishes its purposes by reaching and affecting its readership.

A final reminder: Writing improves only through practice. The worker who awaits a magical transformation into a talented and prolific author will inevitably be disappointed. For some people, writing will never be enjoyable or easy; for most of us, however, it is a necessity. Most practitioners can develop the capability to write carefully, appropriately, clearly, and directly—and these simple skills, as we have seen, are crucial for increasing the effectiveness of written communication.

32. Work Guides

National Health Council, National Assembly of National Voluntary Health and Social Welfare Organizations, United Way of America

PREPARING FINANCIAL STATEMENTS

THE OPERATING STATEMENTS

Contributors and others concerned with the financial needs and management of charitable organizations are interested primarily in the support an agency receives from different sources and what it does with it—i.e., the expenses of operating the agency's service programs and other activities. The operating statement formats developed for uniform financial reporting by voluntary health and welfare organizations are the first two exhibits given below: Exhibit A, Statement of Support, Revenue, and Expenses and Changes in Fund Balances and Exhibit B, Statement of Functional Expenses. The statements are illustrative, . . . and it is not expected that all agencies will require the same number of classifications, since operations differ from agency to agency.

A brief review of these statements indicates that they differ from formats of operating statements in general use by

commercial organizations. This [article] will examine, primarily for the benefit of the voluntary agencies that are called upon to prepare them, the format of each of the exhibits and the reasons behind it.

Many organizations also prepare special reports for purposes other than public reporting. A prime example is the special project report, which organizations submit to funding agencies (government agencies, foundations, etc.) to account for funds received for particular programs.

These reports vary considerably in format and content, depending on the funding agency's requirements, from a simple listing of support and/or revenue and expenses to detailed printed prescribed forms such as specified by government agencies.

In some instances, a funding agency may require an organization to furnish a special report pursuant to specified accounting procedures that may be at variance with generally accepted accounting principles. For example, a funding agency may require that the special report be prepared on a cash basis.

Conceivably, the costs of a special project could be the same as those of an existing function. In such an event, the development of the costs of the project is accomplished through the regular functionalizing process without having to develop them specifically. If this is not the case, it may be necessary to sort the costs individually by analyzing expense accounts. It is preferable, however, unless the project's activity is too limited to justify it, to install a separate coding procedure to direct the flow of costs routinely from the point of original entry in the books to expense accounts that separate the particular special project costs from those of other activities. This facilitates the preparation of the special project report.

Exhibit A, Statement of Support, Revenue, and Expenses and Changes in Fund Balances

As indicated by its title, Exhibit A is simply an *all-inclusive, multi-column statement*. Reflected in the first part are public support, revenue, expenses and results of operations for each of four Fund groups: the Current Unrestricted Fund, Current Restricted Fund, Land, Building and Equipment Fund, and Endowment Fund. The second part comprises Other Changes in Fund Balances for each of these Funds, i.e., interfund transfers and any other direct increases or decreases of the Fund balances during the year, Fund balances at the beginning of the year, and at an end of the year the Fund balance for each Fund. Agencies are required to report all their public support, revenue, expenses and other changes in Fund balances applicable to the year of the report in this statement. Each of the major sections of Exhibit A is examined below.

Public Support Section. This section is divided into two parts: public support received directly and public support received indirectly. Each is defined later. The term "public support"—comprising contributions of various kinds, special events, legacies and bequests, amounts received from federated and nonfederated fund-raising campaigns, etc.—represents charitable *giving* by the public in support of a voluntary agency. By contrast, the items grouped under other revenue comprise amounts *earned* by an agency through dues, fees, sales, investments and other income-producing activities. The fees and grants from governmental agencies classification groups together support and revenue from only one source: governmental agencies.

Cash donations and pledges from the public usually constitute the major source of public support for voluntary health and welfare organizations. Whether received directly as an unrestricted gift, a restricted gift for operating purposes, a restricted gift for the acquisition of fixed assets, an endowment (the income from which provides operating revenue), or indirectly received through an agency which provides fund-raising services for participating organizations, support and capital additions are essential to the continuity of the organization.

While most support is generally in the form of cash, there are instances where other means of making a contribution are used. Thus, ... contributions may take the form of donated services, property, equipment and materials, which can be included in support if certain criteria are met. These forms of gifts, when properly valued, represent the equivalent of cash in reporting support.

However, if donations (including pledges) received during the year are specified by the donor for use in future periods, these amounts should be recorded as deferred credits in the balance sheet of the appropriate Fund and recorded as public support only in the year in which they may be used. In the absence of clear evidençe as to a specified year, donations and pledges should be recorded as public support in the year made.

Public Support Received Directly. This subdivision of support received from the public is to be used to report all support received by an agency as a result of its own efforts—i.e., not through another organization.

Public Support Received Indirectly. The reason for the segregation of public support received indirectly, as shown in Exhibit A, is to be found in many readers' concern that the operating statements of a voluntary agency relate fund-raising efforts to funds raised. It is difficult, and in some instances impossible, for an agency to ascertain and report fund-raising expenses associated with public support received indirectly through other organizations. Segregation of indirect support as shown in Exhibit A accomplishes two objectives:

1. The reader is placed on notice by both the grouping and by the notes or parenthetic references to the associated fund-raising expenses that Exhibit A does not include, in the fund-raising expenses shown under supporting services, *all* the fund-raising expenses incurred in obtaining the public support reported in the exhibit.
2. It points up separately the public support received directly by an agency through its own efforts alone or under its direct supervision.

Fees and Grants from Governmental Agencies Section. The increasing number of Federal and other governmental agencies that grant funds to health and welfare organizations to carry out programs for which the agencies are responsible, or pay them fees for services rendered, makes it desirable to report this source of funding as a separate classification. The funds received may be support and/or revenue, depending on the basis for payment by the governmental agency.

Revenue. The revenue caption does not appear on Exhibit A because of the way the statement is structured. The illustrated format shows support under the public support caption. The fees and grants from governmental agencies caption includes both support and revenue. Since revenue is included in fees and grants from governmental agencies, it follows that additional revenue would have to be classified under the other revenue caption. Organizations that do not receive fees and grants from governmental agencies, but do receive revenue, would use the Revenue caption instead of Other Revenue.

Other Revenue Section. "Revenue" is a concept that people in all walks of life use and in a general way understand, with normally no necessity to be very precise about its meanings. Standardization of accounting and financial reporting by voluntary health and welfare agencies clearly requires that the concept be applied with some precision. Revenue represents amounts earned and covers various forms.

The other revenue caption covers three types:

1. Gross revenue (without deduction of any costs or expenses) from *service* activities—e.g., dues and fees for services.
2. Revenue from *sales* activities (that include no direct personal services to individual patients and clients), or from sales of publications and materials to affiliated organizations and others. In some cases, it may be appropriate to report such revenues net of direct costs

(such as printing and mailing costs for publications), which should be disclosed parenthetically.

3. Investment income, gains and losses on investment transactions and other non-service and nonsales related revenue.

Exhibit A was designed to report revenue from program services as Other Revenue and costs of these services as program expenses.

Support and Revenue to be Excluded from Exhibit A. There are types of revenue that are *not* to be reported as either public support or other revenue; included are the "in-and-out" receipts that an agency is to account for as custodian funds and the portion of the proceeds of sales of investments or other assets that corresponds to their costs or other value. . . .

Expense Section. The expense section was designed to include all of an agency's expenses. First are the amounts spent by an agency in providing the services for which it has been organized and exists—the expenses of *program services.* The second classification contains the expenses an agency incurs to provide the administrative and fund-raising services that support and make possible its service programs—i.e., the expenses of its *supporting services.* Purchases of securities or other assets for investment or of fixed assets for agency use are to be excluded from Exhibit A expenses as they are merely changes in the form of assets, not expenses.

A third expense classification covers payments to affiliated organizations for unspecified purposes—e.g., those by local organizations to state/national affiliates. These payments will normally be used by the affiliate for program services, management and general and fund-raising expenses, but it is generally not proper for the paying affiliate to make an allocation of such payments to specific expense captions.

The format of the expense section of Exhibit A was developed to present expenses information as simply and concisely as possible. Accordingly, it shows the total expenses of individual program and supporting service functions; it is, in a sense, a *functional expense* report. Further, it shows the extent the Funds incurred functional expenses. Thus, typically, most of the functional expenses represent costs financed by the Current Unrestricted Fund and are therefore reported in that Fund column. To a lesser extent, expenses appear in the column for the Current Restricted Fund. In each situation, expenses comprise costs other than depreciation of building and equipment. The revised *Standards* requires that depreciation on fixed assets held for use be reported entirely in the Land, Building and Equipment Fund, since it represents a cost applicable to the use of fixed assets.

By way of explanation, Exhibit A, Statement of Support, Revenue, and Expenses and Changes in Fund Balances, derives its functional expenses from Exhibit B, the Statement of Functional Expenses. Thus, the total expenses of Exhibit B, $438,200, are reflected in the totals on Exhibit A of program services, $315,400, and supporting services, $122,800. These amounts, added together on Exhibit A with payments to national organizations, $282,400, make up the final total of expenses of $720,600.

The total of Exhibit B's program services, $315,400, are allocated on Exhibit A to the Current Unrestricted Fund, $297,-600; the Current Restricted Fund, $15,500; and the Land, Building and Equipment Fund, $2,300. Supporting services, $122,800, are allocated to Current Unrestricted Fund, $120,900, and the Land, Building and Equipment Fund,

$1,900. It is of note that depreciation, $3,400 (Exhibit B), is allocated entirely, as mentioned earlier, to the Land, Building and Equipment Fund on Exhibit A. The figure, $4,200, shown in the Fund includes this depreciation, $3,400, and an additional $800 representing the cost of raising $7,200 in contributions to building fund appearing in the support section of Exhibit A.

Many contributors are also interested in the objects of an agency's expenses—how much it spent for salaries, for rent, for staff traveling, etc. In reporting to the public, voluntary agencies should therefore also provide a statement showing the composition of their functional expenses totals according to the immediate objects of the expenses. Exhibit B, Statement of Functional Expenses, has been designed for this purpose and is discussed in the last part of this chapter.

Other Changes in Fund Balances Section. This section provides for the reporting of changes affecting Fund balances other than public support, fees and grants from governmental agencies, other revenue, and expenses. There are only a few types of transactions that can be properly reported here. Probably the most common is the transfer from the Current Unrestricted Fund to the Land, Building and Equipment Fund of unrestricted resources that have been used to purchase fixed assets for agency operations. Because resources of a Fund other than the Land, Building and Equipment Fund were used, it is necessary to transfer an amount equal to these resources—i.e., unrestricted—to the Land, Building and Equipment Fund from the Current Unrestricted Fund.

A second type of transfer that might properly be shown in this section would be the transfer to the Current Unrestricted Fund of part or all of the realized gains on endowment funds. Transfers of these gains from the Endowment Fund to the Current Unrestricted Fund must be shown in other changes in Fund balances.

A third type of transfer to be reported in other changes in Fund balances is the transfer that needs to be made from the Endowment Fund to the appropriate Fund —e.g., Current Unrestricted Fund—when the restrictions on the particular endowment lapse and the related investment assets are released.

A fourth type of change in the Fund balance is the return to the donor of part or all of a restricted grant. This occurs when a grant is made, and either the donor requests a refund (an unlikely event), or an unexpended balance remains after all the conditions of the grant are met and a refund is required.

Fund Balances, End of Year Line. This is the final line of Exhibit A, reflecting the amounts on hand at the end of the year in the four Fund balances, after giving effect to public support, fees and grants from governmental agencies, other revenue, expenses, other changes in Fund balances and to the four respective Fund balances of the beginning of the year.

Expanding the Detail of Exhibit A. Uniformity in financial reporting to the public by voluntary health and welfare agencies clearly requires that their financial statements be uniform in format as well as content. To the extent that they are needed by a given agency, the account classification shown in Exhibit A and the order of presentation should be adhered to. Explanatory material provided in parenthetic notes in Exhibit A and in the other financial statements, as well as in Notes to Financial Statements must be adapted, of course, to the requirements of particular agencies. Some agencies may want to expand particular items of public support, other revenue, and expenses. For instance, fees and grants from governmental agencies might be expanded as follows:

Fees and grants from governmental agencies:
 Fees for services:
  City and county agencies .... $XXX
  State agencies XXX

  Total fees XXX
 Grant for child care cost study XXX

  Total fees and grants from
   governmental agencies .... $XXX

As long as the proper title and corresponding total of the expanded classification are shown, amplification of the exhibit is quite acceptable.

Exhibit B, Statement of Functional Expenses

Exhibit B has been designed to help those reading the financial statements of a voluntary agency obtain a general understanding of the kinds of expenses included in each *functional expense category* shown in Exhibit A. Exhibit B shows, in separate columns, how the total expenses of each function were built up from expenses for specific objects—e.g., salaries, materials, telephone and telegraph, etc. The functional expense categories for program services will vary from one organization to another, depending upon the type of services rendered. For some organizations, a single program service category may be adequate to indicate the services provided.

The number of *object expense classifications* has been purposely limited. Exhibit B is designed to present the major types of expenses included in each functional category, while avoiding burdensome detail. The detail shown in the statement will vary from one organization to another. The statement should, however, contain sufficient detail to enable the reader to gain a general understanding of the nature of the costs of carrying out the organization's activities. The level of detail shown in Exhibit B would generally provide this understanding.

. . . Compilation of functional expense totals acceptable for reporting to the public will require that agencies apply rational methods of functional allocation to individual types of expenses and, in some instances, to individual expenses. Exhibit B requires that all costs related to building occupancy be included in occupancy, all costs related to travel in travel, etc.

Object expense grouping requires that the occasional expenses that may fall into two or more object expense classifications be coded, at the time they are first recorded, to show the object classifications in which they should be included. Thus, for example, premiums entered in an insurance column in an agency's cash disbursement journal might be coded numerically, as entered, to indicate whether they were for *employee* health insurance, for fire insurance on the agency's *buildings* or for *travel* insurance.

Included in Exhibit B at the bottom of the statement, below the total of all other expenses, is depreciation of buildings and equipment. Depreciation is distributed to functions by methods of allocation. . . .

ILLUSTRATIVE FINANCIAL STATEMENTS

The revised *Standards* provides uniform accounting and financial reporting procedures sufficiently detailed and extensive to meet the reporting needs, at one extreme, of small local agencies and, at the other, of multi-million-dollar, national associations. The preceding chapters have necessarily attempted to treat the wide variations in sources of support and revenue and types of Funds and balance sheet accounts of the large voluntary health and welfare organizations. Illustrative forms of financial statements for public reporting reflecting these accounting standards are presented in the following pages. They represent a single set of financial statements of a medium-sized. affiliated voluntary organization. In the preparation of combined financial statements for all affiliated entities of an organization, whether at the state or national level, transactions between the entities would be eliminated. Accordingly, the captions in Exhibits A and B regarding sharing of contributions, sales of materials and services, etc. would not appear in combined financial statements.

The public support and revenue classification of Exhibit A illustrates more accounts than an agency is likely to need. All organizations—of whatever size, whether at the local, state or national level, and whether affiliated or fully independent—may present statements simplified to meet their own requirements by the omission of those items not applicable to their operations. On the other hand, the accounts in other revenue, expenses and other classifications may prove inadequate for some large and complex organizations. As previously suggested, organizations in designing their financial statements may choose to supplement or expand categories shown in the illustrated statements to suit their needs. At the same time, they should conform this supplementation and expansion with the classifications and categories of the illustrated statements.

Regardless of its size or the simplicity of its financial structure, every agency seeking to conform its annual financial reports to the standards presented here should include, in one report, at least the three forms of statements illustrated:
1. Statement of Support, Revenue, and Expenses and Changes in Fund Balances,

2. Statement of Functional Expenses, and
3. Balance Sheet.
Notes to Financial Statements [follow these examples.]

The illustrated forms of these first two statements, Exhibits A and B, are columnar. An explanation of the transposition of expenses from Exhibit B to Exhibit A appears in the Expense Section discussion of [The Operating Statement above].

As to the balance sheet, two formats are provided, Exhibit C, the conventional style of separate balance sheets for each fund and as an alternative, Exhibit D, the columnar format, in view of its use by government agencies and many nonprofit organizations.

Obviously, expenses appearing on Exhibit A, in particular program services and supporting services, are derived from Exhibit B. In this regard, an explanation on the transposition of these expenses, including depreciation, from Exhibit B to Exhibit A is provided in [the discussion of The Operating Statement].

A Statement of Changes in Financial Position, as discussed in the Accounting Principles Board Opinion No. 19, is not generally required, since the information normally presented in such a statement is readily available in the Statement of Support, Revenue, and Expenses and Changes in Fund Balances.

Agencies should include notes to their financial statements that provide any additional information needed for fair presentation, such as significant accounting policies, mortgage agreements, pension plans, contingent liabilities, etc. In every case, the standard of public financial reporting to follow is to report all significant facts necessary to make an organization's financial statements fully informative and not misleading. It is thus considered desirable (and in many states is required) that, to fulfill its obligation to the contributing public, the accounts of a voluntary health or welfare organization be audited annually, in accordance with generally accepted auditing standards, by independent public accountants.

Voluntary agencies should include in their published financial statements separate columns showing comparative totals of the preceding year. Their repetition in an agency's current statements may be expected to improve a reader's confidence in the report and his grasp of its significance.

It should be noted that the amounts shown in the accompanying statements have been included *for illustrative purposes only.* No attempt has been made to conform them to relationships exhibited by financial data of any group of voluntary agencies or to suggest particular relationships. Modifications to the illustrated financial statements should be made to fit the facts and circumstances of each specific organization.

EXHIBIT A
Voluntary Health and Welfare Service
State Affiliate, Inc.

Statement of Support, Revenue, and Expenses and Changes in Fund Balances
Year ended December 31, 19X2, with Comparative Totals for 19X1

	19X2					
	Current Funds		Land, Building and Equipment Fund	Endowment Fund	Total All Funds	
	Unrestricted	Restricted			19X2	19X1
Public support and revenue:						
Public support—						
Received directly—						
Contributions (net of estimated uncollectible pledges of $19,500 in 19X2 and $15,000 in 19X1)	$658,900	$16,200	$ —	$ 200	$675,300	$709,800
Contributions to building fund	—	—	7,200	—	7,200	15,000
Special events (net of direct benefit costs of $18,000 in 19X2 and $16,300 in 19X1)	10,400	—	—	—	10,400	9,200
Legacies and bequests	9,200	—	—	400	9,600	12,000
Total received directly	$678,500	$16,200	$ 7,200	$ 600	$702,500	$746,000
Received indirectly—						
Collected through local member units	$ 1,000	$ —	$ —	$ —	$ 1,000	$ 1,000
Contributed by associated organizations (net of their related fund-raising expenses estimated at $500 in 19X2 and $150 in 19X1)	2,000	—	—	—	2,000	6,000
Allocated by federated fund-raising organizations (net of their related fund-raising expenses estimated at $2,300 in 19X2 and $2,200 in 19X1)	23,500	—	—	—	23,500	22,000
Allocated by unassociated and nonfederated fund-raising organizations (net of fund-raising costs)	1,000	—	—	—	1,000	1,000
Total received indirectly	$ 27,500	$ —	$ —	$ —	$ 27,500	$ 30,000
Total support from the public	$706,000	$ 16,200	$ 7,200	$ 600	$730,000	$776,000

	19X2					
	Current Funds		Land, Building and Equipment Fund	Endowment Fund	Total All Funds	
	Unrestricted	Restricted			19X2	19X1
Fees and grants from governmental agencies	$ —	$ 300	$ —	$ —	$ 300	$ 300
Other revenue—						
Membership dues—individuals	$ 500	$ —	$ —	$ —	$ 500	$ 400
Assessments and dues—local member units ....:..	1,100	—	—	—	1,100	700
Program service fees and net incidental revenue of $80	1,000	—	—	—	1,000	800
Sales of materials and services to local member units (net of direct expenses of $1,000 in 19X2 and $700 in 19X1)	300	—	—	—	300	200
Sales to public (net of direct expenses of $800 in 19X2 and $700 in 19X1) ...	100	—	—	—	100	100
Investment income	9,800	700	—	—	10,500	9,100
Gains on investment transactions	20,000	—	—	2,500	22,500	27,500
Miscellaneous revenue	2,800	—	—	—	2,800	3,600
Total other revenue	$ 35,600	$ 700	$ —	$ 2,500	$ 38,800	$ 42,400
Total public support and revenue	$741,600	$ 17,200	$ 7,200	$ 3,100	$769,100	$818,700
Expenses:						
Program services—						
Program A	$125,700	$ 15,500	$ 200	$ —	$141,400	$136,500
Program B	53,900	—	500	—	54,400	48,500
Program C	61,200	—	600	—	61,800	51,600
Program D	56,800	—	1,000	—	57,800	48,600
Total program services	$297,600	$ 15,500	$ 2,300	$ —	$315,400	$285,200
Supporting services—						
Management and general	$ 56,700	$ —	$ 700	$ —	$ 57,400	$ 63,800
Fund raising	64,200	—	1,200	—	65,400	54,600
Total supporting services	$120,900	$ —	$ 1,900	$ —	$122,800	$118,400
Payments to national organization (Note 9)	$282,400	$ —	$ —	$ —	$282,400	$310,400
Total expenses	$700,900	$ 15,500	$ 4,200	$ —	$720,600	$714,000
Excess of public support and revenue over expenses	$ 40,700	$ 1,700	$ 3,000	$ 3,100		
Other changes in fund balances:						
Property and equipment acquisitions from unrestricted funds.............................	(1,700)	—	1,700	—		
Transfer of realized endowment fund appreciation (Note 2)............................	10,000	—	—	(10,000)		
Returned to donor	—	(800)	—	—		
Fund balances, beginning of year	536,100	12,300	64,900	201,700		
Fund balances, end of year	$585,100	$ 13,200	$ 69,600	$ 194,800		

EXHIBIT B
Voluntary Health and Welfare Service
State Affiliate, Inc.
Statement of Functional Expenses
Year ended December 31, 19X2 with Comparative Totals for 19X1

						Supporting Services			Total Program and Supporting Services Expenses	
	Program Services					Management and General	Fund Raising	Total		
	Program A	Program B	Program C	Program D	Total				19X2	19X1
Salaries .... $	4,500	$29,100	$25,100	$26,900	$85,600	$33,100	$36,800	$69,900	$155,500	$143,300
Employee benefits	400	1,400	1,400	1,400	4,600	2,200	1,500	3,700	8,300	7,500
Payroll taxes, etc.	200	1,600	1,300	1,400	4,500	1,800	1,800	3,600	8,100	7,500
Total salaries and related expenses .... $	5,100	$32,100	$27,800	$29,700	$94,700	$37,100	$40,100	$77,200	$171,900	$158,300
Professional fees	100	1,000	300	800	2,200	2,600	800	3,400	5,600	5,300
Supplies ....,	200	1,300	1,300	1,300	4,100	1,800	1,700	3,500	7,600	7,100
Telephone	200	1,300	1,000	1,100	3,600	1,500	2,300	3,800	7,400	6,800
Postage and shipping	200	1,700	1,300	900	4,100	1,300	3,000	4,300	8,400	8,000
Occupancy	250	1,300	1,100	1,250	3,900	1,500	1,350	2,850	6,750	6,300
Rental and maintenance of equipment	250	1,300	1,100	1,250	3,900	1,500	1,350	2,850	6,750	6,300
Printing and publications	100	2,400	1,400	400	4,300	300	1,600	1,900	6,200	5,800
Travel	300	2,200	2,000	2,200	6,700	2,300	3,000	5,300	12,000	11,300
Conferences, conventions & meetings	800	1,900	7,100	2,000	11,800	5,200	7,700	12,900	24,700	15,600
Specific assistance to individuals ....,	400	5,600	4,300	1,100	11,400	—	—	—	11,400	18,400
Membership dues	—	500	—	—	500	—	—	—	500	500
Awards and grants— To National Headquarters	10,000	—	—	—	10,000	—	—	—	10,000	—
To individuals and other organizations	123,200	900	11,900	14,400	150,400	—	—	—	150,400	144,300
Miscellaneous	100	400	600	400	1,500	1,600	2,100	3,700	5,200	6,400
Total before depreciation ...	$141,200	$53,900	$61,200	$56,800	$313,100	$56,700	$65,000	$121,700	$434,800	$400,400
Depreciation of buildings and equipment	200	500	600	1,000	2,300	700	400	1,100	3,400	3,200
Total functional expenses	$141,400	$54,400	$61,800	$57,800	$315,400	$57,400	$65,400	$122,800	$438,200	$403,600

See accompanying notes to financial statements.

EXHIBIT C
Voluntary Health And Welfare Service
State Affiliate, Inc.
Balance Sheets
December 31, 19X2 and 19X1

Assets	19X2	19X1	Liabilities and Fund Balances	19X2	19X1

CURRENT FUNDS

Unrestricted

Assets	19X2	19X1	Liabilities and Fund Balances	19X2	19X1
Cash	$220,700	$242,500	Accounts payable and accrued expenses	$14,800	$13,900
Short-term investments—at cost, which is approximately market value	100,000	100,000	Research grants (Note 3)	59,600	61,600
			Support and revenue designated for future periods	24,500	21,900
Accounts receivable, less allowance for uncollectibles of $1,000 and $500	15,000	9,000	Total liabilities and deferred revenues	$98,900	$97,400
Pledges receivable, less allowance for uncollectibles of $10,500 and $9,200	47,500	36,300	Fund balances: Designated by the governing board for —		
Materials for sale or use, at cost or market, whichever is lower	7,000	6,100	Long-term investments	$280,000	$230,000
			Purchases of new equipment	10,000	—
Prepaid expenses and deferred charges	13,800	9,600	Research purposes (Note 3)	115,200	174,800
Board-designated long-term investments (Note 2)	280,000	230,000	Undesignated, available for general activities	179,900	131,300
			Total Fund balances	$585,100	$536,100
	$684,000	$633,500		$684,000	$633,500

Restricted

Assets	19X2	19X1	Liabilities and Fund Balances	19X2	19X1
Cash	$ 300	$ 500	Fund balances:		
Short-term investments—at cost, which is approximately market value	7,100	7,200	Designated by donors for — Professional education	$ 8,400	$ —
Grants receivable	5,800	4,600	Research grants	4,800	12,300
	$ 13,200	$ 12,300		$13,200	$12,300

LAND, BUILDING AND EQUIPMENT FUND

Assets	19X2	19X1	Liabilities and Fund Balances	19X2	19X1
Cash	$ 300	$ 200	6% mortgage payable, due 19—	$ 3,200	$ 3,600
Short-term investments—at cost, which is approximately market value	17,700	14,500	Fund balances — Expended	$ 48,400	$ 47,700
Pledges receivable, less allowance for uncollectibles of $750 and $500	3,200	2,500	Unexpended—restricted (Note 4)	21,200	17,200
Land, buildings and equipment, at cost, less accumulated depreciation of $29,600 and $26,200 (Note 5)	51,600	51,300	Total Fund balances	$ 69,600	$ 64,900
	$ 72,800	$ 68,500		$ 72,800	$ 68,500

ENDOWMENT FUND

Assets	19X2	19X1	Liabilities and Fund Balances	19X2	19X1
Cash	$ 400	$ 1,000	Fund balance	$194,800	$201,700
Investments (Note 2)	194,400	200,700			
	$194,800	$201,700		$194,800	$201,700

See accompanying notes to financial statements.

EXHIBIT D (an alternate format to Exhibit C)
Voluntary Health And Welfare Service,
State Affiliate, Inc.
Balance Sheet
December 31, 19X2

	Current Funds		Land, Building and Equip-ment Fund	Endow-ment Fund	Total All Funds	
	Unre-stricted	Re-stricted			19X2	19X1
ASSETS						
Cash	$220,700	$ 300	$ 300	$ 400	$221,700	
Short-term investments—at cost, which is approximately market value	100,000	7,100	17,700	—	124,800	
Accounts receivable, less allowance for uncollectibles of $1,000	15,000	—	—	—	15,000	
Pledges receivable, less allowance for uncollectibles of $10,500 Unrestricted Fund and $750 Land, Building and Equipment Fund	47,500	—	3,200	—	50,700	
Grants receivable	—	5,800	—	—	5,800	
Materials for sale or use—at cost or market, whichever is lower	7,000	—	—	—	7,000	
Prepaid expenses and deferred charges	13,800	—	—	—	13,800	
Board-designated long-term investments (Note 2)	280,00	—	—	—	280,000	
Endowment Fund investments (Note 2)	—	—	—	194,400	194,400	
Land, buildings and equipment—at cost, less accumulated depreciation of $29,600 (Note 5)	—	—	51,600	—	51,600	
Total assets	$684,000	$ 13,200	$ 72,800	$194,800	$964,800	
LIABILITIES AND FUND BALANCES						
Liabilities:						
Accounts payable and accrued expenses	$14,800	$ —	$ —	$ —	$14,800	
Research grants (Note 3)	59,600	—	—	—	59,600	
Support and revenue designated for future periods	24,500	—	—	—	24,500	
6% mortgage payable, due 19—	—	—	3,200	—	3,200	
Total liabilities and deferred revenues	98,900	—	3,200	—	102,100	
Fund balances:						
Current unrestricted, designated by the governing board for—						
Long-term investments	280,000	—	—	—	280,000	
Purchases of new equipment	10,000	—	—	—	10,000	
Research purposes (Note 3)	115,200	—	—	—	115,200	
Current unrestricted, available for general activities	179,900	—	—	—	179,900	
Current restricted, designated by donors for—						
Professional education	—	8,400	—	—	8,400	
Research grants	—	4,800	—	—	4,800	
Land, Building and Equipment Fund—						
Expended	—	—	48,400	—	48,400	
Unexpended—restricted (Note 4)	—	—	21,200	—	21,200	
Endowment Fund	—	—	—	194,800	194,800	
Total fund balances	585,100	13,200	69,600	194,800	862,700	
Total liabilities and fund balances	$684,000	$13,200	$72,800	$194,800	$964,800	

For comparison purposes, balance sheet of December 31, 19X1 is attached.

See accompanying notes to financial statements.

Voluntary Health and Welfare Service, State
Affiliate, Inc.
Notes to Financial Statements
December 31, 19X2

1. *Summary of Significant Accounting Policies*
—The Service follows the practice of capitalizing all expenditures for land, buildings and equipment in excess of $150; the fair value of donated fixed assets is similarly capitalized. Depreciation is provided over the estimated useful lives of the assets. Investments are stated at cost. All contributions are considered available for unrestricted use, unless specifically restricted by the donor. Pledges are recorded in the balance sheet as received, and allowances are provided for amounts estimated as uncollectible. Policies concerning donated material and services are described in Note 6.

2. *Investments*—All investments are in marketable common stocks and bonds. Market values and unrealized appreciation (depreciation) at December 31, 19X2 and 19X1, are summarized as follows:

	December 31, 19X2		December 31, 19X1	
	Quoted Market Value	Un-realized Apprecia-tion	Quoted Market Value	Un-realized Apprecia-tion (Depre-ciation)
Current Unrestricted Fund, Board-designated long-term investments:				
Common stocks	$160,000	$10,000	$105,000	$(5,000)
Corporate bonds	135,000	5,000	130,000	10,000
	$295,000	$15,000	$235,000	$ 5,000
Endowment Fund:				
Common stocks	$113,000	$3,000	$114,000	$(6,000)
Corporate bonds	86,400	2,000	78,700	(2,000)
	$199,400	$5,000	$192,700	$(8,000)

Interfund transfers include $10,000 for 19X2, which represents the portion of the realized appreciation ($2,500 realized in the current year and $7,500 realized in prior years) in endowment funds that (under the laws of a state) were designated by the governing board for unrestricted operations. At December 31, 19X2, $20,000 of accumulated realized appreciation was available in endowment funds, which the governing board may, if it deems prudent, also transfer to the Current Unrestricted Fund.

3. *Research Grants*—The Service's awards for research grants-in-aid generally cover a period of one to three years, subject to annual renewals at the option of the governing board. At December 31, 19X1, $174,800 had been designated by the board for research grants. Of this figure, $59,600 was awarded at December 31, 19X2, leaving $115,200 as designated on that date.

4. *Proposed Research Center*—The XYZ Foundation has contributed $5,000 to the Service with the stipulations that it be used for the construction of a research center and that construction of the facilities begin within four years. The Service is considering the construction of a research center, the cost of which would approximate $200,000. If the governing board approves the construction of these facilities, it is contemplated that its cost would be financed by a special fund drive.

5. *Land, Building and Equipment and Depreciation*—Depreciation of buildings and equipment is provided on a straight-line basis over the estimated useful lives of the assets (2% per year for buildings, 5% for

medical research equipment and office furniture and equipment, and 30% for automobile). At December 31, 19X2 and 19X1, the costs for such assets were:

	19X2	19X1
Land	$ 7,600	$ 7,600
Buildings	32,400	32,400
Medical research equipment	33,600	31,200
Office furniture and equipment	4,600	3,300
Automobile	3,000	3,000
Total	$81,200	$77,500
Less accumulated depreciation	29,600	26,200
	$51,600	$51,300

6. *Donated Materials and Services*—Donated materials and equipment are reflected as contributions in the accompanying statements at their estimated values at date of receipt. No amounts have been reflected in the statements for donated services, since no objective basis is available to measure the value of such services. Nevertheless, a substantial number of volunteers have donated significant amounts of their time in the organization's program services and its fundraising campaigns.

7. *Pension Plans*—The organization has a noncontributory plan covering substantially all of its employees. Pension expenses for the current year and the prior year were $——— and $———, respectively, which includes amortization of prior service cost over ——— ——— year period. At December 31, 19X2, the actuarially computed value of the vested benefits in the plan exceeded the Fund balance of the plan by approximately $——— —. The Service's policy is to fund pension cost accrued.

8. *Leased Facilities*— At December 31, 19X2, the organization used five buildings for its community service programs. Three are leased on a year-to-year basis at a total annual cost of approximately $2,000. The remaining two buildings are leased for the next twenty years at a total annual rental of $3,000. The long-term lease commitment on these is $60,000.

9. *Sharing of Public Support*—In accordance with the affiliation agreement with National, up to 40% of total unrestricted support from the public may be shared with National as determined by the affiliate's Board of Directors. Once designated, such amounts are used as directed by the National Board of Directors for National programs of research, education and community services and for supporting, management and general, and fund-raising expenses.

33.   Work Guides   **Richard A. Kaplowitz**   **STEPS IN THE SEARCH PROCESS: FINDING TOP STAFF**

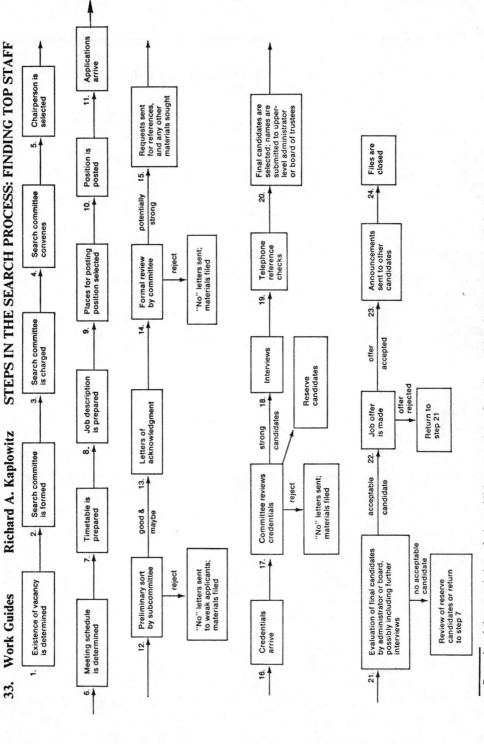

Reproduced by permission of the publisher, American Council on Education, Washington, D.C. From Richard A. Kaplowitz, *Selecting Academic Administrators: The Search Committee,* © 1973, pp. 14—15.

405

34. Work Guides

John D. Ingalls

A CHECKLIST OF ITEMS TO CONSIDER IN ARRANGING A MEETING

Physical Surroundings	Human and Interpersonal Relations	Organizational
Space	Welcoming	Policy
Lighting	Comfort setting	Structure
Acoustics/Outside noise	Informality	Clientele
Decor	Warm-up exercise	Policy and structure committee
Temperature	Democratic leadership	Meeting announcements
Ventilation	Interpersonal relations	Informational literature
Seating: Comfort/ Position	Handling VIPs	Program theme
Seating arrangements/ Grouping/Mobility/ Rest/Change	Mutual planning	Advertising
Refreshments	Assessing needs	Poster, displays
Writing materials	Formulating objectives	Exhibits
Ash trays	Designing and implement- ing activities	Budget and finance
Rest rooms	Evaluating	Publish agenda and closing time
Audiovisual aids	Closing exercise	Frequency of scheduled meetings
Coat racks	Close on time (option to stay)	
Parking		
Traffic directions		
Name tags or cards		
Records/Addresses, etc.		

From *Trainers Guide to Andragogy*, by John D. Ingalls, U.S. Department of Health, Education and Welfare, May 1973.

League of Women Voters of the United States

SIMPLIFIED PARLIAMENTARY PROCEDURE

I. ORDER OF BUSINESS

1. The meeting is "called to order" by the president.
2. The minutes of the preceding meeting are read by the secretary.
   a. May be approved as read.
   b. May be approved with additions or corrections.
3. Monthly statement of treasurer is "Received as read and filed for audit." (Chair so states.)
4. Reports of standing committees are called for by the president.
5. Reports of special committees are called for by the president.
6. Unfinished business is next in order at the call of the chair or of the meeting.
7. New business.
8. The program:—The program is part of the meeting; the president "presides" throughout, but the program chairman makes report.
9. Adjournment.

II. DUTIES OF A PRESIDENT

1. To preside at all meetings.
2. Keep calm at all times.
3. Talk no more than necessary while presiding.
4. Have agenda for meeting before him and proceed in a businesslike manner.
5. Have a working knowledge of parliamentary law and a thorough understanding of the constitution and by-laws of the organization.
6. Keep a list of committees on table while presiding.
7. Refrain from entering the debate of questions before the assembly. If it is essential that this be done, the vice-president should be placed in the chair. A president is not permitted to resume the chair until after the vote has been taken on the question under discussion.
8. Extend every courtesy to the opponents of a motion, even though the motion is one that the presiding officer favors.
9. Always appear at the rostrum a few minutes before the time the meeting is to be called to order. When the time arrives, note whether a quorum is present; if so, call the meeting to order, and declare "a quorum is present."

III. OTHER OFFICIALS

Vice-President

The vice-president of an organization is the one who acts in the place of the president, whenever needed. In case of resignation or death of the president, the vice-president automatically becomes the president unless the by-laws provide other methods.

In official meetings, the vice-president should preside in the *absence* of the president or whenever the president temporarily vacates the chair.

If the president should be absent for a long period, the vice-president may exercise all duties of the president except to change or modify rules made by the president.

The vice-president cannot fill vacancies where the by-laws state that such vacancies shall be filled by the president.

In case of resignation or death of the president, and the vice-president does not care to assume the office of president, the *vice-president must resign.*

The office of vice-president becomes vacant when the vice-president assumes the office of president. If there are several vice-presidents, they automatically move up to the higher office leaving the lower office vacant. This office should be filled as instructed by the by-laws or authorized parliamentary authority.

In the absence of the president, the vice-president is *not* "ex-officio" a member of any committee.

Secretary

The secretary should issue all calls or notices of meetings and should write such letters as the board of directors or executive committee may designate.

The secretary should keep a neat and careful record of all business done in the meetings, with the exact wording of every motion and whether it was lost or carried. Brief extracts from speeches, if important, may be recorded but *no comment of any kind, favorable or unfavorable, should be made.* The minutes should show the names of persons appointed to committees and it is the duty of the secretary to notify all persons nominated or elected on any committee.

The secretary should be on hand a few minutes before a meeting is called to order. He should have the minute book of the organization with him so that reference can be made to minutes of past meetings.

The secretary should always have a copy of the by-laws; standing rules; book of parliamentary procedure endorsed by the organization; list of members or clubs; a list of unfinished business, copy of which should be given the presiding officer.

Minutes

The minutes of an organization should contain a record of what *is done and not what is said.*

Minutes should contain:

1. Date, place and time of meeting.
2. Whether it is a regular or special meeting.
3. Name of person presiding.
4. Name of secretary. (In small boards, the names of those present should be recorded.)
5. All *main* motions, whether adopted or rejected.
6. The names of the persons making the motions; the name of the seconder need not be recorded.
7. Points of order and appeals, whether sustained or lost.
8. A motion which was withdrawn should not be recorded.

Treasurer

The treasurer of any organization is the custodian of its funds and receives and disburses them upon authority from the organization, the board, executive committee or the finance or budget committees. A treasurer should be bonded.

The organization should authorize the medium by which bills are paid (whether by check or by cash and by whom) and should either approve the budget or authorize the executive committee or the board of directors to do so. A chairman or an officer or member should get permission from the president or board to make an expenditure.

No treasurer should accept bills for payment, such as for postage, traveling expenses, etc., from a chairman unless receipts are enclosed.

The treasurer should make a monthly statement and a report once a year, or upon the request of board or parent body during the year. The annual report should be audited. An auditor's report should be presented following the treasurer's report. The presiding officer states to the assembly that to adopt the report of the auditor (if carried) has the effect of accepting the treasurer's report.

Committees

Committees have no authority except that which is granted by the constitution or by vote of the organization. Unless otherwise provided, the person first named or the one receiving the largest number of votes is its chairman. *A committee has no right to incur any debt or involve the organization in any way unless given full authority to do so.*

Under no consideration should one or more members of a committee go ahead with the business without action by a quorum; usually a *majority* of the committee, being present. Failure to observe these rules renders such action "the action of individuals" and subject to "censure," "suits," etc.

IV. PRINCIPAL MOTIONS

General Statement: When a motion has been made, seconded and stated by the chair, the assembly is not at liberty to consider any other business until this motion has been disposed of. If the motion is long and involved the chairman asks the mover to hand it in writing to the secretary. The mover cannot withdraw his motion after it has been stated by the chair. In general all important motions should be seconded, which may be done without rising or addressing the chair.

1. To Amend: This motion is "to change, add, or omit *words*" in the *original main motion,* and is debatable, majority vote.

   To Amend the Amendment: This is a motion to change, add, or omit *words* in the *first amendment;* debatable, majority vote.

   Method: The first vote is on changing *words* of second amendment, the *second* vote (if first vote adopts change) on first amendment *as* changed; the *third* vote is on adopting main motion as changed.

2. To Commit: When a motion becomes involved through amendments or when it is wise to investigate a question more carefully, it may be moved to commit the motion to a committee for further consideration. Debatable—Amendable—Committee must make report on such question.

3. To Lay on the Table: The object of this motion is to postpone the subject under discussion in such a way that it can be taken up at some time in the near future when a motion "to take from the table" would be in order. These motions are not debatable or amendable: majority vote.

4. To Postpone: A motion to postpone the question before the assembly to some future time is in order, except when a speaker has the floor. Debatable: majority vote.

5. To Adjourn: This motion is always in order except:

   a. When a speaker has the floor.

   b. When a vote is being taken.

   c. After it has just been voted down.

   d. When the assembly is in the midst

of some business which cannot be abruptly stopped.

Under all the above circumstances, the motion is not debatable.

When the motion is made to adjourn to a definite place and time, it is debatable.

6. To Reconsider: The motion to reconsider a motion that was carried or lost is in order if made on the *same* day or the next calendar day, but must be made by one who voted with the prevailing side. No question can be twice reconsidered. Debatable: majority vote.

Requires 2 votes: First on whether it should be reconsidered. Second on original motion after reconsideration.

7. The Previous Question: Is to close debate on the pending question. This motion may be made when debate becomes long drawn out. It is not debatable. The form is "Mr. (Madam) Chairman, I move the previous question." The chairman then asks, "Shall debate be closed and the question *now* be put?" If this be adopted by a two-thirds vote, the question before the assembly is immediately voted upon.

8. Point of Order: This motion is always in order, but can be used only to present an objection to a ruling of the chair or some method of parliamentary procedure. The form is "Mr. (Madam) Chairman, I rise to a point of order." The Chairman: "Please state your point of order." After the member has stated his objection, the chair answers:

a. "Your point of order is sustained" or

b. "Your point of order is denied."

If any member is not satisfied he may appeal from the decision of the chair. The chairman then addresses the assembly, "Shall the decision of the chair be sustained?" This is debatable and the presiding officer may discuss it without leaving the chair. Voted on like any other motion: majority or tie vote sustains the decision of chair. Requires a majority of "no" votes to reverse decision of the chair.

V. NOMINATIONS, ELECTIONS, AND TERM OF OFFICE

General Henry M. Robert, author of *Robert's Rules of Order,* says: "In the election of the officers of a society it is more usual to have the nominations made by a committee—when the committee makes its report, which consists of a ticket (a ticket is one name for each office to be filled by ballot), the chair asks, 'Are there any other nominations?'—at which time they may be made from the floor. The committee's nominations are treated just as if made by members from the floor, *no vote being taken on accepting them.*"

If nominations are made from the floor, these names are added to those submitted by the nominating committee. Neither nominations by the committee nor nominations from the floor require a second or adoption by vote, but are acted upon in the election ballot. Nominations are never seconded except as a complimentary endorsement of candidates not known to the assembly. This is rarely done except in national meetings where candidates assemble from all parts of the country.

A nominating ballot is NOT an elective ballot: (is not necessary or desirable where a nominating committee operates.)

When nominations are completed the assembly proceeds to the election, voting by the method prescribed in the constitution and by-laws. The usual method in permanent societies is by ballot, the balloting continued until the offices are filled. If a member is in good standing in the organization and receives a majority of the votes cast in the elective ballot, (or plurality if by-laws so provide), he is then declared to be legally elected to fill the office even though he has not been nominated from the floor or by the nominating committee.

A motion may be made to close nominations but this motion is not in order until the assembly has been given reasonable time to add further nominations to those already made. It is an undebatable main motion, incidental to the nominations. It may be amended as to the time of closing nominations, but have no other subsidiary motion applied to it because it deprives members of one of their rights. It requires a *two-thirds* vote. The motion to reopen nominations is undebatable and requires a *majority* vote. It may also be amended as to time, but no other subsidiary motion applies.

The chair should remind the members that the nominating committee has endeavored to present as sure a ticket as possible, but it is now their privilege to name a candidate for any or all of the offices to be filled, and that they still have the opportunity of casting a ballot, for any eligible members, whether nominated or not.

General Robert says: "Each member may vote for any eligible person whether nominated or not."

A member may withdraw his name if placed in nomination, announcing that if elected he would not be able to serve, but he cannot "withdraw in favor of another member."

Kinds of Voting—Majority vote means more than half the votes cast, ignoring blanks, and a plurality vote is the largest of two or more numbers. A plurality vote never adopts a motion or elects a member to office except by virtue of a special rule previously adopted in the constitution or by-laws. In an election a candidate has a plurality when he has a larger vote than any other candidate.

The Chair Votes—When the vote is by ballot the president writes his ballot, and casts it with the rest.

On a tie vote the motion is lost. If a majority of *one* the chair, (if a member of the assembly), may vote with the minority and make it a tie, and declare the motion "lost" *unless the vote is by ballot.*

In the event of a tie vote by ballot, balloting must continue until a candidate receives a majority. (Unless by-laws provide for plurality.)

To move "that an election be made unanimous," is a mistaken courtesy, as it forces those who did not vote for the candidate to unwillingly submit to the transferring of their vote, thus making it appeaɪ to be unanimous, when it is not:—one negative response causes such a motion to be "lost."

An election takes effect immediately following the completion of the annual business unless the by-laws specify some other date.

This does not mean that officers are tᴏ assume office *at this meeting,* for the duties of the outgoing officers are not completed for the year until after the adjournment of the annual session and all business relating to the annual meeting has been perfected.

Balloting—It is the duty of a chairman of elections to see that ballots are prepared in advance of the meeting and pencils are ready for the election. The tellers shall count the ballots. The chairman of elections reads the report, giving the numbeɪ of votes for each person, whether nominated or "written-in" on the ballot. The presiding officer then "declares" who have been elected.

A formal "Installation" may be arɪ ranged, but office does not depend on installation but on election, (or appointmenᴛ if so provided in by-laws).

VI. DECORUM

Probably the most serious defect in most meetings is the lack of reasonable decorum. Good order must be maintained if business is to be carried out. Courtesy would demand that there should be no whispering or commotion while any speaker has the floor. Do not speak too frequently. Beware of personalities. State *facts* rather than what you think or believe. Nothing so mars the dignity of a meeting as the sharp retort or angry voice.

Speak while motion is pending, not after vote has been taken or *after the meeting is over.*

36. Work Guides

The Association of Junior Leagues

HOW DOES YOUR NEWS SHEET RATE?

The News Sheet should be the organization's means of keeping members well informed and interested. How effectively does your News Sheet do this job?

A good way to check the quality of your News Sheet is to use the standards which follow for an evaluation. You may find that the rating process will bring useful suggestions for improvement.

I. COVER
   a. Does cover have name of the organization? (It should) — Yes—— No——
   b. Does cover have date of issue? (It should) — Yes—— No——
   c. Does the News Sheet look interesting enough to read right now? — Yes—— No——
   d. Does cover tell of something important—in a direct and interesting way? — Good—— Fair—— Poor——

e. Is the cover layout attractive, clear, and uncluttered? — Good—— Fair—— Poor——

II. APPEARANCE
   a. Does the News Sheet look neat, attractive, and provocative? — Good—— Fair—— Poor——
   b. Do headings and placement of stories reflect their comparative importance? — Good—— Fair—— Poor——
   c. Is the type clear and easily read? — Good—— Fair—— Poor——
   d. Are layout and/or illustrations effective? — Good—— Fair—— Poor—
   e. Do the pictures and headlines balance the copy? — Good—— Fair—— Poor——

III. CONTENT
   a. Does the News Sheet indicate the scope of the organization's activities? — Good—— Fair—— Poor——

b. Is the News Sheet aimed at the member rather than the leader? Good—— Fair—— Poor——

c. Does the News Sheet convey to the reader the people who are responsible for carrying out the program and projects? Good—— Fair—— Poor——

d. Does the News Sheet contain a schedule of activities for the coming month? Yes—— No——

e. Is there a "masthead" box on one of the inside pages giving the name and address of the Editor and News Sheet staff, and the year's dates of issue of the News Sheet? Yes—— No——

f. Is national news included? Yes—— No——

g. Is the space used to the best advantage (i.e., if the News Sheet is short, does it avoid wasting space with irrelevant matter)? Good—— Fair—— Poor——

IV. STYLE

a. Is the News Sheet lively without being "cute"? Good—— Fair—— Poor——

b. Is the style readable, direct, and to the point? Good—— Fair—— Poor——

c. Will the language appeal to the average reader? Good—— Fair—— Poor——

d. Are the headings pertinent? Good—— Fair—— Poor——

e. Does the News Sheet avoid such faults as wordiness, exhortations, scolding, generalizations? Good—— Fair—— Poor——

f. Are articles so edited as to avoid monotony? Good—— Fair—— Poor——

g. Are meetings and other organization activities made to sound attractive? Good—— Fair—— Poor——

V. TONE

a. In general, does the News Sheet give a good impression of the organization? Good—— Fair—— Poor——

b. Does it create a feeling of pride in the organization and its leadership? Good—— Fair—— Poor——

c. Does it reflect a feeling of the membership working together toward fulfillment of the organization's programs? Good—— Fair—— Poor——

d. Does the News Sheet convey to the reader the people who are responsible for carrying out the program and project? Good—— Fair—— Poor——

37. Work Guides

Milan J. Dluhy

CREATING ORGANIZATIONAL SUCCESS:
A SUBURBAN HOMEOWNER'S ASSOCIATION

I. INTRODUCTION

Voluntary organizations in communities which possess few ostensible resources but still successfully achieve their goals may serve as useful models for other kinds of organizations which seek to maximize their impact by adopting certain combinations of strategies and tactics. One type of voluntary organization which has been relatively successful over the past 20 years is the homeowner's association which is most frequently found in middle-class suburban communities. The important thing about this kind of organization is that it is purely voluntary and it possesses few resources outside of the time which its members are willing to spend on various endeavors. For example, they have no professional staff, a limited budget, few direct ties with other groups outside of their community, yet they have been quite successful in achieving their goals.

The purpose of this article will be to explore the organization, goals, strategies, and tactics of homeowner's associations in order to gain insight into what aspects of these organizations contribute to successful goal attainment. Knowledge of this sort will contribute to a broader understanding of the range of strategies and tactics available to organizations which attempt to influence the direction in which communities are moving in contemporary

urban society. A secondary purpose of this article will be to provide a descriptive account of one of the more salient political groups which has been directly responsible for shaping the suburban environments in which larger and larger numbers of people are living. As the contemporary American landscape shifts to the suburban portion of our metropolitan areas, we need to assess whether those groups that have participated in shaping this environment offer relevant examples of successful citizen involvement which can be transferred to other organizations and settings.

II. CREATING SUCCESS

Homeowner's associations are voluntary citizen groups made up largely of residential property owners. They seem to emerge in middle-class suburbs where key issues affecting individual neighborhoods arise. In this respect, these organizations are defensive in that they respond to issues or decisions being made by formal governmental authorities which residents feel will be detrimental to their interests. More specifically, homeowner's associations represent clearly defined geographic areas within a suburban community. They are oriented toward their "territory" or "turf" and seek to maintain the social character and economic viability of their neighborhoods. For example, a homeowner's association may react swiftly and effectively to any plans to rezone land surrounding their

Source: Unpublished, Milan J. Dluhy, "Creative Organizational Success: A Case Study of a Suburban Homeowner's Association."

single family residential neighborhoods. Attempts to build apartments, industry, or businesses too close to these neighborhoods are viewed as unreasonable encroachments on the vested interests of property owners. These organizations are defensive in that they fear that changes of this sort will lessen their property values or bring in certain kinds of undesirable land uses or certain people who do not share their desire for a safe, protected living environment free of traffic problems, noise, pollution, crime, etc. Additionally, new residents who do not come from the same social or economic background as the current residents or who do not possess a comparable set of values or life styles are frowned upon.

Another way of characterizing the residents of these neighborhoods is that they are protectionist in outlook. Protectionism is manifested by the desire to maintain the status quo and preserve the existing nature of the area. Homeowner's associations are developed in an effort to reflect these goals in the political arenas of suburbia. The organization's strategy is to counter all attempts by formal governmental authorities to change their placid, residential neighborhood. Therefore, the organization pays close attention to the decision-making processes in the community that might produce decisions which would alter the character of their neighborhoods. Close monitoring of these decision-making processes is the mechanism used to maximize the goals of the residents.

Given this perspective, it is important to note in a discussion of organizational strategies and tactics that homeowner's associations are not necessarily trying to promote change in the community by aggressively initiating a set of policies, programs, or decisions, but rather they are seeking to maintain the status quo through efforts aimed at *vetoing* or *nullifying* actions of governmental authorities which are perceived to be contrary to the interests of the property owners who currently reside in these areas.

While the overall strategy of homeowner's associations is that of monitoring key decision-making processes within the community, the tactics used by these groups give further insight into what creates successful organizational activity. To shed light on these tactics, reference will be made to the behavior of homeowner's associations in one suburban community. The setting is a suburban community which is located in one of the largest metropolitan areas in this country. The interesting thing is that this community has gone from a population of approximately 10,000 at the end of World War II to 100,000 in 1970. While there is some heavy industry in the community and a few scattered commercial settlements, the predominant amount of land is taken up by single family homes which are located in various subdivisions throughout the community. In terms of income and occupation, the community is solidly middle class with a white-collar labor force. In turn, its residents, by and large, are knowledgeable people who participate on a regular basis in government and a variety of voluntary organizations. Rates of turnout in elections are quite high and most public meetings are well attended. The profile of a middle-class community whose residents show an active interest in the affairs of the community is not atypical of various research which has also shown the participation rates and membership in organizations to be quite high in these kinds of communities. The expectation of substantial citizen involvement is therefore quite consistent with what might be predicted based on our knowledge of the variables which most commonly affect the levels of political and social participation.

As this community has grown over the last 20 years, an important trend in its residential development has been the building of the classical suburban subdivision developments in which a builder secures a rather large tract of land and then proceeds to build anywhere from 50 to 400 units. Custom-built homes on individual lots are almost nonexistent so that the community looks like a series of subdivisions connected by the system of roads and highways in the community. In fact, the most noticeable thing about these subdivisions is that they are relatively autonomous areas in both a physical and psychological sense. For example, residents, when asked what part of the community they come from, will say that they come from "Burning Hills," "Georgetown," or 'Maple Gardens." These names were orginally designated by the builder of the subdivision and now serve as a way of identifying neighborhoods within the community. Thus, the original subdivisions become neighborhoods whose identity persists over time.

The importance of these subdivisions is that the larger ones have developed their own Homeowner's Associations. These associations, as indicated earlier, seek to protect the nature of the subdivisions. In fact, there are currently 48 Homeowner's Associations throughout the community. Each association meets regularly, elects officers, discusses issues and takes positions, endorses political candidates, and sends representatives to public meetings. A particularly successful tactic used has been the packing of public meetings with members who object to a particular proposal which is being considered. During the public participation part of the meeting they are extremely vocal and often present petitions to the public officials. In addition, they speak as an organization which represents a substantial number of property owners. Elected officials, in particular, find vocal protest by a large number of people hard to contend with and often clearly see the consequences of taking a public position contrary to the interests of the members of the association present. Threats of retaliation at the polls is the most effective technique of persuading these officials to honor the requests of the citizens.

A concrete example will further illustrate the utilization of this tactic. The city council recently was considering a petition to rezone a tract of land from single family residential to multiple family residential. Two subdivisions abutting this tract of land were composed entirely of single family homes. The two Homeowner's Associations representing these areas became aware of the fact that a public hearing was going to be held on this rezoning. The officers of the two associations circulated a petition opposing the rezoning, had their individual members call individual councilmen voicing the position of the association, and made sure that about 100 people attended the council meeting at which the decision was to be made. The atmosphere of the public meeting dramatizes the pressure tactics that the association used so adroitly. Different speeches were made by property owners voicing opposition to apartments in their area. In a number of instances, threats directed toward individual councilmen were made indicating that a vote for rezoning would result in the lack of political support at the next election. It is fair to say that the sheer numbers and outspoken nature of the audience intimidated many of the council. While this tactic may be viewed as useful, it is also necessary to point out that the threats of lack of political support were very real since most of the Homeowner's Associations actually endorsed candidates in the local nonpartisan elections. Further, many of the members of the association had served as cadres of campaign workers in local elections. One last point of interest is that a number of elected and appointed public officials started as members and officers of these associations before gaining public office. In fact, they used the associations as stepping stones to higher office. Once in office, these officials relied upon the association for continued political support.

Within the last five years, the 48 Homeowner's Associations formed a federation and elected a centralized set of officers. Now when an issue of importance to one association comes up and they need additional support, the federation provides them with the endorsement of all the associations plus the manpower to call officials, pack meetings, and circulate petitions. The key thing is that in a community with no formal political parties, the Homeowner's Associations serve as a vehicle for representing the views of property owners throughout the area. The tactics associated with monitoring decision-making processes suggest that these organizations play an important role as a "watchdog" of what public officials do. They continue to be quite powerful and influential as long as issues on which they can gain almost immediate consensus come up and as long as the people in these associations have a direct stake in the outcome of certain decisions.

III. CONCLUSION

This case of successful organizational strategy and tactics reflects some points which apply in a larger context. First, consensus on goals on the part of an organization allows it to mobilize its members swiftly when actions contrary to the organization are anticipated. The visibility of land use issues and the direct stake that each resident has in the outcome makes an organized reaction easier to accomplish. Second, an organization which meets regularly, discusses issues, elects officers, and keeps abreast of decision-making processes can be readily informed of actions that might be contrary to the membership's interests. Since this awareness is manifested through a vetoing and nullifying strategy rather than a strategy promoting a particular change, the organization need only kill a decision at one stage in the decision-making process and need not effectively maneuver a change through a whole series of stages, each of which requires a strategy and a set of tactics appropriate to the consensus that is needed to get something done. In this respect, negative or defensive groups only need to be successful at one rather than many stages in the decision-making process. Here the tactics of political pressure, packing meetings, and generating petitions are necessary only occasionally. This, in turn, does not put a great deal of strain on the organization's resources.

Third, the Homeowner's Associations discussed in this case show considerable evidence of moving beyond just monitoring decision-making processes. Their long-range effectiveness is now based on their ability to form coalitions with other associations so that they have added political strength. Additionally, the endorsement of political candidates as well as having members of the organization run for political office or gain appointment to key commissions and groups in the community puts the associations in the position not only of influencing the process but also of gaining control of that process. In an evolutionary sense, what started as "grass-roots" organizational activity now shows evidence of being far more potent as these organizations seek to capture key decision-making processes by having their own member as part of the formal processes.

However, it does seem important to note that Homeowner's Associations would not be where they are today without the many years of hard work and mobilization of members that has characterized the organization's efforts over the years.

Given this perspective it seems reasonable to conclude that other voluntary organizations with few ostensible resources can also be successful as long as they have a clear consensus on goals, a nullifying or vetoing strategy, a cadre of members willing to exert pressure, and the ability to demonstrate to elected and appointed officials the political consequences of making decisions contrary to their interests. This set of conditions is not always present but, when it is, the chances of organizational success are good.

The challenge to citizens groups and their leaders is to engineer the climate so that it is receptive to the interests of organizations. And here the choice of appropriate strategies and tactics is critical. The case study of Homeowner's Associations has shown that success does not come overnight but as a result of many efforts aimed at building organizations, managing their activities, monitoring decision-making processes, developing coalitions, and endorsing and running candidates for elective office. Strategies and tactics are transferable if people recognize that fundamentally institutions and political bodies respond to pressure, particularly where the political consequences of inaction are clearly stated and demonstrated periodically.

Bibliography

Chapter I. Assessing the Situation

Cheever, Julia. *Your Community and Beyond: An Information and Action Guide*. Palo Alto, Calif.: Page-Fickli, 1975.

> Readings and survey instruments suggest approaches to assessing urban conditions in such areas as food, housing, health care, education, media, justice, work, and transportation.

Gibson, Janice. *Experiencing the Inner City*. New York: Harper and Row, 1973.

> With brief introductory material, this manual offers a wide range of instruments for the practitioner or student (especially one new to the inner city) trying to get a handle on urban problems—housing, health needs, employment, education, justice, and the courts.

Hamburg, Jill, et al. *Where It's At: A Research Guide for Community Organizing*. 1967. (Available from Department of Social Justice, National Council of Churches, 475 Riverside Drive, New York, N.Y. 10027).

> Generally useful (if somewhat dated) guide for digging into (and organizing around) inner-city problems, from the perspectives of the poor and minority oppressed.

Jones, W. Ron. *Finding Community: A Guide to Community Research and Action*. Palo Alto, Calif.: James Freel, 1971.

> Readings and survey instruments offer approaches to assessing urban conditions in such areas as food, health, schools, housing, welfare, and ecology.

League of Women Voters. *You and Your National Government: The Invisible Partnership*. Washington, D.C., 1962.

> Discusses the legislative, executive, and judicial branches of the federal government. Special attention is given to the legislative process: how a bill becomes law. There is some discussion of the role of the citizen, and a short bibliography.

League of Women Voters Education Fund. *Election Check-up: Monitoring Registration and Voting*. Washington, D.C., 1973.

> Provides guidance to those interested in determining the honesty and accuracy of election procedures in their communities. The booklet discusses the occasions when

monitoring the electoral process is indicated, recruiting people to help, pertinent laws and court decisions, briefing and training monitors, and analyzing the data collected. It includes useful checklists for on-site registration monitors and election day monitors.

League of Women Voters Education Fund. *Know Your Community, 1972; Know Your County, 1974; Know Your Schools, 1974; Know Your State, 1974.*

Four useful guides for those who need to know more about various branches of local and state government, including how to identify problems and workable solutions. Useful for those who want to prepare descriptions or analyses of their cities, counties, public schools, or state governments.

League of Women Voters Education Fund. *What Ever Happened to Open Housing? A Handbook for Fair Housing Monitors.* Washington, D.C., 1974.

Discusses the rules and regulations governing open housing, how to judge who is complying with them and what to do about noncompliance. Includes sample forms for monitoring affirmative fair housing marketing plans.

National Board, Young Women's Christian Association. *Look Beneath the Surface of the Community.* New York, 1974.

This booklet examines various sources of information, the kinds of information that may be needed, some principles of interviewing useful in gathering information, and ways of sharing findings.

Poplin, Dennis. *Communities.* New York: Macmillan, 1972.

A useful, comprehensive approach to looking at the whole idea of community, with particular attention to the range and variety of perspectives available.

Warren, Roland L. *Studying Your Community.* New York: Russell Sage Foundation, 1955.

A comprehensive guide to the gathering of information about local communities prepared by a sociologist specializing in community studies. Covers most segments of community life, including economics, government, housing, education, recreation, religion, income maintenance, social services, health, the media, etc., as well as provisions for special groups such as the handicapped and farm workers. Attention is given to the processes of community organization and planning and conducting a community survey.

Chapter 11.   Planning with the Community

Alexander, Robert C., and Nenno, Mary K. *A NAHRO Guide for Preparing a Local Housing Assistance Plan.* Washington, D.C.: National Association of Housing and Redevelopment Officials, 1975.

Provides details for local planners in preparing a local housing assistance plan under the terms of the Housing and Community Development Act of 1974.

Gilbert, Neil, and Specht, Harry. *Dimensions of Social Welfare Policy.* Englewood Cliffs, N.J.: Prentice-Hall, 1974.

Solid, well-written approach to social welfare policy analysis, especially useful in offering a framework for analysis and exploring choices in the process of policy formulation.

Kahn, Alfred J. *Theory and Practice of Social Planning and Studies in Social Policy and Planning.* New York: Russell Sage Foundation, 1969.

Provides an extensive discussion of the social planning process. The companion volume (STUDIES . . .) offers a series of case studies in social planning, including planning in the fields of poverty, delinquency, income security, community development, mental health, and social services.

Levine, Robert A. *Public Planning: Failure and Redirection.* New York: Basic Books, 1972.

Levine identifies difficulties in public planning, including case studies in public assistance, urban renewal, and community action, and identifies conditions that seem to make plans work better. His general conclusion is that systems which decentralize decision-making, utilize marketlike incentives, or force competition among administrative units tend to improve plans and programs.

Lippitt, Ronald, Watson, Jeanne, and Westley, Bruce. *The Dynamics of Planned Change: A Comparative Study of Principles and Techniques.* New York: Harcourt Brace and World, 1958.

A detailed study of the process of planned change from a social-psychological perspective, with special attention to the role of the change agent in the context of planning community change.

Maffin, Robert W., Silverman, Edward, and Sosson, Deena. *Chart Book for Plotting a Local Community Development Course Under the Housing and Community Development Act of 1974.* Washington, D.C.: National Association of Housing and Redevelopment Officials, 1975.

Essentially, a detailed guide to planning under the 1974 act for use by community development personnel in local governments.

Marris, Peter, and Rein, Martin. *The Dilemmas of Social Reform: Poverty and Community Action in the United States.* (2nd ed.) Chicago: Aldine Publishing Co., 1973.

Detailed case studies of community action in the 1960s with an emphasis on the problems that emerged and the ways they were dealt with in the planning and action process.

Mayer, Robert R. *Social Planning and Social Change.* Englewood Cliffs, N.J.: Prentice-Hall, 1972.

Mayer applies planning theory and conceptual models to the problem of inducing social change. He focuses upon changes aimed at helping people through changes in social structure, and discusses specific cases illustrating change through modifying (1) membership, (2) roles, and (3) statuses. He develops a theory of social structural change and discusses social planning in relation to it.

Morris, Robert, and Binstock, Robert H., with Martin Rein. *Feasible Planning for Social Change.* New York: Columbia University Press, 1966.

Provides a model for social planning by changing the policies of formal organizations, from the perspective of planners with limited influence. Planning is regarded as a process of choice among goals and policies, overcoming resistance to preferred goals, and influencing the dominant factions in organizations by mobilizing resources that can exercise the type of influence necessary to goal attainment.

National Board, Young Women's Christian Association. *Program Planning in the YWCA.* New York, 1975.

This manual provides a step-by-step guide to program planning that has wider application than the YWCA. Phases in the program planning process are discussed, together with steps in each phase. Emphasis is placed on member participation in the process. Seven tools for program planning are included, as well as a case example of the program-planning process.

Taber, Merlin, et al. *Handbook for Community Professionals: An Approach for Planning and Action.* Springfield, Ill.: Charles C. Thomas, 1972.

A cookbook approach to moving a plan from concept to action, heavily illustrated with instruments included.

Chapter III.   Organizing for Change

Alinsky, Saul. *Rules for Radicals.* New York: Random (Vintage), 1971.

Tough, hard-hitting guide to the basic components of organizing for social change. Clear and specific.

Bailey, Robert, Jr. *Radicals in Urban Politics: The Alinsky Approach.* Chicago: University of Chicago Press, 1974.

A research-oriented case study of South Austin organization (Chicago) which throws light on strategic and tactical reasons for the successes (and failures) of Alinsky-sponsored "people's organizations."

Bailis, Lawrence. *Bread or Justice.* Lexington, Mass.: D.C. Heath, 1974.

A case study of the Massachusetts Welfare Rights Organization, especially good on organizing strategy and tactics.

Brager, George, and Specht, Harry. *Community Organizing.* New York: Columbia University Press, 1973.

Emphasizes principles of community work. Especially valuable are sections on constituency organizing and tactics of influencing change targets.

Cooperative League of the U.S.A. *The Buying Club,* n.d. Cooperative League of the U.S.A. *Moving Ahead with Group Action,* n.d.

Fish, John. *Black Power/White Control.* Princeton, N.J.: Princeton University Press, 1973.

An extensive and detailed description of Chicago's Woodlawn Organization with special attention to uses (and limitations) of conflict.

Grosser, Charles. *New Directions in Community Organization.* New York: Praeger, 1976.

A useful review of the development of community organization practice, with special attention to the programs and techniques of the 1960s and 1970s.

Helmreich, William. *The Black Crusaders: A Case Study of a Black Militant Organization.* New York: Harper and Row, 1973.

Particularly useful is the extensive consideration of the relationship between organizational structure and the change approaches and techniques utilized by the Crusaders.

Huenefeld, John. *The Community Activist's Handbook.* Boston: Beacon Press, 1970.

A nice little guide to building a citizen's organization, from the bottom up.

Kramer, Ralph, and Specht, Harry, eds. *Readings in Community Organization Practice* (2nd ed.). Englewood Cliffs, N.J.: Prentice-Hall, 1975.

This comprehensive collection gives attention to community and organizational analysis as well as the processes of directed change. A number of articles offer perspectives on involving citizens on their own behalf.

League of Women Voters Education Fund. *Getting It All Together: The Politics of Organizational Partnership.* Washington, D.C., 1971.

Discusses the problems of groups working together to achieve common purposes, the search for common ground, kinds of groups that may be brought together, establishing contacts with other groups, planning together, choosing the right structure for working together, and selecting appropriate action.

League of Women Voters Education Fund. *The Politics of Change.* Washington, D.C., 1972.

Discusses the concepts and questions to ask in planning community change. This booklet includes a discussion of community analysis, community goals and ways of identifying them, choosing an issue, and organizing for change. A short but useful discussion.

Rothman, Jack, Erlich, John, and Teresa, Joseph. *Promoting Innovation and Change in Organizations and Communities.* New York: John Wiley, 1976.

Detailed description and practitioner's guide to basic organizing techniques: establishing innovations, changing organizational goals, stimulating participation, and increasing the effectiveness of role performance.

Source Collective, The. *Source Catalog: Communities/Housing.* Chicago: Swallow Press, 1972.

Excellent guide, with extensive lists of resources, to organizing around housing and tenant rights.

Chapter IV.   Exercising Influence

Fellows, Margaret M., and Koenig, Stella A. *Tested Methods of Raising Money for Churches, Colleges and Health and Welfare Agencies.* New York: Harper & Bros., 1959.

Includes guidance in raising funds by mail, reaching big givers and foundations, maintaining support over time, building and maintaining lists of potential givers, and information on how to evaluate the results of fund-raising campaigns.

Lawrence, William C., and Snyder, Eloise. *A Guide to Grantsmanship for Area Planners in Aging.* Ann Arbor, Michigan: Project TAP (Institute of Gerontology and the School of Social Work Continuing Education Program, co-sponsors), 1974.

Covers the search for sources, developing details about the grant-giving interests of located sources, developing proposals including problems of writing proposals. Also includes a short bibliography.

League of Women Voters Education Fund. *Going to Court in the Public Interest: A Guide for Community Groups.* Washington, D.C., 1973.

A brief guide for those interested in class action litigation, which discusses the decision to litigate, managing on a small budget, choosing a lawyer, working with the lawyer, and understanding the courts. A glossary of frequently used legal terms is included, together with a list of national organizations involved in litigation.

League of Women Voters Education Fund. *Removing Administrative Obstacles to Voting.* Washington, D.C., 1972.

Discusses the problem, how to develop a plan for overcoming the obstacles, various approaches including public education, utilizing the media, administrative action, litigation, and building community organizations and coalitions that can take a hand in the problem.

League of Women Voters Education Fund. *Shaking the Money Tree.* Washington, D.C., 1969.

A short pamphlet describing the purpose, methods, and additional tips on raising money. Includes a brief bibliography.

League of Women Voters Education Fund. *When You Write to Washington: A Guide for Citizen Action Including Congressional Directory 1975–76.* Washington, D.C., 1975.

A short, step-by-step guide which discusses why, when, how, and what to write, together with a set of "do's" and "don'ts." Included is a list of the names of senators and congressmen arranged by states and congressional districts, together with a list of Senate, House, and Joint Committees and their members.

Lewis, Marianna O., et al. (eds.). *The Foundation Directory* (Edition 5). New York: The Foundation Center (distributed by Columbia University Press), 1975.

Provides detailed information by type, location, and nature of programs supported. A standard reference work found in most libraries.

Richan, Willard C., and Rosenberg, Marvin. *The Advo-Kit: A Self-Administered Training Program for the Social Worker Advocate.* Philadelphia, 1971. (Available from the first author at 1500 N. Broad St. Philadelphia, Pa. 19121)

A six-step training package prepared by a member of the faculty of Temple University's School of Social Work and his colleague. The units are: (1) Setting Up Positive Expectations, (2) Casing the Target System, (3) Making the Case, (4) Making Demands, (5) Building Alliances, and (6) Do It!

Seymour, Harold J. *Designs for Fund Raising.* New York: McGraw Hill, 1966.

A guide to fund raising used by some voluntary associations in social welfare.

U.S. Office of Management and Budget. *Catalog of Federal Domestic Assistance.* Washington, D.C., 1972.

Published and updated periodically, the catalog provides detailed information on federal programs classified by function (e.g., community development, consumer protection, health, housing, income security, social services, etc.). Indexed in several ways to aid in finding programs and grant sources of interest, it also includes information on the regional and local offices of federal agencies

Chapter V. Administering Programs

Child Welfare League of America, Inc. *Guide for Board Organization in Social Agencies.* New York, 1975.

Discusses the purpose of a board, its organization and bylaws, functions of various committees, channels of communication, the executive director, the evaluation of the agency's program and operations, financial accounting, etc. The booklet also contains a short bibliography.

Dail, Hilda Lee. *Let's Try a Workshop with Teen Women.* New York: National Board of the YWCA, 1974.

A short guide to organizing and operating a workshop, including a discussion of the details of arrangements and techniques to use in conducting the workshop to facilitate communication and discussion.

Ehlers, Walter, Austin, Michael, and Prothero, Jon. *Administration for the Human Services.* New York: Harper and Row, 1976.

Strong programmed text which offers the basics in administration for the beginner.

Etzioni, Amitai. *Modern Organizations.* Englewood Cliffs, N.J.: Prentice-Hall, 1964.

In 120 pages lays out the major components of organizational bureaucracies with liberal illustration of concepts.

League of Women Voters Education Fund. *The Budget Process from the Bureaucrat's Side of the Desk.* Washington, D.C., 1974.

A companion to *The Citizen and the Budget Process,* this booklet explains, in ordinary language, accounting terms and processes. It explains how the citizen may get data to understand the budget, how to analyze a budget, and some tips on getting answers to questions and influencing the budget-making process in city government.

League of Women Voters Education Fund. *The Citizen and the Budget Process: Opening Up the System.* Washington, D.C., 1974.

The focus is on city government budgets and their understanding, how they reflect priorities, sources of income, targets of expenditure with a special note on the property tax. There is substantial discussion of change in the budget process, its context, strategies, and tools for change. A sample city budget designed for citizen understanding is included, as well as three brief case examples.

League of Women Voters Education Fund. *Making It Work: A Guide to Training Election Workers.* Washington, D.C., 1973.

Contains principles that are easily generalizable to other types of training. There is a useful insert, entitled "A Guide for Election Day Operations," which discusses three systems—voting machines, punch card, and paper ballots, together with the activities and problems that may arise with each.

National Board, Young Women's Christian Association. *Financial Administration Manual for the YWCA.* New York, 1975.

Readily adapted for use by other organizations, this manual provides detailed guidance in many aspects of financial administration.

National Board, Young Women's Christian Association. *A Primer of Parliamentary Procedure.* New York, 1968.

Discusses the order of business, motions, voting, elections, hints to the president and to members. Somewhat more detailed than the selection included in this volume on the same subject.

National Board, Young Women's Christian Association. *The Role of the Board of Directors in a Community YWCA.* New York, 1969.

Discusses the responsibilities of the board, its composition including officers, structural relations of the board, board-staff relations, and training board members.

National Council of Young Men's Christian Associations. *The Executive Director's Responsibility as a Business Manager in a Health and Welfare Agency.* New York, 1974.

Discusses the executive's accountability, executive controls, selecting control points, setting standards, establishing a cost effectiveness plan, cost accounting, fee setting, budgeting techniques, etc.

Wright, Sara-Alyce P. *Guide for Training Y-Teen Club Advisers.* New York: National Board, YWCA, 1962.

> Provides a step-by-step guide for recruiting, orienting, training, supervising, evaluating, and giving recognition to volunteers. Although focused on the YWCA, its principles are easily generalized to other organizations.

Chapter VI.   Evaluating Programs

Caro, Francis, ed. *Readings in Evaluation Research.* New York: Russell Sage, 1971.

> A good collection of articles, especially helpful in dealing with some of the most problematic aspects of evaluation.

Mager, Robert. *Goal Analysis.* Belmont, Calif.: Fearon Publishers, 1972.

> A delightful little book which humorously suggests ways of defining important but abstract goals ("fuzzies") so that the performances which lead to them can be identified.

Moursund, Janet. *Evaluation: An Introduction to Research Design.* Belmont, Calif.: Wadsworth, 1973.

> Useful nonstatistical approach to the basic problems involved in constructing and carrying out evaluative research.

Mullen, Edward, Dumpson, James, and associates, eds. *Evaluation of Social Intervention.* San Francisco: Jossey-Bass, 1972.

> These 14 articles review recent experimental evaluations of social work intervention. The recommendations for changing programs are especially interesting.

Rossi, Peter, and Williams, Walter, eds. *Evaluating Social Programs.* Palisades, N.Y.: Seminar Press, 1972.

> This reader offers major attention to the factors which have hindered sound and useful evaluative research.

Suchman, Edward. *Evaluative Research.* New York: Russell Sage, 1967.

> A basic work in the field of evaluation, most of it still very much to the point.

Tripodi, Tony, Fellin, Phillip, and Epstein, Irwin. *Social Program Evaluation.* Itasca, Ill.: F. E. Peacock, 1971.

> Short, straightforward approach, especially useful for administrators concerned about program evaluation.

Weiss, Carol, ed. *Evaluating Action Programs.* Boston: Allyn and Bacon, 1972.

> A comprehensive set of 20 readings covering a broad range of topics in social action and education.

Weiss, Carol. *Evaluation Research.* Englewood Cliffs, N.J.: Prentice-Hall, 1972.

> One of the best short introductions to methods of assessing program effectiveness. Excellent bibliography.

Selected Organizations which Publish Relevant Materials

Child Welfare League of America, Inc., 67 Irvine Place, New York, N.Y. 10003.
Cooperative League of the U.S.A., 1828 L Street, N.W., Washington, D.C. 20036.

Family Service Association of America, 44 East 23 St., New York, N.Y. 10010.

League of Women Voters of the United States, 1730 M Street, N.W., Washington, D.C. 20036.

The National Assembly of National Voluntary Health and Social Welfare Organizations, Inc., 345 East 46 Street, New York, N.Y. 10017.

National Association of Social Workers, 1425 H Street, N.W., Washington, D.C. 20005.

National Board of the Young Men's Christian Associations, 291 Broadway, New York, N.Y. 10007.

National Board of the Young Women's Christian Association, 600 Lexington Avenue New York, N.Y. 10022.

National Council on Aging, Inc., 1828 L Street, N.W., Washington, D.C. 20036.

National Federation of Settlements and Neighborhood Centers, 232 Madison Avenue, New York, N.Y. 10016.

National Urban League, 500 East 62 Street, New York, N.Y. 10021.

United Way of America, 801 North Fairfax St., Alexandria, Virginia 22314.

John L. Erlich and **Fred M. Cox**

Name Index

Abarbanel, Karin, 62,65
Adams, R. N., 318n
Aldrich, Nelson, 316n
Alexander, Pearlie, 185
Alinsky, Saul, 153, 196
Alvarez, Ann Rosegrant, 375, 377
Andrew,Gwen, 320n
Anthony, Susan B., 188
Aronson, Sidney H., 314n, 324n

Bailis, Lawrence, 155
Baker, H. R., 334n
Banfield, Edward C., 196
Bealer, Robert C., 318n
Beals, Ralph L., 325n
Beaubien, Anne, 16, 56, 356n
Beer, Samuel, 7n 12
Bell, Philip, 188
Bigman, Stanley K., 325n
Binstock, Robert H., 196
Black, Henry Campbell, 63
Blalock, Hubert M., Jr., 373
Bloedorn, Jack, 68, 81
Blood, J. W., 298
Blumer, Herbert, 316n
Bowditch, Henry, 187
Bowles, Elinor, 253, 280
Brager, George, 9, 12, 153n, 245n, 251
Brim, Orville G., Jr., 325
Brown, William Wells, 188
Buckley, Clair A., 298
Burkley, Walter, 81n

Campbell, Ambrosine, 184
Campbell, D. T., 369, 370
Caper, Philip, 189
Caplan, Nathan, 317n
Caro, Francis G., 320n
Carter, Jimmy, 7
Cartwright, Dorwin, 250n, 252
Channing, William Ellery, 187–188
Christensen, Nellie, 185
Clasen, Robert, 311, 365
Connor, Alan N., 197, 245, 279n
Cooley, Charles H., 38

Cox, Fred M., 1, 16, 198, 245n, 248n, 251, 376

Dahl, Robert A., 252
Davidoff, Paul, 207n
de la Isla, Jaime, 197, 245, 246n, 247n, 250n, 251, 379n
Dluhy, Milan, 375, 414
Douglass, Frederick, 187, 188
Douglass, Richard, 311, 353
Duhl, Leonard, 318
Dyer, Henry S., 348, 352

Epstein, Irwin, 310
Epstein, Joseph, 7, 12
Erlich, John L., 1, 155, 156, 157, 181, 245n, 251, 311,
Etzioni, Amitai, 341

Fairweather, George W., 314
Fellin, Phillip, 310
Fourre, James P., 298
Fox, George, 190
Freeman, Howard E., 314, 347, 352
French, John R. P., 250, 252
Friedlander, William, 66, 81

Gandhi, Mohandas, 192
Gantt, Henry, 293
Gil, David G., 350, 352
Golovin, N. E., 81n
Gora, 188
Gottman, John, 311, 365
Gould, Julius, 63
Gouldner, Alvin, 318n
Griffith, Arthur, 192
Grimke, Sarah, 187

Haber, Alan, 84n
Hamilton, Edith, 318n
Hasenfeld, Yeheskel, 16, 42, 68, 69
Hernon, Peter, 58, 64
Herzog, Elizabeth, 316n
Hoffer, Joe R., 254, 287, 298
Hooper, Isaac, 187
Howe, Irving, 8, 12

Subject Index

THE BOOK MANUFACTURE

Tactics and Techniques of Community Practice was typeset, printed and bound by R. R. Donnelley & Sons Company, Elgin, Illinois, and Crawfordsville, Indiana. The cover design is by Charles Kling, the internal design by the F. E. Peacock Publishers, Inc., art department. The type is Times Roman.